'Phillips' account of persecution as a dynamic of genocide reaches into the histories of Europe and North America exposing the ideological and religious roots of mass violence. The story is meticulously assembled as it portrays the populist political uses of persecution to eradicate the threatening Other. This history of persecution is a moral reckoning and warning'.

Christopher Davey, *Binghamton University, SUNY, USA*

Persecution and Genocide

This volume offers an unparalleled range of comparative studies considering both persecution and genocide across two thousand years of history from Rome to Nazi Germany, and spanning Europe, Asia, Africa, and the Americas.

Topics covered include the persecution of religious minorities in the ancient world and late antiquity, the medieval roots of modern antisemitism, the early modern witch-hunts, the emergence of racial ideologies and their relationship to slavery, colonialism, Russian and Soviet mass deportations, the Armenian genocide, and the Holocaust. It also introduces students to significant, but less well known, episodes, such as the Albigensian Crusade and the massacres and forced expulsions suffered by the Circassians at the hands of imperial Russia in the 1860s, as the world entered an 'age of genocide'.

By exploring the ideological motivations of the perpetrators, the book invites students to engage with the moral complexities of the past and to reflect upon our own situation today as the 'legatees of two thousand years of persecution'. Gervase Phillips's book is the ideal introduction to the subject for anyone interested in the long and complex history of human persecution.

Gervase Phillips is Principal Lecturer in History at Manchester Metropolitan University. He is a historian of conflict, persecution, genocide, and slavery. His previous publications include *The Anglo-Scots Wars, 1513–1550* (1999).

Persecution and Genocide

A History

Gervase Phillips

Routledge
Taylor & Francis Group

LONDON AND NEW YORK

Designed cover image: Expulsion of the inhabitants from Carcassonne in 1209.
Image taken from *Grandes Chroniques de France. Expulsion of the Cathars, circa 1415.*
Workshop of Master of Boucicaut. Niday Picture Library / Alamy Stock Photo

First published 2025
by Routledge
4 Park Square, Milton Park, Abingdon, Oxon OX14 4RN

and by Routledge
605 Third Avenue, New York, NY 10158

Routledge is an imprint of the Taylor & Francis Group, an informa business

© 2025 Gervase Phillips

British Library Cataloguing-in-Publication Data
A catalogue record for this book is available from the British Library

ISBN: 978-0-415-69570-1 (hbk)
ISBN: 978-0-415-69571-8 (pbk)
ISBN: 978-1-003-49433-1 (ebk)

DOI: 10.4324/9781003494331

Typeset in Sabon
by Newgen Publishing UK

Contents

Maps

Acknowledgements

I am grateful to friends and colleagues who kindly commented on draft chapters of this book, or otherwise offered support and advice. To Kathryn Hurlock and Ben Edwards, *dioch yn fawr*. To Andy Crome, Jenny Cromwell, and Laura Sandy, thanks very much indeed. Christopher P. Davey and an anonymous reviewer contributed invaluable comments and suggestions on the original manuscript. Any remaining errors are, of course, my own. The genesis of the book lies in my teaching, especially *Rise of Persecuting Society*, a core unit for over a quarter of a century for first-year history students at MMU, originally conceived by my late colleague Lesley Ling. The staff at Taylor and Francis, in particular Eve Setch and Georgia Lloyd, have extended the greatest patience towards me over several years. That, too, is much appreciated.

The publishers are grateful to Esther Gilbert for granting permission to reuse the map 'Expulsions 1000–1500' from the ninth edition of *The Routledge Atlas of Jewish History* by Martin Gilbert. www.martingilb ert.com/

Introduction

> Look at the facts of the world. You see a continual and progressive triumph of the right. I do not pretend to understand the moral universe; the arc is a long one, my eye reaches but little ways; I cannot calculate the curve and complete the figure by the experience of sight; I can divine it by conscience. And from what I see I am sure it bends towards justice.[1]

These words were spoken by the Unitarian minister and abolitionist Theodore Parker, to his congregation in Boston, Massachusetts, in 1853. His was one of the crescendo of voices then rising in the United States in opposition to slavery. He boldly predicted the 'ruin' of the 'slave power', the planter class who held four million people in bondage in the southern states and who seemed, when he spoke, to be tightening their grip on government in Washington. Parker did not live to see his prediction come true. He died in 1860. In 1861, fearing their loss of influence in Washington, and the consequent threat to their 'peculiar institution' (slavery), the 'slave power' attempted to lead their states out of the Union. By so doing, they triggered the American Civil War. By 1865, they were defeated. Through a combination of self-emancipation and political action, culminating in the 13th Amendment to the US Constitution, the enslaved were freed. The 'arc' of the 'moral universe' appeared to have bent sharply 'towards justice'.

It is, perhaps, unsurprising that such an inspiring ideal, with simple imagery so clearly evoked, and apparently so swiftly vindicated by 'the triumph of the right', has proved enduring. Of course, Parker's name is not so well remembered today. It was Martin Luther King Jr., campaigning for the civil rights of those descended from emancipated slaves, who re-crafted his rhetoric into a succinct and forceful proclamation. On 16 August 1967 in Atlanta, Georgia, he delivered a speech to the Southern Christian Leadership Conference, entitled 'Where Do We Go from Here?' He opened his final paragraph with the phrase 'Let us realize that the arc of the moral universe is long, but it bends toward justice'.[2] These sentiments have continued to inspire. They are invoked by many advocates of progressive social policies, notably by Barack Obama, president of the United States (2009–2017).[3] While few have since expressed the sentiment as eloquently as Parker or

DOI: 10.4324/9781003494331-1

King, the notion that history unfolds as a 'progressive triumph of the right' retains a powerful hold on popular understanding of the past. Indeed, even some academics perpetuate this idea, by suggesting that groups or individuals whose actions they approve of stood 'on the right side of history'.[4]

Regrettably, this is not because the 'facts of the world' really support such a conclusion. After all, we live today in what Samantha Power, US ambassador to the United Nations (2013–2017), has described as the 'age of genocide'.[5] This age, it might be suggested, opened with the massacres, enslavement, and destruction of indigenous polities and cultures that were a recurrent feature of settler colonialism. It reached a portentous inflection point with the deportations by which imperial Russia denuded Circassia, in the Caucasus, of a population of two million people in 1864. The demographic engineering of loyal and homogeneous populations through mass murder and forced depopulation on an unprecedented scale and as a matter of state policy had been inaugurated within Eurasia. Over the next century, some nation states, driven by the pitiless modern ideologies of ethno-nationalism or Marxist-Leninism, and aided by the ruthless potential of statist bureaucracy, strove to transform the continent into a hecatomb.

Uncounted millions have been persecuted in this murderous epoch. If the 'moral arc' of the universe 'bends towards justice', then how exactly did we find ourselves here? The grim persistence and re-occurrence of persecution and genocide into the present century demands we attempt to find an answer for that question. In doing so, we must grapple with the disquieting historicity of our 'moral universe' too. We should not merely recount or strive to simply understand this forbidding history of inhumanity; we should, as historians, be prepared to judge and, if necessary, to condemn. In the words of the genocide scholar and historiographer Donald Bloxham, persecutors 'need to be judged morally as relevantly discerning beings'.[6]

Yet, in judging, we cannot eschew complexity or ambiguity. Consider the French philosopher and jurist Jean Bodin (*c.*1529–1596), a distinguished figure in the intellectual history of the sixteenth century. He is best remembered for his work on political sovereignty and his advocacy of both religious tolerance and a strong central state. He believed this would end internal civil wars and ensure that all subjects of the crown would enjoy the protection of the law. This subject led him inevitably to touch on themes relevant to persecution. In 1571, a Genoese merchant had arrived in Toulouse, where Bodin lived and worked. The merchant's entourage included an enslaved man. The local magistrates freed him without hesitation. Bodin commented approvingly, 'that the slaves of strangers so soon as they set foot in Fraunce become franke and free'. Slavery, he asserted, was 'directly contrary to human nature'.[7] Bodin's stance against slavery invites our admiration; here, surely was a man who stood 'on the right side of history'.

And yet Bodin was also a leading authority on demonology, author of a hugely influential work on the subject, *On the Demon-mania of Witches* (1580). He advocated the death penalty for acts of witchcraft that were committed, he believed, by traitors to God and enemies of the faithful. Age should not spare those accused; even children should be executed (although he was willing to concede that if 'penitent' they might be strangled before being burned). Judges who failed to execute a convicted witch – and those accused of witchcraft were almost always guilty – should themselves be executed. Anonymous denunciations should be encouraged and, for such an exceptionally evil crime, established legal due process (or 'the strict forms of law', as Bodin had it) should be put aside, for it simply shielded the malefactor.[8]

It was not inevitable that Bodin should hold such views; he was not the pliant, unthinking creation of some over-arching historical 'context'. He had vocal contemporaries such as the Jesuit Friedrich Spee, who urged that a compassionate Christianity should determine the treatment of those accused of witchcraft, most of whom, Spee believed, were wholly innocent of the charge. Similarly, members of the Roman Inquisition repeatedly clashed with the papacy when they argued that the questionable injunction of Exodus 22:18, that witches were to be killed, should not be read literally.[9] Bodin's position, thus, represented a conscious, discerning moral choice. Those, like Bodin, who so successfully propagated belief in a phantasm, a widespread Satanic witch cult posing an existential threat to godly communities, thus bear a fearsome responsibility for the 60,000 lives extinguished in the ensuing trials. The principled ally of the enslaved was a bloody-minded persecutor of folk accused of witchcraft.

The point here is not simply about the challenges inherent in trying to understand one historical figure's conflicted *weltanschauung* (world view) in its moral context. The same difficulty in determining the curve of any puta-tive moral arc arises when we consider entire societies historically. Bodin's dismissal of slavery in 1571 as 'contrary to human nature' was not unique, or even unusual. An English court had refused a Muscovite slave entry into the country in 1567. In 1596, a Dutch court in Zeeland freed a hundred enslaved Africans who had been shipped into the port of Middelburg. In western Europe, at least, slavery and other forms of involuntary servitude such as serfdom, were dying out, rejected as unnatural.[10] And yet, *at that same time*, European merchants, financiers, ship-owners, explorers, adventurers, even monarchs, were fashioning the Atlantic slave trade into the largest involun-tary forced migration in history. Some 12 million Africans were transported in the most brutal and inhumane of conditions to the Americas. If they survived the voyage, they were condemned to a usually brief and tormented life of exhausting and debilitating labour as chattel slaves. Their children inherited their status.

Here we see established legal, ethical, or customary protections for the lives and well-being of individuals ignored, to allow persecution to take place. William Palmer, an historian of Tudor policy in Ireland and early English colonialism, has tellingly applied the concept of 'moral regression' to such episodes.[11] It is particularly important for two reasons.

Firstly, much of the current public debate about the past features arguments about the dangers of 'presentism': anachronistically projecting our ethical standards onto historical societies. For example, in the case of the memorialisation of 'great men' who were also slaveholders, the US presidential historian Joseph Ellis has argued that we should not impose '[contemporary] norms on men who lived in another time'.[12] It is an important argument; 'presentism' can indeed distort our understanding of the past. And yet, if Jean Bodin could condemn slavery as 'contrary to human nature' in 1571, what excuse can enlightened Virginian planters such as George Washington or Thomas Jefferson have had for holding others as slaves two centuries later? If there is a context to be invoked here to explain the presence of racialised chattel slavery in eighteenth-century Virginia, it is the moral regression so often inherent in colonialism.[13] We cannot simply assume that modern people are morally superior beings to those discerning individuals who lived before us, and that we should, thus, not ask awkward questions about the motives that drove their actions and behaviours.

The second compelling reason for studying acts of moral regression is, therefore, to seek answers to those awkward questions. Why would a society, composed of folk generally no more cruel, fanatical, or incapable of ethical reflection than we are today, choose to persecute others, to physically harm, to dispossess, to enslave, and to drive into exile? Why, in the most extreme cases, does persecution turn to genocide, the impulse to destroy a people entirely? The overarching answers to those questions offered here will be rooted firmly in ideologies, defined in this case as the belief systems, primarily religious, cultural, and political, that shape social and political acts.

It will also be argued that such prejudicial belief systems have exhibited the most extraordinary longevity, with the cultural transmission of hatreds and bigotry linking patterns of persecution across centuries. The economic historians Nico Voigtländer and Hans-Joachim Voth have compared the later history of German towns where Jews were massacred in the years 1348–1350 (scapegoated for outbreaks of the Black Death) to towns where no medieval pogroms had occurred. The sites of medieval persecution saw higher incidences of violent antisemitism in the 1920s. They also showed higher levels of support for the Nazis in the 1930s.[14] Studying the history of persecution is a profound and necessary reminder of the tight grasp that the past exerts on modern societies.

This emphasis on ideology is not to deny the significance of more material factors (essentially, those rooted in economics and the ensuing structures of power and exploitation) in the history of persecution. Here, these will be fully acknowledged where they are pertinent. Yet rarely can material interests be invoked without acknowledging how fundamentally they themselves were shaped by ideology. Clearly the economics of the emerging market-oriented, profit-driven colonial economy, centred around the labour-intensive plantation, was a major factor in the scale and brutality of the Atlantic slave trade. Yet a simple answer of 'greed' will not explain the 'moral regression' that fixed chains onto Africans *whilst* they were being struck from the limbs of Europeans. To understand how that manifestation of greed was made possible, we must understand why Africans were regarded differently: the 'symbolic blackness' that the Abrahamic religions associated with sin and evil; the long-established notion (again shared across the Abrahamic religions) that Africans were naturally servile and 'cursed' to enslavement; the developing ideology of 'blood purity' and consequent evolution of the idea of race in medieval Europe, before Columbus had even set foot in the Americas.[15]

Explanations of persecution that foreground material causes have been enormously valuable and illuminating. Yet they also have clear limitations. Noel D. Johnson and Mark Koyama, in *Persecution and Toleration: The Long Road to Religious Freedom* (Cambridge, Cambridge University Press, 2019), offer a compelling study of the mistreatment of religious minorities and those accused of witchcraft in medieval and early modern Europe. They emphasise the concrete material realities of politics and economics. The relative fiscal weakness (essentially the inability to raise sufficient revenue to rule effectively) of the pre-modern state, and the consequent political need for legitimisation by the Church to underpin rulers' claims to authority, serves as their fundamental explanation for persecution.

For example, according to Johnson and Koyama, weak political authority in thirteenth-century Languedoc (in southern France) allowed religious dissent, much of it critical of the venality and corruption of the Catholic Church, to flourish. This dissent was stigmatised as 'heresy', which justified 'intervention by the French monarchy'. The ensuing Albigensian Crusade (1209–1229) against the alleged heretics 'burnished the orthodox credentials of the kings of France', legitimising their authority in the eyes of the Church and their fractious subjects. Such episodes of persecution only ended, Johnson and Koyama suggest, when modern nation states emerged over the course of the seventeenth and eighteenth centuries. These had an advanced fiscal capacity and were therefore strong enough to impose their authority throughout their realms while being less dependent on religion as a source of legitimacy. Diverse religious views could, thus, then be tolerated.[16]

This paradigm is then applied across other instances of persecution, such as the medieval expulsion of Jewish communities from western European kingdoms. Their approach provides many genuine insights. Their explanation for the decline of the witch-hunts, noting how wayward local courts were brought more firmly within centralised legal systems that safeguarded due process, is persuasive. Yet their paradigm, like other theoretical models of historical causation, is also prone to both oversimplification and factual inaccuracy.

For example, the French crown was initially reluctant to involve itself in the Albigensian Crusade. In 1207, King Philip II Augustus had rebuffed the papacy's request to lead a crusade against the heretics of Languedoc. The crusading army that marched south in 1209 and waged a brutal campaign of massacre and conquest was not a royal army seeking religious legitimisation for its political authority. Many of those who 'took the cross' may well have fought for material gain: loot from stormed cities, land seized from exiled 'protectors' of heretics. But they fought a holy war too. They were penitents as well as warriors, seeking spiritual rewards. At Easter 1211, Theobald, count of Bar-le-Duc and Luxembourg, arranged the division of his inheritance 'when, for the love of God, we had taken the sign of the holy cross against the Albigensian heretics and were about to set off on our pilgrimage'.[17]

Their violence was righteous violence. We cannot understand what drove them to persecute unless we understand the specific ideological motivations of the crusading movement.

The crusade's legacy was seminal in ideological terms too. It was followed by an almost century-long campaign of religious pacification conducted by clerical inquisitors, that systematically extirpated surviving networks of dissidents and ran individual heretics to ground. For Mark Gregory Pegg, the Albigensian Crusade thus 'ushered genocide into the West by linking divine salvation to mass murder'.[18]

This emphasis on ideology as the principal factor to be considered in understanding instances of persecution and genocide, and the transmission of ancient hatreds and prejudices across centuries, has shaped the structure and content of this book. Given the potential scope of the topic, no attempt has been made to write a comprehensive history of persecution and genocide as global phenomena. The content will focus mainly on Eurasia, from antiquity until the Holocaust, the paradigmatic genocide of modernity. Due attention is given to Africa and the Americas where the currents of race, slavery, and colonisation dictate. There is perhaps some further justification for this approach in that the murderous ideologies whose genesis is described herein arguably became the most productive of persecution globally. The legacies of racialised thinking and colonialism underpinning the Rwandan genocide (1994), or the appalling litany of crimes against humanity committed by Marxist-Leninist regimes in Asia in the 1960s and 1970s, offer testimony to that.[19]

Each chapter will explore the belief systems that shaped the motives of the persecutors, while also discussing the character and extent of that persecution. As the case is being made that ostensibly modern persecutory ideologies, such as political antisemitism or race, have, in fact, very deep and ancient roots, the text is organised chronologically.

The first three chapters consider the ancient world. This opens with an examination of the persecution of Christians within the Roman Empire. These were victims firstly of popular prejudice against their novel and illicit superstition, and then, sporadically within the third century, of hostility from a state keen to bind society through uniform religious practices. The second chapter charts how, as Christianity itself became the dominant religion of the empire, its traditions of pacifism were compromised by internal schisms and doctrinal conflicts combined with the political realities of wielding worldly authority. In response, a Christian theory of righteous persecution would emerge, epitomised by the words of St Augustine: 'at times, then, one who suffers persecution is unjust, and one who persecutes is just', and that 'it is not true that nothing is accomplished when it is accomplished with violence'.[20] Chapter 3 considers the implications of this for pagans. While the process of Christianising the empire was largely achieved through a gradualist policy of persuasion and voluntary conversion, coercion did become a factor in the closing years of the late fourth century. A militant strain of Christianity, rooted in a belligerent tradition of cosmic warfare and the aggressive pursuit of martyrdom, asserted its presence in conflicts with alleged heretics, schismatics, and those who maintained the traditional cults.

In chapters 4, 5, and 6, we shall consider the persecution of some of medieval and early modern Christendom's supposed internal enemies: Jews, heretics, and witches. Jews were for centuries safeguarded by secular and ecclesiastical authorities, for theologians argued that it was God's will that they survive as a distinct people. From the late eleventh century, their position became more vulnerable as traditional protections were abandoned. Religious fervour associated with crusading, intellectual trends that questioned Jewish humanity, and an escalating popular stigmatisation fuelled massacre and exile. In the Iberian Peninsula, emerging notions of 'blood purity' saw anti-Jewish prejudice mutate from a religious to a pseudo-biological prejudice that extended to Christians of Jewish descent. This was one strand in the evolution of ideologies of race.

At much the same time as the position of Europe's Jewish communities became more precarious, other groups, prominently those accused of heresy, also became targets of persecution. Indeed, the medievalist Robert Moore has argued that this era saw the 'rise of persecuting society', shaped to extend the authority of an emerging class of clerical bureaucrats and the Church and sovereigns they served. This created a legacy of the systematic persecution of minorities that has endured until our own times.[21] Chapter 5 will focus on the most notorious episode of the war on heresy: the Albigensian Crusade (1209–1229). While acknowledging the manifold material interests that contributed to the conflict, it will be argued here that the spiritual challenge of heresy to orthodox religion was very real. The peculiar cruelty associated with the war was underpinned by the already well-entrenched belief that persecution could be 'righteous'.[22]

During the final stages of the Albigensian Crusade, legally innovative inquisitorial procedures were developed to identify and prosecute alleged heretics. This saw the accused denounced and condemned on hearsay, denied established due process and, from 1252, subject to the 'vexation' of the body: torture. The subsequent adoption of such procedures by secular courts was one factor that allowed the early modern witch-hunts to claim so many victims, the subject of Chapter 6. Yet the context of those procedures must be understood. Medieval scepticism towards the reality of witchcraft and magic had given way in many to a dogmatic and murderous delusion that took the lives of 60,000 people, 1428–1782. While the pattern of this persecution was marked by strong regional variations and varying degrees of intensity over time, the potential for the hunts existed because of the emergence within Europe of a novel belief in the early fifteenth century: the emergence of a Satanic conspiracy of heretical witches, dedicated to the overthrow of Christendom, who wrought genuine harm through malevolent magic.

The nature of the witch-hunts was often inflected by stereotypes around gender. Not all the victims were women. Yet the overall profile of those accused is suggestive of how deeply rooted cultural stereotypes about the inherent characteristics of certain groups shape persecution. The assumption that weak and licentious women were naturally more susceptible to the wiles of Satan made them, according to Jean Bodin's calculations, fifty times more likely than men to commit witchcraft. And thus 75 per cent of those executed for witchcraft were women.[23]

Race, the subject of Chapter 7, is another particularly powerful example of such deeply rooted stereotyping. Although it is tempting to see ideologies of race as essentially modern legitimisations of the political and economic basis of plantation slavery and colonialism, it will be argued here that their origins are to be found in antiquity and the medieval world. 'Proto-racial' ideologies can be discerned in the habit of relating environment to (inheritable) national characteristics; in the symbolic meanings that were attached to skin pigmentation; in notions of innate nobility, blood descent, and purity; in the customary belief in the inherently servile nature of sub-Saharan Africans shared across Judaism, Islam, and Christianity, and perpetuated by the practice of slavery in North Africa and the Mediterranean littoral. The ideological foundations of the Atlantic slave system's brutal labour regime were laid long before Columbus set foot in the Americas and ushered in Europe's age of overseas empires.

In the final three chapters, we look at modern genocides, firstly in the context of settler colonialism, then within the Russian, Soviet and Ottoman empires. The final chapter will chronicle the Holocaust, the destruction of European Jewry.

The relationship between European overseas colonialism and genocide is a contentious one. Here it will be argued that the mass mortality of indigenous populations that invariably accompanied settler colonialism was not simply an unfortunate corollary of the spread of novel diseases. Epidemics took hold in intentionally inflicted circumstances that left targeted populations vulnerable: armed conflict, dispossession, destruction of crops, enslavement. Warfare in the context of settler colonialism was frequently conducted with an especial brutality. Established European norms around the fate of prisoners and the treatment of non-combatants, for example, were often laid aside. Ironically, this moral regression would ultimately rebound onto Europe. The most ruthless tools of colonialism, such as the concentration camp, or the targeting of disloyal populations for extirpation, would be adopted by the authoritarian and totalitarian regimes that shaped the continent's murderous twentieth century.

Europe's overseas empires were not the only laboratories for twentieth-century patterns of persecution and genocide. In 1864, two million Circassians were subjected to massacre and expulsion from their Caucasian homelands (contemporaries wrote of a land that had been 'dispeopled') by the Russian authorities.[24] The Russian Empire and its Soviet successor state would thereafter repeatedly engage in the violent demographic engineering of loyal populations, especially in border and frontier regions. Massacre, forced migration, political repression, and punitive manipulation of food supplies in periods of famine became the means by which paranoid regimes responded to largely imaginary threats to their security. The tsarist emphasis on 'Russification' gave way for some years to a Marxist-Leninist stress on purging supposed counter-revolutionary elements. Yet, after 1933, it would again be non-Russian populations – Ukrainians, Kalmyks, Volga Germans, Tartars, Chechens – that once again became the objects of a murderous suspicion.

The rise of ethno-nationalism proved a similar dynamic inside the Ottoman Empire. The governing mechanisms that had once facilitated co-existence within a multi-ethnic, multi-faith empire broke down in the latter decades of the nineteenth century. Subject peoples sought equal political rights or even greater autonomy, threatening the integrity of the empire. Predatory 'great powers', posing as the protectors of minority rights, circled menacingly. Territory was lost to war. Millions of Muslim Ottoman subjects were driven from their homes in the Balkans and the Caucasus. *Ittihadism* (unionism), the exclusionary and nationalist ideology of the 'Young Turks', emerged in this atmosphere of existential crisis. The empire's subject Christian populations – Armenians, Assyrians, Orthodox Greeks – were subject to political repression, massacre and ultimately, during the First World War, to genocide.

The Turkish republic that emerged from the ordeal of that global conflict proved remarkably successful in challenging the post-war order envisaged by the victorious allied powers. At Lausanne in 1923, it won grudging international acceptance of borders achieved by massacre and population expulsion. This created a dangerous precedent for other revisionist powers, notably Nazi Germany. Genocidal potential was inherent in the 25-point programme issue by Hitler's *Nationalsozialistische Deutsche Arbeiterpartei* in February 1920. This was a potent mix of *Völkisch* ethno-nationalism, radical antisemitism, and a commitment to the revanchist re-drawing of eastern European borders on putatively racial lines. Chapter 10 charts the development of the Holocaust. It considers the transition from the 'cold pogrom' of the 1930s, designed to drive German Jews from their homeland, to the waging of annihilatory racial warfare within the broader context of the second global conflict.[25] The Holocaust became the paradigmatic genocide of the twentieth century.

The definition of 'genocide' remains a particularly contentious issue. It is, first and foremost, a legal term. Raphaël Lemkin, the Polish lawyer who coined the word in 1944, subsequently worked with two other international legal scholars, the Romanian Vespasian V. Pella, and the Frenchman Henri Donnediue de Vabres, to formulate the United Nations Convention on Genocide, adopted in 1948:[26]

> In the present Convention, genocide means any of the following acts committed with intent to destroy, in whole or in part, a national, ethnical, racial or religious group, as such:
>
> 1. Killing members of the group;
> 2. Causing serious bodily or mental harm to members of the group;
> 3. Deliberately inflicting on the group conditions of life calculated to bring about its physical destruction in whole or in part;
> 4. Imposing measures intended to prevent births within the group;
> 5. Forcibly transferring children of the group to another group.

This definition has been criticised as being, on the one hand, too narrow. It excluded political or social groups, thereby creating a legal 'blind spot' for the annihilation of, for example, 'kulaks' (an allegedly reactionary, wealthy peasant class) in the Soviet Union.[27] On the other hand, elements of the definition, such as 'causing serious bodily or mental harm to members of the group', are very broad and widely applicable. That raises the risk of rendering the word 'genocide', as Michael Ignatieff has suggested, 'worn and debased, casually hurled at every outrage, every violence, even applied to events where no death ... occurs'.[28]

During the 1990s, against a backdrop of war crimes trials arising from the break-up of Yugoslavia (1991–1995) and the genocide in Rwanda (1994), international criminal law underwent significant developments. William Schabas noted that the 'atrophied concept of crimes against humanity emerged as the best legal tool to address atrocities', while the crime of genocide 'remains essentially reserved for the clearest cases of physical destruction of national, ethnic, racial or religious groups'.[29] Some have urged that historians should adopt a similarly focused and precise definition. Steven T. Katz has advocated a stringent definition of genocide as 'an intentional action aimed at the complete physical eradication of a people'.[30]

While the case for this kind of precision in the use of the word is strong, it also raises problems. Historians must reckon with the *longue durée*. A focus on mass killing may confine the use of the word 'genocide' to specific events occurring within a narrow chronological span. This may not fully reflect the fate of a targeted group. For example, indigenous peoples such as the Pequot of Massachusetts were victims of annihilatory massacres during the initial phases of colonisation. The scattered survivors, and their children, were then enslaved, exiled, or subject to forced assimilationist policies. The destruction of the Pequot thus involved both physical massacres intended to eliminate them and subsequent measures towards survivors (and succeeding generations) that aimed to ensure they had no future as a distinct people. Genocide could be an attritional process, extending over time.[31]

Lemkin himself understood genocide to have had two phases. In the first, the 'national pattern' of the oppressed group was destroyed. In the second phase, the 'national pattern' of the oppressor was imposed, either on a territory and those portions of the oppressed allowed to remain, or on land denuded of its original inhabitants and settled by colonists.[32] Historians would do well to retain this insight. The definition of genocide employed in this book will, therefore, be based upon Lemkin's conception as expressed in the 1948 UN Convention, but extended to include political and social groups. It will also draw on the notion of genocide as a process. In the first stage, this is marked by mass murder, or by 'deliberately inflicting on the group conditions of life calculated to bring about its physical destruction in whole or in part'. Thereafter genocides have proceeded by measures to complete 'the disintegration of the political and social institutions, of culture, language, national feelings, religion, and the economic existence' of targeted groups.[33]

It is necessary to make these qualifications to the 1948 definition. Indeed, A. Dirk Moses has argued forcefully that the very concept of genocide itself is problematic. Lemkin suggested that he had recognised a recurrent, if hitherto nameless, historical phenomenon. Moses, however, has argued that genocide is a highly contingent artifice born of the circumstances of the Second World War. The Holocaust serves as its functional archetype. The conceptual triumph of the idea of genocide, symbolised by the 1948 Convention, supplanted older and, in many respects broader and more versatile, formulations such as 'crimes against humanity'. By so doing, it created a hierarchy of international criminality, in which genocide stands as the 'crime of crimes'. This has created a potentially more permissive environment for other offences against civilians which attract less odium. They may even be justified tendentiously as 'military necessity', for example within a putative counter-insurgency campaign, or as political in intent and, thus, outside the legal definition of genocide.[34]

The concept of genocide, de-politicised and narrowly understood as primarily driven by irrational racial or ethnic hatreds, therefore occludes a range of other culpable acts of persecutory political or strategic mass violence against non-combatants: mass internment, indiscriminate aerial bombardment, partition and forced deportations, starvation through blockade, elimination of suspect political or cultural groups. In place of genocide, Moses thus proposes criminalising such 'permanent security' measures. These have arisen when fearful and paranoid authorities held a group 'collectively guilty and attacked [it] pre-emptively ... as a potential security risk', one that is therefore eliminated '*in toto* for reasons of state'.[35]

Here, the problem of genocide will be addressed by broadening the scope of the concept to include political and social groups and by considering it in its close relationship to the related concept of persecution. Although the subject of persecution has been of abiding interest to historians, they have shown less concern for offering a precise definition than international lawyers and human rights activists. The word is used in the 1951 United Nations Convention Relating to the Status of Refugees, which stipulates 'a well foundered fear of persecution' as a necessary condition for eligibility for refugee status. Yet the convention includes no definition. This, inevitably, has led to some debate.[36] Perhaps the most useful attempt to meet the need for a clear definition has been made by the legal scholar Jaakko Kuosmanen. He has argued that persecution is best understood as the 'simultaneous occurrence' of three core components: 'asymmetrical and systemic threat, severe and sustained harm, and unjust discriminatory targeting'.[37]

This suggestion works well historically. 'Asymmetrical and systemic threat' conveys the necessary disparity between the powerful and the vulnerable, and the control by the former of the means of initiating widespread ('systemic') persecution, such as the courts or policing institutions or simple preponderance in armed force. 'Severe and sustained harm' creates a threshold of torments above prejudice, discrimination, or harassment: imprisonment, destruction of livelihood, torture, execution, massacre, forced deportation. Such severe harms, or the threat thereof, are relentless; the persecuted lack the basic security over time 'to live a minimally decent life'.[38] 'Unjust and discriminatory targeting' highlights the delineation of persons or groups to be subject to harm on account of characteristics over which they have little or no control: race, ethnicity, nationality, class, gender, sexual orientation, religious or philosophical affiliation, and political beliefs. The latter categories might be disguised or disowned publicly. Yet they are at the core of many individuals' psychological being, and their substance is thus hard to abandon. Besides, as the relentless pursuit of 'crypto-Jews' in fifteenth-century Spain or 'counter-revolutionaries' in Stalin's USSR demonstrates, for some groups conformity, feigned or sincere, has been no safeguard against persecution.

As Kuosmanen notes, it is the simultaneous occurrence of all three components that gives persecution its distinct character. Thus, for example, Christians in the Roman Empire before 313 CE, Jews in medieval Europe, or Armenians in the nineteenth-century Ottoman Empire were vulnerable minorities, often the subject of unjust and discriminatory treatment. Yet they were persecuted only during those episodes when they were also subjected to severe and sustained harm. The circumstances in which this dangerous combination occurs defy easy categorisation. Highly centralised states have often proved particularly effective agents of persecution, because of the resources and institutions they can bring to bear against the target group. Yet weak states have proved generative of persecution too. Along the violent frontiers of far-flung empires, on plantations where the enslaver's word was law, in distant provinces where the sovereign was but a name, wayward local authorities, or even the popular hostility of the mob, could drive persecution.

Genocide fits squarely into this schema; all three of Kuosmanen's core components have been present in episodes of genocide. In broad terms, genocide is distinguishable from other forms of persecution in the matter of intent. *Génocidaires* seek to destroy their target. Other persecutors have pursued a range of objectives: to discipline and punish, to unify, to govern, to dispossess, to enslave, even ostensibly (in the case of some 'righteous persecutors') to save those they target. Yet studying varying instances of persecution together reminds the historian that maintaining such sharp and clear definitional distinctions can prove difficult. Persecution occurs in a complex and shifting historical landscape, between a desire to forge conformity and a desire to annihilate, through which we can chart a twisted path from the amphitheatres to Auschwitz.

Notes

1 Theodore Parker, 'On the Culture of the Religious Powers', *The Collected Works of Theodore Parker*, Volume 2, edited by Frances Power Cobbe (London: Trübner & Co., 1863), p.48.

2 Martin Luther King Jr., 'Where Do We Go from Here?', 16 August 1967, https://kinginstitute.stanford.edu/where-do-we-go-here [Accessed 17/08/2023].

3 Steven M. Studebaker, *A Pentecostal Political Theology for American Renewal: Spirit of the Kingdoms, Citizens of the Cities* (New York: Palgrave Macmillan, 2016), pp.202–203.

4 See, for example, Wenxian Zhang, 'Standing Up Against Racial Discrimination: Progressive Americans and the Chinese Exclusion Act in the Late Nineteenth Century', *Phylon*, 56 (2019), p.27.

5 Samantha Power, *A Problem from Hell: America and the Age of Genocide* (New York: Basic Books, 2002).

6 Donald Bloxham, *History & Morality* (Oxford: Oxford University Press, 2020), p.235.

7 Jean Bodin, *The Six Books of a Common-Weale*, translated by Richard Knolles (London: Adam Islip impensis G. Bishop, 1606), pp.42–44.

8 Quoted in H.C. Lea (ed.), *Materials Toward a History of Witchcraft* (Philadelphia: University of Philadelphia Press, 1939), p.573.

9 Tamar Herziz, 'Witchcraft Prosecutions in Italy', in Brian P. Levack (ed.), *Oxford Handbook of Witchcraft* (Oxford, Oxford University Press, 2013), pp.249–267; Friedrich Spee von Langenfeld, *Cautio Criminalis, or a Book of Witch Trials*, translated by Marcus Hellyer (Charlottesville: University of Virginia Press, 2003).

10 Robin Blackburn, *The Making of New World Slavery from the Baroque to the Modern, 1492–1800* (London: Verso: 1997), p.61; David Brion Davis, *The Problem of Slavery in Western Culture* (Oxford: Oxford University Press, 1966), pp.108–114.

11 William Palmer, 'Fables of Conquest: Moral Regression in the Early Modern English State and Empire', *Journal for Early Modern Cultural Studies*, 19 (2019), pp.162–198.

12 Quoted in Michael Hirsh, 'If America Grappled Honestly with their History, Would Any Monuments be Left Standing?' *Foreign Policy*, https://foreignpolicy.com/2020/06/24/america-statues-monuments-washington-jefferson/ [accessed 19 August 2023].

13 Allen Buchanan and Russell Powell, 'Toward a Naturalistic Theory of Moral Progress', *Ethics*, 126 (2016), p.1003.

14 Nico Voigtländer and Hans-Joachim Voth, 'Persecution Perpetuated: The Medieval Origins of Anti-Semitic Violence in Nazi Germany', *Quarterly Journal of Economics*, 127 (2012), pp.1339–1392.

15 Gay L. Byron, *Symbolic Blackness and Ethnic Difference in Early Christian Literature* (London: Routledge, 2002); Geraldine Heng, *The Invention of Race in the European Middle Ages* (Cambridge: Cambridge University Press, 2018).

16 Noel D. Johnson and Mark Koyama, *Persecution and Toleration: The Long Road to Religious Freedom* (Cambridge, Cambridge University Press, 2019), pp.60–64.

17 Daniel Power, 'Who Went on the Albigensian Crusade?', *English Historical Review*, 128 (2013), p.1075.

18 Mark Gregory Pegg, *A Most Holy War: The Albigensian Crusade and the Battle for Christendom* (Oxford: Oxford University Press, 2008), p.188.

19 The established literature on post-World War II genocide is extensive. For overviews, see Adam Jones, *Genocide: A Comprehensive Introduction* (New York, NY: Routledge, 2023); Ben Kiernan, *Blood and Soil: A World History of Genocide and Extermination from Sparta to Darfur* (New Haven, CT: Yale University Press, 2007); Samuel Totten and William S. Parsons (eds), *Century of Genocide: Critical Essays and Eyewitness Accounts* (London: Routledge 1997); Benjamin A. Valentino, *Final Solutions: Mass Killing and Genocide in the 20th Century* (Ithaca, NY: Cornell University Press, 2004).

20 St Augustine, Letter 93.8, *The Works of St Augustine: Letters 1–99*, translated by Roland Teske, edited by John Rotelle (New York: New City Press, 2001), p.382; Letter 138.2, quoted in Herbert Deane, *The Political and Social Ideas of St Augustine* (New York: Columbia University Press, 1963), p.165. See also Gillian Clark, 'Desires of the Hangman: Augustine on Legitimized Violence', in H.A. Drake (ed.), *Violence in Late Antiquity* (Aldershot: Ashgate, 2006), pp.137–146.

21 Robert Moore, *The Formation of a Persecuting Society* (Oxford: Blackwell, 2007).

22 Christine Caldwell Ames, *Righteous Persecution: Inquisition, Dominicans and Christianity in the Middle Ages* (Philadelphia: University of Pennsylvania Press, 2009).

23 Lyndal Roper, *Witch Craze: Terror and Fantasy in Baroque Germany* (New Haven, CT: Yale University Press, 2004), pp.17–18; Alison Rowlands, 'Witchcraft and Gender in Early Modern Europe', in Brian Levack (ed.), *The Oxford Handbook of Witchcraft in Early Modern Europe and Colonial America* (Oxford: Oxford University Press, 2013), p.449.

24 'Fate of the Circassians', *The Examiner*, No. 2942, 8 June 1864, p.1.

25 George J. Walmer, 'German Fury: The Old Roots of the New German Nationalism', *The Sewanee Review*, 42 (1934), p.37.

26 Dominik J. Schaller and Jürgen Zimmerer (eds), 'Introduction', *The Origins of Genocide – Raphaël Lemkin as a Historian of Mass Violence* (London: Routledge: 2009), p.5.

27 Beth Van Schaack, 'The Crime of Political Genocide: Repairing the Genocide Convention's Blind Spot', *Yale Law Journal*, 106 (1997), pp.2259–2291.

28 Michael Ignatieff, quoted in Barbara Green, 'Stalinist Terror and the Question of Genocide', in Alan S. Rosenbaum (ed.), *Is the Holocaust Unique?* (Boulder, CO: Westview Press, 1995), p.171.

29 William A Schabas, 'The Law and Genocide', in Donald Bloxham and A. Dirk Moses (eds), *The Oxford Handbook of Genocide Studies* (Oxford: Oxford University Press, 2010), pp.123–141

30 Steven T. Katz, 'The Pequot War Reconsidered', *The New England Quarterly*, 64 (1991), p.213.

31 Michael Freeman, 'Puritans and Pequots: The Question of Genocide', *The New England Quarterly*, 68 (1995), pp.278–293.

32 Raphaël Lemkin, *Axis Rule in Occupied Europe: Laws of Occupation, Analysis of Government, Proposals for Redress* (New York: Columbia University Press, 1944), p.79

33 Lemkin, *Axis Rule in Occupied Europe*, p.79.

34 A. Dirk Moses, *The Problems of Genocide: Permanent Security and the Language of Transgression* (Cambridge: Cambridge University Press, 2021), pp.25–26, pp.201–239.

35 Moses, *Problems of Genocide*, pp.274–275, 511.

36 For discussion, see Jacqueline Bhabha, 'Boundaries in the Field of Human Rights: International Gatekeepers? The Tension between Asylum Advocacy and Human Rights', *Harvard Human Rights Journal*, 15 (2002), pp.155–181; Stephen B. Young, 'Who is a Refugee? A Theory of Persecution', *In Defense of the Alien*, 5 (1982), pp. 38–52.

37 Jaakko Kuosmanen, 'What's So Special About Persecution?', *Ethical Theory and Moral Practice*, 17 (2014), pp.129–140.

38 Kuosmanen, 'What's So Special About Persecution?', p.135.

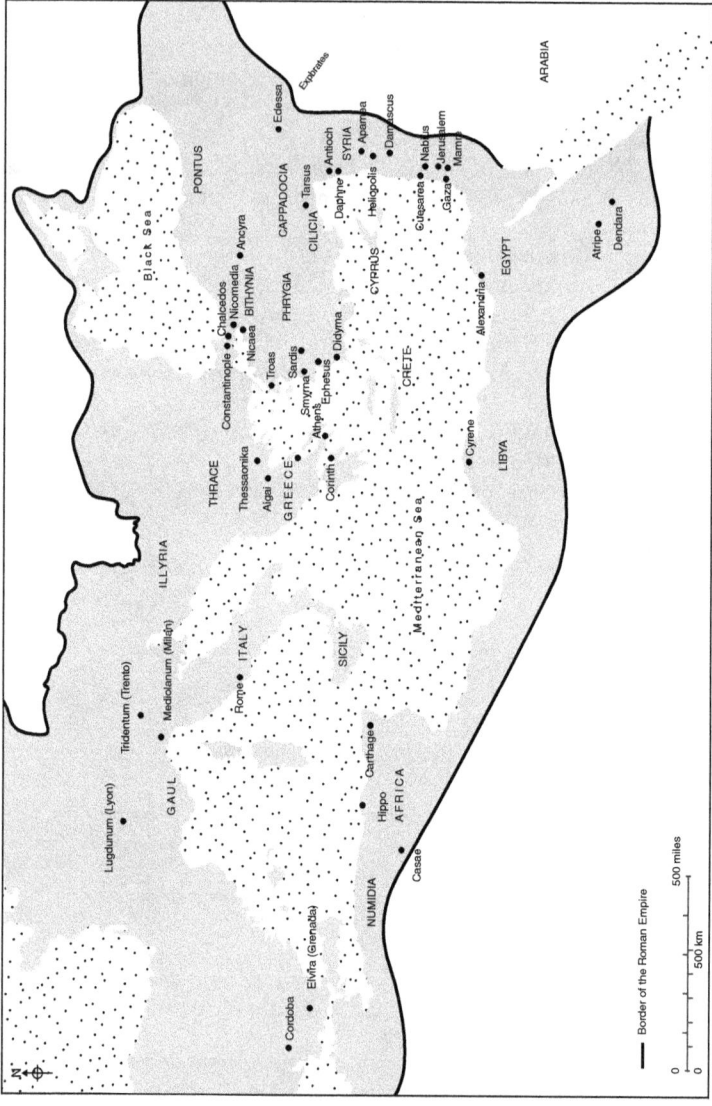

Map 1.1 Early Christianity and the Roman Empire.

1 'Your Cruelty Is Our Glory'

The Roman Persecution of Christians, 64–313 CE

In one of the most memorable passages bequeathed to us by a Roman author, the historian Suetonius wrote how, as a great fire consumed Rome in the year 64 CE, the emperor Nero had watched the conflagration from a tower. Delighting in 'the beauty of the flames' and, inspired by the spectacle before him, he sang lustily of the fall of Troy. According to Suetonius, however, this was really the least culpable aspect of the emperor's behaviour, for 'as if he were upset by the ugliness of the old buildings and the narrow and twisting streets', it was Nero who had set fire to the city in the first place.[1]

Whether the allegation was true or not was, ultimately, of less importance than the fact that so many believed it to be so. Tacitus, generally regarded as Rome's most gifted historian, had also heard talk of Nero's responsibility for the catastrophe. He was driven, it was said, by his desire to found a new imperial city, bearing his own name. Yet Tacitus himself dismissed this charge as a 'nasty rumour' and pointed to the 'emperor's largesse' in caring for refugees, compensating property owners for lost buildings and giving grants to those engaged in rebuilding the devastated city. Nonetheless, reports continued to circulate of mysterious men who had been seen setting the fires and fanning the flames that had raged for six days and seven nights. These, the people whispered, were surely Nero's hirelings. Neither the emperor's charity nor his pious appeasement of the deities Vulcan, Ceres, Proserpina, and Juno (whose disfavour seemed manifest in the scale of the disaster) could put a stop to the circulation of these damaging tales. According to Tacitus, 'to dispel the gossip Nero therefore found culprits on whom he inflicted the most exotic punishments'.[2]

If the allegation is true, then Nero selected these unfortunate scapegoats wisely, choosing to divert blame for the alleged arson onto a small, obscure, and friendless religious sect only recently established in Rome but against whom popular sentiment was already evident. They belonged to a novel and foreign cult, a 'pernicious superstition' associated with magic and doom-laden prophecies that drew people away from the proper worship of their ancestral gods and time-honoured rituals.[3]

DOI: 10.4324/9781003494331-2

Ugly gossip swirled around them: they met in secret to commit crimes that Tacitus and his compatriots regarded as *flagitia* (particularly shameful offences), including *maleficium* (wrongdoing wrought through magic), ritual infant sacrifice, cannibalism, and incest. They were, supposedly, atheists who believed malevolent demons not gods inhabited the city's temples. They withdrew from civil life, disdaining sacrifice, refusing to swear oaths or pay homage to local deities, activities that were central to the maintenance of the social fabric in Roman cities. Their beliefs were sanctified neither by history nor custom. The founder of their sect was a common criminal, crucified just a few years before, during the reign of Tiberius. They preyed on the gullible, especially women, the poor, and slaves, and encouraged them to despise life and revel in a cult of death that joyfully preached the imminent end of the world. They were troublemakers, fire-starters, obstinate and unbending. They were, according to Tacitus, 'those whom the common people call Christians'. That dark constellation of distortions and untruths formed the basis of a powerful stereotype that shaped wider society's attitudes towards Christians for almost three centuries: they were dangerous, anti-social *hostes humani generis* (enemies of mankind), and therefore deserving of persecution.[4]

The fate of those unfortunate Christians of Rome arrested by Nero still has the power to horrify: 'covered with hides of wild beasts, they perished by being torn to pieces by dogs; or they would be fastened to crosses and, when daylight had gone, burned to provide lighting at night'. The emperor opened his own gardens to the public for these grim spectacles, provided circus entertainments to accompany the executions and, characteristic of his taste for theatricality, strolled amiably among the plebeian crowds dressed as a charioteer. In the end, 'guilty though these people were and deserving exemplary punishment, pity for them began to well up because it was felt that they were being exterminated not for the public good, but to gratify one man's cruelty'.[5]

Yet, if compassion for the victims of Nero's cruelty eventually brought this episode to a conclusion, a fearsome precedent seemed to have been set. Almost 150 years later, the North African church father Tertullian (*c.*160–*c.*225 CE) was writing at a time of renewed violence against those who shared his faith. He tried to shame the local Roman authorities by pointing out that it was that most despised of emperors who had initiated the persecutions: 'consult your histories; you will there find that Nero was the first who assailed with the imperial sword the Christian sect … '. He noted, too, that 'under Nero [Christianity] was ruthlessly condemned … Now, although every other institution which existed under Nero has been destroyed, yet this of ours has firmly remained … '.[6]

Tertullian was not content with simply associating the persecutors with the hated Nero. He taunted them with the unshakable faith of their victims. They faced execution with an unflinching courage, even though they could easily have saved themselves through a simple act of sacrifice to an idol.

Neither public humiliation nor appalling physical suffering could compel these martyrs to deny their devotion to the risen Christ and commit idolatry. For Christians, the objective in their struggles in the torture chambers and the arenas was clear. Their enemies sought not, primarily, to kill them but to force them to renounce their faith. Faithfulness unto death was thus victory over persecution. As Tertullian defiantly proclaimed to those who tormented Christians, 'your cruelty is our glory ... the oftener we are mown down by you, the more in number we grow; the blood of Christians is seed'.[7]

The first great Christian historian Eusebius, bishop of Caesarea (c.260–339 CE), placed a similar stress on persecution and martyrdom as central to the experience of the early Church. He organised his account of the nascent religion's first three centuries around the 'widespread, bitter, and recurrent campaigns launched by unbelievers against the divine message'. These campaigns persisted until the edict of toleration issued by the emperor Constantine in 313 CE.[8]

Yet modern historians have been more circumspect. Theodor Mommsen established that there had been no specific law against Christianity. Persecution of Christians had been sporadic and localised for the first two hundred years of the Church's existence. Only in the third century did imperial policy result in empire-wide persecution of Christians. Later historians, such as A.N. Sherwin-White and G.E.M. de Ste. Croix, built upon Mommsen's insights. They emphasised the significance of regional authority. They pointed to the operation of the Roman judicial process of *cognitio extra ordinaria*, investigations outside the common law. These allowed governors in the provinces, having assumed the delegated authority of the emperor himself, to act as magistrates, taking responsibility for legal cases. They summoned the accused to court, conducted the trials and handed down judgments without recourse to established legal formalities. The extent of persecution of Christians, therefore, was largely dependent on the attitudes of these provincial Roman officials. Other scholars, such as W.H.C. Frend and Joyce Salisbury, have also stressed that Christians were not merely passive victims of persecution but were intransigent in the face of demands for religious compromise and even actively inclined to provoke and seek martyrdom. In the eyes of the authorities, their very obstinacy merited punishment.[9]

Although Tertullian blamed Nero for establishing the warrant for persecution in 64 CE, hostility towards the sect was already well established by then. The negative stereotype of Christians was forged initially from its association with radical Judaism. Persecution, in this sense, had a political root. In this view, Jesus had been a felon, rightfully executed on the authority of the Roman governor Pontius Pilate. Jesus had emerged from Galilee, an unhappy region that bred bandits and rebels. He had taught that the establishment of God's kingdom on earth was imminent and would supplant earthly empires. He himself had overturned the money changers' tables in the Temple courtyard in Jerusalem. He numbered a known Zealot (Jewish nationalist insurgent), Simon Zelotes, among his closest followers.[10]

After his crucifixion, his disciples maintained this politically charged posture and thus continued to be viewed as a threat to the Romans and the local elites through whom they ruled: the Temple authorities in Jerusalem and the Judaean client-king Herod Agrippa. Peter and the other apostles had declared within the Temple precinct, 'We must obey God rather than any human authority'.[11] The apostle Stephen was eventually dragged by a mob from a confrontation with the High Priest Caiaphas and stoned to death. Sometime later, around 40 CE, at just the time that the label 'Christian' was gaining currency, 'King Herod [Agrippa] laid violent hands upon some who belonged to the Church ... [and] had James, the brother of John, killed with the sword'.[12]

For a few years, the strong association of Christianity with political disloyalty and civic disorder would be reinforced by the proselytising activities of itinerant apostles. These stirred up dissension both within Jewish communities and between Jewish communities and their neighbours, wherever they preached. They travelled through a fractious world; its population ethnically and religiously diverse but culturally dominated by the Greeks and politically by the Romans. The example of Paul is instructive. As he visited synagogues on his travels, he clashed repeatedly with the local Jewish authorities. His attitude towards gentile converts, who he assured were not obliged to follow the Mosaic Law, gave the appearance of apostasy on his own part. Furthermore, Paul loudly dismissed the rites of the wider polytheist communities as 'worthless things', thus jeopardising the (generally uneasy) civic peace between Jews, Greeks, and Romans in eastern cities. The reaction was predictable and brutal: 'Five times I have received from the Jews the forty lashes minus one. Three times I was beaten with rods. Once I received a stoning'.[13]

Yet the challenge to authority posed by the first followers of Jesus would soon dissipate. The sect moved away from its radical, rural Galilean roots and won converts among gentiles and imperial-minded, urban, Greek-speaking Jews. It reached Rome by about the year 50 CE.[14] Most early Christian writing portrayed the Messiah as a pacific figure whose kingdom was otherworldly. He was no rebel, these accounts suggested. He had died the innocent victim of the Jewish Temple authorities and the Jerusalem mob, rather than of earthly Roman justice.[15] The apostle Paul, himself a Roman citizen, urged his co-religionists to loyalty to empire: 'let every person be subject to the governing authorities; for there is no authority except from God, and those authorities that exist have been instituted by God. Therefore whoever resists authority resists what God has appointed'.[16]

He also echoed socially conservative Greco-Roman assumptions concerning patriarchy and hierarchy: 'I want you to understand that Christ is the head of every man, and the husband is the head of his wife'.[17] Later Christian writers would continue to stress their place within established Roman society. Tertullian, for example, lamented that Christians should ever 'be denied the name of Roman'. He emphasised their profound sense of social obligation: 'We are the same to emperors as to our ordinary neighbours. For we are equally forbidden to wish ill, to do ill, to speak ill, to think ill, of all men'.[18] Thus, neither socially nor politically did Christianity pose any explicit threat to order, peace, or tax collection, the three priorities of Roman colonial administrators.

Nor was Christian monotheism, often widely perceived as the root cause of their persecution, necessarily an insurmountable obstacle to coexistence with polytheistic neighbours. Christianity's break with Judaism was neither swift nor clean. Indeed, we should speak of Christianities in this era, rather than Christianity. The small Jewish movement that had once centred on the figure of Jesus developed along several diverging trajectories in the decades that followed his crucifixion. It is likely, for example, that Jewish-Christian communities (observant of the Mosaic Law but accepting Jesus as the Messiah) survived in Rome's eastern provinces until the coming of Islam in the seventh century. Even in the western provinces, there is strong evidence for close and harmonious relations between some Jewish and Christian communities into the fourth century, with individuals attending both church and synagogue.[19]

Nonetheless, an alternative current, culturally Hellenic, drawing converts from gentile communities, and characterised by an increasingly Judaeophobic tone, was also developing by an early date, being apparent (and strongly reinforced) by the destruction of the Temple in Jerusalem at the climax of the Judaean revolt against Rome in 70 CE.[20] This current itself was far from unitary. One element would, eventually, emerge as hegemonic and claim legitimacy as being both catholic (universal) and orthodox (right-thinking). Alternative traditions would be branded heretical, from the Greek word for 'choice', but signifying, in this instance, the wrong choice. Yet the varied strands of this broad current did share a movement away from Jewish roots and towards syncretism with Greco-Roman belief systems. This much is apparent in the first verses of the Gospel of John: 'In the beginning was the Word, and the Word was with God … And the Word became flesh'.[21]

John was the last to be written of what would eventually become the canonical gospels, probably composed in the final decade of the first century CE. It differed both in narrative detail and in Christology from the three synoptic gospels of Matthew, Mark, and Luke, which drew on an earlier, now lost, common source. The Jesus of the synoptic gospels was essentially a charismatic prophet, healer, miracle worker, and holy man from Galilee, preaching the imminent establishment of God's kingdom on earth. He was, thus, a very Jewish figure. The Christ of John was an eternal and universal saviour, the temporarily fleshly incarnation of God's eternal creative 'Word' (or 'reason' – in the original Greek, the term is logos). As an emanation from the supreme God, he could be easily understood within the Hellenist and, consequently Roman, philosophical traditions.[22]

Many Romans inclined to a particular form of polytheism that we can term 'henotheism': belief in a supreme god (usually Jupiter), from whom all emanated and who presided over a pantheon of lesser supernatural beings.

For some, the many and diverse deities found in the world were simply different aspects or facets of the one pre-eminent god. A similar intellectual framework was being incorporated into nascent Christianity by the end of the first century, notwithstanding its putative monotheism. Indeed, the boundaries between henotheism (sometimes referred to as 'soft monotheism') and monotheism were, and in some respects still are, very blurred. Many practising monotheists also posit the existence of a range of supernatural beings subordinate to the supreme deity: angels, saints capable of intercession or, on the other hand, demons and devils.[23]

As it spread throughout the Mediterranean world, early Christianity developed within that spiritual grey area of overlapping henotheism and monotheism. This space was also occupied by an increasing number of other Romans and Greeks who favoured the worship of 'a single, remote, and abstract deity in preference to the anthropomorphic figures' of conventional mythologies.[24] Indeed one can detect very suggestive congruent lines of thought. Sometime around 210 CE, Tertullian wrote an early defence of Trinitarian doctrine, which he described as 'the mystery ... which distributes the Unity into a Trinity, placing in their order the three persons – the Father, the Son and the Holy Ghost'. In Rome, in 244 CE, the philosopher Plotinus established a Neo-Platonist school that posited the cosmological doctrine of three hypostases: the one ultimate source from which all emanates, a creative reason (word or *logos*), and a divine spirit that was active in the realms of thought and the material world.[25]

Thus, we can see how Christianity developed as a Hellenised eastern cult, based upon a cosmology that might have been easily fully incorporated into Greco-Roman *religio* (by which is meant a broad sense of the divine and of human obligations towards it). In the second century, some Christian teachers, notably Valentinus and Basilides, began to attach especial significance to *gnosis* – esoteric, mystical knowledge of God and destiny – revealed only to members of their particular sects. They abandoned strict monotheism, believing that the corrupt and sinful material world was the creation of a lesser god, a demiurge, derived by a series of emanations from the supreme, and purely good, divine being. Marcion, teaching in 140 CE, also rejected strict monotheism. He regarded the creator God of the Old Testament as the demiurge, while the God of the New Testament was the pure and benevolent supreme deity. He believed that the Christian Church was not the inheritor of the Jewish tradition, but had become infected with Jewish ideas. He rejected the Old Testament wholesale and accepted as canonical only ten of the Epistles of St Paul and an edited version of Luke's gospel, stripped of its most explicitly Jewish elements.[26]

Marcion was excommunicated by the Church in Rome in 144 CE and those whose ideas developed in similar ways were, similarly, deemed heretical. It is tempting, therefore, to regard them as aberrations from the development of a mainstream of resolutely monotheistic Christian thought. However, bearing in mind the extent to which the Pauline Church was also shaped by

Greco-Roman philosophy, and the long internal debates it endured about the precise nature of Christ's divinity and the (subordinate?) relationship of the Son to the Father, it might be suggested that Marcion and the Gnostics merely represented the advance guard of Christianity's march into the henotheistic Roman pantheon. Yet that march was never completed. Most Christians remained monotheists, perceived as unbending outsiders to true *religio* and thus a potential source of threat.

Indeed, despite the growing commonalties, the boundaries between Christianity and Roman *religio* were drawn with ever greater clarity. This ensured that Christians continued to be subject to periodic bouts of persecution. Whatever their social, political, or theological views, their unsavoury reputation endured, and they continued to be, as Tacitus explained, 'people hated for their shameful offences'.[27]

In one respect, Christian behaviour may have contributed to perpetuating this reputation. As the early Church developed, it was often riven by intense personal rivalries, arguments over internal structures, and competition for leadership. There is some evidence that Christians occasionally denounced other Christians to the authorities, in pursuit of these prosaic internal quarrels. One early second-century martyr, Ignatius, Patriarch of Antioch, appears to have been betrayed to the Roman authorities by members of his own community. It is striking that Celsus, a second-century philosopher and critic of Christianity, sneered at the early Church as 'a colony of bats coming forth from a lair, or frogs sitting in council around a swamp, or worms holding an assembly in a corner of filth, arguing with one another about which of them are of worse character'.[28]

Such unseemly disputes can only have reinforced the suspicions many Romans felt towards novel cults and religious innovations. The sociologist of religion Bryan Wilson has explored the peculiar social and political tensions created by new religious movements. He has noted that pre-modern societies have characteristically 'ordered their affairs with reference to the past' and thus 'tradition becomes the touchstone, ensuring the wisdom and safety of particular arrangements'.[29] This observation is true, to an especial degree, of the Romans. The historian Dio Cassius (*c.*150–235 CE) urged his readers:

> Those who attempt to distort our religion with strange rites you should abhor and punish not merely for the sake of the gods (for if a man despises these he will not pay honour to any other being), but because such men by bringing in new divinities in the place of the old, persuade many to adopt foreign practices from which spring up conspiracies, factions and cabals ... .[30]

The connection Dio Cassius made between religious practice and political factionalism should not surprise us. A profound sense of divine immanence permeated the Roman world. Ritual activity around a multitude of altars, shrines, and sacred idols dominated public and private activities and shaped the geography of cities and the rhythm of lives. The author Livy once reminded his compatriots:

> ... our city owed its foundation to augury [divination of the will of the gods] ... There is no place in it that is not filled with religious associations and divine power. There are as many dates for religious ceremonies as there are places in which they are performed.[31]

Adherence to ancient rites underpinned what Romans understood as *pax deorum*: the 'peace of the gods'. Through honouring their sacred obligations, Romans won the favour of the deities who ensured that crops would flourish and that the people of the empire would be spared catastrophe. Religious deviation threatened that favour. Maximin Daia, a fourth-century persecutor of Christians, justified his actions to the people of the port city of Tyre by reminding them of a series of recent wars, earthquakes, floods, and storms: 'And all of them happened at once as a result of the fatal error implicit in the empty folly of these immoral people, when it enslaved their minds and by its shameful deeds came near to making the entire world suffer'.[32]

For the statesman and lawyer Cicero, Roman society itself would collapse without traditional piety: 'if reverence for the gods is removed, trust and the social bond between men and the uniquely pre-eminent virtue of justice will disappear'.[33]

This does not mean that Roman *religio* was incapable of change but that change had to be rooted in tradition and with respect paid to established deities. For example, the Romans effectively colonised the spiritual world of conquered peoples either by syncretism, in which native deities were equated with their own familiar gods and goddesses, or by ritually appropriating them, as was the case with Cybele (also known as *Magna Mater*, 'the Great Mother'), a goddess long worshipped across Asia Minor. The goddess, immanent within a sacred stone, was physically transported to Rome by the Senate in 205 BCE so she might aid the city in its war with Carthage. Her cult was enduringly popular for centuries, but was safely Romanised, for citizens were forbidden from worshipping her in the ecstatic native 'Phrygian' style. Roman law-makers took a particularly dim view of the self-castration, in emulation of her consort Attis, practised by the cult's priests, the *galli*.[34]

In contrast, when new or foreign cults began to flourish outside the bounds of traditional *religio*, they were derided as *superstitio*. This term signified the irrational credulity of their adherents, their alien origins, their association with excess and immorality, and their potential for fostering political subversion. Such cults were occasionally subject to brutal suppression. In 186 BCE, the Senate had acted against the cult of Bacchus, a Greek god, known also to the Romans as Dionysus. The Bacchanalia was denounced as a *coniuratio* (a conspiracy based on oath-taking), allegedly led by assorted foreigners (Greeks, northern Italians, and other immigrant groups), who sought to ensnare respectable young Roman men and women in a web of sexual excess, fraud, and murder. Some 7,000 individuals were identified as belonging to the conspiracy. Arrests and trials followed; 'more were put to death than were imprisoned'.[35]

Secretive, foreign, novel Christianity, too, was associated with similar *flagitia*, especially shocking offences: sorcery, sexual debauchery, incest, cannibalism, and ritual human sacrifice. Historians such as Henry Chadwick have implied that such allegations were specific to Christians, probably arising from misunderstood talk about universal love and the Eucharist.[36] Yet the similarities with the supposed offences of the Bacchants suggests instead that there was a long-standing trope of religious transgression that was deployed and re-deployed against suspect emerging cults, provoking persecution. Indeed, Celsus drew quite explicit parallels between the 'irrational' beliefs of various sectaries. He linked Christians with the frenzied devotees of the eastern gods Mithras and Sabazius, and with those who skulked about in graveyards and at crossroads at night invoking Hecate, the dark goddess of magic and incantation.[37]

Given time, it was not impossible for a *superstitio* to acquire a degree of respectability and find a place within proper *religio*. During the politically unstable years of the 50s BCE, another foreign cult, that of the Egyptian goddess Isis, had been suppressed in Rome. Yet, in 43 CE, the emperor Claudius himself would inaugurate a temple dedicated to Isis on Rome's sacred Campus Martius. Evidence from the 'Villa of the Mysteries' in Pompeii is suggestive of the worship of Bacchus/Dionysus in 50–60 CE.[38]

There were, however, obstacles to Christianity's acceptance, beyond the ill-repute of its adherents. Bacchus, Isis, Serapis, and Mithras may have been foreign, but all had established pedigrees. For a people who 'ordered their affairs with reference to the past', this was an important qualification. To Roman eyes, Christianity lacked the legitimacy conferred by tradition. Indeed, Christianity appeared to be apostasy from Judaism. Roman and Greek attitudes towards Judaism as a faith were complex. In the cities of the eastern Mediterranean, local ethnic conflict frequently manifested itself as a clash between Jewish monotheism and Hellenic polytheism. Popular prejudice aside, however, imperial policy was tolerant of the practice of Judaism by those who were born Jews, and characteristically respectful of its antiquity.[39] Christians tried to lay claim to that antiquity as the inheritors of the Jewish tradition. Yet the continued survival of an extensive Jewish population still faithful to the Mosaic Law (perhaps numbering six million in the second century) suggested that the ancient tradition was still strong. Christians appeared to have abandoned the Law of Moses and, unforgivably in Roman eyes, turned their backs on the past.[40]

Christianity was not simply rootless in time. It had no specific link to a particular city or nation either. Romans accepted religious diversity as a manifestation of the divine will that different peoples worship according to their own distinct rites. Yet Christianity was a proselytising faith that won converts from all communities, with no ethnic basis. Furthermore, it was an exclusive form of worship; one could worship Isis and still do reverence to the other gods. Christianity demanded that adherents not merely accepted Christ but, perforce, deny the traditional gods of their people as well. The internal organisation of the Church, based around the authority of bishops, created an alternative and disruptive focus of social loyalties. Similarly, proselytising sometimes created problems for Judaism too. In short, foreign rites and *superstitio* might be tolerated when practised by others. However, the Romans regarded the abandonment of one's own gods as an action tantamount to treason, particularly if the converts were drawn from the wealthy and the high-ranking. The emperor Domitian (r.81–96 CE) appears to have been drawn into a conflict with the monotheistic faiths over precisely thus issue. He executed his cousin Flavius Clemens and his wife Flavia for 'atheism'. The historian Dio Cassius was clear that this charge was levelled at those 'who were drifting into Jewish ways'.[41]

During the first two centuries of its existence, therefore, Christianity existed, in the eyes of most Romans as a *superstitio*: a disreputable novel belief system that took people away from the proper forms of reverence towards their time-honoured deities. As such, it was the object of considerable popular hostility for this behaviour, as we have noted, endangered the *pax deorum*. Christians failed to fulfil ritual obligations towards the gods and joyfully prophesised an imminent and fiery end to the world, as evidenced in the late first-century Book of Revelation. They thus seemed to invite divine retribution onto the hapless communities that sheltered them. This made them obvious scapegoats for natural disasters. Tertullian had long noted this tendency, lamenting that 'if the Tiber rises as high as the city walls, if the Nile does not send its waters up over the fields, if the heavens give no rain, if there is an earthquake, if there is famine or pestilence, straightway the cry is "Away with the Christians to the Lion!"'[42]

Popular prejudice aside, however, the attitude of imperial authority during this early period was marked by an overriding concern for the maintenance of law and order in the provinces, not the suppression of religious dissidents. This was made clear in a famous exchange of letters in c.110–112 CE, between Pliny the Younger, then governor of Bithynia (in modern Turkey), and the emperor Trajan. Pliny sought advice on how he should treat those denounced to him as Christians. Bithynia was, at the time, plagued by both the activities of clandestine political societies and a worrying falling away of religious observance and sacrifice, for which local temple authorities were quick to blame Christians. Pliny acted decisively to deal with both issues.

For those who confessed the name of Christian and who refused, when asked three times in succession, to renounce their faith (signified by cursing Christ and making offerings to the gods and an idol of the emperor), the punishment had been death. Yet the number of the accused was growing. The governor admitted he knew of no legal precedent for dealing with them. That they met before dawn in secretive gatherings he acknowledged, but he clearly did not associate them with the fractious political groups he was busy suppressing. He tortured two Christian enslaved women ('deaconesses' in the Church) and found no evidence supporting allegations of *flagitia*. Those who clung doggedly to their superstition he executed without compulsion: 'for I was in no doubt, whatever it was they were confessing, that their obstinacy and their inflexible stubbornness should at any rate be punished'. He was puzzled as to how he should treat lapsed Christians and what further action he should take in response to the anonymous denunciations of others.

Trajan reassured Pliny that the actions he had taken were correct and instructed him that those who had lapsed or were prepared to renounce their beliefs were to be freed. In future, he was to ignore anonymous denunciations of Christians. They were to be punished if they came before him and would not bend in the obstinate profession of their faith, but he was not to seek them out.[43]

To the extent that there was a coherent imperial policy towards Christians before 249 CE, Trajan's rescript to Pliny fairly summed it up. His successor Hadrian (r.117–138 CE) would largely echo its tone in his rescript to Minucius Fundanus, governor of Asia, who sought legal advice in response to mob violence against Christians:

> [I]f the provincials can so clearly establish their case against the Christians that they can sustain it in a court of law, let them resort to this procedure only, and not rely on petitions or mere clamour ... But if anyone starts such proceedings in the hope of financial reward, then for goodness sake arrest him for his shabby trick and see that he gets his deserts.[44]

Not every governor was scrupulous in heeding such advice and, thus, the most savage outbreaks of persecution appear to have occurred episodically, on occasions when pliant local authority could be swayed by popular hostility towards Christians. A bloody outbreak occurred at Lugdunum (modern Lyons), in the province of Gaul, in 177 CE, during the reign of Marcus Aurelius. Eusebius described how the Christians were subjected to an escalating degree of social prejudice: '[we were] debarred from houses, baths, and the forum'. Exclusion soon turned to crowd violence: 'noisy abuse, blows, dragging along the ground, plundering, stoning, imprisonment, and everything that an infuriated mob does to hated enemies'. Rather than act against the mob, the provincial governor ordered soldiers from the local garrison to arrest the (non-Christian) slaves of some of the accused and coerced them into alleging incest and cannibalism against their masters. Word of these accusations quickly spread as rumour, that most powerful ally of prejudice, was deployed to chilling effect. The violence was now cloaked in a sense of moral outrage: 'people all raged like wild beasts against us, so that even those who because of blood-relationship had previously exercised restraint now turned on us, grinding their teeth with fury'.[45]

A veneer of legal procedure was then brought to bear to give legitimacy to shedding of blood. Initially, Christians were dragged before the tribune who commanded the local garrison and the city magistrates. Later, the provincial governor himself presided over the examinations. Those who confessed the name of Christian were tortured, to force them to abandon their faith, to extract further confessions of having committed criminal offences or, indeed, in the expectation that they would die from their injuries, thus avoiding the necessity of demonstrating their guilt of any crime. Some succumbed and denied Christ, others endured. Blandina, an enslaved woman subjected to appalling and prolonged torture, would simply utter the words 'I am a Christian: we do nothing to be ashamed of'.[46]

The governor, having sought instructions from the emperor, eventually received letters broadly repeating the rescripts of Trajan and Hadrian. Those who had recanted were to be freed. Of those who clung stubbornly to their faith, the Roman citizens were to be beheaded and the rest thrown to the wild beasts in the city's amphitheatre. Organised as a grotesque public spectacle, the executions combined the passing of the death sentence with the further humiliation and prior torture of the victims. Two, Sanctus and Maturus, 'were again taken through the whole series of punishments', running a gauntlet of whips and enduring 'every torment that the frenzied mob howled for' before being forced into an iron chair, heated over a fire, '[w]hich roasted their flesh and suffocated them with the reek'. The fury of the crowd was not abated even by the deaths of their victims. They refused to allow the burial of the dead, who numbered over forty. For six days, the corpses were subjected to 'insult and the open sky', before being burned to ashes and dumped in the Rhône.[47]

Such episodes demonstrate how Christianity's dark and threatening reputation sustained a hostile popular sentiment against them. Yet this was usually constrained by the authorities. Violent persecution was comparatively rare and never extensive enough to threaten the existence of Christianity. The church in Lugdunum survived this attack, just as the church in Smyrna weathered a similar incident the previous decade, even though they had lost their spiritual leader, the 86-year-old Bishop Polycarp. Three years after the deaths of the 'Gallic Martyrs', 12 Christians were executed in Scillium, North Africa. The circumstances were familiar. They confessed the name of Christ and refused to partake in local civic religious ceremonies. Yet the North African Church continued to thrive.

However, we should not underestimate the significance of persecution and martyrdom in shaping a fundamental ideology that would reinforce Christians' sense of their own distinctness: the conviction that their lives were dedicated to an ongoing struggle against evil. We owe our knowledge of events at Lugdunum, and similar episodes of persecution, to the careful preservation of eyewitness testimonies: the *Acts of the Martyrs*. Such stories were preserved (and in some cases fabricated) because they exerted a powerful influence on early Christian congregations. They included the most graphic descriptions of the tortures inflicted upon the bodies of martyrs and yet asserted that their unconquerable faith had invariably defied scourges, flames, blades, and the claws and teeth of savage animals. The martyr (the word derived from the Greek for 'witness'), who voluntarily accepted suffering and death in this world in the expectation of a glorious afterlife, thus became an ideal type, as an example for all Christians, even in their everyday lives.[48]

This was true not least because the violence of the arena, while claiming only a tiny minority of Christian lives, was understood as a particularly dramatic manifestation of their conflict not with human enemies but with Satan, a struggle in which all Christians partook. Thus, the letters that the survivors of the Lugdunum congregation wrote are clear about who was responsible for their Church's plight: 'the adversary swooped upon us with all his might'. Their human persecutors were mere dupes 'ensnared by Satan'. Martyrs were soldiers for Christ who 'charged into the fight, standing up to every kind of abuse or punishment'.[49]

Whether they had personally experienced persecution or not, all of Christ's followers came to identify profoundly with the reality of that struggle against Satan and the demonic agents of his power on earth. Inevitably, this worldview also shaped their attitude towards the religious duties performed by their neighbours, who were not merely perceived as misguided but demonically inspired or possessed. As Tertullian wrote, 'You think that others [besides the one God], too, are gods, whom we know to be devils'. And it was through traditional ritual that these idol-dwelling devils waged war on righteousness:

> ... the principal crime of the human race, the highest guilt charged upon the world, the whole procuring cause of judgment, is idolatry ... the demons and the spirits of the angelic apostates would turn into idolatry all the elements ... in opposition to God.[50]

Elaine Pagels has noted that embracing Christianity meant '[taking] sides in a war that allows no neutral ground'.[51]

Such certainties created a barrier between the practice of Christianity and Rome's ancestral rites. Moreover, that barrier did not simply separate them from the altars of the 'heathens'. Christians distanced themselves socially too, striving to avoid any activity that might compromise their faith: 'will there be peace in [a Christian's] soul when there is eager strife there for a charioteer? And with his eye fixed on the bites of the bears and the sponge-nets of the net fighters, can he be moved by compassion?' Risking the censure that accompanied social isolation, they shunned the theatre, the racetrack, and the amphitheatre for reasons that echoed their refusal to sacrifice: 'how monstrous it is to go from God's Church to the devil's – from the sky to the sty'.[52]

This overwhelming personal commitment to struggle against Satan, combined with martyrdom's promise of posthumous fame and spiritual reward, made Christians unwilling to compromise in the face of compulsion and thus they risked the escalation of initially limited confrontations with the authorities into active and deadly persecution. Moreover, the courage (or, to their enemies, intransigence) displayed by Christians in the face of such persecution manifested itself, in some cases, not simply as a willingness to accept death but as a positive enthusiasm for martyrdom. The *Acts of the Martyrs* record instance after instance of confrontation between baffled and frustrated authority and joyful victims. Christian acceptance of their fate reinforced the grim impression of the early Church as a death cult. Arrius Antonius, a Roman governor of the province of Asia, was confronted by 'the whole Christians of the province in one united band', who 'presented themselves before his judgement seat' and loudly and insistently confessed the name of Christ. Having executed a number without having stifled the clamour, an exasperated Arrius finally declared 'You miserable wretches, if you want to die, you have cliffs to leap from and ropes to hang by'.[53]

The close relationship between suicide and voluntary martyrdom, that Arrius's ill-tempered remark highlighted, was a matter of fierce controversy within the Church itself. Yet it should be noted that even those who most strongly criticised voluntary martyrdom, such as Cyprian, Bishop of Carthage, nevertheless themselves could also accept death with a similar courage, if in a more stoic manner. St Cyprian died in the arena in 258 CE.

By then, Christian persecution had entered a new and foreboding phase, as the faith increasingly found itself in conflict with imperial policy. In 202 CE, the emperor Septimius Severus issued an edict hostile to both Judaism and Christianity. To a considerable degree, this edict followed established precedents. It was not an explicit attack on the practice of these belief systems by existing worshippers. It forbade conversion. It followed an unsettled period of domestic conflict between rival claimants to the throne. There had also been a foreign war with Rome's eastern neighbour Parthia (during which Judaeans were accused of disloyalty) and an outbreak of noisy, apocalyptic fervour among some Christian communities. These appear to have provoked localised outbreaks of persecution between the years 195–213 CE. In the emperor's native North Africa, the winning of high-status converts to Christianity may have been construed as a particular affront to the Greco-Egyptian god Serapis, of whom Severus himself was an adherent.[54]

The edict, therefore, might best be understood as a conventional attempt to restore the *pax deorum*. Yet historians such as Frend have stressed its essentially novel dimensions: it was, notionally, an empire-wide policy governing religious observance, setting a dangerous precedent for later emperors to follow during a century of increased centralisation of power and concomitant emphasis on loyalty and social cohesion, demonstrated through collective ritual activity. In practice, the Severian edict seemed to have the most adverse impact on Christianity. Indeed, Eusebius provides evidence that some Christians escaped persecution by conversion to Judaism, implying that the latter faith was not being targeted by provincial authorities.[55]

Yet, across the empire, in Alexandria, Corinth, Carthage, and in Rome itself, wealthy Christians were beaten, beheaded, burned, and thrown to the beasts in the arena. *The Acts of the Martyrs* provide telling evidence, too, of how the nature of persecution was gendered. High-status Christian women were subjected to sexual shaming in a sadistic and back-handed testimony to the Christian emphasis on chastity: in Alexandria, Potamiaena was threatened with rape at the hands of gladiators; in Carthage, Perpetua and Felicitas, who had very recently and very obviously just given birth, were initially thrown naked into the arena, an act that shocked even the jeering crowd that had gathered to watch them tortured and executed. Later in the century, we are told of Christian women sentenced by magistrates to be paraded naked in brothels.[56]

The Severian persecution, like those before it, was an episode of limited scope and duration, over by 203 CE. Localised attacks on Christians continued to take place in Africa and Asia. The emperor himself does not seem to have harboured personal animosity towards Christians. According to Tertullian, his infant son and heir Caracalla had a Christian wet-nurse and he found employment in his palace for a Christian steward, Proculus Torpaion, who had once cured him of some illness by anointing him with holy oils.[57] Yet the broader context of the persecution, the centralising and unifying tendencies of the imperial state in the third century, was one that continued to threaten Christian communities.

In 212 CE, Severus's son and successor, Caracalla, issued an edict that granted Roman citizenship to practically all free, male subjects of the empire. He explicitly justified this 'great and pious' act as an act of thanks and homage towards Rome's old and immortal gods. He thus linked citizenship with participation in civic ritual activity, inevitably setting Christianity at odds with Roman authority. Their position was more physically dangerous too. Caracalla's political drive for cohesion and uniformity was matched by an increase in the number of agencies of social control that continued after his death. The third century saw the growth of policing institutions throughout the empire and the consequently enhanced capacity for the Roman state to intrude into the lives of provincials. Christian communities now had to contend with the attention of garrison soldiers, night watchmen and the *diôgmitai* ('pursuers') employed by local *eirenarchs* (officials charged with keeping the peace).[58]

The very existence of these institutions almost certainly heightened the possibility of conflict between Christians and their neighbours. The act of policing communities would have focused attention on activities and gatherings that previously might hitherto have gone unremarked. The *Acts of Cyprian* recorded court proceedings of the mid-third century that indicate searches not only for bishops but for presbyters (church elders), as well as prohibitions on assemblies and on entering cemeteries. All were indicative of a more active and pervasive policing of daily life in Roman cities that generated persecution. Trajan's injunction to Pliny not to seek out Christians appears, a century on, to have become a dead letter.[59]

Indeed, the successive misfortunes that afflicted the empire during the third century, including civil wars, barbarian incursions in both east and west, plagues, and a protracted economic depression, created a peculiarly fertile environment for the persecution of a wayward, minority religious sect. Yet this was not simply a question of scapegoating. As Mark Levene has illustrated, empires in crisis grasp for unity in the face of disruption.[60] In the twentieth century, that unity was often defined by ethnicity or putative race. The Roman worldview demanded a unified ritual response to disaster. To be efficacious, this required the participation of *all* Romans, a category that, post-Caracalla, included all free Christians.

Furthermore, considering the increasing power that the emperor could now wield throughout the empire to compel participation in civic worship and to punish the recalcitrant, it becomes clear why the third century produced so many Christian martyrs. The danger to Christians was not constant; persecution remained sporadic. Yet now, whenever an emperor did choose actively to promote traditional religious obligations, his reach was long and his grasp tight. The stigmas of illegitimacy and misanthropy that clung to Christians in the eyes of their neighbours had political value in the cause of increasing the power of the imperial centre. The mid-century persecutions during the reigns of Decius and Valerian illustrate the point well.

The edict of Decius issued in late 249 CE required of all Roman subjects a specific cult act: blood sacrifice. It stipulated that they engage in sacrifice to their traditional gods (whoever they might be in their city or province); that they partake of the sacrificial meat, and that they swear that they had always sacrificed. Despite its apparent conservatism, J.B. Rives has pointed to two key religious innovations evident in Decian policy. Firstly, and indicative of the centralising tendencies of the third century, imperial authority was now being exercised over local and civic religious systems in the insistence that sacrifice was required. Secondly, individual participation was being demanded in collective acts of worships that, hitherto, had probably been easy enough to avoid. While belief systems and the precise deities being worshipped remained varied across the empire, the act of sacrifice itself could be universalised, effectively creating a unified Roman religion, and this may have been the emperor's motivation. Christians may not have been the specific target of this policy but were, perhaps, seen as symptomatic of a wider problem: the general decline of the act of sacrifice.[61]

Indeed, non-Christians may have suffered for their consciences under Decius too. There was a strong Roman philosophical tradition opposed to blood sacrifice, found, for example, in the works of Porphyry, who argued in favour of vegetarianism, and the poet Lucretius (*c.*94–55 BCE) who thought true piety did not require 'showering the altars with the blood of beasts'.[62] Yet, for a traditionalist such as Decius, the act was central to securing *pax deorum*. Two further elements of the Decian persecution linked it firmly to the growth in imperial authority. One is the employment of bureaucratic mechanisms to monitor compliance. Provincial census registers were used to determine who should sacrifice by especially appointed local commissions.

Once individuals had performed the requisite act before a magistrate, they were issued with a *libelli*, a papyrus certificate. The second is the use of policing institutions to identify and detain dissidents; the bishops of Rome and Antioch were arrested and subsequently executed within weeks of the edict's promulgation.[63]

Nevertheless, local circumstances still dictated enforcement of the edict and thus its impact on Christians who would not sacrifice was strikingly inconsistent. Some provincial officials were reluctant to punish those who refused to comply; they accepted bribes, or allowed a mere sprinkling of grain on an altar to pass for 'sacrifice'. Confessors – those who proclaimed their Christianity – were subject to a range of coercive devices: torture, confiscation of property, banishment, consignment to the mines, and prolonged detention in dark, filthy cells. Even within one city, the individual experiences of Christians could vary tremendously. Cyprian, Bishop of Carthage, was forced to flee and many of those who confessed their Christianity in that city were imprisoned and brutalised to coerce them into making a sacrifice. Yet, strangely, while they were detained, priests were allowed to visit them and celebrate Mass. The mob, however, showed less forbearance than the magistrates, and other Christians were stoned to death in the streets.[64]

The persecution itself, like those that had gone before, was limited in duration. Decius himself was killed in battle with the Goths in 251 CE. Cyprian was able to return to his home city and grapple with the problem of how those who had lapsed in the face of persecution should be reconciled to their faith. That problem would only be magnified by the revival of persecution in 257 CE by the emperor Valerian.

The Valerian persecution appears to have been more explicitly directed against Christians than its Decian forerunner. Yet it seems to have shared the same basic pious concern with universalising religious practice for the well-being of the empire. It placed a particularly strong emphasis on individual participation in cultic rites through acts of *supplicationes*, ritual adoration before altars and idols.[65] Valerian had been emperor since 253 CE but initially made no move against Christians. Then, in 257 CE, he issued an edict that compelled Church officials, bishops, priests, and deacons, to take some part in these rites.

This renewed concern with the empire-wide fulfilment of religious obligations was probably prompted by the escalating series of disastrous events that had convulsed the empire since Decius's death in battle. In the west, barbarian armies had raided into Italy, Dacia, and Greece. In the east, a revived Persian Empire under the Sassanid dynasty had captured the city of Dura-Europos. Rumours circulated that when the Goths had pushed into Pontus, on the southern coast of the Black Sea, in 255 CE, some local Christians had rallied to their standards, serving as guides and spies, and joining them in the looting of property. Ritual supplication to the gods, who seemed to be wavering in their support of Rome, and a clear demonstration of Christian loyalty, were thus required.[66]

This first edict (the exact words of which are lost) seemed, as was the case with the Decian precedent, designed to put pressure on Christians to conform to traditional rites without necessarily inflicting the harshest of punishments. Its focus was on the clergy, with the logic presumably being that congregations would soon follow their bishops to the altars, if the latter could be persuaded to sacrifice. Cyprian of Carthage, for example, was, in the first instance, arrested and detained but not executed. Yet others were not so fortunate; in Numidia, many Christian clergymen were condemned to the mines, and they would later be followed by ordinary Christians, men, women, and children. Conditions in the mines were appalling enough that such treatment was effectively a death sentence.[67]

These measures were not enough to satisfy the emperor, whose first efforts appear to have bred only frustration, for it appeared that few Christians had lapsed and offered sacrifices. In 258 CE, he issued a second edict, extending its reach to include all wealthy Christians. This edict may thus reflect the growing presence of Christians among the most influential sections of society and their success at limiting the impact of Valerian's initial measures against the Church. Now the state moved swiftly and brutally against its victims. Bishop Sixtus of Rome and four of his deacons were tracked down to the local catacombs and executed while the city prefects targeted their congregation, seizing property and killing clergy. In Carthage, Cyprian was tried before the proconsul Galerius Maximus, who sentenced the bishop to death, justifying his execution with these words:

> You have long lived an irreligious life, and have drawn together a number of men by an unlawful association, and professed yourself an open enemy to the gods and the religion of Rome; and the pious, most sacred and august Emperors, Valerian and Gallienus [his son] ... .[68]

Unlawful, hostile to the gods, and disloyal – these were the essential substance of the allegations against third-century Christianity and, as had been the case under Decius, the evidence suggests that the judicial procedures against high-ranking clergy and wealthy laymen and women escalated into more general massacres. Three hundred 'holy martyrs' are said to have been burned in a limekiln at Massa Candida, some thirty miles from Carthage, having refused to offer incense to Jupiter.[69]

The Valerian persecution ended in similar circumstances to that of Decius. The emperor was defeated in battle against the Persians and lived out his days as a slave of his enemy, Shapur I. His son Gallienus immediately ceased the persecution of Christians and restored all the property that had been seized from them. This act ushered in a four-decade long period of peace, prosperity and, very probably, successful growth through proselytising, for the Christian Church within the empire. It did not, however, mark the end of Christianity's conflict with the Roman state; the final, the most protracted, and bloodiest episode was yet to come: the Great Persecution of 303–313 CE instigated by the emperor Diocletian.

The central role of Diocletian in this persecution is a reminder of how significant the attitude of individual emperors towards the Church was in instigating persecution. Clearly not all emperors were hostile to Christianity. Nor did they all respond in the same way to the various crises they faced when in power, by demanding, on pain of punishment, that citizens return to traditional rites. The growth of the Roman state had left Christians vulnerable, but it was the active choice of particularly hostile emperors that filled the prisons and the torture chambers, fed the beasts in the arenas, seized property, and consigned the faithful to the executioner or to lingering deaths in the mines. In the cases of Septimius Severus, Decius, and Valerian, we may reconstruct the intent of their policies with some confidence. Yet the paucity of the surviving evidence allows for only speculation into the personal sentiments that shaped their religious preferences and guided their decision making. In the case of Diocletian, we have some highly suggestive accounts from contemporaries of a man conscious of the intervention of the gods in the material world and fearful of their disfavour. The persecution he initiated reminds us that terrible cruelty can be driven by devout and sincere (if unbending) sentiments of piety.

Proclaimed emperor by the army in 284 CE, Diocletian swiftly proved to be an energetic and determined reformer, imposing price controls, raising tax revenues, and fortifying border zones. He also sought to manage the burdensome responsibilities of ruling a far-flung empire by dividing imperial power between four men, the *tetrarchy*. He exercised personal rule in the eastern empire, while Maximian was installed as his co-ruler in the west. Both men took the title 'Augustus'. Each appointed a deputy, who took the title 'Caesar': Galerius in the east and Constantius in the west.[70]

Yet, such practical innovations aside, Diocletian's political and religious instincts were strongly traditional. Although publicly he exhibited no animus against Christians for the first 19 years of his reign, he shared with Decius and Valerian a commitment to the promotion of traditional deities and rites. As he reformed provincial administration so, too, he rebuilt temples and revived flagging cultic practices. Court ceremonials acquired increasingly sacred and ritual dimensions. Ancestral Roman virtues were promoted; coins carried the dedication 'To the Genius of the Roman People', and especial reverence was demanded towards Jupiter Optimus Maximus as the pre-eminent deity of proper *religio*. It was an atmosphere in which Christians were surely vulnerable even if, for almost two decades, they had been left in peace.[71]

Diocletian's willingness to persecute became manifest in 297 CE. The initial victims were not Christians but followers of the Persian religious teacher Mani (c.216–76 CE). His doctrine of a primeval struggle between light and darkness had proved attractive to many inside the Roman Empire and Manichaeans were particularly numerous in the Asian and African provinces.

Not simply foreign and novel, Manichaeism was strongly identified with Persia, Rome's great rival in the east with whom Diocletian was, at that very moment, at war. As W.H.C. Frend has observed, this successful proselytising creed was seen as an 'enemy assault under colour of religion'. The assault was met with the execution by fire of the cult's leaders, the burning of their scriptures, and condemnation of their followers to the mines. Yet this was not simply a war measure. The imperial edict that accompanied the persecution was a firm statement of the emperor's religious conservatism: '[I]t is the greatest crime to wish to undo what once has been fixed and established by antiquity and holds to its course and is possessed of proper status'.[72]

The precise trigger for the persecution of the Christians reflected Diocletian's personal awe of the gods and sensitivity to their active involvement in human affairs. Our closest witness to the emperor was Lactantius (c.250–c.325 CE), a Christian and teacher of rhetoric at the imperial court. He described how, at a public divination ceremony in Antioch, a priest had declared that the gods were refusing to make their will known because of the presence of profane individuals who had obstructed the rituals. The furious emperor had no trouble identifying the culprits: Christians in his own entourage who had crossed themselves during the ceremony. These he ordered to sacrifice or be scourged.[73]

This incident occurred against a background of escalating tension between the army (whose morale and cohesion were sustained by traditional religious rites) and Christians. Some Christians refused to serve at all, despite the military threats to the empire, reinforcing their reputation for disloyalty. Others, already serving in the army, refused to take part in ceremonial activity. The problem was particularly acute in the east, in areas under the authority of Galerius. At first, he merely forced the resignation of Christians from the legions. By 301 CE, his attitude had hardened. Eusebius of Caesarea, who lived through these days, recorded 'with the Christians in the army the persecution began'. A strong tradition suggests that among the victims was the martyr St George, possibly a soldier beheaded at Lydda in Palestine.[74]

There was already, at this time, an active intellectual challenge to Christianity under way, which some historians, such as Frend, have interpreted as a deliberate and influential propaganda campaign that prepared the ground for active persecution. This included some relatively crude devices, such as the Acts of Pilate, a fabricated account justifying the execution of Christ, which was apparently widely taught to schoolchildren in the east. More sophisticated was the work usually attributed to the formidable Neo-Platonist philosopher Porphyry. Through the scrupulous application of the methods of literary criticism, he highlighted inconsistencies and geographical inaccuracies in the scriptures, undermined some key prophetic literature and, while always respectful of the figure of Christ himself, portrayed the apostles and the evangelists as quarrelsome and unscrupulous forgers.[75]

Yet Diocletian himself, although enraged by what he saw as the impiety of Christians, and urged on by Galerius, was for some time hesitant to enact a general empire-wide persecution. Again, it was a personal religious experience that changed his mind. In February 303 CE, Lactantius tells us, the Oracle of Apollo at Didyma expressed hostility towards Christianity and this persuaded Diocletian to act. His first edicts ordered the destruction of churches, the burning of scripture, dismissal of high-ranking Christians from public service, and the arrest of bishops and priests, who could be pressured into making sacrifices before the altars. He also sought to strip Christians of legal protection for their persons and their property by requiring that anyone who presented themselves in the courts, as a plaintiff, defendant, or witness, make a sacrifice.[76]

The constancy of many Christians, manifest in their responses to these first edicts, was probably the chief dynamic in the subsequent and swift escalation of the persecution to include torture, execution, and massacre, eventually claiming perhaps 3,500 lives.[77] Eusebius records:

> ... when the edict against the Churches was issued at Nicomedia and posted up in a conspicuous place ... a well-known person, by worldly-standards of pre-eminence ... was so stirred up by religious enthusiasm and carried away by burning faith that he promptly seized it and tore it to sheds, as something unholy and utterly profane.

He was executed, and those who followed his example of defiance shared his fate. Imprisoned priests and bishops 'bore up heroically under horrible tortures'. The aim was always to secure participation in a rite of sacrifice; some of those who had been brutalised 'might be dragged a long way by [the] feet' and then 'forcibly propelled by others and brought to the disgusting, unholy sacrifice'. Not all proved strong; Eusebius was scornful of 'souls numbed with cowardice' who 'succumbed to the first onslaught'.[78]

It was in this sense, perhaps, that the persecutors enjoyed some success. Those who surrendered copies of the scriptures to be burned (termed *traditors*) or offered sacrifices often included high-ranking Church men. The legacy of their actions would be a source of bitter schism within the early Church long after the persecution itself was over. That many faltered is unsurprising; the escalation of the horror unleashed appalling savagery and sadism. Eusebius, who witnessed many of the martyrdoms himself, described Christians being crucified, thrown to the beasts of the arena, burned, beheaded, starved, and 'torn to bits from head to foot with potsherds like claws'. These actions continued 'year after year' and 'there were occasions when on a single day a hundred men as well as women and little children were killed'.[79]

Yet the persecutors' intent to coerce Christians to return to the 'institutions of the ancients' (as Galerius would one day express his motivation) manifestly failed. Although estimates of the proportion of the population that was Christian by 303 CE remain speculative (perhaps as high as 16 per cent), there were far too many to suppress through terror, execution, torture, or imprisonment. More tellingly, they seemed to have enjoyed a considerable measure of support from their neighbours and fellow citizens. Even the courts participated in protecting some Christians, such as where non-Christians were granted power of attorney to represent Christians legally and offered sacrifices on their behalf.[80] Popular prejudice had once been the central catalyst for persecution. It would now seem that popular sympathy at the local level, born perhaps of familiarity with long-established, peaceful Christian communities, and the general drift towards monotheism, was the central factor in ending it.

In the west, the persecution was largely limited to the closure of churches and the burning of scripture, and even these limited measures appeared to have effectively ended by 306 CE. In the east Diocletian, sick and weary, resigned in 305 CE, leaving Galerius and his 'Caesar', Maximin Daia, to pursue Christians with a renewed ferocity for a further six years. Yet in 311 CE, Galerius too, suffering a slow and protracted death from disease, acknowledged his failure and issued a proclamation ending the persecution. Crucially, this edict of toleration recognised Christian prayer for the well-being of the empire as a legitimate substitute for sacrifice, signalling that Christianity was no longer to be regarded as a dangerous *superstitio*.[81]

It would be in the west, however, that Christianity's future was determined. In 306 CE, Constantius, the Augustus of the west, had died in York. His soldiers had proclaimed his son Constantine as emperor. His religious beliefs had long inclined him to the worship of a supreme deity, and he had offered especial devotion at times to Apollo and then to Sol Invictus, the 'unconquerable sun'. In 312 CE, on the eve of the battle of Milvian Bridge, the contest that would secure his rule in Rome, one tradition recounts that he experienced a religious vision as he slept. The next morning, he ordered his soldiers to emblazon their shields with a Christogram. And it was to the Christian God that he subsequently attributed his ensuing victory.

The following year, 313 CE, Constantine met with Licinius, the Augustus of the east, in Milan. Together they issued an edict granting 'both to Christians and to all men the freedom to follow whatever religion each one wished'. The popular cultural shift from stigmatisation of Christians to broad sympathy underpinned the force of this edict. That was the essential prerequisite for the subsequent state adoption of Christianity. Yet the edict was of immense importance in signalling the new emperor's intent. Constantine did not merely tolerate Christianity; he actively promoted the faith that had brought him triumph. Licinius, on the other hand, soon stood accused of renewed persecution. Constantine returned to the field at the head of an army and, in 324 CE, won another resounding victory over his eastern rival, securing the empire both for himself and, ultimately, for Christianity.[82]

It was in Antioch that the disciples were first called 'Christians' some time around the year 40 CE. Specifically, they were called *Christiani*, 'followers of Christ', a Latin expression that tells us that the name was applied by the Roman colonial authorities. And it was meant 'in no friendly spirit'.[83] Emerging from Rome's volatile eastern provinces and initially associated with criminality and disloyalty, nascent Christianity quickly acquired an unwholesome reputation. Even as the faith moved away from its radical Judaean roots, to be shaped by wider Hellenic culture and cosmologies, that dark reputation endured. Christians were the subject of vile and shocking rumours, making them convenient scapegoats for (and to many pious individuals the actual cause of) fires, earthquakes, floods, and famines.

Their thirst for martyrdom and the apocalyptic content of their preaching combined with their refusal to offer reverence to gods they believed to be malevolent demons fostered their reputation for hating mankind. For their wary neighbours, these credulous adherents of an alien and novel superstition threatened both the bonds of civil society and *pax deorum*. Periodically popular hatred for the sect would erupt into violent, but localised, persecution. In the third century, emperors sought a greater degree of imperial cohesion through the forging of a unity Roman religion organised around practices such as blood sacrifice, judged by Christians to be idolatrous. They could not cooperate and thus persecution became empire wide.

Yet a parallel religious trend was quietly shaping the spiritual destiny of the empire too. A belief in the worship of a pre-eminent deity inclined the pious towards henotheism, if not monotheism. In the figure of Constantine, that tradition would be united with Christianity, ending the persecution, and ensuring for the Church not just peace but political patronage. How, then, would Christians wield power? And how would those polytheists, henotheists, and heretics whose practices they believed to be Satanically inspired, fare under that authority?

Notes

1 Suetonius, *The Lives of the Caesars*, Chapter 38, translated by Catherine Edwards (Oxford: Oxford University Press: 2008), p.217.

2 Tacitus, *The Annals*, Book 15, Chapters 38–44, translated by J.C. Yardley (Oxford: Oxford University Press, 2008), pp.356–360; cf. Brent Shaw, 'The Myth of the Neronian Persecutions', *Journal of Roman Studies*, 105 (2015), pp.73–100.

3 L.F. Janssen, '"*Superstitio*" and the Persecution of the Christians', *Vigiliae Christianae*, 33 (1979), pp.131–159.

4 Tacitus, *The Annals*, Chapter 44, p.360; David Shotter, *Nero* (Abingdon: Routledge, 2005), pp.59–60; Robert Louis Wilken, *The Christians as the Romans Saw Them* (New Haven, CT: Yale University Press, 2003), pp.17–21.

5 Tacitus, *The Annals*, Chapter 44, p.360.

6 Tertullian, *To the Nations*, Chapter 7; *To Scapula*, Chapter 5, in *The Ante-Nicene Fathers*, Volume III, translated and edited by Rev. Alexander Roberts, Sir James Donaldson and Arthur Cleveland Coxe (New York: Cosimo, 2007), pp.22, 107, 114.

7 Tertullian, *Apology*, Chapters 5, 50, in Roberts et al., *The Ante-Nicene Fathers*, p.55.

8 Eusebius, *The History of the Church from Christ to Constantine*, Book 1, Chapter 1, translated and edited by G.A. Williamson and Andrew Louth (London: Penguin, 1989), p.1.

9 G.E.M. de Ste. Croix, 'Why were the Early Christians Persecuted?', *Past and Present*, 26 (1963),pp. 6–38; W.H.C. Frend, *Martyrdom and Persecution in the Early Church* (London: James Clarke, 2008); A.N. Sherwin-White, 'The Early Persecutions and Roman Law Again', *Journal of Theology Studies*, 3 (1952), pp.199–213; Joyce Salisbury, *The Blood of Martyrs* (London: Routledge, 2004).

10 Luke VI:15. All Biblical quotations are from *The Bible: New Revised Standard Version*, Anglicised edition (Oxford: Oxford University Press, 1985); Allen Brent, *A Political History of Early Christianity* (London: T & T Clark, 2009), pp.1–31.

11 The Acts of the Apostles 5:29.

12 Acts 7:58–60; 12:2.

13 Acts 14:15; 2 Corinthians 11:24–25.

14 Bernard Green, *Christianity in Rome: The First Three Centuries* (London: T&T Clark, 2010), p.22.

15 S.G.F. Brandon, *The Trial of Jesus of Nazareth* (New York, NY: Dorset Press, 1988), pp.140–150; Geza Vermes, *The Passion* (London: Penguin, 2005), pp.118–119; Elaine Pagels, *The Origins of Satan: How Christians Demonised Jews, Pagans and Heretics* (New York: Vintage, 1996), pp.1–34.

16 Romans 13:1, 13:2.

17 1 Corinthians 11:2.

18 Tertullian, *Apology*, Chapter 36, pp.44–45.

19 Paula Fredriksen, 'What Parting of the Ways? Jews, Gentiles, and the Ancient Mediterranean City', in Adam Becker and Annette Yoshiko Reed (eds), *The Ways that Never Parted: Jews and Christians in Late Antiquity and the Early Middle Ages* (Minneapolis, MN: Fortress Press, 2007), pp.35–64. See also Daniel Boyarin, *Border Lines: The Partition of Judaeo-Christianity* (Philadelphia: University of Pennsylvania Press, 2006).

20 See James Dunn, *The Parting of the Ways between Christianity and Judaism and Their Significance for the Character of Christianity* (London: SCM Press, 2006).

21 John 1:1, 1:14.

22 See Geza Vermes, *Christian Beginnings from Nazareth to Nicaea AD 30–325* (London: Allen Lane, 2012), pp.115–133.

23 Anthony F.C. Wallace, *Religion: An Anthropological View* (New York: Random House, 1966), pp.71–73; Gillian Clark, *Christianity and Roman Society* (Cambridge: Cambridge University Press, 2004), Kindle edition, location 537.

24 Jan Bremmer, 'How Do We Explain the Quiet Demise of Graeco-Roman Religion? An Essay', *Numen*, 68 (2021), pp.230–271; Stephen Mitchell, 'The Cult of Theos Hypsistos between Pagans, Jews and Christians', in Polymnia Athanassiadi and Michael Frede (eds), *Pagan Monotheism in Late Antiquity* (Oxford: Oxford University Press, 2002), p.92.

25 Tertullian, *Against Praxeas*, Chapter II, p.598; Charles Freeman, *The Closing of the Western Mind: The Rise of Faith and the Fall of Reason* (London: Random House, 2002), pp.73–74.

26 M.J. Edwards, 'Gnostics and Valentinians in the Church Fathers', *Journal of Theological Studies*, 40 (1989), pp. 26–47; Einar Thomassen, 'Orthodoxy and Heresy in Second-Century Rome', *Harvard Theological Review*, 97 (2004), pp.241–256.

27 Tacitus, *The Annals*, Book 15, Chapter 44, p.360.

28 James Corke-Webster, 'By Whom Were Early Christians Persecuted?' *Past & Present*, Advanced article (2023), pp.25–32, 41 https://doi.org/10.1093/pastj/gtac 041. accessed 16 March 2024.

29 Bryan Wilson, *Religion in Sociological Perspective* (Oxford: Oxford University Press, 1982), p.121.

30 Quoted in Frend, *Martyrdom and Persecution*, p.117.

31 Livy, *The Rise of Rome*, Book 4, Chapter 52, translated by T.J. Luce (Oxford: Oxford University Press, 1998), p.337.

32 Eusebius, *The History of the Church*, Book 9, Chapter 7, p.288.

33 Cicero, *The Nature of the Gods*, Book 1, Chapter 4, translated by P.G. Nash (Oxford: Oxford University Press, 2008), p.4.

34 Clifford Ando, *The Matter of the Gods: Religion and the Roman Empire* (Berkeley: University of California Press, 2008), pp.25–26; Mary Beard, John North, and Simon Price, *Religions of Rome*, Volume 1 (Cambridge: Cambridge University Press, 1998), pp.164–165.

35 Livy, *The Dawn of the Roman Empires*, Books 31–40, Book 39, Chapters 8–19, translated by J.C. Yardley (Oxford: Oxford University Press, 2000), pp.429–441.

36 Henry Chadwick, *The Early Church* (London: Penguin, 1993), p.26.

37 Molly Whittaker, *Jews and Christians: Graeco-Roman Views* (Cambridge: Cambridge University Press, 1984), p.179.

38 Beard et al., *Religions of Rome*, pp.161–163; Christian R. Raschle, 'The Expulsion of Isis Worshippers and Astrologers from Rome in the Late Republic and Early Empire', in Jitse H.F. Dijkstra and Christian R. Raschle (eds), *Religious Violence in the Ancient World From Classical Athens to Late Antiquity* (Cambridge: Cambridge University Press, 2020), pp.87–105; Valerie Warrior, *Roman Religion* (Cambridge: Cambridge University Press, 2007), pp.79–92.

39 James S. McLaren, 'Jews and the Imperial Cult: From Augustus to Domitian', *Journal for the Study of the New Testament*, 27 (2005), pp.262–269; Peter Schäfer, *Judeophobia: Attitudes toward the Jews in the Ancient World* (Cambridge, MA: Harvard University Press, 1997), pp.136–160; Lee I.A. Levine, 'Judaism from the Destruction of Jerusalem to the end of the Second Jewish Revolt: 70–135 CE', in Hershal Shanks (ed.), *Christianity and Rabbinic Judaism* (Washington, DC: SPCK, 1993), pp.125–149.

40 Wilken, *The Christians as the Romans Saw Them*, pp.112–117.

41 John Gager, *The Origins of Anti-Semitism: Attitudes Toward Judaism in Christian and Pagan Antiquity* (Oxford: Oxford University Press, 1985), p.60.

42 Tertullian, *Apology*, Chapter 40, p.47.

43 Gaius Pliny to the emperor Trajan, late 111 (?) and Trajan to Pliny, late 111 (?), in Pliny the Younger, *Complete Letters*, Book Ten, 96 and 97, translated by P.G. Walsh (Oxford: Oxford University Press), 2009, pp.278–280.

44 Quoted in Eusebius, *History of the Church*, Book 4, Chapter 9, p.112.

45 Eusebius, *History of the Church*, Book 5, Chapter 1, pp.139–141.

46 Quoted in Eusebius, *History of the Church*, Book 5, Chapter 1, p.141.

47 Eusebius, *History of the Church*, Book 5, Chapter 1, pp.142–148.

48 G.W. Bowerstock, *Martyrdom and Rome* (Cambridge: Cambridge University Press, 1995); Daniel Boyarim, *Martyrdom and the Making of Christianity and Judaism* (Stanford, CA: Stanford University Press, 1999).

49 Eusebius, *History of the Church*, Book 5, Chapter 1, pp.139–148.

50 Tertullian, *To Scapula*, Chapter 2, p.105; *On Idolatry*, Chapters I and IV, pp.61–62.
51 Pagels, *Origins of Satan*, p.28.
52 Tertullian, *The Shows*, Chapter 25, pp.89–90.
53 Bowerstock, *Martyrdom and Rome*, pp.1, 59–74.
54 Frend, *Martyrdom and Persecution*, pp.320–322; J.G. Davies, 'Was the Devotion of Septimius Severus to Serapis the Cause of the Persecution of 202–3?', *Journal of Theological Studies*, 5 (1954), pp.73–76.
55 Eusebius, *History of the Church*, Book 6, Chapter 12, p.190.
56 Eusebius, *History of the Church*, Book 6, Chapter 3, pp.183–185; Herbert Musurillo (ed.), *The Acts of the Christian Martyrs* (Oxford: Clarendon Press, 1972), pp.107–131; Bowerstock, *Martyrdom and Rome*, pp.53–54.
57 Tertullian, *To Scapula*, Chapter 4, p.107.
58 Christopher J. Fuhrman, *Policing the Roman Empire: Soldiers, Administration and the Public Order* (Oxford: Oxford University Press, 2012), pp.164–168; Beard et al., *Religions of Rome*, p.241.
59 Reinhard Selinger, *The Mid-Third Century Persecutions of Decius and Valerian* (Frankfurt am Main: Peter Lang, 2004), p.85.
60 Mark Levene, 'Why Is the Twentieth Century the Century of Genocide?', *Journal of World History*, 11 (2000), p.320.
61 J.B. Rives, 'The Decree of Decius and the Religion of Empire', *Journal of Roman Studies*, 89 (1999), pp.135–154; J.B. Rives, 'Animal Sacrifice and the Roman Persecution of Christians (Second to Third Centuries)', in Dijkstra and Raschle (eds), *Religious Violence in the Ancient World*, pp.177–202.
62 Beard et. al., *Religions of Rome*, p.278; Warrior, *Roman Religion*, p.23.
63 Rives, 'The Decree of Decius and the Religion of Empire', pp.135–154.
64 Selinger, *The Mid-Third Century Persecutions of Decius and Valerian*, pp.77–78.
65 Christopher J. Haas, 'Imperial Religious Policy and Valerian's Persecution of the Church, AD 257–260', in Everett Ferguson (ed.), *Church and State in the Early Church* (New York: Garland, 1993), pp.155–166.
66 Frend, *Martyrdom and Persecution*, pp.423–425.
67 Selinger, *The Mid-Third Century Persecutions*, pp.83–89.
68 Quoted in Frend, *Martyrdom and Persecution*, p.427
69 Selinger, *The Mid-Third Century Persecutions*, pp.83–93. Frend, *Martyrdom and Persecution*, pp.427–428.
70 Robert Louis Wilken, *The First Thousand Years: A Global History of Christianity* (New Haven, CT: Yale University Press, 2012), p.76
71 Frend, *Martyrdom and Persecution*, pp.477–480; Beard et al., *Religions of Rome*, pp.241–242.
72 Frend, *Martyrdom and Persecution*, pp.478, 488.
73 P.S. Davies, 'The Origins and Purpose of the Persecution of AD 303', *Journal of Theological Studies*, 40 (1989), p.90.
74 Henry Summerson, 'George (*d. c.*303?)', *Oxford Dictionary of National Biography*, Oxford University Press, 2004; online edn, May 2010 www.oxford dnb.com/view/article/60304, accessed 24 March 2013.
75 Wilken, *The Christians as the Romans saw Them*, pp.126–163.
76 Frend, *Martyrdom and Persecution*, p.491.
77 Frend, *Martyrdom and Persecution*, p.537.

78 Eusebius, *History of the Church*, Book 8, Chapters 6–16, p.261.
79 Eusebius, *History of the Church*, Book 8, Chapters 2–16, pp.258–277.
80 Rodney Stark, *The Rise of Christianity* (New York: Harper Collins, 1997), p.13.
81 Wilken, *The First Thousand Years*, pp.80–81.
82 Paul Stephenson, *Constantine: Unconquered Emperor, Christian Victor* (London: Quarus, 2009), pp.113–190.
83 Acts 11:26; Diarmaid MacCulloch, *A History of Christianity* (London: Penguin, 2010), p.110.

2 'More Ruthless Than the Tyrant, More Bloody Than the Executioner'

Christianising the Roman Empire and Forging a Theory of Persecution, 313 CE–*c.*430 CE

Early in the third century, the African church father Tertullian urged upon Scapula, proconsul of the Roman province of Africa and persecutor of Christians, the view that

> … it is a fundamental human right, a privilege of nature, that every man should worship according to his own convictions: one man's religion neither harms nor helps another man. It is assuredly no part of religion to compel religion – to which free-will and not force should lead us.[1]

One hundred years later, in 313 CE, the eastern emperor Licinius and his western counterpart, and recent convert to Christianity, Constantine met in Milan and transformed Tertullian's admirable sentiment into imperial policy. The circular Licinius subsequently issued to his provincial governors granted 'both to Christians and to all men the freedom to follow whatever religion each one wished, in order that whatever divinity there is in the seat of heaven may be appeased and made propitious'.[2]

For Christians, the Edict of Milan is justly celebrated as marking a pivotal moment in their history, signifying the end of imperial persecution, and ushering in an age of peace for the faithful and growing influence for the Church. And yet, despite its provision that 'all men' should be at liberty to follow whatever religion they wished, the edict is not celebrated as a pivotal moment in the establishment of freedom of worship. This is hardly surprising. Gaze forward one hundred years from 313 CE and one sees the temples in ruins, the idols smashed, and the religious liberties of both non-Christians and dissident Christians drastically curtailed by law. In the streets of riot-torn cities and on the floors of temples and churches alike, the blood of believers and unbelievers had freely flowed. Seemingly, persecution in the name of a universal faith had triumphed over the true promise of Milan.

For some, such an outcome seemed inevitable. Steeped in the notion of an ongoing cosmic battle against evil and profoundly influenced by the combative martyr tradition forged before 313 CE, Christian authors have, for centuries, portrayed the history of the early Church as a bitter contest with

DOI: 10.4324/9781003494331-3

'a dying paganism' in which Christians were locked in 'a death struggle in which heathenism should be worsted'.[3] The ascendancy gained in the fourth century was, thus, merely the righteous and triumphant culmination of the battles fought by Christ's martyred soldiers in Roman arenas.

Even academic historians more sympathetic to Greco-Roman religious traditions and less inclined to an uncritical acceptance of Christian triumphalism have often shared a similar perspective. The adherents of an exclusive monotheistic faith, who conceived of themselves as warring against the forces of Satan, would, once they had achieved political power, inevitably fight their battle to a victorious conclusion. For Arnaldo Momigliano, the fourth century thus witnessed a clear-cut contest between paganism and Christianity, as political and spiritual loyalties were effectively merged: 'in religious terms one can easily see that Christianity was bound to insist on the parallelism between the unity of the empire and the unity of the Christian Church'.[4] Similarly Dennis Groh has commented on memories of martyrdoms during the Diocletian persecution 'sealing the fate' of all other religions in the empire: '[Christians] adopted a "never again" attitude ... and, when the opportunity arose, sought to make Christianity the only legally permitted religion'.[5]

This interpretation is undoubtedly correct to stress the role of the twin ideologies of martyrdom and cosmic struggle in shaping the attitudes of some Christian towards others in the fourth century and, thus, in fostering persecution. However, it also rather overestimates how influential those ideologies were, at least at the beginning of the century, and thus presents the Church's intolerance as somehow its inescapable destiny. Yet in 313 CE, Christianity was not a monolithic faith and much of its wide appeal lay in characteristics that militated strongly against persecution: forgiveness, charity, mercy, compassion. Again, it is worth remembering another of Tertullian's (contestable but no doubt heartfelt) claims: 'it is peculiar to Christians alone to love those that hate them'.[6] Influential survivors of the Great Persecution preached religious tolerance. Lactantius, drawing on the ancient authority of Cicero, argued that the recourse to force could only pollute true religion, for God valued inner convictions, devotion, faith, and love, not empty ritual compliance.[7]

Some scholars have, thus, challenged the notion that fourth-century Christians were bound to persecute and have pointed to an alternative tradition, one that forsook violence and that rejected the notion that faith could be compelled. For historians such as H.A. Drake, Michael Gaddis, and Thomas Sizgorich, the key to understanding the persecution of the fourth century is to recognise that Christianity was not intolerant but that, over the course of that century, the movement came to be dominated by militants who were willing to commit violence in the name of faith. Rejecting Tertullian, they accepted coercion as a legitimate means of ensuring religious conformity.[8] The rise of this militant devotion was not inevitable in 313 CE but contingent on subsequent events: religious conflicts within Christianity itself, the competition for both secular and ecclesiastical authority, and the resilience of that wide and diverse collection of still vibrant local cultic practices that Christians had, by the fourth century, come to sneer at as 'paganism' (from the Latin *paganus*, signifying both a backward rusticity and a civilian status, as opposed to the soldiers of Christ, who grew strongest in the cities).[9]

Inevitably, the figure of the emperor Constantine looms large over the debates concerning intolerance and persecution during the establishment of a Christian empire. Few figures have attracted such attention from scholars. Few have proved so enduringly elusive. In particular, the nature and sincerity of his religious convictions and his attitude towards paganism remain subjects of controversy. For T.D. Barnes, Constantine conceived of himself as the protector of Christians everywhere and was driven by a genuinely devout desire to make Christianity the official religion of the empire. This policy required that he not merely identified his own faith strongly with the state but that he actively suppressed pagan cults. H.A. Drake, however, portrayed the new emperor as a consensus-builder, primarily seeking a stable and prosperous empire. He was himself spiritually committed to Christianity but essentially tolerant towards other faiths. Yet he was caught in a political alliance with Christian bishops who would eventually draw him and his successors into violent confrontations with heretics, schismatics (those who challenged the Church's authority but not its doctrine), pagans, and Jews. Paul Stephenson portrays Constantine in a similar fashion, working towards a united Christian empire but broadly tolerant, recoiling from the futile model of persecution that he had witnessed fail under Diocletian.[10]

Much of the difficulty in reaching a consensus about Constantine's own role in fomenting persecution lies in the intractable methodological problems facing his historians. Any examination of the unspoken depths and sincerity of a person's spiritual beliefs is beset by inherent uncertainties. Besides, the fragmentary and partial nature of the surviving evidence leaves us unsure about important issues of context. For example, we do not know for sure how widespread and influential Christianity was at the point of his conversion. If the congregations were large and the bishops already wielded wide and compelling social authority, then Constantine may have been attracted to the faith by rather worldly, political considerations. If Christianity was still a weak, vulnerable, and marginal minority cult, then it would imply genuine commitment on the convert's part. At present the evidence is not conclusive either way.

Judging the concrete realities of Constantine's religious policies has also proved difficult. Much of the documentary record is tendentious, polemical, and contradictory. For example, Constantine's admiring contemporary biographer and Christian apologist, Eusebius, insisted that in the wake of military victory in the east in 324 CE, he had moved swiftly to ban blood sacrifice. The pagan orator Libanius of Antioch, in a late fourth-century speech to emperor Theodosius I, was adamant that he had not done so. Constantine's personal revulsion towards blood sacrifice is attested. He spoke of recoiling with horror from such practices and of his loathing for 'their foul and detestable odours', which, like other Christians and some pagans, he may have believed attracted malevolent *daemons*.[11] Yet he is unlikely to have pursued an outright ban of a ritual activity that was important to the lives of so many of his subjects. To do so would have been to court disobedience, riot, and disorder. A plausible explanation is that Eusebius overemphasised, but did not invent, an actual imperial prohibition issued to discourage an abominated practice. As was often the case with late Roman imperial edicts, this was done without the expectation that this prohibition would necessarily be rigorously enforced at a local level. The immediate aim, it would seem, was deterrence. The eventual objective was to create an atmosphere in which the old cults would wither without recourse to active persecution.[12]

Given that the ultimate desired outcome appears to have been that paganism would eventually be supplanted by Christianity, it might be inappropriate to characterise this policy using the modern expression 'religious toleration'. Toleration may signal disapproval, but it also denotes acceptance. Indeed, in modern societies it often implies legal and social equality. By that definition, Constantine's hope for the eventual, but orderly, extirpation of paganism, and his creation of a hostile environment for its practice, can hardly be described as tolerant. The word 'forbearance' has been offered as a more suitable alternative, as it captures the sense that the emperor was prepared to endure for the time being the existence of rites he abhorred.[13]

During Constantine's reign, only a handful of pagan temples are known to have been destroyed. Two of these were demolished because they occupied locations particularly sacred to Christians. One was at Mamre, an ancient cultic centre but familiar to Christians from the Old Testament. The other was a temple of Aphrodite 'polluting' the alleged site of the crucifixion in Jerusalem and thus cleared from the land to make way for the Church of the Holy Sepulchre. Two other temples of Aphrodite, one at Heliopolis and the other at Aphaca, were shut down because they had outraged public decency. Both had become centres of ritualised prostitution. Three other temples appear to have fallen victim to a violent, unsanctioned backlash by militant Christians against their erstwhile pagan tormentors. At Antioch and Didyma, oracles of Apollo were destroyed, their prophets tortured. At Aigai, the shrine of the demigod and healer Asclepius was razed to the ground.[14]

Other temples were subject to less destructive attacks. Altars and idols were smashed, rituals and processions were disrupted, worshippers and priests assaulted. Yet these were not the actions of Church or state but of individuals or small groups of militant Christians bent on a glorious self-destruction. These acts of violence were, in short, suicide attacks against Satan's host, launched by the most combative soldiers of Christ, to win the crown of martyrdom. In a spirit of joyful eagerness for death, zealous Christians engaged in violence to provoke a violent response. Evidence suggests that this was already a common occurrence during the Great Persecution. Bishops at the Council of Elvira in Spain in 300 CE, believed martyrdom should be endured, even embraced, but not pursued. Anxious less such provocative acts intensify persecution in their cities, they decreed quite explicitly that those killed in retaliation for smashing pagan idols were to be denied the name of martyr. That many bishops had to remind militant elements of their congregations of this judgement throughout the fourth century demonstrates that the practice persisted and represented an ugly reimagining of the concept of martyrdom as a justification for initiating acts of aggression against others.[15]

Yet, for most of the fourth century, such actions did not constitute persecution by religious or secular authorities. Both bishops and the emperor strove to put an end to such violence while creating an environment in which idols and sacrificial rituals played less and less a role in public life. In a letter circulated in the provinces most affected by attacks on temples, Constantine's rhetoric towards pagans was marked by invective. Noting that some Christians had proclaimed that 'the traditional practices of the temples and the authority of darkness have been removed', he lamented that this was not so: 'I would have recommended this very thing to all people, were it not that the violent rebelliousness of villainous error is so deeply ingrained in the souls of some, to the detriment of the common good'. Yet in his response to this pagan 'rebelliousness' and 'villainy', he counselled forbearance not violence. In passages of the letter in which he directly addressed God, he wrote:

> ... it is my earnest desire that, for the well-being of the world and for the benefit of all, your people shall enjoy peace and remain undisturbed. Let those who are in error joyfully receive the benefits of peace and tranquillity in the same way as the believers. For the sweet taste of shared benefits itself has the power to restore them and lead them on the right path.[16]

In the meantime, Constantine enacted an essentially gradualist policy, designed to reduce the role of traditional rites, especially animal sacrifice, in public life and to undermine the economic foundations of cult activity. Municipal taxes were diverted away from the old festivals. Temple funds and landholdings were confiscated to pay for the emperor's own building projects and to obtain the bullion necessary to stabilise his currency. The traditional priesthoods lost prestige, authority, and income. Altars fell dark. Temples grew silent. In some cities, offering animal sacrifice in public became an act of daring. Conversion to Christianity, in contrast, promised both spiritual and material rewards. The carrot-and-stick elements of Constantine's policy can be well illustrated by considering the coastal settlement of Maiouma, the port suburb of the city of Gaza. Although pagan cults were strong in that region, the population of Maiouma converted en masse to Christianity. In consequence, the emperor raised their home to the status of a city, granting them local autonomy and, crucially, control of their harbour duties and other associated incomes. Stubbornly pagan Gaza, on the other hand, lost both authority and revenue.[17]

We might thus conclude that, in the first decade of his reign, Constantine stood within a threshold between Christianity and pagan henotheism. The expectation was that he and his empire would move progressively towards a more Christian identity in time, without recourse to religious coercion. This is evident, too, in the architecture of his 'new Rome', the empire's new eastern capital, Constantinople. When its defensive walls had been traced out in late 324 CE, on the site of the existing small Greek city of Byzantium, the initial plans included three or four Christian churches, but religious provision was made for all citizens, including a temple dedicated to the Fortune of Rome. A statue of the emperor, in the guise of Sol Invictus, was placed prominently upon a column in the city's new forum, maintaining the cultic link between the emperor and the divine.[18]

He retained, too, among his imperial titles that of *pontifex maximus* (chief priest of the traditional cults in Rome) and would be baptised a Christian only on his deathbed in 337 CE. This, however, was not unusual. Baptism was considered a definitive and unrepeatable washing away of sin and was thus commonly undertaken at the end of life. Evidence for his own spiritual commitment to the Christian God was manifest early in his reign. In a Good Friday sermon entitled 'To the Assembly of the Saints', and probably dating to 317 CE, Constantine '[entreated] the favour of Christ with holy prayers and constant supplications, that he would continue to us our present blessings'.[19]

Sunday, the Christian Sabbath, was declared a public holiday in 321 CE. The emperor evidently saw himself as one of Christ's apostles; the statues of the others would ring his tomb, and he had hoped that their actual mortal remains would lie alongside his. He possessed a powerful sense of mission in the apostolic tradition, dedicating his reign to propagating Christian belief among the people and forging the governing institutions of a universal Christian empire. He was, thus, both emperor and 'a sort of bishop'.[20]

Indeed, one central dynamic in his embracing of Christianity, and his evolving policy towards religious difference, would be his relationship with the bishops. They would eventually prove to be pivotal figures in the growth of Christian militancy. In the early years of Christianity, bishops (in Greek, *episkopos* or overseers) had taken their place alongside presbyters (elders) and deacons in governing the affairs of local churches. Clement of Rome's epistle to the church in Corinth, written in about 95 CE, established that the authority of these three offices had been inherited directly from Christ's apostles.[21]

Yet a more hierarchical system of Church government quickly evolved. This was based upon the bishops' increasingly exclusive claim to the apostolic succession, which granted them singular authority over Christians in a particular town or city. In about 115 CE, Ignatius, the bishop of Antioch, arrested and travelling to his martyrdom in Rome, wrote to a number of churches scattered across the Roman province of Asia urging the faithful to show loyalty and obedience to their bishop: 'You are clearly obliged to look upon the bishop as the Lord himself'.[22]

Ignatius saw the role of the bishop as a patron and protector to the poor, to widows and slaves. He was also to be a guardian of orthodoxy, responsible for internal discipline, scriptural teaching, and controlling baptisms. This central-isation of authority would prevent the Church fragmenting. It would counter the divisive influence of itinerant and independently minded preachers and forge common doctrine at periodic synods, or councils, of bishops. Eventually, over the course of the fourth and fifth centuries, the creation of this hierarchy of authority within the Church would extend into the ranks of the bishops themselves. The bishop in each provincial capital, referred to as the metro-politan bishop, was acknowledged as the head of the entire Church within that province. Five such metropolitan sees would ultimately acquire influence over the whole Church: Constantinople, Rome, Alexandria, Antioch, and Jerusalem. Their bishops were considered the heads of the Christian family and would be addressed as patriarch or pope ('papa'). In the west, the latter would one day become the exclusive title of the bishop of Rome, who claimed a primacy based upon a direct apostolic succession from St Peter and St Paul, both reputedly martyred in the city during the reign of Nero.[23]

Socially influential, politically astute, and well connected, the bishops 'constituted the effective power of the church' and would become Constantine's most important allies after 313 CE, gradually displacing the old senatorial class and becoming key arbiters of political authority within the empire.[24] As the partner of the imperial state, the Church began to receive extraor-dinarily generous patronage. The reverse of forbearance towards a despised and impoverished paganism was the active promotion of Christianity at the local level. This was achieved through relieving bishops and their clergy of the burden of paying taxes or from having to take on onerous and usually expensive public offices. Small and moderately sized, but frequently very ornate, churches proliferated, indicating how even low-ranking clergy were able to benefit in the changed environment. The most visible manifestations of this novel imperial dispensation, however, were the larger and magnificent churches, the basilicas, paid for by the emperor: in Rome Saint Peter's, in Antioch a golden-domed octagon, and in Jerusalem the Church of the Holy Sepulchre.

Yet these awe-inspiring arguments in stone did not just preach the faith, they spoke too of the new political realities. Alongside the houses of worship stood audience halls, where bishops presided as judges, reflecting Constantine's wish that they be the exclusive arbiter in disputes between Christians and, in some cases, between Christians and pagans.[25] There were warehouses too, where food and clothes for the poor could be stockpiled, and broad courtyards, where alms could be distributed, banquets held, and the faithful assemble. Since bishops extended their charity to the (always present and always numerous) urban sick and the poor, they rapidly built up their social authority through patronage in the wider community.[26]

There was a spiritual price to be paid for this worldly authority. At Elvira in 300 CE, bishops had used their influence within their own communities to restrain violence. Their new roles within secular society fundamentally changed that equation. They, and indeed any Christians in positions that carried political or judicial responsibilities, inevitably faced pressure to compromise on some tenets of their faith, such as the commitment to turn the other cheek. Criminals had to be punished and frontiers had to be defended from barbarian incursions. The unruly and riotous urban populace of larger towns and cities had to be restrained or, in times of famine or social stress, they might well torch the homes of unpopular local officials. Abstaining from violence was not a practical option. Even exercising restraint would have proved difficult in practice.

The legal protections from state violence that Roman citizens had once enjoyed under the republic had been continually eroded for three centuries under the rule of emperors. The Roman judicial code continued to become more severe under Constantine, with over sixty offences subject to the death penalty by the end of his reign. Brutal punishments, executions, mutilations, and beatings were applied with less and less distinction being made for rank or status. Litigation passed from jury trials to criminal courts before individual judges who passed sentence without checks on excessive cruelty in punishment. The Roman penal code, in short, was savage, and enforcing it made men savage too.[27] Bishops such as Augustine of Hippo found ideological means to reconcile Christian pacifism with Roman legal notions. The Old Testament, for example, provided plentiful examples of God's providence violently punishing the criminal and the sinful. So long as violence was not motivated by greed or cruelty, it might thus be just and righteous.[28]

Yet the growing willingness of bishops to employ violence was not merely a response to their temporal duties. Crucially, it was driven by internal conflicts within the Church itself. Some of these clashes were ugly contests for worldly status and authority. Others stemmed from heart-felt doctrinal differences. Some reflected the lingering and divisive legacy of the persecutions. Whatever drove the disputes, the first victims of Christian persecution during the reign of Constantine would be other Christians. The scale and duration of these conflicts could escalate dramatically because bishops had an impressive capacity to mobilise popular support in pursuit of their quarrels. The chronically underemployed urban poor were tied to them by the distribution of alms. So too were a host of lesser clergymen, by oaths of obedience. Others were the bishops' direct employees, such as the *parabalini* (medical orderlies) of Alexandria and the *fossores* (gravediggers) of Rome.[29]

Whatever their official titles implied, these latter groups frequently served as little more than hired muscle in bloody local conflicts. The riotous mobs of Greco-Roman cities could thus become private armies. The fourth-century historian Ammianus Marcellinus recorded how, in 366 CE, two bitter clerical rivals, Damasus and Ursinus, 'whose passionate ambition to seize the Episcopal throne passed all bounds', clashed in Rome. Their adherents fought for days in the streets and public buildings. Civil authority melted away; the hapless urban prefect fled the city. Damasus's private army of thugs ultimately prevailed but at some cost: 'it is certain that in the basilica of Sicininus, where Christians assemble for worship, 137 corpses were found on a single day'.[30] Violence had thus become a tool of episcopal politics.

Theological disagreements proved just as liable to end in bloodshed. The emperor hoped that Christian monotheism would unify the diverse peoples of the Roman world: a universal Church for a universal empire. Yet, ironically, monotheism had a greater potential for provoking fierce religious divisions and persecution than henotheism or polytheism. Belief in a number of gods accommodated pluralism. Differences in opinion and styles of worship could be held equally legitimate, and thus limited the fractious consequences of theological disagreements. These could be a matter for debate not bloodshed. However, attempting to universalise monotheism, as Garth Fowden has noted, 'tends to focus divinity and ignite debate by forcing all the faithful, with their infinite varieties of religious thought and behaviour, into the same mould, which sooner or later must break'.[31] This was the unforeseen problem Constantine encountered and that would foster persecution notwithstanding Christian injunctions against religious coercion. The quest for universality generated a struggle to define and enforce religious orthodoxy and to stigmatise, and ultimately persecute, those labelled as heretics.

Although Constantine seemed initially unaware of it, this process was already underway before the fourth century. The early Church had promoted internal unity and discipline, chiefly through the authority of the bishops and the broad acceptance of a common canon of scripture, the New Testament, established by the late second century. Some clearly identifiable dissident groups, for example those who explicitly rejected monotheism, such as the Marcionites and the Gnostics, had been denounced as heretical and excluded from the Church. Others were threatening not because of their theology, but because they challenged the position of the bishops. The followers of a Phrygian priest, and recent convert from paganism, named Montanus and two women prophets, Maximilla and Priscilla, had orthodox attitudes towards the one God and his son Christ, but had nevertheless been driven from the Church. Montanists exhibited a passionate commitment to the Paraclete (Holy Spirit) which manifested itself in ecstatic, frenzied worship, vigorous ascetic practices (such as fasting and other forms of self-denial), and new revelations delivered via prophecies and visions. Such charismatic preachers (including, prominently, women) offered a direct link to God and drew to them many Christians. They thus threatened the patriarchal authority of the bishops and their claim to be the sole legitimate arbiters of orthodoxy.[32] The reality, at the opening of the fourth century, was that Christianity still embraced a range of incompatible beliefs and structures of authority that hampered the drive to create a universal Church.

In one sense, the universal Church could cope well with, indeed benefit from, diversity of belief or commitment. Within a broad and welcoming

Sunday congregation, room could be found even for the lukewarm convert or the sincere but ignorant former pagan as they were educated in Christianity. Catechumens, those new to the faith, were found a place within the Church as they went through an extensive religious instruction before baptism. This process eased conversion. At another level though, within the clergy, the Church's message had to be consistent, or its faith would seem incoherent. Here diversity of opinion was far more dangerous. Disagreement on basic theological issues was incompatible with a universal Church and was thus productive of militancy and persecution.

Among the most corrosive of these differences in opinion concerned the very nature of Christ and his relationship to God. It had not been unusual among some early Christian theologians to emphasise a degree of distinction within the Holy Trinity. The unity of God was to be understood in its fullest sense as the unity of God the Father. The Son and the Holy Spirit were divine in a lesser sense. The influential Alexandrian biblical critic and scholar Origen (*c*.185–*c*.254 CE), for example, had apparently argued upon these lines and concluded that the Holy Trinity was a hierarchy of Father, Son, and Holy Ghost. This view was commonplace as late as 300 CE. Indeed, it may even have been the mainstream teaching of the Greek-speaking Church. Some went on from this position to argue that the Son was a product of the creation by the Father, and, thus, they were not of the same substance.[33]

Critics of this theology recognised that it was shaped by pagan philosophy, particularly that of the Neo-Platonists. This school suggested that the one immutable and unknowable source from which all else emanates (God) had a mediator, a less-than-fully divine emanation as it were, who might be present in the material world: the *Logos* (the reasoning power or 'Word' of God), identified by some Christian thinkers as being incarnated in Jesus of Nazareth. Such a position was attractive and useful to Christians living amongst educated pagans, for it made sense of some of the new religion's most outlandish claims such as an immutable and perfect God's presence on a changeable and corrupting earth, or that God could suffer and die on the cross. Christianity could thus be made intellectually respectable and shed the taint of superstition.

Yet in denying Christ's full divinity and in portraying him as a part of God's creation, this understanding of the nature of Christ threatened the very integrity of the faith. Christians worshipped Christ; if Christ was not fully divine, then they were worshipping something other than God. Or, to put it another way, they had lapsed into idolatry. The issue could not, therefore, have been more serious, for as Alistair McGrath has commented, it represented 'the subversion of [Christianity's] inward identity' and thus raised again the possibility of its submersion into an idolatrous sea of paganism.[34]

At the time of Constantine's conversion, the most articulate and well-known proponent of the subordinate nature of Christ was an Alexandrian priest, Arius (*c*.260–336 CE). His most determined and influential opponent was Athanasius (*c*.296–373 CE), first as secretary to bishop Alexander of

Alexandria and, following the death of Alexander in 328 CE, as his successor to the bishopric. For Athanasius, the incarnation of the *Logos* was God entering the material world to achieve the salvation of humankind and overcome death. Father, Son, and Holy Ghost were *homoousios:* of the same substance, coeternal and coequal.

The rival teachings of Arius had been condemned at a synod in Alexandria in *c.*320 CE, but the beliefs he had espoused remained widespread and Arius's own reputation ensured their continued propagation. Within the Church, the issue was all-consuming: the eternal souls of erring individual Christians were imperilled and, in the minds of many, the faith itself risked corruption by pagan (and thus Satanically inspired) belief systems. For Constantine, now encountering the unforeseen divisive consequences of attempting to universalise a far-from-uniform religion, the issue was, initially, a simple inconvenience. Driven by his desire for harmony and consensus, he first dismissed the dispute as 'extremely trivial and quite unworthy of such controversy'.[35] He soon realised he was mistaken.

To forge a consensus, the emperor summoned a general synod at Nicaea in 325 CE. Here, Athanasius's formulation of *homoousios* was accepted as orthodoxy and Arius himself was anathematised. Yet this proved an escalation, not an end of the controversy. Thanks to the influence of the sympathetic Eusebius, bishop of Nicomedia, at court, Arius had swiftly returned to favour. For the next sixty years, the two parties would compete for the right to define orthodoxy within the empire. Constantine himself wavered in his allegiances. Arius had enjoyed a brief welcome back into the fold, but by 331 CE the emperor had grasped the theological danger to Christian monotheism posed by Arianism. Denouncing Arius as a 'Porphyrian' (a follower of the Neo-Platonist philosopher who would have assimilated Christ into the pagan pantheon), he declared the wayward priest an enemy of the Church and ordered his writings burned.[36]

Yet there was no victory for Athanasius either. Accused of corruption and the use of excessive violence against dissident Christian sects in Egypt, he was himself excommunicated in 335 CE and was forced into exile the following year. Welcomed in the city of Rome and broadly supported in the Latin-speaking west, Athanasius was able to recover his see, although he never held it securely and was periodically re-exiled. Arius himself had died in 336 CE, but the doctrine associated with his name was often ascendant within the empire, particularly during the reign of Constantine's son, the resolutely Arian Constantius, from 350 CE until his death in 361 CE. It was not until the reign of the emperor Theodosius I, that the First Council of Constantinople in 381 CE finally ratified the Nicene Creed of 325 CE, its assertion of the coeternal and consubstantial nature of Father and Son and its anti-Arian anathemas.[37]

In terms of the history of persecution, the Arian controversy is significant primarily as a catalyst for militancy and religious violence. Although both parties at times tried to assume for themselves the mantle of the martyrs and accused their opponents of committing atrocities against them, as a conflict conducted largely between powerful and influential Christians, it lacked the asymmetrical characteristic of persecution. Bloodshed there was. Both sides engaged in inflammatory public preaching to mobilise lay support and, in so doing, forced ordinary Christians to confront and clarify their own, perhaps hitherto ill-defined, beliefs and to self-identify with one or other of the antagonistic camps. On both sides of the debate, bishops could call upon those tied to them by patronage for support. Charismatic preachers could rally large numbers to their cause through impassioned sermons and fiery polemics. Arius himself composed ballads to reach 'sailors, millers, travellers, and ... the unlearned'.[38]

Lay Christians could not avoid the contest, for the very notion of legitimate and orthodox faith was at stake, touching the individual's personal relationship with God. Some were drawn to Arianism by the attractive idea that Christ's less-than-wholly-divine nature could thus be emulated; all the faithful could become Sons of God. For others, no suggestion could be more impious than this, an assault on Christ's 'indescribable dignity', drawing its strength from despised pagan philosophies.[39] Inevitably, the aggressive rhetoric heard in the basilicas provoked rioting in the streets and the *agora* of cities across the eastern Mediterranean, as rival mobs clashed for control of public and ritual spaces: 'people rising against people ... cutting down one another', as Eusebius of Caesarea lamented.[40] The quest for harmony through a universal faith had, ironically, fomented violence, in defiance of Christianity's traditions of compassion.

The Arian controversy was perhaps the most widespread of the Church's internal battles but was only one of several conflicts that radicalised opinion, promoted militancy and, ultimately, fostered persecution. Schism in North Africa played a particularly significant role in transforming the nature of martyrdom from a willingness to die for one's faith into a willingness to harm and to kill others. Against the background of a wearying, drawn-out 'sacred trench warfare' between schismatics and the Church authorities, even those who had once argued that compulsion could play no part in true faith came to believe that violence might be sanctioned as a disciplinary measure.[41]

Such an attitude blazed a trial for the righteous persecutors and the moralising aggressors who might thereafter claim that their violence was enacted for the good of their victims or the protection of society, or both. St Augustine (354–430 CE), bishop of Hippo and a theologian who would profoundly shape western theology for centuries, was initially an opponent of physical compulsion of religious dissenters. Ultimately, however, he reconciled the use of force with scriptural authority. He cited such examples as the blinding of Paul on the road to Damascus: 'he who was first Saul and afterwards Paul was forced to come to know and to hold onto the truth by the great violence of Christ who compelled him'.[42] Thus Augustine could conclude that 'at times, then, one who suffers persecution is unjust, and one who persecutes is just'.[43] To understand how he reached this conclusion, which was of profound significance in the history of persecution, it is necessary to consider the precise challenges that faced the early Church in North Africa.

At the heart of the strife that rent Christian communities apart in Roman North Africa were acts of betrayal committed during the persecutions of the third and early fourth centuries. Those rigorist Christians who passionately venerated the memory of the imprisoned and tortured confessors and the local martyrs, such as Cyprian, Perpetua, Felicitas, who had died in the arenas, harboured a lingering bitterness towards the Roman state, identifying it with the Antichrist, the beast of the Book of Revelation. They were unforgiving, too, of those who had lapsed and sacrificed at pagan altars but who later wanted to return to the Church. And they held in utter contempt the *traditores*, clergymen who had meekly complied when soldiers and magistrates had demanded they hand over the scriptures, the very word of God, to be burned. After the ascent of Constantine, such rigorists sought a pure Church composed only of an elect untainted by treason. Sects with similar views existed across the empire and were sometimes referred to by the Greek words *Katharoi*: 'purists'.[44]

Their avowed exclusivity inevitably generated friction with those of their co-religionists who favoured a universal Church, open to all. They were more moderate in their attitudes towards the lapsed and sought to appease the Roman state, heeding Paul's injunction that earthly authority had been instituted by God. In North Africa, Augustine chided the rigorists:

> ... you imagine you escape the weeds before the time of the harvest, because you are nothing but weeds. For if you were grain, you would tolerate the weeds that are mixed in and would not split yourself off from the crop of Christ [who said] 'Allow them both to grow until the harvest'.

The truly righteous would thus wait upon the harvest of the Last Judgement. In the meantime, they 'endure for the good of unity what they hate for the good of justice in order that the name of Christ might not suffer the blasphemy of horrid schisms'.[45]

Even before the Great Persecution had ended, the two factions had come to blows. In 304 CE, Christians had arrived in Carthage from the countryside to bring comfort, food, and drink to imprisoned confessors, who were being deliberately starved to death. They were set upon by armed men, the hirelings of the city's bishop Mensurius and his deacon Caecilian, beaten, whipped, and driven away from the gaol. Mensurius's precise motivation is unclear. He may simply have been trying to appease the Roman authorities, and thus protect the rest of his congregation, by upholding the law. Alternatively, he may have feared the confessors themselves. They were charismatic and spiritually powerful individuals, who wielded tremendous influence over Christian communities, an alternative and unruly source of authority to the established clerical hierarchy. Indeed, before they finally succumbed to hunger, the martyrs in their cells had issued an excommunication of all who associated with the bishop and his deacon.

When Mensurius died in 311 CE, Caecilian was chosen as his successor. Yet, because of his close association with Mensurius, and because one of those who had consecrated him as bishop was a *traditore*, he was unacceptable to the rigorists. They elected their own rival bishop, Majorinus. Caecilian and his followers would win the support of the imperial government and most of the churches outside of Africa. For this reason, they claimed the name *katholikos*, 'Catholic', or universal, Church.[46]

On the death of the rigorist bishop Majorinus, he was succeeded by Donatus. His Catholic opponents thus pejoratively labelled his followers 'Donatists' and denounced them as heretics, for their insistence on the rebaptism of former Catholics entering their congregations. Donatists considered that sacraments such as baptism could only be administered by morally unimpeachable priests. Catholics viewed this insistence as heresy because they held the validity of sacraments to be independent of the character of the priest who administered them. Their efficacy was dependent upon divine grace not mere human merit.[47]

The controversy was complicated by regional tensions. The bishops of the neighbouring province of Numidia, into which the schism spread, threw their weight behind the Donatists partly because of their jealousy of the authority wielded by the bishopric of Carthage. There may, too, have been an ethnic element to the division. Donatism drew the bulk of its supporters from the indigenous Berber population. Catholicism was strongest among Roman colonists. Some historians, notably W.H.C. Frend, have suggested that socio-economic factors also fostered physical aggression and persecution in North Africa. A group called the Circumcellions were, by the 340s CE, the most militant wing of the Donatists, ransacking both Catholic churches and pagan temples, intimidating travellers and beating Catholic priests, sometimes to death. Frend, contentiously, has suggested that they were agrarian rebels, and their cause was the cause of the angry and dispossessed rural poor.[48]

However, we should not lose sight of the fact that the Donatist controversy primarily reflected conscious and explicit differences in religious opinion rather than latent anti-colonialism, class grievances, or unspoken parochial tensions. The Circumcellions were probably a rather loose grouping of men and women drawn originally from socially marginalised, itinerant harvesting gangs, for whom a career as 'holy fighter' presented new opportunities for employment.[49] Yet they were united not by worldly, material objectives, but by their spiritual beliefs. This can be seen in the nature of their violence. Catholic churches and basilicas would be seized (or 're-claimed' as the Donatists would see it) and everything touched by the tainted hand of the Catholic priest would be destroyed: altars smashed, chalices melted down, images whitewashed, even the consecrated host thrown to the dogs. One favoured method of assaulting the priests themselves was to throw a caustic mixture of vinegar and powdered lime into their eyes, plunging into permanent darkness those whom the Donatists considered had turned away from God's light. Their violence thus had a powerful symbolism, redolent of their essentially religious motivation.[50]

Over the course of the controversy, both sides claimed to be the victims of persecution and accused the other of instigating the violence. Both did harm to the other and both discriminated against the other on grounds of their religious beliefs. However, the contest only became clearly asymmetrical when imperial forces intervened. In 313 CE, the rival factions had initially appealed to the emperor to settle their dispute. In response, Constantine had arranged two synods, the first in Rome later that year, the second a year later, in Arles in Gaul. Both supported the claim of Caecilian, to the fury of the Donatists. It would, therefore, be easy to dismiss their ensuing recourse to rioting and civil disorder as an ill-tempered reaction to an imperial decision that had gone against them, costing them the bishopric and its associated authority and revenue.

Yet this was not a simple schism, a quarrel over authority within the Church. Constantine's merging of the roles of emperor and bishop in his own person, and his ongoing project with the bishops to create a universal Christianity would have soon alienated the North African rigorists anyway. The emperor's association of the Church with the imperial state required Christians to cooperate with a government that had recently been the brutal agent of (to their minds) Satanically inspired persecution. His fostering of an inclusive Church, embracing saints and sinners, the devout and the lukewarm, suspect converts who hid their paganism beneath a veneer of Christianity, threatened to contaminate the spiritual purity of congregations. In 346 CE, Donatus himself posed the crucial question: 'What has the emperor to do with the church?' It seemed to his followers that the persecutions had, in fact, never stopped. Caecilian was 'more ruthless than the tyrant, more bloody than the executioner'.[51]

And Satan himself, frustrated in his efforts employing the brute force of the Roman state, was now using guile and deception to turn Christians from the path of righteousness. The imperially backed hierarchy and their clergy were his tricksters. The Donatists thus looked back to the tradition of those slaughtered in the arenas and to the Maccabees, Jewish priests who had died for God, and proclaimed themselves the true 'Church of the Martyrs'. Yet they were not passive martyrs who triumphed by enduring the violence inflicted by others in arenas and prisons. These soldiers of Christ fought their good fight in churches and temples, on country roads and city streets. The ideology of martyrdom had shifted subtly but portentously. Martyrs did not simply endure torture and die for God; now they killed, maimed, and terrorised in his name too.[52]

The alliance of Church and imperial authority would prove equally combative. The emperor was clearly frustrated by, and did not understand, Donatist intransigence. He began to see them as being of unstable mind, engaged in a vile seduction to turn the laity against the holy Church. Since their rioting posed a threat to public order, he authorised judicial proceedings against them in May 317 CE and dispatched imperial troops to Africa to assist his bishops. However, Constantine did not pursue a simple strategy of persecution. He offered funding to Donatist congregations willing to take communion with their Catholic neighbours. Catholic clergymen strove to win over their opponents through theological debate and inspiring sermons (and Donatist clergy did the same).

Yet the ancillary, if sporadic, use of physical coercion drove the wedge deeper between the communities and propelled militancy to the fore. Mindful of the heritage of state persecution, Donatist sources emphasised the violence: 'homes are encircled with battle standards ... threats of proscriptions are launched against the rich. Sacraments are profaned ... Holy virgins defiled, priests of God slaughtered'. As armed men seized Donatist places of worship, at least one major massacre was perpetrated: 'everyone kept their eyes tight shut while each age group and sex was killed, cut down in the midst of the basilica'. The bishop of Avioccala was summoned to Carthage and executed. Yet the bloodshed simply stiffened Donatist resolve and reinforced their commitment both to martyrdom, 'to be killed by the enemy in our combat is triumph', and to the ongoing struggle against Satan, 'who denies that such deeds have the children of the Devil as their authors? What diligence by the serpent! So many evils let loose!'[53]

Constantine recognised his error. In May 321 CE, he wrote to the bishops and laity of the Church in Africa, regretting his use of force and conceding that it had not restored peace and unity. He withdrew his soldiers and ordered an end to judicial coercion of the Donatists, while he waited on heaven to reveal a more effective solution.[54] For the next two decades, the rival Christian Churches in Africa coexisted in relative peace. Violence was more rhetorical than actual. Both sides pursued vigorous propaganda campaigns, utilising sermons, religious chants, and even popular song to demonise their opponents, yet many cities and towns simultaneously maintained both Catholic and Donatist congregations.[55]

Escalation into persecution was usually a consequence of the imperial state's periodic intrusion into North African affairs. After Constantine's death, in 337 CE, he was succeeded by his sons. In the west, in 346 CE, Constans revived the carrot-and-stick policy towards Christian dissidents his father had once vainly pursued. He dispatched the imperial commissioner Macarius, who offered money to loyal congregations (to Donatists a crude attempt at bribery), but who was also backed up by troops whose purpose was to enforce a new edict of unity. When in late 347 CE a party of Donatist bishops travelled to negotiate with Macarius, one was immediately killed, another subsequently executed, and others exiled. More arrests followed. In a Carthaginian torture chamber, 'a war was waged' between a Donatist martyr Maximian, 'a soldier of Christ', and the 'soldiers of the devil'. Maximian was followed to a 'triumphant death' by his companion

Isaac. Before he died, however, Isaac experienced a vision in which he gouged out the eyes of the emperor, a symbolic call to the 'Church of the Martyrs' yet again reinforcing the notion that holy violence might be inflicted not simply endured.[56]

The creation of new martyrs who inspired an increasingly militant band of holy warriors seemed to have eventually taught Constans the same lesson that his father had learned (and Diocletian before him): persecution did not bring order or unity. Indeed, by fostering militancy on both sides, it entrenched division. He swiftly ended his campaign of coercion and Catholics and Donatists returned to an uneasy coexistence, punctuated by sporadic outbreaks of inter-communal violence, for half a century. Even when the co-emperors Arcadius (r.395–408 CE) and Honorius (r.395–423 CE) returned to a policy of repression to restore unity to the African Church, they initially concentrated primarily on using civil and economic constraints rather than physical force. Yet gradually state and Church came to accept the legitimacy of violent coercion, including persecution, as a means of disciplining schematics and those denounced as heretics. This shift in attitude is important not only because it illustrates how, by the end of the fourth century, man clearly no longer had the 'freedom to follow whatever religion his wished', but also because immensely influential figures such as Augustine came to sanction religious violence in the name of orthodoxy.

Ironically, Augustine himself had benefitted from the general religious forbearance of the fourth century. His father was a pagan but his mother a Christian, and he was raised in that faith. Yet in his youth, he had felt no strong commitment to the Church. Aged around twenty, he adopted Manichaeism, a Persian religion that saw Jesus Christ as one of a number of prophets, alongside Buddha and Mani, sent to help human souls in the struggle between good and evil. Highly educated and enormously gifted, he held a number of teaching posts in Carthage, Rome, and finally Milan. He was drawn to much classical learning, especially Plato and the Neo-Platonist philosophers Plotinus and Porphyry.[57]

Yet, at much the same time that he discovered Neo-Platonism, he underwent a profound conversion experience. In 387 CE, he was baptised a Christian. He returned to Africa and when visiting Hippo in 391 CE he was, rather against his own inclinations, ordained a priest at the behest of an admiring populace. In 395 CE, he became bishop.[58] A prolific author, he wielded his pen against pagans, the Manichaeans, and the British heretic Pelagius (who rejected the notion of original sin and believed in the freedom of humans to earn salvation by their own efforts apart from God's grace). As a North African bishop, the most significant controversy for Augustine was that with the Donatists. The written word and the sermon were his instruments of choice and he initially argued against violence. Around 395 CE, he wrote in a conciliatory letter to Maximinus, the Donatist bishop of Siniti in Numidia: 'let us deal with reason; let us deal with the authorities of the divine scriptures; as quiet and peaceful as we can be ... '.[59]

Yet soon Augustine would abandon this position and accept that the state was justified in enforcing religious unity. This dramatic change in attitude seems to have been motivated in large measure by the evidence that, on this occasion, coercion was working, and true faith could be compelled. He had been initially concerned that Donatists forced to take communion with Catholics would simply feign compliance and pollute the Church through this deception. Yet in a letter written sometime after 405 CE to Festus, a Roman official and prominent Catholic layman, he acknowledged of former Donatists in his congregation, 'though some are thought to be pretending because they crossed over to us out of fear of authority, they are later in some temptations shown to be the sort of person who are better than certain others who were Catholics at earlier date'. From this he then concluded 'it is not true that nothing is accomplished when it is accomplished with violence'.[60]

It is difficult to explain why this final episode of persecution appeared to have more success than those under Constantine and Constans. One major difference was that by 400 CE the Donatist Church was itself riven by internal schisms and, rather ironically, the militant Donatist Bishop Primianist now struggled to unify his own flock. The task was further complicated by the involvement of many Donatists in a revolt against Honorius in 397–398 CE. They were pursued for disloyalty as well as heresy. The Church of the Martyrs was thus more vulnerable and less cohesive than it had been in the past. With their confidence badly shaken many Donatists could now be chivvied back into communion with Catholics. 'Oh, if I could show you how many sincere Catholics we now have from the Circumcellions! They condemn their former life and wretched error … ', wrote an enthused Augustine.[61]

Having witnessed the (apparent) efficacy of coercion in these circumstances, it was at this point that Augustine now concluded that 'at times, then, one who suffers persecution is unjust, and one who persecutes is just'. Motivation and the exercise of restraint were, however, crucial distinctions:

> … it is clear that the evil have always persecuted the good and the good have always persecuted the evil: the former by harming them unjustly, the latter by showing concern for them through discipline; the former savagely, the latter in moderation; the former in the service of desire, the latter in that of love.

He offered the analogy of a parent confronting the behaviour of a wayward child: 'for the correction of a son, even with some sternness, there is assuredly no diminution of a father's love'.[62]

Augustine's sincerity in these beliefs should not be doubted, for he urged restraint even in the punishment of captured Circumcellions, many guilty of terrible acts against Catholics: 'fulfil, Christian judge, the duty of an affectionate father; let your indignation against their crimes be tempered by considerations of humanity'. Rather than the rack to stretch or iron claws to 'furrow their flesh' or flames to scorch them, he suggested '[beat] them with rods – a mode of correction used by schoolmasters, and by parents themselves in chastising children ... '.[63]

His attitude towards the legitimacy of (restrained) corporal punishment was a part of a broader acceptance of the inevitability of conflict in the material world: 'among sects, among Jews, Pagans, Christians, heretics are wars, frequent wars ... '. Indeed, he would live to see the sack of Rome in 410 CE by the Visigoths and his own city, Hippo, was under siege by the Vandals (themselves Arian Christians who persecuted Catholic and Donatist alike), when he died in 430 CE. Christians were thus, he concluded, presented with the necessity of self-defence from external enemies and wrongdoers in their own communities. Thus, the pacifism of many of his fellow Christians was not part 'of religious minds but of timorous minds'. Pacifists would sinfully accept subjugation to injustice and refused to follow the example of Moses and the prophets in visiting righteous retribution on evildoers. So long as their cause was just, and they fought not for love of violence, vengeful cruelty, greed, or lust for power, then 'good men undertake wars'.[64] For Augustine and an increasing number of his fellow Christians, violence could be holy. Persecution could be righteous.

As Herbert Deane has noted, such ideas were not inherently characteristic of the faith but represented 'a pronounced change from the beliefs of the early Christian Church, and they mark a significant milestone in the process of relativizing and accommodating Christ's teachings to the imperatives of earthly existence ... '.[65] The Christian Church was not innately intolerant; the survivors of the Great Persecution urged forgiveness. Constantine would endure the survival of rites he despised, while actively promoting the spread of Christianity. Persecution was rejected. However, the demands of worldly authority, wielded for example by bishops or Christians in prominent civic offices, required a pragmatic acceptance of the use of punishment or armed force. The contests within the Church itself, as the emperor tried to forge a unified faith from a range of widely divergent beliefs, turned into a bitter struggle over orthodoxy and heresy.

In this febrile atmosphere, the cosmological battle in which devout Christians believed themselves engaged took on new and portentous dimensions. Martyrdom itself had evolved into a concept that required the faithful to not merely endure the violence of Satan's agents but justified instigating aggression and in carrying the fight to the enemy in his corrupted basilicas, dark synagogues, and idol-strewn temples. Where the application of force proved successful, it taught an ugly lesson. In North Africa, the final collapse of the Donatists drove many of their opponents to conclude that disciplinary violence was necessary and could indeed result in sincere Christians. Violence had triumphed and that triumph was to have a powerful legacy. It spawned a rationale that justified coercion and the physical punishment of human bodies in the name of faith and spiritual discipline. That rationale is best summed up in the words of Augustine: 'at times, then, one who suffers persecution is unjust, and one who persecutes is just', and that 'it is not true that nothing is accomplished when it is accomplished with violence'. This was essentially the Christian theory of persecution that would legitimise religious violence for centuries to come.[66]

Notes

1 Tertullian, *To Scapula*, Chapter 2, in *The Ante-Nicene Fathers*, Volume III, translated and edited by Alexander Roberts, James Donaldson, and Arthur Cleveland Coxe (New York: Cosimo, 2007), p.105.

2 H.A. Drake, *Constantine and the Bishops: The Politics of Intolerance* (Baltimore, MD: Johns Hopkins University Press, 2002), p.194.

3 Bernard Reynolds, *The Early Persecutions and the Martyrs of the First Three Centuries* (London: National Society's Depository, 1897), pp.14–15.

4 Arnaldo Momigliano, 'The Disadvantages of Monotheism for a Universal State', *Classical Philology*, 81 (1986), p.286.

5 Dennis E. Groh, 'The Religion of the Empire: Christianity from Constantine to the Arab Conquest', in Hershal Shanks (ed.), *Christianity and Rabbinic Judaism* (Washington, DC: SPCK, 1993), p.268.

6 Tertullian, *To Scapula*, Chapter 2, p.105.

7 Charles Freeman, AD 381: *Heretics, Pagans and the Christian State* (London: Pimlico, 2009), p.37.

8 H.A. Drake, 'Lambs into Lions: Explaining early Christian Intolerance', *Past & Present*, 153 (1996), pp.3–36; Michael Gaddis, *There is No Crime for Those Who Have Christ: Religious Violence in the Christian Roman Empire* (Berkeley: University of California Press, 2005); Thomas Sizgorich, *Violence and Belief in Late Antiquity: Militant Devotion in Christianity and Islam* (Philadelphia: University of Pennsylvania Press), 2009.

9 A.D. Lee (ed.), *Pagans and Christians in Late Antiquity* (London: Routledge, 2000), p.10.

10 T.D. Barnes, *Constantine and Eusebius* (Cambridge, MA: Harvard University Press, 1981), pp.212, 97, 224, 247; Drake, *Constantine and the Bishops*, pp.235–272; Paul Stephenson, *Constantine: Unconquered Emperor, Christian Victor* (London: Quarus, 2009), pp.303–307.

11 Scott Bradbury, 'Constantine and the Problem of Anti-Pagan Legislation in the Fourth Century', *Classical Philology*, 89 (1994), p.129.

12 John Curran, 'Constantine and the Ancient Cults of Rome', *Greece and Rome*, 43 (1996), pp.68–80.

13 Maijastina Kahlos, *Forbearance and Compulsion: The Rhetoric of Religious Tolerance and Intolerance in Late Antiquity* (London: Duckworth, 2009), pp.6–8.

14 Robin Lane Fox, *Pagans and Christians in the Mediterranean World* (London: Viking, 1986), pp.670–671; Bradbury, 'Constantine and the Problem of Anti-Pagan Legislation in the Fourth Century', p.123.

15 Gaddis, *There is No Crime*, pp.174–179.

16 Quotes from 'Constantine's Changing Attitude towards Paganism', in Lee (ed.), *Pagans and Christians in Late Antiquity*, pp.86–87.

17 Christopher Jones, *Between Pagan and Christian* (Cambridge, MA.: Harvard University Press, 2014), p.100.

18 Stephenson, *Constantine*, pp.201–203.

19 Groh, 'The Religion of the Empire', p.268; T.D. Barnes, 'The Emperor Constantine's Good Friday Sermon', *Journal of Theological Studies*, 27 (1976), p.423.

20 Garth Fowden, *Empire to Commonwealth: Consequences of Monotheism in Late Antiquity* (Princeton, NJ.: Princeton University Press, 1993), pp.90–91.

21 Clement of Rome, First Epistle to the Corinthians, Chapter 42, in Henry Bettenson and Chris Maunder (eds), *Documents of the Christian Church* (Oxford: Oxford University Press, 1999), pp.68–69.

22 Charles Freeman, *A New History of Early Christianity* (New Haven, CT: Yale University Press, 2011), p.116.

23 Harry Boer, *A Short History of the Early Church* (Grand Rapids, MI: William B. Eerdmans, 1976), pp.31–32, 68–70; P.G. Maxwell-Stuart, *Chronicle of the Popes* (London: Thames & Hudson, 2006), p.8.

24 Drake, *Constantine and the Bishops*, pp.109–110.

25 *Sirmondian Constitutiones* 1 in Lee (ed.), *Pagans and Christians*, pp.218–220.

26 Peter Brown, *The Rise of Western Christendom* (London: Blackwell, 2008), p.30 and *Power and Persuasion in Late Antiquity: Towards a Christian Empire* (Madison: University of Wisconsin Press, 1992), p.102.

27 Ramsey MacMullen, *Changes in the Roman Empire: Essays in the Ordinary* (Princeton, NJ.: Princeton University Press, 1990), pp.204–217.

28 Frederick H. Russell, *The Just War in the Middle Ages* (Cambridge: Cambridge University Press, 1975), pp.16–17.

29 Brown, *Power and Persuasion*, pp.102–103.

30 Ammanius Marcellinus, *The Later Roman Empire, AD 354–378*, translated by Walter Hamilton (London: Penguin, 1986), pp.335–336.

31 Fowden, *Empire to Commonwealth*, pp.106–107.

32 Frederick C. Klawiter, 'The Role of Martyrdom and Persecution in Developing the Priestly Authority of Women in Early Christianity: A Case Study of Montanism', *Church History*, 49 (1980), pp.251–261.

33 Freeman, *New History of Early Christianity*, p.194.

34 Alistair McGrath, *Heresy* (London: SPCK, 2009), pp.140–152.

35 Stephenson, *Constantine*, pp.265–66.

36 Drake, *Constantine*, pp.262–263.

37 L.W. Barnard, 'Athanasius and the Roman State', *Latomus*, 36 (1977), pp. 422–437; Walt Stevenson, 'Exiling Bishops: The Policy of Constantius II', *Dumbarton Oaks Papers*, 68 (2014), pp.7–27.

38 Carlos R. Galvao-Sobrinho, 'Embodied Theologies: Christian Identity and Violence in Alexandria in the Early Arian Controversy', in H.A. Drake (ed.), *Violence in Late Antiquity* (Farnham: Ashgate, 2006), p.327.

39 Galvao-Sobrinho, 'Embodied Theologies', pp.321–332.

40 Quoted in Galvao-Sobrinho, 'Embodied Theologies', p.323.

41 Brent Shaw, *Sacred Violence: African Christians and Sectarian Hatred in the Age of Augustine* (Cambridge: Cambridge University Press, 2011), p.314.

42 St Augustine, Letter 93.5, *The Works of St Augustine: Letters 1–99*, translated by Roland Teske, edited by John Rotelle (New York: New City Press, 2001), p.380.

43 St Augustine, Letter 93.8, p.382, and Letter 138.2, quoted in Herbert Deane, *The Political and Social Ideas of St Augustine* (New York: Columbia University Press, 1963), p.165. See also Gillian Clark, 'Desires of the Hangman: Augustine on Legitimized Violence', in Drake (ed.), *Violence in Late Antiquity*, pp.137–146.

44 Christopher Jones, *Between Pagan and Christian* (Cambridge, MA: Harvard University Press, 2014), p.147.

45 St Augustine, Letters 43.21, 76.2, 89.5, in *Works of St Augustine*, pp.168, 298, 361–362; Shaw, *Sacred Violence*, pp.66–82.

46 Gaddis, *There is No Crime*, p.52.

47 Maureen Tilley (ed.), *Donatist Martyr Stories: The Church in Conflict in Roman North Africa* (Liverpool: Liverpool University Press, 1996), pp.25–39; McGrath, *Heresy*, pp.158–159.

48 W.H.C. Frend, *The Early Church* (London: SCM Press, 1982), pp.153–154.

49 Shaw, *Sacred Violence*, pp.630–659.

50 McGrath, *Heresy*, pp.152–155; Gaddis, *There is No Crime*, pp.103–130.

51 *The Acts of the Abitinian Martyrs*, in Tilley, *Donastist Martyr Stories*, p.45.

52 Daniel Boyarin, *Dying for God: Martyrdom and the Making of Christianity and Judaism* (Stanford, CA: Stanford University Press, 1999), p.66; Joyce Salisbury, *The Blood of Martyrs: Unintended Consequences of Ancient Violence* (London: Routledge, 2004), pp.155–163.

53 'A Sermon on the Passion of Saints Donatus and Advocatus', in Tilley (ed.), *Donastist Martyr Stories*, pp.51–60.

54 Tilley (ed.), *Donastist Martyr Stories*, p.xxxii.

55 Shaw, *Sacred Violence*, pp.441–489.

56 'The Passion of Maximian and Isaac', in Tilley (ed.), *Donastist Martyr Stories*, pp.60–75; Gaddis, *There is No Crime*, pp.103–105.

57 St Augustine, *City of God*, Book 8, Chapter 5, translated by Henry Bettenson (London: Penguin, 2003), p.304.

58 For biographies, see Peter Brown, *Augustine of Hippo* (Berkeley: University of California Press, 2000), and Henry Chadwick, *Augustine of Hippo: A Life* (Oxford: Oxford University Press, 2009).

59 St Augustine, Letter 23, in *Works of St Augustine*, p.67.

60 St Augustine, Letter 89.7, in *Works of St Augustine*, pp.362–363.

61 St Augustine, Letter 93.2, in *Works of St Augustine*, p.378; Frend, *The Early Church*, pp.203–204.

62 St Augustine, Letter 93.8, in *Works of St Augustine*, p.382; and Letter 138.2, quoted in Herbert Deane, *The Political and Social Ideas of St Augustine* (New York: Columbia University Press, 1963), p.165.

63 St Augustine, Letter 133.2, quoted in Gaddis, *There is No Crime*, p.142. See also, Peter Iver Kaufman, 'Augustine's Punishments', *Harvard Theological Review*, 109 (2016), pp. 550–566.

64 Quoted in Deane, *Political & Social Ideas of Augustine*, p.161.

65 Deane, *Political & Social Ideas of Augustine*, p.226. See also P.R.L. Brown, 'St Augustine's Attitude to Religious Coercion', *Journal of Roman Studies*, 54 (1964), pp.107–116.

66 Perez Zagorin, *How the Idea of Religious Toleration Came to the West* (Princeton, NJ: Princeton University Press, 2003), p.16.

3 'Peace for the Gods of Our Forefathers'

Pagans Between Persecution and Forbearance, 313–529 CE

By the early fifth century, powerful Christians had come to terms with the twin realities of wielding secular authority and of enforcing discipline within their own Church. In the latter case, the reluctance to engage in physical coercion to compel belief had given way to an acceptance of the necessity, and indeed justice, of violence as a disciplinary measure. As with the schismatic Donatists of North Africa, the first to be 'justly persecuted' were other, if wayward, Christians. Yet this shifting attitude towards the legitimacy and efficacy of persecution would, in time, affect pagans too, for the conflicts between Christians drew them in, even though they took no direct role. The initial imperial policy of 'forbearance' towards paganism would thus eventually be compromised. The militancy born of internal conflicts within the Church combined with anxieties concerning the resilience of the old cultic practices, and their threatened resurgence during the reign of Julian the Apostate (r.361–365 CE), would ensure the triumph of the ideology of righteous persecution.

Although not inevitable, the policy of active persecution of pagans had deep roots. When, in 331 CE, the emperor Constantine had condemned the Christian heretic Arius as a 'Porphyrian', he was inescapably identifying that philosopher and his tradition as a threat to Christianity. All copies of Porphyry's book *Against the Christians* were ordered to be consumed by the flames alongside those of Arius. Even considered against the background of Constantine's general religious 'forbearance', book burning was, in itself, a form of ideological violence, a powerful ritual which left only ashes of what had once seemed dangerous or subversive. In the recent pagan past, Manichaean texts, Christian scriptures, works of divination, and *grimoires* of magical spells had often been subject to this rite of purification. Under Constantine, book burning became a tool by which orthodox Christianity proclaimed its spiritual ascendency over both heretical and pagan beliefs.[1]

If the burning of sacred texts and works of philosophy did pagans no physical harm and did not violate too strongly the policy of forbearance, it nevertheless contributed to the growth of an officially sanctioned discriminatory atmosphere in which hostility towards non-Christians flourished and

DOI: 10.4324/9781003494331-4

found new outlets. One was the reinterpretation of long-established Roman laws, particularly those against the practice of harmful magic and private divination. This targeted elements of pagan worship without outlawing belief systems themselves.

Constantine thus decreed that no *haruspex* (interpreters of portents, especially abnormalities in the intestines of sacrificed animals) should enter a private house on pain of death at the stake. The householder would face proscription and deportation. Such legislation was not wholly without precedent. Private, as opposed to public, divination of the future was long considered self-interested and inherently subversive. Three centuries earlier, the emperor Tiberius had also outlawed the practice.[2] Over the course of the fourth century, however, the definition of what constituted harmful magic was expanded and the pursuit of such alleged wrongdoers became more active.[3] After Constantine's death in 337 CE, his sons pursued this policy with some rigour. Under Constantius II (r.337–361 CE), or so the contemporary historian Ammianus Marcellinus alleged:

> If anyone consulted a soothsayer because he had heard a shrewmouse squeak or met a weasel or encountered any similar omen, or if he used an old wives' charm to relieve pain, a practice which even medical authority allows, he was denounced through some agency which he could not guess, brought to trial and punished with death.[4]

Those practising magic and other traditional rites such as blood sacrifice were particularly vulnerable in this worsening climate because paganism was such a diverse phenomenon. Many pagans were themselves hostile to what they, too, regarded as dangerous *superstitio*, including cursing, spellcasting, fortune telling, and drenching altars in animal blood. Indeed, there was, within Greco-Roman *religio*, a long tradition of opinion critical of animal sacrifice, stretching back to Pythagoras in the sixth century BCE.[5]

In the third century CE, this view had gained increasing popularity thanks largely to the influence of Neo-Pythagorean thought and, likewise, those Neo-Platonic philosophers who favoured a spiritual sacrifice over one of blood, such as Porphyry. He argued that the supreme god should be worshipped 'through pure silence and pure thoughts', while for 'his off-spring, the intelligible gods, it is necessary to add the verbalised hymn'. To the prosaic deities of farm, field, and local cult, offerings of 'first fruit' and grateful celebrations were owed. Blood, however, was a noxious offering, fit only for *daemons*. These, in common with Christians, Porphyry believed were essentially malevolent beings, drawn to impure souls tainted by the consumption of sacrificial meat. Thus, the ritual activity of many pagans of the third and fourth centuries, particularly those of a philosophical inclination, closely paralleled Christian practices. They featured daily divine services and the increased use of lamps, incense, and hymns. Blood sacrifice may no longer have been the dominant rite.[6]

Although the book burning may have given the prescient food for thought, many pagan worshippers would have failed to identify any threat in the condemnation of magic or blood sacrifice. Indeed, they may have approved such measures. Thus, when in the early 340s Constantius moved yet further to stifle such established ritual activities, he did so not in the name of the Christian Church but, explicitly, as part of a campaign against practices that were potentially harmful to all: 'let there be an end to superstition, let the madness of sacrifice be done away with'. Making a canny appeal to that Roman love of the past, Constantius consciously reassured his subjects that his rooting out of such superstition was not a threat to their traditions:

> ... it is our wish that the temple buildings located outside the city walls should remain untouched and undamaged. For since certain plays, circus spectacles, and competitions have their origin from some of these temples, it is not appropriate to pull them down when they provide the Roman people with performances of traditional entertainments.[7]

Similarly, on his one visit to Rome itself, in 357 CE, Constantius had toured the city, paying special attention to the temple of Rome, the shrine of Tarpeian Jupiter, 'beside which all else is like earth compared to heaven', and the Pantheon 'spread like a self-contained district under its high and lovely dome'.[8] This was a clear demonstration of the distance between the emperor and those militant Christians then urging him in the strongest terms to cast down such buildings. In 346 CE, for example, Firmicus Maternus, formerly a pagan henotheist but now a zealous convert to Christianity, had urged upon Constantius and his brother Constans 'the annihilation of idolatry and the destruction of the profane temples', and adjured them to 'persecute root and branch the crime of idol worship'.[9]

Understood in that context, the significance of the emperor's admiring visits to Rome's temples is manifest: he was not going to 'persecute root and branch'. Yet, reassuring as such gestures might have been, they had a profound, if latent, objective. Constantius was gently redefining ancient rites: festivals, plays, and competitions that had once been loaded with ritual significance were now merely 'traditional entertainment'. Magnificent temples were stone monuments to Roman greatness and heritage, a fitting legacy even for a Christian empire. Subtle prejudice, rather than outright persecution, was thus still the imperial policy. Only when a sense of a unified pagan identity had developed, and in turn catalysed radical militancy among Christians, would the battle lines of persecution between two clearly defined and oppositional belief systems become more visible. Then intolerant voices that echoed that of Firmicus Maternus's would begin to be heeded.

The pivotal figure in this development would be the emperor Julian (332–63 CE), remembered to Christian historiography as Julian the Apostate. He was the nephew of Constantine, raised a Christian but who, when he found himself sole emperor in 361 CE, revealed himself to be the champion of the old gods and of the Greco-Roman mythic and philosophical heritages. He hoped to unify the varied streams of pagan traditions under the title of 'Hellenic religion'. While his use of the word 'Hellenic' in this context emphasised the glories of Greece's ancient civilisation, he dismissed Christians as 'Galileans', followers of a rootless and novel cult, born in an obscure corner of a back-ward and troublesome province.[10]

It has often been suggested, and with some force, that the probable basis of Julian's rejection of Christianity was very personal. When Constantine had died, his three sons – Constantine II, Constantius, and Constans – had secured the imperial succession by murdering potential rivals. Among their victims were Julian's father and elder brothers. The sons of Constantine themselves had soon turned upon one another. Constantine II died in a foray against the lands of Constans in 340 CE. Constans himself fell to an assassin in 350 CE, leaving Constantius as sole emperor. The family of Constantine the Great had proved themselves to be poor models of Christian compassion, as the young Julian, just six when he was robbed of his father, seemed to have noted. Ammianus Marcellinus would later comment that 'experience had taught him that no wild beasts are such dangerous enemies to man as Christians are to one another'.[11]

Yet Julian was not simply pursuing a personal feud against 'the Galileans'. In his youth, he had been well-educated in classical literature and philosophy whilst a student in Athens. He had also, apparently, there been secretly initiated into one of the Greek mystery cults (which were, thus, clearly con-tinuing to attract new adherents in the 350s CE). In religion, he inclined to a sincere henotheism, while intellectually his surviving writing betrays a strong Neo-Platonist influence. His knowledge of Christian scripture made him a formidable and well-informed critic of that faith. He was able, for example, to point to contradictions in the gospel accounts of Christ's life and to con-trast the angry, tribal God of the Old Testament with the compassionate and universal God of the New Testament. His polemical text *Contra Galilaeos* (*Against the Christians*) was thus a sophisticated work that not only attacked Christianity but defended a sound and ancient political principle: in a vast empire comprised of diverse populations, religious pluralism, rather than a universal religion, was the most appropriate means of securing harmony and concord:

> Since in the father of all, things are complete and all things are one, while in the separate deities one quality or another predominates, therefore Ares rules over warlike nations, Athene over those that are wise as well as warlike, Hermes over those whom are more shrewd than adventurous; and in short the nations over which the gods preside follow each the essen-tial character of their proper god.[12]

Beyond being an intellectually formidable critic of Christianity, Julian was an energetic and charismatic leader too. Constantius had made him his deputy

Caesar in the west, to deal with barbarian incursions into Gaul while he dealt with the Persian threat in the east. Julian quickly proved himself as a general and was consequently proclaimed Augustus, supreme emperor, by his legions in 360 CE. The following year, Constantius hurried west to meet this challenge but died before the fate of the empire could be decided on the field of battle.

As undisputed emperor, Julian was then able to announce his 'Hellenism' publicly and embark on a policy calculated to reverse Christianity's growing ascendancy. Christians swiftly accused him of being a persecutor of the faithful. However, in regard to religious coercion, Julian outwardly seemed as hesitant as his uncle Constantine. Publicly, he reiterated Constantine's emphasis on forbearance and harmony:

> ... he summoned to the palace the Christian bishops, who were far from united being of one mind, together with their flocks, who were no less divided ... and warned them in polite terms to lay aside their differences and allow every man to practice his belief boldly without hindrance.

Yet Ammianus Marcellinus, who recorded this warning, ascribed to it a more subtle motive than is at first apparent: '[Julian] knew that toleration would intensify [Christian] divisions and that henceforth he would no longer have to fear a unanimous public opinion'.[13] This episode suggests that Julian intended to be very active in rolling back the tide of Christianity. Besides his classic application of the principle of divide and conquer, the emperor withdrew the financial privileges that Constantine had granted the Church. He demanded the return of land and property that had once belonged to pagan shrines. He also forbade Christians from teaching Hellenic literature, history, and philosophy.[14]

While perhaps falling short of serious harm, this was not a trivial matter. A good classical education, or *paideia*, was now as important to ambitious and status-conscious Christians as it was to pagans. *Paideia* allowed individuals access to power and influence, for it imparted a sense of social identity, a culture, and an idealised code of behaviour (courteous, self-controlled, commanding but benevolent) that bonded the wealthy and qualified a cultivated elite to rule.[15] Julian's edict against Christian teachers thus posed a dilemma for wealthy Christians: entrust the education of their children to pagans (and risk the influence they might wield), or see them denied the opportunity to pursue public office. Even some of those who admired Julian felt that this was an unwarranted policy. Ammianus Marcellinus, himself a pagan, wrote 'he was guilty of one harsh act which should be buried in lasting oblivion; he banned adherents of Christianity from practising as teachers of rhetoric or literature'.[16]

The emperor may have stopped well short of making martyrs, but he struck at Christianity in other ways, using his own knowledge of the religion to advantage. He prevented Christians from becoming provincial governors, 'for their law forbids them to use the sword against offenders worthy of capital punishment'.[17] He confiscated the property of Christians in Edessa, justifying his action by citing their religion's call to renounce material wealth. He planned a yet more decisive act too, an 'argument in stone' that would strike at the very credibility of Christianity. Although he displayed no great sympathy towards Judaism as such, he understood the significance of Jerusalem to both of the monotheistic faiths. In 362 CE, Julian thus set about rebuilding Judaism's sacred Temple, razed by Vespasian in 70 CE. Had the project been completed, it would have contradicted Christ's own prophecy concerning the permanence of the Temple's destruction and thus discredited Christian claims that they, not the Jews, were the legitimate inheritors of Israel.[18]

Julian's religious policy appears to have renewed confidence among many pagans. Temples were rebuilt, traditional rites performed publically. An inscription from Casae in Numidia (North Africa) described him as 'restorer of freedom and of the Roman Religion'. In Ma'ayan Barukh, in the Jordan Valley, he was commemorated as 'the restorer of the temples'. In Thessalonika, he was 'one most beloved of God', and 'renewer of sacred rites'.[19] To the horror of 'real Christians', large numbers of those who (it now transpired) had converted for material or social advantage and 'who preferred the riches and honour of this world to the true felicity', now 'sacrificed without hesitation'.[20]

Yet there were limits on how much Julian could achieve. He berated his own co-religionists for the lack of revived Hellenism's progress. He urged pagans to emulate both Jews and Christians in their practice of charity towards the needy. At the same time, he asked Hellenes not to tolerate priests who frequented the games or the taverns, or who engaged in 'disreputable' or 'unbecoming' trades.[21] Yet many 'Hellenes' thought Julian an unconvincing moral exemplar, particularly because of his commitment to the odious rites of blood sacrifice, which he practised on an unprecedented scale. Again, it is noteworthy that the broadly sympathetic Ammianus Marcellinus was critical on this point:

> ... the victims with whose blood he drenched the altars of the gods were all too numerous. On occasion he sacrificed a hundred bulls and countless flocks of other animals, as well as white birds, for which he combed land and sea.[22]

Such noxious hecatombs fostered immorality:

> ... the result was seen in the intemperate habits of the troops, who were gorged with meat and demoralised by a craving for drink, so that almost every day some of them were carried through the streets to their quarters on the shoulders of passers-by after debauches in the temples.[23]

Julian's policies also promoted *superstitio*: 'anyone who professed a knowledge of divination, whether qualified or not, was allowed to consult oracles and examine entrails ... all this without any sort of restriction or the observance of prescribed rules'.[24]

Whatever the successes or otherwise of Julian's pagan revivalism, the atmosphere he created, quite literally in cities where people walked through a fog of reeking sacrificial smoke and could taste the blood in the air, fostered violence. For Christians, that death-scented haze concealed malevolent *daemons*. The promotion of blood sacrifice called to mind the memory of persecutions at the hands of the heathen, where unwillingness to sacrifice had been the test that condemned them. Julian's withdrawal of patronage from the Church and his discriminatory policies against Christians indicated that the imperial state might again become an agent of Satan. The humiliation and loss of status inflicted upon the faithful thus far was bad enough, but how long before participation in sacrifice by all was, once more, demanded?

In the face of this threat to their eternal souls, religious forbearance no longer seemed such a wise or practical response. The militant call for an end to the temples and a purging of their *daemons* was now being heeded by more and more. When Amachius, governor of Phrygia (in modern Turkey) ordered the reopening of a temple in the city of Merum, local Christians assaulted the building and smashed the statues within. Amachius responded in a peculiarly heavy-handed manner. Three men were arrested and ordered to sacrifice. They refused, so the governor had them tortured and executed. Three more names were added to the list of the martyrs. Tales circulated alleging that pagans had attacked Christians and practised 'certain abominable mysteries' in which children were sacrificed and their flesh tasted (these, of course, were familiar allegations that had once been levelled at Christians). For many Christians, it seemed that the persecutions had indeed begun again.[25] In fact, this was not Julian's policy, but local clashes affected his judgement too. On 22 October 362, the temple of Apollo at Daphne in Syria was burned to the ground. Pagans blamed Christian arsonists and Julian, in fury, retaliated by closing the largest church in nearby Antioch.

For their part, many pagans found that same sacrificial smoke a heady vapour, granting licence not just to their rites but to a more active resistance to (what they saw as) Christian provocations. Bishop Mark of Arethusa in Syria, who had (illegally) demolished a temple during the reign of Constantius, was attacked and tortured by local pagans. In Palestine, pagans had targeted Christian cult sites, excavating relics associated with John the Baptist and the prophet Elijah. These were then burned and desecrated by the admixture of animal bones, a gross and infuriating insult to the soldiers of Christ. In 362 CE, a rampaging pagan mob had murdered the unpopular bishop George and two of his officials, Dracontius and Diodorus, who had threatened the temples and altars of Alexandria.[26]

Julian must bear much culpability for the rise of militancy on both sides. Had he genuinely ruled in a Constantinian spirit of religious forbearance and commitment to social harmony, he would surely have brought the full force of his authority down on the rioters of Alexandria. Ammianus Marcellinus insisted that he was furious about George's death but, tellingly, he allowed himself to be placated and merely issued a strongly worded rebuke. He then took personal possession of George's magnificent and valuable library. Across the empire, his policies crystallised and deepened divisions and undermined the very religious pluralism he claimed to promote. He aimed to set Christian against Christian, Jew against Christian, and foster a resurgent and cohesive 'Hellenism' which would, at the very least, marginalise the divided and discredited 'Galileans'. How rapidly the situation of the empire's Christians might have deteriorated further under Julian's rule can only be a matter of speculation. In 363 CE, he turned his attention to foreign policy and resolved to eliminate Rome's greatest military rival in the east: Sassanian Persia. He was deep inside Persian territory when he was fatally wounded during a cavalry skirmish.[27]

Thus ended the imperial dynasty foundered by Constantine. Julian's successor was Jovian, one of his officers, proclaimed emperor by the army in the east. Besides the painful necessity of negotiating a humiliating peace with the Persians, the Christian Jovian tried also to defend the principle of religious pluralism and limit the damage his predecessor's divisive policies had caused. The fundamental principles of the policy of forbearance were to be maintained by his successors, the co-emperors of east and west: Valentinian I (r.364–375 CE); Valens (r.364–378 CE); Gratian (r.375–383 CE); Valentinian II (r.375–392 CE) and, in the early years of his reign at least, Theodosius I (r.379–395 CE). The imperial ban on blood sacrifice was restored but, as the unpopularity of Julian's attempts to revive the practice indicate, many pagans opposed the ritual slaughter of animals themselves by this point. Augustine of Hippo characterised the pagan worshippers of North Africa in the 370s and 380s CE as offering incense, not blood, in their rituals.[28]

The primary religious concern of these Christian emperors seems to have remained ending divisive heresy and schism within their own Church. In 381 CE, the Council of Constantinople, convened by Theodosius, established the orthodoxy of the Nicene Creed and ushered in new laws against Arianism and other assorted heresies. This imposed an authoritarian and dogmatic definition of 'God' upon the empire, brooking no alternative ways of understanding the divine. Charles Freeman has identified this as a pivotal moment in European intellectual history, denying for centuries to come the 'freedom to speculate on what might or might not exist beyond the material world'.[29] In the long term, this view may be correct but the immediate impact on pagans, at least, was probably actually quite limited.

Just a year later in 382 CE, the co-emperors Gratian, Valentinian, and Theodosius issued a rescript (edict) protecting a temple (its precise location is unclear) and instructing the provincial authorities to 'maintain all celebration of festivals' there. The need for the emperors to act in this manner clearly implied some threat to the temple. Almost certainly that threat came from local Christians. That the emperors acted swiftly to put a stop to any violence or iconoclasm demonstrated their rejection of religious coercion. Yet they were careful to find a workable formula to justify the continued existence of the temple and its idols that would sooth Christian anxieties:

> We have decided ... to allow the temple, consecrated once in the presence of large crowds and now still frequented by people, in which there are said to be images which deserve to be judged for their artistic worth rather than their religious associations, to continue to be open ... But this opportunity to enter the temple is not to be taken as giving permission for the performance of sacrifices, which is prohibited there.[30]

So long as no animal blood was spilt, pagans were thus free to visit their temple and celebrate their festivals. Local Christians, on the other hand, could be reassured that the building was essentially an art gallery, not a *daemon*-infested nest of idolators. Like Constantius before them, the co-emperors were subtly redefining key elements of paganism to render them harmless and, indeed, make them worthy of preservation. Religious idols were now works of art, that all could admire. Violence and disorder were headed off wherever possible; religious coercion was still rejected by the state.

The apparent harshness of many of Theodosius's laws and the savagery of the penalties they stipulated, in regard to both Christian heresies and the pagan practice of sacrifice, has given an impression of a clear break with Constantine's gradualist and consensual approach towards fostering Christian orthodoxy. Yet this impression is misleading; there is much evidence to suggest that the purpose of such laws was to frighten not to punish. These were heavy-handed nudges towards conversion perhaps, but not, as yet, persecutory.

Allan Cameron has pointed to the prominent Christian sources that understood, and endorsed, imperial policy as aiming not to persecute the erring but to win their hearts and minds. For example, Gregory of Nazianzus (c.330–390 CE), appointed bishop of Constantinople in 381 CE, summarised Theodosius's policy in these terms:

> I do not consider it good practice to coerce people instead of persuading them ... Whatever is done against one's will, under the threat of force is like an arrow tied back, or a river dammed in on every side of its channel. Given the opportunity it rejects its restraining force. What is done willingly, on the other hand is done steadfastly for all time. It is made fast by the unbreakable bonds of love. The emperor, it seems to me, keeps this in mind, and to this extent keeps fear within bounds, winning over everybody gently and setting up voluntary action as the unwritten law of persuasion.

Writing in about 378/9 CE, John Chrysostom (*c*.347–407 CE), who would also become the bishop of Constantinople, stressed the same point:

> No one has ever made war on [pagans]. Nor are Christians allowed to use force or violence to combat error. They must provide for the salvation of men by persuasion, speech and gentleness. That is why no Christian could ever issue decrees against you such as the devil-worshippers issued against us.[31]

There is evidence that these sentiments were taken wholly seriously by Christians who lived by the injunction to love those who wronged them and to forgive those who sinned against them. In May 397 CE, near Tridentum in northern Italy, three Christian priests, who had possibly done no more than attempt to persuade recent converts against participating in traditional harvest rituals, were murdered by a pagan mob.[32] When the murderers were identified, a local Christian bishop appealed successfully to the emperor for clemency on their behalf. The most powerful bishops of northern Italy at that time – Vigilius of Trento, Chromatius of Aquileia, Gaudentius of Brixia, even the forceful Ambrose of Milan – remained committed to the dissemination of charity and the persuasive power of the sermon as the best routes to win converts and they too were wary of idol smashing and violent confrontations with pagans.[33]

Indeed, when considering the context of such confrontations, it should be borne in mind that the distinctions between pagans, Christians, and Jews were not always clear-cut, and religious identities were fluid. While our documentary sources, for the most part authored by educated and committed Christians, were keen to stress distinct boundaries between religious communities, the material evidence uncovered by archaeologists often tells a much more complex story. Christians and Jews were sometimes buried in the same cemeteries, especially in the eastern provinces of the Roman Empire. Dedications to the cult of *Theos Hypsistos* (Highest God) demonstrated the merging of the spirituality of monotheistic pagans (especially the 'God-fearers', who had long been attracted to the synagogue without embracing fully the Mosaic Law), Jews, and Christians. This was probably the route by which the solar halo made its way from the worship of Apollo, the sun god, into Christian iconography.[34]

In this environment of mutable religious identities, the Christian Church was well-placed to win new adherents without recourse to coercion. The universal ethos of the early Church made a gradual, non-confrontational transition from paganism to Christianity possible. Many nominal Christians continued to wear amulets, watch for signs and omens, attend the games and the chariot races (both activities that had strong ritual overtones), and partake in ancient festivals for a very long time to come. The persistence of such practices would often cause some churchmen much frustration. In 494/5 CE, the bishop of Rome (either Felix II or his successor Gelasius I), was trying to prohibit Christians from taking part in the *Lupercalia*, a boisterous and popular rite of early spring that apparently involved nudity, light flagellation, and much running about. The local nobility protested the ban, on the religiously suspect grounds that not performing the ceremony endangered the city. Yet this exchange demonstrates not conflict but the efficacy of Constantine's original gradualist and conservative policy of forbearance and gently paced conversion. Those taking part in the *Lupercalia* would, overwhelmingly, have described themselves as Christians.[35]

Indeed, notwithstanding the antagonism of some individual churchmen, the Church pursued for centuries an institutional strategy of making concessions to the existing and traditional practices of popular cults. In 596 CE, Pope Gregory the Great sent the missionary Augustine, later the first bishop of Canterbury, to Britain to convert the Anglo-Saxons who had settled there after the fall of Rome's empire in the west. He was specifically instructed to preserve the sites of pagan sanctuaries and maintain their feast days but to dedicate them to the Christian Church and its saints.

This policy sustained aspects of pagan worship too. Across the empire and beyond, wherever missionary activity took Christians, local shrines to patron deities could be reassigned to martyrs who would become local patron saints. Saints were held to be close to God, yet accessible to humans, whose nature they shared, much like the semi-divine and deified figures of the pagan pantheons, such as Aesculapius the Healer, the hero Hercules, or the emperor Augustus. Saints, like demigods and deified emperors, were venerated through prayers and even ritual offerings and, it was believed, could intercede with the divine on behalf of the pious, the sick, and the suffering. The cult of the saints and of their holy relics would become a powerful and enduring feature of Christianity; essentially, it was the means by which pagan henotheism was preserved. This was far from the only mechanism by which paganism was assimilated into a nascent Christendom. Even the names of the old gods (Latin and Germanic) would persist in the minds of the people, for they continued to name days of the week after them.[36]

Once again, the best word to describe this policy is 'forbearance'. The Church would endure for the time being what it ultimately hoped to correct. Many converts from paganism, and indeed the generations to follow, may have been, in the eyes of their priests, ignorant and superstitious. Yet once they were within the congregation, they could be chided from the pulpit and lectured on their errors. Thus, in many cities and provinces, gradual and non-coercive religious syncretism won out, albeit ultimately on very Christian terms. As this process unfolded, Alan Cameron notes, 'as long as there was no public sacrifice, down to the 390s, Christian governments were sensible enough not to be too concerned about what people thought, said or did in private'.[37]

Nor were pagans barred from high office, as Christians effectively had been under Julian. Themistius (*c.*317–*c.*389 CE), pagan head of the Senate in Constantinople, gave wise counsel for over thirty years to Christian emperors from Constantius II (r.337–361 CE) to Theodosius I (r.379–395 CE). Themistius was representative of that ancient tradition of the philosopher, or man of *paideia*, who was free to speak truth to power at the imperial court. His religious beliefs appeared to be no obstacle to a long and distinguished career. This was true of many others too, such as the Roman senator, proconsul, restorer of temples, and staunch defender of the traditional rites, Vettius Agorius Praetextatus, who died in 384 CE.[38]

However, this gradual and largely consensual transition to Christianity is not the whole story. In the final two decades of the fourth century, persecution, too, would play its part in the collapse of paganism and the end of religious pluralism. Membership of the Church encompassed a spectrum of beliefs. At one extreme were the amulet-wearing and festival-going recent converts and the 'crypto-pagans' whose faith was feigned, either for social advancement or to avoid social censure. At the other end of the spectrum were those who still perceived of themselves as soldiers of Christ and inheritors of the martyr tradition: militant, unbending, and watchful for Satan's guile and trickery as he sought to subvert the Church.

For the most part, the Church had, since Constantine, tried to control their excesses. For example, bishops condemned attacks on temples and synagogues and denied the crown of martyrdom to those who sought death at the hands of unbelievers by committing such acts. Yet, after Julian, a more strident and intolerant Christianity was coming to the fore in some cities and provinces of the empire. Sermons laced with invective, open mockery of pagan festivals and idols, and personal denunciations could quickly poison relations between religious communities. Insult and polemic often became the dominant mode of discourse in religious exchanges. On hearing of the death of Praetextatus, the influential biblical scholar Jerome (*c.*345–420 CE) simply announced that he had most certainly gone straight to Hell.[39]

In spite of imperial policy, this vituperative attitude offered little room for manoeuvre for the beleaguered defenders of pluralism, and fostered prejudice. It was now pagan apologists, such as Themistius, who were echoing the second-century Christian Tertullian's call for tolerance most insistently, surely an indication of their threatened and minority status. In 364 CE, in a speech delivered in the emperor's presence, Themistius argued that it was the natural tendency of men to follow different paths to God; religious pluralism not uniformity represented the will of the divine. Tellingly, he pointed to the variety of beliefs found within Christianity to illustrate this point.[40]

It is worth taking a moment to examine both the potential of an intellectual defence of this religious pluralism, based on Hellenic thought, and the reasons for its eventual failure. As a philosopher, Themistius was aware of how much common ground existed between Christianity and paganism. For example, influential Christian writers such as Origen of Alexandria had ensured a permanent place for Plato's doctrines within Christian theology. Thus, the perfect and eternal 'forms' that Plato believed existed in a reality far higher than the shadowy, imperfect perceptions experienced in the material world, were understood by Christians to be the creative thoughts of their God, who could be identified with Plato's notion of an ultimate 'Good'. Similarly, Plato's teacher, Socrates, was widely respected by Christians. His 'noble death' after an unjust condemnation offered a parallel to the story of Christ and a model for martyrs.[41]

For pagan apologists like Themistius, therefore, the belief in Plato's ineffable, supreme deity, shared between themselves and Christians, offered an apparently secure foundation for an intellectual plea for tolerance. Similarly, the mutual recognition of the inscrutability of a transcendental God seemed a sound case against religious coercion, for no one could claim to understand, fully and truly, God's will. Yet, in the wake of the apostate emperor Julian, fewer Christians would be receptive to such arguments (even though they had once been made by as respected a father of the Church as Tertullian). Many Christian citizens were thus turning their backs on the policy of forbearance, even while emperors tried to sustain it. Influential Christians were not interested in philosophical debates in the Greek tradition about the nature of the divine, for their scriptures had revealed the truth and their certain faith trumped doubt-provoking reason. It was another of Tertullian's aphorisms that now acquired the status of a Christian maxim: 'what has Athens to do with Jerusalem?'[42]

For Christians, the appropriation of Athenian figures such as Plato or Socrates was important in establishing their claim to Greco-Roman tradition, and probably made conversion much easier for pagan monotheists and henotheists who shared a characteristic respect for the Hellenic past. Yet this appropriation did not extend to the actual philosophical methods associated with the schools of Athens. Hellenised Jewish philosophers, such as Philo of Alexandria, in the first century CE and Numenius a century later, had argued that some Greek thinkers were worthy of the greatest respect and had genuine insight of the divine. Yet they also suggested that those Greeks had discovered nothing that was not already apparent in Jewish holy scriptures. As Numenius put it, 'Who is Plato if not Moses speaking Greek?'[43] Philo and Numenius became important figures for many Christian theologians too, notably Origen of Alexandria, allowing them to portray individuals such as Plato and Socrates as useful teachers and moral exemplars for Christians, but without endorsing pagan philosophy.

Thus, ultimately, those pagan apologists who tried to establish a reasoned defence of religious pluralism found Christians unwilling to admit the possibility of shared truths or that there was any room for debate. Augustine of Hippo, while acknowledging how close Platonists were to Christians in their beliefs about the supreme God, condemned them outright for their denial of Christ's resurrection and divinity, and for countenancing polytheism. Nor was he willing to discuss such matters with unbelievers, 'all ... issues of Christian doctrine are widely discussed ... but it is faith which opens the approach to them for the intellect, and lack of faith closes it'. In short, those without the correct beliefs to begin with could never acquire true knowledge.[44]

It is in this context that we should understand the dismissive Christian response to calls for tolerance from pagans such as Themistius, or the Roman senator Symmachus who, in 384 CE, unsuccessfully requested of the emperor Valentinian II the return of the Altar to Victory, removed by Gratian in 382 CE, to the Roman Senate:

> ... we request peace for the gods of our forefathers, for our patron deities. Whatever each person worships, it is reasonable to think of them as one. We see the same stars, the sky is shared by all, the same world surrounds us. What does it matter what wisdom a person uses to seek for the truth? It is not possible to attain to so sublime a mystery by one route alone. But these are matters for debate by men at leisure; we offer you now prayers, not a battle.[45]

Yet an assertive militant form of Christianity would not debate with those who lacked their faith and was now indeed shaping up for a battle. If this was not evident in imperial policy, it was reflected in the violence that increasingly flared up in some cities, towns, and provinces around the Mediterranean. In 386 CE, Marcellus, bishop of Apamea in Syria, had soldiers and labourers demolish the Temple of Zeus in that city, apparently with the support of the praetorian prefect Maternus Cynegius, the emperor's representative in the east. For a bishop with powerful political allies to embark on such a campaign was a grim indicator of the rise of Christian-led persecution. Syria's pagans were not passive in response; when Marcellus next assaulted a temple, in nearby Aulon, he was captured and burned alive.[46]

Yet the attacks on the temples did not cease. Cynegius himself had undertaken a tour of the eastern provinces. With him travelled a body of monks. These were the black-robed, hymn-singing, shock-troops of militant Christianity and they smashed up shrines and temples wherever they marched. In Antioch, a prominent pagan citizen called Libanius denounced their unlawful excesses in a letter to the eastern emperor Theodosius:

> You have neither closed the temples nor banned entrance to them. From the temples and altars you have banished neither fire nor incense nor the offering of other perfumes. But ... these people, Sire, while the law yet remains in force, hasten to attack the temples with sticks and stones and bars of iron, and in some cases, disdaining these with hands and feet. Then utter desolation followers, with the stripping of roofs, demolition of walls, the tearing down of statues and the overthrow of altars, and the priests must either keep quiet or die ... They sweep across the countryside like rivers in spate, and by ravaging the temples, they ravage the estates, for wherever they tear out a temple from an estate, that estate is blinded and lies murdered.[47]

Although it is not certain if Theodosius ever received this appeal, he clearly shared some of the concerns Libanius voiced. In 386 CE, he expressed a preference for a pagan to be overseer of Egypt's temples, since a Christian could not be expected to protect them. On Cynegius's death in 388 CE, the emperor replaced him with Tatianus, an aristocratic pagan. In late 390 CE, he ruled that those troublesome monks should return to the deserts or some 'great empty space', well away from temples and shrines. The problem at this stage, however, was, as Charles Freeman noted, 'the emperor was acting to preserve temples just as his officials were destroying them'.[48]

Christian militancy probably owed its rise chiefly to the fears provoked by Julian and the consequent sense that the Church was not yet safe; the struggle with Satan was not won and the adversary might yet seize again earthly power to threaten the faithful. The lingering legacy of Julian's reign is captured well in the response of Ambrose, bishop of Milan, to the plea of Symmachus for the return of the Altar of Victory to the Senate and the restoration of public funds to the Vestal Virgins and the traditional priesthoods:

> These people complaining about expenses are the ones who never spared our blood, who even destroyed church buildings. These people asking you [Valentinian II] to grant them privileges, too, are the ones who denied us, in Julian's recent law, the ordinary rights to speak and teach ... .[49]

Militancy too, grew perhaps from a sense that Christianity, despite its impressive growth, remained in an active competition for souls. For instance, the cult of *Theos Hypsistos*, the Highest God, 'not admitting a name, known by many names', had developed into a dynamic and attractive synergy of pagan monotheism, Judaism, and Christianity, and was strong across the eastern Mediterranean until well into the fifth century.[50] In the same region, a contemporary group called the *Caelicolae* was denounced for 'Judaising' (either successfully winning converts from Christianity to Judaism, or practising Christianity in a manner adjudged too Jewish). At pagan oracles and shrines, the end of Christianity was being predicted. Augustine of Hippo railed against the 'worshippers of false gods' who, having despaired at the failure of the physical persecution of Christians, now disseminated a slanderous prophecy that the Apostle Peter 'used sorcery to ensure that the name of Christ should be worshipped for 365 years, and on completion of that number of years it should come to an immediate end'.[51]

Thus, even as Christianity flourished and grew, gradually establishing both spiritual and political hegemony, that sense of cosmic struggle and the ongoing conflict with evil did not merely persist, but acquired a new purchase on the hearts and minds of many of the faithful, including bishops. Like Augustine in Hippo, even the once pacifically inclined were coming to accept that 'at times, then, one who suffers persecution is unjust, and one who persecutes is just', and that religious coercion could in fact save souls.[52]

Moving beyond a consideration of the religious legislation preserved in the documentary record, there is material evidence that also points clearly to instances of persecution. The archaeology of religious hatred offers powerful clues but poses difficult questions too. The mute testimony of razed buildings, smashed altars, and defaced idols is often compelling in itself. Temples across Egypt bear such scars. At the Dendara complex, a colossal expenditure of time and physical effort must have been put into hacking and hammering away at the depictions of deities – the statues and relief carvings that iconoclasts targeted – from walls and columns up to 17.2m high and precincts covering 3200m². Only the sheer scale of the buildings prevented complete obliteration. Smaller sites were easier targets. In Lower Slaughter, in Gloucestershire, Britain, excavation of what had once been a rural shrine uncovered altars, votive tablets, and two statues of deities, both deliberately beheaded, and all thrown down a well. The subterranean cult shrines of the god Mithras seem to have been particular targets across the empire. At a site near Strasbourg-Koenigshoffen, a huge relief carved in stone, over 4m high and 2.46m wide, was splintered into fragments in what must again have been a sustained, deliberate, and physically demanding effort.[53]

It is clear, therefore, that acts of destructive violence occurred within pagan temples and shrines at specific sites in both the east and west of the empire on an extensive scale. However, exactly when these rampages happened is not always apparent nor is the identity of the perpetrators: invading barbarian armies, the rioting poor, frenzied religious mobs? And if Christians were responsible, does that necessarily reveal persecution of a pagan minority? Among the most zealous and militant of fourth-century Christians were converts from paganism, such as Firmicus Maternus, who had urged the destruction of the temples upon the emperors in 346 CE. Thus, might a ruined temple have been the handiwork of a formerly pagan community, consensually ridding itself of the profane, demon-haunted sites of its earlier errors?

Yet those awkward questions can, in probability, be answered. The uniformity of the tools used and consistency of technique in attacking particular sites, such as Dendara, suggest an organised and sustained effort, not the sudden action of passing invaders or rioters. The quite deliberate targeting of the heads or faces of deities when other representations, decorative motifs of animals for example, were often ignored, points strongly to a religious motivation. So too do the Christian crosses sometimes carved deeply onto the walls of slighted pagan shrines. The archaeological context of the finds often provides sound information for dating the destruction of temples. The well at Lower Slaughter, for example, was fourth century. Just occasionally too, a grim discovery points to physical violence against humans associated with the destruction of temples and shrines. At the site of a temple of Mithras in Sarrebourg, France, the skeleton of a man in his thirties was discovered, hands chained and with large fragments of a smashed cult relief piled upon him. The victim had been placed, quite deliberately one must conclude, at the base of an idol that had been broken and inverted. A pagan martyr, one is tempted to speculate, killed for defending the altars of his gods? In the most detailed and forensic survey of the archaeological evidence from this period yet written, Eberhard Sauer has concluded that such events occurred but were probably exceptional and overall little blood was spilled. Nevertheless, he argues persuasively that militant Christian interventionism, particularly in the form of physically destructive attacks on temples and shrines, played a key role in the decline of paganism in the late fourth century.[54]

The evidence considered in whole therefore presents a somewhat contrasting picture. Emperors, alongside many influential bishops and Christian theologians, generally rejected persecution and the efficacy of religious coercion. Across the empire, it is *likely* that Christianisation proceeded gradually and peacefully, assimilating and preserving aspects of pagan practice along the way, a phenomenon exemplified in the cult of saints (and, by the fifth century, the emergence of the cult of Mary the Blessed Virgin), which made the Christian Church a hospitable home for those whose religious tendencies veered towards henotheism. Yet in some locales, religious change does appear to have been wrought through violence.

In order to understand why Christianisation proceeded peacefully in some places and was associated with persecution in others, it is necessary to bear in mind the nature of the Roman Empire and the limitations on the power wielded by the state. Despite the centralisation of the third century, and the quest for increased social and religious conformity that had accompanied it, the Roman state remained fundamentally weak in the provinces. Roman emperors could only restrain (or conversely promote) persecution to a rather limited degree. The empire was ruled through regional and provincial elites and thus it was largely local not imperial circumstances that shaped relations between religious communities. The Donatist controversy, for example, while it ultimately had profound implications for wider Christian attitudes towards religious coercion, was very much a North African contest. It was driven by the province's recent history of persecution, personal rivalries for authority, and the existence of particularly strong and influential rigorist congregations. W.H.C. Frend has also suggested peculiar ethnic and social dimensions, with the indigenous agrarian poor challenging the wealthy Roman colonial elite.[55]

Similarly, peculiar local circumstances appear to have been the spur for instances of Christian persecution of pagans. This was not inherent to Christianisation; it was not universal, and it was not driven by an (actually rather weak) central state. Persecution was born of local antagonisms and driven by local personalities. This is not to deny that imperial policy had some effect at local level. Successive legislative acts from Constantine onwards had been designed to create an environment that was unfavourable to the long-term survival of paganism. In some instances, they fostered an atmosphere that was permissive of active hostility towards the shrines and temples of the old gods and to their adherents. This occurred most often where provincial officials or clergy held militant views, and where local conditions were already confrontational and inter-communal relations volatile.

As a case study, events in the Egyptian city of Alexandria illustrate the circumstances that generated intense local persecution well. The ethnically heterogeneous city had a long history of civil disorder. Its majority Greek population was particularly determined to defend its local hegemonic status, by violent means if necessary. This had led to bloody clashes with, in particular, a Jewish population eager to exercise the full rights of urban citizenship. Inevitably, this confrontation, although fundamentally about ethnicity and representation in city politics, had taken on a marked religious dimension.

In 38 CE, Greek mobs, besides attacking Jews in the streets, broke into synagogues and placed statues of the divine Emperor Gaius (Caligula) inside. They were using the cult worship of the emperor as a political weapon; Jews could neither tolerate such idols in their place of worship, nor could they destroy or remove them without committing sacrilege in the eyes of the Roman authorities. Thereafter hostility generally simmered, periodically boiling over into violence. In 115 CE, Jewish communities across Egypt and North Africa, apparently rallying to the call of a messianic leader, had fought with their Greek neighbours, gaining some temporary ascendancy in rural areas but finally were defeated in the cities, notably Alexandria.[56] City politics, religion, and communal violence had, thus, long been intertwined in Alexandria to an unusual degree.

In the fourth century, the rise of Christianity had added yet a further dynamic to this conflicted cityscape. But the Christians were not simply another urban faction competing for political or economic advantage. Their fractious theological debates had a peculiar tendency to descend into acts of wanton violence.[57] Thus, in keeping with Alexandria's riotous traditions, Christians there had fought frequent street battles among themselves, especially over the Arian controversy. They had clashed with pagans too. The new metropolitan bishop George and two of his officials, Dracontius and Diodorus, had aroused pagan fears after their arrival in the city in 357 CE. The city was at that time peculiarly tense and fractured along religious lines; pagans had sacked and desecrated the city's main Christian church the previous year.[58]

With epic tactlessness, George had barely set foot in the city when he archly and publicly wondered for how much longer the Serapeum, the temple of the city's protecting deity Serapis, would stand. He had then prohibited public sacrifice. Soon after, Dracontius had overturned an altar in the city's mint and Diodorus had cropped the curls of some boys in the street because he thought long hair was 'an aspect of the worship of the gods'.[59]

In 362 CE, when Julian had arrested and executed military commanders in Egypt for alleged treason, a mob took the opportunity to deal with the bishop George. He was beaten to death in the street. Dracontius and Diodorus shared his fate. Interestingly, the city's Christians did nothing to save or avenge the bishop. Their acquiescence in his murder is a telling reminder of the complex syndrome of prejudice that characterised religious persecution in this age. George was an Arian and ruled the Christians of Alexandria (many of whom were loyal still to that great enemy of Arianism, the then-exiled bishop Athanasius) with a heavy hand. They may too have looked forward to the destruction of the city's temples and altars, but, in the meantime, they did not mourn the death of the heretic. Some of them were probably in the mob that killed him.[60]

An uneasy truce was subsequently maintained between the competing faiths of Alexandria for the next twenty years. Bishop Athanasius returned to the city but had little reason to follow the fatal example of George's policy of open hostility to the temples. Although the Christian Church probably now enjoyed a clear majority among the population, a sort of urban balance of power was maintained by an informal alliance between pagans, Jews, and Arian Christians that checked any arbitrary abuse of power by Athanasius.[61] In 385 CE, the old patriarch died. Leadership of the Alexandrian Church passed to his secretary, Theophilus. As the city's bishop, it would be Theophilus who would preside over one of the most dramatic and significant of violent confrontations between Christians and pagans in late antiquity: the fall of the Serapeum.

Although this event would have far-reaching and symbolic consequences, it was the product of volatile local circumstances and a fateful but unplanned discovery. Tensions had been heightened by recent events beyond Alexandria. Before his death in 388 CE, the militantly Christian praetorian prefect Maternus Cynegius, presumably accompanied by his black-robed, iron-bar-wielding monks, had twice visited Egypt. He had closed temples and reinforced prohibitions on sacrifice. Theophilus may well have been emboldened by this display of power by a strong-minded provincial official. Recent imperial legislation may have boosted his confidence to act against the temples yet further. Beginning in February 391 CE, the emperor Theodosius issued another series of prohibitions forbidding blood sacrifice and fining officials who entered temples. The latter provision was something of a novelty. In all likelihood, it was aimed at easy-going Christian officials who, as part of their civic duties, had been taking part in cultic rites and festivals, and, by so doing, had offended their more hard-line co-religionists. These had then complained to the emperor.[62]

It was open, however, to a tendentious interpretation as a licence to move against the temples themselves. Whatever its precise provisions and notwithstanding the lack of rigour with which it may have been enforced in some far-flung provinces, imperial religious legislation had thus created an environment that was antagonistic to pagan cults. Locally, the militant, the ambitious, and the ruthless could exploit this atmosphere to pursue the politics of confrontation and rabble-rousing. Theophilus grew more belligerent. Alexandria's pagans were correspondingly angry, fearful, and suspicious.

Fate then chose to make an unfortunate intervention. In 391 CE, while renovating a church, labourers broke into an older subterranean cult shrine beneath this site, now surrendered to Christianity. This sanctuary still contained idols and ritual objects. For Theophilus, the message conveyed by these pathetic relics, abandoned beneath a living, thriving Christian house of worship proved too tempting to resist. Not fearing to provoke, indeed seemingly intent in engaging in an overt display of triumphalism, the bishop had the relics paraded through the city's *agora* (an open space for public assembly) where they were roundly mocked and ridiculed by a boisterous Christian crowd. Alexandria's uneasy truce ended there and then. Pagans, outraged by the sacrilege, gathered, and attacked the taunting despoilers of their holy places. Fighting ebbed and flowed in the streets surrounding the *agora* with much loss of life before the pagans sought refuge in the Serapeum, a solidly built and imposing complex, comprising not just a temple and its precinct but a large and famous library too (its significance was as much political and cultural as religious). Vengeful Christians laid siege.

It is interesting to note that Alexandria's intellectual elites were at the heart of this violence. Among the Serapeum's defenders, three well-respected pagan teachers – Olympius, Ammonius, and Helladius – were particularly prominent. Helladius would later, while in exile, boast of having personally killed nine Christians during the rioting. The influence these men wielded may well have played an important role in the peculiarly aggressive response to the parade in the *agora*. Most of those who have written of these events blame Theophilus for the violence, but there were clearly rabble-rousers amongst the pagans too. The ancient sources assert of the tall and handsome Olympius that no one could resist the words that 'flowed from his holy mouth'.[63] It is possible therefore that they had purposefully mobilised many of their students for this combative defence of Hellenism. The Christians numbered some similarly high-brow rioters among their number, including a teacher of rhetoric called Gessius. He was seized during a pagan sortie from the temple. Dragged inside, he was tortured and then crucified.

The local authorities were confronted by a protracted stand-off that seemed likely to end in considerable bloodshed. Romanus, Count of Egypt, and Evagrius, the *praefectus augustalis* responsible for the upkeep of law in the province, appealed to the emperor himself for guidance. Theodosius was probably anxious for a peaceful solution. The previous year he had courted infamy when he had ordered the massacre of around 7,000 thousand inhabitants of the Greek city of Thessalonika, who had rioted and killed the commander of the local garrison. It is likely that the slaughter had gone far beyond what he had originally intended. He had been greatly shamed by the event. Bishop Ambrose of Milan had chided him for his lack of patience and quick temper, and Theodosius had travelled to his cathedral to perform due penance. His response to the crisis in Alexandria was, thus, to a degree measured. Yet it was a catastrophic blow to the pagans, nevertheless.

The imperial rescript granted amnesty to those in the Serapeum, while proclaiming those Christians they had killed to be martyrs. The specific cults involved in the violence, primarily that of Serapis, were to be suppressed. Hearing these words read out, the pagans fled away. The Christians cheered. The temple was overrun. After a moment of fearful, awe-struck hesitation, the magnificent chryselephantine statue of Serapis (composed of diverse materials, including gold and ivory, assembled on a wooden framework) was toppled and hacked to pieces. Theophilus, once more, would exploit the opportunity for a public demonstration of Christian triumph. Portions of the statue were thrown onto celebratory bonfires all over the city. He then established a monastery on the site of the Serapeum. Emperor Theodosius had endorsed this humiliation of the enfeebled pagan deity. He had signalled that he had now abandoned the Hellenistic and pharaonic tradition of imperial divinity and recognised the overarching spiritual authority of the Christian bishops. Cultic sites would now be correspondingly more vulnerable to religious violence.[64]

In a telling congruence of contingent events, a political struggle for the future of the empire would then deal another blow to pagan hopes for tolerance and push Theodosius towards a more repressive religious policy. In early 392 CE, the youthful western emperor, Valentinian II, had attempted to assert his authority over the man who wielded real power over the west, Arbogast, the commander of his legions. Arbogast was a Frankish chieftain, a barbarian from beyond the empire's borders. So were most of his soldiers, recruited into an over-stretched Roman army, desperately in need of skilled recruits. Valentinian's brave effort to control these unruly allies ended swiftly, with his suspicious death in May 392 CE. Arbogast then raised an unassuming and little-known Roman teacher of rhetoric, Eugenius, to the imperial purple, as a convenient puppet. For the eastern emperor Theodosius, this was a serious political threat: a rival for supremacy rising in the west. Such a challenge was far from unprecedented in Roman history. Theodosius had dealt with another such usurper as recently as 388 CE.

Unfortunately, the contest with Arbogast acquired an unwarranted religious significance. Eugenius was certainly a Christian and it is possible Arbogast was too, although contemporary Christian writers, such as Paulinus, Ambrose's deacon and later biographer, denounced him as a pagan. Similarly, an important political ally of Arbogast, the Roman senator Virius Nicomachus Flavianus, was portrayed in Christian sources as a fanatical and dangerous pagan, who had allegedly threatened to restore the cults of Rome, stable horses in the basilica of Milan, and conscript the clergy into his army.[65]

This was propaganda, but it appears to have been effective. Theodosius's religious legislation now moved more firmly against a range of elements of pagan worship. In November 392 CE, he addressed a new law to the recently appointed, and militantly Christian, praetorian prefect in the east, Flavius Rufinus. This law reiterated sanctions against blood sacrifice (punishable by death), but also imposed fines and confiscation on those who worshipped their *lares* (household gods) with fire, offered wine to their *genius* (spiritual double) or perfumes to their *panates*, the gods of their pantries. Lighting ceremonial lamps, wafting incense, hanging garlands, decorating trees with ribbon and altars with grass, all common elements of private, domestic worship, now became crimes.[66]

This was a far more stringent and intrusive anti-pagan measure than those passed since the reign of Constantine. Explaining the exact cause of this shift is difficult. Speculatively, the (imagined) revival of the pagan cause in the west and the riotous disorder of Alexandria may have played some part. Alongside this novel intrusion into the spiritual world of private citizens, yet further laws against public cult were enacted. To troublesome Alexandria, Theodosius sent a second rescript to Evagrius and Romanus which looked like a 'thorough-going eradication of public paganism within the city'. All the temples were to be closed and no one was to revere shrines or 'attempt anything with reference to the gods or the sacred rites'.[67]

The eastern emperor's main concern remained the political threat that had arisen in the west. He finally met Arbogast's army on 4 September 394 CE, near the Frigidus, a river close to the city of Aquilea in northern Italy. He won a decisive victory. Christian authors continued to suggest that the battle had been a genuinely existential crisis for their faith. Theodosius's victory was thus yet further evidence of God's favour in the ongoing cosmological struggle with a demonically inspired paganism. For example, having described how a divine wind had secured the victory by tearing the javelins from the hands of the emperor's enemies during the fighting, Augustine of Hippo went on to celebrate how Theodosius then 'cast down the images of Jupiter which had been supposedly consecrated against him'.[68]

This tendentious interpretation of the barbarian Arbogast's bid for power in the west demonstrates the extent to which the militant Christian conception of an ongoing cosmological warfare was coming to dominate mainstream opinion within the wider Church. Combined with the acceptance of physical, bodily coercion as a legitimate means of saving souls, this combative posture posed a significant and unprecedented threat to paganism in the final years of the fourth century.

Theodosius himself died in 395 CE. Although, until the very last years of his reign, his own religious policy had not differed substantially from the forbearance practised by Constantine, his legacy was marked: a climate of opinion in which militant Christians, including powerful bishops and court officials and provincial administrators could, if they so chose, act without restraint against those outside the church. In 399 CE, two high-ranking officials, Counts Jovius and Gaudentius, toured Africa, smashing statues and demolishing temples. In Carthage, they closed a major cult site, the temple of Juno Caelestis, much to the delight of the bishop Augustine, who regarded this as an instance of just persecution and a fulfilment of God's will.[69]

Yet, even bearing that the potential for such persecution now existed, the evidence also suggests, once again, that simply because legislation had been passed does not mean that it was necessarily enforced. Gradualism continued to be the reality of policies designed to make Christians out of pagans. It was not until the year 529 CE, over two centuries on from the accession of Constantine, that the emperor Justinian actually passed laws demanding that 'those who have not yet been baptised must come forward'.[70] Patterns of persecution of pagans in the fifth and sixth centuries suggest that Christianisation proceeded peacefully in most places and aggressively in some, as had been the case in the preceding century. The influence of a particularly charismatic individual remained an important factor in initiating local persecution. For example, one prominent figure in early fifth-century Egypt was Shenoute (*c.355–c.466* CE), the legendarily long-lived abbot of the monastery of Atripe. He was the scourge of heretics and a despoiler of temples, who carried the war against idols to those remote corners of the countryside where pagan practices lingered longest.[71]

Yet many pagans seemed to have abandoned their traditional beliefs from the 390s CE onwards, not as a direct and fearful response to coercion and the destruction of their temples, but rather because their gods seemed so impotent in the face of such attacks. In Alexandria, it was reported that when the head of defeated Serapis was carried through the streets it was mocked even by former adherents. Similarly, when predictions that the Nile would not rise and water the land because of the sacrilege committed by Christians were sharply contradicted by rather heavy flooding, pagans began to sneer that 'the river, like an old man or fool, could not control his waters'.[72]

At the same time, across the Romano-Hellenic world, Christian miracles were well attested by the most credible authorities. Augustine himself recalled 'a miracle that happened at Milan while I was there, when a blind man had his sight restored … A great crowd had assembled to see the bodies of the martyrs Protasius and Gervasius and the miracle took place before all those witnesses'.[73] The old gods were powerless. The God of the Christians worked wonders. Conversion was a rational response.

However, some adherents of the ancient cults could be stubbornly persistent in their faith. They were now more vulnerable in the face of militant Christianity and a growing minority status, but they remained a visible presence in communities around the Roman world for a long time to come, notwithstanding the assertion of the co-emperors Honorius and Theodosius II, in 423 CE, that there were no longer any pagans.[74] Even some of those involved in the most violent confrontations continued to practise their beliefs relatively freely in the changed climate following Theodosius's death. Helladius and Ammonius, leaders of the doomed defence of the Serapeum, both fled Alexandria and settled, without apparent problem, in the imperial capital, Constantinople. There they openly taught Hellenism and (more discretely) served as priests in the cults of Zeus/Ammon and Thoth/Hermes respectively.[75]

Elsewhere, pagans and paganism continued to wield some influence. When, in 410 CE, a barbarian army of Visigoths under King Alaric was bearing down on Rome, negotiations took place between Pope Innocent I and pagan priests, as the latter offered to perform certain rites that had apparently saved another city from destruction. The priests found a firm supporter in the city's pagan prefect Pompeianus. Pope Innocent, too, was apparently tempted but insisted that the rites take place in secret. The pagans, on the other hand, argued that the ceremonies would not work unless they were conducted in public and involved the full participation of the Senate. The rites did not therefore take place (and Rome was sacked by Alaric), but the conversation itself was evident of the hold that the old beliefs could still have, even on popes and prefects.[76]

In Alexandria, paganism persisted after the fall of the Serapeum. Yet it remained, too, a most volatile city, where forbearance might turn to persecution with a shocking rapidity. An appalling and infamous murder in 415 CE would demonstrate both the threat of violence that now hovered over pagan communities, but also the very local and contingent factors that remained the principal catalysts in turning a hostile climate of opinion into the actual shedding of blood. The victim of the murder was the philosopher Hypatia (*c.*355–415 CE). Her killers, who hacked her to death with shards of broken pottery, were a Christian mob. They justified their appalling savagery on the grounds of their horror of *superstitio*. Hypatia, they howled, was a sorceress, an active practitioner of magic and an agent of Satan, wielding an unholy power over the city and, crucially, its prefect, Orestes. Yet the philosopher was widely renowned for her moral and intellectual authority, chastity, ethical courage, and commitment to pluralism. Her cruel murder might therefore be seen as emblematic of Christian fanaticism and the inevitability of persecution in the name of the faith. The actual circumstances of her death, however, reveal a far more complex story, that centred on an ugly struggle for worldly, not spiritual, authority.[77]

Hypatia was a central figure in the power politics of Alexandria not because she held a position of authority herself, but because she wielded considerable influence across all of that troubled city's communities. In Constantinople, the Christian historian Socrates Scholasticus paid her a handsome tribute while explaining her importance:

[Hypatia] made such attainments in literature and science as to far surpass all the philosophers of her own time ... On account of the self-possession and ease of manner which she had acquired in consequence of the cultivation of her mind she not infrequently appeared in public in the company of the magistrates. Neither did she feel abashed in coming to an assembly of men. For all men on account of her extraordinary dignity and virtue admired her the more.[78]

Her lectures drew large crowds, but she was closest to a devoted circle of pupils, both pagan and Christian, that she gathered around her from the 380s CE onwards. These students were, in general, representative of the wealthy elite of Romano-Greek society. They went on from their studies to secure important positions, while maintaining close contact with their former teacher. At least two of them, the brothers Synesius and Euoptius of Cyrene, became bishops.

Furthermore, when high-ranking imperial officials arrived in Alexandria, they too attended her lectures and sought her counsel. In 412 CE, the city's new prefect, Orestes, disembarked after a voyage from Constantinople and seems to have quickly forged a productive working relationship with Hypatia, frequently seeking her advice on political and municipal matters. Orestes, like many of her circle, was a Christian, but his friendship with the pagan philosopher should cause no surprise. Hypatia was fulfilling a well-established public role in Romano-Greek cities, that of the philosopher who could speak truth to power, exercising the right known as *parrhésia* (freedom of speech). It was the weight her opinion carried, especially with Orestes, rather than her religious beliefs, that sealed her fate.[79]

Orestes himself was struggling to maintain his own position. He represented the old ruling class of empire, of good family and education, and appointed to secular authority as the direct representative of the emperor. The rival he found in Alexandria, on the other hand, was a figure of the new order, the rising class of ecclesiastical power brokers that was breaking the hold of the old senatorial caste on government: Patriarch Cyril (d.444 CE), nephew and successor to Theophilus. The two men seemed first to have clashed following Cyril's high-handed and provocative treatment of the leaders of Alexandria's Jewish community. He had threatened them with the severest penalties after they had denounced one of his men to the new prefect as a troublemaker. In febrile Alexandria, these angry words quickly developed into street battles.

Christian authors blamed the Jews for instigating the actual violence, but there is no doubt that it was the Jewish community that suffered the gravest losses. The patriarch, through his considerable patronage network, could mobilise a significant proportion of Alexandria's population to fight his battles. He was also able to call upon the muscle of the *parabalini* (supposedly 'hospital attendants'), whom he directly employed and the zealous monks from the nearby monasteries of Nitria. Their numbers proved overwhelming and by the time the fighting had died down, all the synagogues of Alexandria were in Cyril's hands. Some were promptly converted into churches. Jewish homes were ransacked. Many families were driven from the city forever. Although 'excessively grieved that a city of such magnitude should have been so suddenly bereft of so large a portion of its population', Orestes was powerless. All he could do in response was to fire off an indignant report to Constantinople while he plotted how to curb the wayward bishop's pretensions.[80]

An attempt at reconciliation brokered by the city's council failed. Cyril arrived ostentatiously flourishing a book of the Gospels at Orestes, seeking a symbolic act of submission to his spiritual authority. Orestes refused to take the book, preserving his status, but thereby laying himself open to the charge of being lukewarm in his faith. Cyril was now able to use religion as a weapon. Shortly after, Orestes was attacked in the street by a mob of five hundred monks from Nitria, denouncing him as a crypto-pagan. One of them, Ammonius, hurled a rock that bloodied the prefect's head. Shamefully, most of his bodyguard fled away. His life would have been in danger, had not a number of public-spirited Alexandrians driven off the monks, apart, that is, from Ammonius who was seized and presented to the prefect. He died soon after under torture. Cyril's cynical attempt to have him then proclaimed a martyr failed to persuade many Alexandrians, who judged the dead monk the author of his own misfortune.[81] Orestes's response to the incident was to forge an alliance with disgruntled elite Christians and pagans, Jewish leaders and Hypatia herself. She was at the centre of an extensive and useful network of patronage of her own, embracing clergy, magistrates, and imperial officials.

For Cyril, this was a potentially dangerous combination, but he could still rely on the religious sensibilities of his followers to counter the emerging threat. Hypatia was, at one and the same time, both the lynchpin of the alliance and its weakest spot. The rumours were soon being spread: the pagan sorceress had bewitched the prefect and drawn him away from the Church. One day in March, 415 CE, as the philosopher was returning to her home, she was waylaid by a Christian mob, driven 'by a fierce and bigoted zeal'.[82]

They dragged her to a church, built on the site of a former temple, where she was murdered and her body burned, an act associated with ritual purification. Cyril, naturally, had been careful to keep some distance between himself and those who bloodied their hands in his cause, but few doubt he was responsible for Hypatia's death. He was clearly the main beneficiary too. Despite imperial censure, he had broken Orestes's faction and now he ruled in Alexandria. Christian crowds hailed him for his righteous victory over the idolators, but they had not been his target. This was a political assassination, wearing the guise of religious persecution.[83]

The confluence of factors – political, religious, social, and personal – that had contributed to Hypatia's murder are a powerful reminder of the contingent nature of specific instances of persecution in late antiquity. There is, however, little disguising the broader context in which the philosopher died. In the early fourth century, the attitude of Constantine and his successors towards non-Christians had been characterised by forbearance and a conservative preference for gradual, peaceful change over coercion and a radical transformation of the religious world. Indeed, much of Christianity's success must be credited to its ultimate capacity for syncretism with henotheistic belief systems and its assimilation of those Greco-Roman traditions which were so important to a past-orientated society. Christian persecution of pagans was, therefore, neither inevitable nor was it the principal mechanism by which the empire was Christianised.

Through most of the fourth century, imperial 'anti-pagan' legislation was chiefly designed to undermine public cult worship, end blood sacrifice, and prevent Christians from having to take part in traditional rites. It did not seek to outlaw private beliefs or domestic worship (except the practice of harmful magic), and there was a general consensus that forced conversion was invalid.

Yet, by the final decade of the fourth century, it seemed as if a warrant for persecution had been granted and that in some volatile provinces and cities, Christianity and paganism clashed violently. Theodosius's final legislation moved beyond the public and into the realm of private, domestic worship. Even when imperial policy remained restrained, the more militant of the emperor's officials and his bishops had exploited a religious climate that became permissive of confrontation to harass pagans and tear down temples and overthrow altars. The same zealous impulses that had driven the evolution of martyrdom into a doctrine that sanctioned holy violence proved very useful to those charismatic rabble-rousers who sought the destruction of the temples. Black-robed monks, singing hymns as they threw rocks and brandished iron bars, or concerned Christian citizens, roused to murderous anger by talk of pagan sorcery, provided the strong-arms that provincial and city authorities needed to pursue their local quarrels. This was true not only of those who persecuted out of genuine, if fanatical, religious commitment, like Maternus Cynegius, but also those, like Cyril of Alexandria, who pursued more worldly contests and merely hid behind claims of righteousness.

Christian intolerance and militancy had flourished partly because of the climate of opinion created by legislation hostile to paganism, however restrained its original objectives and however weakly it had been enacted. It had also been catalysed by the tumultuous events that separated Licinius and Constantine's edict of Milan in 313 CE, promising 'all men the freedom to follow whatever religion each one wished', from the death of Hypatia a century later. The compromise with the worldly and ugly imperatives of political authority, the bitter and radicalising internal conflicts with heretics and schismatics, the frightened backlash to the existential threats posed by pagan resilience and, in particular, the reign of Julian the Apostate, all ultimately compromised the Church's commitment to the policy of forbearance.

Yet, in all probability, it was that policy that had delivered the most converts. For that reason, the character of the Church would be marked for centuries to come by its strong pagan heritage. Indeed, the cult of saints and the Blessed Virgin Mary became intrinsic to the practice of Christianity until the Reformation. Other, less welcome, pagan practices survived too. In a late sixth-century sermon, the bishop Martin of Braga in Galicia (in modern Portugal) berated his rustic congregation for lighting ceremonial flames at certain rocks, trees, and crossroads. They also observed signs and omens and practiced divination, dropped offerings of wine and bread in springs, cast spells and could occasionally be heard to invoke the names of the old gods as they worked. The sermon proved so pertinent to clerical needs it was widely copied and translated, a testimony to the widespread persistence of 'pagan' practices. Elements of it were apparent in a sermon delivered by an English abbot, Aelfric of Eynsham, in about 1000, over four hundred years after it was originally written.[84]

Ultimately, the Church had preserved as much as it had destroyed and had won more souls through persuasion than persecution. This triumph had left only one other faith widely practised and resilient in the European successor states to the Roman Empire: Judaism. And the story of medieval Europe's Jewish communities would reveal once more the complex and contingent nature of religious persecution.

Notes

1 Daniel Sarefield, 'Book Burning in the Christian Roman Empire', in H.A. Drake (ed.), *Violence in Late Antiquity* (Farnham: Ashgate, 2006), pp.287–296.

2 Mary Beard, John North, and Simon Price, *Religions of Rome*, Volume 1 (Cambridge: Cambridge University Press, 1998), p.231.

3 Peter Brown, 'Religious Coercion in the Later Roman Empire: The Case of North Africa', *History*, 48 (1963), p.287; A.A. Barb, 'The Survival of the Magic Arts', in Arnaldo Momigliano (ed.), *The Conflict Between Paganism and Christianity in the Fourth Century* (Oxford: Clarendon Press, 1963), pp.100–125.

4 Ammianus Marcellinus, *The Later Roman Empire (AD 354–378)*, Book 16, Chapter 8, translated by Walter Hamilton (London: Penguin, 1986), pp.96–97.

5 Beard et al., *Religions of Rome*, Volume 1, p.229.

6 Porphyry, 'On Abstinence from Animal Food', in A.D. Lee (ed.), *Pagans and Christians in Late Antiquity* (London: Routledge, 2000), pp.32–33; Scott Bradbury, 'Julian's Pagan Revival and the Decline of Blood Sacrifice', *Phoenix*, 49, 4 (1995), pp.334–337.

7 *Laws on Pagan Practices in the 340s preserved in the Theodosian Code 16.10.2–3*, in Lee (ed.), *Pagans and Christians*, pp.96–97.

8 Ammianus Marcellinus, *Later Roman Empire*, Book 16, Chapter 10 in Hamilton (trans.), pp.101–102.

9 Quoted in Ramsey Macdonald, *Christianity & Paganism in the Fourth to Eighth Centuries* (New Haven, CT: Yale University Press, 1997), pp.13–14.

10 Julian, Letters 84 and 89, in Lee (ed.), *Pagans & Christians*, p.97.

11 Ammianus Marcellinus, *Later Roman Empire*, Book 22, Chapter 5, in Hamilton (trans.), p.239.

12 Quoted in Charles Freeman, *The Closing of the Western Mind: The Rise of Faith and the Fall of Reason* (London: Pimlico, 2003), pp.186–187.

13 Ammianus Marcellinus, *Later Roman Empire*, Book 22, Chapter 5, in Hamilton (trans.), p.239

14 Julian, *Letter 61C*, in Lee (ed.), *Pagans and Christians*, pp.102–104.

15 Peter Brown, *Power and Persuasion in Late Antiquity* (Madison: University of Wisconsin Press, 1992), pp.35–70.

16 Ammianus Marcellinus, Book 22, Chapter 10, in Hamilton (trans.), p.246.

17 Socrates Scholasticus, *The Ecclesiastical History*, Book 3, Chapter 13 (Wilmington, NC: Nuvision, 2007), p.144.

18 Clifford Ando, 'Pagan Apologetics and Christian Intolerance in the Ages of Themistius and Augustine', *Journal of Early Christian Studies*, 4 (1996), p.181; Jacob Neusner, *Judaism and Christianity in the Age of Constantine* (Chicago, IL: University of Chicago Press,1987), pp.16–17, 81–85; Isaiah Gafni, 'The World

of the Talmud: From the Mishnah to the Arab Conquest', in Hershal Shanks (ed.), *Christianity and Rabbinic Judaism* (Washington, DC: SPCK, 1993), pp.240–244.

19 'Epigraphic Evidence for Julian's Religious Policies', in Lee (ed.), *Pagans and Christians*, pp.104–105.

20 Socrates Scholasticus, *Ecclesiastical History*, Book 3, Chapter 13, p.144.

21 Julian, Letter 84, in Lee (ed.), *Pagans and Christians*, pp.97–98.

22 Ammianus Marcellinus, Book 22, Chapter 12, in Hamilton (trans.), pp.248–249.

23 Ammianus Marcellinus, Book 22, Chapter 12, in Hamilton (trans.), pp.248–249.

24 Ammianus Marcellinus, Book 22, Chapter 12, in Hamilton (trans.), pp.248–249.

25 Socrates Scholasticus, *Ecclesiastical History*, Book 3, Chapter 13, p.145; Michael Gaddis, *There is No Crime for Those who Have Christ: Religious Violence in the Christian Roman Empire* (Berkeley: University of California Press, 2005), pp.92–93.

26 Gaddis, *There is No Crime*, pp.94–95.

27 Ammianus Marcellinus, Book 23, Chapter 1; Book 25, Chapter 3, in Hamilton (trans.), pp.255–256, 292–294.

28 Alan Cameron, *The Last Pagans of Rome* (Oxford: Oxford University Press, 2011), p.67.

29 Charles Freeman, *AD 381: Heretics, Pagans and the Christian State* (London: Pimlico, 2008), pp.102–103

30 Theodosian Code 16.10.8, in Lee (ed.), *Pagans and Christians*, p.113.

31 Gregory of Nazianzus and John Chrysostom, quoted in Cameron, *Last Pagans of Rome*, pp.70–71.

32 Michele Renee Salzman, 'Pagan-Christian Religious Violence', in H.A. Drake (ed.) *Violence in Antiquity* (Ashgate: Farnham, 2006), pp.267–273.

33 Salzman, 'Pagan-Christian Religious Violence', p.272.

34 Stephen Mitchell, 'The Cult of Theos Hypsistos between Pagans, Jews and Christians', in Polymnia Athanassiadi and Michael Frede (eds), *Pagan Monotheism in Late Antiquity* (Oxford: Oxford University Press, 1999), p.124.

35 Galerius 'Letter Against the Lupercalia', in Beard et al. (eds), *Religions of Rome*, Volume 2, pp.123–124. See also Pierre Chuvin, *A Chronicle of the Last Pagans* (Cambridge, MA: Harvard University Press, 1990), pp.119–149.

36 Christopher Jones, *Between Pagan and Christian* (Cambridge, MA: Harvard University Press, 2014), pp.99–101, 123.

37 Cameron, *Last Pagans of Rome*, p.67.

38 Peter Brown, *Power and Persuasion in Late Antiquity* (Madison: University of Wisconsin Press, 1992), pp. 35–70.

39 Freeman, *Closing of the Western Mind*, p.236.

40 Clifford Ando, 'Pagan Apologetics and Christian Intolerance', p.179.

41 Candida Moss, *The Myth of Persecution: How Early Christians Invented a Story of Martyrdom* (New York, NY.: Harper Collins, 2013), pp.60–61.

42 Tertullian, 'On Prescription Against Heretics', Chapter 7, in *The Ante-Nicene Fathers*, Volume III, translated and edited by Alexander Roberts, James Donaldson, and Arthur Cleveland Coxe (New York: Cosimo, 2007), p.246.

43 Freeman, *Closing of the Western Mind*, p.71; Maren R. Niehoff, 'Philo's Views on Paganism', in Graham Stanton and Guy Stroumsa (eds), *Tolerance and Intolerance in early Judaism and Christianity* (Cambridge: Cambridge University Press, 1998), pp.135–158.

44 Ando, 'Pagan Apologetics and Christian Intolerance', pp.194–197

45 Symmachus, 'Memorandum 3.3–10', in Lee (ed.), *Pagans and Christians*, p.117. For a full account, see Cameron, *The Last Pagans of Rome*, pp.33–56.

46 Chuvin, *Chronicle of the Last Pagans*, pp.59–60.

47 Libanius, 'In Defence of Temples', in Lee (ed.), *Pagans and Christians*, pp.121–122. On the violence of monks, see Fabrizio Vecoli, 'Violence and Monks: From a Mystical Concept to an Intolerant Practice (Fourth to Fifth Century)', in Jitse H.F. Dijkstra and Christian R. Raschle (eds), *Religious Violence in the Ancient World from Classical Athens to Late Antiquity*, Cambridge: Cambridge University Press, 2020, pp.306–322.

48 Freeman, AD 381, pp.119–120.

49 Ambrose, 'Letter 72, 3–4', in Lee (ed.), *Pagans and Christians*, p.118.

50 Sven Günther, 'A New Document for Theos Hypsistos', *Zeitschrift für Papyrologie und Epigraphik*, 212 (2019), pp. 158–160; Julia Ustinova, 'The "Thiasoi" of Theos Hypsistos in Tanais', *History of Religions*, 31 (1991), pp.150–180.

51 Augustine, *City of God*, Book 18, Chapter 54, pp.838–839; Mitchell, 'The Cult of Theos Hypsistos between Pagans, Jews and Christians', pp.81–148.

52 St Augustine, Letter 93.8, p.382, and Letter 138.2, quoted in Herbert Deane, *The Political and Social Ideas of St Augustine* (New York: Columbia University Press, 1963), p.165.

53 Eberhard Sauer, *The Archaeology of Religious Hatred in the Roman and Early Medieval World* (Stroud: The History Press, 2003), pp.59, 79–80, 89–96.

54 Sauer, *Archaeology of Religious Hatred*, pp.157–159, 165–173.

55 W.H.C. Frend, *The Early Church* (London: SCM Press, 1982), pp.153–154.

56 James S. McLaren, 'Jews and the Imperial Cult: From Augustus to Domitian', *Journal for the Study of the New Testament*, 27 (2005), pp.262–269; Peter Schäfer, *Judeophobia: Attitudes toward the Jews in the Ancient World* (Cambridge, MA: Harvard University Press, 1997), pp.136–160; Lee I.A. Levine, 'Judaism from the Destruction of Jerusalem to the End of the Second Jewish Revolt: 70–135 ce', in Hershal Shanks (ed.), *Christianity and Rabbinic Judaism* (Washington, DC: SPCK, 1993), pp.125–149.

57 Richard Lim, 'Religious Disputation and Social Disorder in Late Antiquity', *Historia: Zeitschrift für Alte Geschichte*, Bd. 44 (1995), pp.204–231.

58 Christopher Haas, *Alexandria in Late Antiquity: Topography and Social Conflict* (Baltimore, MD: Johns Hopkins University Press, 1997), p.283.

59 Haas, *Alexandria in Late Antiquity*, p.288.

60 Ammianus Marcellinus, Book 22, Chapters 11 and 13, in Hamilton (trans.), pp.246–250; Haas, *Alexandria in Late Antiquity*, pp.286–294.

61 Hass, *Alexandria in Late Antiquity*, pp.159–160.

62 Cameron, *The Last Pagans*, p.62.

63 Hass, *Alexandria in Late Antiquity*, p.164.

64 This account of the fall of the Serapeum is drawn from John H.F. Dijkstra, 'Crowd Behaviour and the Destruction of the Serapeum at Alexandria, 391/392 CE', in Dijkstra and Raschle (eds), *Religious Violence in the Ancient World*, pp.286–305; Maria Dzielska, *Hypathia of Alexandria* (Cambridge, MA.: Harvard University Press, 1995), pp.79–82; Hass, *Alexandria in Late Antiquity*, pp.160–166, and John F. Shean, 'The Destruction of the Serapeum in 391: Religious Violence and Intolerance in an Imperial Age', *Journal of Religion and Violence*, 9 (2021), pp.149–170.

65 Cameron, *The Last Pagans of Rome*, p.84.

66 Cameron, *The Last Pagans of Rome*, pp.74–92; Chuvin, *Chronicle of the Last Pagans*, pp.69–72.

67 Haas, *Alexandria*, p.166.

68 Augustine, *City of God*, Book 5, Chapter 20, p.222.

69 Freeman, AD *381*, p.130; Paula Fredriksen, *Augustine and the Jews* (New Haven, CT: Yale University Press, 2010), pp.340–341.

70 Chuvin, *Chronicle of the Last Pagans*, p.133.

71 'Christianisation in Rural Egypt from Besa, Life of Shenoute', in Lee (ed), *Pagans and Christians*, pp.137–138.

72 Haas, *Alexandria in Late Antiquity*, p.167.

73 Augustine, *City of God*, Book 22, Chapter 8, p.1038; Ramsey Macmullen, *Christianity & Paganism* (New Haven, CT: Yale University Press, 1997), pp.93–97

74 Chuvin, *Chronicle of the Last Pagans*, p.79.

75 Alan Cameron, 'Wandering Poets: A Literary Movement in Byzantine Egypt', *Historia: Zeitschrift für Alte Geschichte*, Bd. 14 (1965), p.474.

76 MacMullen, *Christianity and Paganism*, p.22; Chuvin, *Chronicle of the Last Pagans*, p.83.

77 My interpretation of the life and death of Hypatia is drawn primarily from Maria Dzielska, *Hypatia of Alexandria*, translated by F. Lyra (Cambridge, MA.: Harvard University Press, 1995).

78 Socrates Scholasticus, *The Ecclesiastical History*, Chapter 15, p.270.

79 Peter Brown, *Power and Persuasion in Late Antiquity*, pp.115–116.

80 Socrates Scholasticus, *Ecclesiastical History*, Chapter 13, p.268.

81 Socrates Scholasticus, *Ecclesiastical History*, Chapter 14, p.269.

82 Socrates Scholasticus, *Ecclesiastical History*, Chapter 15, p.270.

83 Dzielaka, *Hypatia of Alexandria*, p.104.

84 Jones, *Between Pagan and Christian*, pp.123–124.

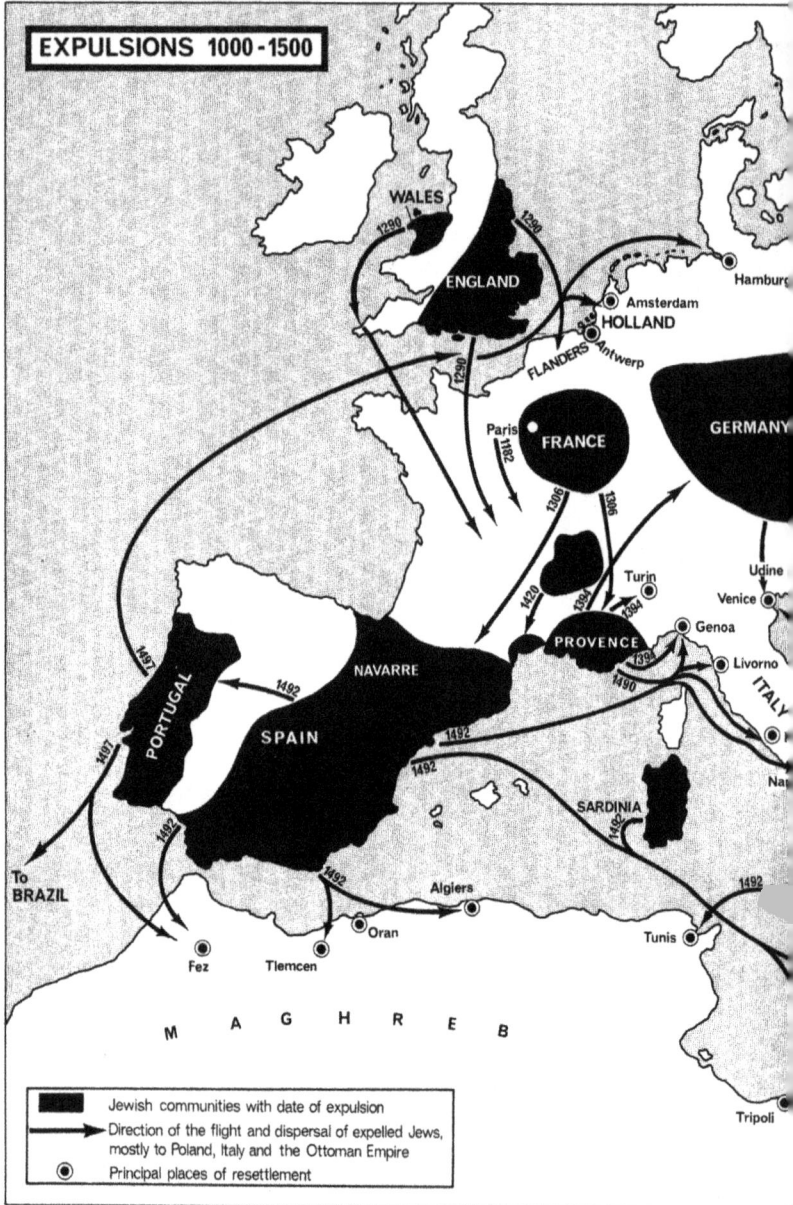

Map 4.1 Expulsions, 1000–1500. From *The Routledge Atlas of Jewish History*, ninth edition, by Martin Gilbert, 2023, copyright Martin Gilbert, 1969. By Routledge. Reproduced by permission of Taylor & Francis Group.

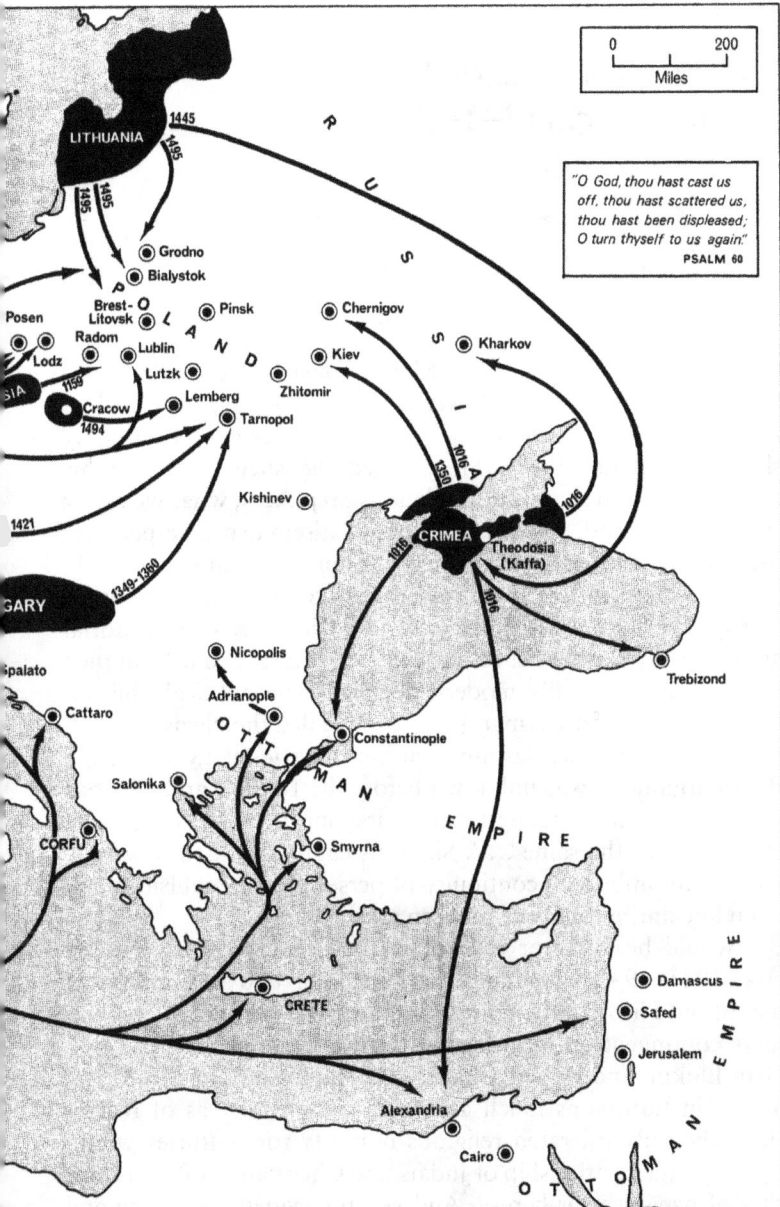

LITHUANIA

1445

1495

1495

1495

RUSSIA

0   200

Miles

"O God, thou hast cast us
off, thou hast scattered us,
thou hast been displeased;
O turn thyself to us again."
PSALM 60

Grodno

Bialystok

Posen

Brest-
Litovsk

Pinsk

Chernigov

Kharkov

Radom

Lublin

Lodz

Lutzk

Kiev

POLAND

1159

Zhitomir

Cracow

Lemberg

1494

Tarnopol

1421

Kishinev

1016

1550

1016

CRIMEA

Theodosia
(Kaffa)

1349-1360

1016

GARY

1016

Spalato

Nicopolis

Adrianople

Trebizond

Cattaro

OTTOMAN

Constantinople

Salonika

EMPIRE

CORFU

Smyrna

Damascus

Safed

CRETE

Jerusalem

Alexandria

OTTOMAN EMPIRE

Cairo

OTTOM

4 'Slay Them Not'

The Medieval Roots of Modern Antisemitism, *c.*313–1492

In 1879, the German journalist Wilhelm Marr popularised the term 'anti-semitism' to characterise his hostility towards Jews. This was, essentially, a political concept. Marr believed that Jews dominated Germany's economy and ruthlessly exploited its people. He rejected the suggestion that his ideology had any connection to medieval religious prejudices, what we might term 'anti-Judaism'.[1] Instead, he insisted upon antisemitism's respectably 'scientific' basis in contemporary racial theory. Supposedly innate 'Jewish' characteristics were transmitted from generation to generation: materialism, misanthropy, lecherousness, impiety, and an innately conspiratorial nature.[2] It has not merely been racist thinkers such as Marr who have argued that antisemitism is an essentially modern doctrine. The political philosopher Hannah Arendt, herself a German Jew who had fled the Nazis in 1933, asserted that 'Antisemitism, a secular nineteenth-century ideology – which in name, though not argument, was unknown before the 1870s – and religious Jew-hatred, inspired by the mutually hostile antagonism of two conflicting creeds, are obviously not the same … '. She thus cautioned against writing a Jewish history 'of an unbroken continuity of persecutions, expulsions and massacres', from late antiquity to the modern era.[3]

Certainly, it would be an error to explain the genocide of six million European Jews, 1941–1945, as simply the climax of two millennium of sustained persecution. Historically, episodes of persecution were in fact episodic and highly contingent on local factors. Hence historians such as Salo Baron, Jonathan Elukin, and Robert Chazan have understood the historical Jewish experience in Europe as much as one of opportunity as of repression.[4] Indeed, as the only tolerated religious minority for centuries within Christendom, the unique relationship of Judaism to Christianity offers a stark contrast to that of paganism or heresy. And yet, the evidence for long and dark continuities cannot be ignored either. The connection between modern 'racist' antisemitism and medieval 'religious' antagonism to Judaism is far stronger than has often been allowed.

In one study, the German economic historians Nico Voigtländer and Hans-Joachim Voth identified four hundred towns that were home to Jewish

DOI: 10.4324/9781003494331-5

communities and were affected by the arrival of the Black Death in the years 1348–1350. Jews were often blamed for the plague and in some cases those medieval Jewish communities were cruelly persecuted. In others, they were spared. Voigtländer and Voth then looked at events in those same towns during the twenty years following Germany's defeat in the First World War They found:

> ... persistence of anti-Semitic attitudes and behavior for more than half a millennium. Localities that burned their Jews in 1348–50 showed mark-edly higher levels of anti-Semitism in the interwar period: attacks on Jews were 6 times more likely in the 1920s in towns and cities with Black Death pogroms; the Nazi Party's share of the vote in 1928 – when it had a strong anti-Jewish focus – was 1.5 times higher; readers' letters to a virulently anti-Semitic Nazi newspaper *(Der Stürmer)* were more frequent; attacks on synagogues during the 'Night of Broken Glass' *(Reichskristallnacht)* in 1938 were more common; and a higher proportion of Jews was deported under the Nazis.[5]

Such persistence suggests that a neat distinction between modern anti-semitism and medieval anti-Judaism would be hard to sustain. The idea of Jews as the conspiratorial enemy of Christian communities emerged in antiquity in the *Adversus Judaeos* (against the Jews) tradition of Christian polemic. The stereotypical 'racial' Jewish characteristics identified by nine-teenth- and twentieth-century antisemites were all well established in popular culture by the end of the fifteenth century. So, indeed, was the 'racial' notion that these traits passed from generation to generation in the bloodline, regardless of religious identity. This is not to suggest that the horrors of the Holocaust were in any sense predetermined centuries earlier. However, any understanding of the twentieth century's paradigmatic genocide must surely acknowledge the historically very deep-rooted prejudices that fuelled such murderous persecution.

It is important, but surprisingly difficult, to determine when exactly the history of a specific hostility towards Jews should begin. Some scholars would look to the pre-Christian world, and see in the attitudes of Egyptians, Greeks, and Romans the origins of an enduring hostility. For Peter Schäfer, the exclusive nature of Jewish monotheism, their sense of being a chosen people, their refusal to intermarry, the legalism of their dietary restrictions and Sabbath observance, the (to Roman eyes particularly) abhorrent prac-tice of circumcision and their proselytism, all marked Jews out in the ancient world for a particular odium. Both the Egyptians (for whom the story of Exodus had been particularly offensive) and the Greeks, he argued, held a crude contempt for Jews as misanthropists and the 'outcasts of humankind'. Roman attitudes were a little more complex. Although sharing much of the Greek attitude towards Judaism, they also displayed a measure of respect for the antiquity of the Jewish religion and their devotion to God. There were, indeed, both Romans and Greeks who were sympathetic monotheists or henotheists (worshippers of a supreme deity), 'God-fearers', who willingly associated themselves with the local synagogue. Some even converted to Judaism. Yet that act itself provoked hatred and anxiety among the mass of Romans. For them, the abandonment of one's own ancestral gods was not merely impious but treasonous.[6]

One can then find ugly prejudices expressed against Jews in antiquity. The politician and lawyer Cicero (106–43 BCE) once reminded a jury of 'the odium of Jewish gold' and 'you know they stick together [and of] how influential they are in informal assemblies'.[7] Beyond hostile sentiments, there is evidence of sectarian violence. In 139 BCE, Jews were expelled from Rome, an event repeated in 19 CE, by the authority of the emperor Tiberius, and again in 41 (or 49) CE by Claudius. The Jewish philosopher Philo recorded that a contentious visit by Herod Agrippa (the unpopular client-king through whom the Romans ruled Judaea) to Alexandria in 38 CE, provoked the Roman prefect Avillius Flaccus to exclude Jews from participation in city politics. A riot ensued during which many Jewish lives were lost. The bodies of victims were dragged through the streets and leading members of the Jewish community were publicly scourged. Mobs of Greeks and Egyptians broke into synagogues and placed statues of the 'divine' emperor Gaius (Caligula) inside. A similar event occurred in Jamnia, in Judaea itself, soon after. On that occasion, the icons and altars placed in their synagogues were destroyed by the city's Jews. This action seems, in turn, to have provoked Gaius's dire (but ultimately abortive) threat to erect a statue of himself inside the Temple of Jerusalem.[8]

Yet, it may be misleading to conclude from such events that a specific and exceptional hostility towards Jews analogous to later prejudices existed. Greeks and Romans exhibited a generalised contempt towards conquered peoples. Cicero's bigotry extended widely. He denounced Egyptians as depraved and their religious beliefs as verging on the demented: 'Who does not know the customs of the Egyptians? Their minds are infected with degraded superstitions ... many monsters and beasts of every sort are held by them sacred to the gods'. In Rome, all immigrants were, for the poet Juvenal, a danger: 'ready to worm their way into the houses of the great and become their masters'. Those from Syria and Anatolia attracted his especial spite: 'they are experts in flattery, dishonest, lecherous and promiscuous. They take over the city with their money'.[9] Jews appear to have been among the objects of a sweeping xenophobia, rather than a particular and distinct prejudice.

Similarly, the fear of foreign belief systems, cults, and superstitions gaining Roman converts was a general one. Even Greek philosophers had, on occasion, been banished from Rome, in 161 and 154 BCE. When Jews were targeted, they were usually not the only victims. In 139 BCE, they were expelled with the city's itinerant astrologers. In 19 CE, when Tiberius again exiled Rome's Jews, they were banished to Sardinia alongside worshippers of Isis. On other occasions, expulsions seem to have less to do specifically with religious activity but rather with some kind of civil disorder of the kind found among immigrant populations in rapidly growing, multi-ethnic imperial cities.[10] Suetonius records that Emperor Claudius (r.41–54 CE) 'expelled the Jews [from Rome] ... since they were constantly making disturbances at the instigation of Chrestus'. Although the identification of this 'Chrestus' is disputed (some suggest it is a reference to Christ and that the problem was thus sectarian conflict within Rome's Jewish community), this expulsion was apparently the response to specific acts of unruly behaviour, rather than the religion or general character of the city's Jews.[11]

The relationship between prejudice towards Jews and prejudice towards other subject peoples was clearly a close one and is thus suggestive that no distinct Judaeophobic tradition existed. Even the rioting in Alexandria in 38 CE, although clearly aimed very specifically at that city's Jewish population, does not necessarily demonstrate the existence of a wider hostility towards them as a people. The conflict in that city arose from disputes over the political status of its Jewish community. Under the emperor Augustus, Alexandria's Jews had been considered as a state within the city state, ruled by their own *ethnarch* (ruler) and with their own courts. They had paid the same poll tax as native Egyptians, a tax from which ethnic Greeks were excused. By the 30s CE, and for reasons that are not altogether clear, there no longer appeared to be a Jewish *ethnarch* and Alexandrian Jews were agitating for *isopoliteia*: equal citizenship with the Greeks. The latter bitterly resented their pretensions. The unfortunate timing of the arrival of the Jewish king Agrippa inflamed the situation. Martin Goodman has concluded that the events in Alexandria were not the result of a wider antipathy towards Jews but 'probably a product of conditions specific to that city'.[12]

A series of tumultuous events over the following decades may have fostered greater antipathy towards Jews. A revolt against the heavy-handed Roman administration broke out in Judaea in 66 CE. This ended with the destruction of the Temple in Jerusalem in 70 CE, by the future emperor Vespasian and his son Titus. Inter-communal riots involving the Jews of the diaspora occurred across Egypt, the neighbouring province of Cyrenaica (modern Libya) and on the island of Cyprus, in 115–117 CE. In 130 CE, the emperor Hadrian founded a new city, Aelia Capitolina, on the site of Jerusalem, provoking a second doomed nationalist revolt, under Shimon Bar Kokhba, in 132–135 CE.

However, there was no collective punishment of Jews and no strong evidence that their legal status changed as a consequence of these conflicts. The annual contribution that they had once sent to maintain the Temple in Jerusalem was now diverted to fill Roman coffers. The lives of most Jews outside of Judaea were undisturbed, even in nearby provinces such as Galilee and Syria.[13] Expressions of prejudices towards Jews still seemed to be closely related to more generalised prejudices against Rome's subject peoples. Writing during the reign of Hadrian, the philosopher Diogenes lumped Jews and Egyptians together, denouncing both as 'the most superstitious of all people' and 'the vilest of all people'.[14]

It is possible that divisions within the Jewish community itself, consequent upon the destruction of the Temple, played some role in fostering a nascent Judaeophobia. Among those scattered by the Judaean wars were the followers of Jesus. Some of these remained firmly within Judaism. In Syria, Christian communities claiming a lineage from the first followers of Jesus long thrived. Some venerated the martyred James, 'brother of Jesus', but faithfully observed the Torah. Such groups, whom we might term 'Jewish-Christians', are known from fragmentary sources and references to their (now lost) scriptures.[15]

Other followers of Jesus were actively seeking gentile converts, and this would ultimately be productive of friction. The Gospel of John, the last of the gospels to be written, sometime between 90–110 CE, was produced in a community heavily influenced by Greek literary and philosophical traditions. These taught the eternal nature and divinity of Christ. This teaching seems to have brought this particular community into conflict with the local synagogue, from which it appears to have been physically expelled. That local conflict was then reflected in the stories the gospel told of Jesus's ministry: 'for this reason the Jews were seeking all the more to kill [Jesus], because he was not only breaking the Sabbath, but was also calling God his own Father, thereby making himself equal to God'.[16]

The Apostle Paul is among the most contentious of figures in this process: a Hellenised Jew, a Pharisee, and a persecutor of the followers of Jesus until his own dramatic and violent conversion on the road to Damascus in the early 30s CE. Paul's proselytising mission was to the gentiles, not to his fellow Jews, and it was undertaken in the expectation of imminent apocalypse. Time was, therefore, of the essence. A protracted debate about the relationship between those who had joined God's covenant through Jesus and those through adherence to the Torah was not necessary. Paul's message was, in these pressing circumstances, simple: through Jesus, gentiles did not need to become Jews to enjoy salvation. At no point did Paul urge Jews themselves to abandon the Torah. He did warn against gentile converts ritualistically aping the formulas and restrictions of the old covenant. Much of his teaching, for example that gentile converts need not be circumcised, inevitably brought him into bitter conflict with other Jews, who disagreed over the obligations that God's chosen people need fulfil. Yet Paul himself, confident that the end of days was at hand, appeared to accept that salvation awaited the faithful of both old and new covenants.[17]

Yet Paul struggled to reconcile the obligations of both old and new covenants. Some gentile converts, such as the community that produced the Gospel of John, guided their new faith away from Judaism and were more open to Hellenising influences. Others embraced the legal obligations of the Torah with fervour and, by so doing, appeared to stifle the spiritual message of Jesus and his sacrifice on the cross. That much of the early conflict ostensibly between 'Christians' and 'Jews' was, in fact, between different kinds of Christians is evident in a careful reading of scripture. Consider the warning in the Book of Revelation 2:9 (dating from *c*.90 CE) against 'the slander of those that say they are Jews and are not, but are a synagogue of Satan'. The targets of this barb were probably gentile converts to Christianity who were rigidly following Jewish law, rather than Jews themselves.

Yet here we begin to discern a central tension that would eventually emerge as Christian Judaeophobia. For some early Christians, those of their co-religionists who drifted wholly into Jewish practice, 'Judaisers', posed as much of a threat to those who, influenced by pagan philosophy and *religio*, moved towards henotheism or polytheism. Both risked destroying the unity and coherence of the early Church. The *adversus Judaeos* tradition thus began with debates *between* Christians. The vilification of Judaism was a rhetorical device by which the boundaries of the Christian faith could be established and policed. This was a gradual and contested process. Those who rejected all Jewish influence, like the dualist Marcion (d. *c*.160 CE), were branded as 'heretics' and excommunicated. The same fate awaited those who drifted too far in the other direction, towards the Torah.

Early Christian diversity did not necessarily lead to conflict. Indeed, on a day-to-day level, it seemed to promote a ready pluralism in some locations: intermarriage with Jews, shared religious festivals, communal observance of both Sabbaths, individuals attending both church and synagogue were all well attested into the fourth century.[18] Yet it did have the potential to generate friction. As the first and then the second generation of followers of Jesus passed away and the Apocalypse no longer seemed so imminent, the question of the long-term relationship between the old and new covenants became more pressing.

For some adherents, their differences could no longer be ignored. Those most interested in preserving the coherence and separateness of Christianity did so by promoting a distinctive, authoritative, and universal dogma that would eventually assume the status of 'orthodoxy'. In some cases, this objective was pursued through a direct, if not necessarily violent, confrontation with Judaism. These confrontations did not merely mark the boundaries between the faiths but, crucially and forcefully, insisted that Christianity had now supplanted Judaism: the two covenants thus became rivals. Rivalry bred hostility.

Sometime in the 140s CE, the gentile convert to Christianity and Christian apologist Justin Martyr was teaching in Rome. In his most celebrated work, *Dialogue with Trypho the Jew*, Justin strove to answer Trypho (an educated Jew who had fled Judaea following the revolt of 135 CE) when the latter had pointed to the contradictory position of those Christians who claimed to accept Jewish scripture but refused to follow the Torah. Justin had responded with the assertion that the demands of Jewish law were meant only for Jews, as a punishment from God. Besides, he observed, Christians had their own specific burdens to bear, including martyrdom for their faith.

The most serious theological disagreement between them concerned the unsettling question of the nature of Christ. Trypho could not accept Jesus as a divine messiah, a concept that threatened the unity of God. Justin could not compromise his belief that Christ was indeed divine, God's *logos* made flesh. Although still accepting the possibility of Jewish salvation, he argued that the old covenant was finished, telling Trypho 'you ought to understand that [the gifts of God's favour] formerly among your nation have been transferred to us'.[19]

There can be no doubting the ideological purpose underpinning Justin's work: he strove to prevent gentile Christians from observing Jewish law lest they go over wholly to Judaism. Vilifying Jews was a central part of his strategy. He alleged that they were not merely wrong-headed, but were themselves guilty of persecuting Christians and had done so ever since they 'had killed the Christ'. It was an ugly charge, soon levelled again in the works of other Church Fathers, such as Tertullian (*c.*160–225 CE) who referred to the 'synagogues of the Jews' as 'fountains of persecution'.[20]

Here then, we are clearly confronted by the emerging *Adversus Judaeos* tradition and the foundations of Judaeophobia. Jews were not simply being portrayed as the adherents of an old and now-abolished covenant with God. They were incapable even of reading their own scriptures properly and therefore blind to the spiritual truths and prophecies of Christ's reign those scriptures contained. They were Christ-killers and active enemies of the Christian faith. In Tertullian's mockery can be seen much of the outline of later stereotypes of Jews: 'scattered abroad, a race of wanderers, exiles from their own land and clime they roam over the whole world without either a human or a heavenly king'.[21]

It should be understood, however, that this bitter language was being employed as much to forge a united Christianity as it was to attack Judaism. For example, when Tertullian attempted to refute the teachings of the Christian heretic Marcion, he needed to demonstrate that the vengeful God of the Old Testament was indeed the same compassionate God of the Christian New Testament. This he could achieve by presenting the Jews as especially wicked, as especially deserving of righteous anger. To demonstrate this peculiar malevolence, throughout his writings he portrayed Jews as denying the prophets, rejecting Jesus, persecuting Christians, as rebels against God. For the Church Fathers, therefore, Judaeophobia was still principally a means of defeating internal enemies within Christianity itself. It was applied to both those who rejected the vengeful God of Israel, such as Marcion, and, at the other end of the spectrum of Christian belief, to 'Judaisers' who embraced the Torah. As David Nirenberg comments, 'anti-Judaism was a tool that could usefully be deployed to almost any problem, a weapon that could be deployed on almost any front', hence its potency and longevity.[22]

The existence of this nascent Judaeophobic tendency within some Christian communities did not, of course, translate into active persecution whilst Christians themselves were a powerless and vulnerable minority. As late as the Council of Elvira, *c.*306 CE, at which the aggression of those militants who actively sought out martyrdom by attacking others was condemned, the emphasis was still on establishing clear boundaries between the faiths. Christian landlords were enjoined not to allow Jews to bless their crops, and clerics and lay people were not to eat with Jews. Such attempts at prohibition indicate that such practices remained common. The apparent efficacy of Jewish ritual blessings, their arcane language, and the mysteries of their rites, combined with the reputed power of their magicians and healers, were known to draw Christians to the synagogues. So long as religious affiliations remained fluid, Christian clergy felt that the Church remained vulnerable, even once Christian emperors were on the throne.[23]

The danger seemed greater still when the pagan Julian the Apostate began his programme of religious reforms in 361 CE, threatening as he did to rebuild the Temple in Jerusalem. Had that project been successful, it would have undermined the claims that many theologians had been making: that God had abandoned the Jews to exile; that Christianity was the new Israel; that the Christian Church was fulfilling the ancient prophecies contained in the Old Testament. It was in the context of this sustained existential fear for the future of the Church that some of the most vitriolic rhetorical attacks on Jews and Judaism were delivered from the pulpit. In 386 CE in Antioch, where Christianity, Judaism, and Hellenism competed vigorously for spiritual loyalties, an anxious presbyter called John Chrysostom (c.347–407 CE), later bishop of Constantinople, felt compelled to heap odium upon the city's Jews. Jews, he preached, sacrificed children to devils. They were 'Christ killers' who were, and always had been, hated by God. They were 'degenerated to the level of dogs'. The synagogue was the haunt of 'rabble, effeminate men and prostitutes'.[24]

In 388 CE, a Christian mob, roused to zealous fury by similar sermons from their bishop, burned down a synagogue in the Syrian city of Callinicum. Emperor Theodosius initially demanded the bishop pay for the reconstruction of the building. It had belonged to peaceful, law-abiding, and tax-paying Roman citizens. Theodosius was in Milan and found himself confronted by that city's formidable bishop, Ambrose. He asked what Theodosius would do if the bishop of Callinicum refused his orders to fund the rebuilding of the synagogue. Would he make him a martyr for his faith? Was he prepared that 'the inheritance acquired by Christians through the fervour of Christ' be handed over to 'unbelievers' so that they might build a 'temple of godlessness'? Theodosius rescinded his order punishing the bishop of Callinicum. The growing vulnerability of Jewish citizens within a Roman empire dominated by a militant Christianity was now apparent. Heretics, pagans, and finally Jews had felt the force of Christianity's acceptance of holy violence. By 400 CE, Judaeophobia had thus established itself as a widespread ideology, capable of translation into active, physical persecution of Jews.[25]

Yet there was to be a crucial difference in the experience of persecution suffered by Jews, and that suffered by heretics and pagans. The latter were to disappear, driven to extinction through a combination of persuasion, assimilation and, ultimately, coercion. Judaism, however, was to survive as the only tolerated religious minority in Christendom. As Jacob Neusner has observed, there were two fundamental reasons why Judaism survived while Christian heresies were extirpated and the old cults died away: 'firstly Christianity permitted it to endure and, second, Israel, the Jewish people, wanted it to'.[26]

Christian permissiveness towards Judaism was rooted in both political and religious attitudes. Although some imperial posts were barred to Jews, the Roman tradition of respect for Jewish citizenship and religious freedom was maintained throughout the fourth century. In 393 CE, five years after the incident at Callinicum, Theodosius firmly asserted that the 'sect of the Jews is forbidden by no law'. In 396 CE, the right of Jews to observe their Sabbath was protected. Jewish clergy, unlike pagan priests, were guaranteed their traditional legal and civil privileges.[27] No aspect of Jewish religious practice was targeted by legislation in the way that blood sacrifice had been criminalised. Nor were synagogues, unlike pagan temples, deprived of income and property over the course of the fourth century. Heresy, the enemy within, was judged more threatening than a superseded Judaism. Thus, the vigour and ferocity with which heretics were pursued far surpassed the, for the most part, rhetorical Christian assaults on Judaism.

Indeed, even in the increasingly militant climate of the late fourth and early fifth centuries, the survival of Jews was important to Christians. Their destruction was not part of God's design and therefore the nature and extent of their persecution would always differ materially from that of other religious minorities and dissidents. The Jews had, Christians acknowledged, once been God's chosen people and could not thus simply be discarded. Marcion and those like-minded heretics who had rejected the Old Testament as the scripture of a lesser god, and who would have denied all connection with Judaism, had been driven from the Church. A sense of Christianity and Judaism as being sibling religions remained strong. Augustine of Hippo reminded his congregation that Jesus and the apostles had lived their lives as observant Jews. In sermons written between 395–398 CE, he preached that heretics were deluded by their own pride and pagans were misled by demons. God, however, was the source of Jewish practice. Their continued obstinate adherence to those practices was their 'mark of Cain', by which God signalled his desire they survive as a distinct people. So, although Augustine came to accept the legitimacy of the physical coercion of heretics and pagans, he did not accept it in regard to Jews. They were to survive within a shared religious community. Their final destiny, as the end of days approached, would be to accept Jesus as the Messiah and earn redemption.[28]

In the meantime, their fate was to exist as a wandering, miserable, despised minority. Yet there was divine purpose here too. Augustine, like so many Christian theologians before him, had debated with pagans, who suggested that Christianity was a novel superstition, and with dualist heretics, who pointed to the apparent contradictions between the Old and New Testaments. He saw that Jews might fulfil an important role in refuting these arguments. Jews carried with them in exile their undeniably ancient scriptures. These scriptures, Christians believed, had prophesied Christ. They thus established both the historical respectability of Christianity and demonstrated the congruence between the Old and the New Testaments: 'It follows that when the

Jews do not believe in our Scriptures, their own Scriptures are fulfilled in them, while they read them with blind eyes'.[29]

For Augustine, therefore, there was both a place and a need for Jews within Christian society and they should not be harmed. Such was God's will, Augustine reasoned, as foretold in Psalms 59: 'Slay them not, lest at some time they forget your law. Scatter them'. Here was laid the foundation for Christian attitudes towards Jews that would endure for centuries to come.[30]

Yet Jews themselves were not simply passive in the face of evolving Christian attitudes. They were architects, too, of their own survival. In the face of Christianity's growing ascendency in the fourth century, Jewish rabbis forged a formidable intellectual and theological response to the claims of the Church. In the 'dual Torah' of written and oral traditions, they found an answer to Christian claims to be the new Israel in their own doctrine of God's will, revealed in a history beginning in Genesis of messianic promise as yet unfulfilled, and of Israel as comprising 'the family, after the flesh, of the founders of Israel'. Thus, a normative Judaism emerged following the conversion of Constantine, with Jews understanding the unfolding history of the world through, and conducting their lives according to, the Torah.[31] This ultimately contributed to a social unity among Jews, and a consequent resilience, that neither disparate paganism nor fractious 'heretics' could match.

This resilience, and the implication that Jews remained the chosen people, inevitably generated friction with the triumphalist and militant Church that had emerged by 400 CE. The Augustinian injunction to 'slay them not' did not prevent episodes of physical persecution of Jews, their banishment from some cities and even incidents of forced conversion, notwithstanding the Church's official disapproval of such acts. As was so often the case with violence between Christians, and between Christians and pagans, peculiar local circumstances drove these occurrences, whatever imperial policy favoured. The weakness of the central state again proved a factor in persecution.

In 418 CE, Severus, bishop of Jamona in Minorca, worked assiduously in his pulpit to poison relations between his congregation and the local Jewish community. His chief target appears to have been a prominent and influential Jewish citizen, Theodorus. He had fulfilled all the duties of the town council in the nearby city of Magona, including that of *defensor civitatis* (chief magistrate), despite that role being technically reserved for Christians. He had been succeeded by his kinsman and co-religionist Caecilianus. Severus aimed to usurp their position and secure his own authority by fostering religious conflict. In February 418 CE, he was finally able to rally militant Christians to his cause by exploiting the power of a martyr's cult: 'some remains of the blessed martyr Stephen' were deposited in the church of Magona and 'now zeal for the faith was consuming our hearts, now the hope of many coming to salvation was aroused'. Hitherto friendly relations with local Jews were transformed into hatred. A riot left the city's synagogue in ashes. In the aftermath, so Severus asserted, hundreds of Minorca's cowed Jews chose conversion and built a church on the site of their former place of worship.[32]

Events in Minorca demonstrated that Jews were both protected and yet vulnerable within the Christian Roman Empire. That vulnerability would be sustained. The rhetoric of the *adversus Judaeos* tradition did not become any less prevalent even as the Church itself became more secure. Indeed, many of the texts within that tradition would be copied, circulated, and appealed to as evidence of Jewish malevolence for centuries to come. The sermons of John Chrysostom, originally reflecting the appeal of Judaism and the peculiar insecurity of Christianity in Antioch in the late fourth century, were soon translated from Greek into Syriac and Latin and widely disseminated. They would demonstrate an impressive historical reach. Six hundred years after John's death, they would be translated into Russian just as the first massacres of Jews in Russian history were taking place, under Prince Vladimir in the grand duchy of Kiev (now Kyiv).[33]

Within a Christendom that both forbore and reviled them, Jews could not escape their unwarranted reputation. Even when their Church was more secure, militant Christian authors continued to find in the rhetoric of Judaeophobia a powerful rallying call to the faithful. At much the same time as the forced conversions were occurring in Minorca, propagandists were still intent on portraying Christians as the victims of Jewish persecution. The ecclesiastical historian Socrates Scholasticus (*c.*380–439 CE), for example, alleged that an innocent Christian child had fallen prey to 'malevolent' Jews:

> At a place named Inmestar, situated between Chalcis and Antioch in Syria, the Jews were amusing themselves in their usual way with a variety of sports. In this way they indulged in many absurdities, and at length impelled by drunkenness they were guilty of scoffing at Christians and even Christ himself; and in derision of the cross and those who put their trust in the Crucified One, they seized a Christian boy, and having bound him to a cross, began to laugh and sneer at him. But in a while becoming so transported with fury they scourged the child until he died under their hands.[34]

We should not, of course, credit much truth to this ugly tale. The accusation of the torture, murder, and even cannibalising, of child victims in orgiastic, drink-fuelled pseudo-ritual activities was a long-established calumny in antiquity. It had been levelled at Christians themselves. As the Carthaginian church father Tertullian had recorded: 'monsters of wickedness, we are accused of observing a holy rite in which we kill a little child and then eat it ... '.[35] That such familiar fables were incorporated early on into the Church's *adversus Judaeos* tradition provides suggestive evidence for how Judaeophobia was sustained.

In the west, as the Roman Empire gave way to the 'barbarian' successor kingdoms over the course of the fifth and sixth centuries, the Church endured and became the most successful vehicle for assimilation of disparate populations. As the secular administrators of the empire disappeared, clerical authority, pre-eminently embodied in the urban bishop, was enhanced. The clergy worked with the new secular power, the warrior elites. The Church, thus, was able to transmit much of Rome's ancient culture intact to what would eventually emerge as the kingdoms of medieval Europe. It was also even able to transmit a sense of shared identity and unity across the fractured territories that had once all been ruled by Rome, a unity based upon the notion that there existed a single community of Christian people: 'Christendom'.

Yet this expedient redefining of membership of the broader community, through religious identity rather than through the political idea of citizenship, was to have unfortunate implications for the Jews of western Christendom. It challenged one protection that had shielded them from persecution: the legal rights due to Roman citizens. Hostile bishops could now move against legally defenceless Jewish communities. In 576 CE, a Gallic bishop 'converted the local Jewish community to Christianity and banished those who refused baptism'.[36]

Such episodes remained isolated and localised. While Judaeophobic sentiment was sustained by the Church, the impulse to actively persecute Jews was still checked by the legacy of Augustine. That legacy itself was revived and reinforced by Pope Gregory the Great (r.590–604 CE). Often referred to as the first medieval pope, it was principally Gregory who established the primacy of the papacy in the west. He was an active leader, ending famine in Rome, defending northern Italy from invading Lombards, strengthening the Church's influence throughout the former provinces of the empire. His writings reveal his conviction that attacks on Jews and their religious practices were sinful. In 598 CE, he upheld a complaint made by the Jews of Salerno against their local bishop, informing the offending cleric that 'just as the Jews should not have license in their synagogues to arrogate anything beyond that permitted by law, so too in those things granted them they should experience no infringement of their rights'. It is a measure of Gregory's lasting influence that this ruling, or papal bull, was reissued by later popes, including five separate occasions between the years 1198 and 1254.[37]

In one respect, however, Gregory's attitude towards the Jews differed from that of Augustine's. He advocated active proselytising and offered rewards and protection to those Jews who willingly accepted baptism. He would, therefore, have been content to see distinct Jewish communities disappear through conversion, so long as this was achieved without coercion or duress. His stance on the need for determined preaching to 'hard-hearted' Jews was driven by his strong belief that Satan worked among them and that they were allied to Antichrist. His position is a reminder that the notion that Christ's soldiers were engaged in an ongoing cosmic war against Satan remained a defining characteristic of Christianity, fostered and sustained by the cult of martyrs, throughout the medieval period.

Yet when we consider the case of the Jews, we can see that this war was no simple dichotomy between good and evil. Heretics and pagans were the allies and dupes of Satan too, yet, having no purpose in the ultimate fulfil-ment of Christian triumph, they were to be hunted down and extirpated utterly. Jews straddled the battle lines of cosmic struggle in a much more complex way; allies of Satan, perhaps, but protected by God and whose *eventual* conversion would signal the end of days. Having this protected, if precarious, place within Christendom, allowed Jewish communities to endure.

They would survive in the long term, too, because of their own resilience. The spiritual unity of rabbinic Jewish communities ensured that the Christian attempts to persuade Jews to convert were generally unsuccessful, even when pursued with the degree of vigour advocated by Gregory the Great. He would lament:

> ... is it not an awful shame to preach futilely to hard hearts, to take the trouble to demonstrate the truth, but to find no compensation for one's efforts – in the conversion of one's listeners? Nevertheless, the ensuing pro-gress of their listeners is a great comfort for preachers.[38]

The expectation of that eventual conversion ensured a place for Jews within the accepted boundaries of Christian communities. Yet hostile sentiment towards Jews also remained immanent within the culture of those communi-ties. Thus, on occasion, assaults, forced conversions, massacres, and exiles, might be successfully portrayed as morally justified when they occurred in response to some perceived act of Jewish infamy. Yet, if Judaism's dark repu-tation provided the common pretext for such events, the actual causes of persecution were still highly contingent on specific, local circumstances and violence was rarely sustained.

The Visigoth kingdom that covered much of the Iberian Peninsula and southern Gaul from the late sixth to the early eight century provides an instructive case study of the factors that led to state-sponsored persecution in one early medieval kingdom. In this instance, the stringently punitive measures taken against Iberian Jews by some Visigoth monarchs appear to have been primarily politically motivated. They reflected a weak grasp on power and the consequent importance of undermining hostile factions among their subjects. The peculiar volatility of the Visigoth kingdom is manifest in the fate of its rulers. Between 589 CE and its final collapse in 711 CE, it was ruled by 18 different kings drawn from 15 separate families. Seven of these monarchs were either deposed or murdered (or both). Rebellions, attempted usurpations, and violently disputed successions were frequent. Against this backdrop of instability, a pattern emerged that saw royal policy towards a large, prosperous, and well-assimilated Jewish population veer dramatically between persecution and patronage, as the throne passed from one king to the next.[39]

For example, in March or February 612 CE, King Sisebut attained the throne following a period when Jews suffered relatively few legal disadvantages. Some had held high political and military rank. Yet the new king enacted a series of legislative assaults on Judaism. Christian slaves were freed from Jewish masters, who were also obliged to give them sufficient property to live independent lives. Jewish proselytism became a capital offence. Former Christians, who had previously converted to Judaism, were obliged to convert back again. Jews were barred from hiring Christian workmen and were expelled from offices that gave them authority over Christians. When Sisebut discovered that his legislation was being flouted, he initiated a yet fiercer programme of forced conversion and exile. This sudden swing towards a persecutory policy, following a long period of forbearance and finally escalating to violent coercion, gives the initial impression of Sisebut as a man motivated by a particular religious fervour.[40]

Certainly, the theological environment during Sisebut's reign would have been conducive to active Judaeophobia. His Iberian contemporary Isidore, bishop of Seville (*c*.560–636 CE), was responsible for writing one of the most influential polemics of the period: *On the Catholic Faith against the Jews*. Isidore shared many of Gregory the Great's assumptions, particularly concerning the alliance between Jews and the Antichrist. Yet he lacked the pope's patience and was not prepared to take comfort in the belief that the eventual Second Coming of Christ would be marked by Jewish conversion to Christianity. Rather, he believed that the Second Coming might actually be hastened *by* the active conversion of the Jews.[41]

Yet he too was committed to persuasion rather than coercion and he steadfastly opposed the extreme measures to which Sisebut ultimately resorted. So too did the majority of Sisebut's bishops. Indeed, not only did they oppose forced conversion but many, for example those who had interests in the slave trade, continued to do business with wealthy and influential Jews and ignored anti-Jewish legislation.[42] This friction between Sisebut and the Church casts some doubt on the notion that the king was actually motivated by piety. Indeed, his manipulation of ecclesiastical appointments and the boasts he made of the worldly and material advantages accruing from being an orthodox king might be described as cynical.[43]

If it was not his individual religious fervour that drove Sisebut to persecute his Jewish subjects, then perhaps it was that cynical search for material advantage. This, however, was unlikely to have been an economic reward. If the king's anti-Jewish laws were enacted, he stood to gain little financially: only if Jews refused to free Christian slaves could their property be seized by the crown, and only if Jewish proselytes refused to return to the Church could they be enslaved and sold. Thus, only by encouraging legal transgression could the monarch realistically have hoped to profit. If this was a policy to raise money, it was, as Bernard Bachrach has observed, 'unnecessarily tortuous and less than efficient'.[44]

The most likely material advantage Sisebut sought through the persecution of the Jews was political. While his policy brought him into conflict with the Church and yielded little financial gain, it would clearly also have done a great deal to undermine the position of an influential Jewish community that had, apparently, become involved in the interminable struggles to secure the throne. Without their Christian workforce, large Jewish-owned agricultural estates would have swiftly collapsed. Driven from high office and unable even to hire Christian labourers and artisans, Jews could build up no networks of patronage and their authority would have declined accordingly. Sisebut, it would appear, was punishing the Jews not because they were Jews, but because they had opposed his claim to the throne.

In the Frankish kingdom to the north of Visigoth Spain, the fate of the Jewish population had also depended very much on their relationship with ruling monarchs. Over the course of the fifth century, the Franks had expanded into the Roman Empire from lands north and east of the Rhine. An early fifth-century chieftain named Merovech had founded the royal dynasty which would ultimately unify a disparate people and give shape to 'Francia'. The most important of the Merovingian kings was Clovis, who converted from paganism to Catholic Christianity in about 500 CE. The Merovingians' Jewish subjects, long-established in the south of what had been the old Roman province of Gaul, suffered for the religiosity of this dynasty, which frequently pursued a policy of forced conversion. In 582 CE, for example, King Chilperic I, ordered the baptism of the Jews.[45]

This policy, however, would not be sustained by the successor dynasty, the Carolingians, who took the throne as close allies of the papacy and under whose rule many Jews thrived economically and achieved high office. Under both the emperor Charlemagne (crowned by Pope Leo III in 800 CE) and his son, Louis the Pious (r.813–40 CE), Jews bore arms and served alongside Christians in the levies that fought the emperors' wars. They held land and farmed successfully. Some were entrusted with important diplomatic missions, including one to Harun al-Rashid, the caliph in Baghdad. They were active as merchants both locally and within the long-distance trading networks stretching around the Mediterranean world.[46]

As the millennium approached, the status of the Jews as Christendom's only tolerated minority seemed secure. Indeed, they not only endured their 'exile' from Jerusalem, many prospered. From the long-established Jewish communities found in the commercial centres of Italy, Iberia, and southern Gaul, adventurous migrants moved north, often with the encouragement of rulers such as the Carolingians, who were keen to catalyse economic developments in their lands by settling skilled merchants in their growing towns and cities. Yet as both the economies and the political structures of these northern kingdoms developed, new and more potentially dangerous challenges to coexistence and forbearance would emerge. The unity of the Carolingian Empire, within which Jews had been protected, was ultimately undermined by a combination of internal factionalism and pressure from eternal enemies.

The crisis facing the empire was dramatic. By the 830s CE, Louis the Pious was faced by both Viking raiders from the north and, from the south, Muslim armies threatening both Francia and Italy. In the east, the danger came from the steppes, the formidable horse armies of the Magyars (Hungarians).

On Louis's death in 840 CE, his succession was disputed by his grandsons. The ensuing civil war lasted three years and ended with the partition of Charlemagne's inheritance. This left some Jewish communities vulnerable. In 876 CE, Archbishop Angesius of Sens expelled all Jews (and, rather mysteriously, all nuns) from the city.[47]

This threat of exile would now hang over Jewish communities, especially in northern Europe. Their communities were only recently established among peoples who thus regarded them as alien and knew of them chiefly through the ugly reputation forged by the *adversus Judaeos* tradition. The Church as a whole, while broadly adhering to the Augustinian injunction to 'slay them not', nevertheless began in some cases to accept the legitimacy of exiling those who refused to accept baptism. This shift in Church policy may also have had its roots in political developments and, in particular, the developing contest between spiritual and worldly authority.

Shortly before his death in 939 CE, Pope Leo VII was involved in correspondence with Frederick, archbishop of Mainz, in the kingdom of Germany concerning the city's Jewish inhabitants. The archbishop had asked whether he should force the Jews to accept baptism or exile them. Leo's response was, on the face of it, wholly conventional. He was astonished that the archbishop was ignorant of ancient canon law which absolutely prohibited forced conversion. Instead, he admonished Frederick to preach with greater diligence and win the Jews over to the Christian faith. He then added, however, that if they did not accept the faith, then they should indeed be expelled from the city. His policy can best be understood in the light of a quarrel he was pursuing with the German king, Otto I. That monarch enjoyed very positive relations with his Jewish subjects, and put much trust in them, for example employing them on important diplomatic missions to the caliph of Muslim Cordoba. He could thus be attacked indirectly through a community that was politically and economically useful to him.[48]

This political context continued to shape the context of Jewish persecution. The title of emperor bestowed upon Charlemagne by Pope Leo III had finally lapsed in 924 CE, as partible inheritance left his heirs in the west controlling ever smaller, and ever less imperial, domains. However, in 962 CE, it would be revived when Otto I was crowned emperor in Rome by Pope John XII (r.955–964 CE). At that moment, the beleaguered and unpopular John had needed Otto's intervention to secure his position and their alliance was mutually convenient. Yet, in the long term, the relationship between this reborn empire and the papacy was to be deeply problematic. The seemingly neat division of temporal and spiritual authority between the two proved instead a source of lasting friction. Antagonism arose, inevitably, from a series of conflicting interests.

Consider, for example, the widespread practise of simony, the buying and selling of clerical offices for profit. This was an important source of revenue for emperors, but a sin in the eyes of the papacy. Emperors, in turn, resented papal claims to supremacy and strove to limit the authority of popes by appointing loyal allies to bishoprics in their own territories. At stake was not only the important temporal question of who should control the wealth and patronage of the Church but also the equally pressing matter of the spiritual well-being of Christendom itself. Reform-minded popes sought to curb abuses such as simony and clerical marriage, remove unsuitable candidates from bishoprics, and improve both the education and moral behaviour of the priesthood, in order to ensure that their congregations received proper pastoral care.

In 1076, the most determined of reformers, Pope Gregory VII, had claimed the right to depose unsuitable monarchs as he sought to curb the power of the emperor Henry IV and revitalise Christian society. Henry was excommunicated twice, in 1076 and again in 1080. Rival kings with papal backing attempted to seize his throne in a long civil war. Henry retaliated by invading Italy in 1084, forcing Gregory to flee and installing his own anti-pope, styled Clement III, in Rome. Gregory died in Salerno the following year. It took the papacy itself some time to recover its authority, even in Italy. Relations with the emperor remained tense. Indeed by 1157, the then-emperor, Frederick I, was referring to his German domains as 'Holy', in a direct counterpart to the pope's claims to spiritual jurisdiction.[49]

Unfortunately for the recently established Jewish communities in German towns, they continued to find themselves caught up in the struggles between emperors and popes. This seems one possible explanation for the (temporary) expulsion of Jews, perceived as allies of the emperor, from Mainz in 1012. Yet the spiritual dimension of the eleventh-century papal reform movement was equally significant. It fostered a desire among many Christians to live the apostolic life, the life of poverty and subjugation to Christ, and to better understand religious doctrine and observance. It represented a 'Christianisation' of society that, in the long term, can only have served to alienate Christians from their 'spiritually blind' Jewish neighbours.[50]

However portentous this development must have been, active persecution remained rare for decades to follow. Western Christendom was itself more secure. In the east, the Magyars had been defeated at the Battle of Lechfield by Otto I in 955 CE. In the west, Viking raiders had turned to settlement, accepted baptism, and been largely assimilated. To the south, papal armies had driven Muslim forces from the Italian mainland by 915 CE. Against a backdrop of demographic and economic growth, northern Europe continued to offer opportunities to Jewish migrants.

For the most part, they enjoyed the protection of the Church. Many bishops continued not only to safeguard Jews but appeared to enjoy warm and friendly relations with them. The deaths of Bishop Adalbero of Metz in 1005, Archbishop Walthard of Magdeburg in 1012 and Archbishop Anno of Cologne in 1075 were all marked by intense mourning within their local Jewish communities. In 1084, Bishop Rudiger of Speyer boasted that he aimed to 'enhance a thousandfold' the glory of his city by settling Jews in it. He set aside a protected area for them to live, unmolested by the 'insolence of the mob'. He granted them freedom to engage in commercial activities, autonomy in their own communal affairs, and the right to carry arms and take their part alongside their Christian neighbours in guarding the city's fortifications.[51]

Nor was it just bishops who encouraged Jewish settlement. A significant Jewish presence was established in England after the Norman conquest of 1066. King William I transferred Jews from Rouen to his new kingdom after his victory; in a council in 1070, he granted them his especial protection and asserted that he would treat their persons and property as his own. The Jewry of Rouen were well established in commerce and, increasingly, in money lending, and their presence would thus be a useful stimulus to the economic development of England.[52]

And yet, before the eleventh century was ended, an unheralded and ferocious series of violent assaults on Jewish communities had been unleashed and a decisive shift in relations between the two religious communities had taken place. The cause of this growing persecution was the re-emergence of a militant dogma of holy war and cosmic struggle that had found its most potent expression in the crusading movement. On 27 November 1095, Pope Urban II (r.1088–99) had preached a sermon at Clermont in France in which he had called upon those Christians who could bear arms to aid their hard-pressed neighbour, the eastern church of Constantinople, against the Muslim Saracens. A well-organised preaching campaign followed. Urban himself spent eight months touring French-speaking lands, while across western Christendom, his bishops and their parish priests took up the message. Yet it was not just the Church's hierarchy that preached God's War. Popular, charismatic preachers, such as Peter the Hermit in Lorraine, inspired all ranks of society with a volatile religious fervour born of an apocalyptical, visionary, and provocative assertion of Christian supremacy.[53]

Those who answered this call were understood to be undertaking a supreme act of penance. As a visible mark of their status, the arms-bearing pilgrims to Jerusalem became *crucesignati* ('signed with the cross'), wearing that symbol prominently on their clothes, or, in some cases, branding it onto their flesh. The contingents began to muster. One band passing through the Rhineland, led by Count Emich of Flonheim, started killing Jews who refused baptism in Speyer on 3 May 1096, the Jewish Sabbath. The bishop of Speyer was swift to intervene, and evacuated the city's Jews to fortified redoubts in the countryside so that only eleven lives were lost. His colleagues in Worms, Mainz, Cologne, Trier, and Metz proved less able, or willing, to afford such protection. In those cities, Jewish communities were destroyed by massacre and forced baptism.[54]

Understanding why those *crucesignati* turned upon these settled Jewish enclaves that, theoretically, enjoyed the protection of the Church, requires an understanding of both the motivations underpinning the Crusades as a whole and of the individuals who joined them. The occupation of Jerusalem by unbelievers was not unacceptable to Christians. They had long lived with the fact. The holy city had been under Muslim rule since it had been conquered in 638 CE, during the initial phase of Islamic expansion. Tales of the maltreatment of Christian pilgrims to the holy sites caused consternation when they circulated, but they had not set armies marching.

However, by the late eleventh century, there had been important shifts in what might be termed the 'strategic balance' between Islam and Christendom that heightened the possibility of military intervention from the west. Firstly, the Byzantine Empire was under severe pressure, having suffered a catastrophic defeat at the hands of the Muslim Seljuk Turks at the Battle of Manzikert in 1074. The Emperor Alexius Commenus (r.1081–1118) had requested assistance and Pope Urban had been receptive to his call. He was alive to the possibility that should he organise successful military aid, it might end the long-running schism between the Latin- and Greek-speaking Churches, with the latter accepting papal supremacy. Secondly, western Christendom was already enjoying military successes against the arms of Islam, fuelling the desire to recover previously lost territory for Christendom. In the Iberian Peninsula, the Christian kingdoms of the north campaigned against the Moors, who had been present since the eighth century. In 1085, Toledo had fallen to Alfonso VI of Castile. In these propitious circumstances, calls to take up the sword against the unbelievers found a receptive audience; when Urban had preached holy war, many of those listening had yelled out 'Deus lo Volt!' ('God wills it!').[55]

This religiously sanctioned violence against unbelievers necessarily imperilled Jews. Claims that churches in Palestine had been desecrated by Muslim rulers at the behest of their Jewish subjects had already been circulating in France and Germany as early as 1007. The notion that Jews were allies of the 'Saracens' (the Arabic-speaking Muslims of the Levant) was thus already established and legitimised attacks upon them. In the 1060s, bishops in Spain had had to act to protect Jewish communities from attack by northern knights arriving to assist in the Reconquista.[56]

Yet in 1096, there was far more to the violence unleashed against Jews than their alleged allegiance to Islam. In some instances, burghers and villagers with no intention of joining the Crusade seemed merely to have taken the opportunity to plunder a vulnerable community. Robbery then escalated into violence. A Hebrew source, the Soloman bar Simson Chronicle, recorded that when Peter the Hermit and his followers first passed through Trier, the Jewish community had provided them with funds and provisions and, in return, had been left unharmed. Emboldened by this precedent however, locals began to extort money on their own account. The beleaguered Jews sought refuge in the bishop's palace but, as more crusaders, including Emich and his band, entered the city, the situation deteriorated further. The bishop, having ineffectually warned the townsfolk against harming the Jews, himself went into hiding. Alone and defenceless, the Jews trapped in the palace were urged to accept baptism. Of those who courageously refused, some took their own lives and the lives of their children. Others were martyred at the hands of their persecutors.[57]

Notwithstanding the ferocity evident in the Rhineland persecutions, these events did not result in the extirpation of Jewish communities. Ecclesiastical and secular authorities had striven (not always successfully, it must be admitted) to protect Jewish communities and the worst atrocities were the consequence of popular hostility, committed by mobs of burghers, peasants, and the least disciplined elements of crusader armies. In 1146, as recruitment for the Second Crusade gathered pace, Jewish communities across France and Germany were again the targets of renewed mob violence. Once again lords and clerics, such as the leading theologian Bernard de Clairvaux, denounced the attacks. It was the same in 1188: as the Third Crusade took shape, German bishops and the emperor Frederick I had to respond quickly to head off trouble in cities such as Mainz.

The most threatening movements were those headed by popular evangelists for the Crusades. Often outside of ecclesiastical control, charismatic preachers linked material poverty to spiritual virtue and thus blurred the distinction between armed pilgrimage and social conflict. When Louis IX of France was captured during a disastrous expedition against Egypt in 1250, a popular movement of 'shepherds and simple people' from across Brabant, Flanders, Hainault, and Picardy, was rallied by the sermons of 'the Master of Hungary'. He was a renegade monk who claimed a visionary mandate from the Virgin Mary to march to Louis's rescue and promised his followers a place in paradise that only the poor could claim. In this, the so-called 'Shepherds' Crusade', the socially radicalising potential of religious enthusiasm was made manifest. Although referred to as 'shepherds' by their contemporaries, and dismissed as a rabble, their number included minor nobles and other well-to-do adherents, suggesting that the movement was comprised of the politically as well as the economically marginalised. By the summer of 1251 these 'shepherds' were attacking wealthy churches, tipping priests into rivers, and demanding that an indolent nobility lead them in arms to the Holy Land. When not placated with food and drink, they turned to banditry. They rioted in Rouen, Orléans, and Bourges. Conspicuously, they also attacked Jews and looted synagogues.[58]

A second Shepherd's Crusade occurred in 1320. The movement was inspired by a vision to a Spanish boy of 17 whose very flesh, it was proclaimed, had been marked with the cross by an angel. Across France, the 'shepherds' rose once more, ostensibly to march against the Moors of Granada. Denied royal support, they sometimes targeted prisons and royal castles. Yet, for the most part, their violence was directed against Jews. These were massacred or forcibly converted across Aquitaine, Languedoc, Navarre, and Aragon. Some townsfolk and priests joined these attacks; Guyard Gui, *sénéschal* of Toulouse, would subsequently execute one cleric who had personally murdered four Jews and plundered their property. In this instance, the persecution of Jews should be understood within a broader socio-political conflict. Jews were not merely convenient scapegoats, against whom popular hostility might be easily roused. They were particularly vulnerable too. Attacks on unarmed and defenceless Jewish communities carried far less risk of lethal retaliation than direct assault on the possessions of the crown or the Church.[59]

Influence-seeking rabble-rousers such as Emich of Flonheim sought to transform an underlying, popular prejudice against Jews into violent physical assaults. Achieving such a transformation depended upon that original prejudice confirming allegations that were both widely accepted as true and so vile that they might rouse ordinary folk to acts of murderous rage. While long reviled as spiritually blind, the stereotypical image of Jews held in Christian minds had further deteriorated from the twelfth century onwards. This deterioration infused a religious prejudice with a murderous potentiality.

One source of this deterioration was intellectual. A renewed and prolific *adversus Judaeos* tradition was being forged in the recently established universities of northern Europe. Scholars such as Anselm of Bec argued that the correctness of the essential doctrines of Christianity could all be demonstrated by the application of reason. And, since human beings were creatures of reason, all humans should, thus, accept Christian doctrines. Anselm and other scholars, such as Peter Abelard who advanced a similar thesis, often made their case in the form of a debate between themselves and a Jewish disputant. These exchanges were often presented as polite and courteous, suggestive that constructive interfaith discussion was still possible at this stage.

Yet the implications of the central argument were dangerous in the extreme: those who refused to accept the putative rationality of Christian doctrines could not be human or, at least, fully human, as humans were essentially rational creatures. Less restrained voices than Anselm or Abelard were keen to make this point explicitly. Peter the Venerable, appointed abbot of Cluny in 1122, wrote 'I know not whether a Jew is a man because he does not cede to human reason ... '. Unable or unwilling to 'cede to reason', the Jew was therefore more akin to beast: 'The ass hears but does not understand; the Jew hears but does not understand'.[60]

The intellectual denial of Jewish humanity was mirrored by a deterioration in the popular image of Europe's Jews. Here, much of the hostility was rooted in politics and economics, but never wholly divorced from religious imperatives. One manifestation of the reformist impulse of the Christian church in the twelfth century was a campaign against usury, which was considered sinful. Yet, with a growing economy, there was a simultaneous pressing need for credit. If Christians were to be debarred from lending money at interest, then Jewish bankers and merchants might continue to fulfil that role.[61]

The English example is illustrative. From 1158 onwards, King Henry II made it increasingly difficult for his Christian subjects to profit from usury. In 1166, for example, he confiscated the estates of the wealthy Flemish moneylender William Cade. In the meantime, two dozen Jewish communities established a sophisticated financial network, connecting London, Norwich, Lincoln, and York, lending money and collecting debts. In England, as in

France, Jews were considered to belong to the crown, and were thus directly under royal jurisdiction and protection. This was a somewhat contingent form of 'protection'. In 1180, Henry confiscated the temptingly large estate of the moneylender Aaron of Lincoln. It did, however, allow them to conduct business in some security.[62]

Yet it also left Jewish communities peculiarly vulnerable to sporadic outbreaks of violent popular hostility. The association of Jews with money-lending furthered the deterioration of their image, reinforcing their reputation as grasping, materialistic, and avaricious. Their relationship with the sovereign also meant that they were often seen as agents of the crown, hence their utility as proxy-targets for attacks on authority, so evident during the Shepherds' Crusades. Rousing mobs against such figures proved all too easy.

During the first year of the reign of England's Richard I, 1189–90, as crusaders gathered to accompany their king on an expedition to recapture Jerusalem, Jews were massacred in London, Norwich, King's Lynn, Lincoln, Stamford, and Bury St Edmunds. In York, Jewish families fled to the small castle to escape a rampaging mob. There they committed suicide as the fortifications were burned around them. The subsequent royal enquiry established that the ringleaders of the massacre – Robert of Ghent, Robert de Turnham, and Richard Malebisse – were all heavily indebted to Jewish moneylenders. As the mob they had incited murdered defenceless people, the ringleaders had ensured that the records of their own debts, held in York Minster, were destroyed.[63]

Alongside the infamy that attached to moneylending as an activity, many other charges frequently levelled against Jewish communities were simply fantastical. In the twelfth and thirteenth centuries, two particularly damaging allegations emerged. One was that Jews re-enacted the supposed crime of deicide by stabbing or otherwise damaging the Eucharist wafer which, according to Catholic doctrine, contained the blood and body of Christ. The other was that Jews were guilty of the ritual murders of Christian children. Once before, centuries earlier, Socrates Scholasticus had made this alleged against the Jews of Inmestar. Before then, it had been made against Christians themselves. It was, however, only from the mid-twelfth century that the charge was established as a peculiarly powerful and recurrent characteristic of hostility towards Jewish communities. In 1150, the Jews of Norwich in England were accused of having murdered an apprentice boy called William, by a local monk, Thomas of Monmouth. His motives for doing so are not wholly clear but pilgrims to the miraculous shrine of 'Saint William the Martyr' soon proved a ready source of cash for his Benedictine priory.[64]

Similar allegations then occurred with depressing regularity throughout medieval Europe. They fuelled massacres and judicial murders, such as the 32 Jewish men and women who, accused of crucifying a Christian child during Passover, were burned to death in Blois in 1171. In Fulda, Germany in 1235, the story acquired a new and peculiarly repellent twist: that the blood of murdered Christian children had been siphoned out for use in ritual medicine.

This 'blood libel' would demonstrate the most astonishing historical reach. In September 1928, rumours circulated in Massena, in upstate New York, that a missing four-year-old (later found safe and well in local woodland) had been kidnapped by local Jews. These had allegedly conspired to drain her blood at the forthcoming celebration of Yom Kippur. In July 1946, 42 Polish Jews, including Holocaust survivors, were massacred by their neighbours in Kielce. The murderers justified their act by insisting that their victims were thirsting for the blood of Christian children. The cultic veneration of children supposedly 'martyred' by Jews was not actually repudiated by the Catholic Church until the Second Vatican Council of 1962–1965.[65]

As Gavin Langmuir has observed, the emergence of such irrational 'chimerical fantasies' was a peculiarly significant event in the history of persecution of the Jews, linking medieval massacres to twentieth-century genocide.[66] These irrational populist fantasies of Jewish malfeasance were all the more dangerous because they took shape alongside an equally portentous shift in the attitude of both religious and royal authority. This would see the gradual rejection of the Augustinian tradition of forbearance towards Jews as a reviled but tolerated non-Christian subject group. This pivotal change was primarily rooted in the ambitions and influence of Innocent III, who became pope in 1198.

Outwardly, Innocent III maintained the Augustinian commitment to Jewish survival within Christian communities. Yet, in striving to forge a unified and obedient Christendom under papal overlordship, he was also keen to ensure the social isolation of Jewish unbelievers. Thus, in 1215 at the Fourth Lateran Council, he established as doctrine what had occurred previously as a local phenomenon: 'That Jews should be distinguished from Christians by dress'. Such distinction might take the form of a cloth 'badge of shame' or characteristic headgear. At Easter, Jews were forbidden to be 'better dressed' than Christians, as this was interpreted as a form of mockery of those who marked the 'holy Passion' by wearing signs of mourning. Innocent also reaffirmed strictures against Jews holding public offices or, indeed, any position that might place them in authority over believers.[67]

Yet the social and economic segregation of Jews would all be rendered unnecessary, if only they would abandon their faith and embrace Christianity. This might be achieved through one of the methods by which Innocent was already confronting popular heresy among Christians in the towns of Languedoc and northern Italy: dispatching talented and charismatic preachers to dispute with the spiritually blind and those in error and win them over for Christ. Inevitably, such a preaching and conversion campaign would become confrontational, if not aggressive.

The mendicant orders, principally the Dominicans and the Franciscans, originally tasked with disputing publicly with heretics and preaching directly to the people in the streets and market squares of villages, towns, and cities, were given the responsibility for winning converts among Jews. To aid their missionary endeavours, many friars learned Hebrew and began to study the Talmud (the compilations that embody the oral teaching of Rabbinic Judaism), so that they might dispute with Jewish scholars more effectively.

In other instances, Jewish converts to Christianity brought knowledge of the Talmud with them. One convert, Nicholas Donin, proved particularly influential. His petitions to Pope Gregory IX argued that the Jews had abandoned 'the law which God gave Moses in writing' and adopted another law (the Talmud) in its place. The content of the Talmud itself was dismissed as matter both 'abusive' and 'unspeakable', including 'blasphemies against God and his Christ' and 'fables about the Blessed Virgin'. If this was the case, the Talmud would be both heretical (regarding biblical Judaism) and blasphemous (towards Christianity). In 1239, Gregory sent letters to archbishops, bishops, and kings across western Christendom, calling for investigations into the Talmud. Inquisitorial proceedings followed. In 1240 in Paris, a clerical court found the Talmud guilty and 24 wagon loads of Jewish manuscripts were subsequently burned.[68]

Yet the danger was not simply restricted to manuscripts. If the Talmud was heretical and blasphemous, then contemporary Jews had been led astray from the Mosaic law. In this case, they were no longer witnesses to the truth of the Bible. Indeed, their presence within Christian communities was potentially harmful. The grounds upon which the Augustinian injunction to forbearance was built was thus brought into question. This can be seen in the works of the leading scholastic philosopher of his age: Thomas Aquinas. He broke with established theological convention that castigated the Jewish 'sages' at the time of Jesus for their spiritual blindness, their failure to recognise that he was the Messiah. Instead, Aquinas asserted, they knew he was the Messiah but had him crucified anyway, in a wilful act of defiance of God. Such a suggestion powerfully reinforced a notion of Jews as Christ-killers, as being guilty of the most heinous of crimes: deicide.[69]

Physical expulsion then became the most significant manifestation of the precariousness of Jewish life. Under the pretext of responding to a ritual murder, Philip II Augustus of France expelled Jews from his personal domains in 1182, confiscating their wealth as he did so. There followed other local expulsions, often followed by recalls, in which Jews were allowed to return. The overarching trend, however, was towards larger-scale and more permanent exile. In 1290, Edward I ended over two centuries of Jewish presence in England, a decision seemingly rooted in both religious antipathy and economic advantage. King Philip IV of France similarly expelled Jews from royal lands, Île-de-France, Poitou, Anjou, Champagne, and Normandy in 1306. In the mid-fourteenth-century, surviving Jewish communities were often blamed for the ravages of the Black Death, spreading the disease by poisoning wells, in conspiracy with Muslims and lepers.[70]

This scapegoating prompted further massacres and expulsions, in southern France, Switzerland and, devastatingly, across much of Germany. In the years 1348–1351, what had become one of the largest Jewish communities on the continent, in the Rhineland, was almost entirely eradicated by fire and exile.

In 1394, Charles VI issued a royal decree that definitively expelled Jews from France. For centuries to come, the locus of Jewish life moved eastward.[71]

The final expulsions of Jews from western Christendom were those from Spain and Portugal in 1492 and 1497 respectively. The fate of the Sephardic Jews, those of the Iberian Peninsula, is particularly significant both in charting the increasingly precarious situation of medieval Jewish communities generally, and in illuminating the link between medieval and modern prejudices. By the fourteenth century, the region was home to one of the largest (perhaps between 3 and 5 per cent of the population) and oldest Jewish communities in Europe (probably established before 300 CE). This would prove no safeguard.[72]

By 1250, the *Reconquista* had brought most of the Iberian Peninsula, except the Muslim kingdom of Grenada, under Christian rule. Yet the history of Iberia had not merely been one of conflict. Under both Muslim and Christian sovereigns, Christian, Jewish, and Muslim populations had coexisted, becoming closely bound culturally, economically, and socially. The twentieth-century Spanish historian Américo Castro coined the term *convivencia* (living together) to describe what he thought of as a distinctive Iberian religious frontier. This term, perhaps, fostered a somewhat rose-tinted vision of a harmonious society, with a ready practice of tolerance. In actuality, rigid hierarchies among the faiths had been maintained; legal and social boundaries were well policed. Indeed, episodes of violent persecution, for example riotous assaults on Jewish communities during Easter week, or the recurrent attacks on Jews under the Muslim Almoravid and Almohad dynasties during the eleventh and twelfth centuries, played a role in sustaining *convivencia*. They reinforced unity among the dominant caste, while allowing for a general forbearance towards the sustained presence of a subordinated and regulated minority, kept firmly in its place by periodic persecution.[73]

Convivencia aside, in many respects the vulnerability of Spanish Jews had grown over the course of the fourteenth century, paralleling wider developments in the rest of Europe. Stereotypes of Jewish malfeasance, such as ritual murder allegations, were well established. The scapegoating of Jews for the ravages of the Black Death that had been seen in Germany, the Low Countries, and southern France was also evidenced by massacres in Barcelona, Cervera, Lleida, and Tàrrega, in 1348. Twenty years later, Henry of Trastámara further inflamed anti-Jewish sentiment for political purposes, during a revolt against his half-brother King Pedro I of Castile (a patron of merchants and maritime traders, who was thus accused of being under undue Jewish influence).

Against this backdrop of contingent events, Dominican and Franciscan friars pursued an active, missionary policy aimed at both Jews and Muslims. Besides genuine religious conviction, pressure to convert was increased by restrictive legislation preventing Jews from practising medicine and restricting their business activities. They were forbidden to sell 'any kind of edible food' to Christians. Stigmatising dress codes and residential segregation in designated Jewish quarters (later termed 'ghettos'; the name derived from the Venetian example established in 1516) were enforced. In 1391, a series of riots and massacres, in Seville, Toledo, Valencia, and Barcelona drove thousands more to convert.[74]

The presence of so many so-called '*conversos*' created peculiar tensions within Christian society. Once Jews had converted, the social and economic barriers that had restricted their lives fell away. By the mid-fifteenth century, a thriving class of 'New Christians' had been created, numbering between 250,000 and a million people. Many now prospered. They took prominent roles in urban authorities and joined the land-owning *hidalgo* class. Some rose to positions of power and authority even within the Church. The *converso* Pablo de Santa Maria became bishop of Burgos. His son Alfonso became bishop of Cartagena. Their presence, in turn, stoked resentment, among 'Old Christians', who disparaged *conversos* as *Marranos* ('swine') and accused them of being crypto-Jews, still secretly adhering to their old religion.[75]

Lineage thus became a central concern of the anti-*conversos*. They began to conceive of Jewishness not as a religious identity but as an inalienable essence carried in the bloodline. In early 1449, rioters protesting against an oppressive tax regime in Toledo targeted both local Jews and *conversos*. To placate the mob, the city's chief magistrate issued a decree that excluded *conversos* and their descendants from holding municipal offices. Toledo's measure was the first of Spain's *limpieza de sangre* (purity of blood) statutes, but other cities, including ones in neighbouring Portugal, would follow suit in the 1460s and 1470s. The concept was denounced by the papacy, as it was a denial of the redemptive power of baptism. Yet it was approved at the time by King Juan II as he struggled to rally popular support. This mutation of a religious prejudice into an identifiably pseudo-biological racial prejudice, was a key moment in the transmission of medieval Judaeophobia into modern antisemitism.[76]

Policing the boundary between the Jewish and the *converso* population remained a pressing concern for both secular and ecclesiastical authorities in Spain. The suspicion was that the presence of unconverted Jews would always tempt *conversos* to 'heretical depravity'. In 1480, Ferdinand of Aragon and Isabella of Castile, whose dynastic marriage had unified Spain, established the Inquisition, having received the permission of the papacy. Initially, this was to investigate charges of 'Judaising' levelled at *conversos*. Under the authority of Isabella's confessor, Tomás de Torquemada, the Inquisition developed into a formidable bureaucracy, soliciting secret denunciations, imprisoning the accused, and resorting to torture when they were slow to confess. The most obdurate of those found guilty, 'relapsed heretics' who had previously reconciled to the Church and had then returned to their error, were surrendered to the 'secular arm' for execution at the stake. More commonly, victims suffered imprisonment, confiscation of property, and an intense social stigma that extended to their families. Convicted prisoners were compelled to take part in humiliating, public *autos-da-fé* (acts of faith), parading barefoot and wearing garish robes, that would then be hung in their parish churches, as a lasting reminder of their infamy.[77]

Although *conversos* rather than Jews were the Inquisition's initial concern, the latter were inevitably drawn into the orbit of its activities. In 1490, an allegation was made that a conspiracy of *converso*s and Jews had stolen a Eucharist for magical purposes, and had kidnapped and crucified a young Christian boy, the so-called 'Holy Child of La Guardia'. No child had been reported missing. No body was ever found. Yet under torture the accused confessed. They went to the stake in November 1491. The usually secretive proceedings of the Inquisition had been abandoned in this instance and the affair had the public character of a show trial. It followed several localised expulsions of Jewish communities, such as from Seville and Córdoba in 1483. There inquisitors had made the case that where unconverted Jews were present, they would conspire with *conversos* to harm the 'Old Christians'.[78]

The case of the Holy Child of La Guardia reinforced that specious argument at the national level. In January 1492, Granada fell, and Ferdinand and Isabella finally completed the *Reconquista*. Under pressure from the Inquisition and striving to create a unified, Catholic realm, the monarchs issued an edict expelling all Jews who refused conversion from Spain in March 1492. Ultimately, probably around 100,000 people were exiled from a land that had been home to their community for over a thousand years.[79]

Some found temporary refuge in neighbouring Portugal. However, the subsequent marriage of King Manuel I to Ferdinand and Isabella's daughter was made conditional on the conversion of Portugal's Jews, or the expulsion of those who refused. In 1497, an edict was issued that gave Jews (and the nation's remaining Muslims) one year to settle their affairs and leave. Yet Manuel was unwilling to lose the financial expertise of so many useful subjects. Many Jews were thus forcibly baptised. Children were separated from their parents to be raised in Christian households. It was an ugly, cynical policy that left a dangerous legacy. In 1536, a Portuguese Inquisition would be established to harry and police the nation's 'New Christians' and their descendants.[80]

At the point at which the Sephardic Jews were expelled from the Iberian Peninsula, all the essential ingredients of modern antisemitism were in place. The stereotype of the 'Jew' as misanthropic, threatening, avaricious, impious, usurious, untrustworthy, and conspiratorial was well established. The ideology of blood purity blurred the distinction between religious and racial prejudice. The habit of belief in chimerical and absurd fantasies of Jewish malfeasance was deeply ingrained. The resulting and enduring prejudice was darkly portentous.

In 1943, as the Nazi Holocaust that would ultimately consume the lives of six million European Jews unfolded, the historian Joshua Trachtenberg would point to the absurdity of the murderous indictments levelled against them. How, for example, 'can one believe that all Jews are at one and the same time Communists and capitalists … ?' 'Why', he would ask, 'are Jews so cordially hated – and feared? By what mysterious legerdemain can a weak, defenceless minority be invested in the public eye with the awesome attributes of omnipotence?'[81] For Trachtenburg, the answer lay in a deep history:

> Modern so-called 'scientific' antisemitism is not an invention of Hitler's. But it was born in Germany during the last century, and it has flourished primarily in Central and Eastern Europe, where medieval ideas and conditions have persisted until this day, and where the medieval conception of the Jew which underlies the prevailing emotional antipathy toward him was and still, is deeply rooted.[82]

The case he made still seems powerfully compelling.

Notes

1 Jacob Katz, *From Prejudice to Destruction: Anti-Semitism, 1700–1933* (Cambridge, MA: Harvard University Press, 1980), pp.260–267.

2 Francisco Bethancourt, *Racisms: From the Crusades to the Twentieth Century* (Princeton, NJ: Princeton University Press, 2013), pp.283–89.

3 Hannah Arendt, *The Origins of Totalitarianism* (New York: Schocken Books, 2004), p.3

4 Jonathan Elukin, *Living Together; Living Apart: Rethinking Jewish-Christian Relations in the Middle Ages* (Princeton, NJ: Princeton University Press, 2007); Robert Chazan, *Reassessing Jewish Life in Medieval Europe* (Cambridge: Cambridge University Press, 2010).

5 Nico Voigtländer and Hans-Joachim Voth, 'Persecution Perpetuated: The Medieval Origins of Anti-Semitic Violence in Nazi Germany', *Quarterly Journal of Economics*, 127 (2012), pp.1339–1392.

6 Peter Schäfer, *Judeophobia: Attitudes Towards the Jews in the Ancient World* (Cambridge, MA: Harvard University Press, 1997), pp.197–211.

7 Cicero quoted in Benjamin Isaac, *The Invention of Racism in Classical Antiquity* (Princeton, NJ: Princeton University Press, 2004), p.454.

8 James S. McLaren, 'Jews and the Imperial Cult: From Augustus to Domitian', *Journal for the Study of the New Testament*, 27 (2005), pp.257–278; Martin Goodman, *Rome & Jerusalem: The Clash of Ancient Civilisations* (London: Penguin, 2008), p.420; Sam Wilkinson, *Caligula* (London: Routledge, 2005), pp.49–61.

9 Quotes from Isaac, *The Invention of Racism*, pp.231–233, 357.

10 Bernard Green, *Christianity in Ancient Rome* (London: Continuum, 2010), p.26; Isaac, *Invention of Racism*, pp.235–239.

11 Suetonius, *The Lives of the Caesars*, Chapter 25, translated by Catherine Edwards (Oxford: Oxford University Press: 2008), p.18.

12 Goodman, *Rome and Jerusalem*, pp.420–421.

13 McLaren, 'Jews and the Imperial Cult', pp.262–269; Schäfer, *Judeophobia*: pp.136–160; Lee I.A. Levine, 'Judaism from the Destruction of Jerusalem to the End of the Second Jewish Revolt: 70–135 CE', in Hershal Shanks (ed.), *Christianity and Rabbinic Judaism* (Washington, DC: SPCK, 1993), pp.125–149.

14 Levine, 'Judaism from the Destruction of Jerusalem', pp.146–147; Goodman, *Rome and Jerusalem*, p.494.

15 Harold W. Attridge, 'Christianity from the Destruction of Jerusalem to Constantine's Adoption of the New Religion: 70–312 CE', in Shanks (ed.), *Christianity and Rabbanic Judaism*, pp.168–169.

16 The Bible, John 5:18

17 John G. Gager, *The Origins of Anti-Semitism* (Oxford: Oxford University Press, 1983), pp.247–264; Lloyd Gaston, 'Paul and the Torah', in Alan T. Davies (ed.), *Antisemitism and the Foundations of Christianity* (Eugene, OR: Wipf and Stock, 2004), pp.48–71; B.A. Pearson, 'I Thessalonians 2: 13–16: A Deutero-Pauline Interpolation', *Harvard Theological Review*, 64 (1971), pp.79–94.

18 Paula Fredriksen, 'What Parting of the Ways? Jews, Gentiles, and the Ancient Mediterranean City', in Adam Becker and Annette Yoshiko Reed (eds), *The Ways that Never Parted: Jews and Christians in Late Antiquity and the Early Middle Ages* (Minneapolis, MN: Fortress Press, 2007), pp.35–64.

19 Charles Freeman, *A New History of Early Christianity* (New Haven, CT: Yale University Press, 2011), pp.136–141.

20 Graham N. Stanton, 'Justin Martyr's Dialogue with Trypho: Group boundaries, "proselytes" and "God-fearers"', in Graham N. Stanton and Guy G. Stroumsa (eds), *Tolerance and Intolerance in Early Judaism and Christianity* (Cambridge: Cambridge University Press, 1998), pp.263–278; Tertullian, *Scorpiace*, Chapter 10, in *The Ante-Nicene Fathers*, Volume III, translated and edited by Alexander Roberts, James Donaldson, and Arthur Cleveland Coxe (New York, NY: Cosimo, 2007), p.643.

21 Tertullian, *Apology*, Chapter 21, in Roberts et al., *The Ante-Nicene Fathers*, p.34.

22 Tertullion, *The Five Books Against Marcion*, in Roberts et al., *The Ante-Nicene Fathers*, pp.269–428; David Nirenberg, *Anti-Judaism: The History of a Way of Thinking* (New York, NY: W.W. Norton, 2013), pp.102–104.

23 W.P. Bowers, 'Jewish Communities in Spain at the Time of Paul the Apostle', *Journal of Theological Studies*, 26 (1975), p.398; Neil B. McLynn, 'Conversion Anxieties: Policing Christian Behaviour in Late Antique Antioch and Hippo', *Archives de Sciences Sociales des Religions*, 63 (2018), pp. 99–116.

24 Robert Wilken, *John Chrysostom and the Jews: Rhetoric and Reality in the Late the Century* (Eugene, OR: Wipf & Stock, 1983), pp.64–94, 116–127.

25 Ambrose, 'Letter 87', in A.D. Lee (ed), *Pagans and Christians in Late Antiquity* (London: Routledge, 2000), pp.159–162.

26 Jacob Neusner, *Judaism & Christianity in the Age of Constantine* (Chicago, IL.: University of Chicago Press, 2007), p.146.

27 Wilken, *John Chrysostom and the Jews*, pp.52–54.

28 Paula Frederiksen, *Augustine and the Jews: A Christian Defense of Jews and Judaism* (New Haven, CT.: Yale University Press, 2010), pp.274–275, 290–314.

29 Saint Augustine, *City of God*, Book 18, Chapter 46, translated by Henry Bettenson (London: Penguin, 1972), pp.827–828; Neusner, *Judaism & Christianity*, pp.146–147.

30 Jeremy Cohen, *The Friars and the Jews: The Evolution of Medieval Anti-Judaism* (Ithaca, NY: Cornell University Press, 1982), pp.20–21.

31 Neusner, *Judaism & Christianity*, pp.148–149.

32 Severus of Minorca, 'Letter Concerning the Jews', in A.D. Lee (ed.), *Pagans and Christians in Late Antiquity* (London: Routledge,2000), pp.163–164.

33 Wilken, *John Chrysostom and the Jews*, pp.161–162.

34 Socrates Scholasticus, *The Ecclesiastical History*, Chapter 16 (Wilmington, NC: Nuvision: 2007), pp.270–271.

35 Tertullian, *Apology*, Chapter 7, in Roberts et al., *The Ante-Nicene Fathers*, p.23.

36 Robert Markus, 'From Rome to the Barbarian Kingdoms (330–700)', in John McManners (ed.), *The Oxford Illustrated History of Christianity* (Oxford: Oxford United Press, 1992), p.85.

37 Alex Novikoff, 'The Middle Ages', in Albert S. Lindemann and Richard S. Levy (eds), *Antisemitism: A History* (Oxford: Oxford University Press, 2010), pp.65–66.

38 Quoted in Novikoff, 'The Middle Ages', p.66.

39 Bernard Bachrach in *Early Medieval Jewish Policy in Western Europe* (Minneapolis: University of Minnesota Press, 1977), pp.3–26 and 'A Reassessment of Visigoth Jewish Policy, 589–711', *American Historical Review*, 78 (1973), pp.11–34.

40 Bachrach, 'A Reassessment of Visigoth Jewish Policy, 589–711', p.16.

41 Bat-sheva Albert, 'Isidore of Seville: His Attitude Towards Judaism and His Impact on Early Medieval Canon Law', *Jewish Quarterly Review*, 80 (1990), pp.207–220.

42 Novikoff, 'The Middle Ages', p.67.

43 Bachrach, 'A Reassessment of Visigoth Jewish Policy, 589–711', p.18.

44 Bachrach, 'A Reassessment of Visigoth Jewish Policy, 589–711', p.18.

45 Norman Roth, 'Bishops and Jews in the Middle Ages', *Catholic Historical Review*, 80 (1994), p.3.

46 Michael McCormick, 'New Light on the "Dark Ages": How the Slave Trade Fuelled the Carolingian Economy', *Past & Present*, 177 (2002), pp.52–54.

47 Roth, 'Bishops and Jews', p.5.

48 Roth, 'Bishops and Jews', p.7.

49 Thomas Renna, 'Papal Approval of Holy Roman Emperors, 1250–1356', *Expositions*, 11 (2017), p.76.

50 Anna Sapir Abulafia, 'The Ideology of Reform and Changing Ideas Concerning Jews in the Works of Rupert of Deutz and Hermannus Quondam Iudeus', *Jewish History*, 7 (1993), pp.43–63.

51 Roth, 'Bishops and Jews', p.8.

52 Robin Mundill, *The King's Jews: Money, Massacre and Exodus in Medieval England* (London: Continuum, 2010), pp.4–5.

53 Marcus Bull, 'The Roots of Lay Enthusiasm for the First Crusade', *History*, 78 (1993), pp.353–372; H.E.J. Cowdrey, 'Pope Urban II's Preaching of the First Crusade', *History*, 55 (1970), pp.177–188.

54 Christopher Tyerman, *God's War: A New History of the Crusades* (London: Penguin, 2007), pp.100–106 and *The Crusades: A Very Short Introduction* (Oxford: Oxford University Press, 2004), pp.12–14; Jonathan Riley-Smith, *The First Crusade and the Idea of Crusading* (London: Continuum, 2009), p.34.

55 Tyerman, *God's War*, p.44.

56 Anna Sapir Abulafia, *Christian-Jewish Relations 1000–1300* (London: Routledge, 2014), p.139.

57 Robert Chazan, '"Let Not a Remnant or a Residue Escape": Millenarian Enthusiasm in the First Crusade', *Speculum*, 84 (2009), pp.295–296; Norman Simms, 'The Unspeakable Agony of Kiddusth ha-shem: Forced Jewish Infanticide during the First and Second Crusades', *Medieval History Journal*, 3 (2000), pp.337–362.

58 Gary Dickson, 'The Advent of the Pastores (1251)', *Revue Belge de Philologie et d'Histoire*, 66 (1988), pp.249–267.

59 David Nirenberg, *Communities of Violence: Persecution of Minorities in the Middle Ages* (Princeton, NJ: Princeton University Press, 1996), pp.43–50; Tyerman, *God's War*, pp.802–805.

60 Quoted in Novikoff, 'The Middle Ages', pp.71–72.

61 Chazan, *Reassessing Jewish Life in Medieval Europe*, p.116.

62 Abulafia, *Christian-Jewish Relations 1000–1300*, pp.90–92.

63 Mundill, *The King's Jews*, pp.75–82.

64 Gavin Langmuir, 'Thomas of Monmouth: Detector of Ritual Murder', *Speculum*, 59 (1984), pp.820–846.

65 Gavin Langmuir, *Towards a Definition of Antisemitism* (Berkley, CA.: University of California Press, 1990), pp.263–271; Marvin Perry and Frederick Schweitzer *Antisemitism: Myth and Hate from Antiquity to the Present* (New York, NY.: Palgrave, 2002), pp.43–72.

66 Langmuir, *Towards a Definition of Antisemitism*, pp.14–15.

67 Jacob Rader Marcus (ed.), *The Jew in the Medieval World: A Sourcebook* (Cincinnati, OH: Hebrew Union College Press, 1990), p.154.

68 Robert Chazan, 'The Condemnation of the Talmud Reconsidered (1239–1248)', *Proceedings of the American Academy for Jewish Research*, 55 (1988), pp.11–30; Cohen, *The Friars and the Jews*, pp.60–68.

69 Cohen, *The Friars and the Jews*, pp.124–125, 147–148.

70 Samuel K. Cohn, Jr., 'The Black Death and the Burning of Jews', *Past & Present*, 196 (2007), pp.3–36.

71 Dan Cohen-Sherbok, *Atlas of Jewish History* (London: Routledge, 1994), pp.91–92; Mundill, *The King's Jews*, pp.156–159.

72 Philippe Wolff, 'The 1391 Pogrom in Spain. Social Crisis or Not?', *Past & Present*, 50 (1971), pp.5–6.

73 Nirenberg, *Communities of Violence*, p.245; Jonathan Ray, 'Beyond Tolerance and Persecution: Reassessing Our Approach to Medieval "Convivencia"', *Jewish Social Studies*, 11, 2 (2005), pp.1–18.

74 'Economic Laws: Spain, 1412, 1432', in John Edwards (ed.), *The Jews in Western Europe 1400–1600* (Manchester: Manchester University Press, 1994), pp.75–77; Norman Roth, 'The Jews of Spain and the Expulsion of 1492', *The Historian*, 55, 1 (1992), pp.17–30; Wolff, 'The 1391 Pogrom in Spain', pp.4–18.

75 Jerome Friedman, 'Jewish Conversion, the Spanish Pure Blood Laws and Reformation: A Revisionist View of Racial and Religious Antisemitism', *The Sixteenth Century Journal*, 18 (1987), pp.5–8; Roth, 'The Jews of Spain', pp.22–23.

76 María Elena Martínez, *Genealogical Fictions: Limpieza de Sangre, Religion and Gender in Colonial Mexico* (Stanford, CA: Stanford University Press, 2008), pp.26–30; 'Racial Laws against Jewish Christians: Spain 1449 and Portugal', in Edwards (ed.), *Jews in Western Europe*, pp.100–101.

77 John Edwards, *Inquisition* (Stroud: The History Press, 2009), pp.85–102.

78 Roth, 'The Jews of Spain and the Expulsion of 1492', pp.26–27.

79 Edwards, *Inquisition*, pp.109–113.

80 Edwards, *Inquisition*, pp.130–135.

81 Joshua Trachtenburg, *The Devil and the Jews: The Medieval Conception of the Jew and Its Relation to Modern Anti-Semitism* (Philadelphia, PA: The Jewish Publication Society, 1993), pp.1–6.

82 Trachtenburg, *The Devil and the Jews*, p.5.

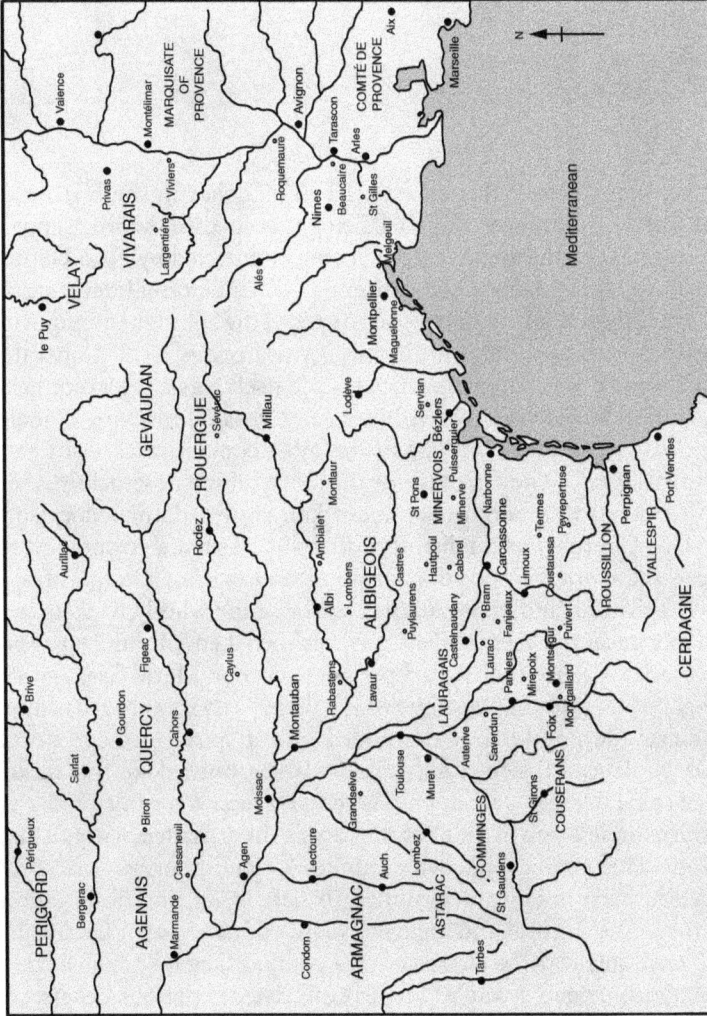

Map 5.1 Languedoc, 1209.

5   'Kill Them All. God Will Know His Own'

The Albigensian Crusade and the Persecution of Heretics, 1209–1321

The Albigensian Crusade has an especial significance in the history of persecution. The Polish lawyer Raphaël Lemkin coined the word 'genocide' in 1944, in response to the atrocities then being committed by Nazi Germany in occupied Europe. He defined the concept as the intentional destruction of a national, ethnical, racial, or religious group and the subsequent imposition of its oppressor's 'national pattern'. Lemkin was anxious to demonstrate that, although his word was a neologism, genocide itself was a recurrent historical phenomenon.[1] He described the Albigensian Crusade, formally launched by Pope Innocent III in 1209, as 'one of the most conclusive cases of genocide in religious history'.[2] The objective of this crusade was, ostensibly, the extirpation of a heretical Church that had taken root in Languedoc (southern France). This Church was dualist. Its adherents posited a cosmology of 'two principles': the eternal opposition of good and evil, of God, whose realm was purely spiritual, and of Satan, the creator of the wholly wicked, material world. More recently, medievalists have echoed Lemkin, and also pointed to the crusade as a seminal act of persecution. For Mark Gregory Pegg, it 'ushered genocide into the West by linking divine salvation to mass murder'.[3]

As the crusade unfolded, it descended into a spiral of disproportionate retaliatory violence. Unrepentant heretics were burned at the stake. The peoples of defiant cities and towns, heretic or not, were put to the sword. Indeed, the complex web of motives that drove the crusaders was not confined to religion. The conflict pitched ambitious, land-hungry northern lords against a southern nobility determined to defend its traditional autonomy and territory. The cultural and linguistic distinctions between Languedoc and the north gave this war the character of a conquest, against which the population fought to defend a way of life, irrespective of religious beliefs.

While the crusaders struggled to master the military challenges of an inglorious war characterised by wearying sieges and sudden ambushes, the Catholic Church refined its techniques of ideological pacification. After the armies had ceased to march, a new mechanism of persecution was forged: 'inquisition'. Papal inquisitors continued the campaign to extirpate heresy. The accused would often be sequestered and examined in secret.

DOI: 10.4324/9781003494331-6

They would not, generally, be informed of the charges against them. They would largely be unable to secure qualified legal defence. Robert Moore has contextualised the Church's repression of alleged heretics in the twelfth and thirteenth centuries as one component of an emerging wider pattern that also targeted Jews, lepers, and homosexuals. This policy, he argued, was designed to extend the authority of a rising class of bureaucrats and functionaries, clerics and courtiers, and the Church and sovereigns they served. It created a legacy of the systematic persecution of minorities that has endured until our own times.[4]

Yet, to establish whether this seminal conflict also constituted a genocide, as Lemkin suggested, would require historians to demonstrate the planned destruction of a discrete population, identified by their religious beliefs: the Cathars. However, that identification has now been called into question. Certainly, the name 'Cathar' is problematic. Although widely used by modern historians, it was applied to heretics in Languedoc only rarely by their contemporaries. As with other titles, such as Manichaean, with which they labelled their opponents, Catholic clergy had learned the name Cathar from patristic texts on heresy written centuries earlier. The people who became the objective of the crusade of 1209 did not refer to themselves as Cathars. They may have self-identified as 'good women' and 'good men', or even as 'good Christians', but those terms were not exclusive to them. The securest option is to refer to them as Albigensians. This was a widely used contemporary appellation, derived from the city of Albi, where the dualist heresy was believed to be particularly strong. Philip II of France had, for instance, written to the pope discussing plans to 'march against the Albigensians' in the winter of 1207–1208. It was, thus, a name imposed by their Catholic enemies, but it usefully distinguishes them from other sects both inside and outside of Languedoc.[5]

However, controversy does not merely surround by what name we should refer to these alleged heretics but extends to the very nature of 'popular heresy'. Conventional historiography has treated the heretics' challenge to the Catholic Church as very real, born of dramatic religious, political, and social change. Western Europe itself was understood as a single Christian polity: Latin Christendom. Here, temporal authority was vested in secular rulers, kings, and emperors, and spiritual authority in the pope and the Catholic Church. Beginning in the eleventh century, Latin Christendom was profoundly transformed by widespread religious revivalism. In Rome, a succession of reform-minded popes, prominent among whom was Gregory VII (r.1073–1085), strove to rid the Church of corruption, such as simony (the sale of clerical offices), secular control of bishoprics and benefices, and the sinful behaviour of venal and unchaste clergy. To achieve this end, however, would require the papacy to exercise an unprecedented authority over Christendom.

This intrusive papacy ultimately generated friction in every sphere of life, from high politics to personal piety. The boundary between secular and spiritual authority was particularly fiercely contested. In 1075, Pope Gregory VII forbade secular rulers from appointing bishops in their own lands and subsequently asserted the papacy's right to depose those sovereigns who defied the Church. There were those monarchs who refused their obedience, most notably Henry IV (1050–1106), ruler of much of Germany, Burgundy, and northern Italy (what would later become known as the Holy Roman Empire). Yet to do so risked personal excommunication and an interdict on their lands that denied most sacraments to their subjects. The papacy became increasingly jealous of its authority, which it wielded like a worldly monarchy. It became more bureaucratic, intolerant, and even warlike, employing and part-funding the armies of allies or raising its own troops in the Papal States.[6]

One of the most dramatic manifestations of these tendencies was the crusading movement. In November 1095, Pope Urban II (c.1035–1099) proclaimed a holy war, calling upon Christians to go to the aid of their co-religionists in the Holy Land, under Muslim rule since 638 CE. Those who swore to undertake this armed pilgrimage 'could substitute this journey for all penance'. This was a promise of salvation earned through acts of 'meritorious violence' that harnessed considerable popular religious enthusiasm.[7] They were to be distinguished by wearing their faith's most cherished symbol, the cross, and would thus be *crucesignati* ('signed with the cross'). From this expression, later historians would derive the word 'crusade'.[8]

The notion of penitential warfare would soon prove equally useful for the papacy in its struggle against internal enemies. For the development of this worldly, monarchical papacy promoted in many lay Christians a critical stance towards the clergy. They desired a return to the basic tenets preached by Christ and his apostles: asceticism, chastity, preaching, and the renunciation of wealth. Their sense of mission was frequently given an urgency by their millenarianism, the belief that the end of the world was imminent. The Church struggled to stifle such dissent against a backdrop of socio-economic change. Latin Christendom's economy was growing, and urbanisation created bustling towns where life was lively, conversations discordant, and thoughts, even on matters sacred, unfettered. Self-taught, unauthorised, but often very charismatic, preachers took to the roads and the marketplaces. Some rejected not only the materialism of the Church and the moral failings of the clergy but also challenged Catholic doctrines that lacked basis in scripture: confession, infant baptism, transubstantiation, purgatory.[9]

The Church would often stigmatise dissent as heresy, but this identification would always be problematic. The dividing line between heresy and orthodoxy was often contingent on the group's relationship with clerical authority. Many of those who rejected material wealth, and wandered from town to town as preachers urging a life of apostolic poverty, remained steadfastly obedient to the Church. They were considered not simply orthodox but praiseworthy. Francis of Assisi (c.1180–1226), the son of a wealthy urban merchant, exchanged his clothes with those of a beggar, disowned his family, and gathered around him a small band of like-minded followers. In 1209, with papal approval, he founded a religious order, the Franciscans, whose wandering friars both practised and preached an apostolic life. Yet Francis never suggested that poverty was a spiritual requirement for all Christians, or even for the clergy. He remained faithful to the Church.

The career of Valdes of Lyons, however, offered a stark contrast. Sometime around 1170, Valdes, also from a rich merchant family, gave his wealth to the poor and started his own career as an itinerant preacher, living off alms and attracting many followers: the 'Waldenses' or 'Poor of Lyons'. Like Francis, Valdes affirmed his orthodox religious beliefs, and his apostolic way of life was initially granted papal approval in 1179. Yet the group's theological ignorance caused some concern, and they were forbidden from preaching. This restriction was ignored and, for this disobedience, the Waldenses were declared heretical in 1184. Valdes himself died at some point between 1205 and 1218. His followers, by now spread over France and established in Germany and Italy, were rent by schism. Some reconciled to the Church. Others grew more radical, asserting their right to preach and insisting that poverty was a spiritual requirement of all Christians. They and similar groups, such as the followers of the fiery preacher Henry of Lausanne who burned crucifixes, wrecked altars, and assaulted clergymen, would be hounded as heretics.[10]

The Albigensians, against whom the papacy ultimately dispatched a crusade, were different because of the suggestion that they had embraced dualism. This had, according to the established historiography, been transmitted to them from the Bulgarian sect known as the Bogomils. They believed in 'the two principles': that Satan (the creator god of the Old Testament, whose authority they thus rejected) had fashioned the false, material world, and that only the soul, imprisoned in sinful flesh, was created by God. Christ was an angel who had only appeared to have physically suffered on the Cross and risen from the tomb. His true significance was his teaching. They rejected the Catholic sacraments and the doctrines of hell, purgatory, transubstantiation, and bodily resurrection. Their spiritual elite were the *perfecti*. These had received the *consolamentum* (the entry of the Holy Spirit by the laying-on of hands), abjured meat and marriage, and preached to the *credentes* (believers). These *credentes*, the rank-and-file of the sect, led less ascetic lives, but would hope to receive the *consolamentum* on their deathbeds.[11]

The Albigensians were not thus guilty of mere 'error', but, to clerical observers they were 'traitors', who, by rejecting the authority of the Church, rejected the authority of Christ too. According to Bonacurses, 'formerly one of their masters', writing around 1176, 'they say the Church was lost [to the Antichrist]' and they 'damn Ambrose, Gregory, Augustine, Jerome and the others together'. By then, the sect was organising its own dioceses and bishops. In 1167, Bishop Mark of Lombardy travelled with 'Papa Niquinta', from Constantinople, to meet Robert of Épernon, bishop of France and Sicard Cellarer, bishop of Albi, at a council in the *castrum* (fortified village) of St-Félix, near Toulouse. There they established three new dioceses in Languedoc: Toulouse, Carcassonne, and Agen.[12] The challenge here was not an erring sect within Catholicism. Far more threateningly, it was a separate Church altogether.

By this time, the Catholic Church was aware of its emerging rival in Languedoc. In 1145, the influential Abbot Bernard of Clairvaux had travelled to the region to correct the doubts spread by Henry of Lausanne. In Toulouse, the reception from the townsfolk was sullen and antagonistic. Alphonse-Jourdain, count of Toulouse, seemed himself a *fautor* (protector) of the arch-heretic Henry. And Henry's anti-clericalism appeared to be redolent of a deeper malaise. The Church had detected the presence of dualists, whom they termed 'Manichaeans'. Bernard preached that the field 'was sown with wicked seed' and that the 'little foxes' of heresy were loose in the 'vineyards of the Lord', threatening the eternal souls of the faithful.[13] He, like many of his fellow churchmen, sought first to debate the misguided and the ignorant and win them back to the fold. Yet, ultimately, a defining quality of heresy would be the obstinacy with which the accused so often clung to their beliefs. The scene was set for escalating confrontation and violent persecution.

This, at least, has been the conventional understanding. There has, however, emerged a radically different interpretation of the conflict that ultimately drove persecution in Languedoc. Historians such as Robert Moore and Mark Gregory Pegg have questioned the existence of an organised Church of dualistic heretics in the late twelfth century. They challenge the idea that scattered groups of alleged heretics, in Languedoc, Germany, or Lombardy, shared any institutional structures with each other or with dualists in the Balkans. Rather, the religious dissent of the age was characterised more by individual doubt and distinct regional religious cultures rather than any sharply delineated, overarching doctrines. In 1164, the Catholic bishop of Albi debated with a group of alleged heretics, who 'chose to be called *boni homines* [good men]', in the village of Lombers. These *boni homines* gave no solid indication of dualist beliefs. They did reject the authority of the Old Testament. They denounced, too, bishops and priests who wore 'gleaming raiment' as 'ravening wolves, hypocrites and seducers'. Nor would they swear oaths. Yet they also expressed an entirely orthodox range of beliefs. When threatened with a judgement of heresy, they readily affirmed their belief in the 'one God' and the Holy Trinity.[14]

Lacking a coherent body of doctrine, formal institutions, or hierarchy of leaders to refute, such vaporous yet persistent dissent was difficult for the Church to counter. Yet clerical bureaucrats strove to assert their authority, suppress criticism, and bring to heel autonomous local cultures. What they needed was a tool by which to securely identify, socially isolate, and criminalise those who raised grievances against the Church. As the bishop of Albi demonstrated at Lombers, an accusation of heresy served this purpose well, bringing the querulous into line and disciplining the broad body of the faithful.

According to this revisionist interpretation, clerics understood the nature of heresy from their education. As scholars in the university in Paris or while working in the scriptoriums of monasteries, they had read descriptions of ancient heresies, including dualism. When allegations of heresy were made against contemporary groups, like the *boni homines* of Lombers, clerics attributed to them the characteristics of heretical groups that had existed centuries before. Those they labelled as Manichaeans or Cathars were understood as part of a tradition of lethal 'spiritual pestilence' spreading infection throughout the body of Christendom and damning souls to eternal torment.[15]

Those historians who have taken this sceptical approach to the nature of popular heresy do not, however, deny that coherent heretical sects did eventually emerge among those the Church persecuted. Yet they see this as a late development. In Languedoc, they suggest, it was only *after* the Albigensian Crusade that appreciable numbers of persecuted Christians had moved towards dualism, embracing the stigma of the heretical identity imposed upon them by the 'ravening wolves' of the Catholic Church. Decades of suffering violent repression in this material world may have played some part in convincing them that they did indeed inhabit the creation of Satan.[16] By this analysis, persecution was not the response to heresy; heresy was the response to persecution.

There are, thus, two conflicting interpretations to explain the origins of the Albigensian Crusade. The traditional account accepts that an organised, heretical dualistic Church existed in Languedoc, and was well established by the latter half of the twelfth century. The response of the Catholic Church was a progression from campaigns of persuasion, by preaching and debating, through to campaigns of violent suppression, by crusade and inquisition. This was a reaction to a genuine threat both to the Church's authority and to the souls of ordinary Catholics who might be infected with heresy. The sceptical challenge to this narrative argues that heresy was an ideological construct. It was born of the criminalisation of devout Christians who chafed at the growing, intrusive power of a clergy that often seemed to them materialist and sinful. Shaped by their experience of persecution, some of these Christians eventually embraced the heretical doctrines they had been stigmatised as holding.

Whatever the differences in terms of causation and chronology, it is worth noting that both traditionalists and sceptics accept that, ultimately, a distinct group was targeted for extirpation. A religious genocide occurred. Both schools of thought therefore recognise the significance of the Albigensian Crusade in shaping institutionalised persecution thereafter. Achieving a further degree of synthesis between the two positions is difficult but not impossible. As the sceptics argue, the overwhelming mass of primary evidence we possess concerning the heretics of Languedoc was written by their tormentors. Descriptions of their theology, their institutions, the arguments they advanced in debates, even the transcriptions of their confessions before inquisitors, were all filtered through the distorting lens of their persecutors' prejudices and beliefs. They cannot be taken at face value. As Lucy Sackville notes, 'the picture of heresy that we receive from texts is a construction of orthodox commentators, rather than a straightforward description'. Yet that construction was not simply born in a university classroom. It derived in large part from actual encounters with heretics and engagement with their doctrines.[17]

In some instances, Catholic clergymen reproduced long sections of contemporary heretical texts, in order to refute them. Durand of Huesca's work *Liber contra manicheos*, for example, contains lengthy sections of a 'Manichaean' treatise that expressed the views of alleged heretics in Albi, Toulouse, and Carcassonne. Durand may have made the connection to ancient Manichaeism, familiar from his own education. Yet the text was, indeed, avowedly dualist. It addressed at length 'two worlds', 'two kingdoms', and a 'twofold creation'. It found 'the present wicked world' to be 'wholly seated in wickedness'. It dates from no later than 1222.[18]

There is other evidence that tends to support the traditional interpretation that an organised dualist Church was long present in Languedoc. We possess, for example, an account of the council of heretical bishops in the *castrum* of St-Félix, near Toulouse in 1167. The surviving copy is preserved in the work of a seventeenth-century antiquarian, Guillaume Besse. He transcribed this from a now-lost document, probably dating from 1223 and produced for the archive of Peter Isarn, (heretical) bishop of Carcassonne. Isarn's copy was itself apparently drawn up from an original document, more contemporaneous to the council itself. The sceptics have suggested that the account is a forgery, either by Besse or by Isarn, seeking to establish his own episcopal lineage and authority. Yet in 1999, at a conference that met specifically to debate its authenticity, experts in the study of medieval language concluded that the original text was 'written at the same time as the events which it describes'.[19]

Similar controversy surrounds other twelfth-century evidence for the spread of dualist heresies in Languedoc. The chronicle of Gervase of Canterbury, compiled around 1188, included a letter written in 1177 by Count Raymond V of Toulouse. In this, he appealed to the abbot of the Cistercians at Cîteaux for assistance in suppressing 'the filth of heresy' in his lands. He stated explicitly that alongside the heretics' abomination of the Eucharist and rejection of bodily resurrection, the 'two principles are introduced'. Moore writes that this letter is 'of questionable authenticity', but offers no evidence for this view. Pegg, on the other hand, treats the petition to the Cistercians as genuine. However, he argues that it was simply a political manoeuvre, by which Raymond hoped to tarnish his local rival Roger II Trencavel of Béziers with the 'stain of heresy'.[20] Both suggestions appear to be attempts to deflect attention away from a reliable contemporary source that explicitly points to the presence of dualists in Languedoc by the 1170s.[21]

The clergy genuinely believed that such heretics posed the direst of threats to the souls of those they infected with their spiritual pestilence: eternal damnation. For Bernard of Clairvaux, preaching in 1145, 'Souls everywhere are snatched away to the dread tribunal, alas, unreconciled by penance, unfortified by Holy Communion ... nor are they allowed to draw near to salvation ... '. The heretic thus committed a crime more heinous than physical murder. The heretic murdered souls.[22] Those who persecuted stubborn heretics who would not repent believed themselves the righteous implements of a just God. For their part, thousands of women and men in Languedoc would prove faithful enough to their own beliefs to go to the stake rather than renounce them. The scene was set for a long, violent, and bloody struggle, with a profound spiritual conflict at its heart.

Yet, while it is necessary to consider these debates surrounding the religious origins of the Albigensian Crusade, there is a danger that, in so doing, other factors that contributed to the escalation of violence may slip from sight. In many respects, Languedoc became the centre of a perfect persecutory storm, as contending parties competed to dominate the region, and spiritual and secular conflicts became intertwined. Between 950 and 1350, Latin Christendom expanded dramatically, effectively doubling in size from its heartlands in France, northern Italy, and western Germany. Peripheral areas were drawn into its political and ecclesiastical framework: Scandinavia, and the Iberian Peninsula in the west, Bohemia, Hungary, Poland, and Livonia to the east. In some instances, such as in Scandinavia, this expansion was achieved peacefully. Existing ruling dynasties established Catholic bishoprics and celebrated the Latin liturgy. Elsewhere, in Livonia for example, the process was effectively one of military conquest and colonisation. This was led by a 'violent and self-directing warrior class', drawn from a restless and fortune-hungry aristocracy.[23]

While Languedoc was not geographically a peripheral region, it was linguistically, socially, and culturally distinct from northern France. The Romance language of the south (which survives today as Occitan) was much closer to Catalan than to the French language spoken by northerners. Southern society was less rigid. The nobles and bourgeois of its bustling, wealthy towns shared alike a taste for luxury and sought to conduct themselves according to a common culture of refined manners and courtesy. The socially exclusive ethos of chivalry, a tripartite fusion of martial and Christian ideals with notions of noble lineage, was developing in northern France and England in the late twelfth century. Yet it was slow to penetrate Languedoc. Tournaments, elsewhere an important mechanism for propagating the values and rituals of chivalry, seem not to have been a characteristic of life for Occitanian nobles.[24]

Jennifer Kolpacoff Deane has also pointed to a 'constellation of factors' that made the religious landscape of the south very different from the north and fostered popular spirituality and anticlericalism. The firm alliance between nobility and clergy evident where royal authority was strong, such as in France or England, and that promoted cooperation in the face of threats to either's power, was far weaker in Languedoc. There, nobles often exhibited greater solidarity with those local folk they perceived as 'good Christians' than with a venal and lax local clergy. The Occitan ideal of *Paratge*, an ethos emphasising the importance of shared inheritance, lineage, and the defence of the rights of family and allies, meant that kinship structures were clannish and loyal. Religious dissent would be protected even if it were not personally embraced.[25]

The actual authority wielded by these courtly southern nobles was attenuated generation by generation. Primogeniture, the mechanism by which great dynasties in the north consolidated their land and wealth, was rare in the south. There, inheritances were usually shared among the children of the nobility. Thus, in the north, noble houses accrued power and constructed extensive networks of regional loyalty. In the south, many may have claimed nobility, but the command they exercised was limited. By 1207, the town of Mirepoix had no less than 35 'co-seigneurs' (lords). The *castra*, fortified village strongholds, of these nobles dotted the landscape. Yet the institution whereby *fiefs* were held in return for military service to a lord was, also, rare in the south. When 'private wars', feuds, and raids, erupted, it was often *routiers* – Gascon, Navarrese, and Catalan mercenaries – who did the fighting. The region was, thus, politically fragmented, and militarily vulnerable. To the predatory men of northern France's 'violent and self-directing warrior class', Languedoc thus looked like an opportunity, ripe for conquest.[26]

The danger was not lost on the greatest households in Languedoc. The counts and viscounts of the south were descended from administrative officials appointed by the emperor Charlemagne (*c.*742–814 CE) to govern his volatile southern frontier. After Charlemagne's death, they had become a hereditary aristocracy. Although theoretically acknowledging the suzerainty of the French crown, they had soon sloughed off its authority. By the tenth century, the south was a landscape of autonomous or semi-autonomous principalities, duchies, and counties.

The most successful ultimately forged kingdoms of their own, such as Aragon. Some of the nobles of Languedoc attempted to emulate their increasingly powerful neighbours. The counts of Toulouse adopted primogeniture and strove to build up networks of allegiances through a rather tenuous system of *conventiae* (agreements) with other landholders. This proved no substitute for power based upon the granting of *fiefs*.[27]

The counts of Toulouse found themselves involved in four levels of dangerous competition. These occurred locally with other Occitan nobles, prominently the Trencavel viscounts of Béziers; on their borders, with the Anglo-Norman Angevin Empire and Aragon, and regionally with the crown of France. Finally, Count Raymond VI of Toulouse clashed with the papacy over the boundaries between spiritual and secular authority (and thus access to tithes and land revenues) within his own dominions. His disputes with the Church would escalate and become entangled with allegations that he was a *fautor* of heretics: he sheltered them and allowed them to preach. While

Raymond's own religious views remained orthodox throughout his life, his conflict with the Church became a central dynamic in the radicalisation of the papacy's policy towards heresy in Languedoc.

In 1198, Pope Innocent III succeeded the 92-year-old Celestine III. Benefitting from a thorough training in canon law, the new pope swiftly proved a determined defender of orthodoxy. Within a year of his accession, he had issued a decree that equated heresy with the offence of treason. This measure, linking spiritual sin to a legal crime, allowed for those who were convicted to be stripped of their property and their children of their inheritance.[28] To pursue his campaign, Innocent expected the active cooperation of secular authorities, for he believed he had been called 'to reign over kings from the throne of glory'. Princes and nobles were his instruments to cure the 'spreading canker' of heresy. Yet in this role, he found the troublesome Raymond VI, and indeed the rest of the southern nobility, wholly wanting. The interests of the papacy and the aggressive warrior nobility of the north were coming into belligerent alignment.[29]

However, it important to recognise that there was no rush to embrace physical persecution. Innocent was no fanatic. His attitude towards heresy is best understood within his sweeping programme of reform. This would be revealed fully at the Fourth Lateran Council in 1215, the most significant ecclesiastical council of the age. There, Innocent strove to redefine confession, the mass, and many other aspects of worship, while also securing clerical control of marriage. He hoped to bring popular cults, the veneration of relics, and preaching under tighter ecclesiastical authority.[30] Combating heresy was a central component of his drive for orthodoxy. He insisted upon proper investigations and trials for alleged offences. He was swift to remind those around him who sought to depose Raymond VI that the count himself had never been proved a heretic.

Steps were taken to reform the Church within Languedoc. Innocent was a patron of charismatic, itinerant preachers who were sworn to poverty, lived on alms, and were free from the interference of slothful, worldly bishops. Nobles were promised indulgences (remission of penalties, either earthly or in purgatory, for their sins) if they drove heretics from their lands. Yet, in the peculiar circumstances of Languedoc's fractured internal politics, they either lacked the authority to do so or they harboured some respect for ascetic religious dissidents. In 1203, frustrated by slow progress, Innocent finally dispatched a capable and determined legate, Peter de Castelnau, to take charge. Peter pilloried the southern clergy, even deposing the bishops of Béziers, Toulouse, and Viviers. He debated and excommunicated heretics and wielded the threat of interdiction against the local nobility. He was a formidable figure.[31]

For his own part, Raymond had, in 1205, sworn to extirpate heresy in his dominions but had failed to follow through on his oath. Confronted by the papal legate, he manoeuvred between submission and defiance. In 1207, he was excommunicated, both as a *fautor* of heretics and as an employer of *routiers*, whose violence towards pilgrims, women, merchants, priests, and ecclesiastical property violated the 'Peace of God'. That violence would now also claim the pope's own legate. His party was ambushed at a river crossing on 15 January 1208, following a bitter meeting with the count of Toulouse. A 'servant of Satan' lanced Peter de Castelnau 'in the ribs from behind', mortally wounding him.[32] It was immediately assumed, although never proven, that the murderer was in the employ of Raymond. A wrathful Pope Innocent III now called for a crusade against the heretics of Languedoc, their lordly *fautors*, and the roving bands of mercenaries who killed at their command.

Innocent did not have to strive hard to justify his embrace of violent persecution once he had taken that decision. Eight centuries on, the Augustinian principle that disciplinary violence could make sincere Christians out of heretics was still axiomatic. The canon lawyer Gratian, writing in about 1140, reaffirmed the propriety of physically coercing those who had strayed to return to orthodoxy. Indeed, he explicitly argued that the necessity of religious persecution was a justification for war.[33] Similarly, Bernard of Clairvaux asserted that those who slayed unbelievers were not guilty of murder but committed a righteous act: 'malicide'.[34] In 1179 at the Second Lateran Council, the 'salutary remedy' offered by disciplinary violence was specifically invoked as a response to the 'loathsome heresy of those that some call Cathars ... in the regions of Albi and Toulouse'.[35]

In November 1207, Innocent had urged King Philip II Augustus of France to strike 'manfully and powerfully' at 'wicked heresy' in the region of Toulouse, for 'wounds which do not respond to poultices must be cut out with steel'.[36] The French king, however, was busy dispossessing England's King John of Normandy, Maine, and Brittany. He would not be distracted. It took the murder of the papal legate to create a forceful imperative for good Christians to heed the pope's renewed call to arms, issued in a Papal Bull of 9 October 1209. The Cistercian monk and chronicler Peter of les Vaux-de-Cernay, who would himself accompany the crusade, captured the mood: 'Forward then soldiers of Christ! Forward, brave recruits to the Christian army! Let the universal cry of grief of the Holy Church arouse you, let pious zeal inspire you to avenge this monstrous crime against your God!'[37]

All who heeded this call and took up arms were offered an indulgence, suspension of their debts, and ecclesiastical protection for their possessions. Many of France's most prominent nobles, including Duke Odo of Burgundy, Hervé de Donzy, Count of Nevers, and Gaucher of Châtillon, Count of St Pol, took the cross. These were very wealthy men and they stood to gain little materially from the conflict. Their reward would be spiritual. However, it is probably worth noting that they would receive the same remission of sins as if they had joined a crusade to the Holy Lands, but at considerably less expense. As Abbot Gervase of Prémontré enthused in a recruiting letter, 'the pilgrimage is not long either in time or in distance'.[38] Three papal legates, two archbishops, and six bishops also led their own retinues into the field. The most important of these was the papal legate Arnaud-Amaury of Cîteaux, who would exercise effective command of the initial campaign.

They were joined by many from the lesser ranks of the nobility, such as Simon de Montfort, who would eventually emerge as the leader of the crusade.[39] Often veterans of fighting in the Holy Land, de Montfort and his peers were, no doubt, motivated by religious belief too. Yet they also looked to establish their own patrimonies in the south. The final element of this formidable and highly motivated force were the *ribalds*, the common crusader pilgrims who rushed to take the cross from across the kingdom of France, from Germany, and from Lombardy. This army, mustered at Lyon by July 1209, was, by contemporary standards, large, perhaps 30,000 strong.[40]

Such strength can be illusory. Tactically, on the battlefield or in siege works, the crusaders would repeatedly demonstrate their superior military capabilities. Yet converting tactical prowess into strategic success long eluded them. The initial campaign was effectively derailed by the canny machinations of Raymond of Toulouse. Alarmed by the army massing on the borders of his lands, Raymond sought reconciliation with the pope. He promised to end his practice of appointing Jews to public offices, disband his mercenaries, and hand over seven of his own castles to the Church. He underwent a humiliating act of public penance after which Innocent restored him to the communion.[41]

Raymond audaciously then took the cross and joined the ranks of the *crucesignati*. Good churchmen railed at the behaviour of 'this deceitful, torturous and perjured man', but he had now unhinged the crusaders' strategy. To the extent that they had had a tangible military objective, it had been the count of Toulouse and his lands. Now that he was their comrade-in-arms, they had to focus their attention elsewhere. They selected Béziers. The viscount of this doomed city was Raymond Roger Trencavel, who happened to be a long-time rival of the count of Toulouse and who had recently rebuffed his plea for a united defence against the invaders.[42]

The crusaders arrived before the walls of the city on 21 July 1209. The viscount and the Jewish community of Béziers (who knew well what they might expect at the hands of a crusader army) had withdrawn to the more heavily fortified city of Carcassonne. Yet the townsfolk, as was common in the burgeoning cities of Languedoc, had a strong sense of municipal independence. On 22 July, the city's militia launched sorties to disrupt the crusaders as they prepared their siege-lines. A French knight was pitched from a bridge and 'cut to pieces'. Outraged and zealous for Christ (and, possibly, loot), the *ribalds* seized clubs, tools, and whatever other weapons were to hand and threw themselves at the fortifications: 'they began to go round the town taking the walls apart stone by stone, they jumped down into the ditches and set to work with picks, and others went to batter and smash down the gates'.[43] Surprised by this unplanned assault, the crusading knights followed in their wake. The startled defenders abandoned their ramparts. The assailants swarmed into the streets. Béziers was doomed.

The massacre that ensued became the most infamous event of the Albigensian Crusade. It was a grim custom of medieval warfare that the lives and property of those sheltering within a fortification who had refused a call to surrender, and would not negotiate, were forfeit.[44] However, in this instance, the attackers could hardly claim to have suffered the privations of months in the siege-lines or to have paid a heavy price in blood in the act of storming the walls that justified this practice. And yet, because this was, by nature, a persecutory war, there was no place for mercy even in a victory so easily won.

It might have been possible to impose some restraint on the exultant *ribalds*, who understood the distinction between heretic and Catholic. According to the Cistercian prior Caesarius of Heisterbach, one paused for guidance from the papal legate Arnaud-Amaury: 'What shall we do, lord? We cannot tell the good from the bad'. His reply rendered the distinction immaterial: 'Kill them all. God will know his own'. This sentiment, whether Arnaud-Amaury actually said it or not, was the inevitable corollary of the Church's belief that the wounds of heresy 'must be cut out with steel'. Those who sheltered heretics, as Canon 27 of the Third Lateran Council stated, were to be anathemised alongside them. Now they were butchered alongside them too. Thousands died.[45]

William of Tudela, although a southern Catholic sympathetic to the crusaders, nevertheless acknowledged the peculiar savagery of what was done:

> And they killed everyone who fled into the church; no cross or altar or crucifix could save them. And these raving beggarly lads, they killed the clergy too, and the women and the children ... God, if it be his will, receive their souls in paradise!

Yet, while placing the blame for the bloodletting on the lowliest elements of the army, William also suggested that this was not an entirely spontaneous act. If the swiftness of Béziers' fall caught the crusader leadership by surprise, it would seem that they had already planned for its outcome:

> The lords ... all agreed that at every castle the army approached, a garrison that refused to surrender should be slaughtered wholesale, once the castle had been taken by storm. They would then meet with no resistance anywhere, as men would be so terrified as what had already happened.[46]

As those who died were heretics and their *fautors*, such exemplary violence was not merely strategically useful, it was righteous. Peter of les Vaux-de-Cernay assured his readers that the citizens of Béziers were 'robbers, lawbreakers, adulterers and thieves of the worst sort, brimful of every kind of sin', before extolling the massacre as 'a splendid example of divine justice and Providence'![47]

The powerful signal sent by the crusaders at Béziers did indeed appear to herald a victorious conclusion to their campaign. The 'blessed warriors of the Lord' had marched swiftly on Carcassonne. The siege was short. The crowded citadel was soon cut off from its water supply. On 15 August, Raymond Roger Trencavel, surrendered both the city and himself, as a hostage. The citizens were spared massacre but lost all else. They were expelled, wearing only 'their shifts and breeches'. Their homes and property were forfeit.[48] Resistance crumpled. Across a disunited south, lords and knights now scrambled to come to terms with the invaders. Towns and cities finally acted against those they identified as heretics; the unrepentant were handed over to secular authorities and consigned to the flames. Only a handful of well-fortified *castra* remained defiant. Those, including many 'perfects' who could not reconcile to the Church, fled the cities and towns, and scattered into the mountains.[49]

Yet, like the very strength of the crusading army, this victory was also an illusion.

The crusaders had no viable strategy to turn this early success into a longer-term refashioning of Languedoc into a land free of heretics and wayward nobles. With an apparent sense of 'mission accomplished', and indulgences won, the crusading army swiftly dwindled. Arnaud-Amaury demanded a 'good lord' be chosen to rule the conquered territories. The leading nobles all declined for 'they had plenty of land in the kingdom of France ... and they did not wish to take another man's inheritance'. This 'sacred business', was then accepted by Simon de Montfort, lauded by admirers as 'a valiant baron, a tough fighting man, wise and experienced'. The less admiring thought him 'cruel and murderous'.[50]

Yet even as southern lords and bishops hurried to pledge their allegiance, the character of the war was changing. Having failed to prevent the occupation, the population of Languedoc would turn to resistance. Like so many military commanders confronted by the complexities of waging a counter-insurgency, de Montfort would soon discover that 'winning battles does not necessarily mean winning wars when those battles are merely prolonging and magnifying strategic error'.[51]

Historically, gaining external support has been a significant factor in sustaining insurgencies.[52] For those committed to reigniting the fight against the crusaders in Languedoc, this support would come from King Peter II of Aragon. Peter claimed suzerainty over Béziers and Carcassonne; Raymond Roger Trencavel had been his vassal. He refused to accept de Montfort's homage as the new viscount of the captured lands. As a powerful and geographically well-placed source of moral, and eventually material, support, Aragon sustained resistance. Raymond Roger, count of Foix, formally gained Peter's protection and by the autumn he and de Montfort 'made vigorous war on each other'.[53]

De Montfort's enemies would not yet risk a direct confrontation in open battle, even against his attenuated army. Yet they could take back what he had won piece by piece. Over the winter of 1209–1210, he lost control of forty castles and *castra*. The character of this protracted and unchivalrous form of war only exacerbated its tendency to cruelty. Gerald of Pépieux was a vassal of de Montfort's hostage Raymond Roger Trencavel. News now reached him that his lord had died in captivity. Trencavel almost certainly succumbed to dysentery, but many believed he had been murdered. Vengefully, Gerald abandoned an earlier agreement with de Montfort and burned down his castle of Puisserguier. Two crusader knights who had surrendered to him were brutally mutilated, their eyes put out and their ears, noses, and upper lips cut off.[54]

Such savagery was not unique to the Albigensian Crusade, but it did become particularly marked during that conflict. It was usually a characteristic of a particular kind of war; rebels against their lawful sovereigns or unbelievers, be they heretic or infidel, might expect such barbarism. In Languedoc, 'the normal chivalric law of arms' operated, at best 'intermittently'.[55] This was in large measure a consequence of the inherently persecutory character of a war waged against heretics and their alleged *fautors*, even amongst a majority Catholic population. Yet other factors drove the cruelty too. As far as de Montfort was concerned, if southern lords like Gerald of Pépieux who had given him pledges of allegiance then reneged, then they were guilty of treason and were treated harshly as rebels. Southerners, with their own traditions of looser alliances based around temporary *conventiae*, probably did not see things that way, thus shaping their understanding of de Montfort as 'a man of blood'.[56]

Massacres thus became a recurrent feature of the conflict driven by both religious and retaliatory impulses. When Minerve fell to the crusaders in 1210, 'a hundred and forty perfected heretics' refused to reconcile with the Church and were executed.[57] Such resolution in the face of an awful death by fire demonstrated how little progress was being made in driving heresy from Languedoc. Indeed, as is characteristic of floundering counterinsurgency campaigns, such victories as Minerve only made more (and more implacable) enemies. Southern lords who had lost lands and titles to the crusaders became *faidits* (the dispossessed). These *faidits* gave southern resistance a die-hard core of warriors who had little left to lose, and much to recover, by fighting on against those occupying their lands. When de Montfort's fortunes rose, the *faidits* withdrew to the forests and the hills, and fought their war in that grey area between partisans and bandits. When southern armies gathered in strength, 'the dispossessed knights [came] out of the greenwood' and joined them.[58]

De Montfort, for his part, could never concentrate sufficient force to achieve lasting victory before a significant portion of his army drifted homewards. The term of service required for a crusader to win his indulgence was just forty days. Most of those who arrived each year at the opening of a campaign season in the spring were 'short-timers', counting the days until 'when it seemed good to them they went home to their countries, having completed their forty days' duty and won their pardons'.[59]

This factor, too, contributed to the bitterness of the warfare of Languedoc. In early 1211, it took De Montfort over a month to capture the town of Lavaur, held by the Lady Girauda and her *faidit* brother Sir Aimery. Although the garrison had finally surrendered, they were denied terms. Sir Aimery and eighty knights were hanged. Four hundred alleged heretics were herded into a meadow and burned to death, with no offer of reconciliation to the Church. Lady Girauda was thrown down a well, with stones then heaped upon her.[60] Her gritty defence had cost de Montfort time he could not spare. He responded with exemplary violence.

His lethal frustration may have reflected his sense of an opportunity slipping away. Raymond VI of Toulouse, faced with unrelenting pressure to drive heretics from his own lands, had abandoned the crusade. In February 1211, he had been excommunicated once more. Now his domains, including Toulouse, were vulnerable. Yet Raymond had rallied the citizens and they had united in fortifying and defending the city against the invaders.[61] De Montfort abandoned an attempted siege in late June, when he could no longer feed his troops.[62] Thereafter, he ravaged southern farmland until, their forty days' service completed, his summer soldiers headed home. Although crusader forces won a sharp tactical victory over the count of Foix at the Battle of Saint-Martin-La-Lande in September, long-term strategic success was still elusive.[63]

For the moment, though, De Montfort now dominated all of Languedoc, save for Toulouse and Montauban. To consolidate his hold, he aimed to transform the south into the image of the north. De Montfort enfeoffed his loyal northern followers with the lands taken from the *faidits*. By the Statute of Pamiers, approved on 1 December 1212, strict restrictions were placed on a lord's rights to divide up his land in his will, and Simon's vassals were obliged to provide military service when summoned. By these northern innovations, he sought to avoid the attenuation of power and the military weaknesses that had plagued the southern nobility. Some concessions to local politics were made. A scattering of southern lords who had consistently demonstrated their loyalty retained their lands and their customs. Taxes were cut, tollgates were removed, and pledges to uphold justice freely were made, in an effort to win the support of the urban *bourgeois*.[64] De Montfort and his lords had arrived as crusaders, but they aimed to stay as *colons*, settler-colonists.

Innocent, beseeched by dispossessed southern nobles, pressured by Peter II of Aragon, and keen to redirect crusader zeal towards Jerusalem, now had to reconsider his position. The fatal alignment between the interests of the papacy and the 'violent and self-directing warrior class' that had catalysed the Albigensian Crusade in 1209 was no longer so clear-cut. In January 1213, the pope formally suspended the privileges of crusaders against the Albigensians. However, the evidence of surviving charters indicates that those who went to fight alongside de Montfort continued to understand their military service as a penitential act and were encouraged in that belief by their local clergy. In June 1213, the Champenois lord Erard de Brienne announced that he was 'about to set off on the Albigensian pilgrimage'. Two months later, the bishop of Toul confirmed the grant of a 'crusader against the Albigensian heretics'. Religious sentiment continued to fuel de Montfort's war of conquest.[65]

It was the magnitude and seeming permanence of this destabilising intrusion into regional politics that finally provoked King Peter II of Aragon to intervene directly into the war. It was a fatal error. He was killed in battle against a numerically inferior but audaciously led force under De Montfort at Muret on 12 September 1213, one of the most decisive tactical victories of its era.[66] Strategically, the situation simply grew more complex for the crusaders. Simon's success had further alarmed the Church, as his military operations had carried over into areas untouched by heresy. In 1215, even Arnaud-Amaury, now installed as the archbishop of Narbonne, slammed this city's gates on a crusading army in a dramatic assertion of the Church's authority.

The circumstances here were particularly telling. Prince Louis, heir to the throne of France, was now fulfilling vows to join the crusade that he had made in 1213. He had brought an army south to campaign alongside de Montfort. Together they finally entered Toulouse, and Simon was proclaimed its count. Louis would soon depart, to launch an abortive invasion of England, yet Languedoc was being pulled ever closer to the growing French realm. This, too, explains the Church's growing ambivalence towards the war in the south.

At the Fourth Lateran Council in November 1215, Innocent judged that the sons of those dispossessed by de Montfort, untainted themselves by heresy, should inherit, at the very least, those of their fathers' lands not actually occupied by the crusaders. That decision may have confirmed the incomers in possession of what they already held, but it gave the nobility of Languedoc, including Raymond VII, heir to Toulouse, cause for hope in a renewed struggle. Young Raymond of Toulouse thus led an army back into the field and took the important garrison of Beaucaire in July 1216. The same month, the architect of the Albigensian Crusade, Innocent III, died. His successor, the politically astute Honorius III, was certainly committed to the idea of crusading but also showed some early willingness to listen to the claims of the dispossessed southern nobility.[67]

So, the *faidits* emerged once more from the greenwoods to ambush isolated crusader garrisons and supply convoys. The citizens of Toulouse conspired with Count Raymond VI. The insurgency re-gathered momentum. De Montfort responded as many modern counterinsurgents have done, riskily expanding the war into adjacent areas from which his elusive enemies drew logistical and political support. In the summer of 1217, he crossed the Rhône and invaded Provence. In his absence, in September, Raymond VI retook Toulouse. It was now late in the campaigning season, but Simon realised he must react quickly. He marched hard for Toulouse and immediately launched his first assault against the defenders. It failed. Simon settled down for a siege. On 25 June 1218, he was struck by a missile from one of the city's mangonels, killing him instantly.[68]

The Albigensian Crusade did not end with the death of Simon de Montfort. Yet his death was most certainly a watershed. Militarily, the campaign would become a war of unification, in which the French crown would assert its sovereignty over Languedoc. Southern armies initially made much ground recovering their territories, even after the deaths of Raymond VI of Toulouse in 1222 and Raymond Roger of Foix, in 1223. In 1224, Simon's heir, Amaury de Montfort, conceded defeat, but took the momentous step of '[resigning] his claim to the territory to the illustrious King of France and appointed him as his successor to all his rights'.[69] Louis VIII had crusaded for the stipulated forty days in the south in 1219, in a gesture to improve his relations with the papacy. When he returned in May 1226, he led an army of unprecedented size, sustained by the wealth of his kingdom. Overawed, no southern army materialised to meet him in the field. Béziers, Carcassonne, Castelnaudary, Puylaurens, Lavaur, and Albi welcomed the king and were garrisoned.[70]

Rather than displacing the local nobility, the crown diplomatically accepted their submissions and protestations of loyalty. One war-weary *faidit*, Sicard de Puylaurens, now declared himself 'drunk with delight' at Louis's arrival, which promised peace at last.[71] When Louis died, succumbing to disease at Montpensier in November 1226, only Toulouse remained defiant. During the minority of his son, Louis IX, the war was maintained by his military governor Humbert de Beaujue. Finally accepting the futility of continuing to struggle against the wealthy and well-resourced French crown, Raymond VII offered his surrender to the royal court in November 1228, marking the end of the Albigensian Crusade.

The subsequent 1229 Treaty of Paris did not end the persecution. In many respects, the peace was mild. Raymond was not wholly dispossessed. However, his daughter, and only child, Joan was betrothed to the king's younger brother, Alphonse of Poitiers. Time would, thus, deliver Toulouse to the French crown. The *faidits*, too, were treated generously so long as they abjured heresy. On that issue, there would be no compromise. Indeed, the Church expected that a chastened southern nobility would now pursue the Albigensians with vigour. Yet the papacy would not depend upon such uncertain allies. Rather than rely on the blunt and undiscriminating use of overwhelming military force, which had so often seen undiscriminating massacres, and which provoked popular opposition to the Church, Innocent III had, at the Fourth Lateran Council (1215), shifted emphasis to the systematic identification of individual heretics and the curing of their spiritual sickness.[72] The developing and evolving procedure of inquisition would thus become the principal instrument for the destruction of the Albigensians.

The method of inquisition, in which the judge himself investigated and presented the charges against a defendant, was becoming the standard procedure in ecclesiastical courts at this time.[73] It was initially devised to allow the Church to pursue cases against corrupt clergymen even when no one had submitted a formal complaint against them. Since individuals who made allegations and then failed to prove their case in court were themselves liable to be punished, this was not an unusual situation. Yet rumours or an informal denunciation of *mala fama* (ill repute), made without risk of legal penalty or the burden of proving a case, could trigger an inquiry. Inquisition was therefore a useful legal innovation to ensure that possible offenders were investigated and, if necessary, punished. However, in the context of heresy, as legal scholar Mirjan Damaška has commented, 'a summary variant of inquisitorial procedure emerged (*inquisitio hereticae pravitatis*) [inquiry into heretical depravity] in which rules favouring defendants withered away like flowers caught by an early frost'.[74]

According to this procedure, inquisitors acted as detective, judge, and jury when investigating those suspected of heresy. Those accused, often on the slenderest of evidence or hearsay, would be examined in secret. The identities of those who had denounced them would not be disclosed. Nor would they be told of the specific charges against them. They would usually face the inquisitor alone; legal representation, while allowed, was discouraged by the threat that the lawyers themselves might be denounced as *fautors*. The priority given to extracting a confession in time legitimised the 'vexation' of the body through torture, the use of which was authorised in 1252, provided it did not cause mutilation, the shedding of blood, or death. The infliction of physical suffering was considered righteous because, as it was expressed by the Fourth Lateran Council, 'the soul is more precious than the body'. If pain brought the accused to understanding of their guilt and subsequent repentance, then it was justified.[75]

Those who confessed and recanted, and cooperated by denouncing others, would receive penances of varying severity and be reconciled to the Church. The obdurate would be handed over to the secular authorities for execution, usually by burning at the stake, for churchmen were themselves prohibited from taking lives.

As those who stood before an inquisitor were practically defenceless, the inquisitorial procedure reliably and swiftly delivered the desired outcomes: it disciplined those who had erred and bought the repentant back into the fold; it generated denunciations, thus exposing networks and communities of heretics; it ensured the deaths of those who stubbornly defied the authority of the Church. It took, however, some time for the procedure to develop into the ruthless mechanism that would shatter the Albigensian heresy. In the first instance, bishops were responsible for pursuing inquisitions. Cardinal Romano Frangipani, a papal legate, had arrived in Toulouse in 1229 with ambitious instructions on how best to police entire communities. These included not simply identifying suspected heretics, but establishing lists of the population of each parish. Thus, regular attendance at confession, individual oaths of orthodoxy, and possible movements to avoid the attention of the authorities could all be monitored. This level of bureaucracy would, eventually, grow into one of the most effective tools of persecution, with long-term ramifications beyond the repression of the Albigensians. Initially, however, those tasked with holding inquisitions lacked both the administrative ability and the will to sustain the repression.[76]

The chronicler William de Puylaurens for example, lamented that the new count of Toulouse soon 'lost his enthusiasm and became cool and remiss, and less hot in pursuing the business of faith and peace'.[77] So, too, the bishops. Mired in local politics and distracted by their other duties, they generally proved lax in the pursuit of heresy. Pope Gregory IX (who had succeeded Honorius III in 1227) had come to understand the need to appoint dedicated preachers as his own deputies to establish inquisitorial tribunals. These inquisitors would be directly accountable to him and not under the potentially enervating influence of local authorities.

While the mechanisms of a formidable instrument of persecution were being assembled, there were early, and disastrous, missteps. The first inquisitors had been appointed to pursue heresies outside of Languedoc. Conrad of Marburg, who had been preaching in Germany since 1227, was given a commission to impose penalties for heresy in 1231. Two years later, Robert le Bougre, a former heretic turned Dominican friar, was granted permission to investigate heresy in northern France. Both proved excessively zealous. The priority of the Church was eradication of heresy, where possible by thorough investigation, the correcting of error, and the curing of spiritual sickness through confession, penance, and a return to the fold. Conrad was soon extracting the most bizarre confessions of demon worship, incest, and rituals involving the kissing of the hindquarters or mouths of toads, cats, or a duck 'the size of an oven'.[78]

Those who found themselves before him but denied any part in such lurid fantasies were handed over to the secular authorities to be burned. Robert also proved very quick to deliver the 'stiff-necked' to the flames. He claimed to be able to identify unbelievers simply by their speech and gestures, so he had no shortage of victims. Both he and Conrad rapidly alienated local bishops who saw their own jurisdiction and authority undermined. Without episcopal protection, Conrad was murdered in 1233. Robert was briefly suspended in 1234 but then allowed to resume his grim campaign. It continued until May 1239, when he was responsible for the burning of over 180 alleged heretics at Mont Aimé in Champagne. Shortly thereafter, he was imprisoned before ending his days performing menial duties in the monastery of Clairvaux.[79]

The possibility of individuals such as Conrad and Robert arising, who abandoned due process and engaged in such excesses, remained a dangerous characteristic of inquisition. Indeed, it was repeated in Languedoc where Pope Gregory again looked to the Dominican order for inquisitors. Dominic de Guzmán (c.1174–1221), a canon at the Spanish cathedral of Osma, had begun preaching in the south as early as 1206. Travelling everywhere by foot, carrying only his books, and living a simple life, he sought to 'use a nail to drive out nails', matching the *perfecti* in their exemplary asceticism and in debate. Once the Albigensian Crusade was underway, the Church's active preaching missions largely faltered against the backdrop of violence, terror, and massacre. Dominic persevered, winning the support of both Bishop Fulk of Toulouse and Simon de Montfort himself.

They granted Dominic properties and revenues, allowing him to establish religious foundations that fulfilled the same kind of community roles as the homes of prominent Albigensians. For example, a convent foundered near Fanjeaux offered 'to receive noble women who had been entrusted to the heretics to be fed and educated by their parents on account of their own poverty'.[80] As Dominic's influence grew, so did the number of his followers: black-robed friars who had taken holy vows but lived among the people. In 1216, Honorius III officially confirmed their status as the mendicant 'Order of Preachers', specifically enjoined to 'walk about and seek those who go astray'.[81]

The Dominicans were, thus, the obvious choice to carry forward the work of inquisition in Languedoc. St Dominic himself had died in 1221. In 1233, the first of his order to be appointed to undertake inquisitions were Pierre Seilha and Guillaume Arnaud in the dioceses of Cahors and Toulouse, and Arnaud Cathalà in Albi. Their initial priority appears to have been to identify heretics and have them executed. In Toulouse, an elderly woman was tricked into confessing on her deathbed and was then carried to a field outside the city and burned. When the inquisitors arrived in Moissac, some chose to flee, either to the mountain stronghold of Montségur, or to their co-religionists in Lombardy. They were condemned in their absence. In Albi, Cathalà did not confine himself to the living. He also condemned the dead. Bodies of alleged heretics were exhumed and burned. The horrified people of Albi rose up and the inquisitor almost died at the hands of an angry mob. Another of the early inquisitors, Guillaume Pelhisson, recorded the resistance that this relentless campaign began to provoke, 'the great lords of the land, the leading knights and townspeople ... defended heretics and concealed them, and struck and wounded and killed their persecutors ... '.[82]

Pelhisson and other clerics inevitably began to single out Raymond VII for criticism. The count himself was still making some efforts to placate the Church, such as offering rewards to those who would denounce others as heretics. Yet the widespread disorder that the inquisitors were provoking was not simply counterproductive in terms of the efforts to win souls back to the faith, but it undermined all local authority. In 1235, Guillaume Arnaud demanded the presence of twelve prominent and respected citizens of Toulouse to answer accusations of heresy. His actions provoked a riot; the Dominican convent which he had made his base was overrun and he fled to Carcassonne. Some of his order were intimidated by this violence, but Arnaud rallied the friars by holding out the promise of martyrdom.

Thus fortified, his deputies in Toulouse repeated the citations against the twelve accused. A second riot ensued. Both the convent and the bishop's palace were sacked. Their occupants were physically, and roughly, carried out of the city.[83]

From the Church's perspective, this first inquisitorial campaign had not been without its successes. In 1236, Raymond Gros an influential *perfecti* who had moved within Albigensian circles for over twenty years surrendered himself. He offered not only his own confession but denounced many others, living and dead, who had undergone 'heretications'. The chronicler Guillaume Pelhisson commented that 'So well and so fully did Raymond Gros confess the doings of heretics and their believers and in so orderly a fashion in with such accuracy, that no one should think it could happen without divine providence'.[84]

The incident demonstrated the potential of inquisitorial procedures for dismantling the communal networks that sustained the Albigensians. Terror at the prospect of an appalling death, the possibility of lighter penances for cooperation, and fear of dispossession that would rob families of their inheritances may all have played some part in convincing some to go before the inquisitors. Yet it was also clear that without the support of the local secular authorities and some mitigation of inquisitorial excesses, then others would remain defiant and resistant. There was a case to be made, and this was probably Raymond's hope, for returning the organisation of inquisitorial tribunals to the bishops.

Yet, as during the crusade, the religious conflict would be decisively shaped by political struggle. In April 1240, Raymond Trencavel, the dispossessed heir to the viscounty of Carcassonne and Béziers, staged an abortive and short-lived revolt. Raymond VII had held aloof from this fighting but was already on a collision course with the French crown. He had, in 1239–1240, been waging a private war against Count Raymond Berengar of Provence, Louis IX's father-in-law. Louis had committed royal troops, whom the count of Toulouse had routed. Subsequently, he had made half-hearted protestations of loyalty to the king and staged a brief and abortive siege of an isolated mountain castle at Montségur, one of the last remaining strongholds of the Albigensians, to prove his faithfulness. However, he was also conspiring with England's Henry III and Hugh de Lusignan, count of La Marche, to launch a joint campaign against King Louis that would overturn the settlement of 1229. The rebellion of 1242 was a wretched failure. Henry of England was defeated by a French army at Taillebourg. The supine de Lusignan broke ranks and made a separate peace with Louis. Raymond was abandoned by his key local ally, Roger of Foix.[85]

The political vicissitudes that accompanied the two rebellions signalled to the Dominicans that they might resume their inquisitions. In May 1242, eleven inquisitors, led by Dominican William Arnold and a Franciscan colleague Stephen of St Thibéry, arrived in the *castra* of Avignonet, just fifty miles from the Albigensian mountain fastness at Montségur. On the night of 28 May, Pierre-Roger of Mirepoix, castellan of that stronghold, seized his chance and led a party of armed men to the village. The friars were massacred in their beds. As with the murder of Peter de Castelnau decades before, this rash and bloody act triggered an escalation of religious persecution.[86]

However, war-weary southern nobles, eager to reconcile with crown and Church, now supported the work of the inquisitors. They handed over suspects and required attendance at sermons. Shortly before his own death in late 1249, the chastened Raymond VII himself had eighty alleged heretics and *fautors* burned at Agen. Royal seneschals and Catholic bishops mobilised armies against heresy without provoking further rebellions. Montségur, the most important centre of Albigensian resistance, fell after a lengthy siege in March 1244. According to legend, two hundred unrepentant prisoners were captured there and executed in the *prat dels crematz* ('field of the burned'), below the castle walls. Québus, the last bastion, smaller and less influential, surrendered in 1255. The Albigensian Church had lost its *fautors*, its bishops had been consigned to the flames, and its adherents were scattered without refuge. Now the inquisitors could complete the process of its eradication.[87]

They quickly established the bureaucratic machinery that would ultimately prove more effective than armies as an instrument for the extirpation of heresy. Inquisitors were given particular territorial jurisdictions, for example, Friar Ferrier, based in Carcassonne and responsible for the ecclesiastical province of Narbonne, or Bernard of Caux in Toulouse, with responsibility for the entire diocese. Acting in their capacity as judges, they would be joined by delegates, often fellow Dominicans for particular cases, and crucially, by notaries and scribes. These recorded every step of an investigation: witness statements, confessions, responses to questions, and sentences of the court. The books they produced were among the most powerful implements of the inquisition. Those whose names appeared in them as penitents could be tracked and monitored. Those named in confessions could be identified as suspected heretics and targeted. Networks of dissidents could then be quickly unravelled and the sustaining community bonds of the Albigensians destroyed. It is a testimony to the effectiveness of this bureaucracy that when pockets of violent resistance flared up, the physical records of inquisitors were frequently targeted, alongside those who carried them. In 1247, a courier and clerk who worked for local inquisitors were ambushed and killed near Narbonne. The registers they carried were burned.[88]

The Dominican order itself gained its first martyr in 1252 when the inquisitor Peter of Verona was murdered in Lombardy, where many Albigensians had sought sanctuary. Felled 'by the swords of the impious', 'Peter Martyr' was canonised the following year. His death blurred the distinction between the martyr and the inquisitor, fuelling the righteous zeal of those who persecuted heretics.[89]

Once again, however, care must be taken not to confuse zeal with fanaticism, or even, necessarily, excess. Inquisitions were not blunt instruments. By 1249, the first of a number of handbooks for inquisitors had been produced. By and large, regular procedures were established and followed. This was the bedrock for their success. The local clergy would announce the imminent arrival of an inquisitor and his retinue to a particular place. Proceedings would then open with 'general preaching', with local officials obliged to ensure attendance. All those who heard the sermon would be required to swear an oath abjuring heresy, plead obedience to the Church, and assist in the apprehension of the guilty. A period of grace might then be offered, perhaps from six to twelve days, during which those who confessed to heresy and told of all they knew might be granted more lenient penalties. Others, those who refused to take the oath, were suspected of heresy or had already been arrested would then be summoned.

Before the inquisition, each would be questioned: have you heard the heretics preach? Have you 'adored' (venerated) a heretic or received the 'consolamentum'? Where? When? With whom? In some cases, the more elderly suspects would reveal networks, familial connections, and communities of heresy stretching back decades. In 1243, Helis of Mazerolles, a noblewoman from an influential family, had told of how, fifty years before, her grandmother and others had openly maintained houses in Fanjeaux and Montréal where heretics had preached. She had named those, living, or now deceased, who had attended, who had 'adored' the preachers, who had genuflected before them, and who had given them food and money to sustain them.[90]

At this time, confession was largely the consequence of relentless psychological and social pressure rather than torture. The reach exercised by the inquisitors made evasion difficult. In Toulouse alone, between 1245 and 1246, some 5,605 witnesses were interrogated. Those suspected of heresy might be held in a grim and dirty confinement, at their own expense. They might be summoned again and again, without sure knowledge of what their accusers knew or could prove. Nor was it simply a question of the fate of the accused themselves. Their relatives suffered too; *fama* (reputation) was an important component of status within medieval societies. The children and grandchildren of dead and unreconciled heretics were barred from holding secular office. Should they become embroiled in legal cases, their *mala fama* (ill repute) was held to be reliable evidence in court. The temptation to confess to something, to end the torment and uncertainty, to spare families from ignominy, and to be treated with a degree of leniency for cooperating fully (especially by naming others), proved hard to resist.[91]

Following confession, those condemned by inquisitors were subject to some form of punishment. Sentences would be proclaimed publicly in a ceremonial performance, prefiguring the grim and spectacular *autos-da-fé* of the later Spanish Inquisition, that clearly demonstrated the inquisitorial tribunals' authority. If the transgressions of the guilty were judged particularly serious, they might be imprisoned for life, again at their own expense and thus imposing a lasting financial burden on their families. Most, though, would be required to undertake some form of penance: making financially exacting charitable donations, public scourging, pilgrimage to some holy place, bearing a visible sign of their guilt in the form of a yellow cloth cross sewed to their clothing. These punishments should not be regarded as minor.

If multiple pilgrimages to distant shrines were demanded, the penalty amounted to a form of banishment, and a dangerous and expensive one too, considering the cost and perils such journeys entailed. Homes where heretical acts had taken places might be demolished. The penitential cross visible on clothes was a powerful means of stigmatising people, exposing them to ignominy, maltreatment, and ostracism, leaving some unable to support themselves. Failure to accept or complete their penances (which were, in theory, undertaken voluntarily) would see a victim back before the inquisitors but facing more serious consequences for their 'relapse'. The most obdurate of the accused, those who refused to confess or recant their beliefs in the face of evidence that their judges found compelling, would be surrendered ('relaxed') to the secular authorities, with a hollow plea for mercy and an expectation that they would die at the stake. The partial surviving records suggest that this was the fate of perhaps 8 or 9 per cent of those sentenced by inquisitors.[92]

That only a comparatively small proportion of those who faced the inquisitors died should in no way mislead us as to the horror of what had unfolded and the suffering that crusade and inquisition had trailed in their wakes. The communities of believers and the networks of houses they operated from were largely dismantled by the mid-thirteenth century. The Albigensians, thereafter, were a fragmented sect of renegades who took to the hills and the greenwoods. The number of women *perfectae*, who had been prominent within the faith, declined noticeably after the fall of Montségur. Women wandering alone or in small groups in remote areas quickly attracted the attention of the authorities. Male *perfecti* became less accessible to the faithful once they had scattered, and their influence waned accordingly. Those who might once have offered protection were no longer able to do so. Amblard Vassal of La Roque Arifat, a knight in the Albigeois, found himself before an inquisitor for sheltering a band of dispossessed men including some *perfecti*. Rather than betray his contacts, he became a *faidit* himself, but was captured and imprisoned in 1274. Lombardy seemed to offer some refuge and many Albigensians fled to northern Italy. Yet they failed to win converts or re-establish their Church and were crushed by the inquisitors by 1300.[93]

When groups were able to revive more extensive local networks, they proved vulnerable to spies and informers. These were often themselves former Albigensians now cooperating actively with local inquisitors, such as the spy Marquesa. Her family had been long associated with heresy, but her depositions in 1243 served inquisitors well in identifying suspects in the region of Carcassonne.[94]

Resistance to the inquisitors flared up periodically, with protests to the king of France from the citizens of Carcassonne and Albi in 1280, 1285, and 1291. Yet, while the inquisitors responded vigorously and ruthlessly to what they characterised as heretical plots, it is likely that these were essentially politically motivated conflicts, directed against the growing and unrestrained power of the tribunals. By the first quarter of the fourteenth century, there were few heretics left to pursue in Languedoc. Documents preserve the names of less than twenty *perfecti* and reveal no trace of coherent church organisation. One last major revival occurred in 1299–1310, in the county of Foix, inspired by the preaching of the Autier brothers, Pierre and Guillaume, who had returned from exile in Lombardy.[95]

They had some local and temporary success, drawing in many sympathetic peasants and artisans to their mission. Yet they soon faced three of the most dedicated and formidable inquisitors: Geoffrey d'Ablis, Bernard Gui, and Jacques Fournier. Guillaume died at the stake in 1309; his brother Pierre, defiant to the last, shared his fate a year later. By the middle of the century, the faith of the Albigensians comprised 'little more than memories'.[96]

Accepting, as the balance of probabilities suggests, that there was an organised and extensive dualist Church present in Languedoc by 1167, then its reduction to mere memories by 1350 confirms Raphaël Lemkin's suggestion that a 'religious genocide' had taken place. The Albigensians had been destroyed, both physically, through massacre, execution, or exile, and spiritually, via an inquisition that triumphantly reasserted Catholic orthodoxy in the region. Furthermore, the crusade had resulted in the imposition of the oppressor's 'national pattern' onto Languedoc. The south's political autonomy and distinct culture was fast eroded as their homeland was firmly subsumed into the kingdom of France.

Yet there had been no rapid or frenzied descent into violence and bloodshed. The papacy had initially sought to drive the 'little foxes' of heresy from the 'vineyards of the Lord' with the cooperation of the local nobility, through preaching to the people, and by debating with erring heresiarchs. The peculiar characteristics of Languedoc, its discordant politics, its fractious nobility, its often venal and ineffective clergy, all frustrated such approaches. When the crusade against the south came, it quickly exhibited the characteristics of 'Holy War'. *Ribalds* and nobles alike showed themselves to be 'men of blood', as they sought personal salvation through acts of violence against others. Their pitiless pilgrimage united the people of Languedoc into a prolonged and determined insurgency. The crusade took on many of the characteristics of a colonial campaign of conquest. The ensuing conflict was largely fought outside the normal established bounds of moral restraint or any chivalric code. This was, thus, a persecutory war both in terms of its origins and conduct.

Placing it within a broader history of persecution, its significance is manifest. Long-established persecutory ideologies, such as the Augustinian principle that violence could be a righteous and effective means of returning heretics to orthodoxy, were reaffirmed. Indeed, the establishment of the crusading movement gave renewed force and vigour to the notion of penitential violence, blurring the distinction between warriors and pilgrims. The most important legacy, however, was the procedure of inquisition. Ecclesiastical tribunals charged with the detection and prosecution of alleged heresy would be deployed again, against communities of alleged Waldensians, 'spiritual' Franciscans, Beguines, and later Lollards in England and Hussites in Bohemia. The apparatus of these tribunals evolved over time, reaching an apogee in organisational sophistication and permanence in early modern institutions, the Roman, Venetian, and Spanish Inquisitions, the latter of which survived until 1834.[97]

Yet it was the essence of how inquisitorial procedures ensured confessions that made this such an important innovation in the history of persecution: the reliance on informers, the examination of suspects in secrecy, the ignorance of the accused of the precise charges or evidence against them, the frequent absence of qualified legal defence, the use of torture, physical or psychological, the incentives to confess and to denounce others. The potency of such procedures as engines of persecution would be illustrated again during the European witch-hunts that began to increase in incidence in the latter half of the fifteenth century. They would reach their apogee in the totalitarian torture states of the twentieth century. As one official slogan in communist China informed prisoners: 'the denunciation of others is a very good method of repentance'.[98]

Notes

1 Dominik J. Schaller and Jürgen Zimmerer, 'Introduction', in Dominik Schaller and Jürgen Zimmerer (eds), *The Origins of Genocide: Raphael Lemkin as a Historian of Mass Violence* (London: Routledge, 2009), p.5.

2 Raphaël Lemkin, *Lemkin on Genocide*, edited by Stephen Leonard Jacobs (Lanham, MD: Lexington Books, 2012), p.71.

3 Mark Gregory Pegg, *A Most Holy War: The Albigensian Crusade and the Battle for Christendom* (Oxford: Oxford University Press, 2008), p.188.

4 Robert Moore, *The Formation of a Persecuting Society* (Oxford: Blackwell, 2007), pp.144–145.

5 Daniel Power, 'Who Went on the Albigensian Crusade?', *The English Historical Review*, 128 (2013), p.1071; Claire Taylor, 'Looking for the "Good Men" in the Languedoc: An Alternative to "Cathars"?', in Antonio Sennis (ed.), *Cathars in Question* (Woodbridge: York Medieval Press, 2016), pp.242–256.

6 Jeffrey Richards, *Sex, Dissidence and Damnation: Minority Groups in the Middle Ages* (Abingdon: Routledge, 1991), p.42; D.P. Waley, 'Papal Armies in the Thirteenth Century', *The English Historical Review*, 72 (1957), pp.1–30.

7 Marcus Bull, 'The Roots of Lay Enthusiasm for the First Crusade', *History*, 78 (1993), pp.353–372.

8 Christopher Tyerman, *The Crusades: A Very Short Introduction* (Oxford: Oxford University Press, 2005), pp.12–13.

9 Andrew Roach, *The Devil's Word: Heresy and Society 1100–1300* (Harlow: Pearson, 2005), pp.34–59; Richards, *Sex, Dissidence and Damnation*, pp.42–45.

10 Christine Caldwell Ames, *Medieval Heresies: Christianity, Judaism and Islam* (Cambridge: Cambridge University Press), 2015, pp.154–158.

11 Bernard Hamilton, 'Wisdom from the East: The Reception by the Cathars of Eastern Dualist Texts', in Peter Biller and Anne Hudson (eds), *Heresy and Literacy,*

1000–1530 (Cambridge: Cambridge University Press, 1994), pp.38–60; Malcolm Lambert, *The Cathars* (Oxford: Blackwell, 1998), pp.19–60.

12 Bonacursus, 'An Exposure of the Heresy of the Cathars, made before the People of Milan', in Walter Wakefield and Austin Evans (eds), *Heresies of the High Middle Ages* (New York: Columbia University Press, 1969), pp.171–173; 'Heretical Council of St-Félix', in John H. Arnold and Peter Biller (eds), *Heresy and Inquisition in France, 1200–1300* (Manchester, Manchester University Press, 2016), pp.16–19.

13 Quoted in Roach, *The Devil's Word: Heresy and Society 1100–1300*, pp.68–72.

14 'A Debate between Catholics and Heretics', in Wakefield and Evans (eds), *Heresies of the High Middle Ages*, pp.190–194.

15 Hilbert Chiu, 'Alan of Lille's Academic Concept of the Manichee', *Journal of Religious History*, 35 (2011), pp.492–506.

16 Julien Théry-Astruc, 'The Heretical Dissidence of the "Good Men" in Albigeois (1276–1329): Localism and Resistance to Roman Clericalism', in Sennis (ed.), *Cathars in Question*, p.81.

17 L.J. Sackville, *Heresy and Heretics in the Thirteenth Century* (Woodbridge: York Medieval Press, 2011), pp.22–25, 154.

18 'A "Manichean" Treatise', in Wakefield and Evans (eds), *Heresies of the High Middle Ages*, pp.496–510. See also Clare Taylor, 'Evidence for Dualism in Inquisitorial Registers of the 1240s: A Contribution to a Debate', *History*, 98 (2013), pp.319–345.

19 Quoted in Bernard Hamilton, 'Cathar Links with the Balkans and Byzantium', in Sennis (ed.), *Cathars in Question*, p.141.

20 Moore, *War on Heresy: Faith and Power in Medieval Europe* (London: Profile Books, 2012), p.192; Pegg, *A Most Holy War*, pp.50–52.

21 Peter Biller, 'Goodbye to Catharism?', in Sennis (ed.), *Cathars in Question*, pp.291–295.

22 Darren Oldridge, *Strange Histories* (London: Routledge, 2018), pp.165–167.

23 Robert Bartlett, *The Making of Europe: Conquest, Colonization and Cultural Change 950–1350* (London: Allen Lane, 1993), p.28.

24 Linda M. Paterson, *The World of the Troubadours: Medieval Occitan Society, c.1100–1300* (Cambridge, Cambridge University Press, 1993), pp.62–89.

25 Jennifer Kolpacoff Deane, *A History of Medieval Heresy and Inquisition* (New York: Rowman & Littlefield, 2011), pp.36–37; Paterson, *World of the Troubadours*, pp.70–71.

26 Michael Costen, *The Cathars and the Albigensian Crusade* (Manchester: Manchester University Press, 1997), pp.43–47; Jonathan Sumption, *The Albigensian Crusade* (London: Faber and Faber, 1978), pp.15–31.

27 Elizabeth M. Hallam and Judith Everard, *Capetian France, 987–1328* (Harlow: Pearson, 2001), pp.68–74.

28 Deane, *Medieval Heresy and Inquisition*, pp.51–52.

29 Sumption, *Albigensian Crusade*, pp.65–68.

30 Jeffrey M. Wayno, 'Rethinking the Fourth Lateran Council of 1215,' *Speculum*, 93 (2018), pp.611–637.

31 Sumption, *Albigensian Crusade*, pp.68–70.

32 Innocent III, '*Ne nos ejus* (10 March 1208)', in Catherine Léglu, Rebecca Rist, and Claire Taylor (eds), *The Cathars and the Albigensian Crusade* (London: Routledge, 2014), p.39.

33 Frederick J. Russell, *The Just War in the Middle Ages* (Cambridge: Cambridge University Press, 1975), p.75.

34 Russell, *Just War in the Middle Age*, p.37.

35 Malcolm Barber, *The Cathars* (London: Pearson, 2000), pp.132–133.

36 Innocent III, 'Inveterata pravitatis heretice (17 November 1207)' in Léglu et al. (eds), *The Albigensian Crusade*, p.36.

37 Peter of les Vaux-de-Cernay [PVC], *The History of the Albigensian Crusade*, translated by W.A. and M.D. Sibly (Woodbridge: Boydell, 1998), p.37.

38 Quoted in Power, 'Who Went on the Albigensian Crusade?', p.1056.

39 Simon de Montfort, 5th Earl of Leicester (*c.*1175–1218), was the father of Simon de Montfort, 6th Earl of Leicester (*c.*1208–1265), remembered in English history for his persecution of Leicester's Jews, and for leading the baronial opposition to Henry III.

40 Lawrence W. Marvin, *The Occitan War: A Military and Political History of the Albigensian Crusade, 1209–1218* (Cambridge: Cambridge University Press, 2008), pp.30–35; Sean McGlynn, *Kill Them All: Cathars and Carnage in the Albigensian Crusade* (Stroud: The History Press, 2015), pp.43–46.

41 PVC, *The Albigensian Crusade*, p.44.

42 PVC, *The Albigensian Crusade*, p.43; Joseph Strayer, *The Albigensian Crusade* (Ann Arbor: University of Michigan Press, 1992), p.56.

43 William of Tudela [WoT], *The Song of the Cathar Wars*, translated by Janet Shirley (Farnham: Ashgate, 1996), *Laisse* [stanza] 19–20, pp.20–21.

44 Richard L. C. Jones, 'Fortification and Sieges in Western Europe', in Maurice Keen (ed.), *Medieval Warfare: A History* (Oxford: Oxford University Press, 1999), pp.182–183.

45 McGlynn, *Kill Them All*, pp.61–72. Laurence W. Marvin, 'War in the South: A First Look at Siege Warfare in the Albigensian Crusade, 1209–1218', *War in History*, Vol. 8 (2001), pp.381–382.

46 WoT, *Song of the Cathar Wars*, *Laisse* 21–22, pp.20–21.

47 PVC, *The Albigensian Crusade*, pp.48–49, 51.

48 William of Puylaurens, *The Chronicle of William of Puylaurens* [CWP], translated by W.A. and M.D. Sibly (Woodbridge: Boydell, 2003), pp.33–34; PVC, *The Albigensian Crusade*, p.54.

49 CWP, Chapter XIV, pp.34–35; Strayer, *Albigensian Crusade*, p.64.

50 WoT and Anonymous Successor [AS], *Song of the Cathar Wars*, *Laisse* 35, p.27; *Laisse* 205, p.172.

51 Robert Thompson, *No Exit from Vietnam* (London: Chatto and Windus, 1969), p.136.

52 David Galula, *Counterinsurgency Warfare: Theory and Practice* (Westport, CT: Praeger, 2006), pp.25–26.

53 WoT, *Song of the Cathar Wars*, *Laisse* 41, pp.29–30.

54 PVC, *The Albigensian Crusade*, pp.73–74.

55 Norman Housley, 'European Warfare, c.1200–1320', in Keen (ed.), *Medieval Warfare*, p.134.

56 AS, *Song*, *Laisse* 205, p.172.

57 PVC, *The Albigensian Crusade*, p.85.

58 AS, *Song*, *Laisse* 153, p.84; Sumption, *Albigensian Crusade*, p.172. Barber, *The Cathars*, pp.61–62.

59 WoT, *Song, Laisse* 126, p.63; Laurence Martin, 'Thirty Nine Days and a Wake-up: The Impact of the Indulgence and the Forty Days' Service on the Albigensian Crusade 1208–1218', *The Historian*, 65 (2002), pp.75–94.

60 WoT, *Song, Laisse* 69, p.42.

61 CWP, Chapter XVII, pp.40–41.

62 WoT, *Song, Laisse* 83, p.47.

63 WoT, *Song, Laisse* 91–106, pp.51–54.

64 Sumption, *Albigensian Crusade*, pp.154–155.

65 Power, 'Who Went on the Albigensian Crusade?', p.1079.

66 Marvin, *The Occitan War*, pp.180–195; McGlynn, *Kill Them All*, pp.165–176.

67 Sumption, *Albigensian Crusade*, pp.178–182.

68 AS, *Song, Laisse* 203, p.122.

69 CWP, Chapter XXXII, p.69.

70 CWP, Chapter XXXIV, pp.73–74.

71 Sumption, *Albigensian Crusade*, p.220.

72 Jennifer Kolpacoff Deane, *A History of Medieval Heresy and Inquisition* (New York: Rowman & Littlefield, 2011), pp.90–92.

73 Henry Ansgar Kelly, 'Inquisition and the Prosecution of Heresy: Misconceptions and Abuses', *Church History*, 58 (1989), pp.439–451.

74 Mirjan Damaška, 'The Quest for Due Process in the Age of Inquisition', *American Journal of Comparative Law*, 60 (2012), p.924.

75 Cristine Caldwell Ames, *Righteous Persecution: Inquisition, Dominicans, and Christianity in the Middle Ages* (Philadelphia: University of Pennsylvania Press, 2009), p.165; Richards, *Sex, Dissidence and Damnation*, p.57.

76 Sumption, *Albigensian Crusade*, p.229.

77 CWP, Chapter XL, p.89.

78 Deane, *Medieval Heresy and Inquisition*, p.97.

79 Roberts, *Sex, Dissidence and Damnation*, p.57.

80 Roach, *The Devil's World*, pp.97–98.

81 Ames, *Righteous Persecution*, p.6.

82 Extract from the *Chronicle of William Pelhisson*, in Léglu et al. (eds), *The Cathars and the Albigensian Crusade*, p.206.

83 Barber, *The Cathars*, pp.177–178.

84 Quoted in Karen Sullivan, 'Disputations Literary and Inquisitorial: The Conversion of the Heretic Sicart of Figueiras,' *Medium Ævum*, 78 (2009), pp.71–72.

85 Costen, *The Cathars and the Albigensian Crusade*, pp.156–157.

86 Costen, *The Cathars and the Albigensian Crusade*, p.157.

87 CWP, Chapter XLIV, pp.107–108.

88 Barber, *The Cathars*, p.193.

89 Ames, *Righteous Persecution*, pp.70–72

90 'Deposition of Helis of Mazerolles, 1243', in *Heresy and Inquisition in France, 1200–1300*, edited and translated by John H. Arnold and Peter Biller (Manchester: Manchester University Press), 2016, pp.337–350; Walter Wakefield, *Heresy, Crusade and Inquisition in Southern France, 1100–1250* (Berkeley: University of California Press, 1974), pp.173–180.

91 Malcolm Lambert, *The Cathars* (Oxford: Blackwell, 1998), p.215; Chris Wickham, '*Fama* and the Law in Twelfth-Century Tuscany', in Thelma Fenster and Daniel Lord Smail (eds), *Fama: The Politics of Talk and Reputation in Medieval Europe* (Ithaca, NY.: Cornell University Press, 2003), pp.15–26.

92 Michael Costens, *The Cathars and the Albigensian Crusade* (Manchester: Manchester University Press, 1997), p.174; Deane, *A History of Medieval Heresy and Inquisition*, pp.113–115.
93 Lambert, *Cathars*, pp.221–222.
94 'Deposition of Marquesa the Spy, 1243', in Arnold and Biller (eds and trans), *Heresy and Inquisition in France, 1200–1300*, pp.332–336.
95 Wakefield, *Heresy, Crusade and Inquisition*, p.89.
96 Wakefield, *Heresy, Crusade and Inquisition*, p.189; Lambert, *Cathars*, pp.230–271.
97 See Richard Kieckhefer, 'The Office of Inquisition and Medieval Heresy: The Transition from Personal to Institutional Jurisdiction', *Journal of Ecclesiastical History*, 46 (1995), pp.36–61; Edward Peters, *Inquisition* (Berkeley: University of California Press, 1989).
98 Quoted in Jean-Louis Margolin, 'China: A Long March into Night', in Stéphanie Courtois et al., *The Black Book of Communism: Crimes, Terror, Repression* (Cambridge, MA: Harvard University Press, 1999), p.505.

6 'Some Fantastic Delusion'

The Witch-hunts in Early Modern Europe, *c*.1420–1782

Around the year 900 CE, Regino, abbot of Prüm, authored a decree: the Canon *Episcopi*. This urged bishops to 'labour with all their strength to uproot thoroughly from their parishes the pernicious art of sorcery and *malefice* [harmful spells]'. In particular, he denounced 'wicked women perverted by the devil, seduced by illusions and phantasm of demons, [who] believe and profess themselves, in the hours of night, to ride upon certain beasts with Diana, the goddess of pagans ... to traverse great spaces of earth'. Such sorcery, he asserted, was not real, but 'dreams and nocturnal visions'. Who, he inquired, 'is so stupid and foolish as to think that all these things which are only done in spirit happen in the body?' Those who persisted in this belief should be 'foully disgraced' and driven from their parishes.[1]

Yet, in 1595, the French judge Nicolas Remy would assert that, although occasional tales of night flights might be 'some fantastic delusion', nevertheless 'witches do in fact fly to and bodily present themselves at their notorious evil assemblies of demons ... '.[2] Nor did Remy feel that practitioners of *malefice* should merely be exiled. He sent at least eight hundred alleged witches to the stake. Overall, between 1428 and 1782, perhaps 60,000 individuals were executed for witchcraft.[3] Scepticism concerning sorcery had given way to a different 'fantastical delusion': witchcraft was a fearful reality to be punished with death. Understanding why this happened is one of the most puzzling problems in the history of persecution.

For the scholars of the Enlightenment, there was an obvious explanation. The French philosopher Voltaire (1694–1778) dismissed the witch-hunts as the product of popular superstition and the egregious bigotry of the clergy. They had ended when an intolerant age gave way to an age of reason. Nineteenth-century historians, such as Henry Charles Lea, reasserted this 'liberal-rationalist' tradition: 'dogmatic theology' had caused the witch-hunts; the 'newer scientific modes of thought' of the Enlightenment had ended them.[4]

This interpretation would not suffice. It did not explain why Regino's scepticism had given way to Remy's delusion. If belief in *maleficium* (witchcraft) was simply the product of pre-Enlightenment superstition, then why

DOI: 10.4324/9781003494331-7

had trials for the crime been rare before the fifteenth century? Nor did it acknowledge that the decline in witch-hunting was well underway decades before the Enlightenment began. Having abandoned the 'liberal-rationalist' tradition, modern historians of the witch-hunts, such as Brian Levack, have adopted 'a multi-causal approach' that recognises a complex interplay of factors to understand why the witch-hunts occurred.[5]

Some were rooted in both popular and elite ideologies: an established folk culture where belief in the potency and ubiquity of magic was deeply ingrained and a novel ideology among educated elites that stressed the reality of demonic and heretical witchcraft. Broader religious change was a factor too, in particular the impact of the Reformation and the imperative to build godly regimes that policed individual piety and morality. Institutionally, the adoption of inquisitorial procedures into secular legal systems proved dangerously conducive to producing confessions, while the weakness of central governments allowed local witch panics to escalate into witch-hunts. Once the popular stereotype of the witch had been established, then contingent factors such as crop failures, outbreaks of disease, or neighbourhood feuds, could also spur witchcraft allegations.

Widespread belief in the reality of witchcraft outlasted the actual witch-hunts by many years. The decline in witch-hunting was rooted more strongly in practical legal and political considerations than in the onset of 'enlightened' thought. By the 1630s, there was a growing doubt about the legal procedures that had secured so many convictions in witchcraft cases. This 'crisis of confidence' caused magistrates and judges to be increasingly reluctant to try alleged witches. At much the same time, the growing authority and fiscal capacity of the early modern state brought unruly local courts in regions where witch-hunting persisted more firmly under centralised control, ensuring greater due process and the safeguarding of the rights of the accused. Legal doubts and politics thus ended the witch-hunts, years before the 'newer scientific modes of thought' challenged widespread belief in witchcraft.

Understanding the witch-hunts within this broad framework, historians are still faced with an intriguing mosaic. The overall picture of a European-wide phenomenon of witch-hunting is clearly discernible, but that whole is comprised of a myriad of smaller incidents, each with its own somewhat irregular form and characteristics. The witch-hunts were essentially sporadic episodes, varying in frequency and intensity from region to region. Attempting to find overarching paradigms to explain the witch-hunts has thus proved challenging, as an examination of the modern historiography demonstrates. In the first instance, it was necessary to clear away some misconceptions, and not merely those of the 'liberal rationalist' tradition.

In the early twentieth century, folklorists, pre-eminently Margaret Murray, had drawn upon a wellspring of romanticism and argued that while witches were neither in league with the Devil nor set on causing harm to others, they were real. They were, according to Murray, a hereditary sect, a surviving pagan fertility cult, whose rites were maligned by an oppressive Church as *maleficium*.[6] Although attracting much popular attention, Murray's work was poor history. Norman Cohn noted that she utilised a very limited range of primary sources, from which she selectively quoted, passing over the fantastical and unbelievable elements of alleged witches' confessions. No substantive case for the existence of a long-standing, organised, and coherent fertility cult was offered beyond assertions and dubious inferences.[7]

Cohn did not, however, reject the significance of pagan, pre-Christian traditions in shaping the stereotype of the witch that emerged in the early modern period. The night flights, for instance, appeared rooted in two ancient traditions. The first was that of the *strix*, the screeching, owl-like creature who flew out in the hours of darkness to feed on the blood of unguarded babies. The second was the belief that some among the common folk joined a powerful female supernatural figure in nocturnal flights. This figure was variously identified by authorities as the goddess Diana, or as Holda (who veered between nurturing sky-mother and vengeful hag), or as Hecate, the goddess of magic. Her entourage, 'the wild hunt' or 'furious hoard', it was asserted, was composed of the souls of the prematurely dead. Evidence suggests that this tradition, with local variations, was deeply rooted in folkways across Europe. Cohn notes the survival in Sicilian villages into the twentieth century of belief in the *donas de fuera* ('ladies from outside'). Sicilian peasants would travel out of their bodies by night to meet with tall, beautiful women, with long shimmering hair, to dance, feast, and bless well-kept households.[8] Julian Goodare has identified a similar fairy cult, the 'seely wights', in sixteenth-century Scotland.[9]

Drawing upon testimony collected by Italian inquisitors in the late sixteenth and early seventeenth centuries, Carlo Ginzburg identified a group of peasant men and women of the Friuli region fated, by being born with the caul (amniotic membrane) still shrouding their bodies, to join the *benandanti* ('good walkers'). These left their bodies at night, perhaps in dreams or a trance-like state, or one induced by hallucinogens. Some then travelled with 'the furious horde'. Most, however, rode great distances to the 'field of Josaphat', on hares, billy-goats, or cocks. There, they deployed in martial companies and engaged in combat with witches to protect their villages and ensure a plentiful harvest.

The story of the *benandanti* is particularly revealing in terms of charting how such ancient folk traditions mutated into the stereotype of the early modern witch. By the time the inquisitors started questioning the Friulian peasants about their beliefs in the 1580s, the malevolent *strix* was already being associated with those who rode out on such nightly cavalcades. Thus, for the inquisitors, the *benandanti* were not magical warriors protecting their communities, but were themselves witches, travelling to demonic sabbaths. By the 1630s, the original tradition had disintegrated, even in the minds of *benandanti*. The original clear distinction between themselves and the witches was largely eroded. Many, in rambling and self-contradictory confessions, affirmed that they had indeed abjured their Christian faith, murdered children by sorcery, and entered pacts with the Devil at orgiastic sabbaths. The *benandanti* had been, literally, demonised.[10]

Other long-standing folk beliefs around magic were also significant in the emergence of the early modern stereotype of the witch. Popular magical traditions provided a mystical armour against the vagaries of fate: ill-fortune in love and business, diseases in people and livestock, crop failure, storms, and unseasonable weather. Amulets, charms, incantations, and spells were characteristic elements of a rich, prosaic, and near-ubiquitous agrarian cosmology. Educated churchmen, like Regino of Prüm, may have railed against the illusory nature and paganism of such practices, but folk magic was neither antagonistic towards nor incompatible with Christianity. It may have had powerful pagan precedents, but it had evolved comfortably with the rising hegemonic monotheism.

Theologians held that the religious merely beseeched God for his aid in a spirit of humble supplication, while sorcerers sinfully sought to command occult forces to do their will. Yet, for lay folk, and even some members of the clergy, a rigid demarcation between liturgy, ritual, and holy relics on the one hand, and charms, incantations, and magical amulets on the other, may not always have been so obvious. In one English necromancer's manual, written *circa* 1532–1539, the author included a spell to identify a thief. This involved immersing a clay ball containing the names of suspects in a vessel of holy water and commanding 'I conjure you holy water, by the Father, the Son and the Holy Spirit, and by St Mary the mother of Our Lord Jesus Christ ... to send up the name who is responsible'.[11]

Communities had their own specialist magical practitioners, cunning men, and wise women, who might offer their services for a fee. These were adept at astrology, fortune telling, recovering lost possessions, identifying thieves, settling debts, manufacturing love charms, and protecting against harmful spells and ill-health. They combined their practical knowledge of herb-lore, midwifery, and meteorology, with their wisdom in conjuration, potions, and spell-casting. Such cunning folk had lived and practised their arts among the people of Europe's villages and towns for centuries, without fear of persecution by the authorities.[12]

Those seeking to understand the onset of witch-hunting, therefore, have looked again at the question of why, from the early 1400s onwards, clerical and secular authorities began to take allegations of *maleficium* so seriously and thus looked askance at all magic users. The answer appears to be found most dramatically in evolving religious ideologies, specifically the rise of demonology among an educated elite. This development had its roots in the preceding centuries.

Theologians had begun to develop a renewed and fearful concern over the activities of the Devil and his demons in the late 1200s. A significant source of these clerical anxieties was the threat to orthodoxy posed by popular heresy, such as the dualism that had sparked the Albigensian Crusade (1209–1229). Magical practices began to take their place in broader discussions of such dissent. In 1320, for example, Pope John XXII consulted ten leading theologians and experts in canon law on whether magic should be considered innately heretical. Such discussions led theologians, inquisitors, and canon lawyers back to the writings of the church fathers of late antiquity. In St Augustine's influential treatise *De doctrina christiana* (*c.*400 CE), he had firmly linked the practice of magic (including pacts, spells, charms, astrology, divination, and medical magic) with paganism. All such 'trifling or noxious superstition [was] constituted on the basis of a perfidious association of men and demons ... '. Thus, no form of magic was legitimate within Christianity.[13]

At this point in time, for medieval churchmen, the popular magic practised by the ignorant common folk was not a pressing concern. Authors who wrote of female enchantresses in medieval texts before the fifteenth century seemed to draw upon classical Mediterranean models, such as Circe, whom they encountered in Homer's *Odyssey*. The 'woman addicted to sorcery' who features in William of Malmesbury's chronicle (*c.*1140), was described as gluttonous, lascivious, and skilled at ancient augury. She was also relatively young and apparently literate, not the rustic hag of later stereotype. Despite practising 'demonical arts', she did not abjure her Christian faith, summoning a monk and a nun for her comfort when death approached.[14]

Describing this individual as a 'witch', as many translators of the Latin chronicle have done, is problematic, as it calls the early modern stereotype too readily to mind. Had such an individual actually lived, her neighbours may have referred to her as a *wicch* or *wichche*. Yet in neither learned texts nor popular medieval folkways had the later stereotype of the quarrelsome, neighbourhood witch, operating as a member of a wider coven in league with Satan, emerged. Indeed, witches were often portrayed as solitary creatures with non-human characteristics, such as iron teeth or red eyes, found in remote locations, deep in forests or cave dwellings, away from others.[15]

The magical practitioners feared the most by medieval authorities were educated sorcerers or necromancers (originally so called because of their invocation of spirits). These were mostly to be found in university towns and at courts. Cecco d'Ascoli was condemned by inquisitors in Florence in 1327 and sent to the stake. He was a *magister*, a university teacher from Bologna, whose special subjects were mathematics and astrology. It was his dogged and unrepentant commitment to the latter that led to his execution as a heretic. While night flights and shape shifting were still largely dismissed as illusions, it was accepted that, through the agency of demons, actual harmful effects might be achieved by magicians. So, when allegations were levelled against supposed sorcerers, such as Bertrand d'Audiran, canon of Agen, in 1326, they were not now held merely to have been deluded by demons. Rather, in invoking them, d'Audiran had achieved effective results: 'terrifying thunder-claps, shaking, lightening, storms, floods, all blows by demons, attacks and the deaths of men and other countless damage'.[16]

In an infamous case in Kilkenny, Ireland, in 1324, Dame Alice Kyteler was accused both of murdering her three husbands and of sorcery. She had, her tormentors alleged, performed magical rites with a demon, Artis Filius, and had carnal relations with an incubus, Robin Artison. Her prosecutor was Richard Ledrede, bishop of Ossory. He, revealingly, had been present at the papal court of Avignon in 1307–1314, when King Philip IV of France had persecuted the Knights Templar. This was a politically inspired sorcery trial; the king had justified his suppression of the powerful and wealthy order by allegations of idolatry and abhorrent sexual practices, and that they had allied themselves with Satan. The specific charge against them was 'heresy'.[17]

Although it was fear of heresy that initially seems to have drawn the attention of theologians and inquisitors to the pursuit of sorcerers, the rise of learned demonology was a significant phenomenon in its own right. There was an influx of ancient magical texts into western Christendom in the thirteenth and fourteenth centuries via increased contact with the Arab world. Particularly influential were the 'Hermetic' texts, attributed to Hermes Trismegistus, reputedly 'the first alchemist after the flood'.[18] In actuality, these were composed between 100 CE and 300 CE, somewhere in North Africa. Philosophical works with much to say on the nature of God and the work of providence, they also concerned themselves with alchemy, astrology, talismans, and magic. For some scholars and theologians, ignorant of their true origins, these works were a divinely inspired 'pre-Christian revelation' and thus a valid and legitimate source of knowledge.[19]

This was a problematic position to maintain, given St Augustine's admonishment that all forms of magic were illicit within Christianity. More specifically, many Hermetic texts suggested means by which demons and spirits could be tempted, manipulated, or compelled, through invocation, possession, or the forging of a pact, to do the bidding of a necromancer. The sophistication and authority of this ancient literature thus allowed for a viable belief in the efficacy of magic. For early medieval clergymen like Regino of Prüm, the credulity of superstitious lay persons had been a source of frustration. Only God was truly capable of supernatural acts, 'miracles', outside of the ordinary operation of the natural world. The demonology of the later medieval period however recognised the potential of 'preternatural' events. These occurred within nature but were abnormal *mira* (artificial marvels) wrought by occult (hidden) forces wielded by an adept practitioner of magical science. In some instances, these marvels were brought about by an understanding of obscure but natural qualities of an object: *magia naturalis* (natural magic). In other cases, they were achieved through the invocation of spirits or demons: *magia daemonica* (demonic magic).[20]

In the universities and monasteries where such ideas were studied, some would accept the legitimacy of, at least, the *magia naturalis* and argue for its rightful place in the acquisition of wisdom. Others, ultimately a majority within the Church, would reject all magic as heretical diabolism: the *crimen magiae* (the crime of magic). Consider, for example, the respective attitudes of Michael Scot (1175–c.1232) and Thomas Aquinas (c.1225–1275). Scot, a mathematician, astrologer, and courtier to Emperor Frederick II, denounced demonic magic as unacceptable. However, he then argued that the wise mage, who 'interprets characters and phylacteries, incantations, dreams and makes ligatures of herbs', could claim his place within Christianity.[21]

For Aquinas, the most influential of the scholastic philosophers, the practice of any of the magical arts invariably depended upon a pact with a demon. Thus, it constituted apostasy from the true faith. Furthermore, this magic wrought via demonic agency was genuinely harmful: 'although the works of demons which appear marvellous to us are not real miracles, they are sometimes nevertheless something real. Thus, the magicians of Pharaoh by the demons' power produced real serpents and frogs'.[22]

Within a century, the twin fears of heresy and sorcery had come to dominate the Church's thinking. Astrology retained a tenuous respectability in some classrooms, but its practitioners always risked accusations of the *crimen magiae*. Scot himself was widely denounced as a sorcerer. He even figured as a character in Dante's *Divine Comedy*'s *Inferno* (1320), wandering eternity with his head twisted round, gazing backwards, in the company of other infamous diviners of antiquity and the Middle Ages.[23] Fears of the activities of sorcerers, chiefly found among the clergy and at courts, drove legal cases against those accused of *maleficum*, such as Cecco d'Ascoli, Bertrand d'Audiran, and Alice Kyteler. Sorcery at this point was still largely an elite crime. Yet there would soon be a growing concern about the traditional magical practices of the common folk too.

This process is well illustrated in the case of Italy in the late fourteenth century. In Florence in 1375, Vieri di Michele Rondinelli, scion of a wealthy merchant family, prosecuted his brother's mistress Caterina for bewitching his sibling and siphoning off the family fortune. Sexual magic figured prominently in other cases too, such as the 1394 case in Poppi, where Nicolosa Vanzi was prosecuted for using sorcery to win the love of her neighbour, Andrea di Spigliato. Although the accused here were ordinary women, these were conventional sorcery trials.[24] They did not fit the later stereotype of the quarrelsome older woman. There was no suggestion of a pact with Satan, or night flights to sabbaths. There was no chain reaction of further denunciations, or active pursuit of other malefactors.

However, within a few years, these characteristics were beginning to appear. In the 1420s, the Franciscan preacher Bernadino de Siena had encouraged the active denunciations of *stregas* (witches). He recorded how, in Rome, probably in 1426, he had initially preached on the dangers of witchcraft to no effect. His audience thought he was 'dreaming it up'. He then applied, in historian Franco Mormando's words, some 'spiritual coercion'. He told his audience that if they withheld information on those practising witchcraft, they would share the burden of sin. One hundred accusers then came forward. Bernadino's notion of who witches were and what they did now bore much in common with the early modern stereotype. He thought older women the most likely to be guilty. He thought they operated collectively, in a conspiracy, and were in league with the Devil. He drew on both elite fears of demonic magic and folkloric tales of *stregas* feasting on children's blood.[25]

In some ways, Bernadino's thoughts on the nature of witchcraft were not fully formed. For example, he doubted the reality of the night flight. Developments further north, contemporaneous with Bernardino's Italian campaigns, set a more long-lasting precedent. Julian Goodare has referred to the western Alps region (what is today western Switzerland, Savoy in France, and the Italian Piedmont) as the cradle of early modern witch beliefs.[26] Here, in particular, the connection between medieval fears of heretics and early modern panics about witches was very apparent. In the early fifteenth century, emerging heresies – the Lollards in England, and the Hussites in Bohemia – were the cause of renewed concern. In the western Alps, the supposed threat came from a more familiar sect, the Waldensians. This group had been founded by Valdes of Lyon in 1170. By the early 1400s, they were known for their anticlericalism and their rejection of many Catholic rites and doctrines, such as purgatory and the efficacy of prayers for the dead.

Alongside the Waldensians, there were also, so it was alleged, 'new sects' composed of witches. These were founded by 'some Christians and perfidious Jews', according to Pope Alexander, in a letter to the inquisitor Pontus Feugeyron, in Avignon in 1409. This conflation of Jews with the 'new sects' would be widespread and long-standing. A stained-class window commissioned in Nuremburg in 1598 depicted the ritual murder of a Christian child by a Jew, assisted by a witch. The 'new sects' were 'sorcerers, diviners, invokers of demons, enchanters, conjurers, superstitious people, augurs [and] practitioners of nefarious and forbidden arts'.[27] The older heretical sects and the alleged new ones were closely associated in the minds of the authorities. By 1430, the word *Vaudoises*, derived either from 'Waldensian' or the Swiss canton of Vaud, was being applied to heretics who caused sickness and death, impotence in men, infertility in women, and crop failures, by magical means. *Vaudoises* came to be synonymous with *sorcières*, the French word for witches.[28]

Alleged *Vaudoises* then became the object of a series of persecutions centred on the Swiss canton of Valais. According to the chronicler Hans Fründ, some two hundred were burned in 1428. Revealingly, in terms of the emergence of the witch stereotype, Fründ would recount how they had shape-shifted into wolves and flown by night on chairs. They had met together to conspire, in the company of an 'evil spirit' and had eaten the flesh of children. They posed an existential threat to all, for they had entered into a conspiratorial pact with Satan, and he had promised them their own laws and that they would 'overcome Christianity'.[29]

Thereafter, persecution of alleged witches became a persistent characteristic of the region. Two women were burned in Fribourg (modern Switzerland) in 1437, followed a year later by a woman and a man. In 1440, four women and a man went to the stake and two other men were broken on the wheel. In 1442, three men and four women were burned. In 1466, in Berne, Hans

Heyman confessed under torture to having being part of a group who had caused two recent avalanches. The next year, 14 women and men, also convicted of witchcraft, were executed in the same city. The investigations that accompanied these trials shaped what would become commonplace methods in witch-hunting. In trial records from 1440 and 1482, mention is made of the shaving of the accused's body to locate incriminating 'witch marks' (moles or lesions).[30]

That the convicted witches were executed is also of significance in understanding the dynamics of the early modern witch-hunts. Until comparatively recently, the injunction in Exodus 22:18, 'thou shall not suffer a witch to live', had not been understood literally by canon lawyers. As Regino of Prüm had urged, those deluded by the illusion of magic were to be driven from their parishes but not executed. This was a valid understanding of the original Hebrew, which might be rendered as 'thou shall not suffer a witch to live within the community'.[31]

The literal reading of Exodus 22:18, that witches were to be executed, was, in common with a more literal reading of scripture generally, a later medieval phenomenon. It was still contested by some in the early modern period. For example, Italian inquisitors were often reluctant to sentence convicted witches, especially repentant, first-time offenders, to death. Bewildered *benandanti* might be pronounced 'lightly' suspect of heresy and sentenced to three years at the oars of a Venetian galley. Members of the Roman Inquisition, established in 1542, clashed with the papacy on this issue more than once. Yet, their position was very much a minority view by then. For most, witchcraft was a *crimen exceptum*, an exceptional Satanic crime against the faithful, for which there could be no pardon. For the French jurist Jean Bodin, 'there is no punishment cruel enough for the wickedness of witchcraft'.[32]

It was not so much these hunts themselves but rather the ideology that they spawned, that gave these early western Alpine cases their long-term legacy. Five roughly contemporaneous authors scripted manuscripts that powerfully shaped belief in the emergence of this terrifying 'new sect' of demonic witches. The Franciscan inquisitor Ponce Feugeyron is generally credited with writing *Errores Gazariorum* (*The Errors of the Heretics*) which made manifest the relationship between the emerging demonic witch cult and earlier fears of heretical sects. It offered its intended readership, inquisitors, and judges, 'a blueprint for interrogations'. Elements of the treatise, such as the luring of victims into the cult by established members, were echoed in subsequent trial records.[33]

Lucerne chronicler Hans Fründ detailed the conspiratorial rites in which the accused had, allegedly, participated. Two other secular writers, Claude Tholosan, magistrate of Briançon, and the poet Martin Le Franc, produced works, *Ut Magorum et Maleficorum Errores* (*Errors of the Magicians and Witches*) and *Le Champion des Dames* (*The Defender of the Ladies*) respectively, that emphasised the supposed susceptibly of women to the wiles of the

Devil. The most influential of the five was Johannes Nider, a Swiss Dominican prior and author of *Formicarius* (*The Ant's Nest*). This was a disturbing satire on human society, that devoted considerable attention to *malefice*, and the ways in which it harmed good Christians: love spells, inspiring hatred, causing impotence, causing disease, and injuring property or livestock.[34] In this literature then, the traditional concerns of folk magic were combined with the elite fears of sorcery. The conflation of the practice of magic with heresy is evident too. Here, therefore, is the nascent ideological basis of the early modern witch-hunts.

Even among those who shaped the stereotype of the early modern witch, there were significant disagreements about the phenomenon. The author of *Errores Gazariorum*, for example, denounced his subjects as 'fiends' who flew by night on brooms, 'stove forks', cats, and goats. Nider, in contrast remained very sceptical on this point. He included a tale in *Formicarius* of a Dominican friar who had sat up all night to watch a woman who claimed to fly in the company of Diana. The woman had rubbed herself with ointment and spoken an incantation. She had then fallen into a writhing, fitful sleep but clearly flew nowhere. Her delusions, the Dominican was able to convince her when she woke, were simply 'the work of demons'. (Today, it has been suggested that the use of hallucinogens, or epilepsy, or sleep paralysis, or psychological conversion disorders, may explain why people believed them-selves bewitched.)[35] Yet, equally, Nider's scepticism had very clear limits. He described some of the earliest versions of the witches' 'sabbath'. Witches may not have flown to these gatherings, but they met, in churches an outraged Nider asserted, to 'renounce Christ and to pay homage to the Devil'.[36]

For many theologians, it was the novelty of the emerging threat that allowed them to disregard the scepticism of the past. The Dominican friar Nicholas Jacquier, in his work *Flagellum Hereticorum Fascinariorum* (*The Scourge of Heretical Bewitchers*) (1458), specifically denied that the deluded women described by Regino of Prüm were the same as the 'modern witches'. For Jacquier, the new defining characteristics were the sabbath, the reality of physical and sexual contact with demons, and the Satanic pact undertaken voluntarily and constituting an act of apostasy. The canon *Episcopi* had, to a great degree, acted as a legal restraint on the pursuit of the *malefica*. Belief in an entirely new sect of demonic witches, unprecedented and unknown to earlier authorities, largely swept that restraint away.[37]

There were always sceptical voices urging caution. Ambrogio Vignati, an Italian jurist of the 1460s, argued that, as the devil was incorporeal, it was simply impossible for him to have physical contact with supposed witches. The suggestion that those who confessed freely to being witches were mentally ill was made around 1500 by the French physician Symphorien Champier.[38] Yet belief in the demonic sect of witches was spreading to an educated but more credulous audience. The introduction of the printing press into Europe, in around 1450, made possible the wider and faster dissemination of learned treatise concerning witchcraft, such as Nider's *Formicarius*, which had initially only been available in manuscript form. Further works on the diabolical witch conspiracy appeared to take advantage of the new medium, most infamously that by the Dominican inquisitor Heinrich Kramer, *Malleus Maleficarum* (*Hammer of the Witches*), first published in 1486.

The overall significance of this work is a matter of some debate for historians. To a degree, the story of its genesis and publication demonstrates the slow pace at which fears of the alleged new sect of witches took hold beyond the Alps. A theology professor at Cologne, Kramer had been appointed as an inquisitor in 1470. Yet he had made little progress in pursuit of *maleficium* cases, due to resistance both from local bishops and the secular authorities. In 1484, he had obtained a bull from the pope to allow him to proceed. This was included in the *Malleus*. It gave papal authority to what was a sometimes repetitive and clumsily structured, but comprehensive, text combining an inquisitor's manual with a broader treatise on witches.[39]

Publication did not result in a renewed surge of witch-hunts. Indeed, in Italy, the number of witch-trials declined in the immediate aftermath of the appearance of Kramer's work. Yet the book would be republished again and again, and it would work its insidious views into the cosmologies of inquisitors, judges, and witch-hunters, both Catholic and Protestant, for two centuries. One of the most dangerous ideas expressed by Kramer, and one that contributed to the ideological structure that sustained the witch-hunts, was his suggestion that those who denied the reality of witchcraft should themselves 'be considered to have been detected in heretical perversity' or, at least, 'strongly suspect of heresy'.[40] Jean Bodin, the French philosopher and demonologist, went even further, affirming in 1579 that 'those who deny the existence of witches are almost always witches themselves'.[41] How many sceptical voices were silenced by this kind of admonition can only be speculated.

Even though the early modern stereotype of the witch soon reached a wider audience, the actual incidence of witch-hunts remained relatively low for some time. Indeed, after 1500, it seems to have declined for a period. The generally accepted explanation is that this hiatus in witch-hunting was due to the initial impact of the Reformation. Protestant reformers strove to restore their churches to their imagined state of early purity, stripping away Catholic 'superstitions' they felt had no basis in scripture. Simultaneously, the Catholic Counter-Reformation undertook a series of internal reforms aimed at reviving the faith, strengthening the papacy, and improving discipline within the *Curia* (the papal court). Between 1517, when reformer Martin Luther supposedly nailed his 95 theses to the door of a church in Wittenburg, to the last session of the Catholic Council of Trent in 1562–3, which ended calls for reconciliation with Protestants, the unity of western Christendom was permanently shattered. With the attention of both ecclesiastical and secular authorities contending with this seismic change, the number of witchcraft prosecutions declined markedly. From around the mid-sixteenth century, the rate had then begun to pick up. The long-term impact of the Reformation would be to usher in the most intense century of the European witch-hunts, *circa* 1550–1650.

For Catholics, the emergence of Protestantism represented a greater threat to Christian unity than even the medieval heresies. Once more, St Augustine's defence of righteous persecution, developed to discipline Donatist separatists in the late fourth century and called upon more recently to justify the physical extirpation of heretics, was widely invoked. And not only by Catholics, for Protestant reformers embraced the theory of just persecution too. In Geneva, John Calvin strove to establish a godly regime, orderly, disciplined, and intolerant of heresy, idolatry, or immorality. In 1553, he orchestrated the execution of the anti-Trinitarian Michael Servetus.[42]

Here the interests of theologians and rulers elided. Early modern monarchs strove to make their authority more absolute and embarked upon ambitious state-building projects. They centralised and bureaucratised their kingdoms, brought unruly nobles to heel, created large professional standing armies, and restructured their finances and tax regimes. The consequent impulse to control the lives and affairs of ordinary subjects also extended to their personal piety and moral purity. Persecution of 'incorrect' religious behaviours promoted both the legitimacy and the authority of the early modern state. State building thus played its part in the witch-hunts.[43]

These godly regimes confronted Satan and his allies. Martin Luther, like so many of his generation, was acutely conscious of the physical agency of the Devil in the world. He recounted how his mother had been tormented by a neighbourhood witch and that his own illnesses were not natural but the result of 'pure sorcery'. He inveighed against *Teuffelshuren* (the Devil's whores), *Wettermacherin* (weather-makers), and shape-shifters who stole milk, *Milchdiebin*: 'there is no compassion to be had for these women; I would burn them all myself, according to law ... '.[44]

The gendered anxieties evident here in Luther's worldview were inherent in Satanic witch beliefs across confessional divides. Witch-hunting was not a deliberate attempt to control or murder women per se. Nor did witch-hunters specifically target midwives or female healers, although their professions made them peculiarly vulnerable to accusations: '[she] who knows how to heal knows how to destroy', affirmed one witness to inquisitors in Modena in 1499.[45] Yet the ugly prejudices of patriarchal society, the belief in women's innate moral weaknesses, licentiousness, and dangerous sexuality, ensured that they were far more vulnerable to suspicions than men. King James VI of Scotland opined that 'as that sexe is frailer than men is, so is it easier to be intrapped in these grosse snares of the Devill'. Jean Bodin believed that women were 'fifty times' more likely than men to be tempted into diabolic witchcraft.[46]

As Christina Larner observed in her account of the Scottish witch-hunts, ideologically both the Reformation and the Counter-Reformation made it more likely that such underlying beliefs would be articulated as lethal allegations. With the age's powerful emphasis on personal piety, adult women, while 'frailer than men', were now held to be less childlike and more fully accountable for their own souls. If they chose to practise witchcraft, then they were to be held responsible for that act.[47]

This Janus-faced combination of believing women to be innately suscep- tible to Satan's wiles, while holding them to the highest standards of personal responsibility for their piety, largely explains why, overall, they constituted some 75 per cent of those executed for *maleficium*. In some regions, up to 90 per cent of the victims of the hunts were women. Evidence derived from profiles of those accused in Scotland, England, Italy, Lorraine, and Germany, suggests that older, outspoken, and assertive women, those furthest removed from masculine perceptions of well-behaved, pious, and respectable femin- inity, were the most likely to be accused.[48]

Witch-hunts were thus highly gendered. Yet they never focused solely on women. Indeed, in some exceptional cases, men had outnumbered women as victims. This had occurred where *maleficium* had become locally associated with a particular male occupational group that enjoyed a potentially unruly autonomy. This, for example, was the case among shepherds in Normandy (who were in the habit of using stolen Eucharists in performing magic), or were seen as dangerous outsiders, such as itinerant magical practitioners in Russia.[49] This serves as a reminder that witch-hunting tended very strongly to be a matter of internal discipline within local communities of co-religionists. Catholics and Protestants tended not to accuse one another of witchcraft, but rather they usually accused neighbours who ostensibly shared their own communion, but whose piety was thought suspect. In Protestant England, for example, cunning folk were sometimes smeared as being papists as well as witches, because Catholicism itself was denounced as a form of sorcery.[50]

Ensuring that their own communities were godly, that their neighbours were true to the faith and alert to the wiles of the Devil, was especially important to those who lived in threatening proximity to the other side of the confessional divide. Similarly, the presence of dissenters of their own faith provoked similar fears. Quakers in seventeenth-century England were often denounced as being agents of Satan and were sometimes subjected to the ordeals of swimming and pricking to prove them witches. In Germany and the Netherlands, both Protestant and Catholic authorities frequently accused Anabaptists of being 'minions of the Devil', and of attending witches' sabbaths. Those areas where religious identity was particularly contested, along borders or in regions that contained sizable religious minor- ities, were thus particularly prone to witch-hunts. This was true of Germany, Switzerland, Franche-Comté, Lorraine, and Poland, all of which had heter- ogenous religious populations.[51]

Yet the allegations of witchcraft made against neighbours did not neces- sarily simply arise from a concern about the behaviour or godliness of others. More complex internal motives may have lurked. The heightened religious tensions of the age promoted, in both Catholics and Protestants, an active consciousness of one's own sins, doubts about personal sanctity, and a desire to demonstrate piety. The projection of an individual's consequent feelings of guilt and unworthiness onto others, by accusing them of the ultimate impiety – entering into a conspiracy with Satan – may well have been a useful outlet for these insecurities. Those already subject to popular prejudices – the socially marginalised, feared and despised – were particularly obvious targets. Bodin, for example, claimed that 'gypsies are generally witches, as has been found by judgements rendered'.[52]

And, in some instances, it was not simply the profound religious changes of the age that were driving this process of guilt projection. Newly emerging socio-economic tensions sometimes transformed the mundane quarrels, personal disputes, and status antagonisms of village life into allegations of *maleficium*. Satanic witchcraft might have been an essentially elite concern, but local personal rivalries were often the triggers for specific instances of persecution. In 1565, in Kolozsvár, Hungary, almost all the victims of one large-scale witch-trial were cunning folk who had been accused of *malefice* by other cunning folk. In witch-trials in the Hungarian towns of Hódmezövásárhely and Nagybánya, midwives accused midwives.[53]

This socio-economic explanation for witch-hunting found particular favour with historians such as Keith Thomas and Alan Macfarlane in the 1970s. They drew upon insights from anthropologists researching African societies such as the Azande. Among the Azande, witch beliefs performed significant social functions in strengthening village solidarity and relieving social strains. Focusing on England in the sixteenth and seventeenth centuries, Thomas and Macfarlane identified intra-communal tensions arising from the rise of an individualistic, market-orientated economy. This undermined the traditional moral economy of agrarian communities, which emphasised mutuality and fairness in transactions and in granting charity. A request for food from an impoverished villager or itinerant beggar, for example, might result in a refusal from a prosperous neighbour. The disappointed supplicant might then utter harsh words, perhaps even a curse. Should that well-to-do neighbour then suffer some misfortune, ill-heath, loss of livestock, or crop failure, then they might level an accusation of witchcraft against the impoverished figure who had importuned them. By doing so, they assuaged their own guilt for defying the older customs of charity and directed communal anger at a marginalised individual who threatened the good order, godliness, and stability of their village.[54]

In some instances, this interpretation seems to offer valuable insights. For example, in 1612, near Pendle in Lancashire, pedlar John Law had met Alizon Device on the road to Trawden Forest. Alizon had either begged for or attempted to buy some pins, but Law had refused the request. She cursed him and, shortly thereafter, Law suffered what appears to have been a stroke.

Believing himself the victim of *malefice*, he named Device as his tormentor. Arrested and interrogated, Device confessed to bewitching Law with the aid of the Devil and named her impoverished grandmother, Elizabeth Southerns, as a witch. Also named were Anne Whittle and members of her family. Anne and Elizabeth were both long-established, competing, magical practitioners, of dubious social repute. Professional rivalry, economic marginalisation, a disputed request for charity, and long-standing quarrels between families, all seem to have fuelled what became one of the few large-scale witch-hunts in English history. Elizabeth succumbed to the miserable conditions in which she was held, dying in her cell in Lancaster Castle. Ten others were convicted and hanged. The episode seemed to expose the prosaic social conflicts that often underpinned the fantastical tales of diabolical familiars, bargains with Satan, spells, and nocturnal sabbaths.[55]

Considering the question of why allegations of *maleficum* were made, Frederick Spee, a Jesuit priest convinced of the innocence of many who had been consigned to the flames, offered a world-weary explanation. He identified four groups who 'continually incite the rulers against witches'. The first were the learned but naïve 'theologians and prelates', who were 'happy in their own speculations' but lacked experience 'in the affairs and wickedness of men'. The second were the lawyers, who 'have gradually noticed that conducting trials is a very lucrative office'. Thirdly, were 'the ignorant and usually jealous and malicious common folk, who everywhere avenge their feuds through defamation'. Finally, there were actual sorcerers, who slyly denounced others 'to remove any suspicion of the crime further from themselves'.[56] Of course, for witch-hunts to take place though, 'the rulers' had to take such denunciations seriously. Witch-hunting was a judicial activity; it required not just denunciation but the active participation of the state and the law courts.

Witches, it is true, occasionally died at the hands of violent, lawless mobs. In England, in 1643, two suspected witches were killed by soldiers, in Newbury, Berkshire and Malmesbury, Wiltshire. This, however, was during a brutal civil war, when the normal operation of civil law was entirely disrupted.[57] For the most part, legitimate authorities actively opposed any mob justice that challenged their own orderly rule. Local courts were sometimes reined in when hunts got out of hand. During a witch panic in 1643–1644, the *Parlement* of Toulouse executed three 'witch-finders' who had been paid by local magistrates to test suspects. At the same time, the *Parlement* of Dijon overturned a number of convictions that had gone through the local courts because of the rabble-rousing activities of other such witch-finders, one of whom was sent as a slave to the galleys.[58]

Over time, this imposition of higher authority over wayward local power structures would play a significant role in ending the witch-hunts. However, until that process played itself out, the involvement of secular courts was a major factor in the persecution of alleged witches. Indeed, secular courts became more prominent in the prosecution of witchcraft cases than either inquisitorial tribunals or ecclesiastical courts. The latter had, traditionally, handled religious offences, including heresy, idolatry, blasphemy, or entering into pacts with demons. Yet *maleficum* was a matter of mixed jurisdiction. Secular courts had handled criminal cases where, allegedly, sorcerers had committed murder by magical means. The crime here had been the homicide rather than the casting of the spells. By the sixteenth century, the fears of this new and conspiratorial sect of Satanic witches that threatened the whole of society had now created a compelling logic for secular authorities to take a more active role in the hunts. Many states therefore eventually enacted specific prohibitions against witchcraft in their criminal codes.

The *Reichstag* (the Imperial Diet of the Holy Roman Empire) did so in 1532. England's Parliament followed suit in 1542, 1563, and 1604, as did Scotland in 1563. In the later sixteenth and early seventeenth centuries, Sweden, Denmark, Norway, and Russia issued similar edicts against witchcraft. France was a rare exception to this trend, but in the east of the country, the rulers of France-Comté, bordering Protestant German states, not only passed specific laws but also presided over several waves of intense persecution, including some of the last large-scale witch-hunts in France, 1657–1660. With the exception of Spain, both inquisitorial tribunals and other ecclesiastical courts would gradually be eclipsed by secular magistrates and officials who often proved more zealous in their pursuit of alleged witches.[59]

The Spanish example bears closer examination. The Spanish Inquisition, unlike its medieval predecessors, was a highly centralised organisation, underpinned by the authority of the Spanish crown and thus wielding considerable power. Originally established in 1478, it had first concerned itself with policing the religious practices of *conversos*, that is, Jews and their descendants who had converted to Christianity. It had then turned its attention to *Moriscoes*, nominally converted Muslims, and, in the sixteenth century, to Protestants. Perhaps with this succession of suspect internal religious minorities to pursue there simply was not the same impetus to hunt witches.

The documentary record is most complete for the country's northern provinces. There, from 1498 to 1610, inquisitorial courts condemned just two dozen witches to death at *autos-da-fé* (the delivery of sentence in matters of faith). Spanish secular courts put hundreds to death over the same period. During one unusually intensive witch-hunt in the Basque country in 1609–1614, an *auto-da-fé* did send several more witches to the stake. Yet the tribunal's junior inquisitor, Alonso de Salazar y Frías, subsequently reviewed the cases of almost 2,000 individuals who had confessed to being witches. Most of these were children and adolescents. His conclusion was that their putative offences were simply imaginary; nothing heretical or physically harmful had actually occurred. Catalonia subsequently witnessed a major witch panic, 1614–1622, that claimed at least 150 victims. Again, this was undertaken by secular authorities, not the Inquisition. A few more isolated cases of executions for witchcraft occurred in the 1620s, but thereafter, while local hunts took place, the only deaths that occurred were at the hands of vigilantes and mobs, not the authorities. Indeed, from about 1550 onwards, the Inquisition had been wrestling control of witch-trials from the secular authorities and the more it did so, the less intense and frequent the hunts in Spain became.[60]

Both the Spanish and the Roman Inquisitions developed a comparatively restrained approach towards alleged witches. Yet, ironically, the adoption of inquisitorial procedures into secular legal systems, widespread across Europe by the sixteenth century, was a powerful factor in perpetuating the witch-hunts. Originally developed in order to combat popular heresy in the thirteenth century, inquisitorial tribunals had very distinct characteristics. Inquisitors investigated allegations, and then acted as both judges and juries. Those accused were generally examined in isolation. If they had been denounced, they were not told the names of those who had accused them. Their reputations in their communities were admissible as evidence against them. They often faced the inquisitor alone. Legal representation, while allowed, was discouraged by the threat that the lawyers themselves might themselves be denounced as heretics or witches. Indeed, in the case of witch-craft allegations, prominent jurists argued that the normal legal safeguards ought to be abandoned to secure convictions. French witch-hunter Jean Bodin wrote, 'if the strict forms of law were adhered to, not one witch in 100,000 would be punished'.[61]

Skilled inquisitors were encouraged to be duplicitous when interviewing suspects, to entrap them. Nicolau Eymeric, a Catalan inquisitor, had written a manual *Directorium inquisitorum* (*Guide to Inquisitors*) in 1376. In it, he advised inquisitors to 'use ruses to catch the heretic in his error'. One example was to inform the suspect that their guilt was already established because their acquaintances had already confessed in full. Confession and repentance were all that was left to them.[62] Priority was given to extracting such a confession, the 'queen of evidence', because it was necessary to secure a conviction. This, in turn, had legitimised the use of torture. This rarely failed to elicit the desired result. Investigators assumed that those who initially endured physical torment could do so only through evil arts. Failure to confess was the sorcery of silence; the accused had 'bewitched herself into taciturnity and hence deserves to be burned alive'.[63]

Tortured, terrified, browbeaten, manipulated, weary, and sometimes ill or deluded, it is small wonder that so many of those accused finally confessed.[64] Among the most moving testimony that has survived from a victim of the witch-hunts is a 1628 letter written by 55-year-old Johannes Junius, *Bürgermeister* of Bamberg, to his daughter, Veronica. His family were the victims of an escalating chain-reaction panic; his wife had been executed for witchcraft the previous year. Junius himself was arrested and tortured, almost certainly in the city's purpose-built *Hexenhaus*. After displaying remarkable fortitude for some time, Junius could endure the pain no longer and confessed to being a witch. He assured Veronica that this confession was 'pure lies': 'innocent I came to jail; innocent I was tortured; innocent I must die'.[65]

One powerful indicator of the significance of inquisitorial procedures in driving intense, chain-reaction witch-hunts is the relative rarity of such events in jurisdictions where they were *not* used. England is the prime example. There trials were conducted before lay jurymen. It was they, rather than those who investigated the offence or presided over the courtroom, that determined their outcome, by delivering the verdict. Trials were public affairs, not secret investigations. Confession was not required to secure conviction. This sometimes resulted in English juries convicting the accused on flimsy hearsay evidence, but it also meant that the systematic use of torture had not established itself in English criminal procedure. This was challenged between *circa* 1540 and 1640, England's 'century of torture'. In those years, the Privy Council had authorised the use of torture more frequently, but overwhelmingly in alleged crimes of state, such as sedition and treason. Torture warrants were only rarely issued to assist in the investigation of non-political crimes, such as homicides or thefts.[66] The appalling instruments of physical cruelty employed during inquisitorial investigations in other states, the *strappado* and the thumbscrew, were not present during investigations of witchcraft in England.

Other forms of torture – the ordeal by water ('swimming' of alleged witches) and sleep deprivation – were sometimes practised by self-appointed witch-finders, such as John Stearne and Matthew Hopkin, in order to generate confessions. They also browbeat and harangued their unfortunate, weary, and frightened victims. With the connivance of local magistrates, they had stoked a witch panic in Essex in 1645–1647, that claimed the lives of over a hundred women and men, an unprecedented event in England. This, however, was during the aforementioned civil war, when the normal operation of civil law had broken down.[67]

Overall, with a population of around 4.4 million in 1600, England witnessed only about some five hundred executions for witchcraft before trials petered out in the latter half of the seventeenth century. This contrasts with far more intense witch-hunting where inquisitorial procedures were employed. In Lorraine and Luxembourg, both with populations of just 300,000, the witch-hunts in each claimed in order of 1,600 victims. Switzerland, with a population of one million, witnessed about 3,500 executions. English witch-hunting had its own characteristics. The emphasis on the role of demonic 'familiars', often taking the form of small animals, in assisting alleged witches, was often prominent (but not wholly unique) to English cases.[68] The method of execution for those convicted, hanging rather than burning, was distinct. Yet the nature of the legal system should probably rank as the most important distinguishing factor, ensuring that the English witch-hunts were comparatively restrained.[69]

Scotland provides an interesting contrast. Current estimates place the country's death toll of convicted witches at around 2,500, while the nation's population was just one million. The majority of the victims died during nationwide panics in 1590–1597, 1629–1630, 1649, and in 1661–1662, when over three hundred witches were executed. Scotland's legal system was, Brian Levack noted, something of a 'hybrid between English and Continental models'. Trials themselves resembled English ones, with relatively independent juries deliberating on a verdict. Judges, though, played a more active role, particularly in the investigation of offences, during which they compiled dossiers of written depositions to be used in evidence. This may not have mattered so much, except that, short of professional judges, Scotland's Privy Council allowed local magistrates, with no formal legal training, to conduct trials for witchcraft. Due process was frequently compromised, and torture applied. High rates of convictions for the offence ensured. Interestingly, a similar situation prevailed in Massachusetts in 1692. There, allegations of *maleficum* made in Salem triggered a chain-reaction hunt that ended with the execution of 20 women and men. The judges who presided over those trials also had no legal training and, like their Scottish counterparts, failed to safeguard due process. They allowed both physical and psychological coercion to be applied to obtain confessions.[70]

Yet it would be the German-speaking regions of the Holy Roman Empire that would come to be known as 'the heartlands of the witch-hunts', accounting for the execution of some 27,000 people, from a total population of 16 million. They executions were frequently the result of large-scale, chain-reaction hunts, where an initial accusation led to an escalating series of denunciations, that might take hundreds of lives in a matter of months. The key to understanding the ferocity of witch persecution within the Holy Roman Empire is the weakness of central authority and subsequent leeway given to the courts, secular and ecclesiastical, of over 2,000 semi-independent territorialities: seven prince-electorates, 43 secular principalities, 32 ecclesiastical principalities, 140 independent lordships, 70 imperial abbacies, four cantons of the Teutonic Order, 75 imperial cities and scores of imperial knights (670 in Swabia, 700 in Franconia, 360 along the Rhineland).[71]

Alongside inquisitional tribunals and ecclesiastical courts, German secular courts began to prosecute witchcraft cases from an early date. In 1446 or 1447, almost one hundred years before the Reichstag had enacted specific provisions against witchcraft in a criminal code, civil authorities in Heidelberg had burned members of an alleged witch sect.[72] As the courts dealing with witchcraft cases were operating at a local level, those conducting investigations were very often personally entwined in the currents of fear and panic, the antagonistic local politics and quarrels, and the influence of rabble-rousers and self-righteous persecutors who drove individual outbreaks of witch-hunting.

The Heidelberg trial provides a strong pointer to how the ideological framework of belief in demonic witchcraft was spread early in German-speaking lands. The city council of Basel had dispatched one of their own experts on the new sects, Peter zum Blech, to assist the authorities in Heidelberg. Much of the formative literature was widely accessible to a German readership too, beyond the clergy. The Lucerne chronicler Hans Fründ, whose account of the Alpine trials of 1428 had done so much to forge the stereotype of the early modern witch, had written in German. He used a late fourteenth-century neologism, *Hexen*, to refer to witches, and *Hexerei* would soon become the standard term for witchcraft across most German-speaking communities.[73]

The extent of actual persecution within the Holy Roman Empire, at least outside the western Alpine region, was limited until the final years of the fifteenth century. The cases initially tended to be small-scale and isolated, such as the two women burned in Berlin in 1446. As has been noted, Heinrich Kramer published *Malleus Maleficarum* in 1486 partly out of frustration at the resistance he had encountered to his attempts to incite witch-hunts. Disturbingly, however, he was subsequently able to claim, in Nuremburg in 1491, that over two hundred witches had been burned due to his inquisitions. Opposition to his activities remained. His Dominican superior Jacob Sprenger (once regarded as a co-author of Kramer's, now understood to have been a bitter foe) appears to have driven him from his province. Yet Sprenger's efforts may have been a futile venture to hold back the tide of persecution. Both ecclesiastical and secular courts were now taking an increased interest in witchcraft.[74]

While the scale and intensity of witch-hunts would not reach their peak until after the mid-sixteenth century, there does appear to have been a notable escalation in persecution inside the Empire between the 1480s and 1520. Wolfgang Behringer has suggested that it was linked to environmental factors, a succession of poor harvests, plague, and livestock murrains. These were devastating events for an agrarian society, and without an understanding of their complex natural causes, the people of early modern Europe searched for scapegoats. For Behringer, this link between severe mortality crises, often exacerbated by human activities such as warfare, was a recurrent factor that stimulated witch-hunts throughout the period (the 1430s, when the witch panics had first emerged, was also a period of crop failure born of climatic change, livestock disease, and conflict). As cities, towns, and villages counted their many dead, and awaited the next misfortune, apocalyptic fears were inevitably stoked. Heinrich Kramer was just one who urged his compatriots to look to the Book of Revelation and understand that this new sect of witches heralded the arrival of the Antichrist.[75]

It was in this fearful context that the Reichstag legislated against *Hexerei* in the *Carolina* criminal code of 1532. For a while, witch-hunts continued to be sporadic and often focused on individuals, such as a maid of the Black Forest burned for supposedly causing the destruction by fire of the town of Schiltach. A further major shift in scale and intensity occurred in 1563, when 63 witches were executed in the imperial city of Wisenstieg. This was followed by an increased incidence across the German-speaking lands, such as Swabia and the Rhineland. From 1581 to 1593, a sustained panic in Trier probably took around a thousand lives. Among them was Dietrich Flade, the vice-governor of the city, rector of the university and one of the highest-ranking victims of the witch persecutions.[76] Again, it is worth noting the correlation of this escalation with a further deterioration in climatic conditions, as heavy rainfalls and an overall drop in temperature associated with the 'little ice age' ruined harvests and destroyed livelihoods. As malnutrition and poverty took their grim toll once more, desperate, angry folk looked for someone to blame.[77]

However, it is important not to overstate environmental factors as a cause of the persecutions, even if they often bred allegations. Many areas that suffered poor harvests and waves of human and animal sickness did not indulge in witch-hunts. In the decentralised empire, local politics, broadly understood, usually determined whether or not a panic actually took place. The ecclesiastical courts often continued to try alleged witches, particularly in cities such as Trier, where temporal as well as spiritual authority was wielded by the elector-archbishop. Elsewhere, it was increasingly secular authorities that took the lead. However, in some cases, they resisted the pressure to pursue witches. In Württemberg, the scholars in the faculty of law at the University of Tübingen urged restraint, as did their colleagues in the law faculty at Heidelberg, capital of the Rhenish Palatinate. In both Württemberg and the Palatinate, rulers reined in local courts and generally prevented the kind of chain-reaction panics that took so many lives elsewhere in the Empire.[78]

Up until the 1630s, this was the exception rather than the rule. Where secular and ecclesiastical authorities agreed on the need to pursue and extinguish these demonic cults, where influential voices – such as the local law and theology faculties – were convinced, too, of the efficacy and necessity of this mission, and where a fearful population cried out for protection against Satan and his acolytes, when their crops failed, their livestock died, and their milk spoiled, then supposed witches burned.

Over four thousand trials occurred in Mecklenburg, where 'justice' was administered by hundreds of petty feudal lords. Similarly, some fifteen hundred trials took place in Thuringia, where jurisdictions were equally fragmented among local dynasties, each a law unto themselves. Actual executions peaked in the 1620s and 1630s. Three hundred died in Würzburg in 1616–1618, followed by a second chain reaction hunt, 1626–1630, that took the lives of a further nine hundred individuals. Six hundred were executed in Bamberg, 1626–1630; 768 in Mainz in 1626–1629. In Cologne, a hunt lasting ten years, 1624–1634, claimed two thousand victims. After Cologne, witch-trials within the Holy Roman Empire became less frequent but no less terrifying when they occurred. Thirty-seven alleged witches were executed in Esslingen in 1662–1665. One hundred and forty young men and boys, followers of the alleged witch and vagabond 'Sorcerer Jack', were condemned to death in Salzburg in 1680. Thereafter witch-trials within the Empire were isolated and rare events, with the last taking place in 1782.[79]

Understanding the drawn-out and convoluted processes which saw the decline of the witch-hunts is almost as difficult as explaining their origins. It is well understood that the intellectual currents of the early Enlightenment, *circa* 1680–1730, had a profound effect on educated belief in such matters as witchcraft, which was consigned to the provincial backwaters of rural superstition. As Liselotte von der Pfalz, Louis XIV's sister-in-law, noted in 1718, 'in Paris people don't believe in witches and we hear nothing about them; at Rouen they believe that witches exist, and there one always hears about them'.[80] Yet it is also now understood that Enlightenment thinking can have played little part in the decline of witch-hunting. That decline had begun in the early years of the seventeenth century, when the rulers, lawyers, and theologians still largely believed (or professed to believe) in the reality of *maleficium*.

Yet 'reason' had its place in the story of witch-hunting's decline. A long-standing and persistent sceptical tradition had cast doubts on the reality of *maleficum* and on the dubious criminal proceedings that generated so many convictions. Dutch humanists, such as Erasmus of Rotterdam, had dismissed belief in witchcraft as mere superstition in the early sixteenth century. Their compatriot, physician Johann Weyer, had argued in his 1563 work *De Praestigiss Daemonum* (*The Devil's Tricks*) that the old women who were so frequently accused of witchcraft, and often confessed to it, were actually suffering from 'melancholy' (what we might think of as mental illness), and were themselves incapable of causing real harm.[81]

In England, Member of Parliament Reginald Scott, also argued, in *The Discoverie of Witchcraft* (1584), that confessing witches were simply deluded. Indeed, he took the radical step of suggesting that a childish superstition was sustained only by 'the tyranicall cruletie of witchmongers and inquisitors'. His contemporary Cornelius Loos, professor of theology in Trier, wrote a bold manuscript, *On True and False Magic*, challenging the legal basis of the trials that had brought such terror to his city.[82]

In 1631, Friedrich Spee, a Jesuit priest who had ministered to women accused of witchcraft in Germany, called for Christian compassion in his treatise *Cautio Criminalis*. While he dutifully professed that he himself believed that 'witches, hags and sorcerers really exist', he criticised the inquisitorial legal procedures and the use of torture that caused the innocent to confess, and the denunciations that inevitably triggered chain-reaction hunts:

> One can hardly say what misery this is if any woman falsely states that she is guilty because of the violence of her pain, since in most courts there are no means available by which she might escape. She is forced to accuse others whom she does not know, whom her questioners not infrequently place in her mouth, or the torturer suggests, or who they have heard are already infamous, or denounced ... And those women must in turn denounce others and they in turn still others and so on.[83]

Spee was always careful to make his case in terms that even the most orthodox believers would struggle to counter: 'The devil can transform himself into an angel of light as scripture testifies [Corinthians 11:12–15] ... therefore the Devil can also represent innocent people ... '. Confessing witches might testify that they saw neighbours cavorting at a sabbath. Putative victims might testify that the woman they denounced as a witch had appeared in spectral form at night to torment them. Yet how could any prudent judge discount the possibility that what these witnesses had actually seen was Satan, in the guise of an innocent? For those who insisted God would never allow Satan to practise such a deception, Spee simply asked, 'How are my adversaries so certain God would not permit it? God allows many more serious things ... namely the deaths of martyrs and infants, the desecration of the sacred host, and similar unspeakable matters'.

Spee did not demand that his readers abandon their beliefs in witchcraft, only that they question the legal procedures that were currently condemning so many to death. His was a 'pious scepticism'.[84]

Such reasoned and theologically respectable arguments were not without effect. Over the long term, they persuaded some judges, rulers, and counsellors to rein in the hunts in their lands. For example, Philipp von Schönborn, archbishop of Mainz, was reputed to have exercised greater caution during witch-trials after having read Cautio Criminalis. Yet for some time, this scepticism struggled to win influence in the face of effective and powerful polemics that continued to stoke fear of the diabolic conspiracy of the witches. Older works, such as the Malleus Maleficarum, were regularly reprinted. New works, by educated authors with practical experience of handling witchcraft cases, reiterated, and reinforced the established beliefs, creating an authoritative body of literature that was difficult to challenge. The French judge and attorney general for Lorraine Nicholas Rémy published Demonolatreiae (Demonolatry) in 1595. It was reprinted eight times, with two German translations. The Jesuit priest Martin Del Rio's work Disquisitionum Magicarum Libri Sex (Six Books of Investigations into Magic) written a few years later, would go through twenty print runs and was translated into French in 1611. Henri Boguet, a judge in Burgundy with a particular expertise in demonic possession, published a popular text in 1602, Discours des sorciers (Discourse on Sorcerers) that eventually ran to eight editions.[85]

The sceptics long struggled to reach the same readership. On publication, Weyer's work was dismissed as 'the ravings of a single heretic'. Loos was imprisoned by the authorities in Trier and forced to recant his views. Scott's book was translated into Dutch, but does not appear to have reached a wider readership beyond England. Spee's compelling plea was written in Latin and was not available in accessible, vernacular translations until the latter half of the seventeenth century. At that point, it began to have a more significant impact. The French translation of 1660, for example, was part of a coordinated propaganda campaign to end the witch panics then occurring in Franche-Comté. Spee's work was also known to have been influential in shaping the edict issued by Frederick William I of Prussia in 1714, that ended the use of torture, forced confessions, and the death penalty in witchcraft cases.[86]

Such statutory decriminalisation, the repealing (or significant revision) of witchcraft laws, came late: in France in 1682, in Britain in 1736, in Poland in 1776, and in Sweden in 1779. By this point, witchcraft trials had largely ceased anyway. When isolated cases did occur, there was now public outrage. The execution of Anna Göldi, the last witch legally executed in Europe, in Glarus, Switzerland, in 1782, was widely denounced as a 'judicial murder'.[87]

The impulse that ended the witch-hunts thus concerned not the reality of the crime but rather reflected the awareness that many of those who had been convicted and executed had been innocent. Rulers, magistrates, and judges became more and more reluctant to try witchcraft cases, more cautious in how they handled those that came to court, and more willing to uphold appeals made by those who had confessed under torture. That long-standing and persistent intellectual tradition that had taken a sceptical look at the investigations and trials of alleged witches finally found an audience. In the aftermath of chain-reaction hunts that seemed to have run out of control, in the Basque Country in 1609–1614, in Cologne, 1624–1634, in Scotland, 1661–1662, and in Salem, Massachusetts in 1692, the authorities recoiled and took stock of the dubious nature of the evidence that had sent so many to their deaths.

H.C. Erik Midelfort and Edward Bever have thus written of a 'crisis of confidence' in the criminal procedures used to secure convictions in witchcraft cases. The kind of 'evidence' that had once encouraged a fatal certainty, was now rejected as unsound. In Denmark, the legal scholar Laurits Nørregard warned that an alleged witch's confession was the last thing anyone in authority should believe. Alongside this faltering confidence in the courts, was a wavering certainty in the scriptural justification for executing witches. Johann Weyer and Reginald Scot had both questioned the literal reading of Exodus 22:18 as demanding the death penalty for witches, echoing earlier concerns expressed by some Spanish and Italian inquisitors. Nor, in fact, was it even clear that 'witch' was a particularly good translation for the Hebrew word *mekhashepa* that appeared in the original verse.[88]

They were not exceptional in asking this kind of sceptical, cautious question of scripture. Indeed, their position was redolent of many early medieval theologians before a dangerous literalism had begun to take hold. Bloodshed among Christians, religious wars, and persecution, had driven some thinkers during the Reformation to urge once more a caution in those who believed that they must condemn others to the flames on the basis of their own understanding of scripture. The French Protestant theologian Sebastian Castellio had published a work questioning the rectitude of persecuting heretics as early as 1553. He had observed that many scriptural passages were obscure and might legitimately be interpreted in different ways. A century on, as the witch-trials declined, such a view grew increasingly common. The dogmatic certainty that had driven the impulse to build a godly, and necessarily intolerant, regime gave way to scepticism that allowed room for doubt. And doubt was incompatible with burning witches. As it penetrated the minds of the judges and magistrates who presided over witch-trials, the number of those trials declined.[89]

A note of caution should be sounded before this doubt is associated too readily with an ensuing rise of 'tolerance'. Traditionally, the Treaty of Westphalia, that ended the Thirty Years War (1618–1648), has been seen as a watershed, with a continent weary of the cost in blood and treasure of a century of religious conflict accepting a grudging forbearance towards others' beliefs. From that point, the Enlightenment philosophers such as Pierre Bayle, with his radical assertion that even atheists could be good citizens, forged the intellectual case for toleration.[90]

Yet Europe's age of religious conflict did not, in fact, end in 1648. Nor did the absolutist state's persecution of religious minorities cease during the early Enlightenment. The most infamous illustration of this point was King Louis XIV of France's campaign against the Protestant Huguenots. This culminated in 1685 in the revocation of the Edict of Nantes that had granted them some rights, ushering in a fresh wave of repression, and helping to spark renewed European-wide conflict in the Nine Years War (1688–1697). As historians such as Alexandra Walsham and Benjamin Kaplan have demonstrated, tolerance as a practice tended to develop initially at community level, as personal contacts tended to erode frightening stereotypes and ordinary folk learned to live together. Kaplan, for example, has pointed to the high incidence of interfaith (Catholic-Protestant) marriages in the Dutch Republic as a powerful mechanism in creating a 'fluid integrated society'.[91]

One might conclude, therefore, that the early modern state, still all too ready to persecute dissident minorities, played little effective part in the decline of witch-hunting. Yet this would be too hasty a conclusion. The growth of the powerful, bureaucratised central state did play a role in reducing the occurrence of witch-trials. This was largely a result of a broader programme to increase the government's authority at the expense of those unchecked local authorities that threatened its untrammelled exercise of sovereignty. The last witch-hunts in towns in rural Würtemberg were thus ended when the government in Stuttgart intervened and sent soldiers to impose control.[92]

Mostly this process was altogether less dramatic. Ultimately, it reflected the fiscal capacity (the ability to raise revenue to pay for, among other things, soldiers) of early modern states. Fiscal capacity allowed those states to strengthen adherence to the rule of law and to enforce standardised and consistent legal procedures. As local courts were brought more firmly within centralised legal systems, the neglect of due process that had previously characterised so many local witch-trials came to an end. In a particularly illuminating case study of France, the economists Noel Johnson and Mark Koyama have demonstrated how, as France's fragmented legal system was brought more firmly under the authority of Paris over the course of the seventeenth century, there was a corresponding decline in the frequency of witch-hunts. Conversely, the witch-hunts persisted longest in weakly governed states, such as Poland or Hungary.[93]

Fears of heretics, sorcerers, and demons had created the ideological basis for the early modern witch-hunts. This was epitomised in the belief in a 'new sect' of witches, who abjured their faith, entered into a pact with Satan and worked harmful *malefice* against their neighbours, that had been established, initially in the western Alps, as early as the 1420s. This ideology eventually challenged the traditional scepticism and restraint concerning the reality of magic and the treatment of those who practised, or were alleged to practise, magic. Folkloric traditions of night flights and fairies, and elite phantasms of the Devil and orgiastic sabbaths, elided into a fatal synthesis.

Personal quarrels, social tensions, prosaic misfortunes, hardships born of environmental crises, and rabble-rousing 'witch-mongers', all generated accusations. The adoption of inquisitorial procedures into civic legal systems produced confessions and further denunciations. The Reformation impulse to forge godly regimes placed an emphasis on individual religious and moral conformity that left many vulnerable to denunciation, often on no stronger basis that their poor reputation within a neighbourhood. The ugly assumptions of a patriarchal society ensured that the majority of the victims were women. Decentralised, fragmented, local court systems, often staffed by untrained magistrates and judges, failed to safeguard due process and often themselves stoked witch panics.

Yet the witch-hunts were not a tidal wave that swept the continent. They varied in intensity and in frequency, and their incidence must be understood in terms of highly variegated circumstances. Intellectually, sceptical voices may have been muted for over a century, shouted down by the hectoring chorus of 'witch-mongers' like Heinrich Kramer. Yet, where due process was respected, and where a strong central authority was committed to maintaining order, witch-hunting had been restrained. As, starting from roughly the 1630s, a 'crisis of confidence' over the legal systems that had generated so many convictions affected experienced judges and magistrates, and as the fiscal capacity of centralised states allowed greater control over local courts, the witch-hunts declined.

The decline of the witch-hunts did not coincide with an emerging age of tolerance. Indeed, contemporaneously to the emergence of the beliefs that drove the witch-hunts, and also drawing on medieval roots, another ideology would emerge that would drive the most destructive forms of persecution of the modern age: slavery, colonialism, and genocide. That ideology was 'race'.

Notes

1 'The Canon (Capitulum) Episcopi', in H.C. Lea (ed.), *Materials Toward a History of Witchcraft*, Volume 1 (Philadelphia: University of Pennsylvania Press, 1939), pp.178–180.
2 Nicholas Remy, 'The Devil's Mark and Flight to the Sabbath', in Brian P. Levack (ed.), *The Witchcraft Sourcebook* (London: Routledge, 2004), p.84.
3 Brian P. Levack, *The Witch-Hunt in Early Modern Europe* (London: Pearson, 1995), p.25.

4 Quoted in Peter Elmer, 'Science, Medicine and Witchcraft', in Jonathan Barry and Owen Davies (eds), *Palgrave Advances in Witchcraft Historiography* (Basingstoke: Palgrave Macmillan, 2007), p.35.

5 Levack, *The Witch-Hunt in Early Modern Europe*, p.3.

6 Margaret Murray, *The Witch-Cult in Western Europe* (Oxford: Oxford University Press, 1921).

7 Norman Cohn, *Europe's Inner Demons: The Demonisation of Christians in Medieval Christendom* (London: Pimlico, 1993), pp.152–161.

8 Cohn, *Europe's Inner Demons*, pp.162–180.

9 Julian Goodare, 'The Cult of the Seely Wights in Scotland', *Folklore*, 123 (2012), pp.198–219.

10 Carlo Ginzberg, *The Night Battles* (Baltimore, MD: Johns Hopkins University Press, 1983).

11 A.A. Barb, 'The Survival of the Magical Arts', in Arnaldo Momigliano (ed.), *The Conflict between Paganism and Christianity in the Fourth Century* (Oxford: Clarendon Press, 1963), pp.100–125; Paul Foreman (attrib.), *The Cambridge Book of Magic: A Tudor Necromancer's Manual*, translated by Francis Young (Cambridge: Texts in Early Modern Magic, 2015), p.71.

12 Keith Thomas, *Religion and the Decline of Magic* (London: Weidenfeld and Nicolson, 1971), pp.252–300.

13 Edward Peters, *The Magician, the Witch and the Law* (Philadelphia: University of Pennsylvania Press, 1978), pp.4–6.

14 William of Malmesbury, 'The Sorceress of Berkeley', in Alan Kors and Edward Peters (eds), *Witchcraft in Europe, 400–1700* (Philadelphia: University of Pennsylvania Press, 2001), pp.70–72.

15 Julian Goodare, *The European Witch-Hunt* (London: Routledge, 2016), p.134.

16 Alain Boureau, *Satan the Heretic: The Birth of Demonology in the Medieval West*, translated by Teresa Lavender Fagan (Chicago, IL: University of Chicago Press, 2006), p.24.

17 Anne Neary, 'The Origins and Character of the Kilkenny Witchcraft Case of 1324', *Proceedings of the Royal Irish Academy: Archaeology, Culture, History, Literature*, 83 (1983), pp.333–350; Julien Théry, 'A Heresy of State: Philip the Fair, the Trial of the "Perfidious Templars" and the Pontificalization of the French Monarchy', *Journal of Medieval Religious Cultures*, 39 (2013), pp.117–148.

18 Michela Pereira, 'Alchemy and Hermeticism: An Introduction to This Issue', *Early Science and Medicine*, 5 (2000), p.117.

19 David Porreca, 'Hermes Trismegitus: William of Auvergne's Mythical Authority', *Archives d'histoire doctrinale et littéraire du Moyen Age*, 67 (2000), pp.143–158; Stanley Jeyaraja Tambiah, *Magic, Science and the Scope of Rationality* (Cambridge: Cambridge University Press, 1990), pp.25–26.

20 Stuart Clark, *Thinking with Demons: The Idea of Witchcraft in Early Modern Europe* (Oxford: Oxford University Press, 1997), p.262.

21 Peters, *The Magician, the Witch and the Law*, pp.85–87.

22 Thomas Aquinas, extract from *Summa Theologiae*, in Kors and Peters (eds), *Witchcraft in Europe*, pp.97–103.

23 Peters, *The Magician, the Witch and the Law*, pp.85–87.

24 Gene A. Brucker, 'Sorcery in Early Renaissance Florence', *Studies in the Renaissance*, 10 (1963), pp.9–10.

25 Franco Mormando, 'Bernardino of Siena, Popular Preacher and Witch-Hunter: A 1426 Witch Trial in Rome', *Fifteenth Century Studies*, 24 (1998), pp.84–118.

26 Goodare, *The European Witch-Hunt*, pp.40–41.

27 'Pope Alexander to Pontus Fougeyron on New Sects (1409)', in Kors and Peters (eds), *Witchcraft in Europe*, p. 153; Lyndal Roper, *The Witch Craze: Terror and Fantasy in Baroque Germany* (New Haven, CT: Yale University Press, 2004,) pp.40–43.

28 Goodare, *The European Witch-Hunt*, pp.45–46.

29 Hans Peter Brodel, 'Fifteenth Century Witch Beliefs', in Brain Levack (ed.), *The Oxford Handbook of Witchcraft in Early Modern Europe and Colonial America* (Oxford: Oxford University Press, 2013), p.39.

30 Lea (ed.), *Material Toward a History of Witchcraft*, Volume 1, pp.248–251.

31 Ronald Hutton, *The Witch: A History of Fear, from Ancient Times to the Present* (New Haven, CT: Yale University Press, 2017), p.52.

32 Joen Bodin, quoted in Lea (ed.), *Materials Toward a History of Witchcraft*, Volume 2, p.573; Ginzburg, *The Night Battles*, p.133; Tamar Herziz, 'Witchcraft Prosecutions in Italy', in Levack (ed.), *Oxford Handbook of Witchcraft*, pp.249–267. Peters, *The Magician, The Witch and the Law*, p.68.

33 Georg Modestin, 'The Metamorphoses of the Anti-Witchcraft Treatise *Errores Gazariorum*', in Julian Goodare, Rita Voltmer, and Liv Helene Willumsen (eds), *Demonology and Witch-Hunting in Early Modern Europe* (London: Routledge, 2020), p.49.

34 Johannes Nider, extract from *Formicarius* in Lea (ed.), *Materials Towards a History of Witchcraft*, Volume 1, p.261.

35 Edward Bever, *The Realities of Witchcraft and Popular Magic in Early Modern Europe* (Basingstoke: Palgrave, 2008), pp.126–127, 143–150; Owen Davies, 'The Nightmare Experience, Sleep Paralysis, and Witchcraft Accusations', *Folklore*, 114 (2003), pp.181–203; Charlotte-Rose Millar, 'Dangers of the Night: The Witch, the Devil, and the "Nightmare" in Early Modern England', *Preternature: Critical and Historical Studies on the Preternatural*, 7 (2018), pp. 154–181.

36 Modestin, 'The Metamorphoses of the Anti-Witchcraft Treatise *Errores Gazariorum*', p.56; Nider, extract from *Formicarius* in Lea, *Materials Towards a History of Witchcraft*, Volume 1, pp.260, 264.

37 Martine Ostorerp, 'Promoter of the Sabbat and Diabolical Realism: Nicolas Jacquier's *Flagellum Hereticorum Fascinariorum*' in Jan Machielsen (ed.), *The Science of Demons: Early Modern Authors Facing Witchcraft and the Devil* (London: Routledge, 2020), pp.41–43.

38 Edward Bever, 'Witchcraft Prosecutions and the Decline of Magic', *Journal of Interdisciplinary History*, 40 (2009), p.266.

39 Hans Peter Broedel, *The 'Malleus Maleficarum' and the Construction of Witchcraft: Theology and Popular Belief* (Manchester: Manchester University Press, 2003); Tamar Herzig, 'The Bestselling Demonologist: Heinrich Institoris's *Malleus Maleficarum*', in Machielsen (ed.), *The Science of Demons*, pp.53–67.

40 Heinrich Kramer, *The Malleus Maleficarum*, edited and translated by P.G. Maxwell-Stuart (Manchester: Manchester University Press, 2007), p.49; Levack, *The Witch-Hunt in Early Modern Europe*, pp.55–56.

41 Quoted in Lea (ed.), *Materials Toward a History of Witchcraft*, Volume 2, p.555.

42 John Coffey, *Persecution and Toleration in Protestant England, 1558–1689* (Harlow: Pearson, 2000), pp.22–23.

43 Christina Larner, *Witchcraft and Religion: The Politics of Popular Belief* (Oxford: Blackwell, 1985), pp.35–67.

44 Kors and Peters (eds), *Witchcraft in Europe*, pp.262–263.

45 Quoted in Ginzburg, *The Night Battles*, p.78.

46 Quoted in Chistina Larner, *Enemies of God: The Witch-Hunt in Scotland* (Oxford: Blackwell, 1983), p.93.
Alison Rowlands, 'Witchcraft and Gender in Early Modern Europe', in Levack (ed.), *Oxford Handbook of Witchcraft*, p.449.

47 Larner, *Enemies of God*, pp.100–101.

48 Lyndal Roper, *Witch Craze: Terror and Fantasy in Baroque Germany* (New Haven, CT: Yale University Press, 2004), pp.17–18.

49 Valerie A. Kivelson, 'Male Witches and Gendered Categories in Seventeenth-Century Russia', *Comparative Studies in Society and History*, 45, 3 (2003), pp.606–631; William Monter, 'Toads and Eucharists: The Male Witches of Normandy, 1564–1660', *French Historical Studies*, 20 (1997), pp.563–595.

50 Alexandra Walsham, *Charitable Hatred: Tolerance and Intolerance in England, 1500–1700* (Manchester: Manchester University Press, 2006), p.146.

51 Levack, *The Witch-Hunts in Early Modern Europe*, pp.114–120; Gary K. Waite, *Eradicating the Devil's Minions: Anabaptists and Witches in Reformation Europe, 1535–1600* (Toronto: University of Toronto Press, 2007); Walsham, *Charitable Hatred*, p.146.

52 Quoted in Lea (ed.), *Materials Toward a History of Witchcraft*, Volume 2, p.573.

53 Ildikó Sz. Ktristóf, 'Witch-Hunting in Early Modern Hungary', in Levack (ed.), *Oxford Handbook of Witchcraft*, pp.350–351.

54 Alan Macfarlane, *Witchcraft in Tudor and Stuart England: A Regional and Comparative Study* (London: Routledge, 1970); E.E. Evans-Pritchard, *Witchcraft Among the Azande* (Oxford, Clarendon Press, 1937); Thomas, *Religion and the Decline of Magic*.

55 Thomas Potts, *The Wonderfull Discouerie of Witches in the Countie of Lancaster* (London: 1613); Stephen Pumfrey, 'Potts, Plots and Politics: James I *Daemonologie* and *The Wonderful Discoverie of Witches*', in Robert Poole (ed.), *The Lancashire Witches: Histories and Stories* (Manchester: Manchester University Press, 2002), pp.31–32.

56 Friedrich Spee van Langenfeld, *Cautio Criminalis, or a Book of Witch Trials*, translated by Marcus Hellyer (Charlottesville: University of Virginia Press, 2003), pp.49–51.

57 Malcolm Gaskell, *Witchfinders: A Seventeenth Century English Tragedy* (London: John Murray, 2005); 'Witchcraft and Evidence in Early Modern England', *Past & Present*, 198 (2008), p.46.

58 Robin Briggs, *Witches and Neighbours: The Social and Cultural Context of European Witchcraft* (London: Blackwell, 2006), p.168; William Monter, 'Witchcraft Trials in France', in Levack (ed.), *Oxford Handbook of Witchcraft*, p.226.

59 Levack, *The Witch-Hunt in Early Modern Europe*, pp.84–90.

60 Lu Ann Homza, 'An Expert Lawyer and Reluctant Demonologist: Alonso de Salazar y Frías, Spanish Inquisitor', in Machielsen (ed.), *The Science of Demons*, pp.299–312; William Monter, 'Witchcraft in Iberia', in Levack (ed.), *Oxford Handbook of Witchcraft*, pp.268–275.

61 Lea (ed.), *Materials Toward a History of Witchcraft*, Volume 2, p.573.

62 Pau Castell Granados, 'The Inquisitor's Demon's: Nicolau Eymeric's *Directorium inquisitorium*', in Machielsen (ed), *The Science of Demons*, pp.19–34.

63 Fredrich Spee van Langenfeld, extract from *Cautio Criminalis* in Kors and Peters (eds), *Witchcraft in Europe*, p.428.

64 Goodare, *The European Witch-Hunt*, pp.208–216.

65 The letter is reproduced in full in Lara Apps and Andrew Gow, *Male Witches in Early Modern Europe* (Manchester: Manchester University Press, 2003), pp.159–165.

66 John H. Langberin, *Torture and the Law of Proof: Europe and England in the Ancien Régime* (Chicago, IL: University of Chicago Press, 1976), pp.73–128.

67 Malcolm Gaskell, *Witchfinders: A Seventeenth Century English Tragedy* (London: John Murray, 2005).

68 Rochelle Rojas, 'The Witches' Accomplice: Toads in Early Modern Navarre', *The Sixteenth Century Journal*, 51 (2020), pp.693–740.

69 Goodare, *The European Witch-Hunt*, pp.400–411.

70 Brian P. Levack, The Decline and End of Witchcraft Prosecutions'" in Levack (ed.), *Oxford Handbook of Witchcraft*, p.438; Brian P. Levack, 'State-Building and Witch-Hunting in Early Modern Europe', in Jonathan Barry, Marianne Hester, and Gareth Roberts (eds), *Witchcraft in Early Modern Europe: Studies in Culture and Belief* (Cambridge: Cambridge University Press, 1996), pp.109–110.

71 Thomas Robisheaux, 'The German Witch Trials', in Levack (ed.), *Oxford Handbook of Witchcraft*, p.180.

72 Modestin, 'Metamorphoses of the *Errores Gaziorum*', pp.57–58.

73 Goodare, *The European Witch-Hunt*, pp.45–46.

74 Wolfgang Behringer, *Witches and Witch-Hunts* (Cambridge: Polity, 2004), pp.76–77; Lea (ed.), *Materials Towards a History of Witchcraft*, Volume 1, p.251.

75 Behringer, *Witches and Witch-Hunts*, pp.68, 77–78.

76 Kors and Peters (eds), *Witchcraft in Europe*, pp.309–318.

77 Christian Pfister, 'Climatic Extremes, Recurrent Crises and Witch-Hunts: Strategies of European Societies in Coping with Exogenous Shocks in the Late Sixteenth and Early Seventeenth Centuries', *The Medieval History Journal*, 10 (2006), pp.33–73.

78 Robisheaux, 'The German Witch Trials', pp.189–190.

79 Behringer, *Witches and Witch-Hunts*, p.109; Robisheaux, 'The German Witch Trials', pp.184–185.

80 Monter, 'The Male Witches of Normandy', p.594.

81 Gary K. Waite, ' "Man is a Devil to Himself,': David Joris and the Rise of a Sceptical Tradition Towards the Devil in Early Modern Netherlands, 1540–1600', *Nederlands archief voor kerkgeschiedenis /Dutch Review of Church History*, 75 (1995), pp.1–30.

82 Reginald Scott, *The Discoverie of Witchcraft* (London: Henry Denham for William Brome, 1584), p.17.

83 Spee van Langenfeld, *Cautio Criminalis*, pp.187–198.

84 Edward Bever, 'Witchcraft Prosecutions and the Decline of Magic', *Journal of Interdisciplinary History*, 40 (2009), p.274; Spee van Langenfeld, *Cautio Criminalis,* pp.219–220.

85 Laveck, *The Witch-Hunt in Early Modern Europe*, pp.56–57.

86 Goodare, *The European Witch-Hunts*, pp.81–82; Kors and Peters (eds), *Witchcraft in Europe*, pp.317–318; Spee van Langenfeld, *Cautio Criminalis*, pp.xxxii–xxxiii.

87 Goodare, *The European Witch-Hunts*, pp.321–322.

88 Edward Bever, 'Witchcraft Prosecutions and the Decline of Magic', pp.263–293; Levack, 'The Decline and End of Witchcraft Prosecution', in *Oxford Handbook of Witchcraft*, pp.429–446.

89 Perez Zagorin, *How the Idea of Religious Toleration Came to the West* (Princeton, NJ: Princeton University Press, 2003), pp.97–144, 285–286.

90 Michael W. Hickson, 'Pierre Bayle and the Secularization of Conscience', *Journal of the History of Ideas*, 79 (2018), pp. 199–220

91 Walsham, *Charitable Hatred*, pp.300–329; Benjamin Kaplan, *Divided by Faith: Religious Conflict and the Practice of Toleration in Early Modern Europe* (Cambridge, MA: Harvard University Press, 2007), pp.267–268.

92 Johannes Dillinger, 'On Politics, State Building and Witch-Hunting', in Levack (ed), *Oxford Handbook of Witchcraft*, p.545.

93 Noel D. Johnson and Mark Koyama, 'Taxes, Lawyers, and the Decline of Witch Trials in France', *Journal of Law & Economics,* 57, 1 (2014), pp.77–112, and *Persecution and Toleration: The Long Road to Religious Freedom* (Cambridge: Cambridge University Press, 2019), pp.214–220.

7   'God's Fire Impressed the Mark of Slavery Upon You'

Race and Slavery, c.1450–1888

In November 1596, one hundred captive African men, women, and children were shipped into the Dutch port of Middelburg. The local authorities promptly freed them, pointedly observing that there was no slavery in the province of Zeeland. This bold act was not untypical of its day. Europeans had become increasingly intolerant of slavery inside their own countries. In 1425, a papal bull had threatened Christians who enslaved their co-religionists with excommunication. By the sixteenth century, monarchs across the emerging nation states of the continent boasted of their subjects' freedoms. Authorities opposed the presence of slaves within their borders. In 1567, an English court refused the entry of a Russian slave into the country. In 1571, magistrates in Toulouse had freed the slave of a visiting Genoese merchant. A witness to that decision, the political philosopher Jean Bodin, asserted that 'the slaves of strangers so soon as they set foot in Fraunce become franke and free'. Indeed, slavery, he argued, was 'directly contrary to human nature', leading the enslaved to ferment 'servile warres' and the enslavers to commit 'so many murders, cruelties and detestable villanies'. Within Europe, the ancient institution of slavery was in decline.[1]

Yet the eventual fate of those who had been brought in chains to Middelburg revealed a striking historical paradox. Just as the peoples of Europe were rejecting slavery within their own borders, they were acquiescing to, or indeed participating in, the enslavement of millions of Africans in their newly established colonies. The established legal and ethical boundaries that had come to govern the lives of the people of early modern England, France, the Netherlands, and Spain, were put aside abroad, to facilitate the persecution of Africans and the indigenous populations of the Americas (Africans will be used here as a convenient shorthand for 'sub-Saharan Africans'). This historical process has been termed 'moral regression'.[2] The captain of the Middelburg slave ship appealed against the decision to free his captives to the *Staten Generaal*, the national assembly, in The Hague. There may have been no slavery in Zeeland, but, after some prevarication, the assembly granted the enslaver permission to do as he wished with his cargo. Nine

DOI: 10.4324/9781003494331-8

of the unfortunate Africans had since died. The others were shipped to the Americas for sale.[3]

They were part of the largest forced migration in history. Over the course of some four hundred years, *circa* 1492–1860, some twelve million people were enslaved in Africa and transported against their will across the Atlantic.[4] There, most of those who survived the horrors of the ocean crossing (and their descendants) would toil relentlessly in violently coercive, agricultural slave labour camps. These 'plantations' were the first great economic engines of modern imperialism, the foundations upon which western global hegemony would ultimately be built. This episode of persecution was distinguished by its four-century duration, its discriminatory racial basis, its sheer human scale (encompassing both the millions transported and their descendants), the pervasive asymmetrical militarised violence with which slave regimes were policed, the brutal and ruthless manner in which unfree labour was exploited, the exposure to material deprivation, and the myriad severe harms to which the enslaved were subjected, including murder, sexual abuse, family separations, torture, and mutilation.

It is tempting to understand the moral regression that facilitated the enslavement of Africans, with all its concomitant horrors, as rooted simply in greed and materialism. According to the Trinidadian historian Eric Williams, writing in 1944, 'Here then is the origin of Negro slavery. The reason was economic, not racial, it had to do not with the color of the laborer, but with the cheapness of the labor'. For Williams, the 'subhuman characteristics [of Africans] so widely pleaded, were only later rationalizations to justify a simple economic fact: that the colonies needed labor and resorted to Negro labor because it was cheapest and best'.[5]

This view was for a long time something of an orthodoxy among historians. And Williams was certainly correct in pointing to the utility of race as a legitimisation of the ruthless exploitative economics of colonialism. It is, however, less clear that ideologies of race were simply 'a later rationalisation', born of modern imperialism. Even before the Atlantic slave trade was established in the latter half of the fifteenth century, Africans were already the objects of powerful stereotypes that characterised them as naturally servile and innately inferior. Such 'proto-racial' beliefs were bound up tightly with well-established religious and cultural prejudices. They help to explain why, at much the same point in history that Europeans were concluding that slavery was 'directly contrary to human nature', they were nevertheless so willing to enslave Africans. The further evolution of racial beliefs in the context of settler colonialism, into a hegemonic political ideology that underpinned white supremacy, ensured that, in the Americas, slavery would survive into the latter half of the nineteenth century. Race slavery would end only when a combination of active resistance by the enslaved and a campaign of political abolitionism made it untenable.

It is, at this point, important to define carefully what is meant here by race and racism.

The essential idea of race is the belief that humankind can be divided into distinct biological categories. According to this belief, the physical, intellectual, and moral characteristics of these different categories of people are fixed, and inherited from generation to generation. Races might be most visibly identified by their phenotype: observable bodily characteristics such as skin pigmentation, skull shape, or hair colour and texture. Yet the most significant differences are held to be inner qualities, such as capacity for reason and for virtue. Racism is the political expression of this belief: some races are superior to others and suited by nature to dominate the inferior races.

The words themselves are of no great antiquity. Race and its European cognates (such as *razza* in Italian or *raça* in Portuguese) first appeared in texts of the late fifteenth century. It originally lacked many of its modern connotations but had some sense of linking biological descent to character. 'Racism' is a yet more recent neologism. Richard Henry Pratt was the first superintendent of Carlisle Indian School, foundered in 1879 to educate Native American children away from the reservations. As an advocate of cultural assimilation, he was a critic of government policies that segregated Native Americans. In 1902, he denounced them as constituting 'racism'. By the 1930s, the word was in common usage, largely in response to the emerging political programme of the Nazis in Germany.[6]

At much the same time, anthropologists, such as Franz Boas in the United States and Ashley Montagu in the United Kingdom, were scientifically debunking the basis of biological race thinking. They demonstrated that differences in phenotype were entirely superficial and were no indicators of heritable traits of character or intellect. As Montagu observed, biological race was a 'myth', a social construct to justify one group's domination of another.[7] That the myth had proved so potent was in part a consequence of just how deeply rooted it was historically.

There were four main strands of pre-modern thought and practice that coalesced into modern racial ideologies: a classical tradition, linking supposedly innate and inheritable characteristics of national groups to their environment; a religious tradition, common to Judaism, Christianity, and Islam, that associated dark skin with sin and held Africans to be the descendants of Ham, cursed to slavery; a European tradition that linked bloodline and breeding to character and nobility, and a practice of slavery along the Iberian frontier of Christendom and Islam that both perpetuated the institution, and created and sustained notions of African servility.

Environmental determination (the supposed effects of climate upon character) and a corollary belief that some peoples were naturally suited to servitude was an intellectual inheritance from ancient Greece. For the philosopher Aristotle (384–322 BCE), heat produced lassitude. Easterners such as the Persians were thus 'endowed with skill and intelligence but are deficient in spirit; and this is why they continue to be peoples of subjects and slaves'. The peoples of northern Europe, in contrast, were shaped by the less hospitable environments in which they lived: '[they] are full of spirit, but deficient in skill and intelligence; and this is why they continue to remain comparatively free but attain no political development and show no capacity for governing others'. The Greeks, Aristotle noted, 'intermediate in geographical position, unite the qualities of both sets of people'. They possessed 'both spirit and intelligence ... and to show a capacity for governing every other people'.[8] Explaining differences between populations in terms of climate remained popular for centuries. The French Enlightenment philosopher Montesquieu made much the same case in 1748.[9]

Since this environmental thesis seeks explanations for differences between peoples based in climate and geography, rather than biological descent, it might seem neither racial nor even proto-racial in character. Yet as Benjamin Isaac has observed, both the Greeks and the Romans seem to have believed that once characteristics had been acquired, then they were indeed passed to subsequent generations, becoming stable and permanent. The effects were invariably detrimental. Ascribing strongly to a belief in the inevitability of decline, the Greeks and Romans do not appear to have believed that a servile Asiatic, or their child, would grow bold and free in a more bracing northern environment.[10] For Aristotle, some peoples were 'natural slaves', incapable of the reasoned, autonomous, practical decision making that would allow them to live truly worthwhile lives. Their reduction to slavery – to live as mere instruments of some master's will – was, thus, no injustice.[11]

It is also likely that classical culture bequeathed to the Abrahamic religions (Judaism, Christianity, and Islam) the association of dark skin with demons, sin, and the spirits of the dead. In Suetonius's account of the life of the emperor Caligula, Ethiopians appear in a nocturnal performance as representatives of the underworld. The author Lucian described being accosted by a demon 'filthy, long-haired and blacker than darkness', that he drove off by bellowing a curse 'in the Egyptian tongue'.[12]

Similarly, in early Christian writings, demons and the Devil are consistently described as appearing as Egyptians, Ethiopians (a generic term for Africans), or simply as black. In the late first-century *Epistles of Barnabas*, the author asserts that 'the way of the black one is crooked and full of cursing ... '. In the late second-century *Acts of Peter*, a demon is described as 'a most evil looking woman, an *Aithiops* not *Aigyptios* [Ethiopian not Egyptian] but altogether black'. Influential early Christian theologians, such as Tertullian, also deployed this useful symbolic colourism. He crafted what Gay L. Byron has referred to as an 'ethno-political rhetoric', in which both *Aegypto* and *Aethiopiae* represented sinful nations threatened with God's judgement for their pagan practices. Fourth- and fifth-century monastic literature from Egypt consistently invoked Ethiopian women as diabolical and sexual threats. One desert-dwelling ascetic was, thus, tempted by 'the work of the devil' in the form of 'an Ethiopian woman, smelly and disgusting in appearance'. This powerful association between blackness, the Devil and sin, linked to a rhetoric that very clearly identified distinct ethnic groups, particularly Ethiopians, is not simply more evidence for the existence of ancient proto-racism. It also serves to warn against that tendency to differentiate sharply between pre-modern religious prejudices and modern racial prejudices. Their deepest roots were entangled.[13]

This powerful symbolic blackness left a legacy for Europe into the medieval period. Skin colour continued to be a powerful signifier in art, iconography, and religious literature. The association between black skin and the Devil, sin, and the inner blackness of the soul, remained strong. Nor was this simply a question of pigmentation; those depicted as the torturers and executors of John the Baptist and Christ, on objects such as the Winchester Psalter (*c*.1150), were frequently portrayed with a clear African phenotype, visible in facial features and hair.[14]

The religio-symbolic meaning attached to black skin was evident in the Muslim world too. 'Ubaydallāh, made governor of Sīstān in 671 CE, and a descendant of one of the Companions of the Prophet, was derided for his partial African descent. In a satire against him, one poet sneered, 'The children of a stinking Nubian black – God put no light in their complexions'.[15] A particular association of Africans with slavery was also established by the seventh century. Once Arab armies had conquered Egypt, 639–642 CE, then *bilād al-Sudan*, 'the land of the blacks', became accessible as a source of abundant labour for domestic service, mining, and large-scale agricultural production. As they were *kuffār*, unbelievers, they could legitimately be captured and enslaved in *jihad*, holy war. The Islamic trans-Saharan and oceanic slave trades probably saw in the region of eleven million transported over a period of 1,300 years, from *c*.600 CE to 1900. The Islamic Republic of Mauritania legally abolished slavery only in 1981, the last country in the world to do so.[16] A proto-racist ideology is evidenced by the very real distinctions between the treatment of enslaved Africans and those of other origins. Two Arabic words were used for those held in bondage. The word *'abd* was the traditional word for *any* slave, but came to be almost wholly associated with Africans. Others were referred to by different terms, prominently *mamlūk*, which, conventionally, had meant 'one who is owned'.[17]

The *'abd* fetched a lower price than the *mamlūk*, who might be ransomed by Christian or Jewish co-religionists or exchanged for a Muslim captive. Yet higher prices, too, seemed to reflect a value placed on fairer complexions. The wealthiest men favoured Circassian or Slavic women as concubines. In turn, Habash (Abyssinian/Ethiopian) women were favoured by well-to-do merchants and traders over darker-skinned Zanj.[18] The *'abd* were, overwhelmingly, bound to menial labour, often of the most dangerous and debasing kind. They toiled in the gold mines of 'Allāqī in Egypt and the copper mines of the Sahara. In Iraq and Persia, they drained marshes, dug ditches, and cleared salt flats in appalling conditions that provoked massive servile insurrections. The most serious, the Zanj Rebellion, lasted over 15 years from 868 to 883 CE, and perhaps 300,000 people died in the fighting.[19]

One of the most significant sources for the ideology of black racial inferiority within Islam was scriptural. However, it was not derived from the Qur'ān but from the Judeo-Christian tradition. The Book of Genesis (9:18–27) recounts the strange story of the curse of Ham: following the flood, Noah had become a farmer and established a vineyard. He became drunk upon the wine he produced and passed out naked in his tent. There, his youngest son, Ham, saw him lying naked and informed his brothers, Shem and Japhet. These, respectfully averting their gaze, covered their father. When Noah awoke and learned of Ham's behaviour, he cursed the descendants of Ham's son, Canaan, to be slaves of the descendants of Shem and Japhet.

Nowhere in scripture was Ham, or his descendants, associated with Africans. Yet a tradition identifying Canaan as the ancestor of dark-skinned people eventually emerged. A fourth-century Syriac Christian treatise, *The Cave of Treasure*, identified Egyptians, Kushites, and Indians as Canaan's descendants. An Arabic translation added 'other blacks' to this list. Once the tradition had passed into Islamic culture, it became a powerful legitimising myth for the enslavement of Africans. The ninth-century scholar Ibn Qutayba gave this version: '[Ham] was a white man having a beautiful face and form. But Allah changed his colour and the colour of his descendants because of his father's curse ... They are the *Sūdan*'.[20]

The tradition linking the curse of Ham to a state of natural servitude inherited by Africans is significant not simply for its role in justifying slavery within Islamic societies, but because it was shared with Christendom and Judaism. Benjamin of Tudela, a Jewish intellectual from Navarre, wrote a chronicle of his travels in Asia and Africa, in 1169–1171. Of those taken in raiding south of Egypt, he wrote, 'there is a people among them [the Egyptians] who [are] like animals ... They go about naked and have not the intelligence of ordinary men ... And these are the black slaves, the sons of Ham'.[21]

That Benjamin was a resident of the Iberian Peninsula was itself significant, for there the practices that shaped modern Atlantic slavery took root. It had been conquered by Islamic invaders from Morocco in 711–18 CE, but by 1248 only Granada remained under Muslim rule. The institution of slavery had survived from antiquity in the region because conflict between Christian and Muslim polities generated captives, 'unbelievers', who could thus legitimately be enslaved. (The Roman Justinian Code that shaped medieval western jurisprudence allowed capture in war, birth to enslaved parents, and self-sale as the legitimate grounds for enslavement.) Furthermore, the Islamic African slave trade was linked to a Mediterranean network that brought both enslaved Slavs (from whom derived the English word 'slaves') and 'black Moors' (Africans) to Spain, from the tenth century.[22]

The Iberian frontier also appears to have been the site of another key conceptual development linking proto-racial to modern racial ideology: the emergence of the notion of *limpieza de sangre* (purity of blood). 'Blood purity' was initially tied primarily to religious identity, offering another sharp reminder of the blurry boundaries between pre-modern religious and putatively modern biological prejudices. The fifteenth century was an age of renewed religious conflict and nation building. Ferdinand II of Aragon and Isabella of Castille united their respective realms in 1479 and then went on to conquer Grenada in 1492. This created a united Spain, with large Muslim and Jewish populations, but where an emerging sense of ethno-national identity was strongly linked to Catholicism. Under pressure, many Jews and Muslims had converted, the so-called 'New Christians'. Yet the (formerly Jewish) *conversos* and the (formerly Muslim) *Moriscos* were often denied either ecclesiastical or secular positions of prestige or high public status, which were reserved for 'Old Christians', those of unimpeachable caste and lineage. *Limpieza de sangre* statutes proliferated across Spain, allowing for legal discrimination against Christians of Jewish or Muslim descent.[23]

The idea of *limpieza de sangre* would be swiftly grafted to the fifteenth century's colour prejudices. Once the colonisation of the 'New World' was under way, statutes were deployed to prevent both those of African and Native American descent from gaining royal or ecclesiastical appointments. The idea of 'whiteness' came to be understood as representing a descent 'uncontaminated' by any admixture of black or native blood. In areas colonised by Spain, an elaborate (if in practice somewhat malleable and negotiable) social hierarchy of *castas* (racial castes) developed, where those of mixed descent were characterised, and their life chances determined, according to their quotient of Spanish, Native American, or African blood. The *mestizo* was the child of a Spanish father and a Native American mother; the *mulatto* of Spanish and African parentage.[24]

Such attention to descent represented, alongside the idea of purity, a long-standing European fascination with lineage, especially that of noble families. Here, too, we can see how cultural prejudices, in this case originally around social class, elided into biological explanations for difference and distinction. Charles de Miramon has noted how in thirteenth-century scholastic literature a discourse connecting innate nobility to blood descent emerged. While the emphasis, inevitably, was on the distinguished characteristics of noble or royal blood, it is interesting to note that the concept also allowed for the inheritance of negative traits. Thus were the children of traitors and heretics subject to legal sanctions for the sins of their parents, condemned by their 'faulty blood' (*sanguine improbato*). From the perspective of proto-racial ideology, the key development was the extension of this blood relationship beyond immediate family. By the early fourteenth century, supposed hereditary virtues became markers of a wider group, a species of fictive kinship with a shared and common identity, characterised by its good blood: the nobility. For de Miramon, 'Hereditary is not the ordered genealogical tree of a pedigree but the more diffuse soul of a group. The notion of race developed out of this legacy'.[25]

Ultimately so too did the modern vocabulary of prejudice. Many in medieval society had a sophisticated understanding of how to breed for desirable characteristics in horses, hawks, and working canines. The earliest recorded use of the word 'race' appears in the context of hunting dogs. Jacques de Brézé, seneschal of Normandy, wrote a poem commemorating a 1481 hunt, in which two pedigree bitches are singled out and praised for the danger they posed to the deer: 'your race is their enemy'. He then adds a seminal corollary: '[hunting is the] nicest possible trade. It should come to nobles by race when they are not soldiering'. In an age of state formation, it should come as no surprise that very soon this politically valuable concept of race was being applied to a yet wider shared fictive kinship group: a people or nation. In a 1552 French Latin dictionary, Robert Estienne suggested that 'race' should be translated as *stirps*, *gens*, or *sanguine* (stock, people/tribe, or bloodline).[26]

Thus, when, in 1441, a Portuguese ship's captain, Antão Gonçalves, violently kidnapped a man and a woman from the West African shoreline, their fate had already been sealed by the colour of their skin: enslavement.[27] The mentality that informed Gonçalves' behaviour in this small, ugly incident was shaped by deep currents, old and new: the religious prejudices that associated African phenotypes with sin and Satan, the licence to enslave 'heathens', and the particular environment of the Iberian Peninsula, a frontier where Christendom and Islam had coexisted, fought, traded, and exchanged ideas, including the notion of the innately servile character of 'black Moors'. There, too, the idea that descent, expressed as blood purity, conferred full membership of a community, had acquired a particular force, applied first to the detriment of those Iberians of Jewish or Muslim heritage, but later to be brought to bear on Africans and the peoples of the Americas. A broader but similar European ideology had also emerged, a species of fictive kinship, in which imagined shared bloodlines came to define peoples and their characteristics: race.

Antão Gonçalves soon returned to the coast of West Africa, in the company of a Portuguese knight, Nuno Tristao. Together they waged war on the unsuspecting inhabitants, landing under cover of darkness to attack peaceful settlements, and finally returning to Portugal with ten more captives. It was a small haul, but enough to impress the heir to the throne, Prince Henry. With his patronage, Lançarote da Ilha, collector of royal taxes in the Algarve port of Lagos, organised a larger expedition. Six armed caravels set out to capture 'black Moors'. They returned on 8 August 1444, unloading 235 forlorn captives on the quay at Lagos, ushering in 'a new era in the social, economic and ideological history' of Europe, Africa and, soon after, the Americas. In 1494, a German traveller, Dr Jerome Münzer, expressed astonishment at the 'really extraordinary' number of enslaved Africans in Lisbon, many of them labouring in the royal iron works.[28]

Just as proto-racial ideologies and the nascent Atlantic slave trade itself pre-dated the 'discovery' of the 'New World', so, too, did the earliest development of the brutal and exploitative economic enterprise, the plantation, that drove demand for African labour. Sidney Mintz has usefully defined the plantation as

> ... a politico-economic invention, a colonial frontier institution, combining non-European slaves and European capital, technology, and managerial skill with territorial control of free or cheap subtropical lands in the mass, monocrop production of agricultural commodities for European markets.[29]

The earliest of such ventures in the Atlantic world were established in Madeira in the mid-1450s, for the production of sugar. The cultivation of sugar cane had itself been learned from Arabic agriculture in the eastern Mediterranean. In the tenth and eleventh centuries, many sugar-producing regions, such as Cyprus, Crete ('Candida'), and Sicily, had come under Christian control. Since the large-scale production of this crop had always depended to some degree on unfree labour, the merchants of Venice and Genoa were soon dealing in Slavic captives. This source of bondspeople ended with the fall of Constantinople to the Ottomans in 1453, cutting the enslavers off from the Black Sea. Yet, as sugar production spread westward, new sources opened up. The original labour force in Madeira was mixed, with free Portuguese migrant labourers a majority up until the mid-sixteenth century. Yet an enslaved workforce was present from the earliest days too: Muslim Moroccans and Berbers, 'Black Moors', and Guanches. The latter were the indigenous people of the Canary Isles, whose colonisation, in the name of Castile, had been initiated by the military adventurer Jean de Bethancourt in 1402.[30]

The treatment of the Guanches was both redolent of the proto-racist assumptions that had already formed and also predictive of the fate of the indigenous peoples of the Americas. They were dismissed by the king of Portugal in 1436 as 'nearly wild men who inhabit the forests [and] are not united by a common religion, nor are they bound by the chains of law ... living like animals'. Thus, papal blessing was received for the mission to civilise and convert the isles and enslave those who resisted the process. As their numbers dwindled, their place on plantations was taken by Africans.[31] Ensured of workers from this source, further experiments in plantation economics followed in the Azores, Fernando Po, and São Tomé. On this latter island, the plantations were worked by captives from the Kongo and Angola. Alongside Capo Verde, São Tomé would emerge as a vital *entrepôt* in the transatlantic trade as demand for enslaved African labour grew.[32]

Slave raiding by Europeans themselves had a limited future in the region; it was fraught with risk, and the European ability to penetrate far inland was limited both by the military strength of local polities and their susceptibility to disease. It was better to establish trade networks, building 'factories' (fortified trading posts) on the coast, such as on the Gold Coast at Elmina (modern Ghana), in 1482. In many cases, the new arrivals could simply join existing trade networks, including those for slaves, established by Muslim merchants. Many of the polities that the European slave traders dealt with were peoples who had converted to Islam, such as the Songhai Empire. These then waged *jihad* against their unbelieving neighbours, generating captives for trade. In other instances, the enslavers were not themselves Muslims, but often neighboured Muslim lands, and had long-established patterns of supplying them with captives, such as the Ashanti, Dahomey, and Oyo.[33]

The violence that so often accompanied enslavement was just one contributing factor to an appalling mortality associated with the Atlantic slave trade. Those taken alive would then endure brutality, sickness, and exhaustion, both en route to and within the coastal slaving forts. Many succumbed. Once the transatlantic slave trade to the Americas was established, the subsequent sea voyage, the 'Middle Passage', itself became a struggle for survival. Victims were packed onto the ships. Each adult had typically only five to seven square feet of deck space, where they spent most of the journey, chained, lying in filth and vomit. Their mortality rates on these 'floating dungeons', as one former crewman described them, varied between 10 and 20 per cent.[34]

The voyage could last two to three months. Fevers and dysentery, the systemic violence used to cow the enslaved, storms, suicidal despair, and inadequate rations: all took their grim toll. In some instances, the enslaved were simply murdered at sea. One hundred and thirty-three sick captives on the slave ship *Zong* in 1781 were drowned on the captain's orders. The ship was short of water, and they were deemed expendable. Indeed, in line with the ruthless commercial logic of the trade, their loss might be made good through an insurance claim. Landfall did not put an end to the suffering and the dying. The process of adjustment to the new environment and the harsh plantation labour regime, known to contemporaries as 'seasoning', took yet more lives. The Jamaican slave-owner and colonial administrator Edward Long calculated that a quarter of those who survived the Middle Passage died within 18 months of their arrival on the island.[35]

One early visitor, in about 1482, to the emerging West African oceanic slaving frontier, including Elmina and Madeira, was the young Genoese navigator Christopher Columbus. A decade later, he crossed the Atlantic and set foot on the island he called Hispaniola (today divided between the Dominican Republic and Haiti). He had sought a trade route to the 'Indies' (South East Asia), but instead had inadvertently stumbled upon a continent whose existence was hitherto unknown to him. His original vision, of establishing monopolistic trading posts with the east, was swiftly put to one side. In its place, he offered his employer, the crown of Castile, what would become the blueprint for the colonisation and economic exploitation of the Americas: expropriation of indigenous peoples and the use of forced labour in large-scale commercial agriculture and the mining of precious metals: 'Here there is only wanting a settlement and the order to the people to do what is required …

So that they are good to be ordered about, to work and sow, and do all that may be necessary',[36] he enthused to their highnesses Ferdinand and Isabella. As he made his case, he explicitly compared the Taínos people of Hispaniola with the Guanches of the Canaries. He situated the future of the 'New World' firmly into the ideological assumptions and economics of the Atlantic system that he had witnessed taking root off the coast of West Africa.[37]

Early experiments to base plantation economies on enslaved Native American labour invariably failed, although the Spanish, Portuguese, and English all attempted them. The demographic collapse of native populations, traumatised by violence, exhausted by the ruthless discipline of plantation work regimes, and exposed to unfamiliar diseases such as smallpox, was the main reason for this. The fate of the Taíno stands as a tragic example. By the 1540s, their population had fallen from perhaps 500,000 to fewer than 500. Other enslaved Native Americans merely shared their fate. An Italian, Girolamo Benzoni, spent 15 years in the Caribbean, 1541–1556, where he witnessed what happened to those who arrived in chains to replace the Taínos. Having commented on the cruelty with which they were treated, branded on face and arms, 'bartered for wine, flour, biscuit, and other requisite things', he then noted: 'although an almost infinite number of the inhabitants of the mainland have been brought to these islands as slaves, they have nearly all since died'.[38]

Horrified by the death tolls and keen to win native souls for Christ, both Spanish and Portuguese clergy vigorously campaigned to end the enslavement of Native Americans. The Portuguese Jesuit António Vieira would secure such legislation in 1655. Yet he, and others like him, such as the sixteenth-century Spanish Dominican friar Bartolomé de las Casas, also favoured the importation of enslaved Africans, to secure bonded labour for the colonies. Their preconceived notions of African servility easily accommodated this apparent contradiction. In one sermon, Vieira urged enslaved Africans to accept their lot: 'God's fire impressed the mark of slavery upon you ... Your vocation is the imitation of Christ's patience'.[39]

While slavery was practised throughout the European colonies of North and South America, it achieved its highest demographic concentration and greatest economic and political significance where agricultural plantations were developed: Brazil, the West Indies, and Britain's southern colonies in North America, later the southern states of the United States. The Spanish and the Portuguese, with their established links to the plantation systems of Madeira, Fernando Po, and São Tomé, were swift to start importing enslaved Africans. The northern European colonists – the English, French, and Dutch – would emulate them. England's first colony had been established at Jamestown, Virginia, in 1607. Its early years were precarious in the extreme, but in 1619 its labour force was augmented by '20 Negars'. These had been traded for supplies to the colony's leaders by an English privateer *White Lion*. The captives had been seized from a Portuguese slaver off the coast of Yucatan (Mexico).[40]

However, Barbados was England's first significant plantation society and became the prototype for those that followed, both in the West Indies and the southern colonies. From 1629 to 1634, its main crop was tobacco. Thereafter, tobacco prices fell and, anyhow, the Barbadian leaf had proved inferior to the Virginian. Barbadian planters briefly experimented with indigo and cotton, but by 1643 had switched decisively to sugar. Hugely profitable, by 1680, sugar accounted for 80 per cent of the island's arable land, 90 per cent of its labour force, and 90 per cent of its export earnings. This was the 'sugar revolution' that shaped agriculture in the British Caribbean for 300 years, with Jamaica coming to dominate production by 1740.[41]

By 1680, the labour force was overwhelmingly enslaved. Up until about 1660, indentured servants (Europeans working out a fixed term of service, three to seven years) had been cheaper than slaves. Yet the costs of importing servants rose steadily. Domestic economic prospects improved, wages grew, and there was less incentive to take the risky step of emigration. As a result, supply contracted. Purchasing indentures became more expensive. To attract white labour, Caribbean planters had to offer better terms, shorter contracts, improved housing and diet, skilled roles rather than back-breaking toil. That, too, drove costs up. Over the same period, the cost of slaves declined. Supply increased. In 1663, the Company of Royal Adventurers of England was charted to supply Barbadian planters with field hands at £17.00 per head, compared to £40.00 in 1638. By the late 1660s, the price of slave labour had fallen yet further to some 35 per cent below the level of the 1640s. The cost of indentured labour increased by over 300 per cent over the same period.[42]

Enslaved labourers offered another advantage, in that they could be driven relentlessly for maximum productivity. Even with the appalling mortality rates associated with the cane fields, an enslaved field hand generally laboured for a year longer than the average indenture lasted. And they worked in highly regimented gangs, sun-up to sun-down, often under the management of ex-soldiers such as the displaced former Royalist cavalier Richard Ligon. He left a vivid account of how disciplined and ruthlessly organised Barbadian plantations had become by the 1650s, when the workforce still consisted of a mixture of 'Christian servants' and 'poor negroes'.[43] They were organised in gangs, each of which was employed in a particular task:

> ... some were to weed, some were to plant, some were to fell wood, some were to cleave it, some were to saw it into boards, some to fetch home, some to cut Canes, Others to attend the Ingenio, Boyling-house, Still-house, and Cureing-house; some for the harvest to cut the Maize ... others to gather Provisions ... and dress it at fit times for their dinners and suppers.

Individual productivity was maximised by a mixture of coercion (physical punishment) and incentives (for example, the possibility of 'promotion' to a materially rewarding supervisory role). The balance between these two, Ligon recorded, was, in general, a reflection on the managerial culture fostered by the planter and his agent, and could thus be 'mercifull' or 'cruell'. The 'cruell' regime would encourage the use of physical violence by overseers, the whip, or worse, to discipline plantation labourers and drive them to yet greater exactions in their work. A 'discreeter' and 'better natur'd' planter would discourage, or at least mitigate, what they deemed to be excessive brutality. It should, of course, be clearly noted that, in this context, the distinction between 'cruell' and 'mercifull' was a relative one, a difference of degree, not kind. No plantation management regime, even the 'better natured' ones, disavowed physical coercion as the basis of ensuring labour discipline and productivity. The infliction of severe harm was intrinsic to slavery.[44]

A similar pattern emerged in the Chesapeake colonies of Virginia and Maryland. Planters there were able to attract indentured servants for longer by offering better prospects, for example, more land after the end of their term. Ultimately, however, the broad cost equation was the same, and slaves began to supplant servants across these colonies from the 1660s onwards.[45] Yet there was more happening here too. The wealthiest Chesapeake planters did not simply respond to market signals. They were a small elite that strove with deliberation to establish and sustain their political and economic dominance. This they achieved at the expense of Native Americans, whose lands they expropriated, as well as poor whites, whose access to resources, especially the best land, they restricted, and the enslaved, whose labour they ruthlessly exploited in clearing and working that stolen land.

Race slavery was integral to this bid for mastery, politically and economically. It provided workers who could be ruthlessly exploited, to a degree to which neither free labour nor indentured servants could have been subject. Pregnant women and nursing mothers would be expected to perform heavy field labour. Young children would tote water, scare birds, or clear trash. Even the oldest slaves, too weak for field work, would assist with the livestock, in the kitchens, or taking care of infants. At Thomas Jefferson's Virginia plantation Monticello, the living quarters were arranged to ensure all made a productive contribution to work. The dwellings of the enslaved were situated close together so that the 'superannuated women', no longer capable of fieldwork, could look after the young children, who themselves were to act as 'nurses' to the infants, freeing their mothers for labouring duties. Everyone worked.[46]

Politically, race also drove a wedge between those who might otherwise have united in opposition to the great planters. Having seized land from Native Americans, they opposed land reform that might have distributed it more widely. They acquired 'headrights' (which secured grants of land) by importing servants and slaves. They exploited the powerful offices they held to bend the laws and safeguard the extensive estates they had amassed. The great planters might, therefore, have expected unified resistance from the dispossessed, the defrauded, and the enchained. However, such potential unity was undermined by race. Patronage and privilege were offered to favoured servants. Aspirational whites might be offered positions as overseers, with the opportunity to purchase slaves of their own.[47] Poor whites would be motivated by the fear of servile insurrection and mobilised in support of the planter regime by mandatory service in slave patrols. Even Native Americans were employed by the slave-holding regime, to hunt runaways and maroons (those who had absconded and formed communities in remote locations). Race was thus a powerful tool for maintaining elite hegemony by setting the exploited against one another.[48]

The potential for a unified opposition to planter hegemony was not a phantasm. In 1676, a recent English immigrant to Virginia, Nathaniel Bacon, had led an abortive rebellion, which had rallied both servants and the enslaved in opposition to the colony's governor Sir William Berkeley. Doubtless Bacon's rebellion focused the minds of the planter elite on the possibility of such a dangerous alliance. Yet by that point, the fostering of racial hostility among poor whites towards Africans was already established. In 1669, Hannah Warwick, an indentured servant, had fled a plantation where she had been under the authority of 'a negro overseer'. She was arrested and tried for running away. Yet she successfully argued that she was not bound to obey a 'negro' and thus was not punished.[49]

While the presence of a 'negro overseer' supervising white labourers suggests there was still a degree of flexibility in the status of Africans at this point, the court's decision was indicative of the hardening of racial attitudes. Indeed, plantation inventories from the 1650s strongly suggest that the wealthiest planters had already made the decision to purchase more enslaved Africans than indentured servants, even though they cost more at that point. This, thus, represents a conscious preference for slavery, rather than an unthinking decision shaped by economics.[50] In Virginia, at least, the relative shifts in labour costs over the 1660s merely catalysed the transformation.

Ideological factors did not simply shape the preference for slaves rather than servants; they sustained the oppression of the enslaved too. While violence was the principle means by which slavery was upheld, planters also developed further tools to control a workforce prone to resistance and flight. Anthony Parent has identified 'an ideology of patriarchism and a strategy of slave proselytism' as key developments to maintain plantation discipline. The former emphasised the formation of society based around the untrammelled supremacy of the father figure – in this instance, the large-scale planter. The latter enjoined a form of Christianity upon the enslaved that stressed obedience to one's enslaver and stoic acceptance of one's lot in life.[51]

In the formative years of plantation slavery in North America, English planters had been loath to allow their slaves to convert, since they justified their enslavement by their 'heathenism'. Richard Ligon had pleaded with one Barbadian planter to allow the baptism of one enslaved man, 'as ingenious, as honest, and as good natur'd poor soul, as ever wore black, or eat green'. The planter had refused because 'being once a Christian, he could no more account him a Slave, and so lose the hold they had of them as Slaves'.[52]

By the early eighteenth century, colonial legislatures had crafted novel laws, breaking with English precedents, to close down such potential routes to freedom. For example, the Virginia slave codes of 1705 stipulated that slaves were all persons 'who were not Christians in their native country … notwithstanding a conversion to Christianity afterwards'. This iniquitous principle was easily extended to their children too, in the unspoken doctrine Rebecca Goetz has termed 'hereditary heathenism'.[53] Such a useful, if morally regressive, legal innovation allowed religion to be bent to the enslavers' purpose. In 1724, the Reverend Hugh Jones observed that 'Christianity encourages and orders them to become more humble and better servants'.[54]

Patriarchism offered a stern and uncompromising framework for hierarchical authority. From the late 1730s onwards, it acquired a somewhat softer edge, in appearance if not reality. Patriarchism gave way, ostensibly, to an ideology of paternalism. This preserved the extended kinship metaphor but placed a greater emphasis on shared obligations and responsibilities. It stressed the putative benefits of dependant status: protection, care in childhood, sickness and ill-health, material well-being. The roots of this change were largely religious. Britain and its North American colonies were, at this moment, swept by religious revivalism: 'the Great Awakening'. Evangelical preachers worked for the Christian reform of society and the rejection of social evils. For many, that reform now included slavery, which John Wesley, the founder of Methodism, denounced roundly as 'the sum of all villainies'.[55]

In 1740, the Anglican cleric George Whitefield, dispatched to South Carolina and the new colony of Georgia, seemed similarly sure of that view. He castigated enslavers in an open letter: 'Your Slaves … work as hard if not harder than the Horses … upon the most trifling Provocation, [they are] cut with Knives, and had Forks thrown into their Flesh'. What he saw of their treatment left Whitefield convinced that the enslaved he encountered across the South would be better off dead. Although unsure of 'whether it be lawful for Christians to buy slaves', he was confident that 'it is sinful, when bought, to use them … as though they were Brutes'.[56] From Whitefield, however, this became a call for better treatment rather than emancipation.

The impact of the Great Awakening on slavery was shaped by its regional and cultural context. In Britain and the northern colonies, it became a wellspring of anti-slavery thought that would develop into the political abolitionism of the late eighteenth century. In the southern colonies, it spawned an enduring legitimising myth of the plantation as a community rather than a slave labour camp. In this vaunted idyll, the planter headed an extended kinship group. This was bound by strong, personal ties and mutuality and set apart from the ugly, exploitative, unfeeling capitalistic 'wage slavery' endured by industrial workers in bleak manufacturing cities. In 1857, Virginian George Fitzhugh would thus denounce factory conditions in England, where, allegedly, children were brutalised, women prostituted, and men 'cruelly beaten with a horsewhip, strap, stick, hammer handle, file, or whatever tool is nearest at hand'. In a slave society, where free and enslaved were bound by ties of mutual obligation, he tendentiously averred, such class conflict would not occur.[57]

By the 1740s and the 1750s, even evangelists in the southern colonies had largely accommodated themselves to slavery. Whitefield himself had acquired a plantation in Georgia by the mid-1740s. He had argued for the extension of slavery into that colony, against the wishes of its original founders, claiming that 'Georgia never can or will be a flourishing province without negroes'. He conceded that blacks 'are brought in a wrong way from their own country', and acknowledged that the barbarism of the Atlantic slave trade was 'not to be approved of'. Yet he declared himself blameless and helpless in that aspect of the institution: '[it] will be carried on whether we will [it] or not; I should think myself highly favoured if I could purchase a good number of them'. Conversion was high on his list of priorities. And it was, he asserted, his Christian duty 'to make their lives comfortable and lay a foundation for breeding up their posterity'.[58]

Having noted the use of religion by enslavers as a means of social control, there is room for considerable scepticism about Whitefield's motives here. Indeed, the historian of persecution must ask whether this putative 'paternalism' genuinely ameliorated the treatment of the enslaved or merely disguised it, as the rhetorical struggle with political abolitionism escalated.

While not denying the realities of brutality and harsh physical discipline inherent in the US South's system of slavery, Eugene Genovese argued that paternalism should be taken seriously. He contrasted the relatively low incidence of servile insurrections in the southern colonies/states of North America, and the high rate of natural population-increase of their enslaved population, with those of the Caribbean and Brazil. These characteristics he attributed to a distinctly southern paternalism. There, he asserts, a genuine sense of mutual dependency emerged that allowed the enslaved to claim certain customary rights, for example, respect for their 'marriages', and family life, or permission to participate in a 'slave economy' of domestic production and exchange. 'Masters' were responsive to these claims because of their own psychological need to see themselves as 'paternalists', as the benevolent heads of extended families, white and black. In return, the enslaved accommodated themselves to their situation and carved out what meaningful lives they could within a world primarily shaped by their enslavers. This possibility of accommodation with the enslavers blunted active resistance to their dominance. The South did not develop the revolutionary tradition so manifest in the Caribbean and Brazil.[59]

This suggestion is particularly important because resistance and insurrection was, ultimately, to play such a central role in ending racial slavery in the Americas. The Haitian Revolution, 1791–1804, the servile insurrection that toppled the wealthiest slave regime in the world, would prove the seminal event. Yet even on the tobacco, rice, and cotton plantations of the American South, relations between the enslaved and enslaver were actually far more conflictual than the model of 'paternalism' allows.

Some few favoured slaves were able to better their condition by forging the kind of reciprocal and mutual bonds with their enslavers that Genovese describes. George Washington's longest serving overseer at his Mount Vernon plantation was an enslaved man, Davy Gray. He lived in larger quarters and ate better than those he supervised in the fields. He even received a small wage. Similarly, a married couple, Will and Kate, were put in charge of Muddy Hole, one of Mount Vernon's constituent farms. Kate was additionally employed as 'grany' [*sic*], caring for the plantation children, for which services she was paid. She also raised and sold livestock, including to Washington.[60]

Yet the relationships that such 'confidential' slaves enjoyed with planters were far from typical. Far more often, the lives of those enslaved on plantations were grim and unremitting battles for survival, even if their enslaver did ostentatiously manifest 'paternalistic' behaviours. Charles Manigault, a Savannah River rice planter, strove to embody the paternalist ideal. In 1845, he instructed an overseer on his Gowrie Plantation to 'be Kind in word & deed to all the Negroes for they have always been accustomed to it'. He would later include this as a stipulation in his contracts with white employees in management roles. He demanded high-quality clothes and goods for his workforce. He distributed these himself, to establish a personal bond with those, he stated again and again, he regarded as part of his 'family'. And then he set them to arduous physical labour in a cruelly unhealthy environment where they suffered a shockingly high mortality rate. Overwork, yellow fever, dysentery, and pneumonia took their inevitable toll. In 1834, an outbreak of cholera killed two-fifths of Gowrie's slaves in a matter of weeks. Lives were destroyed, families shattered, bodies broken. No personal bond had been forged. During the Civil War (1861–1865), the enslaved at Gowrie sacked the 'big house' before fleeing to Union lines.[61]

Indeed, even in the cases of those trusted 'confidential' slaves who appeared to enjoy the patronage of the planter, we should not assume that outward compliance signified a deeper accommodation with enslavement. When the British sloop-of-war HMS *Savage* appeared in the Potomac off Mount Vernon in early 1781, the captain offered freedom to those who would abandon the plantation. The 17 people who seized this offer were led by one of Washington's relatively privileged enslaved overseers.[62]

Similarly, outward expressions of 'paternalistic' behaviours by planters often blurred more self-interested motives. Even before the abolition of the (legal) Atlantic slave trade in 1807, many planters had made the simple economic calculation that encouraging slave marriages and family life increased their own wealth. Thomas Jefferson once wrote to an overseer that he 'consider[s] the labor of a breeding woman as no object, and that a child raised every 2. years is of more profit than the crop of the best laboring man … it is not [women's] labor, but their increase which is the first consideration with us'.[63]

This form of 'profit' was not achieved simply by encouraging the enslaved to have families. Enslaved women were defenceless before institutionalised rape and sexual abuse. The formerly enslaved Mary Ester Peterson was born to a 15-year-old mother, whose enslaver had three sons. The brothers 'came in ... threw her down ... and tied her ... so she couldn't struggle, and one after the other used her as long as they wanted for the whole afternoon'.[64]

Encouraging families was also a useful means of exerting control and discouraging flight. One Louisiana planter wrote in 1750, 'it is necessary that the Negroes have wives, and you ought to know that nothing attaches them so much to a plantation as children'.[65] These were coldly calculated assessments, based on the twin imperatives of order and profit derived from the commodification of humans.

Perhaps the strongest indicator of the very real limits of planter 'paternalism' in the American South was their willingness to break those family attachments when it suited them to do so. With no legal protections, families endured the agonies of enforced separation for many reasons. Estates might be divided between heirs on the death of a planter. A planter who had purchased more land might send away some of his workforce to establish a new plantation. If a plantation failed, and they were ultimately business enterprises, then their assets might be sold off to cover their debts. Indeed, a financially struggling planter might make the decision to sell off some of 'his people' to fend off financial difficulties. The enslaved were valuable capital assets and were frequently used as collateral on loans or mortgaged. This allowed planters to purchase more land and more slaves, fuelling the further growth of slavery itself. The enslaved were, in Bonnie Martin's words, 'worked financially as well as physically', with all the risks and uncertainty that entailed. This ugly reality was, in fact, a very long way removed from the 'land-orientated world of medieval Europe', that Eugene Genovese believed 'forged the traditional paternalist ideology to which the southern slaveholders fell heir'.[66]

Such ruthless speculative behaviour was most apparent when 'gentleman planters' chose to participate in the internal slave trade, profiting by selling off individuals with little regard for their families. Michael Tadman has established that some 60 to 70 per cent of all interregional movement of slaves within the United States in the years 1820–1860 was accounted for by the internal slave trade, not planter migration. The cotton boom in the lower South created an insatiable demand for field hands. Virginia planters, their soils depleted, and looking for some alternative to growing tobacco, seized upon the opportunities presented by this demand. Consequently, in the upper South in the 1850s, a third of first marriages were broken by forced separation and nearly 50 per cent of enslaved children would lose touch with at least one parent. This cruelty was not forced upon reluctant 'paternalists'; it was born of their 'fundamental racist insensitivity' combined with the temptation to profit.[67]

The other pervasive threat that haunted the lives of the enslaved, always present, and often realised, was physical violence. The peculiar severity with which the enslaved were driven to this unrelenting work was frequently commented upon. In the 1790s, the House of Commons heard from witnesses reporting from the West Indies. They recounted seeing women pausing from fieldwork to suckle their children 'roused from that situation by a severe blow from a cart-whip'. The whip used was a 'plaited cow-skin with a thick, string lash'. Use of this 'formidable implement' sometimes proved lethal, either during the punishment or thereafter, through 'mortification' of the savage wounds that had been inflicted. Driven by this violence, labourers were pushed to their physical limits. Some of those who toiled in the processing mills worked 18-hour shifts, on occasion collapsing in exhaustion and losing hands and arms to the machinery.[68]

Solomon Northup, enslaved for twelve years on Louisiana plantations, 1841–1853, left a particularly compelling first-hand memoir of the experience of the enslaved. Of labour management, he recalled 'the fastest hoer takes the lead row. If [someone] passes him, he is whipped. If one falls behind or is a moment idle, he is whipped. In fact, the lash is flying from morning until night'.[69] There was no place of sanctuary from such brutality. As Thavolia Glymph has demonstrated, the 'big house' was expected to be as relentlessly productive as the fields. Those who laboured there were subject to the same violent discipline. Enslaved in Alabama, Mandy Cooper recalled how she was punished for having failed to churn milk fast enough, 'three white women beat me from angah [anger] because they had no butter for their biscuits and cornbread. Miss Burton used a heavy board while missus used a whip'.[70]

Inevitably, such violence was not confined to driving productivity: it permeated society. 'Extraordinary punishments', inflicted with 'malice, fury and all the worst passion of the human mind' were recorded. One Jamaican planter was known to drop hot lead onto his victims, '[destroying] by severity forty out of sixty Negros in three years'. Others restrained their bondspeople in spiked collars, that gagged their mouths and prevented them from lying down, while their bodies were laden with weights and chains. An overseer in Grenada killed a man by throwing him into a boiling vat of cane juice. A 'mistress' almost beat to death a young girl who she had forced into prostitution, for failing to earn enough money.[71]

Since the legal framework that was established around racial slavery was more concerned with safeguarding the institution than protecting its victims, those who meted out extraordinary violence to the enslaved had little fear of any consequences. In North America, English law was simply set aside, and new precedents established. A Virginian overseer, Andrew Byrn, was tried in 1729 for the homicide of an enslaved man who 'died by means of the correction given him for running away'. He was initially 'convicted of the murder of a Negro Slave under his care', and thus 'sentenced to death'. Yet Virginia's ruling council then intervened and recommended that Byrn be shown mercy. Yet mercy was not their real concern. They feared that executing a white overseer for killing an enslaved person would 'stir up the Negroes to contempt of their Masters and Overseers, which may attend with dangerous consequences for this colony, where the Negroes are so numerous'.[72]

Planters themselves might have had more reason to restrain the violence, either because of the emotional damage it did to their own self-image as benevolent paternalists, or because of the physical damage it caused to their property. Yet many, especially in the Caribbean, were absentees who lived in Britain. They were in no position to intervene one way or the other on behalf of their workers. Even on continental North America, day-to-day management was very often left in the hands of overseers. Planters may have been resident at other properties, or they may have retreated to a coastal dwelling in the heat of the summer. On large contiguous estates, like Mount Vernon, the land may have been divided into smaller farms, each with an overseer in charge. So, myths of paternalistic planters aside, those enslaved on plantations worked far more regularly under overseers than under those who actually owned them.[73]

If, as was often the case, these overseers were paid in 'shares' (portions of the crop produced by those they supervised), then they had a peculiar incentive to drive the field hands hard and cruelly. Planters, in turn, frequently denounced their overseers for their brutality, ignorance, and dishonesty. Thomas Jefferson even dismissed 'that seculum of beings called overseers' as the 'last and lowest' class of Virginian society. Yet, despite such rhetoric, so long as they returned a healthy profit, planters proved in practice reluctant to restrain those who wielded the whip. George Washington clashed repeatedly with Hyland Crow, one of the overseers at Mount Vernon, over the latter's brutality. Yet he did not dismiss Crow. Rather he increased his wages for two consecutive years because of the crop yields he had delivered. Only when Crow had the pertinacity to demand yet higher pay did Washington begin to question the desirability of employing him further.[74]

The centrality of violence to racial slavery was not simply a matter of driving high productivity. It also functioned 'to keep enslaved Africans quiescent'.[75] The policing of the institution, whether considered within the confines of a single plantation, or in the manner in which the slaveholding, colonial regimes worked to preserve white racial supremacy across the Americas, took on some of the characteristics of a war. Those familiar with slavery in the ancient world will know of the Greek historian Plutarch's claim that the Spartans randomly murdered members of their enslaved Helot population who dared to travel at night. By daylight, some strong and vigorous Helot worker might also be arbitrarily singled out for an exemplary execution. To legitimise these acts the *ephors* (Sparta's senior magistrates) formally declared war on the Helots each year.[76]

While lacking the formal declaration of war, the situation in the Americas was not, in actuality, so very different. Richard Ligon had sought to allay fears of insurrection in Barbados in the 1650s by emphasising the significance of military power in subduing the enslaved: 'seeing the mustering of our men and hearing their gunshot (than which nothing is more terrible to them) their spirits are subjected to so low a condition, as they dare not look up to any bold attempt'.[77]

The plantation colonies were militarised societies, organised for collective violence. In 1704, South Carolinian enslavers had recognised that 'the colony needed two military forces: a militia to repel foreign enemies, and a patrol to leave behind as a deterrent against slave revolts'. Such armed slave patrols, in which all white men were liable for service, were permanently established, in times of 'peace' as well as when invasion threatened, or rumours of insurrection swirled.[78] The violence they enacted often seems as random and arbitrary as that supposedly unleashed by the Spartans against the Helots. On Christmas Eve 1808, an enslaved man called Joe was visiting his wife on a neighbouring plantation in Westmoreland County, Virginia. Armed patrollers stormed the cabin and shot him dead.[79] In Brazil, a dedicated unit, the *Regimento dos Capitães-do-Mato*, was established that pursued fugitives from the sugar fields and spearheaded attacks on *quilombos*, the communities of runaways that were often established in Brazil's frontier region.[80]

One peculiar characteristic of the quasi-military nature of plantation regimes was the systematic use of aggressive dogs, specifically bloodhounds bred for the task, not merely to pursue those fleeing enslavement but to torture and punish the defiant. Louisianan David Barrow recorded in his diary how he had set hounds upon one man who had attempted to escape his plantation: 'dogs soon tore him naked, took him home before the negro[es] at dark & made the dogs give him another overhauling'.[81] In Cuba, the authorities maintained a permanent unit of dog-handlers, the *Chasseurs del Rey*, to police the plantations. Cuban dogs and handlers were frequently hired out to other slave-holding regimes suppressing maroons or confronted by revolt: the British in Jamaica in 1795–1796, the French in Haiti in 1802, the Americans in Florida in 1835–1842. As Sara E. Johnson has noted, 'the axis of Spanish, French, British, and North American slave-holding powers in the region collaborated in subduing non-white enemy combatants, using canine warfare techniques that dated back to the Spanish conquest of the Americas'.[82]

Understanding American slavery as, essentially, a form of conflict helps also to illuminate its ultimate demise. For, despite all the odds against them, this war was not wholly one-sided. The enslaved forged a tradition of resistance. Patterns of resistance varied over time and place. Those colonies, such as Brazil or Jamaica, where mortality rates were highest, natural population growth low, and the enslaved workforce was maintained by imports of Africans – disproportionately young men, often prisoners of war – were the most volatile. On continental North America, in the Chesapeake and Carolinas, and later the expanding cotton frontier in the deep South, where the creole (American-born) population outnumbered the African-born, rebellion was rarer and smaller scale. Ties of family and a greater awareness of the obstacles facing the fugitive or the rebel, prompted alternative patterns of resistance: temporary flight (*petit marronage*), sabotage, exercise of bodily autonomy (extending to abortion, infanticide, and suicide), or a persistent, calculated degree of intransigence and non-cooperation.[83]

Wider demographics were a factor too. Where the enslaved population outnumbered the free, then collective, organised resistance was more likely. Again, continental North America was the exception here. Only in South Carolina were the enslaved a slight majority, but not to the extent that countered the oppressive presence of slave patrols, militia, and an ever-vigilant white population. Indeed, even where the enslaved substantially outnumbered the free, the simple fact the slave-holding regimes were essentially permanently organised to wage war against the enslaved meant that conflicts with such regimes would always be asymmetrical. This largely ensured their security for centuries.

The Haitian Revolution (1791–1804) proved exceptional, affecting the complete political, economic, and social transformation of the French sugar-producing colony of Saint Domingue into an independent black state. This success was largely a consequence of the Haitian Revolution's 'symbiotic relationship' with the French Revolution (1789–1799), which undercut the slaveholders' capacity to resist a mass insurrection, under the capable leadership of Toussaint Louverture and Jean-Jacques Dessalines.[84] Yet, although exceptional in its immediate outcome, the Haitian example might be understood within a wider interpretative framework, in which the history of slave resistance is not simply dismissed as broadly one of recurrent failure. Understanding resistance, and its relationship with political abolitionism, provides one key to understanding plantation slavery's ultimate demise.

Hilary Beckles has suggested a three-stage structural model by which to chart the '200-years war' against slavery in the British West Indies. This model can quite readily accommodate the wider Caribbean, Brazil, and the American South. The earliest stage, 1500–1750, was a volatile period during which the plantations were first established, a time of fluid, frontier conditions where many were able to escape their bondage. During the second stage, 1750–c.1800, plantation societies had matured into slave societies, and the demographics of the enslaved workforce had significantly changed. The odds were then stacked very significantly against the plantation rebel and the runaway. Yet wars and revolutions, in the Americas and Europe, would give those determined to be free their opportunities. By seizing those chances, they would help undermine the institution of plantation slavery itself. During the final stage, c.1804–1838, the impact of the successful Haitian Revolution combined with the rising tide of political abolitionism in the European metropoles of slave-holding colonies, would create a final and fatal 'general crisis in plantation slavery'.[85]

During that first stage, 1500–1750, the majority of enslaved Africans were disproportionately young and male, often captive warriors enslaved in conflicts in Africa. The politico-military framework and institutions that supported plantation slavery had not fully developed. Widespread resistance was thus common. In general, this involved the enslaved organising in groups, frequently led by an individual with some military experience in Africa, who aimed not to challenge slavery itself, but effectively to fight their own way to freedom. For example, in 1739, during the Stono Revolt in South Carolina, a mixed group of American- and African-born rebels, apparently led by recently enslaved African prisoners of war, set out to fight their way from the British colony to Spanish Florida, where they had been promised their freedom.[86]

That daring flight failed; the fugitives were chased down by overwhelming numbers of militia. Elsewhere, however, other escapees successfully established autonomous maroon (in Brazil, *quilombo*) communities, in isolated areas within colonies. The longevity and size of some of these communities, and their role as a source of ongoing challenge to planter regimes, makes maroons and *quilombolas* significant, if often unheralded, actors in the story of how the chains of New World slavery were weakened.

The Palmares Republic, in the Pernambuco district of Brazil, originated in the amalgamation of several small isolated *quilombo* in the early seventeenth century. Eventually, it had a total population of some 20,000 people. This 'African state' was only finally subjugated after an independent existence of almost a century. In 1695, a large army financed by the Portuguese crown was recruited especially for the task. The longest-surviving maroon communities were those established in Jamaica and the Dutch colony of Surinam. They successfully defended their freedom and remain conscious of their distinct heritage to this day. Both groups proved superlative exponents of asymmetrical 'bush warfare'. Captain J.G. Stedman of the Dutch army commented that the Surinamese leaders, against whom he had served for five years, possessed 'a masterly trait of generalship ... as would have done honour to any European commander'.[87]

By the latter half of the eighteenth century, as plantation societies matured, the creole population increased, creating bonds of family that militated against risking all in rebellion. Militias, slave patrols, and other quasi-military formations embodied the advantage that the slaveholders had come to wield in any confrontation with rebels. Rebellions became more desperate acts, escape even less certain. There were, however, strong continuities too. The 1760 uprising in Jamaica was led by recently enslaved Africans, most prominently Tacky, an experienced commander of the Gold Coast Coromantee people. As with many such dramatic acts of resistance in this period, the instruments of oppression proved too strong. In this instance, crucially, the forces arraigned against the rebels included both free blacks serving in a colonial militia and local maroons. In return for some measure of freedom and forbearance for themselves, these groups would assist in defending the institution of slavery. American slaveholders proved skilled and pragmatic practitioners of the strategy of divide and conquer.[88]

Where the politico-military framework that supported plantation slavery was itself threatened by external forces, the rebel and the runaway had the greatest opportunities. In an era of revolutionary conflict, violent challenges to the *ancien regime* thus created the potential for successful resistance. This was evident during the American War of Independence (1775–1783). Not only did the conflict disrupt the normal mechanisms by which the enslaved population was policed, but the British offered freedom (to those owned by rebel planters at least) as a strategy. Over the course of the war, perhaps as many as a hundred thousand attempted self-emancipation through flight to British lines. British defeat ultimately ensured that only a proportion, such as the 3,500 evacuated from New York to Canada by Sir Guy Carleton, achieved this. Yet these events demonstrated in no uncertain terms that the enslaved were alive to wider political developments in the Atlantic world, and very conscious of slavery's vulnerability in a revolutionary age. As the Reverend Henry Muhlenberg, a Philadelphian minister, confided to his diary during the war, the enslaved 'secretly wished that the British army might win, for then all Negro slaves will gain their freedom'.[89]

Notwithstanding British defeat, the war had a transformative effect on the British Empire's relationship to slavery in the Atlantic world. While moral sentiment against slavery had been growing among religious groups such as Quakers and evangelical Anglicans, after 1783, the loss of the 13 American colonies caused a wider re-evaluation of imperial policy and principles. Defeat threatened the legitimacy of the empire and reform became a matter of pressing concern. A virtuous opposition to slavery (especially in contra-distinction to those colonial rebels who cried for their own liberty while enslaving others) became an attractive position for politicians eager to reaffirm their empire's inherent worth. The Society for the Abolition of the Slave Trade was founded in 1787. Abolitionist sentiment was thus transformed into a pragmatic, political programme.[90]

Those who led the campaign in Parliament against the pro-slavery 'West India interest', such as Thomas Clarkson, William Wilberforce, Granville Sharp, would initially distance themselves from the bloodshed of insurrection. Understanding the ideological position of these individuals is important in the story of abolitionism. Few historians now accept the case made by scholars such as Lowell J. Ragatz or Eric Williams that British abolitionism was driven primarily by material interests. They argued that the protectionist, mercantilist plantation colonies of the British Caribbean were in terminal economic decline by the late eighteenth century. As such they were a drag on the nation's prosperity. Under a cloak of humanitarianism, abolitionism thus advanced the cause of Britain's manufacturers: free-market, free-labour, industrial capitalists.[91] Economic historians, such as Seymour Drescher, have, however, since demonstrated the buoyant prosperity of Caribbean slave colonies well into the early nineteenth century. Abolitionism was thus an act of economic self-harm.[92]

Its essential idealism must therefore be taken seriously. British abolitionism arose from a complex synthesis of factors. These included the post-Revolutionary War crisis of imperial legitimacy, the long-standing Anglo-American debates about natural rights and the struggle for freedom against tyranny, and the growing conviction that slavery was prevented by English law (the popular understanding of the 1772 judgment of the Court of King's Bench that had freed the enslaved African James Somerset).[93] In particular, awareness of sin and a heavy burden of guilt motivated abolitionists, who were predominantly evangelicals who took their Christianity, and the prospect of divine retribution against their nation, very seriously. Abolitionism might be understood as an 'ideology of atonement'; after Parliament abolished the Atlantic slave trade in 1807, one relieved British poet wrote that '[God's] wrath subsides' and 'all his frowns recede'.[94]

The initial preference of those campaigning to end slavery through legislation was to avoid further violence. Ultimately, however, the political campaign against slavery and the physical resistance offered by the enslaved themselves would become mutually reinforcing. The Haitian Revolution (1791–1804) was a pivotal event. Prior to this, the focus of those who resisted enslavement had principally been their own escape. In Haiti, slavery itself was abolished. The rest of the Americas would follow.

By 1791, Saint Domingue was the wealthiest plantation economy in the Americas, with an enslaved population of 500,000, 40,000 whites and 30,000 free 'people of colour'. Many of the latter were themselves slave owners but were also subject to legal discrimination and racial prejudice. The sugar and coffee plantations were ruthlessly exploitative, but volatile too. The proportion of African-born labourers was high. A strong tradition of *marronage* forged bonds between these recent arrivals and the creole population, and fostered resistance. The vibrant spiritual practices of Vodun aided in the mobilisation and organisation of some rebel groups.[95] The wider context was the French Revolution, which divided white society, brought radicals sympathetic to abolitionism to positions of authority, and politicised the 'people of colour', as they demanded political equality.

For the two years following the outbreak of widespread revolts in August 1791, a complex pattern of shifting allegiances obscured the direction of the insurrection. Some rebel groups were tempted by Spanish offers of land, arms, and their own freedom to fight for monarchism and the old order. Many of the wealthier 'people of colour', having secured political equality for themselves in 1792, were opposed to any further threat to slavery. In 1793, however, facing invasion from Britain and Spain, Léger-Félicité Sonthonax, the Civil Commissioner commanding several thousand French troops in the colony, issued a local declaration of emancipation, to win over support from the rebels. Sonthonax was a member of the French abolitionist society, the *Société des Amis des Noirs*, and his actions might best be understood as a confluence of principle and pragmatism.[96] The following year, pressured into a more radical position by the presence of elected black deputies from Saint

Domingue, such as Jean-Baptiste Bellay, the National Convention in Paris followed suit. This rallied key rebel leaders, including Toussaint Louverture, to revolutionary France's cause.

Years of bitter warfare followed, which saw both British and Spanish military interventions defeated, and slavery ended across the colony. By 1800, Louverture was recognised as the colony's governor. Loyalty to France, however, would end with the rise of Napoleon Bonaparte. Seeking to re-enslave the people and restore white supremacy, Bonaparte's soldiers waged a savage campaign of re-conquest. Louverture died in a French dungeon in 1803. His second-in-command, Jean-Jacques Dessalines, led his compatriots in the final stage of the revolution: the war of independence (1802–1804). Once more, the fighting was marked by ferocity on both sides, before the French were finally driven out. The Republic of Haiti (the name was that once used by the long-disappeared indigenous population) was declared in 1804.[97]

The scale of bloodshed and atrocity that had accompanied the revolution was staggering. In excess of 200,000 Haitians died; France lost around 50,000 military casualties (most to yellow fever rather than battle) and some 30,000 colonists. Many of the latter were massacred in the very final stages of the revolution. All possibility of coexistence had seemingly been destroyed by the manifest determination of French commanders such as Rochambeau to extirpate all rebels. Dessalines argued that the only way to finally defeat slavery was to kill the entire white population, a paradigmatic example of what has been termed a 'subaltern genocide': the extermination of a ruling group by a subordinated one.[98]

Unsurprisingly, many abolitionists recoiled from the horror that had unfolded. Pro-slavery ideologues capitalised on stereotypes of African savagery and the opportunity to allege that abolitionist agitation had only inflamed the rebels. In the United States, Thomas Jefferson disparaged the Haitian revolutionaries not as torch bearers of liberty but as 'Cannibals of the terrible republic'.[99] Yet the fear that this contempt masked, and that Jefferson shared with slaveholders across the Americas, was a recognition that the foundations of plantation slavery were shaking. Political abolitionists soon saw this too. In 1824, the British writer Elizabeth Heyrick dismissed passive schemes for gradual emancipation and cited the Haitian Revolution as a precedent for 'immediatism'. As the American abolitionist, and former slave, Frederick Douglass asserted, Haiti was 'the original pioneer emancipator of the nineteenth century'.[100]

Having won their own freedom, the Haitians were able to provide further direct assistance in the growing campaign against slavery. In 1816, they provided arms, munitions, and hundreds of volunteer fighters to Simón Bolívar. He would go on to defeat the Spanish Empire in the Americas and set in train the emancipation of the enslaved in Spain's former colonies. In other cases, it was their example that counted. Rebels in Cuba in 1812 flew Haitian flags and wore Haitian hats. In 1816, during a major rising in Barbados, one leader, Nanny Grigg, urged her fellow rebels to fight for freedom 'the way they did in Saint Domingo'. In the United States, some degree of Haitian inspiration has been cited for both the sophisticated Gabriel plot of 1800, that sought to seize Richmond and capture Virginia's governor, James Monroe, and the march on New Orleans by several hundred rebels in 1811. Some signs of Haitian influence were also evident in the largely Muslim-inspired Mâle revolt in Brazil in 1835. Strikingly, these plots and insurrections aimed not at attaining freedom merely for those who participated, but for greater, revolutionary change. This is what Haiti had unleashed.[101]

Although those campaigning politically for abolition had initially striven to distance themselves from rebellion and violence, the revolutionary character of resistance could not be ignored. The British abolitionists had first targeted the Atlantic slave trade. After this was finally abolished in 1807, it was hoped that the conditions endured by the enslaved in the Caribbean would improve. Without recourse to fresh imports, planters would have an incentive to better the circumstances of those who laboured for them. Slavery itself might simply wither away, displaced by the inexorable rise of wage labour that so many abolitionists championed as the key to progress. However, it soon became clear that slavery remained both entrenched and brutal after 1807, pointing to the possibility that revolution might become inevitable.

The abolitionists shifted their rhetoric. They countered planter narratives of servile savagery by pointing to the manifest exercise of restraint by early nineteenth-century plantation rebels. During the Demerara rising of 1823, no plantation property was destroyed. In other instances, where there had been extensive economic damage, the rebels had nevertheless shown no desire to commit massacres. Hundreds of Barbadian rebels were executed during and after the 1816 rising. Only one white civilian and one black British soldier had been killed. In Demerara, 12,000 rebels seized sixty plantations, but only two or three white men died. The Baptist War (so-called because of the alleged influence of non-conformist preachers over the enslaved population), in Jamaica in 1831–1832, cost the lives of only 14 whites. The authorities, however, were responsible for the deaths of some 540 enslaved Jamaicans. Evidence now given before a Select Committee of the House of Commons stressed planter cruelty towards a Christian people who struck out only in self-defence. The instability and violence, and what it might mean for British authority and prosperity, further underscored the case for freedom.[102]

The British Empire finally abolished slavery in the Emancipation Act of 1833, a moment that portended the end of slavery across the Americas. It held out longest where the plantations remained most profitable. In the United States, the debate over slavery's expansion into the western territories acquired after the war with Mexico (1846–1848) would finally trigger the South's attempt to secede from the Union in 1861. During the ensuing Civil War (1861–1865), tens of thousands of the enslaved 'self-emancipated' and escaped into Northern lines. They could not be returned to bondage, to labour for traitors to the Union, so their fate had to be addressed. They thereby transformed a war to prevent secession into a war to end slavery.

Lincoln's somewhat limited Emancipation Proclamation of 1863, freeing only the slaves of those in active rebellion, was followed by the Thirteenth Amendment that finally outlawed slavery in December 1865.[103] The last bastions were Cuba and Brazil, who finally ended almost four centuries of legal chattel slavery in the Americas in, respectively, 1886 and 1888.[104]

Yet the end of slavery by no means signalled the end of persecution on the grounds of race. Notwithstanding the close and darkly symbiotic relationship between the growth of plantation slavery and the hardening of proto-racial ideologies into modern racism, the latter thrived, even after the former fell. Race had acquired a new scientific respectability; if it could no longer justify enslavement, it could still provide a justifying myth for European dominance through formal and informal empire of the rest of the globe. By law and custom, race justified grotesque inequalities in power and wealth. And worse. Over the course of the next century, it would become one of the ideological mainstays of the most extreme manifestations of persecution yet seen in history, during the age of genocide.

Notes

1 Jean Bodin, *The Six Books of a Common-Weale*, translated by Richard Knolles (London: Adam Islip impensis G. Bishop, 1606), pp.42–44; Robin Blackburn, *The Making of New World Slavery From the Baroque to the Modern, 1492–1800* (London: Verso: 1997), p.61. David Brion Davis, *The Problem of Slavery in Western Culture* (Oxford: Oxford University Press, 1966), pp.108–114.

2 William Palmer, 'Fables of Conquest: Moral Regression in the Early Modern English State and Empire', *Journal for Early Modern Cultural Studies*, 19 (2019), pp.162–198.

3 Dienke Hondius, 'Black Africans in Seventeenth-Century Amsterdam', *Renaissance and Reformation / Renaissance et Réforme*, 31 (2008), pp.88–89.

4 The precise figure is elusive. See Paul E. Lovejoy, 'The Volume of the Atlantic Slave Trade: A Synthesis', *Journal of African History*, 23 (1982), p.496.

5 Eric Williams, *Capitalism and Slavery* (Chapel Hill: University of North Carolina Press, 1944), p.14.

6 George M. Fredrickson, *Racism: A Short History* (Princeton, NJ: Princeton University Press, 2002), p.5; K. Tsianina Lomawaima and Jeffrey Ostler, 'Reconsidering Richard Henry Pratt: Cultural Genocide and Native Liberation in an Era of Racial Oppression', *Journal of American Indian Education*, 57 (2018), pp.79–10; Naomi Zack, *Philosophy of Race: An Introduction* (Cham, Switzerland: Palgrave Macmillan, 2018), p.149.

7 Franz Boas, 'Changes in the Bodily Form of Descendants of Immigrants', *American Anthropologist*, 14 (1912), pp.530–562; Ashley Montagu, *Man's Most Dangerous Myth: The Fallacy of Race* (Oxford: Oxford University Press, 1942).

8 Quoted in Martin Harvey, 'Deliberation and Natural Slavery', *Social Theory and Practice*, 27 (2001), p.58.

9 Anthony Pagden, 'The Peopling of the New World', in Miriam Eliav-Feldon, Benjamin Isaac, and Joseph Ziegler (eds), *The Origins of Racism in the West* (Cambridge: Cambridge University Press, 2009), p.297.

10 Benjamin Isaac, 'Racism: A Rationalisation of Prejudice in Greece and Rome', in Eliav-Feldon et al. (eds), *The Origins of Racism in the West*, p.43.

11 Malcolm Heath, 'Aristotle on Natural Slavery', *Phronesis*, 53 (2008), pp.243–270.

12 Gay L. Byron, *Symbolic Blackness and Ethnic Difference in Early Christian Literature* (London: Routledge, 2002), pp.37–38.

13 Byron, *Symbolic Blackness*, pp.44–47, 70–73.

14 Geraldine Heng, *The Invention of Race in the European Middle Ages* (Cambridge: Cambridge University Press, 2018), pp.181–256.

15 John Alembillah Azumah, *The Legacy of Arab-Islam in Africa* (Oxford: One World, 2001), p.137.

16 Ralph Austen 'The 19th Century Islamic Slave Trade from East Africa (Swahili and Red Sea Coasts): A Tentative Census', *Slavery and Abolition*, 9 (1988), pp.21–44; Ronald Segal, *Islam's Black Slaves* (London: Atlantic Book, 2001), pp.56–57, 204–213; Human Rights Watch, 'World Report: Mauritania Events of 2020', www.hrw.org/world-report/2021/country-chapters/mauritania [accessed 5 November 2022].

17 Bernard Lewis, *Race and Slavery in the Middle East: An Historical Enquiry* (Oxford: Oxford University Press, 1990), pp.63–65.

18 Hannah Barker, 'Reconnecting with the Homeland: Black Sea Slaves in Mamluk Biographical Dictionaries', *Medieval Prosopography*, 30 (2015), pp.87–104.

19 Ghada Hashem Talhami, 'The Zanj Rebellion Reconsidered', *International Journal of African Historical Studies*, 10 (1977), pp.443–461; Segal, *Islam's Black Slaves*, pp.42–46.

20 David Goldenberg, *The Curse of Ham: Race and Slavery in Early Judaism, Christianity and Islam* (Princeton, NJ.: Princeton University Press, 2003), pp.26–40, 172–174; Ibn Qutayba, quoted in Bruce S. Hall, *A History of Race in Muslim West Africa* (Cambridge: Cambridge University Press, 2014), p.47.

21 Goldenberg, *Curse of Ham*, p.175; James H. Sweet, 'The Iberian Roots of American Racist Thought', *William and Mary Quarterly*, 54 (1997), pp.151–152.

22 Alice Rio, *Slavery After Rome, 500–1100* (Oxford: Oxford University Press, 2017), pp.24–28.

23 Francisco Bethancourt, *Racisms: From the Crusades to the Twentieth Century* (Princeton, NJ: Princeton University Press, 2013), pp.138–151; Frederickson, *Racism*, pp.22–23.

24 Bethancourt, *Racisms*, pp.163–180; Brooke N. Newman, 'Blood Fictions, Maternal Inheritance, and the Legacies of Colonial Slavery', *Women's Studies Quarterly*, 48 (2020), pp.27–44.

25 Charles de Miramon, 'The Invention of the Concept of Race', in Eliav-Feldon et al. (eds), *Origins of Racism in the West*, p.212.

26 De Miramon, 'The Invention of the Concept of Race', pp.200–201.

27 A.J.R. Russell-Wood, 'Iberian Expansion and the Issue of Black Slavery: Changing Portuguese Attitudes, 1440–1770', *American Historical Review*, 83 (1978), p.16.

28 Joaquim Romero Magalhães, 'Africans, Indians, and Slavery in Portugal', *Portuguese Studies*, 13 (1997), p.144; Russell-Wood, 'Iberian Expansion', p.16.

29 Sidney Mintz, 'Caribbean Society', *International Encyclopedia of the Social Sciences*, David L. Sills (ed.), Volume 2 (New York: Macmillan, 1968), p.311.

30 Blackburn, *Making of New World Slavery*, pp.108–112.

31 Blackburn, *Making of New World Slavery*, pp.62–63.

32 Toby Green, *The Rise of the Trans-Atlantic Slave Trade* (Cambridge: Cambridge University Press, 2012), pp.178–179; William D. Phillips, 'The Old World Background of Slavery in the Americas', in Barbara L. Solow (ed.), *Slavery and the Rise of the Atlantic System* (Cambridge: Cambridge University Press, 1991), pp.50–51.

33 Azumah, *Legacy of Arab-Islam in Africa*, pp.119–123; A. Norman Klein, 'Slavery and Akan Origins?', *Ethnohistory*, 41 (1994), pp.627–656.

34 Quoted in Marcus Rediker, *The Slave Ship: A Human History* (London: John Murray, 2007), p.156.

35 Herbert S. Klein, *The Atlantic Slave Trade* (Cambridge: Cambridge University Press, 2010), pp.132–161; Jeremy Krikler, 'A Chain of Murder in the Slave Trade: A Wider Context of the Zong Massacre', *International Review of Social History*, 57 (2012), pp.393–415; Sowande' Mustakeem, ' "I Never Have Such a Sickly Ship Before": Diet, Disease, and Mortality in 18th-Century Atlantic Slaving Voyages', *Journal of African American History*, 93 (2008), pp.474–496.

36 Christopher Columbus, 'Journal of the First Voyage of Columbus', in Clement Markham (ed.), *Journal of Christopher Columbus (during his first voyage, 1492–93) and documents relating to the Voyage of John Cabot and Gasper Corte Real* (London: Hakluyt Society, 1893), p.114.

37 Barbara L. Solow, 'Capitalism and Slavery in the Exceedingly Long Run', in Barbara L. Solow and Stanley L. Engerman (eds), *British Capitalism & Caribbean Slavery: The Legacy of Eric Williams* (Cambridge: Cambridge University Press, 1987), pp.62–63.

38 David Brion Davis, *Inhuman Bondage: The Rise and Fall of New World Slavery* (Oxford: Oxford University Press, 2006), p.98; Jack D. Forbes, *Black Africans and Native Americans* (Oxford: Blackwells, 1988), pp.32–35.

39 Quoted in Blackburn, *Making of New World Slavery*, p.185. José Eisenberg, 'António Vieira and the Justification of Indian Slavery', *Luso-Brazilian Review*, 40 (2003), pp.89–95; Francis A. Dutra, 'The Vieira Family and the Order of Christ', *Luso-Brazilian Review*, 40 (2003), p.24.

40 Casandra Newby-Alexander, 'The Arrival of the First Africans to English North America', *Virginia Magazine of History and Biography*, 127 (2019), p.189.

41 Russell R. Menard, 'Plantation Empire: How Sugar and Tobacco Planters Built Their Industries and Raised an Empire', *Agricultural History*, 81 (2007), pp.309–332.

42 Hilary McD. Beckles and Andrew Downes, 'The Economics of Transition to the Black Labor System in Barbados, 1630–1680', *Journal of Interdisciplinary History*, 18, 2 (1987), pp.225–247.

43 Richard Ligon, *A True and Exact History of the Island of Barbados* (London: Humphrey Mosely, 1657), p.114.

44 Ligon, *A True and Exact History*, pp.44, 114.

45 John C. Coombs, 'The Phases of Conversion: A New Chronology for the Rise of Slavery in Early Virginia', *William and Mary Quarterly*, 68 (2011), pp.332–360; David Galenson, *White Servitude in Colonial America* (Cambridge: Cambridge University Press, 1981); Russell Menard, 'From Servants to Slaves: The Transformation of the Chesapeake Labor System', *Southern Studies*, 16 (1997), pp.362–390.

46 Stephen B. Hodin, 'The Mechanisms of Monticello: Saving Labor in Jefferson's America', *Journal of the Early Republic*, 26 (2006), pp.388–389.

47 Laura Sandy, 'Slave Owning Overseers in Eighteenth-Century Virginia and South Carolina', *Slavery & Abolition*, 38 (2017), pp.459–474.

48 Anthony Parent, *Foul Means: The Formation of a Slave Society in Virginia, 1660–1740* (Chapel Hill: University of North Carolina Press, 2003), p.172.

49 A. Leon Higginbotham, *In the Matter of Color: Race and the American Legal Process: The Colonial Period* (Oxford: Oxford University Press, 1978), pp.29–30; H. McIlwaine (ed.), *Minutes of the Council and General Court of Virginia, 1622–1632 and 1670–1676* (Richmond, VA: Richmond Colonial Press, 1924), p.513.

50 Coombs, 'The Phases of Conversion', pp.347–348.

51 Parent, *Foul Means*, p.2.

52 Ligon, *A True and Exact History*, p.50.

53 Rebecca Goetz, *The Baptism of Early Virginia: How Christianity Created Race* (Baltimore, MD: Johns Hopkins University Press, 2012), pp.86–111.

54 Parent, *Foul Means*, pp.2, 250.

55 Quoted in William Moister, *Africa Past and Present* (London: Hodder & Stoughton, 1879), p.144.

56 Allan Gallay, 'The Origins of Slaveholders' Paternalism: George Whitefield, the Bryan Family, and the Great Awakening in the South', *Journal of Southern History*, 53 (1987), p.381.

57 David Donald, 'The Proslavery Argument Reconsidered', *Journal of Southern History*, 37 (1971), p.5.

58 Galley, 'Origins of Slaveholders' Paternalism', p.391.

59 Eugene Genovese, *Roll, Jordan, Roll. The World the Slaves Made* (New York: Pantheon Books, 1975).

60 Laura Sandy and Gervase Phillips, ' "Known To Be Equal to the Management": The Modernising Planter and the Enslaved Overseer', *Journal of Global Slavery*, 6 (2021), pp.169–172.

61 Jeffrey R. Young, 'Ideology and Death on a Savannah River Rice Plantation, 1833–1867: Paternalism amidst 'a Good Supply of Disease and Pain', *Journal of Southern History*, 59 (1993), pp.673–706.

62 Sandy and Phillips, ' "Known To Be Equal to the Management" ', p.170.

63 Hodin, 'The Mechanisms of Monticello', pp.388–389.

64 Quoted in Wilma King, ' "Prematurely Knowing of Evil Things": The Sexual Abuse of African American Girls and Women in Slavery and Freedom', *Journal of African American History*, 99, 3 (2014), p.174.

65 Genovese, *Roll, Jordan, Roll*, p.452.

66 Genovese, *Roll, Jordan, Roll*, p.5; Bonnie Martin, 'Slavery's Invisible Engine: Mortgaging Human Property', *Journal of Southern History*, 76 (2010), p.866.

67 Michael Tadman, *Speculators and Slaves: Masters, Traders and Slaves in the Old South* (Madison: University of Wisconsin Press, 1980), p.111.

68 *Remarks on the Methods of Procuring Slaves with a Short Account of Their Treatment in the West-Indies, &c.* (London: Darton & Harvey, 1793), p.1.

69 Quoted in David Brion Davis, *Inhuman Bondage: The Rise and Fall of Slavery in the New World* (Oxford: Oxford University Press, 2006), p.199.

70 Thavolia Glymph, *Out of the House of Bondage: The Transformation of the Plantation Household* (Cambridge: Cambridge University Press, 2003), p.32.

71 *Remarks on the Methods of Procuring Slaves*, p.1.

72 Laura Sandy, *The Overseers of Early American Slavery: Supervisors, Enslaved Labourers, and the Plantation Enterprise* (New York: Routledge, 2020), p.29.

73 Sandy, *Overseers*, pp.19–60.

74 Sandy, *Overseers*, pp.6, 197–198.

75 Trevour Bernard, *Planters, Merchants and Slaves* (Chicago, IL: University of Chicago Press, 2019), p.134.

76 James T. Chambers, 'On Messenian and Laconian Helots in the Fifth Century BC', *The Historian*, 40 (1978), p.271.

77 Ligon, *True and Exact History*, p.46

78 Sally E. Hadden, *Slave Patrols: Law and Violence in Virginia and the Carolinas* (Cambridge, MA: Harvard University Press, 2001), pp.19–20.

79 Gervase Phillips and Laura Sandy, 'Slavery and the "American Way of War", 1607–1861', *Comparative Studies in Society and History*, 63 (2021), p.846.

80 Herbert S. Klein and Francisco Vidal Luna, *Slavery in Brazil* (Cambridge: Cambridge University Press, 2011), p.199.

81 John Hope Franklin and Loren Schweninger, *Runaway Slaves: Rebels on the Plantation* (Oxford: Oxford University Press, 1999), pp.161–162.

82 Sara E. Johnson, ' "You Should Give them Blacks to Eat": Waging Inter-American Wars of Torture and Terror', *American Quarterly*, 61 (2009), p.67; Gervase Phillips, 'The Employment of War Dogs in the Medieval and Early Modern West', *British Journal for Military History*, 7 (2021), pp.15–18.

83 Stephanie M.H. Camp, 'The Pleasures of Resistance: Enslaved Women and Body Politics in the Plantation South, 1830–1861', *Journal of Southern History*, 68 (2002), pp.533–572; Kelly Houston Jones, ' "A Rough, Saucy Set of Hands to Manage": Slave Resistance in Arkansas', *Arkansas Historical Quarterly*, 71 (2012), pp.1–21.

84 Franklin W. Knight, 'The Haitian Revolution', *American Historical Review*, 105 (2000), p.106.

85 Hilary Beckles, 'Caribbean Anti-Slavery: The Self-Liberation Ethos of Enslaved Blacks', *Journal of Caribbean History*, 22 (1988), pp.1–19.

86 John K. Thornton, 'African Dimensions of the Stono Rebellion', *American Historical Review*, 96 (1991), pp.1101–1113.

87 Klein and Luna, *Slavery in Brazil*, pp.196–197; J.G. Stedman, 'Guerrilla Warfare: A European Soldier's View', in Richard Price (ed.), *Maroon Societies: Rebel Slave Communities in the Americas* (Baltimore, MD: Johns Hopkins University Press, 1996), p.311.

88 Vincent Brown, *Tacky's Revolt: The Story of an Atlantic Slave War* (Cambridge, MA: Harvard University Press, 2020); Gary Sellick, 'Black Skin, Red Coats: the Carolina Corps and Nationalism in the Revolutionary British Caribbean', *Slavery & Abolition*, 39 (2018), pp.459–478.

89 Quoted in Gregory J.W. Urwin, 'When Freedom Wore a Red Coat: How Cornwallis' 1781 Campaign Threatened the Revolution in Virginia', *Army History*, 68 (2008), p.13.

90 Christopher L. Brown, *Moral Capital: Foundations of British Abolitionism* (Chapel Hill: University of North Carolina Press, 2006).

91 Lowell J. Ragatz, *The Fall of the Planter Class in the British West Indies, 1763–1833* (New York: Century Co., 1928); Eric Williams, *Capitalism and Slavery* (Chapel Hill: University of North Carolina Press, 1944).

92 Seymour Drescher, *Econocide: British Slavery in the Era of Abolition* (Pittsburgh, PA: University of Pittsburgh Press, 1977).

93 Wiliam Palmer, 'How Ideology Works: Historians and the Case of British Abolitionism', *Historical Journal*, 52 (2009), pp. 1039–1051.

94 John Coffey, '"Tremble, Britannia!": Fear, Providence and the Abolition of the Slave Trade, 1758–1807', *English Historical Review*, 127 (2012), pp. 844–881.

95 Crystal Nicole Eddins, 'Runaways, Repertoires, and Repression: *Marronage* and the Haitian Revolution, 1766–1791', *Journal of Haitian Studies*, 25 (2019), pp.4–38.

96 Dannelle Gutarra, 'The Discourses of Sonthonax's Mission in Saint-Domingue: The Coda to the Abolition of Slavery', *French Colonial History*, 17 (2017), pp. 81–102.

97 This brief account is drawn primarily form Laurent Dubois, *Avengers of the New World: The Story of the Haitian Revolution* (Cambridge, MA: Harvard University Press, 2005).

98 Philip R. Girard, 'Caribbean Genocide: Racial War in Haiti, 1802–4', *Patterns of Prejudice*, 39 (2005), pp.138–161.

99 Arthur Scherr, 'Jefferson's "Cannibals" Revisited: A Closer Look at His Notorious Phrase', *Journal of Southern History*, 77 (2011), p.252.

100 Quoted in David Brion Davis, *Inhuman Bondage: The Rise and Fall of Slavery in the New World* (Oxford: Oxford University Press, 2006), p.158; Marilyn Walker, 'Gendering Transatlantic Anti-Slavery History', *The Eighteenth Century*, 57 (2016), p.404.

101 Robin Blackburn, 'Haiti, Slavery, and the Age of the Democratic Revolution', *William and Mary Quarterly*, 63 (2006), pp.643–674; Davis, *Inhuman Bondage*, pp.157–174; Gerald Mullin, *Flight and Rebellion: Slave Resistance in Eighteenth-Century Virginia* (Oxford: Oxford University Press, 1972), pp.140–163.

102 Davis, *Inhuman Bondage*, pp.205–229; Gelien Matthews, *Caribbean Slave Revolts and the British Abolitionist Movement* (Baton Rouge: Louisiana State University Press, 2012), pp.180–183.

103 Karen Cook Bell, 'Self-Emancipating Women, Civil War, and the Union Army in Southern Louisiana and Lowcountry Georgia, 1861–1865', *Journal of African American History*, 101 (2016), pp.1–22; James Oakes, *The Radical and the Republican: Frederick Douglass, Abraham Lincoln and the Triumph of Anti-Slavery Politics* (London: Norton, 2007).

104 Christopher Schmidt-Nowara, 'Empires against Emancipation: Spain, Brazil, and the Abolition of Slavery', *Review (Fernand Braudel Center)*, 31 (2008), pp.101–119.

8 'How Godly a Deed It Is to Overthrow So Wicked a Race'

Genocide and Colonialism, 1492–1908

In a radio broadcast of 24 August 1941, Britain's Prime Minister Winston Churchill reflected on some of the darkest days of the Second World War. The occupied nations of continental Europe were 'stunned and pinioned', while Italy, Hungary, Romania, and Bulgaria had thrown in their lot with Nazi Germany and become 'jackals of the tiger'. On 22 June, the Axis armies had unleashed their assault on the Soviet Union, heralding a descent into barbarism. Operation Barbarossa was not simply an invasion; it was a campaign of annihilation. Churchill informed his listeners that 'whole districts are being exterminated. Scores of thousands, literally scores of thousands of executions in cold blood are being perpetrated by the German police troops'. This was 'merciless butchery' with 'famine and pestilence [following] in the bloody ruts of Hitler's tanks'. He concluded that 'We are in the presence of a crime without a name'.[1] That crime would soon be given a name: genocide.

Raphaël Lemkin was a Polish lawyer, born in Bezwodene in 1900, to a Jewish farming family. He would lose 49 relatives, including his parents and a brother, to the Nazi destruction of European Jewry, what his co-religionists would call the *Shoah* (catastrophe), and the world would remember as the Holocaust (originally meaning a burned sacrifice). In 1944, having himself escaped eastern Europe and found safety in New York, Lemkin would coin the neologism 'genocide', from the Greek *genos* (which he translated as 'race' or 'tribe') and the Latin *cide* (killing).[2] While the immediate tragic context was clear, his concern was always much wider than contemporary events. Although the crime's name was new, Lemkin argued that he was simply recognising a recurrent historical phenomenon. His purpose was to ensure that it had no future.

He would later claim that his concern for persecuted groups had been stirred in childhood, when he had read Henry Sienkiewicz's 1896 novel *Quo Vadis*. This contained vivid descriptions of Emperor Nero's cruelty towards early Christians. He had, thereafter, sought out other examples: the Huguenots in France, the Moors of Spain, the Aztecs of Mexico. Yet this was not simply a matter of distant history. Lemkin was shocked by the slaughter of

DOI: 10.4324/9781003494331-9

the Armenians by Ottoman authorities during the First World War. He noted, too, massacres of Christian Assyrians by Iraqi troops in 1933. By then, he was a qualified lawyer advocating for new statutory offences in international law, concerning both physical attacks on minorities and the destruction of their cultural heritages. His position was very much informed by the work of established proponents of legal innovations that would facilitate humanitarian intervention and criminalise statist aggression, such as the Romanian Vespasian V. Pella, and the Frenchman Henri Donnediue de Vabres.[3]

His focus on such legal protection for groups arose from his profound belief in the intrinsic value of the collectives that produced the culture which in turn gave human lives meaning. As he explained in 1946:

> Cultural considerations speak for international protection of national, religious and racial groups. Our whole cultural heritage is a product of the contributions of all nations. We can best understand this when we realize how impoverished our culture would be if the peoples doomed by Germany, such as the Jews, had not been permitted to create the Bible, or to give birth to an Einstein, a Spinoza; if the Poles had not had the opportunity to give to the world a Copernicus, a Chopin, a Curie; the Czechs, a Huss, a Dvorak; the Greeks, a Plato and a Socrates; the Russians, a Tolstoy and a Shostakovich.[4]

His own experiences of war honed his idealism into the cause to which he devoted the remainder of his life: 'outlawing the destruction of peoples'. By so doing, he hoped to contribute to a novel innovation in international law. This would allow for the punishment of those who sought to destroy particular racial, ethnic, or religious groups, even if that entailed curtailing the sovereignty of individual nation states. For Lemkin, state sovereignty could only legitimately be 'directed towards the welfare of people'. It could not 'be conceived as the right to kill millions of innocent people'.[5] Thus, Lemkin's innovative legal framework envisaged not merely the punishment of those guilty of genocide, but also establishing a responsibility for intervention by the international community into the affairs of sovereign states, to prevent genocides from occurring.

The new paradigm that went beyond punishing wartime atrocities to protect persecuted groups from their own governments, even in peacetime, was swiftly appreciated by a wider audience. The shortcomings of existing international law became apparent at the 1945–1946 Nuremberg trials. Although the word 'genocide' had achieved enough currency by this point to be mentioned in the indictments of Nazi war criminals, it was not yet enshrined in international law. As such, it did not figure in any verdicts. The atrocities that were indicted were essentially war crimes conventionally understood. Thus, only those offences that took place after the invasion of Poland in September 1939 were considered. Overall, the charges of waging aggressive war or committing crimes against humanity (which did not specify direction against a particular national, ethnic, or racial group) were emphasised above the persecution of minorities.[6]

Trygve Lie was the first General Secretary of the United Nations, established in 1945 to maintain international peace and security. He invited Lemkin to work with those two other respected legal scholars Pella and de Vabres to draft an international criminal code against genocide. The final agreed version of the UN Genocide Convention was ratified by the UN on 10 December 1948 and came into effect on 12 January 1951.[7]

Yet, even as the convention was being drafted, fundamental disagreements over the precise definition and scope of the word 'genocide' had emerged, with profound consequences for the final text. In the first instance, therefore, it is worth paying full attention to Raphaël Lemkin's original conceptualisation. His initial definition, in *Axis Rule in Occupied Europe*, was as follows:

> By 'genocide' we mean the destruction of a nation or an ethnic group ... Generally speaking, genocide does not necessarily mean the immediate destruction of a nation, except when accomplished by mass killings of all members of a nation. It is intended rather to signify a coordinated plan of different actions aiming at the destruction of essential foundations of the life of national groups, with the aim of annihilating the groups themselves. The objectives of such a plan would be the disintegration of the political and social institutions, of culture, language, national feelings, religion, and the economic existence of national groups, and the destruction of the personal security, liberty, health, dignity, and even the lives of the individuals belonging to such groups. Genocide is directed against the national group as an entity, and the actions involved are directed against the national group as an entity, and the actions involved are directed against individuals, not in their individual capacity, but as members of the national group.[8]

He went on to explain that genocide had two phases. In the first, the 'national pattern' of the oppressed group was destroyed. In the second phase, the 'national pattern' of the oppressor was imposed, either on a territory and those portions of the oppressed allowed to remain, or on land denuded of its original inhabitants and settled by colonists.

While this particular passage identified the target of genocide as either a 'nation' or an 'ethnic group', Lemkin's writing more generally reveal that he understood 'the human cosmos' to consist of five groups: national, racial, religious, ethnic, and political.[9] Lemkin's original formulation was, thus, sweepingly broad; it was after all a response to Nazi occupation policies across the whole of western and eastern Europe. This was valuable because it recognised genocide was not simply a matter of deliberate 'mass killings'. It might be committed through the 'violent undermining' of the cultural and economic foundations of a group's existence over time, or by the creation of material conditions leading to rapid population decline through 'natural' causes, such as disease. Yet, as a practical basis for international law, it would need considerable refinement.

Conversely, there was also a risky narrowness to Lemkin's original conception. This stemmed from his central emphasis on protecting 'groups'. It might be questioned whether complex modern societies were composed of such readily identifiable, neatly demarcated, and bounded groups, to which specific cultures or interests could be attributed. Indeed, the reification of such groups might be dangerous, since this was a favoured tool of rabble-rousers and demagogues, used to inflame the mob against erstwhile neighbours and compatriots. German Jews had been among the most assimilated in Europe until the Nazis robbed them of their German identities and stigmatised them collectively as alien, corrupting, and threatening.[10]

What, however, made the point about the narrowness of Lemkin's original definition around protected groups more serious was that the text agreed in the UN Genocide Convention was narrower still. The discussions leading to the adoption of that text was conducted against the backdrop of the nascent Cold War. Controversies soon emerged. These included the identification of the groups that qualified for protection, the question of whether destruction had to be intentional to qualify as genocide, and whether cultural genocide should be included at all. Lemkin himself retreated from his original position that political groups should be included, arguing that they lacked 'permanency and the specific characteristics of the other groups referred to', and that the Convention 'should not run the risk of failure by introducing ideas on which the world is deeply divided'. The pressure to exclude political groups came most forcefully from the Soviet Union. Yet there was a wider concern, even within some democracies, that their inclusion might too readily draw the international community into the internal affairs of nation states.[11]

It was the western powers that were chiefly opposed to the inclusion of cultural genocide. European colonial powers, and nations born in settler colonialism, such as the US, Australia, and Canada, had all engaged in assimilationist policies that undermined the cultural and economic foundations of the lives of indigenous peoples. The UN Convention on Genocide thus fell short of Lemkin's original conception:[12]

> In the present Convention, genocide means any of the following acts committed with intent to destroy, in whole or in part, a national, ethnical, racial or religious group, as such:
>
> 1. Killing members of the group;
> 2. Causing serious bodily or mental harm to members of the group;
> 3. Deliberately inflicting on the group conditions of life calculated to bring about its physical destruction in whole or in part;
> 4. Imposing measures intended to prevent births within the group;
> 5. Forcibly transferring children of the group to another group.

Chronicling examples of genocide from the modern era, in the light of both Lemkin's original definition and the UN Convention on Genocide, reveals just why it remains so difficult to characterise with precision the essential nature of the crime, and why the definition of genocide remains contested.

Such a chronicle must start with empire. Linking colonialism to geno-cide invites controversy. That the process of empire building, particularly when associated with the establishment and growth of settler colonies, was associated with the deaths of millions of indigenous peoples and the destruc-tion of their political, social, and cultural institutions, is manifest.

Whether this necessarily occurred as a consequence of 'intent to destroy' is moot. Yet underpinning European colonialism was an ideology of supremacy rooted in proto-racial thinking, religious scruple, and notions of the natural right of the civilised to rule over the savage or the barbarian that traced their lineage to antiquity. Colonisers may have argued bitterly over the degree to which this ideology justified the violent dispossession, massacre, or enslave-ment of indigenous populations, but its fundamental assumptions went unchallenged for centuries.

The central ideological dynamics of European supremacism were captured in the early years of overseas colonialism at the 1550–1551 Valladolid debates. The protagonists were Juan Ginés de Sepúlveda, lawyer and humanist philosopher, and the Dominican friar Bartolomé de Las Casas. Sepúlveda defended the violent manner of the Spanish conquest by redefining the established medieval understanding of 'just war' to incorporate conflict with those he deemed to be barbarians (a useful act of 'moral regression'). Drawing on the Greek philosopher Aristotle, he invoked the violation of 'natural law' as just grounds for war. He understood 'natural law' to be 'right reason and inclination to duty and to accept the obligations of virtue' combined with a capacity for 'discerning the good and just from the bad and unjust'. Barbarians, through their (alleged) acts of idolatry, human sacrifice, cannibalism, and cruelty in war, had violated 'natural law'. Their subjugation was, thus, just: 'the *dominium* of the perfect over the imperfect, the strong over the weak, superior virtue over vice most applicable to those barbarians called Indians [Native Americans]'.[13]

He added the suggestion that the saving of souls resulting from the ensuing conversion of the 'Indians' further justified the means used to accomplish the ends. In this, he echoed St Augustine's remark that 'it is not true that nothing is accomplished when it is accomplished with violence'. And he prefigured the arguments of a later generation of apologists for empire, such as the lib-eral philosopher John Stuart Mill who justified the harshness of British rule in India in similar terms: 'despotism is a legitimate mode of government in dealing with barbarians, provided the end be their improvement'.[14]

Las Casas, who had already published an eviscerating critique of the atrocities committed by his compatriots in the Americas, made a spirited rejoinder to Sepúlveda. He observed that in terms of violating 'natural law', that the Spanish themselves 'in the absolutely inhuman things they have done to those nations [of the Americas] have surpassed all other barbarians'. He went on to reject that the ends of conversion justified the means of conquest. Brutality resulted only in suffering and provoked resistance: 'Anything should be tolerated to avoid waging war, the sea of all evil ... for this is not helpful to the spread of the gospel'.[15]

Yet even Las Casas never abandoned the fundamental assumptions of European supremacism. Keen that Native Americans were not subject to forced labour, he advocated for the enslavement of Africans instead, ascribing to the established proto-racist belief that they adjusted better to that condition. His condescending and assimilationist vision for the indigenous population was shaped by his belief that they should abandon their 'barbarous, fierce and depraved' customs under ecclesiastical tutelage. Whatever moral qualms he eventually voiced over African slavery or the original dispossession of native land, he, too, embodied 'the logic of colonialism'.[16] That logic always contained the potential for persecution and genocide.

Consider the Americas as an example. It is now generally accepted that the total population of the continents probably stood at around 60 million. North America (excluding Mexico and Central America) was around seven million in 1492, the year Columbus arrived on the island of Hispaniola.[17] Over the course of the next two centuries, a demographic catastrophe unfolded. Indigenous populations across North and South America fell by perhaps 95 per cent overall. Cultures, cities, complex large-scale polities, and even languages were lost. Much ink has been spilled debating the raw statistics, especially around the exact size of the pre-contact population. The evidence is too partial and fragmentary for much more than informed guesswork. This has allowed for some tendentious dismissals of the fate of native peoples. For North America, especially, diminishing both the aggregate population and the rate of the decline served to not disturb triumphalist narratives of the conquest and settling of an untamed, and basically empty, wilderness. However, recent new evidence derived from the study of a large dataset of prehistoric and contemporary mitochondrial DNA samples has confirmed that a dramatic, severe, and widespread 'contraction' in population occurred in the aftermath of 'first contact' with Europeans.[18]

But was this genocide? The question largely hinges on whether there was an *intent* to destroy. By far the most significant factor driving the catastrophic mortality rates was disease. Epidemics of such infections as smallpox, measles, and influenza ravaged indigenous communities. These were new pathogens to the Americas, carried by Europeans and requiring only fleeting contact to have devastating, and unplanned, consequences. Thomas Moreton visited the English Plymouth colony, in Massachusetts, shortly after its establishment in 1620. He stumbled across a deserted native village littered with human remains. Noting the care and ceremony that the local peoples normally attached to the disposal of their dead, he understood what had happened. Those few who had not succumbed to a disease that had taken hold suddenly and killed quickly, had simply fled away. Like many of his generation, he saw the work of providence in this tragedy: 'the hand of God fell heavily upon them, with such a mortall stroake that they died on heaps'. In particular, he thought the people of that village had suffered a divine retribution for an attack on a party of French fur traders who had landed on a nearby shore some years earlier. Five had been taken captive; the rest had been killed. One of those captives probably harboured the pathogen that subsequently proved so lethal.[19]

Modern epidemiologists would attribute its devastating impact not to divine anger, but to the fact that the natives had no previous exposure to infections carried by Europeans and Africans, and were consequently immunologically compromised. These were, thus, 'virgin soil epidemics' and that, it has been suggested, is a key to understanding the staggering post-contact collapse in population.[20] However, the disastrous consequences of European colonisation on indigenous populations cannot simply be dismissed as an unfortunate, and essentially unintentional, corollary of their lack of immunity to unfamiliar diseases.

Revealingly, the impact of novel diseases was not uniform across the Americas. There were dramatic variations. The population of the Taíno of the Greater Antilles islands fell from perhaps 500,000 in 1496 to fewer than 500 in 1570, following first contact with Europeans. In contrast, the population of the Navajo, of the southwest of the North American continent, actually grew following contact with the Spanish in the 1600s. Then, there were a few thousand. Today there are 300,000. Understanding *why* diseases had such variable outcomes on different groups necessitates considering wider geographic, social, political, and economic factors. In many instances, consideration of these reveals a very real intent to do harm on the part of the colonisers.[21]

To a degree, there were factors outside anyone's control that explain variation in mortality rates. The Taíno were a densely settled, sedentary, and insular population, who lived in large villages. They practised an intensive form of agriculture, including irrigation and soil-enrichment schemes, that required much organised labour. Such population centres suffered greatly due to epidemics, especially where the mechanics of contagion were not understood, and the sick were not quarantined. In contrast, the Navajo lived semi-sedentary lives and followed a mixed economy of hunting and planting. The acquisition of Spanish livestock, especially sheep, and the development of pastoralism, was a positive boon for them. They lived in remote, semi-arid areas, unattractive to European settlers, in small, dispersed kinship groups. When epidemics reached them, they hit them hard, but they did so less frequently and with less risk of widespread contagion. They thus suffered less than even their near neighbours, the pueblo-dwelling Hopi.[22]

Yet there was another significant difference, the one that doomed the Taíno. That was the nature of their contact with Europeans. Columbus himself had attempted to establish commercial sugar plantations on Hispaniola

in the earliest days of colonisation, enslaving the local population to provide the necessary labour. That experiment failed because of the ensuing
mortality rates. And that was not simply a question of immunity. Disease
took its staggering toll of the population as the people were enfeebled by
enslavement, poverty, malnutrition, overwork, and brutality. These were the
consequences of a deliberate policy that aimed to destroy autonomous native
societies and reduce their former members to slaves, with, in Lemkin's terms,
the oppressor's national pattern (government, religion, culture, and economic
and legal systems) then imposed upon them.[23]

Similar processes were repeated across much of North America. For
example, after the establishment of an English colony in South Carolina in
1670, the colonists had forged a military alliance with local tribes, such as the
Yamasee. These they encouraged to launch slave-raiding expeditions against
native peoples under Spanish paramountcy in neighbouring Florida. This
policy served three purposes: it drew the powerful Yamasee into a dependent
trading relationship with the English; it undermined a rival colonial power
by harming those under their ostensible protection, and it provided a supply
of slaves who could be put to work on the Carolinians' plantations or be
traded on to New England and the Caribbean. Crucially, it also catalysed
and magnified the impact of disease. Between 1699 to 1712, epidemics of
influenza, typhus, measles, and smallpox had struck the war-ravaged communities with devastating force. The raiding parties and their captives had
become the primary vectors for spreading the lethal pathogens, affecting
both the Yamasee and those they enslaved. By 1706, the native population
from Spanish Florida had been reduced from about 25,000 to just 400,
sheltering within the fortifications of St Augustine.[24] In such circumstances,
the epidemics must be considered as an inevitable consequence of a deliberate
colonial policy that aimed at the extirpation of specific tribal groups. The
case for considering this as genocide would seem strong.

Thus, while the staggering indigenous population decline caused by disease in the Americas after 1492 cannot, *tout court*, be regarded as genocide, specific episodes, where epidemics took hold as the result of deliberate
harmful policies, probably ought to be. A similar point might be made about
warfare in North America too. While not all conflicts between colonisers and
Native Americans were genocidal in intent, some clearly were.

They drew on an ugly 'old world' precedent. During military campaigns
in Ireland in the sixteenth and seventeenth centuries, the English had come
to practise a form of 'unlimited' warfare. They dismissed their Irish enemies
as 'savages' or 'barbarians' who were, therefore, outside the prevailing moral
restraints exercised during conventional wars. The English thus destroyed
the material resources upon which the targeted populations depended for
survival. They targeted non-combatants. They massacred prisoners. In late
1574, the Earl of Essex drove Irish men, women, and children from their
Ulster homes into barren winter woodlands, knowing full well they would
freeze or starve. His compatriot Edward Barkley commented, 'How godly a

deed it is to overthrow so wicked a race the world may judge: for my part I think there cannot be a greater sacrifice to God'.[25]

There were a number of factors that gave rise to the peculiar cruelty with which the English waged war in Ireland. Fears that Catholic powers might invade their own realm via Ireland gave the conflict an existential quality for Protestant Englishmen. It was a peculiarly difficult conflict to wage. The guerrilla tactics employed so effectively by Irish forces were both frustrating, exhausting, and terrifying. Unable to bring their elusive enemy to battle, the campaigns dragged on, and the hungry, ragged, and fearful soldiery despaired of seeing their homes again. An enemy who would not stand his ground but would strike and disappear, English soldiers concluded, was cowardly and not worthy of respect. The Irish themselves seemed utterly alien by language, dress, and habits. So, the English soldiers ruthlessly wielded fire and sword with little discrimination against those they dismissed as a 'wicked race', combatants or otherwise.[26]

In essence, these circumstances would be re-created in colonial contexts, such as North America. In their earliest years, the colonies perched on the edge of extinction. The Native Americans, like the Irish, pursued a baffling, frightening and, to the colonists' eyes, dishonourable 'skulking' way of war, based on stealth and ambush. Such an enemy could be swiftly dismissed as treacherous, savage, and wicked, fit only for extirpation. Some campaigns were thus genocidal. During the Pequot War of 1636–1637, several hundred inhabitants of one village on the Mystic River were massacred, without regard to age or gender. The remainder of the tribe was relentlessly pursued; men of an age capable of bearing arms were executed, women and children enslaved, either by the English or their indigenous allies, the Narragansetts and Mohegans.[27]

That warfare had the potential to become genocide in this context should not surprise. Although the scale of these conflicts was small, sometimes involving just a few hundred combatants, they exhibited many of the key characteristics of what military historians have termed 'total wars'. These can be characterised by the mobilisation en masse of populations as either soldiers or labourers; the wholesale deployment of cultural and economic resources to sustain the will and means to fight and the legitimisation of targeting the *entirety* of an enemy population, combatant, and non-combatant.

Metacom's (or Kings Philip's War) of 1675–1676 saw a majority of adult males mobilised on both sides: the Wampanoags and the English colonists in the (still precarious) Plymouth settlement. There was no meaningful distinction between home and military front; settlements were themselves frequently battlegrounds. All laboured to support the war bands and militia regiments, even providing sustenance for winter campaigns, unusual in the period. Cultural resources as well as military and economic ones were mobilised in support of the war effort. The colonists castigated their enemies, on pages and from pulpits, as allies of Satan and irredeemably savage; in the words of one New England poet, 'Monsters shapt and fac'd like men'. The campaign was conducted with the aim of extirpating the Wampanoag nation as an entity. Of their pre-war population of 12,000, 4,000 were killed or sold into slavery. The survivors were scattered and placed under the authority of the colonists' allies, such as the Mohegans.[28]

These early episodes established a grim precedent. As John Grenier has noted, 'violence directed systematically against non-combatants through irregular means, from the start, has been a central part of America's way of war'.[29] And therefore 'deliberately inflicting on the group conditions of life calculated to bring about its physical destruction in whole or in part', simply became a characteristic of warfare against Native Americans. George Washington dispatched a punitive force to campaign against Iroquois tribes allied to the British during the War of Independence in 1779. He instructed the commander, General John Sullivan, that his 'immediate objects' were 'the total destruction and devastation of their settlements'. Villages were torched, crops destroyed, peach and apple trees girdled. The Iroquois fled, but were relentlessly pursued by smallpox, exposure, and starvation. Thousands died. Within half a century, the victor's national pattern was imposed: a million Americans had settled upon their former lands.[30]

This expansionism was not simply fuelled by materialistic greed for land, although that was plentifully evident. It was ideological too. The revolutionary generation believed that the future of the new republic depended upon the existence of a politically independent property-owning class of white men: small farmers, planters, and artisans. These would be the experimental nation's best defence against aristocracy and despotism. This propertied class, the bulwark of American freedom, thus needed land. For Americans, therefore, expansionism aimed to create, in Thomas Jefferson's words, an 'empire for liberty'. Such an empire felt entitled to the land hitherto unproductively occupied by those dismissed as irredeemable savages.[31]

These acts of dispossession and concurrent genocidal colonialist violence were recurrent features of empire building from the sixteenth to the twentieth centuries. The examples are legion, if often overlooked: the annihilation of the Aboriginal people of Tasmania, 1803–1847 by British settlers; the destruction of tribal groups loyal to Emir Abd al-Qadir by the French military in Algeria, 1832–1847; the extirpation of tribal nomadism in Cyrenaica, 1911–1931, where, at one point, the Italian authorities had incarcerated half the population in concentration camps.[32]

In many instances, these episodes cannot simply be associated with the original destruction of native groups' national pattern (Lemkin's first phase of genocide). Conquest, within a colonial and post-colonial context, might best be understood as a cyclical phenomenon, with each reoccurrence having genocidal potential.

Consider, for example, the Maya of Guatemala. The Spanish conquest began in 1524, but took over a century to complete. The invaders struggled to overcome a series of small but determined groups, in terrain that suited the defenders. The vicious, protracted warfare that ensued was accompanied by the inevitable massacres and epidemics, causing a catastrophic collapse in population. Once subdued, their own political and economic institutions destroyed, the surviving Maya were resettled in *congegación*, where the Spanish ruling elite imposed their national pattern. These new villages provided them with a pool of workers for their *encomienda* system of coerced labour. Yet Maya communities proved remarkably resilient, adopting many aspects of Hispanic culture while retaining the essence of their own. Such dynamism led to a tradition of resistance, such as the Tzeltal rebellion of 1712, which was driven by a heady combination of peasant material grievances and Christian messianic fervour. Such uprisings invariably provoked a heavy-handed military response, and the bloody drama of conquest was re-enacted as they were crushed.[33]

This process did not end with Guatemala's independence in 1821. As was often the case, de-colonisation simply left power in the hands of the old colonial elites, or their allies. The power structures that had underpinned colonial forms of exploitation and oppression remained, and therefore so did the potential for genocide.[34] In the late nineteenth century, Guatemalan conservative regimes used forced labour schemes, debt peonage, and vagrancy laws to, once more, destroy Mayan autonomy and impose a new market-oriented national pattern, geared to the needs of coffee planters. The cycle of re-conquest continued into the twentieth century. During the 1980s, one million Maya were driven from their homes, as the government engaged in 'counterinsurgency' operations against communist guerrillas. These made no distinction between revolutionaries and peaceful villages. 'Indian' became synonymous with 'subversives', thus facilitating the same genocidal ferocity once witnessed in sixteenth-century Ireland or seventeenth-century Virginia.[35]

While, overwhelmingly, it has been indigenous peoples such as the Maya who have been the victims of colonial genocides, it should be noted that resistance to colonisation sometimes also demonstrated what Nicholas Robins has described as a 'genocidal impulse'. For example, in 1680 the Pueblo Indians, of what is now New Mexico, rose in a well-organised and efficiently executed rebellion that eliminated the Spanish presence in their lands. The Pueblo had first contact with the Spanish Empire in 1538. As they had been subjugated, they had experienced population decline through disease and war, demands for forced labour, and sustained assaults on their religion and culture, principally by the Franciscan missionaries who had dominated the economic and political life of the province since 1616. Their situation had been made worse by a series of droughts and by predation on their settlements by semi-nomadic peoples, the Navajo and the Apache. These had recently acquired horses, becoming a militarily formidable enemy. Punitive slaving expeditions against them by the Spanish tended to only escalate, rather than mitigate, the violence. A number of desperate, uncoordinated, and rapidly extinguished revolts by the Pueblo had taken place over the 1600s.

The 1680 rebellion was different. Inspired by religious visions and aiming to restore Pueblo autonomy, its leader Popé, insisted that the insurgents 'put an end to as many [Spanish] as possible, sparing neither men, women, children nor missionaries'.[36] Forging a high level of cooperation across several communities and maintaining secrecy until the last moment, the 1680 rebellion was, in the short term, successful. After fierce fighting, those Spaniards who were not killed, fled. For twelve years, they had no presence in the Rio Grande basin. Their national pattern was obliterated; churches and mission stations were destroyed, and Pueblo culture and ritual reinstated. Popé's millenarian vision of a native utopia, however, was not fulfilled. Drought, internal dissension, and continued conflict with the Navajo and Apache saw to that. The Spanish re-conquered the area in 1692.

Robins has suggested that such genocidal insurgencies were a recurrent phenomenon in American colonialism. As evidence, he chronicles two other episodes. The first of these was the Great Rebellion of 1780–1782. This began as a local uprising in 'upper Peru' (modern Bolivia), but subsequently developed into the most significant threat to the Spanish Empire in the Americas before the wars of independence. The leaders of this rebellion, such as Túpac Amaru and Túpac Catari, shared Popé's utopian millenarianism, and commitment to destroying the Spanish colonialists root and branch. Secondly, Robins considers the Caste War which began in 1847, on the Yucatán Peninsula, in post-independence Mexico. Cecilio Chi led local Maya in a series of attacks against towns and haciendas with the intention of eliminating those of Spanish descent and allegiance in the region. The Maya were able to establish a separatist community, Chan Santa Cruz, that did not acknowledge Mexican suzerainty until 1915. Robins acknowledges that these rebellions did not result in the total extirpation of the Hispanic Spanish populations. In the Caste War, many Hispanics were enslaved rather than killed. Some fought on the Mayan side. Yet these movements 'sought the practical elimination of a people, culture, language and, to varying degrees, belief system'. He concludes that the rebellions thus constitute 'retributive genocides'.[37]

In the final stages of the Haitian Revolution, 1791–1804, the fighting had become so bitter and the cycle of atrocities and massacres so destructive that both the French, attempting to re-impose their rule on the island, and the Haitians, fighting to prevent their re-enslavement, explicitly pursued genocidal strategies. The French commander Charles Leclerc informed Paris that 'I will have to fight a war of extermination', because the rebellious slaves had been 'living like brigands for ten years' and could never be made to work again. After his death in November 1802, his successor, Donatien Rochambeau, expressed the same sentiments, 'we must exterminate all the armed Blacks, the farm labourers and their chiefs ... without this we will lose our colonies ... '.[38]

Together, yellow fever and implacable Haitian resistance had defeated the French. In 1804, the victorious Haitian commander, Jean-Jacques Dessalines, vowed both to 'give a just example of the vengeance that may be exacted by a proud people', and to ensure there would be no future attempt to renew the war: 'May they shudder when they approach our coastline ... '. He ordered that the thousands of French people still on the island – soldiers, planters, *petits blancs* (the urban poor) – be killed, and not sparing the women and children.[39]

The notion of such 'retributive genocides', or 'subaltern genocides' as they are sometimes referred to, is a controversial one. Given that the insurgents usually lacked the preponderance of power that is generally associated with the capacity for genocide, it might be argued that it is an inappropriate frame of reference for such wars of resistance. Gary Clayton Anderson asks, 'Can genocide be applied where oppressed people rebel against their oppressors? If that expansive definition were to be accepted, where would the line be drawn and would not the term genocide lose all meaning?'[40] Yet, in terms of the 1948 UN Convention on Genocide, it is difficult to avoid the conclusion that the rebels, having achieved a local asymmetrical advantage, did indeed target a national group for destruction and proceeded by killing them or by 'causing them serious bodily or mental harm'.

Lemkin himself was conscious of the significance of colonialism in the history of genocide, but was also ambivalent about the relationship. He identified very clear instances that he thought genocidal. These included the Belgian colonisation of the Congo, where some 50 per cent of the population died, 1886–1908; the massacres and forced removals of Aboriginal peoples from Tasmania by British settler colonists, 1827–1831, and the systematic extermination of the Herero and Nama peoples in German South-West Africa (modern Namibia), 1904–1908. The appalling, rapacious crimes committed in the Belgian Congo were not driven by the imperatives of unlimited, unconventional warfare, or even a desire to wipe out indigenous peoples. They were essentially economic in their rationale, consequent upon the violent enslavement of the Congolese and the brutal work regimes on the colony's rubber plantations. Yet for Lemkin, such a policy clearly aimed at the 'disintegration of the political and social institutions ... and the economic existence of national groups, and the destruction of the personal security, liberty, health, dignity, and even the lives of the individuals belonging to such groups'. Thus, it too constituted genocide.[41]

Lemkin, however, tended to see such imperial genocides as atypical rather than characteristic, even in settler colonialism, where the coloniser's national pattern was invariably imposed. He shared some of the ugly prevailing stereotypes of indigenous societies. In the case of the Congo, for example, he blamed Belgium's native Congolese auxiliaries, 'an unorganised and disorderly rabble of savages', for many of the worst excesses of the regime there. Overall, he seems to have accepted Europeans' self-proclaimed civilising mission as potentially beneficial to native groups. In particular, imperialism was a potent vehicle for bringing more and more of the world under the remit of international law, which Lemkin saw as the principal instrument for preventing future genocides.[42]

This ambivalence towards colonialism's relationship to genocides was, and remained for some time, particularly apparent in the matter of cultural genocide. Although a determined proponent of the idea that assaults on the cultural lives of groups constituted genocide, Lemkin nevertheless accepted that cultures were dynamic. They would change, through a process of 'diffusion', resulting from exposure to external intercultural exchange. In such cases, a native group's culture might 'become weaker and may disintegrate entirely when exposed to strong outside influences'. Such change, however, Lemkin thought, should arise from the autonomous acquisition of external institutions and cultural forms, and was not to be imposed coercively.[43]

Liberal imperialists pursued policies that were designed to promote such cultural acquisition and catalyse the transformation of indigenous cultures. Yet they trod a fine line when they did so. For example, in Australia, Canada, and the United States, indigenous children were taken from their families to receive a 'civilising' education in white adoptive families, residential schools, or some such institution. Despite the very clear provision in the 1948 UN convention prohibiting the forced removal of children from one group to another, these policies persisted into the 1970s. Only comparatively recently has there been official acknowledgement that these measures could, as a 1997 Australian government inquiry put it, 'properly be labelled "genocidal"'.[44]

This suggestion has been accompanied by much controversy at the very notion that liberal democracies might have committed genocides through assimilationist policies intended, so their instigators insisted, to improve the lives of indigenous peoples. Such policies, however, ought to be considered in their broader and deeper historical context. As Pauline Wakeham has observed, prevailing understanding of genocide has tended to focus on the 'prioritization of time-intense direct violence enacted with explicitly declared intent'.[45] Thus, an event such as the extirpation of the Pequot during the war of 1636–1637, and in particular the massacre of combatants and non-combatants alike at the village on the Mystic River, might be clearly identifiable as genocide. Yet such a conception tends to obscure the longer-term processes, unfolding over generations, by which indigenous societies have been destroyed, and replaced by a coloniser's national pattern.

These processes may have moved through initial settler violence, subsequent repression, implementation of economic and social policies designed, explicitly or implicitly, to undermine traditional ways of living, forced relocation, through to assimilationist policies such as removing children from their communities for a 'civilising' education. Reconceptualising genocide as a potentially *longue durée* and attritional phenomenon would clarify its applicability to colonialism considerably. The summary of the 2019 Canadian *National Inquiry into Missing and Murdered Indigenous Women and Girls: A Legal Analysis of Genocide*, recommended this approach, concluding:

> … colonial destruction of Indigenous peoples has taken place insidiously and over centuries. The intent to destroy Indigenous peoples in Canada was implemented gradually and intermittently, using varied tactics against distinct Indigenous communities. These acts and omissions affected their

rights to life and security, but also numerous economic, cultural and social rights. In addition to the lethal conduct, the non-lethal tactics used were no less destructive and fall within the scope of the crime of genocide. These policies fluctuated in time and space, and in different incarnations, are still ongoing. Without a clear start or end date to encompass these genocidal policies, colonial genocide does not conform with popular notions of genocide as a determinate, quantifiable event.[46]

However, besides recognising colonial genocide's peculiar long-term and attritional characteristics, it is important to note the close relationship between some episodes and related events that subsequently occurred in Europe. This is most apparent in the systematic campaigns of physical annihilation, often waged under the guise of war or counterinsurgency. The genocide of the Herero and Nama in German South-West Africa, 1904–1908, has been singled out as especially portentous.

In many respects, this conflict, although undoubtedly very brutal, largely resembled other colonial precedents. The Germans presence dated only to 1884. Twenty years later, their settlers were still thin on the ground, less than 5,000 in total. Many lived on isolated and remote farms, far from the capital of Windhoek, and were acutely conscious of their vulnerability. The colony's governor, Theodor Leutwein, had suppressed some outbreaks of armed resistance and attempted to assert control through indirect rule, in a manner familiar to the French or British. He initially fostered the support of both Samuel Maharero, the paramount chief of the Herero, and Hendrick Witboi of the Nama. Yet these two men would subsequently lead their peoples in revolt. Robbed of their lands, impoverished, subject to forced labour, and enraged by the legal impunity with which German colonists committed murders, rapes, and assaults, first the Herero, in January 1904, and then the Nama, the following September, had struck back.[47]

The ensuing military campaigns followed a familiar pattern of doomed indigenous resistance. The insurgents initially achieved a degree of surprise, isolating military garrisons and outposts, severing transport and communication links, and attacking farms. Lethal violence was carefully targeted: women and children, Africans from other tribes, missionaries, and non-German Europeans were spared. The colonists' dead, overwhelmingly adult, male farmers, numbered 123. The response showed no such restraint. Leutwein was sidelined, and command given to the newly arrived General Lothar von Trotha. Commanding thousands of professional soldiers, supported by machine guns and modern artillery, he inflicted a decisive defeat on the Herero at the Battle of Waterberg, 11 August 1904. The whole tribe – men, women, children – had assembled hoping to negotiate terms. Instead, the survivors were driven towards the barren, waterless Omaheke Desert.

The pursuit was relentless and brutal. Stragglers and the abandoned wounded were put to death, regardless of age or sex. As the survivors fled into the desert, access to waterholes was sealed off. Thirst killed those who escaped bullets and bayonets. On 2 October, von Trotha issued the infamous *Schrecklichkeit* (frightfulness) order: the Hereros were no longer German subjects; men were to be shot on sight, women and children driven back into the desert. Explaining this policy to his superior in Germany, General Alfred von Schlieffen, he rejected the view that the Hereros were 'necessary raw material' to labour in the colony, 'the nation as such must be annihilated or if this is not possible from a military standpoint then they must be driven from the land'.[48]

The Nama, having witnessed the fate of the Hereros at Waterberg, pursued a guerrilla campaign, which some bands successfully sustained until late 1907. Yet they, too, would be offered no negotiated settlement and were pursued relentlessly. To a degree, von Trotha's policy of extermination was ameliorated. Von Schlieffen, together with Germany's Chancellor Bernhard von Bülow, countermanded von Trotha's *Schrecklichkeit* order. The chancellor did so on economic, political, and humanitarian grounds. Von Schlieffen merely thought it impractical. Yet their intervention had little impact. Hereros and Namas were now able to surrender, but, once they did so, they were confined to concentration camps. These were a recent 'imperial-military invention', already utilised by the Spanish in Cuba in 1895–1898, the US in the Philippines 1899–1902, and the British in South Africa, 1899–1902. They were intended to separate guerrillas from their civilian logistical and intelligence networks. Mortality rates from disease, malnutrition, and exposure in incompetently administered camps were shockingly high. In the German case, peculiarly meagre rations combined with heavy forced labour, for women and children as well as men, added to the death rates. At the inhospitable Shark Island Camp, some 2,000 Nama prisoners died, 1906–1907, a mortality rate of 77.5 per cent.[49]

The camps had largely continued von Trotha's policy of annihilation, by other means. By 1908, about half of the Nama's pre-war population of 20,000 were dead. The Herero had lost perhaps 60,000 from a pre-war population of 75,000–80,000. Their traditional ways of life were destroyed. The survivors were forbidden from owning land or cattle. Adult males were compelled to carry passes. All were subject to vagrancy laws that effectively reduced them to a permanent class of unfree labourers, exploited by white farmers and disciplined by the whip.

The destruction of the Herero and Nama has assumed a particular signifi-cance in scholarship on genocide as a distinct step on the road to Auschwitz. Jürgen Zimmerer has argued that the conflict was 'a prelude to the Holocaust' and stood 'at a decisive interface, between the massacres carried out by groups of settlers and local militias on the American and Australian frontiers and the quasi-industrial methods of carrying out mass murder in the Third Reich'.[50]

In this analysis, Zimmerer echoes the suggestion made in 1947 by the political philosopher Hannah Arendt that 'some of the fundamental aspects' of European colonialism in the years 1884–1914, 'appear so close to [twen-tieth century] totalitarian phenomena' that the period might be considered

'a preparatory stage for coming catastrophes'.[51] Arendt's contemporaries
Frantz Fanon and W.E.B. Dubois also pointed to the precedents set by colonialism. Dubois wrote:

> ... there was no Nazi atrocity – concentration camps, wholesale maiming
> and murder, defilement of women, or ghastly blasphemy of children –
> which the Christian civilization of Europe had not long been practicing
> against colored folks in all parts of the world in the name of and for the
> defense of a Superior Race born to rule the world.[52]

Specifically, in terms of the Herero and Nama genocides, Zimmerer has identified a number of characteristics as foreshadowing the Holocaust. Previous
genocidal massacres, he argued, had generally been committed by colonists or
local militias, at the edges of empire, where the authority of the central state
was weak and unable to restrain settler violence. In contrast, in South-West
Africa, the German state had taken the lead in the process. It had broken
'the ultimate taboo' with a concrete policy of exterminating entire peoples,
facilitated by the formidable bureaucracy of a modern state and actioned
by professional soldiers. Once this taboo was broken, it was 'imaginable' to
conceive the eradication of specific groups, from Africans to 'Jews, Sinti and
Roma, homosexuals and the handicapped'.[53]

Other scholars have also stressed the place of the South-West African
genocide as a wellspring of exterminatory ideologies. Isabel Hull pointed to
the role of evolving German military doctrine, wherein the objective of annihilation of the enemy's armies (*Vernichtung*) tended towards conflation with
the annihilation of the enemy *tout court*. This, Hull argues, fostered an institutional propensity for 'final solutions'. This tendency was not necessarily
unique to the German military. Other armies had behaved similarly in the
colonial context. The fatal difference was that in Imperial Germany, a conservative constitution had left the army far less accountable to civilian oversight, or susceptible to intervention by politicians. Without such restraint, the
culture became ingrained and more likely to sway future strategy.[54]

Benjamin Madley drew attention to the geographer Friedrich Ratzel who
coined the term *Lebensraum* (living space). Ratzel argued that 'superior
cultures' invariably destroyed 'inferior cultures' in battles for *Lebensraum*.
He was a founding member of the expansionist Pan-German League and
Africa figured prominently in his dark vision of existential cultural conflicts,
outlined in his 1897 work *Political Geography*. Rudolf Hess appears to have
introduced Hitler to this text whilst the latter was incarcerated in Landsberg
Prison in 1924. Hitler looked to eastern Europe rather than Africa as the
proper objective of German colonialism, but the concept of *Lebensraum* was
central to his own conception of a war of annihilation.[55]

Perhaps, however, the most telling dimension of the link between the
genocides in South-West Africa and the Holocaust was the centrality of
ideologies of race. By the early twentieth century, these were evolving from

legitimising systems of political and economic domination to justifying far more radical policies of exclusion or extermination. Europeans had ascribed inherently servile characteristics to Africans even before the establishment of the Atlantic slave trade in the mid-fifteenth century. The subsequent rise of plantation slavery in the Americas hardened loose, malleable racial thinking into a hegemonic racist ideology that underpinned white supremacy. In the eighteenth century, Enlightenment thinkers gave this legitimising myth of white racial superiority a patina of intellectual respectability. Thus, for example, in 1737, the Swedish naturalist Carl Linnaeus theorised the existence of four human races, which he ordered hierarchically by skin colour: white Europeans, red Americans, yellow Asiatics, black Africans. Skin pigmentation betokened supposed starker distinctions in inherited intellectual and psychological characteristics. The European was ingenious and law-abiding, the American irascible and custom-bound, the Asiatic melancholic and opinionated, the African lazy and servile. The European was, thus, the most apt to rule.[56]

In the nineteenth century, such theorising developed into a pseudo-science, taught in universities, and widely propagated in society. The most pernicious manifestation of this was Social Darwinism. Ideologues such as the Victorian sociologist Herbert Spencer applied Darwinian principles of natural selection, and the notion of 'survival of the fittest', to human groups. History thus became the story of past struggles between competing races. And the future, it was thus argued, would belong to those peoples who exhibited the greatest fitness for survival.[57]

In turn arose the study of human hereditary, or eugenics. This essentially proposed selective breeding to 'improve' the fitness of the racial 'stock'. In Germany, eugenics, or *Rassenhygiene* (race hygiene) was an established, academically respectable field by the time of the conflict in South-West Africa. The anthropologist Eugen Fischer arrived in the colony in 1908, especially to study the physical and intellectual characteristics of children of the Baster people. These were of particular interest to Fischer because they were *Mischling* (of mixed ancestry) descended from European settlers and African women (the name Baster derived from the Dutch *bastaard*). Fischer's tendentious conclusions was that the admixture of African blood to European stock inevitably resulted in physically and mentally inferior offspring. 'Miscegenation' thus was the wellspring of racial degeneration. In this context, race was no longer merely a question of who should rule, but of who should be allowed to survive and propagate.[58]

While it is unclear if Hitler read Fischer's work, the latter contributed significantly to the eugenicist thinking that undoubtedly influenced him. He, and other prominent Nazis such as Heinrich Himmler, considered the German *volk* to be almost synonymous with the so-called 'Aryan' race. According to the pseudo-history of nineteenth-century racist ideologues such as Arthur de Gobineau, the Aryans were the 'branch of the white people' responsible for all 'the great human civilisations'.[59] The future of humanity thus lay in the protection, and indeed biological perfection, of the German *volk*. Eugenics would be the tool to achieve this end, through the Nazi *Aktion T4* programme of murdering the disabled and implementing policies to prevent reproduction among supposedly inferior 'asocial' stock (such as habitual criminals, prostitutes, and alcoholics). Race mixing, though, posed the gravest threat; for Hitler, 'the sin against blood and the race are the original sin in the world and the end of humanity which surrenders to it'. The greatest threat to the racial purity of the German *volk* were the Jews, whom the Nazis believed to be locked in an epoch-spanning Darwinian struggle for existence with the Aryans.[60]

These points of contact between the genocides of the Herero and the Nama, and the Holocaust demonstrate the significance of colonial conflicts to understanding many of the ideological impulses that drove twentieth-century genocides.[61] Yet it would be a mistake to draw overly deterministic conclusions. Colonialism did not lead inevitably to later genocides. Indeed, those nations with the longest history of colonial violence, such as France or Britain, did not go on to commit genocides in the twentieth century. Their practice of imperial rule was still culpably brutal, as events in Kenya, 1952–1960, or Algeria, 1954–1962, readily attest. The mass incarceration, use of torture, and collective punishments they employed against allegedly disloyal populations certainly 'approached the borderline between extreme repression and the partial destruction of society'.[62] They were persecutory, but they stopped short of the intentional wholesale annihilation of peoples. By the twentieth century, they had come to depend upon economic development of colonial societies, and the fostering of a westernised, indigenous elite, as the basis of their rule.

Nor, in the German case, should we walk a straight road from Windhoek to Auschwitz. Whatever striking ideological commonalities emerge, from the rhetoric of *Lebensraum* to a radical, exterminatory form of racism, there is no evidence that events in German South-West Africa *directly* shaped or influenced Nazi policy. Africa had ceased to figure in German politics because Germany had ceased to be a colonial power after the First World War. That conflict, combined with the impact of a worldwide recession, was a national and demographic catastrophe that had shifted the nation onto a new and dark trajectory.[63] And by then, other dangerous precedents had occurred on the Eurasian continent itself.

Notes

1 Winston Churchill, Radio Broadcast, 24 August 1941, www.ibiblio.org/pha/timeline/410824awp.html [accessed 28 April 2023].

2 Raphaël Lemkin, *Axis Rule in Occupied Europe: Laws of Occupation, Analysis of Government, Proposals for Redress* (New York: Columbia University Press, 1944), p.79.

3 A. Dirk Moses, *The Problems of Genocide: Permanent Security and the Language of Transgression* (Cambridge: Cambridge University Press, 2021), pp.150–157;

Johann Justus Vasel, ' "In the Beginning, There Was No Word ..." ', *European Journal of International Law*, 29 (2019), p.1053.

4 Quoted in Matthew Lippman, 'The Drafting of the 1948 Convention on the Prevention and Punishment of the Crime of Genocide', *Boston University International Law Journal*, 3 (1985), p.3.

5 Quoted in Dominik J. Schaller and Jürgen Zimmerer (eds), 'Introduction', *The Origins of Genocide – Raphaël Lemkin as a Historian of Mass Violence*, (London: Routledge, 2009), p.3.

6 Lippman, 'The Drafting of the 1948 Convention', p.5.

7 Adam Jones, *Genocide: A Comprehensive Introduction* (London: Routledge, 2006), p.364; Schaller and Zimmerer (eds), *The Origins of Genocide*, p.5.

8 Lemkin, *Axis Rule in Occupied Europe*, p.79.

9 Raphaël Lemkin, *Lemkin on Genocide*, edited by Steven L. Jacobs (Lanham, MD: Lexington Books, 2012), p.3.

10 A. Dirk Moses, 'Lemkin, Culture, and the Concept of Genocide', in Donald Bloxham and A. Dirk Moses (eds), *The Oxford Handbook of Genocide Studies* (Oxford: Oxford University Press, 2010), pp.22–25; Martin Shaw, *What is Genocide?* (Cambridge: Polity Press, 2007), p.20.

11 Quoted in Lippman, 'The Drafting of the 1948 Convention', p.11; Beth van Schaack, 'The Crime of Political Genocide: Repairing the Genocide Convention's Blind Spot', *Yale Law Journal*, 106 (1997), pp.2259–2291.

12 Ann Curthoys and John Docker, 'Defining Genocide', in Dan Stone (ed.), *The Historiography of Genocide* (New York: Palgrave Macmillan, 2010), pp.13–14.

13 Daniel R. Brunstetter and Dana Zartner, 'Just War against Barbarians: Revisiting the Valladolid Debates between Sepúlveda and Las Casas', *Political Studies*, 59 (2011), pp.736–737.

14 St Augustine, Letter 89.7, *The Works of St Augustine: Letters 1–99*, translated by Roland Teske, edited by John Rotelle (New York: New City Press, 2001), pp.362–363; Mill quoted in Mark Tunick, 'Tolerant Imperialism: John Stuart Mill's Defense of British Rule in India', *Review of Politics*, 68 (2006), p.595.

15 Brunstetter and Zartner, 'Just War against Barbarians ', pp.739–745.

16 Asselin Charles, 'Colonial Discourse Since Christopher Columbus', *Journal of Black Studies*, 26 (1996), pp.140–142.

17 John D. Daniels, 'The Indian Population of North America in 1492', *William and Mary Quarterly*, 49 (1992), pp.298–320; Russell Thornton, 'Native American Demographic and Tribal Survival into the Twenty-first Century', *American Studies*, 46 (2005), pp.23–38.

18 Brendan D. O'Fallon and Lars Fehren-Schmitz, 'Native Americans Experienced a Strong Population Bottleneck Coincident With European Contact', *Proceedings of the National Academy of Sciences of the United States of America*, 108 (2011), pp.20444–20448.

19 Thomas Moreton, *New English Canaan* (Amsterdam: Jason Fredbrick Stam, 1637), pp.22–24.

20 Alfred W. Crosby, 'Virgin Soil Epidemics as a Factor in the Aboriginal Depopulation in America', *William and Mary Quarterly*, 33 (1976), pp.289–299.

21 Ronan Arthur and Jared Diamond, 'Understanding Tribal Fates', *Science*, 334 (2011), pp.911–912; David S. Jones, 'Virgin Soils Revisited', *William and Mary Quarterly*, 60 (2003), pp.703–742.

22 Arthur and Diamond, 'Understanding Tribal Fates', p.912; Marsha Weisiger, 'The Origins of Navajo Pastoralism', *Journal of the Southwest*, 46 (2004), pp.253–282; Samuel M. Wilson, 'Surviving European Colonization in the Caribbean', *Revista de Arqueología Americana*, 12 (1997), p.150.

23 David Brion Davis, *Inhuman Bondage: The Rise and Fall of New World Slavery* (Oxford: Oxford University Press, 2006), p.98; Jack D. Forbes, *Black Africans and Native Americans* (Oxford: Blackwells, 1988), pp.32–35.

24 Eric Bowne, '"Carrying awaye their Corne and Children", The Effects of Westo Slave Raids on the Indians of the Lower South', in Robbie Ethridge and Sheri M. Shuck-Hall (eds), *Mapping the Mississippian Shatter Zone: The Colonial Indian Slave Trade and Regional Instability in the American South* (Lincoln: University of Nebraska Press, 2009), p.105; Paul Kelton, '"Shattered and Infected": Epidemics and the Origins of the Yamasee War, 1696–1715', in Ethridge and Shuck-Hall (eds), pp.312–332; John E. Worth, 'Razing Florida: The Indian Slave Trade and the Devastation of Spanish Florida, 1659–1715', in Ethridge and Shuck-Hall (eds), pp.295–311.

25 Quoted in William Palmer, 'Fables of Conquest: Moral Regression in the Early Modern English State and Empire', *Journal for Early Modern Cultural Studies*, 19 (2019), p.167. For the Irish precedent in early American warfare, see John Grenier, *The First Way of War: American War Making on the Frontier* (Cambridge: Cambridge University Press, 2005), pp.102–104; Wayne E. Lee, *Barbarians and Brothers: Anglo-American Warfare, 1500–1865* (Oxford: Oxford University Press, 2011), pp.36–64.

26 William Palmer, 'Toward a New Moral Understanding of the Tudor Conquest of Ireland', *Historical Reflections / Réflexions Historiques*, 45 (2019), pp.1–21.

27 Ronald Dale Karr, '"Why Should You Be So Furious?": The Violence of the Pequot War', *Journal of American History*, 85 (1998), pp.876–909; Patrick M. Malone, *The Skulking Way of War: Technology and Tactics Among the New England Indians* (Seattle, WA: Madison, 1991).

28 Matthew S. Muelbauer and David J. Ulbrich, *Ways of War: American Military History from the Colonial Era to the Twenty-First Century* (New York, NY.: Routledge, 2014), pp.33–35; Benjamin Thompson, quoted in Alden T. Vaughan, 'From White Man to Redskin: Changing Anglo-American Perceptions of the American Indian', *American Historical Review* 87 (1982), p.941.

29 Grenier, *First Way of War*, p.224.

30 Barbara Alice Mann, *George Washington's War on Native America* (Lincoln: University of Nebraska Press, 2008), pp.51–110.

31 Jeffrey Ostler, *Surviving Genocide: Native Nations and the United States from the American Revolution to Bleeding Kansas* (New Haven, CT: Yale University Press, 2019), pp.85–86.

32 Chamyl Boutaleb, 'Heroes and Villains: An Algerian Review of Tocqueville and Emir Abd al-Qadir', *Review of Middle East Studies*, 45 (2011), pp.44–49; Alexander De Grand, 'Mussolini's Follies: Fascism in Its Imperial and Racist Phase, 1935–1940', *Contemporary European History*, 13 (2004), pp.127–147; Benjamin Madley, 'From Terror to Genocide: Britain's Tasmanian Penal Colony and Australia's History Wars', *Journal of British Studies*, 47 (2008), pp.77–106.

33 Robert Wasserstrom, 'Ethnic Violence and Indigenous Protest: The Tzeltal (Maya) Rebellion of 1712', *Journal of Latin American Studies*, 12 (1980), pp.1–19.

34 Herbert Ekwe-Ekwe, *Biafra Revisited* (Reading: African Renaissance: 2006), pp.1–17.

35 Richard N. Adams, 'The Conquest Tradition of Mesoamerica', *The Americas*, 46 (1989), pp.119–136; W. George Lovell, 'Surviving Conquest: The Maya of Guatemala in Historical Perspective', *Latin American Research Review*, 23 (1988), pp.25–57.

36 Quoted in Nicholas A. Robins, *Native Insurgencies and the Genocidal Impulse in the Americas* (Bloomington: Indiana University Press, 2005), p.28.

37 Robins, *Native Insurgencies and the Genocidal Impulse*, pp.164–172.

38 Quoted in Phillippe R. Girard, 'Caribbean Genocide: Racial War in Haiti, 1802–4', in Dirk Moses and Dan Stone (eds), *Colonialism and Genocide* (London: Routledge: 2007), p.61.

39 Girard, 'Caribbean Genocide: Racial War in Haiti, 1802–4', p.43.

40 Gary Clayton Anderson, 'Review of *Native Insurgencies and the Genocidal Impulse in the Americas* by Nicholas A. Robins', *Journal of American History*, 93 (2007), p.1254.

41 Dominik J. Schaller, 'Raphael Lemkin's View of European Colonial Rule in Africa: Between Condemnation and Admiration', in Schaller and Zimmerer (eds), *The Origins of Genocide*, p.91.

42 Dirk Moses, 'Lemkin, Culture, and the Concept of Genocide', p.27; Schaller, 'Raphael Lemkin's View of European Colonial Rule in Africa', pp.91–92.

43 Dirk Moses, 'Lemkin, Culture, and the Concept of Genocide', pp.27–28.

44 Quoted in Madley, 'From Terror to Genocide', p.77. See also Katherine Ellinghaus, 'Indigenous Assimilation and Absorption in the United States and Australia', *Pacific Historical Review*, 75 (2006), pp.563–585; Anthony J. Hall, 'A National or International Crime? Canada's Indian Residential Schools and the Genocide Convention', *Genocide Studies International*, 12 (2018), pp.72–91; Margaret D. Jacobs, 'Remembering the "Forgotten Child": The American Indian Child Welfare Crisis of the 1960s and 1970s', *American Indian Quarterly*, 37 (2013), pp.136–159.

45 Pauline Wakeham, 'The Slow Violence of Settler Colonialism: Genocide, Attrition, and the Long Emergency of Invasion', *Journal of Genocide Research,* 24 (2022), p.338.

46 Quoted in Wakeham, 'The Slow Violence of Settler Colonialism', pp.340–341.

47 Jürgen Zimmerer, 'The Model Colony?' in Zimmerer and Zeller (eds), *Genocide in German South-West Africa*, translated by Edward Neather (Monmouth: Merlin Press, 2008), pp.19–40.

48 John Bridgeman and Leslie J. Worley, 'Genocide of the Hereros', in Samuel Totten and William S. Parsons (eds), *Century of Genocide* (London: Routledge: 1997), pp.28–29.

49 Casper Wulf Wrichsen, 'Forced Labour in the Concentration Camp on Shark Island', in Zimmerer and Zeller (eds), *Genocide in German South-West Africa*, pp.84–99; Isabel K. Hull, 'Military Culture and "Final Solutions" in the Colonies', in Robert Gellately and Ben Kiernan (eds), *The Spectre of Genocide* (Cambridge: Cambridge University Press, 2003), pp.157–158.

50 Jürgen Zimmerer, 'War, Concentration Camps and Genocide in South-West Africa: The First German Genocide', in Zimmerer and Zeller (eds), *Genocide in German South-West Africa*, p.59.

51 Hannah Arendt, *The Origins of Totalitarianism* (New York: Schocken Books, 2004), p.167.
52 Quoted in Robert Gerwarth and Stephan Malinowski, 'Hannah Arendt's Ghosts: Reflections on the Disputable Path from Windhoek to Auschwitz', *Central European History*, 42, (2009), p.280.
53 Zimmerer, 'War, Concentration Camps and Genocide in South-West Africa', pp.58–60.
54 Hull, 'Military Culture and "Final Solutions" in the Colonies', pp.160–162.
55 Benjamin Madley, 'From Africa to Auschwitz: How German South-West Africa Incubated Ideas and Methods Adopted and Developed by the Nazis in Eastern Europe', *European History Quarterly*, 35 (2005), pp.429–464.
56 Ivan Hannaford, *Race: The History of an Idea in the West* (Baltimore, MD: Johns Hopkins University Press, 1996), pp.204–205.
57 Francisco Bethencourt, *Racisms: From the Crusades to the Twentieth Century* (Princeton, NJ: Princeton University Press, 2013), pp.300–308.
58 Madley, 'From Africa to Auschwitz', pp.453–456.
59 Arthur de Gobineau, *Gobineau: Selected Political Writings*, edited by Michael D. Biddiss (London: Jonathan Cape, 1970), pp.142–144.
60 Quoted in Richard Weikart, *Hitler's Ethic: The Nazi Pursuit of Evolutionary Progress* (New York: Palgrave Macmillan, 2009), p.139.
61 A. Dirk Moses, 'Conceptual Blockages and Definitional Dilemmas in the "Racial Century": Genocides of Indigenous Peoples and the Holocaust', in Moses and Stone (eds), *Colonialism and Genocide*, pp.148–180.
62 Martin Shaw, 'Britain and Genocide: Historical and Contemporary Parameters of National Responsibility', *Review of International Studies*, 37 (2011), p.2427.
63 Gerwarth and Malinowski, 'Hannah Arendt's Ghosts', pp.279–300.

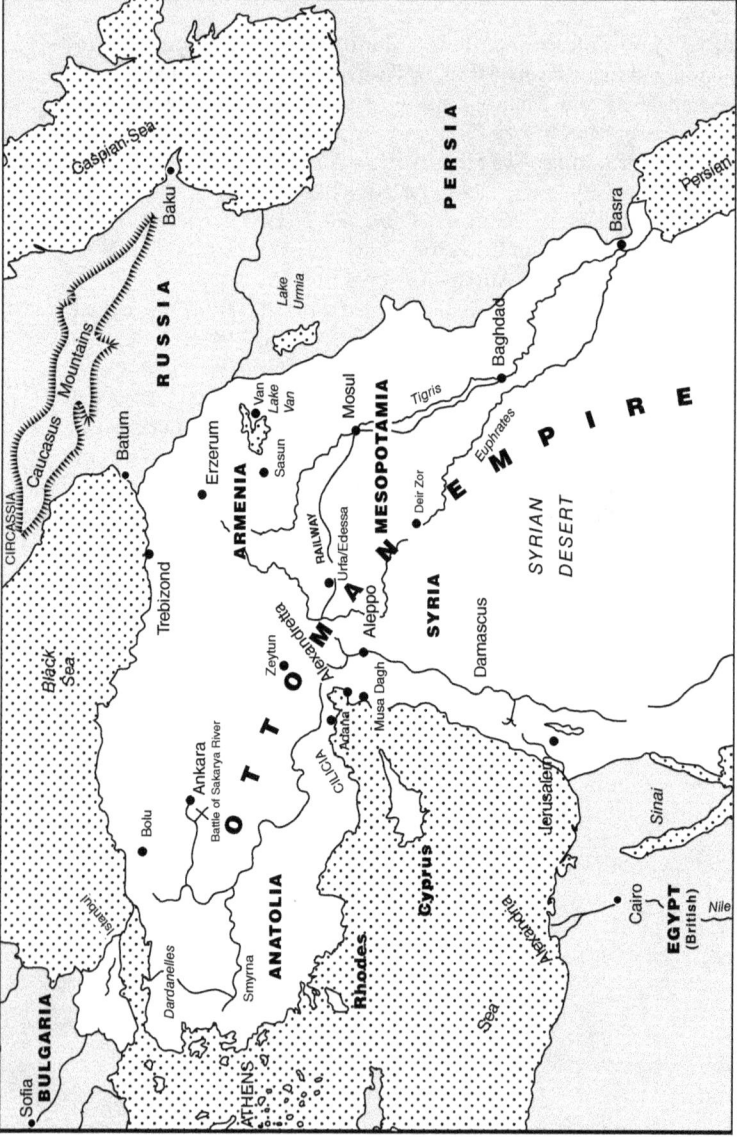

Map 9.1 The Ottoman Empire and Caucasian Frontier, 1914.

9 'More Unpitying Than Pestilence or Fire'

Genocides in the Ottoman, Russian, and Soviet Empires, 1864–1945

On 18 June 1864, readers of the British weekly periodical *The Examiner* were informed of startling news: 'The Caucasus has been dispeopled, not figuratively, or comparatively, or politically, but actually and literally by a ukase [decree] more unpitying than pestilence or fire'.[1] This was slightly misleading. It was not the whole of the Caucasus that had been 'dispeopled' by the tsar's decree. However, a region of some 55,663 square kilometres, an area greater in size than Denmark, had, indeed, been denuded of its population, about two million Muslim Circassians. After stubbornly resisting Russian encroachment for nearly a century, they had finally succumbed in the face of impossible odds.

The Russians had conquered other peoples before and absorbed them into their empire. And they had violently repressed rebels and insurgents, until they had accepted Russian rule. Yet what they now did to the Circassians was without precedent. At least a million died: massacred, starved, frozen or succumbing to epidemics. The survivors were exiled; 150,000 were resettled internally, within the vastness of Russia. The remainder, over half a million, were deported to the Ottoman Empire.[2]

While offering sanctuary to their co-religionists, the Ottomans were woefully unprepared for the influx of desperate refugees. A British journalist in Istanbul wrote that 'the helpless and destitute state of these unhappy beings surpasses in misery and horror anything I have seen recorded in connexion with suffering humanity'.[3] And yet, over the next hundred years, such scenes of 'misery and horror' would be repeated, again and again. The 'dispeopling' of Circassia foreshadowed the fearful scale and ruthless statism of twentieth-century Eurasian genocides. Nationalism would tear the old empires apart, along fault lines of ethnicity. States would abandon policies toward minorities of assimilation or subordination and choose instead extirpation. War and revolution would escalate repression into massacre and expulsion. Borders would be redrawn by genocides and ethnic cleansing. The international community would condemn the inhumanity, and then cravenly accept the new maps. Whether driven by ideologies of imperialism, ethno-nationalism, or Marxist-Leninism, statist mass murder and persecution would claim untold

DOI: 10.4324/9781003494331-10

millions of victims. Russia, its successor state, the Soviet Union, and the Ottoman Empire would lead the way.

During the First World War, between 800,000 and 1.5 million Armenians – Christian subjects of the Ottoman Empire – were killed by their own government. This had been accomplished either directly through massacre, or as the result of exposure, exhaustion, starvation, and disease, during brutally conducted forced deportations. Although, in terms of numbers, the Armenians were the main victims, other Christian groups, such as the Assyrians, were also targeted. Displaced communities of Assyrians continued to suffer massacres into the 1930s, drawing the attention of Raphaël Lemkin. For some historians, such as Philip Jenkins, this process was the seminal event in the emergence of radical, exterminatory patterns of twentieth-century persecution: 'the modern concept of genocide as a uniquely horrible act demanding international sanctions has its roots in the thoroughly successful movements to eradicate Middle Eastern Christians ... '.[4]

The persecution of the Ottoman Empire's Christian minorities, chiefly Armenians and Assyrians but eventually including the Greek Orthodox population too, is usually understood as occurring in three stages. The first of these comprised a series of massacres of Armenians in the period 1894–1896, puzzling in that such a long-established, historically loyal Ottoman population should then be subject to such treatment. This was followed by a period of relative peace, punctuated by sporadic incidents of violent repression, such as a massacre at Adana in 1909. The second stage, 1915–1916, saw the planned and systematic destruction of Armenian and Assyrian populations. Genocide occurred in the context of the First World War. This conflict has been understood as having either radicalised Ottoman policy towards its Christian minorities, or providing a pretext for the brutal acceleration of an unfolding thirty-year project to 'Turkify' the Ottoman Empire.[5] Finally, between 1919 and 1924, as the disintegrating empire endured partial occupation by Allied forces and invasion by Greece, inter-ethnic conflict led to further massacres, deportations, and forced population exchanges.

The Armenians were the first people to adopt Christianity as their state religion, converting from Zoroastrianism sometime between 301 and 314 CE. They had been under the rule of 'the Sublime Porte' (as the Ottoman government was often known) since the fifteenth century. Although Islam was the state religion of the empire, both Christian and Jewish Ottoman subjects were generally permitted to practise their faiths. The people of each minority religion or sect within the empire were organised as groups known as *millets*. Headed by a patriarch, answerable directly to the sultan, each *millet* was allowed considerable autonomy in both religious and civil affairs, such as education, marriage, and property rights. This was religious forbearance not equality. The *dhimmi*, non-Muslims living under Islamic sovereignty, were liable for the *jizya* poll tax and subject to extensive discrimination. They could not bear arms, ride horses, or even wear the same clothing as Muslims. They could nor build or repair their churches and synagogues without permission. Their manner towards Muslims was expected to be deferential. If they observed these terms, they might live in peace, as the Armenians, long known *as millet-i sadika* (the loyal *millet*), did for centuries.[6]

Persecution of Christian minorities arose as the *millet* system unravelled over the course of the nineteenth century. This was caused by a number of factors: competition for land with traditionally pastoralist tribes, especially the Kurds, who were transitioning to more sedentary lifestyles; an internal political reform programme that aimed at promoting a civil and political equality which ultimately proved unacceptable to the majority Muslim population; the emergence of conflicting nationalist visions for the Ottoman state's future, one of which was the formation of an ethno-religious state, with a homogeneous Turkish and Islamic population; a geopolitical crisis, with territory lost, Muslim communities massacred and exiled, and consequent profound fears stemming from an existential threat of imperial dismemberment.

Millions of Muslim refugees, the *Muhacirs*, were forced to flee persecution in the Balkans and from the Caucasus. In the latter area, the expansionist Russians had engaged extensively in massacres and forced migrations. The fate of the Circassians has already been noted. A fresh wave of refugees, over 300,000, arrived in Ottoman lands in the wake of the Balkan Wars, 1912–1913, and they too had suffered terribly, not just from war and massacre, but also from the ravages of hunger and disease. Once in Anatolia, they and the other *Muhacirs* competed with the established Christian population for land, as well as introducing a peculiarly strong anti-Christian element into Ottoman politics.[7]

The relationship between the Armenians and their Kurdish neighbours in eastern Anatolia had also shifted in the early nineteenth century. The local Kurdish lords had long exacted taxes from the Armenian peasantry but, valuing them as productive farmers, had largely protected them. In the mid-nineteenth century, the Ottoman state had moved to curtail local rebellions and assert stronger central authority. The old ruling class had been driven into exile. In their place, new chiefs arose, who were less tolerant of Christianity and greedy to seize land, as their people gradually adopted settled agriculture. Well-armed and well-mounted, these behaved in an increasingly predatory fashion towards the vulnerable, unarmed Armenians.

It had long been the practice of Kurdish tribes to winter in Armenian settlements, supported by the Christian peasantry. Now they frequently despoiled the villages as they left, abducting Armenian women, killing those who resisted them. The reactionary Sultan Abdülhamid II (r.1876–1909) came to regard the Kurds as useful regional allies as he sought to hold his fractious empire together. He organised the tribes into a light cavalry militia, the *Hamidiye*. He also promoted a pan-Islamist, fundamentalist religious ideology, that appealed to both Kurds and many ordinary Turks. These would become central instruments in the persecution of Armenians.[8]

The Armenians themselves responded to the changing circumstances of the nineteenth century in a number of ways. Many chose emigration. Some left the

Ottoman Empire for areas of the Caucasus now controlled by the Russians, forging what the Ottoman authorities regarded as a dangerous link with a hostile foreign power. Others migrated internally. Educated, skilled Armenians thrived in Ottoman cities, as artisans, merchants, and entrepreneurs. In some regions, such as Cilicia, in southern Anatolia, wealthy Armenians were buying up land from impoverished and indebted Muslims. Inevitably, their prosperity, alongside their roles as landlords and moneylenders, invited a hostile resentment. One major factor in driving the persecution of Armenians was the revulsion many Muslim subjects of the empire felt on seeing *dhimmi* achieving wealth and a measure of social and political equality. An astute American diplomat compared their reactions to that of white southerners in the United States, faced by the steps towards equality made by emancipated African Americans after the American Civil War.[9]

Politics, too, became a route by which some Armenians sought to challenge their degraded status. Working through the established institutions of the *millet* proved futile; the sultan denied its mandate to act in wider economic or social matters. Indeed, as a British journalist observed, Abdülhamid had 'ceased to listen to the Patriarch and ignored the Constitution previously granted to the national church'.[10] Long established rights and privileges were abolished. Armenians across the empire were being imprisoned and plundered.

Frustrated reformers thus turned to new political organisations, the *Hnchak* and *Dashnaksutiun* parties, founded in 1887 and 1890, respectively. The *Hnchak* sought an independent homeland; the *Dashnaksutiun*, greater autonomy within the empire. These were avowedly revolutionary organisations, socialist and nationalist, strongly influenced by contemporary Russian models. They advocated violence alongside appeals to the international community as strategies, both guaranteed to alarm the Ottoman authorities. Neither party enjoyed particularly widespread support among the masses. Wealthy Armenians, generally committed to achieving gradual change within the established structures of empire, were themselves targeted by the revolutionaries. The Armenian peasantry, on the other hand, was far from achieving a revolutionary consciousness. They might appreciate the actions of Armenian fighters who defended them from the predation of their neighbours, but all too often became the victims of indiscriminate, heavy-handed state retaliation for bombings and assassinations in which they had no part.[11]

At much the same time, constitutionalist parties were emerging among the Muslim communities of the empire too. In a decree issued in 1856, as part of the *Tanzimat* reform programme, steps had been taken towards modernising and secularising the state, including a rhetoric of equality for non-Muslim subjects. The reform impulse had encountered a significant obstacle, when the conservative and absolutist Sultan Abdülhamid II came to power. Opposition groups that continued to press for change, known as the 'Young Turks', gradually coalesced to form the Committee of Union and Progress (CUP). In some instances, they stood on common ground with the *Dashnaksutiun*, sharing a goal to reform and modernise the Ottoman state on a European model.

Yet the 'Young Turks' were acutely aware of the looming external threats to the empire. The disastrous events of 1878 – defeat at the hands of the Russians, and the loss of Bosnia, Herzegovina, Serbia, Rumania, Bulgaria, Kars, and Cyprus – posed an unprecedented crisis for the empire. Internal rebellion by subject Christian peoples had been a major factor. Furthermore, the minorities question gave the great powers useful, and self-interested, leverage as they competed to secure influence in the empire's domestic politics. At the 1878 Treaty of Berlin, an international covenant was signed, designed to compel the Porte to undertake reform in the provinces with high Armenian populations. Very little effort was ever made to ensure compliance with these measures, but the damage was done. The Armenians thus became an object of suspicion among other Ottoman subjects. Repeated international pressure of this nature, culminating in the Reform Act imposed on the Ottomans in February 1914, was understood by the Young Turks as an ultimately existential threat. With the historic territory of Armenia now forming the heartlands of the Ottoman Empire, any advance they made towards regional autonomy was seen to pose the direst of dangers. The CUP came to pursue a radical and exclusionary nationalist ideological vision known as *Ittihadism* (Unionism): a homogeneous population, defined by its shared Islamic and Turkish-speaking identity.[12]

All of these frictions played some role in the massacres of Armenians that took place in 1894–1896. The first clash occurred in the mountainous eastern district of Sasun. By 1894, the farmers of Sasun were suffering the predatory attentions of local Kurdish tribes, as well as receiving demands for taxes from the central government. In this remote area, the Armenians had exercised a degree of autonomy. For this reason, the *Hnchak* had established a presence among them. The villages could, thus, mobilise *fedayi*, an armed militia. They refused to pay their taxes until the government offered effective security from Kurdish attacks. The *fedayi* first fended off the local tribesmen. In Istanbul, the sultan feared revolution. He dispatched both regular army units and the *Hamidiye* to crush Armenian resistance. Over the course of August and September, some 8,000 Armenian men were killed; women were raped and abducted, and land and homes despoiled. A British report concluded, 'There was no insurrection, as was reported in Constantinople [Istanbul]; The villagers simply took up arms to defend themselves against the Kurds'.[13]

That same lethally disproportionate response was evident a year later, following a demonstration organised by *Hnchak* in Istanbul itself. The international context is important here in understanding Abdülhamid's actions. Following the Sasun revolt, Britain, France, and Russia pressured the Ottomans to finally enact the measures agreed in 1878 to protect Christian minorities. *Hnchak* leaders sensed an opportunity to draw the great powers into internal Ottoman politics, with a rowdy demonstration in the capital in September 1895. They were met by soldiers, police, and an armed mob. Many of the marchers were killed, as were other Armenians resident in the city, who had taken no part in the demonstration.

This clash triggered anti-Armenian riots, first in urban areas, beginning in Trabzon on the Black Sea coast. This was not simply an opportunity for slaughter but for economic gain; a witness reported that 'every shop of an Armenian in the market was gutted and the victors ... gutted themselves with spoils'.[14] Similar episodes of massacre and plundering occurred in Maraş, Harput, Diyarbekir, and Urfa, where some 8,000 died, including 3,000 burned to death in the city's cathedral where they had sought sanctuary. The violence spread to outlying towns and villages too. It was orchestrated in such a way as to break communal bonds as much as to kill. Forced conversions occurred. At Içme, for example, Armenians were taken one by one from the church in which they sheltered. Those who refused to renounce their faith were shot. Women and girls were sexually assaulted. The missionary Caleb Gates noted that 'when zaptiehs [policemen] come, the Turks give to each an Armenian woman for the night'.[15]

Most communities were defenceless; no *fedayi* or revolutionaries were present. Only at Van and mountainous Zeytun was serious armed resistance attempted. This was largely a reaction to the ongoing massacres; the Ottoman authorities presented it as further evidence of revolutionary provocation.[16]

However, in August 1896, the *Dashnaksutiun* recklessly provided the authorities with a pretext for further violence. They staged a high-profile armed seizure of the Imperial Ottoman Bank in Istanbul. Several guards were killed, and foreign nationals taken hostage. With the world's attention focused upon them, they demanded autonomy for six historically Armenian provinces. The hope that the great powers would intervene was a horrendous miscalculation. Russia, Britain, and France might loudly proclaim themselves the protectors of Christian minorities, but their fears of upsetting the fragile balance of power in the east, or of facilitating a rival profiting at Ottoman expense, stayed their hands. Retaliation fell indiscriminately on Armenians across the empire. Troops and police stood aside while armed mobs (with iron bars and knives allegedly supplied by the authorities) murdered some 4,000–5,000 Armenians in the streets and houses of the capital. Further massacres ensued, as at Eğin, where some 2,000 Armenians died, and a thousand homes were torched.[17]

By the autumn of 1896, the Sublime Porte was acting to curb the violence and local authorities generally came to heel. The massacres of the 1890s are generally understood to have been, in Donald Bloxham's words 'a "cull" of a proto-national element, including terrorization and expropriation, with a neo-conservative religious backlash against an "inferior" ", upstart religious group'.[18] Ottoman record keeping was in no sense adequate to allow a final toll of the dead. Estimates range from a low figure of 50,000 to as many as 300,000.[19] One English correspondent of *The Times* resident in Istanbul opined that Abdülhamid bore principal responsibility for the bloodletting and 'that in some parts of the Empire ... he was exterminating [the Armenian] race'.[20] Yet the extent to which the massacres were centrally directed and planned is not clear. Directives issued from the Porte to local authorities were often couched in ambiguities, and considerable discretion was left to officials on the ground.

Yet, while it may thus be possible to query the existence of a genocidal intent on the part of the Porte at this point, a portentous shift in relations between the Ottoman state and its Armenian subjects had certainly occurred. An ideological framework for genocide had been established. The Armenians were blamed for their own fate; violence against them was explained by their revolutionary activities and the putative threat they thus posed to Muslim neighbours. Those who continue to offer mitigation for Ottoman policies still advance this argument, what Robert Melson has termed 'the provocation thesis'.[21]

Despite the general lack of a revolutionary consciousness among the majority of Armenians and the disproportionate, arbitrary, and indiscriminate nature of the punitive measures, this notion of Armenian provocation was widely credited. It helps explain why so many ordinary people were willing to participate in the violence. *The Times* Istanbul correspondent suggested that the Porte's control of the Turkish-language newspapers, and censorship of political publications, had allowed it to shape the populace's perceptions:

> The Turks in the interior who have massacred so many thousands of helpless Armenians [had been] worked up to a high pitch of fanatical excitement ... and justified their acts on the grounds they were engaged in a holy war – in which it was their duty to kill and plunder.[22]

Committed to using pan-Islamism to inspire loyalty to the empire, Abdülhamid had indeed promoted the idea that his Muslim subjects 'look upon attacks against Christians as the fulfilment of a religious duty'.[23] Thus Kurds, Circassians, and Arabs had joined with Turks in attacking Armenians. Religious scholars, the *Ulemah*, and their students, had been prominent in many of the massacres. Women had ululated as their husbands and sons slaughtered their neighbours.[24] From Istanbul, *The Times* correspondent attempted to capture the gist of the 'feelings of the Turks' he spoke to towards the Armenians:

> We have nursed this people in our arms for centuries. We have protected them and conferred all sorts of favours upon them. They have lived with us and grown rich among us, and now, without reason, they turn upon us and wish to murder us and destroy the Empire ... Such ingratitude deserves the severest punishment. As they have created a state of war, we are justified by our religion in killing them and seizing their property.[25]

While the scale and intensity of violence against the Armenians abated after 1896, this ideological basis, combining political, religious, and economic motives for persecution, only intensified. In July 1908, the CUP seized political power in a coup that made the position of Christian minorities yet more vulnerable. In April 1909, reactionary elements, affronted by constitutional changes that had allowed Christian minorities greater rights, turned on Armenians and other Christians in the city of Adana and its vicinity. Local authorities, troops and police had joined with the mob in attacking Christians. Some 20,000 Armenians and 1,270 Assyrians were killed. In this province, Cilicia, many Armenians had acquired arms, and some 2,000 Muslims died too.[26]

Although the massacre at Adana had been instigated by conservative opponents of the 'Young Turks', they themselves proved no allies to the victims. Their putative policy was secularisation of the state, yet they relied on Islam to maintain loyalty among an ethnically diverse but majority Muslim population. That state was to be dominated by Turks. The leaders of the CUP all had close family connections to the threatened European peripheries of the Ottoman Empire. By 1913, power was in the hands of a triumvirate of *pashas*: Mehmed Talât, the Interior Minister, originally from Thrace; Ismail Enver, Minister of War, whose father was from Macedonia, and Ahmed Cemal, Minister of the Marine and Governor of Syria, who was born on Lesbos. They were acutely conscious of the dangers of internal subversion, and the predatory stance of the European powers, and were familiar with the western ideology of an exclusionary ethno-nationalism. The deteriorating international situation, the losses of Libya to Italy, 1911–12, and in the Balkan Wars, 1912–1913, only heightened their sense of crisis. It shaped policy too. The CUP was behind a campaign of harassment that displaced Ottoman Greeks and Bulgarians from the coastal and border areas in the west. In October 1914, they took the momentous decision to enter the First World War as allies of Germany, in a gamble that they hoped would be the empire's salvation.[27]

How the *Ittihadist* project to create a highly centralised, modern state, with a homogenous, Turkish-speaking Muslim population might have unfolded had the Ottoman Empire not entered the global conflict is impossible to say. Yet the conditions of war quickly escalated internal levels of violence. Early on, massacres of Armenians had occurred at Artvin, Ardahan, and Ardanuç. In February 1915, Armenian soldiers in the Ottoman Army had been disarmed and transferred to labour battalions. Initially exploited to perform the most arduous manual tasks, such as road building, they would, eventually, be massacred. Local deportations had occurred the same month in Cilicia, following rumours that the British were preparing to land in the vicinity. Donald Bloxham has described the Ottoman trajectory towards genocide as 'cumulative radicalisation' (borrowing that phrase from Hans Mommsen's description of the Nazi path towards the 'final solution'). He argues that what began with these more limited regional measures up until

May 1915, had transformed by the summer of that year into 'a crystallized policy of empire-wide killing and death-by-attrition'.[28]

A deteriorating military situation appears to have been a major catalyst in escalating this internal persecution. In late December 1914, Enver Pasha had launched an offensive against the Russians on the Caucasian front, his strategy driven by the pan-Turanist dream of uniting all the Turkic speaking peoples. Poorly clothed and poorly supplied, Ottoman troops had attacked in mountainous terrain during blizzards, only to be routed by a Russian counter-attack at Sarikamiş. By January 1915, the Russian Army was poised to advance into Anatolia. The presence of Armenian soldiers – some recruited in the Russian Caucasus, some refugees from Anatolia – in their ranks was well noted by the Ottomans. Enver Pasha was quick to allege Armenian disloyalty as the cause of his failure. The Russian victory encouraged Britain and France to conduct an amphibious strike to capture the Dardanelles and threaten Istanbul. Their forces first landed on the Gallipoli peninsula on 25 April 1915.[29]

Five days earlier, Armenian *fedayi* had taken control of the city of Van. This was in response to local massacres of Armenian men of military age that, according to the US ambassador Henry Morgenthau, had seen 24,000 murdered in just three days. For six weeks, they held Ottoman forces at bay, until relieved by the advancing Russians. Muslim towns and villages suffered atrocities under their occupation. The empire faced a dire prospect, and policy towards the Armenians grew correspondingly harsher.[30]

On 24 April, prominent and influential Armenians were arrested en masse in Istanbul. Thereafter, Talât Pasha sent orders to regional authorities to act similarly to decapitate local Armenian leadership, forestalling organised resistance. During May and June, the extent and scale of deportations of Armenian settlements increased. From eastern frontier zones, such as around Van and Erzerum, conceivably threatened by a Russian advance, deportees were driven southwards on foot. Yet the deportations were not confined to the war zones; populations from the west and north, from cities such as Bolu, 72 miles inland, were also forced onto the roads south towards Aleppo. Their land, farms, homes, and businesses were expropriated and redistributed to Muslims. These measures were not only to change the demographics of Anatolia, but were designed to create an exclusively Muslim economy too.[31]

The men were either massacred early on, or conscripted into 'labour battalions', from which they would never return. So, for the most part, the deportees were women and children. They can have constituted no real threat to Ottoman security. Still, the deportations were carried out with a brutality calculated to kill. The missionary Dr Martin Niepage 'heard with horror that a new phase of Armenian massacres had begun ... which aimed at exterminating, root and branch, the intelligent, industrious, and progressive Armenian nation, and at transferring its property to Turkish hands'. Exhausted, starved, tormented by thirst, and wracked by dysentery and typhus, '[the deportees] are driven on and on from one place to another. The thousands shrink to hundreds and the hundreds to tiny remnants, and even these remnants are driven on till the last is dead'. Along the way, they were subject to robbery, rape, and murderous assault. A German engineer reported 'corpses of violated women lying about naked in heaps on the railway embankment at Tell-Abiad and Ras-el-Ain'.[32] In June 1915, the Habsburg ambassador to Istanbul, Johann Markgraf Pallavicini, reported that the Ottoman Minister of the Interior was 'destroying the alien elements' in the empire and that 'River basins, lakes, valleys and caves are filled with corpses. The streams of the Euphrates and the Tigris take down decaying corpses'.[33]

Understanding the Armenian genocide confronts us with fundamental questions of definition, intent, and process. These are made more complex, because the atrocities were committed behind a smokescreen of official obfuscation and misdirection at the time, followed by a subsequent purging of incriminating government records. Turkey, the successor state to the Ottoman Empire, maintains a policy of denying that genocide occurred. In their official narrative, the massacres are portrayed as local inter-ethnic strife that affected all communities. The deportations, it is argued, were a necessary war measure, designed to secure Ottoman lines of communication, running through a disloyal population, from guerrilla attacks. Subsequent deaths by disease, exposure, starvation, or attacks on deportees were committed by predatory tribesmen, the consequences, supposedly, of lawlessness, poor planning, or maladministration, not premeditation or design. Sympathetic western academics have been enlisted to help propagate this narrative. Their works mimic scholarship, citing archival sources, extensively footnoted, and positively reviewed by like-minded peers. Yet the case rests upon the highly selective use of evidence, the editing and mis-transcription of primary sources, failure to subject those sources to due critical analysis, and tendentious justifications at odds with easily demonstrable facts.[34]

Denial is part of the process of genocide. It began whilst the atrocities were in progress. Talât Pasha took steps to try and prevent missionaries and foreign diplomats from gathering evidence of the slaughter. When he heard that 'foreign officers' were finding, and photographing, the bodies of Armenians strewn across the deportation routes, he issued 'very important' orders to local officials to 'have these corpses buried at once and do not allow them to be left near the roads'. He also instructed anyone passing accounts and photographs of Armenian suffering to the American Consul be stopped: 'Dangerous people of this kind must be arrested and suppressed'.[35]

Yet the scale and clear central organisation of what was happening could not be hidden. Major General James F. Harbord, part of a US military mission to Anatolia in 1919, soon established that:

Massacres and deportations were organized in the spring of 1915 under definite system, the soldiers going from town to town. The official reports of the Turkish Government show 1,100,000 as having been deported.

Young men were first summoned to the government building in each village and then marched out and killed. The women, the old men, and children were, after a few days, deported to what Talaat Pasha called 'agricultural colonies,' from the high, cool, breeze-swept plateau of Armenia to the malarial flats of the Euphrates and the burning sands of Syria and Arabia.[36]

Talât Pasha's description of the destination of the deportations as 'agricultural colonies' is characteristic of the official language often employed to disguise reality. There were no 'agricultural colonies'. The survivors of the marches were simply abandoned at desolate desert locations, such as Deir Zor in Syria, where some 350,000 Armenians eventually perished. In some communications, Talât himself was far more candid about what was happening. On 16 September 1915, he informed the prefecture of Aleppo:

You have already been advised that the Government ... has decided to destroy completely all the indicated persons [Armenians] living in Turkey. All who oppose this decision and command cannot remain on the official staff of the empire. Their existence must come to an end, however tragic the means may be; and no regard must be paid to either age or sex, or to conscientious scruples.[37]

Deir Zor was immediately behind the positions of the Ottoman Sixth Army, further giving the lie to the claim that Armenians were being deported away from vulnerable military lines of communications. Organised armed resistance was infrequent. At Van, 65,000 Armenians were ultimately able to evacuate with the Russians. At Dersim, in April 1915, Armenians were joined in resistance by local Kurds, provoked by marauding soldiers and possibly aware of the longer-term implications of 'Turkification' for their own people. Several thousand Armenians were also rescued by the French Navy near Antioch, after holding Ottoman soldiers at bay for six weeks at Musa Dagh, in late 1915. Other instances of resistance such as at Edessa and Shabin-Karahisar, were quickly suppressed. For the most part, the Armenian population was unarmed. The same was true for another Christian minority targeted for destruction at the same time: the Assyrians. Despite having no history of making demands for national autonomy or engaging in revolutionary activity, and posing no discernible threat to Ottoman logistics, they, too, were targeted for deportation and destruction. A quarter of a million Assyrians, half the population, died 1914–1919.[38]

Participation in this process of destruction was widespread. Soldiers, police, *Hamidiye*, and local populations conspired to assault the doomed caravans of deportees. A survivor from Konia recalled:

The soldiers would come and give us a bad time. Others from the hills and mountains would come and snatch girls and baggage, or whatever they could. You scream 'Gendarme, gendarme,' but they would not help, because they were all together in this ... They had brought some deportees on the cliff. They would tie them, shoot them and throw them in the river. There were gendarmes among them, civilians and soldiers.[39]

Prominent among those preying on the deportees were members of the *Teşkilati Mahusa,* the 'Special Organisation'. The presence of this para-military organisation, recruited from gendarmes, tribesmen, *Muhacirs,* and convicts, once again highlights the state's role in the genocide. Thirty thousand strong, it had been foundered in 1911, on the initiative of Enver Pasha. Its original purpose was waging guerrilla war against the Italians in Libya and, in 1913, during the Balkan conflicts. In 1915, it was given a new objective: 'the destruction of the deportee convoys, for which purpose the S.O. maintained close contact with the CUP'. Talât Pasha thus had his willing executioners: 'butchers of human beings, consorting gallowbirds, and gendarmes with bloody hands and eyes'.[40]

As a corollary, it is worth noting the heavy hand of the authorities in overcoming any resistance among the Muslim population to the measures being taken against the Armenians and Assyrians. Such resistance was treated as treason. In Diyarbekir, two low-ranking officials who had 'taken issue with the ... governor's handling of the Armenian deportations' were hanged. Higher ranks who objected to the massacres were dismissed from their posts, as happened to General Hüseyin Celal, Governor of Aleppo. Ordinary Muslims who might take pity on their Christian neighbours were deterred from doing so. The Third Army's General Mahmut Kâmil threatened to hang anyone who sheltered an Armenian and to torch their home. Even citizens of neutral or allied powers, were cowed. The humili-ating 'capitulations' that had guaranteed foreigners some immunity from Ottoman law were abrogated in October 1914. Niepage noted that 'a Swiss engineer was to have been brought before a court-martial because he had distributed bread ... to the starving Armenian women and children in a convoy of exiles'.[41]

While the ugly principles of 'Social Darwinism' had been part of the ideo-logical education of leading members of the CUP, their ethno-nationalism largely lacked an emphasis on biological race and blood purity.[42] This rendered Armenian women and children vulnerable to abduction and enforced conversion; tens of thousands were coercively assimilated into the community of their persecutors. Aghavni, a young Armenian woman, was lying close to death on the banks of the Euphrates at Deir Zor when she was found by two elderly Turks. She was nursed back to health, to be the wife of a son '[when he] returns from the army'. Another survivor recalled how, as a young boy, he had been separated from his grandmother:

... while we sat to eat, the gendarmes came to take money from us. Also, the villagers began appearing and taking away young children. They would grab them and holding them by the hand lead them away. Someone came and took my hand too.[43]

The experiences of the abducted women and children varied markedly. The fortunate were essentially adopted into Muslim families. Most were reduced to slavery. Some of the women and girls were sold on five or six times and were scattered as far afield as the slave markets of Arabia, Tunisia, and Algeria.[44] Known among their persecutors as the *kiliç artiği*, the 'remnants of the sword', many were tattooed on their faces and bodies as a stark visual signifier of the eradication of their identity. Aghavni Kabakian was just eight years old when she was disfigured with tribal markings by her kidnappers, a family of the nomadic Nawar people: 'I was one of those little Armenian girls with rosy cheeks who had carved on her forehead the entire tragedy of her race'. She later escaped her captivity but her sister, eventually married to a Muslim Arab to whom she bore seven children, was, like thousands of other such 'remnants', 'forever lost to our family and our race'.[45]

By spring 1916, the deportations had wound down. Few Armenians remained in the interior. Yet what some contemporaries referred to as the 'de-Christianing of Asia Minor' was far from over.[46] The shifting fortunes of war now largely dictated the situation. In 1918, following the collapse of imperial Russia, the Ottomans were able to resume the strategic offensive and push into the Caucasus. Much of the land they occupied was populated by Armenians, who were subject to a fresh round of massacres. Subsequently, the defeat of the Ottoman Empire itself plunged Anatolia into cruel inter-ethnic conflict in which civilians of all communities suffered. By the time the Allies signed an armistice with the Ottoman Empire on 30 October 1918, Talât, Enver, and Cemal, alongside other leading figures of the CUP and the Special Organisation, had fled the country, fearing punishment for war crimes. They did not long escape their past: Talât (in Berlin in 1921) and Cemal (in Georgia in 1922) were assassinated by vengeful Armenian gunmen. Enver died in a hail of machine-gun bullets in a skirmish with a Red Army unit in Turkestan in 1922.[47]

There were partial and short-lived occupations of Anatolia by the British, French, and Italians, who struggled to contain the violence. In 1920, the Greeks launched an ill-starred invasion, asserting irredentist claims to Anatolian territory, on the basis of the large and ancient Greek population resident there. The invaders were halted in the late summer of 1921 at the Battle of the Sakarya River and driven back to the west. Harnessing a revitalised Turkish nationalism, the victor of Sakarya River, Mustafa Kemal (Atatürk), would go on to establish the modern Turkish republic, overturning the sultanate in 1922. Anatolia's Greek communities followed the surviving Armenians into exile.

The closing stages of the Greco-Turkish War were bitter in the extreme. Both sides committed atrocities against civilians. The Greek military position finally collapsed under pressure from Mustafa Kemal in August 1922.

On 9 September, Turkish troops entered the city of Smyrna (modern Izmir). Fires were started in the Greek and Armenian quarters. The city was swiftly consumed by the conflagration. Harassed and pursued by soldiers, the people fled to the harbour, in the hope of evacuation by the Allied ships at anchor there. A witness on a British vessel recalled:

> The scene that followed on the fire defies description. The people flocked to the quayside, which was not many yards distant from the blazing houses ... The poor wretches went frantic in their efforts to be the first to escape by the boats, many trying to swim out to the vessels anchored in the harbour. In many cases they were drowned and numberless lives were lost.[48]

Mustafa Kemal's victory over the Greeks allowed him to overturn the humiliating provisions of the 1920 Treaty of Sèvres, that had seen the Ottoman Empire cede territory to the Allies and consent to the establishment of occupation zones. Terms were renegotiated at Lausanne in 1923. Under a convention agreed there, the minorities question was to be settled by a population exchange. About 1.25 million Greeks left Anatolia for Greece; 356,000 Turks travelled in the opposite direction. By 1924, the Christian presence in Anatolia had thus dropped from around 20 per cent of the population in 1914 to around 2 per cent. The final stage of this process was by the agreement of the international community. A critical British journalist complained:

> The astounding fact appears to be that what the Turks were unable to do at the height of their power, they are doing now after a supposed defeat at the hands of the Christian nations of Europe. They are *dechristianising* western Asia Minor, one of the very nurseries of Christianity, and that with the consent – we had almost said with the *help* – of Christian Europe.[49]

Indeed, the unfolding of events in the wake of the First World War gave a sort of legitimacy to the brutal engineering of loyal populations by nation states. The policy of 'population exchange' agreed at Lausanne was a vindication for ethno-nationalism and a mask for genocidal deportations. So, too, was the tacit acceptance of an Anatolia devoid of Armenians.[50]

There had been an attempt at justice for the massacred and the exiled. As early as 24 May 1915, as the Armenian genocide had gathered pace, the Allies had jointly warned the Ottoman authorities that they would be legally held accountable for the atrocities. In so doing, they invoked the 1907 Hague Convention, which had striven to 'lessen the evils of war' by binding combatants to 'the principles of international law as established by the usages among nations, by the laws of humanity and the exigencies of the public conscience'.[51] The 1920 Treaty of Sèvres had included provisions for military tribunals to prosecute Ottoman officials accused of crimes against both the Armenians and British prisoners of war. Yet talk of establishing an international tribunal to pursue these cases came to nothing. Part of the problem stemmed from the difficult legal question of whether it was possible, under existing international law, to prosecute officials for wartime crimes committed against their own subjects.[52]

In the end, it was left to the Ottoman government itself to take responsibility for holding the war crimes trials. The recently appointed Grand Vizier, Damad Ferid Pasha, persuaded the British to take this path, assuring them that 'I do not wish – perish the thought – to make light of these crimes, which were such as to make the human conscience tremble forever. I am even less inclined to diminish the guilt of the authors of this great tragedy'.[53] Yet the trials proceeded at a slow pace. In Istanbul, some high-profile prisoners were released from custody.

Frustrated, the British transferred 600 prisoners into their own custody in Malta, but to little effect. Between 1919 and 1922, a series of courts martial did take place in Istanbul. These produced plentiful and detailed evidence of the fate of the Armenians, and where responsibility lay. Yet they resulted in only three 'middle level civil servants' being executed for 'crimes against humanity'. Harsh sentences were also passed, futilely, on leading figures of the CUP, tried *in absentia*. The proceedings, and the government that supported them, were increasingly unpopular among Turks. Concurrently, the war with Greece was fuelling a nationalist backlash. The war-weary British, faced with renewed fighting against the Turks and struggling with their response to the Russian Revolution, chose realpolitik over the pursuit of justice. They exchanged the prisoners held in Malta for British hostages taken by Mustafa Kamel's triumphant nationalist forces. His new Turkish Republic had no interest in pursuing trials any further.[54]

There was a strange coda to the Istanbul war trials. The 1923 Treaty of Lausanne effectively sanctioned new political borders established by genocide and population expulsions.[55] It also contained this declaration:

Full and complete amnesty shall be respectively granted by the Turkish Government and by the Greek Government for all crimes or offences committed during the same period [1 August 1914–20 November 1922] which were evidently connected with the political events which have taken place during that period.[56]

This sweeping amnesty, like the abandonment of the earlier war crimes trials, should be considered in the context of realpolitik. However, this was a truly dangerous precedent. As Raphaël Lemkin observed, 'A nation was killed and the guilty persons set free'.[57] Adolf Hitler noted this outcome too. As he planned his annihilatory war on Poland in 1939, he asked his generals rhetorically, 'Who still talks nowadays about the extermination of the Armenians?'[58] The international legal scholar David Matas concluded, 'There is a direct linkage between the failure to prosecute the crimes against humanity before World War II and their commission during World War II'.[59]

The Russian authorities had faced no consequence for their murderous forced expulsions either. Over the course of the late nineteenth century, mass deportation became something of a routine imperial policy. The shift from assimilation to expulsion of conquered populations was driven primarily by concerns for the security of the empire in the wake of defeat in the Crimean War (1853–1856), and by a recognition of the implacable hostility of some subject peoples, including Caucasian Muslims, towards Russian rule.[60]

The nursery of the new policy of mass deportation was Russian colonialism in the Caucasus. Its adolescence took place on the European borders of empire, targeting 'unreliable elements'. Prominent amongst these were Jews. In an emancipatory age, Russian Jews had made important strides towards civil and political equality. Not unlike the Armenians, that progress provoked among resentful neighbours a violent prejudice. This was manifested in vicious attacks on their communities: the pogroms of 1881–1882 and 1905–1906. During the opening months of the First World War, hundreds of thousands of Jews were forced by the military to leave their homes and were relocated away from the war zones. The deportations were frequently conducted in a fashion reminiscent of a pogrom. The attempts to rationalise these acts were feeble. That Yiddish was 'close to German' and thus a language of spies and traitors was excuse enough. Inevitably, the tsar's subjects of German descent, farming in the border zones, were subject to the same treatment.[61]

The statist policy of destroying communities through mass deportation reached its terrible maturity under the Soviet Union, the successor empire to tsarist Russia. The first target, in 1919–1920, were the Cossacks. These were a distinct social group with an emerging quasi-ethnic identity. Originally, they were militarised frontier communities who had enjoyed special privileges and a degree of autonomy as they spearheaded Russian colonisation of the Pontic-Caspian steppes and the Caucasus. That position was threatened by the Bolsheviks. Cossacks gravitated towards the Whites, the counter-revolutionaries. Lenin thus denounced them as class enemies. A Bolshevik party directive of January 1919 had ordered officials to 'conduct *mass terror* against wealthy Cossacks, extirpating them totally; to conduct merciless mass terror against all those Cossacks who participated, directly or indirectly, in the struggle against Soviet power'.[62]

In late 1920, 45,000 Terek Cossacks were rounded up and deported. Families were dismembered. The men were sent to labour in the coalfields of the Donets Basin. The women and children were scattered and isolated across towns further north. The new Soviet national pattern was imposed upon their former lands. Their *stanitsy* (towns) were renamed and settled by non-Cossacks, or razed to their ground.[63] The inherited brutality of established tsarist practice was now leavened with callous revolutionary zeal; 'when we are reproached with cruelty, we wonder how people can forget the most elementary Marxism,' crowed Lenin.[64]

Within a decade, so-called 'de-Cossackization' was followed by 'de-Kulakization'. Alleged class enemies, the kulaks, those designated as wealthy peasants, were scheduled for 'liquidation'. The group targeted for destruction here was essentially a stratum of peasant society resistant to Soviet economics: the collectivisation of farms and the state's procurement of their grain. Those denounced as kulaks were often the most productive peasant farmers, with a little more livestock, and a few more acres, than their neighbours. Yet their stigmatisation, as the 'avaricious, beastly, and bloated' enemy of the people, was political rather than economic in nature and allowed for their persecution. Those who escaped the firing squads were subjected to the now well-established forced migration. In 1930–1932, five million men, women and children were deported to the east. There, cowed and subdued, they provided much of the labour for Stalin's first Five-Year Plan to colonise and develop Siberia, the far north, the Urals, and Kazakhstan.[65]

The ruthless political repression of putative 'class' enemies might seem distinct from genocide. A limitation of Lemkin's definition, at least as given form in the 1948 convention, may be apparent here. Yet the distinction between putative counter-revolutionary activity and ethnicity or nationality became very blurred in the Soviet Union. The Bolsheviks themselves had well understood the threat that nationalism posed for their revolution and had sought, instead, to harness such particularism. National groups were granted their own (supposedly autonomous) territories, taking their place within the Soviet 'family' of nations. Lenin insisted upon the abandonment of the hated imperial policy of Russification and the primacy of the Russian language in education, law, and politics. Yet over the 1920s, this indigenisation often promoted a sense of separate identity. By 1933, the Georgian Stalin sought greater centralisation of power.[66]

A return to chauvinistic Russian hegemony was his chosen tool. The encouragement of national cultures and national cadres was withdrawn. Entire peoples would become politically suspect once more. This was perhaps most apparent in the case of Ukraine, where peasant resistance to Soviet agricultural policies fused with nationalism. As a party functionary complained, 'the Ukrainian village is the most complex village because of its profound national character and its kulaks'.[67] Here, Stalin deployed starvation to overcome resistance to sovietisation.

Famine, born of forced collectivisation, excessive state procurement of grain, and the disruption of traditional agricultural practices, had struck across the Soviet Union in 1931. By the summer of 1932, Stalin had convinced himself that, at every level, including within the Communist Party, disloyal Ukrainians were intent on starving cities and stifling exports. He complained to his lackey Lazar Kaganovitch, 'We are in danger of losing Ukraine', which was infested with 'nationalist agents and Polish spies'. Consequently, he intentionally amplified the famine in the Ukraine, violently requisitioning all available wheat, including the seed grain vital for the following year's crop. As people starved, the government collection target for 1932 was set at

32 per cent higher than the previous year. Roadblocks ringed cities and millions of Ukrainians were physically prevented from fleeing the famine-struck areas. That this fate was being deliberately inflicted to bring a recalcitrant population to heel was revealed in official communications. One party secretary callously complained in March 1933 that 'The unsatisfactory course of sowing in many areas shows that famine hasn't still taught reason to many *kolkhozniks* [peasants on the collective farms]'.[68]

This policy of deliberate starvation was combined with the arrest of Ukrainian officials and intellectuals, and mass terror. Between August 1932 and December 1933, 125,000 peasants were arrested for taking a few ears of corn or rye ('socialist property') for themselves from the fields. Of these, 5,400 were sentenced to death. Entire villages that failed to meet their targets were punished by deportation. In 1931, the gulags received 71,236 deportees. In 1932, the number soared to 268,091. Of the (at least) six million Soviet citizens who had died of starvation by 1933, about four million were from the Ukraine and North Caucasus, the regions where Stalin deliberately made famine conditions worse. Ukrainians remember this genocide as the *Holodomor*: death by hunger.[69]

Among those deported in 1933 were 60,000 Kuban Cossacks. In one sense, their fate reflected that of the Terek Cossacks in 1920. Yet they were also explicitly denounced as 'Ukrainian nationalists', demonstrating the clear ethnic, rather than putative class, basis of their persecution. This would set a pattern.[70]

That same tendency to equate political disloyalty with some specific ethnicities was manifested in the resurgence of the mass deportations after 1935. Up until the outbreak of the Second World War, suspicion focused on border areas, as it had under the last tsar. From the western borders of Europe, Soviet citizens of Finnish, Latvian, Estonian, Polish, Romanian, or German descent were rounded up and deported eastwards, to Kazakhstan, Siberia, and Tajikistan. In the Soviet Far East, 172,000 ethnic Koreans, who had settled around Vladivostok and Khabarovsk, came under suspicion as Soviet relations with Japan deteriorated. They were uprooted, and sent to Uzbekistan and Kazakhstan, 'for the first time [under the Soviets], the totality of a national minority ... was deported ... '.[71]

After September 1939, the territories annexed by the USSR following the Soviet-German non-aggression pact were subject to the same policy. Members of the 'dominant classes' (intellectuals, military officers, industrialists, landowners, policemen) were arrested and executed. The Polish Army was a particular concern. Lavrenti Beria, Stalin's Minister of Internal Affairs, established a new 'Directorate of Prisoners of War', within the People's Commissariat of Internal Affairs (the NKVD secret police). The rank-and-file prisoners were dispatched to forced labour. The officers, tried at special courts and found guilty of 'resisting the international worker's movement', were liquidated: 4,404 executed in the Katyń Forest, 3,896 at NKVD headquarters in Kharkiv, 6,287 at Kalinin. Again, terror was accompanied by mass deportations of Poles, Ukrainians, and Belarusians. Jews, too, were disproportionately represented among those arrested and transported. In four large-scale waves of deportations between February 1940 and May 1941, between 300,000 and 340,000 were sent to labour in the harsh environments of northern Russia, the Urals, and Siberia.[72]

Following the Nazi invasion of the Soviet Union on 22 June 1941, the Second World War provided Stalin with a convenient pretext for further mass deportations. Eight national groups were deported to Siberia and Central Asia: Volga Germans in September 1941; Karachai of the north Caucasus in October–November 1943; Kalmyks of the Caspian steppe in December 1943; Caucasian Chechens, Ingush, and Balkars, in February–April 1944; Crimean Tartars in May 1944, and Meskhetians in November 1944 (Meskhetia was a region of the Caucasus, its population of mixed Turkic, Greek, Armenian, and Georgian descent). Even with the war against Hitler raging, Stalin devoted considerable resources to this endeavour. The NKVD employed 119,000 troops to police the deportations of early 1944. Probably two million people were forcibly transferred by rail and truck from their homelands. About half of them were under 16 years of age. They could carry little or nothing with them; there was little or nothing waiting for them when they arrived. D.P. Pyurveev, once president of the Autonomous Republic of Kalmykia, wrote of his people: 'They have lost all their cattle. They arrived in Siberia with nothing at all ... [Those] working on the collective farms receive almost nothing at all, since even the original workers on the farms cannot feed themselves'.[73]

Understanding why these deportations took place underscores the essential continuity with the imperialism of the nineteenth century. On the face of it, the deportations may look like responses to the Nazi invasion. The expulsion of the Volga Germans from a frontier zone might be cast as a preventative measure, taken to remove a potentially disloyal population from where they might do harm. This might seem not so very different, in intent if not the violence of its execution, from the internment of Japanese Americans in the United States in 1942. The deportations of the other targeted populations were justified because of their alleged collaboration, or acquiescence towards collaboration, during periods of occupation by Axis forces. Yet there is a deeper history here, one that ties together these people, and explains why they were the object of a particular suspicion and liable to collective punishment. All had arrived relatively recently under Russian hegemony. All had resisted Russification.

The Kalmyks were a nomadic people of Mongolian stock. In 1771, much of their population chose exile rather than submit to encroaching Russian authority. Those who stayed had clung to their traditional way of life. By providing tsarist armies with excellent light cavalry in wartime, they established a position analogous to that of the Cossacks. The Crimean Peninsula was annexed at much the same time: 1783. Its Tartar people were descendants of the Golden Horde, remembered by Russians as having imposed 'the Mongol yoke' upon them. A long history of enmity was deeply rooted on both sides. In contrast, the Volga Germans had chosen Russian rule. They had settled in the late eighteenth and early nineteenth centuries, at the invitation of the crown. It was hoped that they would transform Russian peasant agriculture. Instead, the Germans had resolutely kept to themselves, living in their own enclaves, maintaining their own ethnic identity. The Muslim Caucasian peoples were the most recently subdued, having fought bitterly against the Russians over the first half of the nineteenth century. Their conquest was piecemeal. The deportations of the Circassians in 1864 might have marked Russia's eventual victory, but there was never much of a peace. As recently as 1929–1930, the Red Army had faced stiff fighting across the North Caucasus to suppress rebellions provoked by the collectivisation of farms.[74]

Neither imperial Russia nor the Soviet Union had achieved an unchallenged dominion over these peoples. They maintained their own languages, religious beliefs, cultures, and traditions, defied central authority, and steadfastly resisted first Russification and then sovietisation. Some had historic links to threatening external powers. So, Stalin made the decision to destroy them as nations. It might be argued that deportation is not genocide. 'Ethnic cleansing', a term that gained currency in the late twentieth century during expulsions of minority populations that took place during the break-up of former Yugoslavia, might better describe the Soviet practice of deportations. However, as Norman Naimark has remarked, 'ethnic cleansing bleeds into genocide, as mass murder is committed in order to rid the land of a people'.[75]

In this instance, the mass murder was primarily achieved through privation and disease, a process that began on the journey itself. One deportee recalled that 'in the tightly shut wagons, people died like flies because of hunger and lack of oxygen, and no one gave us anything to eat or drink'. Some deportees travelled for up to 24 days. On arrival, survivors were scattered among collective farms or factories, the bonds of their original communities sundered. Few had decent shelter; of 31,000 families deported to Kirgizstan in late 1944, only 5,000 were housed. Nine hundred families were crammed into 18 apartments at one state farm. Sanitation was 'extremely poor', deportees lacked suitable clothes, even shoes in many cases. Despite the high proportion of young people among the deportees, mortality rates were appallingly high. Of the 228,392 people transported from the Crimea in 1944, 44,887 had died by October 1948. Only 6,564 births had been recorded among those deportees in the same period. Two of the acts stipulated in the 1948 definition of genocide are clearly applicable here: 'Deliberately inflicting on the group conditions of life calculated to bring about its physical destruction in whole or in part', and 'Imposing measures intended to prevent births within the group'.[76]

The Soviet regime had no need of extermination camps like Treblinka. For the Soviets, unlike the National Socialists in Germany, nations, like classes, were considered 'sociohistorical groups with a shared consciousness and not racial-biological groups'.[77] It was not necessary to kill every last member of a targeted group to destroy their national and cultural identities. It was enough that many should die, and the rest be terrorised and scattered, far from their native land. There, to use Lemkin's original formulation of genocide, a new national pattern was imposed. Russian colonists farmed their fields and changed the names of their villages and towns. The Autonomous Republic of the Crimea disappeared. In its place was the Crimean *oblast* (region) of the Russian Federation (gifted to Ukraine in 1954 by Nikita Khrushchev). After 1944, no Soviet map showed the Kalmyk Autonomous Socialist Republic. Where its capital city, Elista, had once stood was located the Russian city of Stenpnoi.[78]

Considered alongside the Armenian experience, the Russian/Soviet examples demonstrate the deep continuities that shaped twentieth-century genocides. Patterns of prejudice established during decades or even centuries of imperial rule stigmatised particular groups, generally distinguished by ethnic and/or religious identity. This would leave them vulnerable to shifts towards more radical policies of violence and exclusion. The methods of engineering loyal populations in contested territories were established within the Russian Empire by the 1860s: mass violence, deportation, death by disease and privation, the sundering of the bonds of family and community, the imposition of the oppressor's national pattern on emptied lands. Pointing to these continuities is not to suggest an overly deterministic explanation of the genocides themselves. The drive to implement such radical exclusionary policies was, in these instances, contingent on the rise to power of those imbued with emerging modern ideologies that stressed extreme chauvinism and conflict: the nationalism of the CUP and the communism of the Soviet Union (combined from the mid-1930s with a resurgent Russian nationalism).

Nor was it simply domestic politics that shaped prejudice into persecution and genocide. Jay Winter suggested that the Armenian genocide should be understood within the context of the potential violence unleashed by total war. This was 'a new kind of war', that 'created the military, political and cultural space in which [genocide] could occur'. This is valuable, but it requires some modification, in particular to acknowledge colonial precedents.

Winter lists five distinguishing characteristics of total war. Firstly, 'crossing the military participation threshold' (above 50 per cent military-age men in arms). Secondly, 'direct and on-going linkages between front and home front' (mobilisation of labour in support of war effort, and civilian understanding of the murderous scale and nature of conflict). Thirdly, 'a redefinition of the military as the cutting edge of the nation at war' (the capacity of an army depended upon the well-being of civilians at home); fourthly, 'the mobilisation of the imagination' (justification of slaughter to a domestic audience through culture and propaganda). Fifthly, 'the cultural preparation of hatred, atrocity and genocide' (demonisation of the enemy through cultural mobilisation). One might add the blurring of the distinction between combatants and noncombatants, and the consequent military targeting of civilian populations and entire economies. Winter specifically rejects pre-modern conflicts, even such ferocious examples as the Peloponnesian Wars or the Thirty Years War, as displaying this full range of characteristics.[79] Yet some pre-modern colonial conflicts did, such as Metacom's War of 1675–1676 in New England.

Of course, the twentieth century's total wars, and the genocides associated with them, were unprecedented in both their scale and capacity for destruction. Yet there had been some precedents for the escalation of violence to genocidal levels during earlier, unrestrained, and existential conflicts, pre-modern 'total wars'. Understanding the relationship of the Armenian and Russian/Soviet genocides to total war is problematic in other ways too. Within the Ottoman Empire, it seems most likely that the war did indeed radicalise Ottoman policy, rather than acting as a pretext for a plan already formulated (although that remains a disputed interpretation). The circumstances of total war made a genocide possible; the military reverses of early 1915 actualised that potential.

The Russian/Soviet cases seem more complex. Some were clearly associated with wars. The colonial campaigns of conquest in the Caucasus appear to have been the laboratory for the deportations, as the fate of the Circassians reveals. It is equally striking though that this policy could be enacted during peacetime, as it was in the 1930s. Even then, it is important to recognise the degree to which the broader international context could shape persecution and genocide. Again, there are some telling pre-modern precedents. In 1609–1614, the *Moriscos*, descendants of Muslims – some sincere Christians, some crypto-Muslims – were expelled from Spain. This was partly because they maintained much of their customs and heritage and partly because they were seen as a potential 'fifth column' for the Ottoman Empire.[80]

In a similar way, the willingness, real or imagined, of the great powers to intervene on behalf of the Armenians from 1878 onwards played a significant role in inciting hatred towards them among their fellow Ottomans. Stalin's paranoia about foreign agents and nationalists ensured that non-Russian peoples, especially in zones bordering unfriendly powers, were particularly targeted. In this example, when a total war did come, this seems more of a pretext for further deportations of suspect populations. The Caucasian peoples were deported in 1943–1944, with the Germans already in retreat. Any meaningful security threat the deported populations had posed was over by that point.

The genocides that occurred within the Ottoman and Russian/Soviet empires in the first half of the century had their own specific legacies. As noted, the sheer awful scale of destruction achievable by modern nation states was one distinctive character of twentieth-century genocides. Efficient bureaucracy was as much a part of this as the weaponry of industrial warfare. Of course, sound administration had been a useful tool of persecution on occasions in the past. The bureaucratisation of performing blood sacrifice, including the issuing of *libelli* (certificates) to those who had done so, helped exposed Christians to the Decian persecutions of 249 CE. The thoroughness of inquisitors' record keeping had brought to light networks of heretics in thirteenth-century Languedoc. Yet these were pale foreshadows of the extent to which modern polities might intrude into every aspect of people's lives. By the twentieth century, those states bent on persecution have possessed means of surveillance and the capacity to project their authority and enforce rules that has been unparalleled in history. Those bureaucrats who were tasked with enforcing the rules, became the modern arbiters of power, with the ability to control the lives of others.

Within the Ottoman Empire, the bureaucracy was well enough developed to give the genocide its systematic, widespread character. Influential Armenians were identified and swiftly arrested first, leaving their communities leaderless. The deportations were ruthlessly organised to a common procedure: army, gendarmes, and the Special Organisation coordinated their actions. The central state, to a considerable degree, maintained both communications with, and authority over, the regional officials. Hatred was propagated among the population at large, ensuring widespread complicity in, or at least acquiescence to, the genocide. Inter-ethnic conflict between Muslims was largely avoided by emphasising common religiosity, masking for the time being the longer-term threat *Ittihadism* posed to non-Turks. (In the 1920s and 1930s, 'tribal populations that do not speak Turkish' and 'people who do not share the Turkish culture', predominantly Kurds, were themselves subjected to 'resettlement laws', and coercive 'denaturalization'.)[81]

Yet this instance of the power of bureaucracy would be immeasurably surpassed by what was achieved in the Soviet Union. Stalin's centralisation of power and his bureaucracy's capacity to intrude into the furthest recesses of people's social and private lives was unprecedented. The Soviet Union came to epitomise 'totalitarianism'. It was characterised by a one-party state, dictatorial rule, and monopolistic control of mass communications and all economic and social organisations. These were combined with secret police, networks of informers, active suppression of dissent, and the effective propagation of a unifying core ideology: Marxist-Leninism. Persecution was immanent within the Soviet system. During the dark years of Stalin's 'Great Terror', 1936–1938, the mass murder of Soviet citizens became quite arbitrary, its extent driven by managerialist quotas and central planning. Dutiful functionaries were simply 'charged with the task of exterminating 10,000 enemies of the people'. And 10,000 victims would thus be shot.[82] Sources of internal conflicts were largely managed, at least until the level of regional and nationalist discontent began to unravel the USSR in the 1980s.[83]

The effectiveness of the totalitarian state as an instrument of persecution also manifested itself in the historically unprecedented scale of the deportations achieved by the Soviets. The cruelty inherent in this can be well illustrated by an example of how the NKVD learned to make them more 'successful' and more 'economical':

Experience gained from transporting the Karachai and Kalmyks has made it possible for us to take certain measures that allowed us to pare back what is needed for convoys and hence ultimately to diminish the number of journeys that need to be made. We now put 45 people into each cattle truck as opposed to the previous 40. By placing the people together with their possessions, we also cut down on the number of trucks required, thus saving 37,548 meters of planks, 11,834 buckets, and 3,400 stoves.[84]

Seemingly mundane, prosaic measures were implemented by bureaucrats apparently devoid of human empathy. They were integral elements in inflicting uncounted levels of misery and death on the deportees. They ensured that deportation was not simply a journey, but an efficient stage in a process of attrition. Stifled bodies gasping for breath, while crowded into filthy cattle trucks, without regard for sanitation or sustenance, on hellish journeys that stretched into days and weeks would be a characteristic, too, of the Holocaust.

Notes

1 'Fate of the Circassians', *The Examiner*, 2942 (8 June 1864), p.1.
2 Stephen D. Shenfield, 'The Circassians: A Forgotten Genocide?', in Mark Levene and Penny Roberts (eds), *The Massacre in History* (Oxford: Berghahn Books, 1999), pp.149–162.
3 'The Circassian Exodus', *The Times*, 9 May 1864, p.11.
4 Taner Akçam, *A Shameful Act: The Armenian Genocide and the Question of Turkish Responsibility* (London: Constable, 2007), pp.199–200; Philip Jenkins, *The Lost History of Christianity: The Thousand-Year Golden Age of the Church in the Middle East, Africa, and Asia* (Oxford: Lion Books: 2009), p.140.
5 For conflicting interpretations, see Donald Bloxham, *The Great Game of Genocide: Imperialism, Nationalism, and the Destruction of the Ottoman Armenians* (Oxford: Oxford University Press, 2005); cf. Benny Morris and Dror Ze'Evi, *The Thirty-Year Genocide: Turkey's Destruction of its Christian Minorities, 1894–1924* (Cambridge, MA: Harvard University Press, 2019).
6 Ronald Grigor Suny, 'Writing Genocide: The Fate of the Ottoman Armenians', in Ronald Grigor Suny, Fatma Müge Göçek, and Norman Naimark (eds), *A Question of Genocide: Armenians and Turks at the End of the Ottoman Empire* (Oxford: Oxford University Press, 2011), p.25; Theo Maarten van Lint, 'The Formation of Armenian Identity in the First Millennium', *Church History and Religious Culture*, 89 (2009), p.269.
7 Justin McCarthy, *Death and Exile: The Ethnic Cleansing of Ottoman Muslims, 1821–1922* (Princeton, NJ: Darwin Press, 1995), pp.23–179; Shenfield, 'The Circassians: A Forgotten Genocide?', pp.149–162.
8 Stephen H. Astourian, 'The Silence of the Land: Agrarian Relations, Ethnicity, and Power', in Suny et al. (eds), *A Question of Genocide*, pp.63–67.
9 Astourian, 'The Silence of the Land', pp.67–81; Morris and Ze'Evi, *The Thirty-Year Genocide*, p.114.
10 'The State of Feeling Among the Turks of Constantinople', *The Times*, 12 November 1895, p.8.

11 Bloxham, *The Great Game of Genocide*, pp.29–69, 49–51.

12 Akçam, *A Shameful Act*, pp.90–92.

13 Robert Melson, 'A Theoretical Inquiry into the Armenian Massacres of 1894–1896', *Comparative Studies in Society and History*, 24 (1982), p.487.

14 Quoted in Morris and Ze'Evi, *The Thirty-Year Genocide*, p.74.

15 Quoted in Morris and Ze'Evi, *The Thirty-Year Genocide*, p.83.

16 Morris and Ze'Evi, *The Thirty-Year Genocide*, pp.98–104.

17 Morris and Ze'Evi, *The Thirty-Year Genocide*, p.108.

18 Bloxham, *The Great Game of Genocide*, p.55.

19 Melson, 'A Theoretical Inquiry into the Armenian Massacres of 1894–1896', p.489.

20 'The State of Feeling Among the Turks of Constantinople', *The Times*, 12 November 1895, p.8.

21 Melson, 'A Theoretical Inquiry into the Armenian Massacres of 1894–1896', pp.493–495.

22 'The State of Feeling Among the Turks of Constantinople', *The Times*, 12 November 1895, p.8.

23 Akçam, *A Shameful Act*, p.34.

24 Morris and Ze'Evi, *The Thirty-Year Genocide*, pp.93–94.

25 'The State of Feeling Among the Turks of Constantinople', *The Times*, 12 November 1895, p.8.

26 Bloxham, *The Great Game of Genocide*, pp.60–62; Morris and Ze'Evi, *The Thirty-Year Genocide*, pp.144–145.

27 Mustafa Aksakal, *The Ottoman Road to War in 1914* (Cambridge: Cambridge University Press, 2008), pp.153–188.

28 Donald Bloxham, 'The Armenian Genocide of 1915–1916: Cumulative Radicalization and the Development of a Destruction Policy', *Past & Present*, 181 (2003), p.143.

29 Michael J. Reynolds, *Shattering Empires: The Clash and Collapse of the Ottoman and Russian Empires, 1908–1918* (Cambridge: Cambridge University Press, 2011), pp.124–139.

30 Henry Morgenthau, *Ambassador Morgenthau's Story* (New York: Doubleday, 1919), p.297.

31 Vahakn N. Dadrian, 'The Preparations for Courts-Martial', in Vahakn N. Dadrian and Taner Akçam (eds) *Judgement in Istanbul: The Armenian Genocide Trials* (Oxford: Berghahn Books, 2011), p.86.

32 Martin Niepage, 'The Armenian Massacres', in Charles F. Horne (ed.), *Source Records of the Great War*, Volume 3 (New York: National Alumni, 1923), pp.161, 164, 167.

33 Quoted in Hannibal Travis, 'The Long Genocide in Upper Mesopotamia: Minority Population Destruction amidst Nation-Building and "International Security"', *Genocide Studies International*, 13 (2019), p.99.

34 Richard G. Hovannisian, 'Denial of the Armenian Genocide 100 Years Later', *Genocide Studies International*, 9 (2015), pp.228–247.

35 'Talât Pasha Dispatches to the Prefecture of Aleppo, 11 December, and 29 December 1915', in Horne (ed.), *Source Records of the Great War*, Volume 3, pp.175–176.

36 James F. Harbord, *Report of the American Military Mission to Armenia* (Washington, DC: Government Printing Office, 1920), p.7.

37 'Talât Pasha Dispatches to the Prefecture of Aleppo', p.175.

38 Akçam, *A Shameful Act*, p.217; Morris and Ze'Evi, *The Thirty-Year Genocide*, pp.242, 373–380.

39 Quoted in Donald E. Miller and Lorna Touryan (eds), *Survivors: An Oral History of the Armenian Genocide* (Berkeley: University of California Press, 1993), pp.90–91.

40 Dadrian, 'The Preparations for Courts-Martial', p.87.

41 Dadrian, 'The Preparations for Courts-Martial', p.88; Niepage, 'The Armenian Massacres', p.169.

42 Vahram Ter-Matevosyan, 'Turkish Experience with Totalitarianism and Fascism: Tracing the Intellectual Origins', *Iran & the Caucasus*, 19 (2015), pp.397–398.

43 Miller and Touryan (eds), *Survivors*, pp.97, 101.

44 Morris and Ze'Evi, *The Thirty-Year Genocide*, p.312.

45 Elyse Semerdjian, *Remnants: Embodied Archives of the Armenian Genocide* (Stanford, CA: Stanford University Press, 2023), p.8, pp.150–155.

46 Reginald Ginns, 'The De-Christianing of Asia Minor', *Blackfriars*, 5 (1924), pp.531–544.

47 Raymond Kévorkian, *The Armenian Genocide: A Complete History* (London: I.B. Tauris, 2006), p.804

48 Ginns, 'The De-Christianing of Asia Minor', p.543.

49 Ginns, 'The De-Christianing of Asia Minor,' p.535; see also Morris and Ze'Evi, *The Thirty-Year Genocide*, p.485.

50 Bloxham, *The Great Game of Genocide*, pp.110–111.

51 Vahakn N. Dadrian, 'History of the Turko-Armenian Conflict', in Dadrian and Akçam (eds) *Judgement in Istanbul,* p.17; Edward G. Elliott, 'The Development of International Law by the Second Hague Conference', *Columbia Law Review*, 8 (1908), p.105.

52 Michelle Tusan, ' "Crimes against Humanity": Human Rights, the British Empire, and the Origins of the Response to the Armenian Genocide', *American Historical Review*, 119 (2014), p.66.

53 Quoted in Kévorkian, *The Armenian Genocide*, p.770.

54 Dadrian, 'The Judicial Liquidation of Some of the Arch Perpetrators by Both CUP and Kemelist Authorities, and the Demise of Other Accomplices', in Dadrian and Akçam (eds) *Judgement in Istanbul*, p.177; Tusan, ' "Crimes against Humanity" ', pp.47–77.

55 Norman M. Naimark, *Fires of Hatred: Ethnic Cleansing in Twentieth-Century Europe* (Cambridge, MA: Harvard University Press, 2001), pp.54–55.

56 'Declaration of Amnesty', *American Journal of International Law*, 18 (1924), pp.92–95.

57 Quoted in Johann Justus Vasel, ' "In the Beginning, There Was No Word … " ', *European Journal of International Law*, 29 (2019), p.1053.

58 Margaret Lavinia Anderson, 'Who Still Talked about the Extermination of the Armenians? German Talk and German Silences', in Suny et al. (eds), *A Question of Genocide*, pp.199–217.

59 David Matas, 'Prosecuting Crimes against Humanity: The Lessons of World War I', *Fordham International Law Journal*, 13 (1989–1990), p.104.

60 Shane O'Rouke, 'Trial Run: The Deportation of the Terek Cossacks 1920', in Richard Bessel and Claudia B. Haake (eds), *Removing Peoples: Forced Removal in the Modern World* (Oxford: Oxford University Press, 2009), p.259.

61 Heinz-Dietrich Löwe, 'Pogroms in Russia: Explanations, Comparisons, Suggestions', *Jewish Social Studies*, 11 (2004), pp.16–24; Nicolas Werth, 'Genocide in the Later Russian Empire and the USSR', in Donald Bloxham and A. Dirk Moses (eds), *The Oxford Handbook of Genocide Studies* (Oxford: Oxford University Press, 2010), pp.386–391.

62 Quoted in Peter Holquist, ' "Conduct Merciless Mass Terror": Decossackization on the Don, 1919', *Cahiers du Monde Russe*, 38 (1997), p.134.

63 Werth, 'Genocide in the Later Russian Empire and the USSR', pp.391–393.

64 Quoted in R.J. Rummel, *Death by Government* (New Brunswick, NJ: Transaction, 1994), p.79.

65 Lynne Viola, 'The Question of the Perpetrator in Soviet History', *Slavic Review*, 72 (2013), p.16.

66 Hennadii Yefimenko and Marta D. Olynyk, 'Bolshevik Language Policy as a Reflection of the Ideas and Practice of Communist Construction, 1919–1933', *Harvard Ukrainian Studies*, 35 (2017–2018), pp.145–167.

67 Quoted in David R. Marples, 'Ethnic Issues in the Famine of 1932–1933 in Ukraine', *Europe-Asia Studies*, 61 (2009), p.513.

68 Andrea Graziosi, 'The Soviet 1931–1933 Famines and the Ukrainian *Holodomor*: Is a New Interpretation Possible, and What Would Its Consequences Be?' *Harvard Ukrainian Studies*, 27 (2004–2005), p.106.

69 Nicolas Werth, 'The Great Famine', in Stéphanie Courtois et al., *The Black Book of Communism: Crimes, Terror, Repression*, translated by Jonathan Murphy and Mark Kramer (Cambridge, MA.: Harvard University Press, 1999), pp.395–398.

70 Terry Martin, 'The Origins of Soviet Ethnic Cleansing', *Journal of Modern History*, 70 (1998), p.847

71 Werth, 'Genocide in the Later Russian Empire and the USSR', p.400.

72 Andrzei and Karel Bartošek, 'Poland, the "Enemy Nation" ', in Courtois et al., *The Black Book of Communism*, pp.370–372.

73 Nicolas Werth, 'The Other Side of Victory', in Courtois et al., *The Black Book of Communism*, pp.221–223.

74 Isabelle Kreindle, 'The Soviet Deported Nationalities: A Summary and an Update', *Soviet Studies*, 38 (1986), pp.387–405; Jeronim Perović, 'Highland Rebels: The North Caucasus During the Stalinist Collectivization Campaign', *Journal of Contemporary History*, 51 (2016), pp.234–260.

75 Naimark, *Fires of Hatred*, pp.3–4.

76 Werth, 'The Other Side of Victory', pp.222–223.

77 Francine Hirsch, 'Race without the Practice of Racial Politics', *Slavic Review*, 61 (2002), p.30.

78 Naimark, *Fields of Hatred*, p.104; Kreindle, 'The Soviet Deported Nationalities', p.393.

79 Jay Winter, 'Under Cover of War: The Armenian Genocide in the Context of Total War', in Robert Gellately and Ben Kiernan (eds), *The Specter of Genocide: Mass Murder in Historical Perspective* (Cambridge: Cambridge University Press, 2003), pp.189–213.

80 Andrew C. Hess, 'The Moriscos: An Ottoman Fifth Column in Sixteenth-Century Spain', *American Historical Review*, 74 (1968), pp.1–25.

81 Soner Çağatay, 'Population Resettlement and Immigration Policies of Interwar Turkey: A Study of Turkish Nationalism', *Turkish Studies Association Bulletin*, 25 (2002), pp.1–24.

82 Rummel, *Death by Government*, pp.80–81.

83 Ronald Grigor Suny, *The Revenge of the Past: Nationalism, Revolution and the Collapse of the Soviet Union* (Stanford, CA: Stanford University Press, 1994).

84 Quoted in Werth, 'The Other Side of Victory', p.221.

10 'The Annihilation of the Jewish Race in Europe'

Persecution and the Holocaust, 1933–1945

In January 1934, American journalist George J. Walmer surveyed how Germany had fared in the year since the new Chancellor, Adolf Hitler of the *Nationalsozialistische Deutsche Arbeiterpartei* (National Socialist Workers Party, NSDAP, or Nazis) had taken office. It had been an ugly twelve months, marked by the thuggery of the party's paramilitaries, the brown-shirted *Sturmabteilung* (storm troopers, or SA), and the persecution of German Jews. Driven from the civil service, their businesses boycotted, subject to social ostracism amidst a barrage of invective that questioned their very right to belong in the country of their birth, 60,000 had already emigrated. Concentration camps and the apparatus of a police state had sprung up. The NSDAP's political opponents had been taken into 'protective custody' and brutalised into compliance. Walmer wondered how this 'renaissance' of a 'barbarian fury' among a people who 'prided themselves, not without reason, on their pre-eminence in science and philosophy, music, and Kultur', could have occurred.[1]

He cannot possibly have imagined how much stronger that fury would grow, and how much it would destroy. In 1939, Hitler would lead his country into a global war that would consume 55 million lives. When he finally took his own life in April 1945, his Third Reich was a defeated ruin. The National Socialist regime had waged his war with a pitiless genocidal determination in eastern Europe, attempting to carve out *Lebensraum* (living room) for the German *Volk* and cleanse the land of 'inferior' races. Within that wider conflict, they had pursued a merciless campaign of extermination against Europe's Jews. Six million would be murdered during what became known as the *Shoah* ('destruction'), or the Holocaust ('burnt sacrifice'). In 1933, the NSDAP had planned to drive German Jews from the Reich. War had transformed that objective into the complete physical annihilation of the Jews in Europe.

Walmer, when attempting to explain this 'renaissance' of 'barbarism', described Germany as an angry, 'thwarted' nation, defeated (through betrayal, so it was supposed, rather than force of arms) in the First World War and dismembered and humiliated at Versailles. There was much truth

DOI: 10.4324/9781003494331-11

to this observation. Yet it will not suffice to explain how the NSDAP came to power. The shattering effects of the Great Depression and the political machinations, and miscalculations, that occurred in 1932 were the crucial proximate reasons for Hitler's rise to the Chancellorship. The swift efficiency with which the NSDAP then constructed a dictatorship, partly based on repression but also building a wide popular support base, allowed them to begin a process of persecution that, under pressure of war, would become a genocide. Theirs was the fury, not the German people's as a whole. Understanding the National Socialist *weltanschauung* (worldview) thus becomes central to explaining the Holocaust: their ambitions to unite all Germans in a Greater Reich; their thirst for *Lebensraum* to ensure the future of the German *Volk*; their embrace of Social Darwinism and the belief that racial struggle was the engine of history; their corollary commitment to 'racial hygiene', and the need to protect the racial purity of the *Volk*. But most of all it is necessary to understand their hatred of Jews. That must be the starting point.

The emancipation of Jews over the course of the nineteenth century had seen medieval barriers to civil and social equality break down. Jews had begun to take their place as full citizens of European states and empires. For some of their fellow citizens, this was not a welcome development. Industrialisation, urbanisation, the rise of market economics, had left many workers and artisans adrift. Conscious of lost status and anxious of their economic precarity, many had looked with suspicion at the once-despised but now-emancipated Jews. Some conservative elements too had come to correlate the emancipation of the Jews with all they feared of an onrushing modernity: increased popular political participation; the decay of old social hierarchies, and a discordant civil society, with Jewish authors, intellectuals, and activists often very visible at its forefront. Finally, the rise of nationalism, provided another fertile source of hostility towards 'alien' Jews. This was especially true of the *Völkisch* ethno-nationalism that conflated language, culture, and putative racial descent with a particular 'soil'.[2] In 1879, the German journalist Wilhelm Marr had dignified these fearful politics with a name: antisemitism.[3]

The weekly newspaper *Der Stürmer* (*The Stormer*) was a particularly poisonous vector of such antisemitism in Weimar and National Socialist Germany. Its ugly motto, emblazoned in blood-red ink on the bottom of its cover, was 'The Jew is Our Misery'. Between its first publication in 1923 and its final issue, in February 1945, it spewed dark fantasies of Jewish malfeasance: global conspiracies; puppet-mastery of corrupt and venal politicians; untrammelled dominance of finance, industry, and the media; authorship of both communism and capitalism, and an existential threat to the racial purity of the German *Volk*. Its crude propaganda invoked stereotypes both ancient and modern. In May 1938, it featured a highly sexualised image of brutishly caricatured Jewish men defiling a naked girl: 'The ritual murder of the non-Jewish peasant girl Esther Solymosi. She was butchered in the synagogue of Tiszaeszlár [in Hungary]'. This was a case from the 1880s. Solymosi, had, in fact, drowned. Before her body had been recovered from a river, local Jews were accused of murdering her and using her blood for their Passover *matzoh*. *Der Stürmer's* editor, NSDAP member Julius Streicher, had characteristically perpetuated the falsehood. His shameless deployment of the medieval 'blood libel', to draw on ancient wellsprings of cultural prejudice against Jews, was not unusual: 'ritual murder [allegations] saw their largest upsurge in the last decades of the nineteenth century, exactly the period when *modern* antisemitism took shape'.[4]

There are good reasons for believing that political antisemitism had been waning in the early 1900s in Germany. The majorities achieved by the Social Democrats and Progressives in the 1912 Reichstag elections suggested that the antisemitism peddled by right-wing parties had lacked appeal to voters. However, the catastrophic events of 1917 and 1918 added a new stimulus to a revived antisemitism. The outcome of the First World War was an inexplicable disaster to most Germans. Their defeat was rooted in military collapse in the field. Yet this was never fully acknowledged or comprehended within Germany. Indeed, senior officers such as Erich Ludendorff began actively fostering the 'stab in the back' legend even before the armistice was signed, masking their own responsibility by scapegoating politicians, alleged Bolsheviks and, inevitably, Jews. The Russian Revolution, threatening to many with its terrifying prospect of the scourge of godless communism ('Judeo-Bolshevism') carried west by a Slavic-Asiatic, and Jewish-controlled, horde, fanned the flames of a resurgent bigotry.[5]

In the decade after the war, around 430 antisemitic associations and societies had operated in Germany. Some 700 antisemitic periodicals were in circulation. The *Protocols of the Elders of Zion*, a notorious, originally Russian, piece of literary fakery was translated into German for the first time in 1920. Purporting to reveal an international Jewish world conspiracy, it sold 120,000 copies. Its influence did not wane, even though it was exposed as a 'crude and theatrical' forgery by *The Times* in 1921.[6]

This was the environment in which the NSDAP had been officially constituted, originally as the *Deutsche Arbeiterpartei* (DAP), in January 1919. The political and cultural milieu from which it first emerged would shape central elements of the party's subsequent programme and appeal. Its early leadership were members of the Thule Society. This was ostensibly an apolitical group, but one steeped in the romantic *Völkisch* nationalist tradition: believers in an ancient Aryan civilisation (centred on the lost northern island of Thule), of which the Germanic *Volk* were the purest inheritors. They postulated an integral, mystical bond between the Germanic *Volk* and their lands: 'blood and soil'. They were prophets of a coming apocalyptic struggle between the superior Aryans and the lesser races. Their antisemitism was radical. Jews were perceived as the most dangerous and cunning of racial foes. They also utterly reviled communism, not simply as a political ideology but, in its Bolshevik manifestation, as a racial and biological threat: a lethal Slavic/Asiatic pathogen, with which conspiratorial Jews hope to infect the

Volk. Besides the pseudo-history, they were drawn to pseudo-science and the occult. Their taste for astrology, runes, and ancient symbolism led them to appropriate such symbols as the swastika. Some of this early DAP leadership cadre, such as founder Anton Drexler, would soon be marginalised. Others – Alfred Rosenberg, Hans Frank, Rudolf Hess – would go on to play leading roles in the Third Reich.[7]

The Thule Society, for all its unsettling radicalism, was hardly more than an elitist discussion group. The *Deutsche Arbeiterpartei* aimed to draw in working- and lower-middle-class activists: factory workers, veterans, artisans, shopkeepers. It leavened its *Völkisch* nationalism with an appealing rhetoric of anti-capitalism (which was also, naturally, presented as a Jewish conspiracy to destroy the *Volk*) and a programme of social welfare measures. These held out a promise of economic security, and a level playing field for small enterprises, to German workers and small businessmen. Essentially, it offered 'a "socialist" alternative to Marxism', calculated to win support from ordinary citizens who considered themselves patriotic Germans.[8]

From November 1918 to August 1919, Germany had been consumed by civil conflict. The government that emerged, the Weimar Republic, struggled to establish its legitimacy. The DAP was merely one of many small parties whose members dismissed Weimar politicians as traitors to the fatherland, complicit in an unjust and humiliating peace. Revolution remained in the air. The government had secured its position by deploying paramilitary units, the *Freikorps*, recruited from the ranks of both veterans and young men who had just missed service in the First World War. These had not merely battled communists in German towns and cities. They had campaigned in the Baltic states against the Bolshevik Red Army, in peculiarly bitter fighting, punctuated by atrocities against prisoners and non-combatants. The presence of such men ensured politics became a brutal business. Many members of Hitler's SA received their political education in the Bavarian *Freikorps Oberland*.[9]

The prosaic politics of the day were conducted in raucous beer-hall meetings and in violent confrontations between ideological rivals. The authorities were as keen to win the war of ideas as the street fighting. It was in that capacity that Adolf Hitler first encountered the DAP. A wounded veteran, he had been employed as an inspector by the Bavarian *Reichswehr* (army), to sway other ex-servicemen away from Bolshevism. He attended a DAP meeting in September 1919 to gauge their position. He was thoroughly unimpressed by the quality of the speakers he heard. Drexler, however, urged him to join them. He prevaricated for two days, for he thought the DAP an 'absurd little organization'. Yet he saw in it, too, a vehicle for his own ambition, for the 'content, the goal, and the road could still be determined, which in the existing political parties was impossible from the outset'. He joined on 16 September 1919.[10]

In truth, the party was hardly a blank slate. The broad direction of the 'road' it had set out upon was clear and Hitler was already a fellow traveller.

He had imbibed *Völkisch* nationalism and radical antisemitism, during his shiftless pre-war years in Vienna, 1908–1913. His Pan-Germanism, with its annexationist designs on land occupied by ethnic Germans far beyond Weimar's borders, chimed with that of the original DAP leadership. And he well understood the importance of winning the active support of working-class and *petit bourgeois* activists. In this regard, he offered the party something novel. He understood how to reach a mass audience. In Vienna, he had seen how Mayor Karl Lueger had mobilised popular support through effective antisemitic demagoguery. Hitler dismissed Lueger's antisemitism as half-hearted and despised his loyalty to the multi-ethnic Habsburg Empire. Yet from him, Hitler learned the value of rhetoric, propaganda, and populism. This, combined with his ruthless ambition, saw him advance quickly within the party.[11]

On 24 February 1920, the newly renamed *Nationalsozialistische Deutsche Arbeiterpartei* issued a 25-point programme, authored by Drexler and Hitler. It is worth considering in some detail, not because the party had any chance of implementing it at that time but because of what it reveals of the NSDAP *weltanschauung* and of how they intended to build a mass movement. It is also significant because elements of it were inherently, if implicitly, genocidal.

Most of the programme comprised (rather vague) populist demands calculated to give the party a broad appeal: all Germans to enjoy equal rights and obligations; all Germans to work for 'the general good'; the abolition of unearned incomes; punishment of war profiteers; nationalisation of large companies; preference for small firms in state contracts; expansion of welfare provision for the old; an end to child labour; enhanced health care for mothers and children; access to higher education for the children of workers; profit sharing from wholesale trade, and land reform. In terms of foreign policy, again, the tone was calculated to cultivate popular, patriotic approval: *Anschluss* (union) 'for all Germans' based upon their right to self-determination, within a 'Greater Germany', and the abolition of the unjust peace treaties of Versailles and St Germain.[12]

Yet this was far from an innocuous platform. It contains dark portents. The phrase 'all Germans' implied union not just with Austrians but including the *Volksdeutsche* (ethnic Germans) of the Sudetenland in Czechoslovakia and the substantial populations in Poland, Hungary, Romania, and Yugoslavia. The creation of a Greater Germany and the revisions of Versailles and St Germain would thus entail the dismembering of other states and the re-drawing of borders.

In the aftermath of the First World War, that was well understood to involve population transfers: families uprooted, long-established communities sundered, the threat, sometimes realised, of massacre. Uncontested borders and loyal populations were achieved through ruthless demographic engineering. For example, over half a million Germans had fled the assimilationist policies of Poland by 1921. Alfred Rosenberg, the influential NSDAP ideologue, was himself an exile from the Baltic. The first, and ultimately most successful, revisionist power to challenge the post-war treaties had been the Turkish republic. In 1923, at Lausanne, Turkey had won international sanction for borders secured by massacres and deportations. The 'exchange' of populations between Greece and Turkey agreed at the same point effectively legitimised ethnic cleansing as a solution to the minorities question.[13]

Once, political systems based upon settled religious or ethnic dominance (of Muslims over Christians in the Ottoman Empire, or Germans and Magyars over Slavs in the Habsburg Empire) had allowed for coexistence. Now, nationalist ideologies preached ethnic exclusivity, of political borders conterminous with demographic borders of shared language, culture, religion, and 'blood' (putative racial descent). The Balkan Wars of 1912–1913 and the First World War had been brutal catalysts of this change. And so, inadvertently, was US President Woodrow Wilson's promise at Versailles of 'self-determination' for formerly subject peoples. It spurred ethno-nationalists to carve out territories violently, in the 'shatter zones' of fallen empires. In the aftermath of the First World War, across eastern Europe and Anatolia, Poles, Russians, Finns, Balts, Austrians, Hungarians, Ukrainians, Slovenians, Croatians, Turks, Greeks, Kurds, and Armenians had fought and killed for blood and soil.[14]

This is an essential context for considering the implications of the NSDAP's own programme of demographic engineering, even in its earliest, ostensibly limited, advocacy of German self-determination. Simply put, in modern Europe, borders were fashioned and refashioned by population transfers and deportations: ethnic cleansing. And, as Norman Naimark has observed, 'both figuratively and literally, ethnic cleansing bleeds into genocide, as mass murder is committed in order to rid the land of a people'.[15]

Two other aspects of the 1920 NSDAP programme are very noteworthy in this regard as well: its colonialism and its antisemitism. It made a demand for 'land and territory (colonies) for the sustenance of our people and colonization for our superfluous population'. This marks the programme as expansionist *beyond* the call for union with the *Volksdeutsche*. It was not a reference to Germany's African and Pacific colonies, lost at Versailles. Advocates of German colonialism were now looking towards eastern Europe. In part, this was a revival of the *Drang nach Osten* ('drive to the east') tradition popularised in the nineteenth century by nationalist historians such as Heinrich von Treitschke. In 1862, he had written of the 'pitiless racial struggle' which Germans had waged from the early thirteenth century onwards against heathen Prussians (originally a Slavic people), Poles, and Lithuanians to secure their eastern lands. There, the soil had been fertilised by 'the most noble German blood', forging a 'magical' link between the land and the Teutonic race. Their conquests were justified as they were the 'bearers of civilisation'.[16]

This tendentious, racialised version of history was familiar to much of the public in Germany. A post-Second World War exploration of the social attitudes of Germans who lived through the NSDAP era by the sociologist

Fritz Süllwold found that 52 per cent of respondents thought that most people in their social circle regarded Slavs as 'an inferior race'. They also saw relationships between Slavs and Germans in the east as essentially conflictual; 75 per cent had reacted with rage to reports of attacks on *Volksdeutsche* in Poland.[17] Such attitudes had been powerfully reinforced by the experiences of many German veterans who had served in *Ober Ost*, occupied territories in the east, during the First World War. Rather than seeing the consequences of war reflected in the ravaged landscapes, filth, and diseases they had encountered, they saw inherent barbarism and chaos. The resistance they encountered to their administrative policies made them grow sceptical that a benign paternalism would suffice to end such primitivism. Instead, they began to conceive of a German mission to bring order, hygiene, and 'civilisation' to the (seemingly) limitless spaces of an eastern Europe 'cleansed' of unworthy races.[18]

Here, too, was a potentially lethal synthesis with the development of German colonial policy in Africa. In German South-West Africa (Namibia), 1904–1908, the authorities had responded to revolts by the Herero and Nama peoples by waging a genocidal war against them. By 1908, about half of the Nama's pre-war population of 20,000 were dead. The Herero lost 60,000 from a pre-war population of 75,000–80,000. Those who still lived were reduced to involuntary servitude on German-owned farms. The German military had manifested an institutional preference for waging annihilatory campaigns in the colonial context, largely without the political restraints that might be brought to bear in, for example, the French or British cases.[19]

By then, both colonial authorities in Africa and imperialistically minded Germans at home had also largely embraced the apogees of radical European racial theorising: Social Darwinism and eugenics. The former was the misguided application of evolutionary theory to human societies. Competition between peoples was presented as the engine of human progress. Ernst Hasse, the leader of the Pan-German League, expressed the view in 1906 that the world belonged to the strong. The weak would disappear: 'The struggle for existence is a natural, rational and [morally] justified process'. In 1897, another (founding) member of the expansionist Pan-German League, the geographer Friedrich Ratzel, expressed essentially the same idea. He coined the word *Lebensraum* – 'living space' – and argued it was vital to secure the land and resources to ensure progress through the expansion of the fittest races. In Hitler's words, as he justified the eastern orientation of his proposed foreign policy, 'only an adequately large space on this earth assures a nation of freedom of existence'.[20]

NSDAP's colonisation of the east was predicated on the establishment of German settlements of healthy peasant stock that would remain entirely separate from whatever portion of the Slavic population was suffered to remain. This would prevent what Hitler referred to as the 'bastardisation' of the supposedly superior race. Eugenics, generally referred to in Germany as *Rassenhygiene* (race hygiene), was the study of human heredity, a corollary to Social Darwinism. Its adherents proposed selective breeding policies to improve racial 'fitness'. These were generally intended to discourage or prevent those deemed less fit from reproducing. 'Miscegenation' was identified as a particular danger, leading to inevitable race degeneracy. Hitler predicted that this would be the destiny of the older European colonial powers; in 300 years' time, 'the last remnants of Frankish blood would be submerged in the developing European-African mulatto state'.[21]

The quest for *Lebensraum* and the ideological emphasis on racial 'hygiene' and conflict as necessary to human progress, would make Slavs, after the Jews, the principal victims of NSDAP genocide. Indeed, the fate of the two was inextricably intertwined, given Hitler's belief that Jews had essentially taken control of Russia via Bolshevism. He also seemed to harbour some notion of carving out a reservation in the east to which Jews could be deported. In 1935, he spoke of their being 'imprisoned in a territory where they can disport themselves according to their nature'.[22]

The centrality of antisemitism to NSDAP ideology was explicit in the 1920 programme. It stipulated that 'only those of German blood ... may be members of the nation. Accordingly, no Jew may be a member of the nation'. It then articulated a series of prohibitions on 'non-Germans': they would not hold the franchise, be permitted to edit, contribute to, or influence, German-language newspapers; they would be subject to 'laws for aliens'. The programme closed by declaring that 'The Party ... combats the Jewish-materialist spirit within and without us ... '.[23]

Hitler thus drew upon the existing reservoir of radical antisemitism while striving to further propagate the politics of hate to a yet wider audience. Streicher joined him in 1922 and began publishing *Der Stürmer* the following year. By then, the party had already acquired its official organ, the *Völkischer Beobachter*. This tended to avoid Streicher's utter crudities and achieved a wider circulation, among a respectable readership. Yet the essential ingredients were the same: a eugenicist-inflected promotion of the Germans as the *Herrenvolk* (master race); contempt for parasitic *Untermenschen* (inferior races), and fear-mongering concerning a Jewish world conspiracy and racial defilement. Early on, therefore, the party had manifested a *weltanschauung* that contained the seeds of genocide and had – tacitly in one instance, explicitly in another – singled out potential targets: Slavs and Jews (there would be others too).

This is not to suggest that, at this point, Hitler had a clear blueprint in mind for the physical destruction of German, less still European, Jewry. Nor did his ascendancy to power seem very likely in 1920. Yet the potentialities already evident in the early 1920s should be recognised. Although Hitler would not have recognised the word, genocide assuredly figured in his calculations. In 1922, he ruminated on the fate of the Armenians during the war. That, he believed, was a warning for what would happen to the Germans if no solution were found to the 'Jewish question'.[24]

Understanding the contingent circumstances that brought Hitler to a point where his ideology might be translated into actions is the next step in charting the path to genocide. Such an opportunity might well have eluded the NSDAP altogether. Hitler's oratory and carefully cultivated appeal as a former front soldier certainly drew new members to the party: 27,000 by 1925, and 178,000 by 1929. However, they did not bring access to power. Impatient and rash, Hitler had attempted a violent *coup d'état*, the Munich Beer Hall Putsch, in 1923. Without the support of the army, and in the face of determined opposition from the authorities, the attempt failed. He spent six months in Landsberg gaol in consequence (where he composed his rambling autobiographical political tract, *Mein Kampf*). In 1925, he reorganised the party. The ranks of the SA swelled. They broke up rival meetings and attacked communists and trade unionists in the streets. While he made headway in the south, he failed to achieve an electoral breakthrough nationally. In the 1928 elections, the party garnered only 810,000 votes and sent just twelve deputies to the Reichstag. In contrast, the Communists won 3.2 million votes and the Social Democrats 9.1 million. A left-liberal coalition, led by the Social Democrats, took office in Berlin.[25]

It was the Wall Street Crash of October 1929, and the ensuing Great Depression, that destroyed this political landscape and gave the NSDAP its opportunity. Heavily dependent on American loans, which were now withdrawn, the German economy staggered. Within two years, a third of German workers were unemployed. The ruling coalition fractured over the correct economic response and collapsed. The president of the Weimar Republic, Paul von Hindenburg, appointed Heinrich Brünning as chancellor. He achieved neither economic nor political stability. In the crisis, parliamentary democracy began to break down. Hindenburg, who had been an aloof figure, took on a more active role. Article 48 of the Weimar Constitution allowed him to bypass the Reichstag entirely. Middle-class voters abandoned the traditional centre parties. Fearful of the resurgent threat of communism, they looked instead to the NSDAP. In the 1930 election, it won 6.4 million votes and returned 107 deputies.[26]

NSDAP official Gregor Strasser had reorganised the party's internal structures, aligning them with electoral districts, facilitating effective campaigns beyond traditional areas of support. As anxious voters looked for an alternative to the old parties, the NSDAP was attractive largely because of an adroit propaganda campaign, headed from 1930 by Joseph Goebbels. This has been described as both cynical and opportunistic. Evasive on solid policy details, the electorate were instead offered reassuring visions of a *Volksgemeinschaft*, a selfless folk community which seemed to promise benefits for all. An almost mystical cult around the figure of Hitler held out a promise of a national saviour. In contrast, members of the leadership cadre now judged too socialist, and likely to alienate middle-class voters, were demoted or excluded from the party. Antisemitism was emphasised where it was thought it would win votes, but downplayed where it elicited a weak response. Similarly, the party would calibrate its anti-Marxist and anti-capitalist posture carefully, to build a *Volksbewegung*, a broad-based popular movement.[27]

Successful as the 1930 election was for the NSDAP, it did not deliver a majority. For as long as he was still chancellor, Brünning largely ignored the Reichstag and ruled by degree, subject to Hindenburg's power of veto. In March 1932, Hitler ran against the revered former Field Marshal Hindenburg, when the latter's term as president expired. He did not win, but he did poll an impressive 13.5 million votes to the incumbent's 19.25 million. Notwithstanding his distaste for the ex-corporal and his rabble-rousing politics, Hindenburg and his coterie now had little choice but to take the NSDAP seriously.

Frustrated by progressive land reforms proposed by Brünning, Hindenburg forced the chancellor to resign, replacing him with Franz von Papen. He accelerated the drift towards authoritarian government, ruling by degree and preparing to restrict voting rights and curtail the power of the Reichstag. Yet he failed to establish a basis of support for his policies. In elections in July 1932, the well-organised NSDAP increased its share of the vote again, polling 13,745,680 and controlling 39 per cent of the Reichstag.[28] The campaign was marked by escalating violence too, with 24 killed and 289 seriously injured in Prussia alone. The nation seemed poised on the brink of open conflict. Papen had courted the NSDAP, but would not accede to Hitler's demand that he would lead any coalition government. Von Papen resigned, to be replaced by General Kurt von Schleicher. Although he made some progress with economic reform, he could not restore political stability either. Another Reichstag election was held in November 1932. This time the NSDAP lost two million votes. Strasser, long associated with the left of the party and frustrated by the turn to the right, resigned. Conscious of this weakening position, and confident that they could now control him, Hindenburg and von Papen agreed to appoint Hitler as chancellor in January 1933.[29]

The circumstances in which Hitler came to power do not indicate that the German electorate, or even the elites who handed him the chancellorship, shared his fatal *weltanschauung*. After the NSDAP made its electoral breakthrough in 1930, the leaders of the Cologne chapter of the Central Association of German Citizens of Jewish Belief observed that 'It certainly would be wrong to equate these 6 ½ million [Nazi] voters with 6 ½ million antisemites'. Rather, the danger they identified was that 'the aversion of the non-antisemitic voters of the Hitler Party against hatred of Jews was not so large as to deny the NSDAP their support'.[30] A longing for political stability, accompanied by economic hardship, rejection of Weimar, a desire for national salvation, and a willingness to tolerate antisemitism and expansionist rhetoric, 'opened the door to barbarism'.[31]

Once that door was opened, Hitler made sure it stayed that way. He acted with a speed and ruthlessness that caught potential opposition flat-footed. A key move was securing control of the police. Hermann Göring, former fighter pilot and long-standing Nazi, was appointed as Prussian Minister of the Interior. He immediately enrolled the SA Brownshirts as auxiliary police officers. Now given an official capacity, they could ransack trade union offices; assault, even murder, communists in the streets, and disrupt Social Democratic meetings. They could also escalate their violence against Jews. Göring had declared that he was 'unwilling to accept the notion that the police are a protection squad for Jewish shops'.[32] Nor were they any protection for the Jewish lawyers beaten and dragged from courtrooms, or Jewish stockbrokers expelled from stock exchanges.

Beyond the legitimisation of the NSDAP paramilitary arm, the architecture of an authoritarian police state was rapidly built. Heinrich Himmler, *Reichsführer* of the elite paramilitary *Schutzstaffel* (SS) – originally Hitler's personal 'protection squad' – was appointed chief of police in 1936. He reorganised the existing political spy units in the police. They became the *Geheime Staatspolizei* (Gestapo), a secret police force who operated without restraint or judicial oversight. The criminal investigative police often proved pre-disposed to the new regime because many shared the NSDAP's belief in eugenics. They viewed criminal behaviour as biological in origin, and that there was a category of unworthy individuals naturally predisposed to habitual criminality: the *Berufsverbrecher*.[33] If any police officers were thought politically unreliable, they were quickly dismissed. Those who remained were subject to NSDAP ideological indoctrination and retrained on military lines. Essentially, they were transformed from being civil servants into military auxiliaries. During the war, they would provide the personnel for the *Ordnungspolizei* (Order Police) that would be at the forefront of the racial war in the occupied territories of the east.[34]

The first of a network of concentration camps was established at Dachau in March 1933. They were originally intended to suppress political dissent, with opponents of the regime taken into what was euphemistically referred to as 'protective custody'. Later, they would also be used to incarcerate prisoners of conscience, Catholic and Protestant clergy, Jehovah's Witnesses, and 'asocials': homosexuals, vagrants, the 'work shy'. They would also become central to the persecution of supposed racial enemies: Jews, and the Roma. The path to repression was considerably eased by the arson attack on the Reichstag, 27 February 1933. Claiming that the communists were responsible, Hitler persuaded Hindenburg to issue a 'temporary' decree suspending civil and political freedoms. The measure was never revoked.[35]

Repression was not the only means by which the NSDAP ensured that it would be able to further its core persecutory policies. Robert Gellately has pointed to Hitler's success in creating a hybrid regime, based upon both fear and popularity. The Third Reich (the successor to the Holy Roman Empire and German Empire of 1871–1918) became, in his words, a 'consensus dictatorship'.[36]

While he had utterly outmanoeuvred the conservatives who thought they might control him, Hitler worked to keep the right onside. The middle classes were receptive to law-and-order campaigns against common criminals, and the suppression of communism. The unsettling, ongoing violence of the Brownshirts was accepted as an ugly but necessary defence of respectable society.[37] The army, an important influence in society, had been planning a revanchist war to overturn Versailles for a decade. Promised rearmament, its leadership was an easy ally to secure.

The Churches were a potential source of opposition. Privately, Hitler despised Christianity.[38] Publicly, he proclaimed his support for 'positive Christianity' (accepting of the NSDAP programme) and asserted that both Catholicism and Protestantism would be pillars of the Third Reich. The Catholic Church had quite successfully steered its parishioners away from the NSDAP under Weimar. Yet it eventually reached a concordat with Hitler, partly to avoid repression and partly because they viewed his government as a bulwark against 'Godless communism'. The Protestant Churches were divided. Pastor Martin Niemöller (incarcerated in concentration camps for seven years) and the theologian Dietrich Bonhoeffer (murdered by the SS in 1945) were prominent dissidents. For the most part, though, fearing communism and the secularisation of society, parish clergy dutifully welcomed SA men to their services. Some attempted to fuse Nazi ideology with Christianity in a German Christian Church, centred on an 'Aryan' Jesus.[39]

The key to understanding support for the NSDAP on the left was economic recovery. Within 18 months of Hitler's appointment as chancellor, unemployment had (apparently) fallen by 60 per cent. This achievement was the result of many factors. Some work-creation schemes initiated by von Papen and von Schleicher were making their impact felt. Spending on rearmament contributed too. New work-creation programmes, such as autobahn construction, played a role. Yet so did a rather cynical manipulation of the statistics, by which some 619,000 of the unemployed were reclassified as 'emergency relief workers'. German workers largely accommodated themselves to a regime that seemed to have achieved an economic miracle.[40]

There was also a potential danger to Hitler from the left-leaning, radical wing of his own party. This was centred on Ernst Röhm, the head of the now three million strong SA. At Himmler's and Göring's urging, Hitler purged the leadership of the Brownshirts on the so-called 'Night of the Long Knives', 30 June–1 July 1934. Röhm was shot.[41]

As Hitler rid the party of unreliable old comrades, he acted decisively to secure those of the future. Through a radically revised school curriculum and involvement in party organisations, German youth was ideologically indoctrinated. Children were inducted into the 'new comradeship' via the *Hitler Jugend* (Hitler Youth) and the *Bund Deutscher Mädel* (League of German Girls). The *Hitler Jugend* grew from 50,000 members in January 1933 to 5.4 million by 1936 (membership became mandatory in 1939). In both the classroom and in extracurricular activities, the members of the youth organisations were subject to a barrage of antisemitic and racist propaganda. It was relentless. One maths question read, 'The Jews are aliens in Germany. In 1933 there were 66,060,000 inhabitants in the German Reich, of whom 499,682 were Jews. What is the per cent of aliens?'[42]

The last parliamentary elections took place in March 1933. The NSDAP won 44 per cent of the vote. Their (soon marginalised) coalition partners, the Nationalist Party, provided enough support to give them a slight majority overall. Combined with the policies of repression and intimidation, this slender mandate proved substantial enough to force through the Enabling Act, which consolidated Hitler's authority, allowing him to rule by decree without reference to Hindenburg or the Reichstag. The aged president died in August 1934. Hitler merged his office with his own, proclaiming himself Führer (leader). The consensual dictatorship had been achieved. (As late as 1949, some German opinion polls indicated that as many as six out of ten respondents still thought that National Socialism was 'a good idea badly carried out'.)[43]

Hitler had stated back in 1919 that the 'final objective' of 'rational anti-semitism', must be 'the removal [Entfernung] of the Jews altogether'.[44] This is now generally understood to mean their removal from the Reich. Yet on his accession to the chancellorship in 1933, he does not appear to have formulated any detailed plans as to how this might be achieved, beyond some discussion of depriving them of their citizenship. It had been the vola-tile SA who had taken the lead, not simply in the street thuggery, but in demanding a boycott of Jewish businesses. As it turned out, the boycott was widely ignored. Of greater significance was the Law for the Restoration of the Professional Civil Service, 7 April 1933. This contained an 'Aryan clause' which sanctioned the 'retirement' of Jewish civil servants. There was some resistance to these measures. Hindenburg demanded, and secured, an exemp-tion for Jewish veterans of the trenches. This, however, was subverted to a degree by a prohibition on their promotion.[45]

In early 1934, the American journalist George J. Walmer aptly described what was then happening to Germany's Jews as a 'cold pogrom', intended to 'compel them to emigrate'.[46] Jewish professionals found it increasingly hard to practise; doctors and dentists were barred from working for public insurance schemes; public-sector workers were dismissed from their posts, and students were forbidden to sit their final exams. Alongside official acts, social ostracism narrowed the bounds of Jewish life. Antisemitic posters and placards appeared on walls. 'Stürmer boxes' appeared in the streets, from which copies of Streicher's poisonous propaganda could be taken free of charge. Clubs and societies, even veterans' associations, encouraged their Jewish members to resign. Public book burnings always included a plen-tiful selection of Jewish authors. In response to this 'cold pogrom', 60,000 German Jews emigrated in 1933–1934. Those emigrants who had owned property generally had to sell it at a loss. All were subject to a punitive 'flight tax', so that their persecution would contribute to the German economy.[47]

It is, of course, very difficult to gauge the extent to which ordinary folk had internalised genuine hostility towards Jews and how many merely outwardly complied in what became an increasingly threatening atmosphere. In 1948, Kurt Grosseman, who had fled Germany in 1933, asked Friedrich Gauss, formerly the highest legal officer in the German Foreign Office, why so many of his compatriots had acquiesced in the persecution. Gauss explained that some feared to lose their position, others to be arrested and sent to a concentration camp, 'and we did not act. We had lost our courage and every concept of morality'.[48]

The SA and the *Gauleiters* (NSDAP regional leaders) were largely responsible for a wave of violence against Jews in that summer of 1935, while economic pressures were also intensified.[49] On 15 September, Hitler promulgated two new antisemitic laws at the NSDAP's annual Nuremberg Rally: The Law for the Protection of German Blood and Honour, and the Reich Citizenship Law. The first of these prohibited marriage and sexual relations between Jews and 'citizens of German blood'. The Reich Citizenship Law robbed German Jews of their citizenship, which was restricted to only those of 'German and kindred blood'. There then followed a somewhat torturous discussion of how, exactly, Jewishness was to be legally defined (by four or three Jewish grandparents) and, for those of mixed descent, how the law affected differing degrees of 'Jewishness'.[50]

The legal status of those robbed of their nationality (not just Jews, but also Roma and Afro-Germans) was that they were now 'subjects' of the Reich, without the rights of citizens but still with obligations towards the state. For as long as Hitler remained concerned about foreign opinion, there was a measure of restraint in the application of the new laws. For example, there were no prosecutions until after the Berlin Olympics of 1936. Yet both the 'cold pogrom' of restrictions on their freedoms and businesses, and the thuggery of the SA continued to make life unbearable for German Jews. A further 67,000 emigrated, 1935–1937.[51]

In November 1937, in a discussion with Goebbels, Hitler had reiterated his objective as the expulsion of Jews, although his ambitions in terms of geographical scope now appeared to have expanded: 'The Jews must get out of Germany, yes out of the whole of Europe. That will take some time yet, but will and must happen'.[52] Over the course of 1938, the programme of 'Aryanisation' was intensified to a point where it plunged Germany's remaining Jews into destitution. They were legally barred from operating businesses or practising their trades. Those who chose to sell their concerns did so at prices set by the state, usually between 30 and 60 per cent of their actual value. Jewish households were compelled to provide detailed inventories of their possessions and property holdings. Access to banking facilities was restricted. Confiscatory taxes destroyed livelihoods and the value of assets. In July, Jews were required to carry special identity cards.[53]

The final act of 1938, the pogrom known as *Kristallnacht* ('night of broken glass',) on 9–10 November, has been seen as a seminal event in the radicalisation of NSDAP antisemitism. It was the most extensive use of violence against German Jews to that date. In October, the regime had expelled 17,000 Polish Jews resident in Germany, against a backdrop of growing violence and physical intimidation. In Paris, Herschel Grynszpan, a 17-year-old Jewish refugee, took revenge by assassinating an official in the German embassy. Goebbels, whose influence with the Führer had been waning, seized upon this as an opportunity to curry favour, and proposed the pogrom to Hitler. Although carefully keeping his distance from a level of violence and destruction that the public may have been uncomfortable with, he verbally agreed: 'Pull back the police. The Jews should be made to feel the full fury of the people'.[54]

This process, with Goebbels taking the initiative to advance a policy that he believed Hitler favoured, and to which he then offered approval, is revealing. In 1934, Werner Willikens, a low-level party functionary, had stated that the Führer could not be expected to issue detailed instructions 'on everything he intends to realise sooner or later'. Therefore, there should be no waiting for specific orders or instructions. Anyone in post in 'the new Germany ... worked best when he has, so to speak, worked towards the Führer'. Ian Kershaw has subsequently identified this notion as key to understanding how the NSDAP dictatorship functioned. The pace and mechanics of the persecution of Europe's Jews would often be driven by those 'working towards the Führer', rather than as a response to detailed instructions.[55]

Kristallnacht had nothing to do with 'the fury of the people'. It was carried out by the SA. They may have mobilised some civilians to join their rampage but this was not a spontaneous expression of violent bigotry. At least ninety Jews were murdered, and hundreds of homes, shops, and synagogues were plundered and destroyed. That many participated only from the very basest of motives, the opportunity for theft and cruelty, is indicated not merely by the robberies, but also by the rape of Jewish girls and women. (In the aftermath, only those who had thus violated the party's sexual mores faced substantive legal penalties, or expulsion from the NSDAP.) Thirty thousand Jewish men were taken into 'protective custody' and brutalised in concentration camps. In the face of much public disquiet, Göring sought to scapegoat the victims, blaming Jewish provocation for the violence. A hefty collective fine was imposed upon the Jewish community. One hundred and fifty thousand more German Jews subsequently emigrated. Indeed, many of those who had been arrested had only been able to secure their release by agreeing to leave the country. As Lucy Dawidowicz observed, by 1938 'emigration' was just a euphemism for 'expulsion'.[56]

The increasing openness of the NSDAP regime's antisemitism should not surprise, given the deteriorating international climate. As Hitler remorselessly steered his country towards war, he reframed the 'Jewish Question' to include not just Germany, but all of Europe. He also made an extraordinarily dark prophecy. On 20 January 1939, he delivered a speech to the Reichstag, in which he stated:

... if the international Jewish financiers in and outside of Europe should succeed in plunging the nations once more into a world war, then the result will not be the Bolshevizing of the earth, and thus the victory of Jewry, but the annihilation of the Jewish race in Europe![57]

Once the war came, it swiftly became clear that it would provide Hitler with opportunities to pursue the ideological imperatives of the NSDAP programme with far greater radicalism. The Law for the Prevention of Offspring with Hereditary Diseases had been an early piece of NSDAP eugenics legislation, passed in 1933. This required the compulsory sterilisation of those suffering from a hereditary condition, including not just physical ailments, but also chronic alcoholism and a usefully vague diagnosis of 'feeble-mindedness'. Such a programme was not unique to Hitler's Germany. Some European countries and the United States had also enacted compulsory sterilisation laws for the hereditarily disabled. However, nowhere was this policy implemented so vigorously as in the Reich. In less than twelve years, about 400,000 individuals were sterilised on the authority of German doctors.[58] It was also only in Germany, under the cover of conflict, that the programme was pursued to its twisted conclusion: euthanasia. In 1935, Hitler's deputy Rudolph Hess had told a physician, 'that if war came, he would pick up and carry out this question of euthanasia', for then 'such a programme could be put into effect more smoothly and readily'.[59]

For a man responsible for so many millions of deaths, it is remarkable that, as far as it is known, Hitler only ever actually signed one document that authorised murder. This was a memo written in October 1939, authorising so-called 'mercy killings' of those judged 'incurably sick'.[60] By so doing, he initiated the *Aktion T4* Programme (derived from its headquarters Tiergartenstrasse 4 in Berlin). He had favoured such a programme for years, having remarked in 1923 that 'the preservation of a nation is more important than the preservation of its unfortunates'.[61] Euthanasia, however, was so abhorrent to the Judeo-Christian ethics of most Germans, that he was careful not to make such views public. His own ethics were rooted in a perverse reading of Darwin: preserving 'life unworthy of life' was an unjustifiable interference in natural selection. War made that interference more harmful because of the disproportionate loss of so many healthy racial comrades at the front. The conflict thus gave the eugenics programme an added urgency.

Overall, some 250,000 physically and mentally disabled individuals, including 5,000 children, were murdered by the medical staff administering *Aktion T4*. The killing was ruthlessly well organised; the victims were transported to one of six killing centres where they were ushered into fake showers and gassed with carbon monoxide. Their bodies were then cremated and a certificate giving a false cause of death sent to their families. Despite the efforts at secrecy, knowledge of the programme became public. Vocal protest, led by the Catholic clergyman Clemens Graf von Galen, led Hitler officially to halt the programme in August 1941. In fact, it continued clandestinely, via lethal injections administered in local hospitals and asylums. Former staff of the T-4 programme found new employment where their experience of gas chambers and crematoria proved useful, in the extermination camps of the Jewish Holocaust.[62]

The conduct of the campaign in Poland similarly betrayed the influence of radical NSDAP ideology on the nature of the war. The objective was the destruction of Poland, the reunion of the *Volksdeutsche* and the territories they occupied with the Reich, and the reduction of what was left to a colony, organised as a strict racial hierarchy. On 22 August, as Joachim Ribbentrop, *Reichminister* of Foreign Affairs, was signing the pact with Stalin that sealed Poland's fate, Hitler urged his generals, 'Have no pity'. The operation was to be conducted in the manner of a colonial-style annihilatory campaign of conquest, with 'the greatest brutality and without mercy'.[63]

The German invasion began on 1 September, with the Soviets crossing the eastern border to occupy their share of the spoils on 17 September. The fighting was over by 6 October. The German frontline units were immediately followed by five mobile SS units, *Einsaztgruppen* (Special Mission Groups) who drew their personnel from the Security Police (SD). Ostensibly their mission was to deal with 'anti-German elements'. The decision had also been taken prior to the invasion that Order Police battalions would also take part in the campaign, ostensibly providing internal security and engaging in anti-partisan operations. These euphemisms covered the reality of their role in terrorising the people into submission and eliminating Poland's leadership: aristocrats, military officers, intellectuals, recalcitrant clergymen, and politicians. They were also to fight the racial war. The 'political soldiers' of the *Einsaztgruppen* and Order Police pursued these aims by making sweeping arrests on the flimsiest of pretexts and summarily executing civilians, without any due process or courts-martial. Jews always numbered disproportionately highly among their victims as the racial re-ordering of eastern Europe began. By December 1939, 50,000 Polish civilians had been murdered, including 7,000 Jews.[64]

The first steps of the Holocaust as a process of systematic mass murder were taken in the earliest days of the war in Poland. A massacre at Ostrów Mazowieck, committed by Police Battalion 91 on 11 November 1939, was an example of what was happening and a portentous sign of what was to come on an even greater scale. A fire had broken out in the town shortly after it was occupied by the Germans. This was immediately attributed to Jewish arsonists. A squad of 'especially brave' men, 'in possession of the necessary toughness', was selected and dispatched to the town. There, these 'brave men' marched their defenceless victims in groups of ten to an execution site and shot them, their bodies tumbling into freshly dug ditches. In all, 364 people were murdered, most of them women and children. Himmler had forged a police organisation with a militarised culture stressing toughness and ruthlessness, and imbued with an ideological belief that they were engaged in an existential race war for the survival of their *volk*. It would prove a useful tool of genocide.[65]

In 1939, some *Wehrmacht* (regular army) officers initially expressed disquiet at the atrocities being committed by the *Einsaztgruppen* and Order Police, fearing that 'brutalisation and moral debasement will spread like a plague', to their own units.[66] Yet such voices were quickly muted. In advance of future campaigns in the east, such as the invasion of the Soviet Union, Hitler issued clear directives to military commanders that 'the *Reichsführer SS* is entrusted on behalf of the Führer with *special tasks* for the preparation of the political administration'. The 'special tasks' were mass murder and the *Wehrmacht* generally proved cooperative and ready to assist. The brutalisation and the moral debasement had indeed spread quickly.[67]

In Poland, the process of racial re-ordering proceeded at pace. The Germans divided the territory they occupied into two parts. Western areas of Poland were annexed into the Reich, creating two new German provinces, Danzig-West Prussia and the Warthegau. These were to be settled by *Volksdeutsche* 'repatriated' to the Reich. The remainder of German-occupied Poland was renamed the *Generalgouvernement* (General Government). Here, Poles, including Jews and Roma, from the west were to be resettled, at least for the time being, while a longer-term concrete policy was formulated. Subsequently, it was to serve as a source of labour, food, and raw materials for the Reich. The governorship was given to the lawyer Hans Frank. This appointment again reveals much about how the Hitler dictatorship functioned. Frank was not an experienced administrator. He was however a veteran of both the First World War and the Bavarian *Frei Korps*. He was an 'old fighter', who had joined the NSDAP in 1919. He was awarded his fiefdom because the Führer could count upon his unquestioning loyalty (or, as his own son memorably put it, because he was 'a slime-hole of a Hitler fanatic').[68]

It was also a characteristic of the Hitler dictatorship that multiple, overlapping, and competing sources of authority were created. The Third Reich has thus been described as 'polycratic', with many centres of power. All may have been 'working towards the Führer', but they were also competing for resources and for influence. This reality shaped the development, pace, and characteristics of genocidal policies during the war. For example, Frank quickly clashed with Himmler over the racial re-ordering of Poland. The scale and speed with which hundreds of thousands of people were being driven from the Warthegau simply threatened to overwhelm Frank's administration. He differed with Himmler, too, over economic priorities within the occupied territories. Forging an expedient alliance with Göring, Frank was able to persuade Hitler to curb the deportation plans over the winter of 1940. Yet this hardly mitigates what was happening: mass shootings, forced deportations, people expelled from their homes with little no notice and with the bare minimum of possessions, transports of families packed onto cattle trucks, without adequate food or water and in freezing conditions. And inadequate accommodation and material provision when they arrived. Ethnic cleansing was bleeding into genocide.[69]

The worst conditions were in the ghettos into which Jews were now being herded. Although often ascribed to an initiative of Reinhard Heydrich, the chief of the SD Security Police, the ghettoisation policy developed somewhat haphazardly. The first was established at Piotrkow Trybunalski as early as

October 1939. In March and April 1940, ghettos were established at Lublin, Kraków, and Łódź. The largest, confining some 350,000 people, was set up in Warsaw, also in April 1940.

Initially, the ghettos had been regarded as a temporary means to segregate Jews until their final expulsion. In June 1940, Heydrich had told Joachim von Ribbentrop, *Reichsminister* of Foreign Affairs, that the 'overall problem' of the 3.25 million Jews in German-occupied territory could 'no longer be solved through emigration'. A 'territorial solution' (mass deportation) was thus now necessary.[70] A persistent notion that Jews might be shipped off to some colony in 'Africa or elsewhere' (Madagascar was a favoured choice for a while) had finally to be abandoned, when it became clear British defeat was not imminent and there would be no access to Africa. The ghettoes thus acquired a degree of permanence and became centres of ruthless exploitation of Jewish labour to support the German war effort. They were also engines of attritional genocide. Meagre rations and insanitary conditions ensured appalling mortality rates as disease and malnutrition took their toll. By June 1941 in the Warsaw ghetto, between 3,500 and 5,500 people died each month.[71]

The next stages in the radicalisation of the Third Reich's genocidal policies would be driven by the contingencies of the war with the Soviet Union. In the spring of 1941, Hitler was giving the impression that he conceived of the expulsion of Jews in their entirety from German-controlled territory as a long-term, post-war project. Indeed, according to Hans Frank, Hitler spoke of it taking 15–20 years to make the General Government *judenfrie* (free of Jews). Adolf Eichmann, head of Gestapo Department IV 4b, with responsibility for Jewish policy in occupied Europe, similarly spoke at this time of making Europe *judenfrei* after the war.[72] Victory was thus a prerequisite for a 'solution of the Jewish question', one predicated on further deportations. Plans for large-scale population transfers depended upon it. Initial areas earmarked for future Jewish occupation included the Pripyat Marshes in Belorussia (now Belarus), or areas of north Russia adjacent to the Arctic Sea.[73]

Operation Barbarossa, the invasion of the Soviet Union launched on 22 June 1941, was, like the war on Poland, planned on the basis that the conflict itself would be annihilatory, and waged without pity or mercy. This created a peculiarly permissive environment in the military zone of operations for an escalation of genocidal atrocities. The Barbarossa Directive, issued 13 May 1941, stipulated that all civilians who 'attacked' German soldiers were to be summarily executed. The definition of 'attack' included distribution of hostile leaflets or failure to follow German orders. By the same directive, soldiers were exempted from prosecution for any offence against the Soviet population that was 'ideologically motivated'. The infamous Commissar Order, issued on 6 June, stipulated that all political commissars, Communist Party functionaries in both the army and civil administration, were to be denied prisoner of war status, and executed.[74]

In this environment, the racial war along the eastern front was quickly initiated. Once again, four *Einsatzgruppen* and battalions of Order Police followed closely in the wake of the frontline units. These became the most proficient exponents of mass murder by shooting. Making flimsy allegations of partisan activity, they executed Jews, Communists, 'commissars', and Roma. The mentally ill were also murdered, so that asylums could be used as hospitals for the army. Early on, some massacres had only targeted men of military age. Yet very quickly, particularly zealous SD officers, such as Freidrich Jeckeln, led the way in expanding the circle of those killed to include women and children. At the Babi Yar Ravine, outside Kyiv, 29–30 September 1941, 37,700 Jewish men, women, and children were murdered by machine-gun fire. They had been told to assemble to be 'resettled'. They had then been marched in batches of 30–40 to the ravine. Other, yet larger, massacres followed. At Odessa, around 50,000 Jews were murdered in October after explosions rocked the city, almost certainly set by the Soviet Secret Police, the NKVD. The perpetrators on that occasion were troops of Germany's ally Romania.[75]

It is an uncomfortable fact that many non-Germans proved 'willing executioners' during the Holocaust. The Romanians massacred between 280,000 and 380,000 Jews in June 1941–1942. This included Romanian Jews; 10,000 were murdered in Bessarabia in June 1941, in 'retaliation' for a Soviet air raid. In some instances, in territories that had recently been occupied by the Soviets, the massacres began at the very point the Germans arrived. At Jedwabne in Poland, 1,600 Jewish men, women, and children were murdered by their neighbours in July 1941. That same month, self-styled Lithuanian partisans assisted German death squads in Vilnius. Some 12,000 Ukrainians acted as auxiliaries to the *Einsatzgruppen* in 1941–1942. In Croatia, the fascist *Ustaša* regime established its own concentration camps and murdered 32,000 Jews, 28,000 Romanies and – the prime target of Croatian genocidal policies – 333,000 Serbs. The motives for complicity in the Holocaust were mixed. Some were rooted in the ethno-nationalism of the age; like *Völkisch* Germans, the perpetrators regarded Jews as immutably alien. Ancient prejudices, based in religion and culture, were also still evident. Yet recent events were very significant too. Some people in those countries that had suffered under Soviet occupation lashed out at their Jewish neighbours, whom they accused of collaboration, because of the well-established myth that Bolshevism was essentially a Jewish ideology.[76]

The *Einsatzgruppen*, their auxiliaries, and their allies, had probably murdered around 1.5 million Soviet Jews by the time they were disbanded in 1943. The circumstances in which they committed their atrocities were utterly primitive in their violence. At Borrisow in Belarus, on 24 October 1941, 6,500 Jews were massacred by German soldiers and Belorussian auxiliaries. A witness described the victims being beaten down the road with iron rods. Women and children 'cried and screamed' as they waited their turn, with the noise of rifles clearly audible. Mass graves had been dug by Russian prisoners of war, and those to be executed were made to lie in these before they were shot: 'the dead and the half-dead were lying pell-mell'. When the bottom row was full, the next batch to be executed were forced to put sand over the bodies and trample it down, before they took their own places in the grave. The Belorussian auxiliaries helped themselves to the possessions of the murdered. They were so drunk and jumpy that German soldiers were advised to stay off the streets because of the danger of random shots. Such dreadful scenes were played out again and again.[77]

In the latter months of 1941, the military situation caused a radical rethink among local Nazi administrators in the occupied territories about long-term Jewish policy. The expectation in June 1941 had been that victory would be swift. The *Wehrmacht* would 'kick in the door' and 'the whole rotten structure' would collapse.[78] Specifically, the mass of the Red Army would be encircled and annihilated west of the Dvina-Dnepr Rivers. That had not been achieved. Despite the scale of their early victories, inflicting over two million casualties on the Soviet forces by September 1941, there was no immediate end to the war in sight. Further offensives would take the *Wehrmacht* to the gates of Moscow, but there they were halted by a Soviet counterattack in December. Any schemes for Heydrich's mooted 'territorial solution', achieved by further deportation of Europe's Jews to the east, had thus to be abandoned for the foreseeable future.

New plans had to be made, in particular, for the future of the ghettos, where disease and starvation were running rampant. Some officials, such as Waldemar Schön, head of the Resettlement Division in Warsaw, were content to let this process run its course. Attrition would contribute to delivering Hitler's eventual goal of a *judenfrie* General Government. Others, such as Dr Ludwig Fisher, governor of the Warsaw district, urged that the ghettos should be properly sustained and developed as a separate slave economy. Productive ghettos would support the immediate priority: the war effort. Given that the war was 'with Jewry in its totality', and that needed to be struck 'destructively' in its 'spawning grounds' to the east, Fisher argued that this was the best way to 'work towards the Führer'.[79] The Führer himself usually failed to offer any concrete resolution to such debates, confining himself to making repeated reminders that he had prophesised that world war would culminate in the 'destruction of Jewry'.[80]

While the frequently acrimonious debate between 'attritionists' and 'productionists' would continue to shape the implementation of policy, the overarching trajectory by late 1941 was working towards making the Führer's prophecy come true sooner rather than later. And this was now not just the case in the military zone of operations. The requirement that all Jews wear identifying Star of David badges had been implemented at a local level in Poland from as early as October 1939. In September 1941, it became the law in Germany and was thereafter emulated across occupied Europe. This act drove the psychological wedge between Jews and non-Jews yet deeper and made their identification and surveillance easier. Helmet Knochen, chief of Security Police in France and Belgium, saw it as 'another step on the road to the Final Solution'.[81]

The transition to systemic mass murder throughout the occupied territories and away from the front was well underway by that point. In August 1941, eastern Galicia was annexed by the General Government. In October, Galician Jews were murdered simply to 'make room' in the Jewish quarter in Stanislau. In November, over 6,000 Belarusian Jews were shot in Minsk. Again, this was done to make room, for 7,000 German Jews deported from the Reich. Sometimes, the problem of how to accommodate the deportees was solved by murdering them; 5,000 German and Austrian Jews were shot on arrival at Kaunas in Lithuania between 25 and 28 November. Shortly thereafter, another thousand German Jews were executed in Riga, on the orders of Friedrich Jeckeln. Himmler, worried that German public opinion might distinguish between the treatment of German Jews and eastern ones, rebuked him for doing so. Yet Jeckeln's actions clearly indicated how key decisions in this regard were effectively devolved. A 'climate of mass murder' was thus established throughout the General Government and the Baltic, even before the construction of the first *Vernichtungslager* (extermination camp) was completed.[82]

Considering the genesis of the extermination camps reveals once more both the place of local initiatives in driving the pace of the Holocaust and the significance of the late summer of 1941 as a seminal period in the transition to a policy of the physical destruction of European Jewry in totality. At the labour camp at Auschwitz, 850 inmates, Russian POWs, and Jews, were murdered in an experimental gas chamber, using a cyanide poison, Zyklon B, in September 1941. Subsequently, a purpose-built killing centre would be constructed at the adjacent site of Birkenau. The camp commandant, Rudolf Höss, explained the development of mass murder by gassing in these terms:

> I always shuddered at the prospect of carrying out extermination by shooting when I thought of the vast numbers concerned and the women and children … I was therefore relieved to think that we were spared all these bloodbaths and the victims would also be spared suffering until their last moment came. Many gruesome scenes are said to have taken place … Many members of the *Einsatzkommandos*, unable to endure wading through blood any longer, had committed suicide. Some had even gone mad.[83]

Similar experiments had been underway at Chełmno, where experts with experience in the T-4 programme developed mobile vans that pumped carbon monoxide exhaust fumes into a sealed passenger compartment, killing the occupants. In September 1941, these were used by *Sonderkommando Lange*, a death squad charged with murdering remaining Jews in southern Warthegau. Chełmno itself became operational as a killing centre in December 1941. Besides their use there, murder vans were also made available to *Einsatzgruppen* in Ukraine and the occupation authorities murdering

Serbian Jews in the camp at Semlin, near Belgrade, in the spring of 1942. The death camp at Bełżec was under construction by October 1941, and became operational the following February. The slave labour camps at Majdanek and Treblinka were converted into extermination camps over the winter of 1941–1942. Sobibór was constructed in March 1942. These camps would make Poland the epicentre of the Holocaust.[84]

The construction of these camps is indicative of the shift to a policy of mass extermination. However, the precise scope of that extermination was still not clearly defined. In September 1941, in Galicia, SS officer Friedrich Katzman ordered the killing of 'superfluous' Jews, that is, those who were not 'productive' for the war effort.[85] The efforts of historians to identify a specific moment when an order was given to proceed with the total and systematic extirpation of all European Jews have proved fruitless. The securest indication that such a policy had been agreed upon remains the Wannsee Conference, 20 January 1942.

This was chaired by Reinhard Heydrich, who had been pushing for the deportation of western European Jews eastward since July 1941. Himmler had now entrusted him with creating the administration and bureaucracy by which to affect 'a Final Solution of the Jewish Question'. That would be the business of Wannsee. The timing of the meeting suggests that a decision 'to proceed with the liquidation of all Jews living in Europe', had been taken in late 1941. Adolf Eichmann, who would play a significant role in the administration of the extermination campaign, was in attendance, as were 14 other senior SS men and NSDAP bureaucrats, including security officers, economists, and lawyers. While the language of Eichmann's minutes was couched in euphemism, the outcome was clear: a scheme for the annihilation of all eleven million European Jews. As an indication of long-term scope, this figure included those in countries yet be defeated, such as Britain, and in neutral countries, including Switzerland, the European portions of Turkey, and Ireland. In the meantime, all Jews in territory under German control would be concentrated in camps in the east. The 'productive' would be worked to death. The 'superfluous' would be murdered immediately.[86]

The scale and intensity of the genocide accelerated rapidly thereafter. The period March 1942 to February 1943 would see the largest death toll of any twelve-month period of the Holocaust: some two million people. Heydrich himself did not live to see the full consequences of his planning; he was assassinated by Czech patriots in Prague in June 1942. The extermination campaign was named *Aktion Reinhard* in his honour. In March, Lublin's Jews had been murdered at Bełżec. Goebbels recorded in his diary:

The Jews are now being pushed out of the *Generalgouvernement*, beginning near Lublin, to the East. A pretty barbaric procedure is being applied here and it is not to be described in any more detail, and not much is left of the Jews themselves ... The former Gauleiter of Vienna [Odilo Globocnik], who is carrying out this action, is doing it pretty prudently ... .[87]

From July to September 1942, 300,000 were transported from the Warsaw ghetto to Treblinka. Those designated as essential workers were granted a brief reprieve. The decision to completely liquidate the Warsaw ghetto was taken in April 1943 but, encountering determined armed resistance from Jewish fighters, this was not achieved until May. A month later, the ghetto of Lviv shared the same fate. The final survivors in Łódź, 70,000 workers, were deported in August 1944. Overall, some three million Polish Jews had been murdered by the end of the war.[88]

The mechanics of mass murder are illustrated by the processes in operation at the *Aktion Reinhard* camps, such as Treblinka. The transportation itself was fatal to many. Victims were packed into cattle trucks, on journeys that might last for days, without sustenance or adequate sanitation. They had been told they were to be resettled and generally would not grasp their fate until it was too late. Once they arrived, the trains were broken down into sections of 20 trucks, each handled sequentially. The survivors were roughly detrained, berated, and beaten. A *Sonderkommando* (special work unit) of Jewish prisoners removed the bodies of the dead from the trucks. Those unable to walk were carried to an 'infirmary', adorned with a prominent red cross (the illusion of resettlement was perpetuated for as long as possible). There, they were immediately shot. A very few of the healthier deportees would be selected for forced labour. The remainder were divided into two groups: men, and women and children. These were made to hand over any money or valuables in their possession. They were then told to strip for showers. Amidst yelling and blows from whips and barking guard dogs, they were driven into the gas chambers. Carbon monoxide was pumped through the 'showerheads'. More than 870,000 Jews were killed in this fashion at Treblinka up to August 1943. Most of those were Poles, but over 100,000 were from Belarus and almost 30,000 from Greece and Slovakia. Some 2,000 Roma were also murdered there.[89]

The fate of the Roma warrants some explanation. Thousands had also been massacred by the *Einsatzgruppen* in the period of mass shootings, 1941–1942. Like Jews, they were held to be a racial threat to the *Volk*. The eugenicist Robert Ritter, a strong influence on NSDAP policy on 'gypsies', described them as 'typical primitives', 'without history' and 'culturally impoverished'.[90] They were also the long-standing victims of marked social prejudices with a reputation for criminality, sexual immorality and, in wartime, spying. Much of this stemmed from their wandering lifestyle. Assimilationist polices that had aimed to transform them into settled German peasants in the nineteenth century had only mixed results. After the NSDAP accession of power, many were victimised in the enforced sterilisation programme. Considerable numbers were incarcerated in concentration camps at Buchenwald, Dachau, Mauthausen, Ravensbrück, and Sachsenhausen.[91]

There was much pressure, from late 1941 onwards, to include Roma in the deportations from German-occupied territories to the east. The pace was again often set by *Gauleiters*, such as Dr Tobias Portschy, of Burgenland in Austria. He seemed to have exhibited a greater hostility towards Roma than towards Jews. He had the 5,000 Roma resident in his region deported to the Łódź ghetto, where most died of disease or malnutrition. Those who survived were gassed at Chełmno. In late 1942, Himmler ordered that all remaining Roma in Poland be concentrated in a segregated camp within the Auschwitz-Birkenau complex. Of these, 5,600 were gassed, and 13,600 died of starvation or disease. The 'Gypsy camp' was liquidated in 1944, to make room for Jewish deportees from Hungary. Overall, probably between 196,000 and 500,000 Roma (20–60 per cent of the total population) died during the *Porrajamos* ('The Devouring'), as they refer to the period from 1933 to 1945.[92]

At Wannsee, Heydrich had boasted that Europe was 'to be combed through from east to west', for Jews.[93] Throughout 1942 and 1943, Himmler and Eichmann pressured Axis powers, collaborationist regimes, and the military authorities in occupied countries to deport Jewish residents. There was some resistance. Although fascist Italy had passed discriminatory antisemitic legislation in 1938, the Italians were reluctant to cooperate with the genocide. Only when Germany occupied much of Italy in 1943 and installed a puppet regime did deportations begin to take place. Some 8,000 of Italy's 40,000 Jews were subsequently murdered. Bulgaria deported 11,343 Jews from territories it had recently occupied in Macedonia and Thrace, but vocal public opposition saved the country's 50,000 Jewish citizens. The Vichy regime was also reluctant to deport French citizens, but quickly assisted in deporting 'alien' Jews. Denmark's King Christian X was a bold advocate for his 8,000 Jewish subjects. Danes generally refused to cooperate with apprehending their fellow citizens. Most Danish Jews were eventually smuggled to Sweden. Elsewhere, authorities cooperated, more or less willingly, or were helpless when German occupation forces conducted round-ups. In Slovakia, the police and fascist Hlinka Guard organised the deportation of 59,000 Jews east in March 1942. Jews from France, Belgium, and the Netherlands began to be transported to Auschwitz-Birkenau in August 1942. By the end of the war, 90,000 French Jews (26 per cent of the pre-war population), 40,000 Belgian Jews (60 per cent) and 105,000 Dutch Jews (75 per cent) had been murdered.[94]

In February 1943, transports from Belarus and Berlin arrived at Auschwitz-Birkenau, which would become the main killing centre, as well as a slave labour camp, as the *Aktion Reinhard* camps were closed that summer. In the following months, transports from occupied Greece began to arrive. The largest Jewish community in Greece – 50,000 strong and one of the most historically significant – was in Salonika (now Thessaloniki). These had been shielded by the Italian occupying authorities, but the Germans had taken over the city in February. Eventually 45,000 of Salonika's Jews would be transported and exterminated at Auschwitz-Birkenau.[95]

There were significant obstacles restricting the extent of Jewish resistance, such as lack of military training and equipment, and the frequent indifference, if not hostility, of their fellow citizens to their fate. Fear of reprisals too, persuaded many that acts of defiance would simply invite massacre. In March 1942, 1,540 Jews of Dolhynov in Belarus were murdered because two Jewish resistance fighters had escaped the ghetto. Besides, lacking full understanding of the totality of the Final Solution, many opted for compliance as the best hope for survival. Yet, over the course of 1943, the process of genocide was disrupted by a number of courageous, if doomed, acts of resistance. There were revolts at both the Sobibór and Treblinka extermination camps. Jewish resistance fighters also struck back at their persecutors during the final days of the Warsaw, Białystok, and Vilna ghettos. In response Himmler ordered a pre-emptive massacre, *Aktion Erntefest* (Operation Harvest Festival), of the 43,000 Jewish workers at Majdanek and the labour camps at Trawniki and Poniatowa on 3 November 1943. In October 1944, 400 *Sonderkommando* at Auschwitz-Birkenau (Jewish prisoners responsible for removing bodies from the gas chambers) staged a desperate revolt and succeeded in blowing up a crematorium. Virtually all were subsequently killed.[96]

For the most part, the overall scale and scope of the killing was dictated by the wider events of the war and the extent of German authority. Heydrich may have nursed ambitions to murder the Jews of Britain, Ireland, and Switzerland, but they remained beyond the Nazi grasp. Similarly in November 1941, Hitler had revealed his now-global aspirations in a conversation with Haj Amin al-Husseini, the Grand Mufti of Jerusalem. He had boldly claimed that when his armies drove south through the Caucasus, 'Germany's objective would then be solely the destruction of the Jewish element residing in the Arab sphere under the protection of British power'.[97] An *Einsatzkommando* was attached to Field Marshal Erwin Rommel's headquarters in North Africa in the summer of 1942. This would have been responsible for killing Jews in Egypt and the Palestine Mandate had Rommel's offensive that year succeeded.[98]

Even as their military effort faltered, the NSDAP hardly wavered in its determination to complete the Final Solution, within its sphere of influence. Their ally Hungary had cooperated in the massacres of non-Hungarian Jews, in Ukraine and in the portion of Yugoslavia they occupied. Yet, even under considerable pressure from Berlin, the Regent Miklós Horthy and his Prime Minister Miklós Kallay refused to deport their own Jewish citizens. Both were convinced by the German defeat at Stalingrad in February 1943 that the war was lost. They began protracted peace negotiations with the Allies. When the Germans learned of this in March 1944, they occupied most of the country. They found many willing collaborators in the ranks of the Hungarian fascist Arrow Cross Party. Beginning in May, 440,000 Hungarian Jews were deported east. Thousands of others died on forced marches into Austria in the closing stages of the war. Overall, 450,000 Hungarian Jews would be murdered, 70 per cent of the pre-war population.[99]

The deported Hungarians were sent to the concentration camp complex at Auschwitz-Birkenau. This was still functioning as both a slave labour facility and a killing centre. Some major German businesses collaborated here with the SS. The chemical giant I.G. Farben exploited 300,000 inmates as labourers, few of whom survived the war, as well as taking part in human medical experiments along with such individuals as the SS physician Josef Mengele. Of the Hungarian deportees, 394,000 were immediately gassed, while the remainder were nearly all worked to death in the labour camps. Transports continued to arrive throughout the summer of 1944, as the NSDAP strove to winnow out as many victims as possible. Jewish deportees even arrived from the Greek islands of Rhodes and Kos, initially convoyed by barge from their homes, despite British naval and air superiority in the Mediterranean.[100] By November, however, it was clear that the Third Reich's deteriorating military position compelled the destruction of the camp. The last executions, of four women who had smuggled explosives to the rebellious *Sonderkommando* in October, occurred in January 1945. By then, two million people had been murdered at Auschwitz.[101]

That was not, however, the end of the Holocaust. The final phase, lasting until April 1945, saw thousands more die as camps' inmates were forced onto 'death marches' to take them out of the path of the advancing Allies. The process was chaotic in the extreme; some inmates were left locked in barracks. In other camps, all who could not walk were shot. On the marches, inmates suffered from exhaustion, exposure, and relentless brutality. Nechama Epstein was among 500 women taken from Bergen-Belsen in the winter of 1944: 'on the way many were shot, those that couldn't walk. We didn't get [anything] to eat. They dragged us from one village to another, from one town to another'. She survived until they reached Theresienstadt (the 'model ghetto', originally established for propaganda purposes). There, the Germans planned to murder them, but the Soviets liberated the camp first, on 8 May 1945. By then, Epstein like many others, was suffering from malnutrition and typhus. She survived. Thousands of others continued to die, even after liberation.[102]

The Holocaust stands at a confluence of the ideologies of persecution we have chronicled thus far. Modern, political antisemitism can trace its deepest roots to the *Adversus Judaeos* (against the Jews) tradition of antiquity and the early Christian Church's struggle to establish its legitimacy and identity. The NSDAP often expressed its racist and eugenicist policies in the idioms of contemporary Social Darwinism, but talk of 'blood and soil' would have been understood well enough by an 'Old Christian' in Toledo in 1449. The Third Reich's internal enemies – witches and heretics recast as trade unionists, communists, social democrats and asocials – were subject to inquisitorial procedures: defenceless as due process was abandoned, denounced, incarcerated, and tortured. The murderous project to re-draw the demographic map of eastern Europe, to dispossess, then enslave, exile, or annihilate, those deemed alien and inferior, was a legacy of both overseas settler colonialism and the recent series of Eurasian massacres and expulsions that had begun with the 'dispeopling' of Circassia in 1864. A people pre-eminent in 'science and philosophy, music, and Kultur', had surrendered to an unimaginable moral regression.

Notes

1 George J. Walmer, 'German Fury: The Old Roots of the New German Nationalism', *The Sewanee Review*, 42 (1934), p.19.
2 William I. Brustein, *Roots of Hate: Anti-Semitisim in Europe before the Holocaust* (Cambridge: Cambridge University Press, 2003); Michael Lerner, *The Socialism of Fools: Anti-Semitism on the Left* (Oakland, CA: Tikkun Books, 1992); Richard S. Levy, 'Political Antisemitism in Germany and Austria, 1848–1914', in Albert S. Lindemann and Richard S. Levy (eds), *Antisemitism: A History* (Oxford: Oxford University Press, 2010), pp.121–135.
3 Jacob Katz, *From Prejudice to Destruction: Anti-Semitism, 1700–1933* (Cambridge, MA: Harvard University Press, 1980), pp.260–267.
4 David I. Kertzer and Gunnar Mokosch, 'The Medieval in the Modern: Nazi and Italian Fascist Use of the Ritual Murder Charge', *Holocaust and Genocide Studies*, 33 (2019), pp.179–181.
5 Brian E. Crim, ' "Our Most Serious Enemy": The Specter of Judeo-Bolshevism in the German Military Community, 1914–1923', *Central European History*, 44 (2011), pp.624–641; Wilhelm Deist, 'The Military Collapse of the German Empire: The Reality Behind the Stab-in-the-Back Myth', *War in History*, 3 (1996), pp.186–207.
6 Lucy S. Dawidowicz, *The War Against the Jews, 1933–45* (London: Penguin, 1977), p.76; 'Jewish World Plot: An Exposure', *The Times*, 16 August 1921, p.9.
7 Eric Kurlander, *Hitler's Monsters: A Supernatural History of the Third Reich* (New Haven, CT: Yale University Press, 2017), pp.34–50.
8 Jay Hatheway, 'The Pre-1920 Origins of the National Socialist German Workers' Party', *Journal of Contemporary History*, 29 (1994), p.248.
9 Robert Gerwarth and John Horne, 'Vectors of Violence: Paramilitarism in Europe after the Great War, 1917–1923', *Journal of Modern History*, 83 (2011), pp.489–512.
10 Quoted in Hatheway, 'The Pre-1920 Origins of the National Socialist German Workers' Party', pp.458–459; Kurlander, *Hitler's Monsters*, p.47.
11 Adolf Hitler, *Mein Kampf*, translated by Ralph Manheim (London: Pimlico: 1992), p.35; Robert S. Wistrich, 'Karl Lueger and the Ambiguities of Viennese Antisemitism', *Jewish Social Studies*, 45 (1983), pp.251–262.
12 'Programme of the NSDAP, 24 February 1920', in Jeremy Noakes and Geoffrey Pridham (eds), *Documents on Nazism, 1919–1945* (London: Jonathan Cape, 1974), pp.37–40.
13 Norman M. Naimark, *Fires of Hatred: Ethnic Cleansing in Twentieth-Century Europe* (Cambridge, MA.: Harvard University Press, 2001), pp.54–55; Dariusz Stola, 'Forced Migrations in Central European History', *International Migration Review*, 26, 2 (1992), pp.324–341.
14 Robert Gerwarth and Uğur Ümit Üngör, 'The Collapse of the Ottoman and Habsburg Empires and the Brutalisation of the Successor States', *Journal of Modern European History / Zeitschrift für moderne europäische Geschichte / Revue d'histoire européenne contemporaine*, 13 (2015), pp.226–248.

15 Naimark, *Fires of Hatred*, pp.3–4.
16 Michael Burleigh and Wolfgang Wippermann, *The Racial State: Germany 1933–1945* (Cambridge: Cambridge University Press, 1991), pp.26–27.
17 Cited in David Furber, 'Near as Far in the Colonies: The Nazi Occupation of Poland', *International History Review*, 26 (2004), pp.549–550.
18 Vejas Liulevicius, *War Land on the Eastern Front: Culture, National Identity, and German Occupation in World War I* (Cambridge: Cambridge University Press, 2000).
19 Isabel K. Hull, 'Military Culture and "Final Solutions" in the Colonies', in Robert Gellately and Ben Kiernan (eds), *The Spectre of Genocide* (Cambridge: Cambridge University Press, 2003), pp.141–162.
20 Hitler, *Mein Kampf*, 587; Richard Weikart, *Hitler's Ethic: The Pursuit of Evolutionary Progress* (New York: Palgrave Macmillan, 2009), pp.35–36, 160–161.
21 Hitler, *Mein Kampf*, p.589; Benjamin Madley, 'From Africa to Auschwitz: How German South West Africa Incubated Ideas and Methods Adopted and Developed by the Nazis in Eastern Europe', *European History Quarterly* 35 (2005), pp.429–464.
22 Quoted in Dawidowicz, *The War Against the Jews*, p.126.
23 'Programme of the NSDAP, 24 February 1920', pp.38–39.
24 Margaret Lavinia Anderson, 'Who Still Talked about the Extermination of the Armenians? German Talk and German Silences', in Ronald Grigor Suny, Fatma Müge Göçek, and Norman Naimark (eds), *A Question of Genocide: Armenians and Turks at the End of the Ottoman Empire* (Oxford: Oxford University Press, 2011), p.216.
25 John Barnhill, 'National Socialist German Workers' Party', in Paul R. Bartrop and Michael Dickerman (eds), *The Holocaust*, Volume 2 (Santa Barbara, CA: ABC-CLIO, 2017), p.455.
26 Richard J. Evans, *The Third Reich in Power 1933–1939* (London: Penguin, 2006), p.8.
27 Peter D. Stachura, 'The Political Strategy of the Nazi Party, 1919–1933', *German Studies Review*, 3 (1980), pp.261–288.
28 Dirk Hänisch, 'Inhalt und Struktur der Datenbank "Wahl- und Sozialdaten der Kreise und Gemeinden des Deutschen Reiches von 1920 bis 1933"', *Historical Social Research / Historische Sozialforschung*, 14 (1989), p.63.
29 Richard Bessel, 'The Nazi Capture of Power', *Journal of Contemporary History*, 39 (2004), pp.180–181; Evans, *The Third Reich in Power*, pp.9–10.
30 Quoted in Bessel, 'The Nazi Capture of Power', p.170.
31 Bessel, 'The Nazi Capture of Power', pp.169–171.
32 Quoted in Bessel, 'The Nazi Capture of Power', p.177.
33 Bessel, 'Nazi Capture of Power', p.180.
34 Edward B. Westermann, *Hitler's Police Battalions: Enforcing Racial War in the East* (Lawrence: University of Kansas Press, 2005), pp.20–57.
35 Evans, *The Third Reich in Power*, pp.20–96.
36 Robert Gellately, 'The Third Reich, the Holocaust, and Visions of Serial Genocide', in Gellately and Kiernan (eds), *The Spectre of Genocide*, p.241.
37 Thomas Childers and Eugene Weiss, 'Voters and Violence: Political Violence and the Limits of National Socialist Mass Mobilization', *German Studies Review*, 13 (1990), pp.481–482.

38 Richard Weikart, *Hitler's Religion* (New York, NY: Regnery History, 2016), pp.28–30.
39 Doris L. Bergen, *Twisted Cross: The German Christian Movement in the Third Reich* (Chapel Hill: University of North Carolina Press, 1996); Susannah Heschel, *The Aryan Jesus: Christian Theologians and the Bible in Nazi Germany* (Princeton, NJ.: Princeton University Press, 2008); Jörg L. Spenkuch and Philipp Tillmann, 'Elite Influence? Religion and the Electoral Success of the Nazis', *American Journal of Political Science*, 62 (2018), pp.19–36.
40 Dan P. Silverman, 'Fantasy and Reality in Nazi Work-Creation Programs, 1933–1936', *Journal of Modern History*, 65 (1993), pp.113–151.
41 Eleanor Hancock, 'The Purge of the SA Reconsidered: "An Old Putschist Trick"?' *Central European History*, 44 (2011), pp.669–683.
42 Urvashi Goutam and Urvashi Gautam, 'Pedagogic Nazi Propaganda', *Proceedings of the Indian History Congress*, 75 (2014), pp.1018–1026.
43 Göran Adamson, 'Nazism and Germany', in Bartrop and Dickerman (eds), *The Holocaust*, Volume 1, p.462.
44 Quoted in Dawidowicz, *The War Against the Jews*, p.43.
45 Burleigh and Wippermann, *The Racial State*, pp.79–80.
46 Walmer, 'German Fury: The Old Roots of the New German Nationalism', p.37.
47 Burleigh and Wippermann, *The Racial State*, pp.80–81; Kertzer and Mokosch, 'The Medieval in the Modern', p.179; Rudolph Stahl, 'Vocational Retraining of Jews in Nazi Germany 1933–1938', *Jewish Social Studies*, 1 (1939), p.190.
48 Kurt R. Grossmann, 'The Final Solution', *Antioch Review*, 15 (1955), p.55.
49 Karl Loewenstein, 'Law in the Third Reich', *Yale Law Journal*, 45 (1936), p.797.
50 Loewenstein, 'Law in the Third Reich', pp.796–797.
51 Stahl, 'Vocational Retraining of Jews in Nazi Germany 1933–1938', p.190.
52 Quoted in Kershaw, *The Nazi Dictatorship* (London: Bloomsbury, 2012), p.108.
53 Eve E. Grimm, 'Aryanization', in Bartrop and Dickerman (eds), *The Holocaust*, Volume 1, pp.47–48; 'Decree on the Changing of Names, 17 August 1938', in Noakes and Pridham (eds), *Documents on Nazism, 1919–1945*, pp.471–472.
54 Quoted in Kershaw, *The Nazi Dictatorship*, p.109.
55 Ian Kershaw, ' "Working Towards the Führer". Reflections on the Nature of the Hitler Dictatorship', *Contemporary European History*, 2 (1993), p.116.
56 Donald McKale, 'A Case of Nazi "Justice": The Punishment of Party Members Involved in the Kristallnacht, 1938', *Jewish Social Studies*, 35 (1973), pp.228–238; Dawidowicz, *The War Against the Jews*, p.142.
57 'Hitler Threatens Destruction of the European Jews in the Event of War', in Noakes and Pridham (eds), *Documents on Nazism, 1919–1945*, pp.485–486.
58 Weikart, *Hitler's Ethic*, p.153.
59 Quoted in Dawidowicz, *War Against the Jews*, p.126.
60 Weikart, *Hitler's Ethic*, p.179.
61 Quoted in Weikart, *Hitler's Ethic*, p.183.
62 Jason C. Engle, 'Euthanasia Programme', in Bartrop and Dickerman (eds) *The Holocaust*, Volume 1, pp.193–194; Beth Griech-Polelle, 'Image of a Churchman-Resister: Bishop von Galen, the Euthanasia Project and the Sermons of Summer 1941', *Journal of Contemporary History*, 36 (2001), pp.41–57.
63 Quoted in Shelley Baranowski, *Nazi Empire: German Colonialism and Imperialism from Bismark to Hitler* (Cambridge: Cambridge University Press, 2011), pp.234–235.

64 Baranowski, *Nazi Empire*, p.237.

65 Westermann, *Hitler's Police Battalions*, pp.143–145, 237–239.

66 'Some Army Attitudes to the SS Atrocities in Poland', in Noakes and Pridham (eds), *Documents on Nazism, 1919–1945*, pp.611–613.

67 'Hitler's Directives for the Administration of Occupied Russia', in Noakes and Pridham (eds), *Documents on Nazism, 1919–1945*, pp.616–617.

68 Baranowski, *Nazi Empire*, pp.244–245; Niklas Frank, quoted in Steven Leonard Jacobs, 'Hans Frank', in Bartrop and Dickerman (eds) *The Holocaust*, Volume 1, p.220.

69 Cristopher Browning, *The Origins of the Final Solution: The Evolution of Nazi Jewish Policy 1939–1942* (London: Arrow Book, 2005), pp.43–63.

70 Quoted in Kershaw, *The Nazi Dictatorship*, p.112.

71 Saul Friedländer, *The Years of Extermination* (London: Weidenfeld & Nicolson, 2007), pp.38–39; Dieter Pohl, 'The Murder of Jews in the General Government', in Ulrich Herbert (ed.), *National Socialist Extermination Policies* (Oxford: Berghahn Books, 2000), pp.85–86.

72 Browning, *The Origins of the Final Solution*, pp.105–106.

73 Pohl, 'The Murder of Jews in the General Government', p.86.

74 Browning, *Ordinary Men*, p.11; David Stahel, *Operation Barbarossa and Germany's Defeat in the East* (Cambridge: Cambridge University Press, 2009), pp.100–101.

75 Donald Bloxham, *The Final Solution* (Oxford: Oxford University, 2009), p.204; Vasyl Doguzov and Svitlana Rusalovs'ka, 'The Massacre of Mental Patients in Ukraine, 1941–1943', *International Journal of Mental Health*, 36, 1 (2007), pp.105–111; Friedländer, *The Years of Extermination*, p.226.

76 Bloxham, *The Final Solution*, pp.92–130; Jan T. Gross, *Neighbours: The Destruction of the Jewish Community in Jedwabne, Poland, 1941* (London: Arrow Books, 2003).

77 'Report on the Execution of Jews in Borrisow, October 24, 1941', in Bartrop and Dickerman (eds) *The Holocaust*, Volume 4, pp.1234–1237.

78 Hitler, quoted in Stephen G. Fritz, *Ostkrieg: Hitler's War of Extermination in the East* (Lexington: University of Kentucky Press, 2011), p.76.

79 Browning, *The Origins of the Final Solution*, pp.151–168.

80 Dawidowicz, *War Against the Jews*, p.148.

81 Quoted in Jessica Evers, 'Yellow Star', in Bartrop and Dickerman (eds) *The Holocaust*, Volume 2, p.731.

82 Bloxham, *The Final Solution*, 214; Christian Gerlach, 'The Wannsee Conference, the Fate of German Jews, and Hitler's Decision in Principle to Exterminate All European Jews', *Journal of Modern History*, 70 (1998), pp.767–769; Pohl, 'The Murder of Jews in the General Government', pp.87–88.

83 Quoted in Fred E. Katz, 'A Sociological Perspective to the Holocaust', *Modern Judaism*, 2 (1982), p.288.

84 Dawidowicz, *War Against the Jews*, pp.175–176.

85 Bloxham, *Final Solution*, p.219.

86 Gerlach, 'The Wannsee Conference', pp.759–812.

87 Quoted in Bertrand Perz, 'Austrian Connection: SS and Police Leader Odilo Globocnik and His Staff in the Lublin District', *Holocaust and Genocide Studies*, 29 (2015), p.400.

88 Dawidowicz, *War Against the Jews*, pp.175–176.

89 Yitzak Arad, *Belzec, Sobibor, Treblinka: The Operation Reinhard Death Camps* (Bloomington: Indiana University Press, 1987), pp.63–104.

90 Quoted in Michael Zimmerman, 'The National Socialist "Solution of the Gypsy Question" ', in Herbert (ed.), *National Socialist Extermination Policies*, p.191.

91 Sybil Milton, 'Holocaust: The Gypsies', in Samuel Totten and William S. Parsons (eds), *Century of Genocide* (London: Routledge, 2009), p.172

92 Guenter Lewy, *The Nazi Persecution of the Gypsies* (Oxford: Oxford University Press, 2000), p.222; Zimmerman, 'The National Socialist "Solution of the Gypsy Question" ', pp.194–204.

93 Quoted in Dawidowicz, *War Against the Jews*, p.177.

94 Dawidowicz, *War Against the Jews*, p.480.

95 Friedländer, *Years of Extermination*, pp.487–490.

96 John M. Cox, 'Jewish Resistance against the Nazism', in Jonathan C. Freidman (ed.), *The Routledge History of the Holocaust* (London: Routledge, 2011), pp.326–336.

97 Quoted in Jeffrey Herf, 'Haj Amin al-Husseini, the Nazis and the Holocaust: The Origins, Nature and Aftereffects of Collaboration', *Jewish Political Studies Review*, 26 (2014), p.18.

98 Gerhard L. Weinberg, 'Ignored and Misunderstood Aspects of the Holocaust', *Historical Reflections / Réflexions Historiques*, 39 (2013), p.9.

99 Dawidowicz, *War Against the Jews*, p.480; Friedländer, *Years of Extermination*, pp.613–619.

100 Friedländer, *Years of Extermination*, p.613.

101 Dawidowicz, *War Against the Jews*, p.191.

102 Testimony of Nechama Epstein, in Donald L. Niewyk, 'Holocaust: The Genocide of the Jews', in Totten and Parsons (eds), *Century of Genocide*, pp.159–160.

Conclusion

To understand the persistence of persecution as a phenomenon in human history, we must move beyond prosaic assumptions about material conflicts for power, wealth, or resources. We must recognise the moral complexities of past societies and the essentially contestable character of the motives of those who persecute. We must question why some were singled out for repression, massacre, or enslavement even when that entailed 'moral regression', the abandoning of a society's customary, legal, religious, or political safeguards of life and well-being. The essential framework for such a study is to probe the ideological beliefs of the persecutor. This does not mean simply invoking hatred, bigotry, or prejudice as explanations for persecution. While both were surely culpable for the harms they caused, the righteous persecutor, in the Augustinian sense, was cast in an altogether different mould from the murderous NSDAP functionary. Whether expressed as explicit political doctrine or more implicitly, in belief systems around culture, custom, religion, or status, the roots of persecution lay in cosmologies or *weltanschauung*. And this, too, is one of the reasons why persecution has persisted; our beliefs and assumptions, including our prejudices, our bigotries, and our righteous certainties, are rooted deeply in history, to a degree we seldom recognise. We are the legatees of two thousand years of persecution.

For the first two centuries of the common era, the persecution of Christians was usually a localised and sporadic phenomenon, driven by popular hostility and the actions of regional authorities rather than imperial policy or law. To a degree, it reflected broader Roman attitudes towards religious innovation and the dangers posed by novel, 'irrational', and foreign *superstitio*. Yet Christianity provoked very specific anxieties and was seen as a particular threat to communities' well-being. Christians were fractious, both amongst themselves and, in the more militant manifestations of the religion, in the active pursuit of martyrdom. Their apocalyptic preaching and stigmatising association with criminality fostered a reputation for hatred of mankind. Their monotheism, while not itself a danger, was combined with their outright refusal to revere any other deities. They would not swear oaths or participate in the rituals that bound civic society, activities that ensured the *pax*

DOI: 10.4324/9781003494331-12

deorum. They became, therefore, both objects of suspicion and convenient scapegoats for fire, flood, famine, or plague.

Persecution only became a matter of imperial policy in the third century. The emperors Septimius Severus, Decius, Valerian, Diocletian, and Galerius all enacted measures that resulted in the persecution of Christians. In part, such measures may have been a targeted response to the increasing success of Christianity in winning high-status converts. In the eyes of these emperors, and indeed many traditionally minded Romans, this act was tantamount to treason. To abandon the gods of one's ancestors was wicked and dangerous folly.

Yet Christians were not always being explicitly singled out. Against a background of political and economic crises, these emperors were seeking to restore the favour of the gods and unify the empire's citizens around mandatory acts of cultic ritual, specifically blood sacrifice. Christians could not participate in such rituals. Behaviours that had, hitherto, merely been frowned upon, such as abstaining from civic rituals, now became criminal. The situation that Christians found themselves in was made worse by the bureaucratisation of the act of sacrifice and the growth of policing institutions. These catalysed a transition from viewing certain behaviours as reprehensible into condemning those behaviours as illegal.

The proclamation of toleration issued by the dying emperor Galerius in 311 CE both legitimised Christianity and implicitly acknowledged the failure of persecution as a means to promote religious conformity. The Edict of Milan, issued in 313 CE by the eastern emperor Licinius and the western emperor Constantine, went further and promised religious freedom. The history of persecution in the fourth century is largely a history of why, ultimately, that promise was not fulfilled.

Constantine, apparently a sincere convert to Christianity, essentially pursued a policy of forbearance towards non-Christians. Violent assaults on temples and idols by those soldiers of Christ seeking martyrdom were condemned by both secular authorities and by the bishops. Instead, the emperor offered encouragement and patronage to Christians and the Christian Church, while starving the pagan temples of funds and discouraging such activities as blood sacrifice. His successors largely followed this lead. The law codes of Theodosius I (r.379–95), seemed to presage an altogether less tolerant religious policy, especially in the intrusive ban on the private worship of *lares* (household gods). Yet he, too, largely rejected outright coercion in matters of belief. The Christianisation of the empire was, for the most part, a gradual and consensual process.

However, by the late fourth century, the atmosphere was changing and there was a turn towards persecution. The more militant strain of Christianity, ready to commit violence in the name of faith, had come to the fore. There were a number of factors for this. One was dissent, schism, and competition for influence within the Church itself. The illusion of monotheism as a means of unifying the citizens of the empire around a shared faith had been quickly shattered by sharply divergent and bitterly contested debates over theology and Christology, such as the Arian controversy. These proved productive of intolerance. The quest for universality generated a struggle to define and enforce religious orthodoxy and to stigmatise, and ultimately persecute, those labelled as heretics.

Christians in positions of authority, especially the bishops, the new power brokers in Roman cities, were also confronted with the harsh (and corrupting) realities of wielding earthly authority. They came to a pragmatic acceptance of the need for the use of force. Some of them did so very enthusiastically and were willing to pursue status through violence. Their private armies of 'gravediggers' and 'hospital attendants' fought street battles in the imperial cities of late antiquity. The brief reign of Julian the Apostate (r.361–365 CE), and his efforts to revive paganism, also provoked a militant Christian backlash. While Christianisation proceeded peacefully in most areas, in others, such as the city of Alexandria, there is evidence for religious persecution tied strongly to local struggles for political authority. An archaeological record of slighted temples and smashed altars hints at similar conflicts elsewhere in the empire.

St Augustine (354–430 CE), bishop of Hippo in North Africa, is a particularly important figure in shaping Christian attitudes towards religious coercion in late antiquity. Initially, he rejected it as inimical to true faith. However, he then witnessed former Donatists, militant schismatics who had broken away from his Church, exhibit genuine devotion after being forced back into communion. Augustine thus came to accept that disciplinary violence could make good Christians. His formulation that one who persecutes may be just, and that one who is persecuted may be unjust, would become an important legitimisation for religious coercion for centuries to come. It is unfortunate that Augustine's clear admonition that such disciplinary violence was ultimately motivated by compassion, to save the souls of those who had strayed, and thus should always be exercised with moderation and restraint, proved less enduring.

Augustine's enormous influence within the western intellectual tradition was also evident in the treatment of Judaism. The position of Jews within Christendom was unique. Unlike either heretics or pagans, they were allowed to practise their own religion. Augustine had urged forbearance. While heretics were deluded by their own pride and pagans were misled by demons, God was the source of Jewish belief. Although in Christian eyes, Jews themselves may have been 'spiritually blind', failing to recognise Jesus as the Messiah, their scriptures contained proof of his status and that Christians were the new Israel. Under this dispensation, although the object of much popular hostility and subject to legal discrimination, both ecclesiastical and royal authorities protected Jewish communities.

Their situation became more precarious from the late eleventh century onwards. The religiosity associated with the Crusades was one factor. Intellectual trends that questioned Jews' capacity for reason (manifested in their stubborn refusal to convert), and therefore their humanity, were another. Capricious secular authorities proved less willing to protect Jewish communities. A crude popular culture stigmatising Jews as responsible for outbreaks of the plague, and accusing them of sacrilege and the ritual murder of Christian children, developed a dangerous persecutory potential. Mob violence, massacres, and exiles followed. By the fifteenth century, the stereotypes of Jewish malfeasance familiar to modern antisemitism were all in place. And the nature of Jewishness had been redefined. What had been seen as a religious identity was now often cast as an inheritable essence, contained in the bloodline. In Spain, laws were passed to prevent formerly Jewish Christians from holding certain ecclesiastical or civil offices. A 'proto-racist' ideology had emerged.

Jews were not the only ones who found themselves cast as Christendom's internal enemies. The Albigensian Crusade (1209–1229) saw Languedoc invaded and conquered by those who 'took the cross', penitential warriors who sought personal salvation through committing acts of righteous violence. This was a seminal episode in the development of institutional persecution in western Europe. To Raphaël Lemkin, it was a 'religious genocide'. Its victims were accused of a dualist heresy, and the local nobility were accused of protecting them. The origins, extent, and character of this heresy remain the subject of historical debate. To a degree, the crusade was driven by the Church's intent to exercise greater control over the spiritual lives of ordinary Catholics and silence dissident, critical voices. Yet the fear of the spiritual contagion of a dangerous heresy was very real, hence the belief that the wounds of heresy 'must be cut out with steel'.

The cruelty and peculiar violence of the ensuing war, however, was not merely the product of religious fervour. The crusade took on the characteristics of a conquest. Land-hungry French knights sought to carve out patrimonies by dispossessing southern nobles conveniently stigmatised as protectors of heretics. Insurgency and counterinsurgency followed, in a bitter campaign marked by massacre and betrayal. Ultimately, only intervention by a French army led by the king would end the fighting. The campaign against heresy was then completed by the development of inquisitorial procedures. Inquisitors, empowered to act as judge, prosecutor, and jury, supported by a formidable bureaucracy, and relying on denunciations and confessions extracted under duress, affected the destruction of the Albigensian heretics.

Inquisitorial procedures would subsequently be widely adopted into secular legal systems in Europe. They became formidable instruments of persecution, evident again during the witch-hunts in the early modern period. Explaining the witch-hunts entails understanding why a long-standing scepticism among the educated towards magic, especially as practised by the peasantry, gave way to a pervasive fear of its potential to do harm. A key development was the emerging belief in a novel form of heresy, a Satanic cult of witches, arising in the early fifteenth century in the western Alps. Elite educated demonology elided with the prosaic magical practices of agrarian communities. Although the witch-hunts were initially slow to spread, they would eventually occur across the continent, reaching their peak in the sixteenth and seventeenth centuries. In particular, where political authority was fragmented, where local courts were unaccountable, and the law was in the hands of untrained magistrates and judges, these fears manifested in the widespread persecution of alleged witches. The highly variable incidence and intensity of these witch-hunts was shaped by an array of factors: neighbourhood quarrels, environmental shocks, the impact of the Reformation, and the nature and operation of established legal procedures.

The witch-hunts began to decline in the first half of the seventeenth century. This was not because belief in the reality of witchcraft itself declined. Rather it was because judges and magistrates acted to protect due process, and the growing fiscal capacity of centralised early modern states allowed greater control over wayward local courts. Loosening the mental grip of a delusional and dangerous ideology, with the capacity to drive persecution, can be a far longer and more challenging process. The history of ideologies of race demonstrates this.

The very long-established stigmatisation of sub-Saharan Africans as inherently servile, within a prejudicial culture shared by Islam and Christendom, was reinforced by the operation of slavery in Africa and the Mediterranean world. The legacy of classical notions of inherent characteristics determined by the environment, and the evolution of beliefs in medieval Europe, concerning lineage, nobility, and 'blood purity', were also important in shaping powerful prejudices. These ideologies might be termed 'proto-racial' in character. When the voracious plantation economies of colonial America demanded labour, these ideologies made it easier to fix chains onto Africans, even as Europeans were rejecting slavery within their own continent.

The mutable medieval ideologies of 'proto-race' would evolve into a more rigid and hegemonic racist ordering of society in the colonies. The 'moral regression' inherent in the Atlantic slave trade would be evident, too, in the brutal and relentlessly exploitative regimes endured by the enslaved on the plantations, to which no European workforce would have been subjected. Only a combination of active resistance and political abolitionism would bring about the end of race slavery in the Americas in the nineteenth century.

During the age of European colonialism, race developed from malleable prejudices and assumptions about inherited characteristics into a hegemonic ideology that legitimised the subordination of colonised peoples. Both Enlightenment thinking and later pseudo-science, gave bigoted racial ideologies a solid veneer of intellectual respectability. Colonisation itself has now become the focus of renewed attention as historians probing the roots of twentieth-century totalitarianism and genocide have looked to earlier empire building outside Europe for precedents. Yet the relationship between colonisation and genocide is a controversial one.

In particular, the question of whether there was 'intent' to destroy a people may be very hard to answer, if, as was the case so often in the Americas, it was disease that caused demographic collapses. Yet to dismiss such mass mortality as an essentially accidental corollary to colonisation is to miss the extent to which epidemics took hold and spread in conditions that settlers intentionally created to harm: war, dispossession, exile, and enslavement. Colonial conflicts also took on peculiarly brutal characteristics. Again, one sees regression from established European standards governing the treatment of non-combatants, prisoners, and the propensity to commit massacres. Considering, too, Raphaël Lemkin's model of genocide as an attritional process – destruction of a group followed by the imposition of the oppressor's 'national pattern' – then the place of modern colonialism in the increasing scale and frequency of genocide becomes apparent. Concentration camps, campaigns of 'total war', and an emergent racism of extirpation (determining not who should rule, but who should live) were born of imperialism.

In continental Eurasian empires, too, emerging ideologies generated conflict and persecution. Ethno-nationalism, centred around a particular culture, language, religion, or putative racial descent, proved especially dangerous. The established structures that had allowed for coexistence in multi-ethnic empires were undercut by subject peoples striving for autonomy and by rulers seeking to preserve their dominance by the pursuit of policies designed to create uniform and loyal populations. The fate of the two million Circassians, subject to massacres and forced deportations at the hands of Russian imperial authorities in 1864, was a portent of the scale and ruthlessness of the demographic engineering by which modern states would fashion loyal populations. They would abandon policies toward minorities of assimilation or even subordination and choose instead extirpation.

The Soviet Union would inherit this policy from its tsarist predecessor. While mobilising the radical and exclusionary ideology of Marxist-Leninism to legitimise assaults on supposed counter-revolutionaries and class enemies, non-Russian populations, Ukrainians, Kalmyks, Volga Germans, Tartars, Chechens, and others, were singled out for attritional genocides. These were pursued through mass execution, calculated exacerbation of famine, forced deportation, and the deliberate infliction 'on the group [of] conditions of life calculated to bring about its physical destruction in whole or in part'. Efficient bureaucracy and the surveillance capacity of modern states would become the prosaic handmaidens of persecution.

In the Ottoman Empire, the nationalistic *Ittihadism* (unionism) of the 'Young Turks' envisaged the Ottoman Empire as a homogeneous, Muslim, and Turkish-speaking nation. While *Ittihadism* was a reform movement, aiming to transform the empire into a modern secular state, it inevitably ran counter to the aspirations of some among the subject peoples of the empire for greater autonomy. The *millet* system that had allowed separate religious communities to coexist for centuries broke down. The loss of Ottoman territory and the violent exile of millions of Muslims from the Balkans and Caucasus, created an atmosphere of existential crisis. This was heightened by the looming threat of intervention by the 'great powers'. In this atmosphere, the empire's subject Christian populations – Armenians, Assyrians, Orthodox Greeks – were subject first to political repression and massacre. Then, under pressure of the First World War, oppression escalated to genocide.

At Lausanne in 1923, the new Turkish Republic won international acceptance of borders created by genocide, thereby creating a dangerous precedent for other revisionist powers, notably Nazi Germany. From its earliest days, Adolf Hitler's *Nationalsozialistische Deutsche Arbeiterpartei* nurtured a genocidal potential. This was evident in the 25-point programme issued by the party in February 1920, containing an ideological commitment to *Völkisch* ethno-nationalism, radical antisemitism, rejection of the Versailles settlement and its corollary, the revanchist re-drawing of eastern European borders on putatively racial lines.

Their radical antisemitism, while catalysed by defeat in 1918, was not shared by the mass of the German population. The NSDAP could only make a political breakthrough in the wake of the Great Depression and backroom dealing with conservative elites that secured Hitler the chancellorship. The majority of those who voted for the NSDAP, or supported them once they were in power, were not motivated by hatred of their Jewish compatriots. They were drawn by other aspects of the NSDAP programme: the promise of political stability, anti-communism, economic reform. Yet they were willing to acquiesce to the party's radical antisemitism. In power, Hitler forged a 'consensus dictatorship', a one-party state, that balanced populism with repression.

From 1933, he was thus able to embark on his ideological campaign against Germany's Jews. Initially, this took the form of a 'cold pogrom' to pressure them to emigrate. German Jews were deprived of their citizenship, their businesses, and their professions. Their social and civic lives were drastically restricted. Prejudice and ostracism were encouraged. The global conflict that opened in 1939 would radicalise NSDAP policies to unimaginable levels of atrocity. Germany waged a ferocious ideological racial war of annihilation in the east. Yet, by late 1941, Soviet resistance made it apparent that expelling Jews, including now the large populations in territories the Germans had conquered, was no longer feasible. Military officers, bureaucrats, and functionaries 'worked towards the Führer', pursuing ever more radical policies to bring about Hitler's prophecy that the war would end in 'the annihilation of the Jewish race in Europe'. Genocide, through mass shootings, gassing, and material hardship and overwork, became their 'Final Solution'.

The recognition of genocide as a legal concept, thanks to the work of Raphaël Lemkin, and adopted in the United Nations Convention of 1948, filled a significant gap in international law. It has not, however, brought 'the age of genocide' to an end. The long, and all too often murderous reach of a history of persecution continues to exercise its grip on the world.

The astonishing persistence of localised patterns of prejudice, as evidenced historically by the relationship between the location of medieval pogroms and incidence of support for the NSDAP in Germany, finds contemporary expression. Consider the example of Spain. Its Jewish population was expelled in 1492. Even today, Jews make up less than 0.05 per cent of Spain's population. There has, thus, not been a meaningful Jewish presence in Spain for over five hundred years. Yet

> ... in a study on Judeophobic attitudes in several European countries that was released towards the end of 2002 by the Anti-Defamation League, Spain came out the worst ... In the Spanish survey, 21 percent of those interviewed were Judeophobic.[1]

This seeming paradox, a living, active prejudice against a long-departed people, may be explained by reference to cultural, religious, and linguistic traditions passed from generation to generation. At rural festivals across Spain, especially at Easter, rituals of persecution are re-enacted; grotesque effigies of 'Jews' are mocked, beaten, even ritually murdered. According to the dictionary of the Spanish Royal Academy (2001 edition), 'a meeting for illicit purposes' is an acceptable definition of the word 'synagogue', and *judiada* may be translated as 'evil action'.[2] This phenomenon is not restricted to anti-semitism. Research in the United States has revealed strong local correlations in southern states between contemporary instances of racial violence linked to voter suppression and the incidence of lynchings of African Americans in the period 1882–1930.[3]

The ideologies that drive such violence can often become quiescent politically, giving the impression of progress. Yet hatreds can simmer for decades or even centuries, sustained within a culture and re-emerging with renewed vitriol when circumstances allow. Although constrained in Europe by the Cold War after the Second World War, ethno-nationalism reasserted itself after the fall of the Soviet Union. As Yugoslavia broke apart and descended into wars of secession (1991–1995), new borders and loyal populations were ruthlessly engineered by violence and forced deportations. The interests of state-building ethno-nationalist politicians and the purveyors of local bigotries elided. Before launching an offensive against the Serbian secessionists of the Krajina region in May 1995, President Franjo Tudjman of the newly independent Republic of Croatia opined that a 12 per cent Serb minority in Croatia was too large, but that half as many might be tolerable. Between 160,000 and 200,000 Serbs were subsequently driven from their homes. The military operation was accompanied by a widespread and tolerated degree of criminality committed against former neighbours: plunder, destruction of private property, murder. Later that year, in July, 8,372 Bosnian Muslim men and boys were massacred in the town of Srebrenica, as part of an endeavour to build a 'Greater Serbia'.[4]

Colonialism, too, has left dangerous legacies. Even after independence, the power structures that had underpinned colonial forms of exploitation and oppression remained, and therefore so did the potential for genocide. In Rwanda, for example, the Belgian colonial authorities had racialised the internal relations of the subject people. 'Hutu' and 'Tutsi' went from being mutable economic and social categories to fixed racial identities. Following independence, they would compete for power. In 1994, a radical nationalist Hutu government would massacre between 500,000 and one million Tutsis and moderate Hutus in a matter of weeks.[5]

The former territories of the Ottoman Empire comprising Upper Mesopotamia (north-west Iraq, north-east Syria, and south-east Turkey), have been described as a 'cradle of genocide'.[6] In 1924, the League of Nations reported ongoing attempts by Turkish authorities aimed at the 'systematic removal of [remaining] Christian populations'. Since then, the region has witnessed a succession of genocides against religious and ethnic minorities, including the Kurds, most notoriously during the Iraqi Anfal campaign of 1988. Assyrian Christian and other religious minorities, such as the Yazidis, Mandaeans, and Shabaks, have been subject to massacre and driven from their homelands by the radical Islamists of ISIS in the mid-2010s.[7]

The radical ideology of Marxist-Leninism has continued to be a driver of persecution too. It provided the intellectual foundations for Stalin's gulags, Mao Zedong's 'Great Leap Forward' (1958–1962), and Cultural Revolution (1966–1976), Pol Pot's Khmer Rouge and the killing fields of the Cambodia genocide (1975–1979). It fuelled wars and repression across Africa and Latin America. At the end of the twentieth century, a French study calculated a human cost of between 85 million and 100 million victims.[8] As the North Korean regime continues to inflict terrible suffering upon its own citizens, and the People's Republic of China escalating persecution of the Uyghur of Xinjiang/East Turkestan, that toll continues to rise. In 2020, the American-Uyghur activist Rushan Abbas observed that '20 million plus Uyghurs are facing genocide in China. Maybe it's too late for them'.[9] The 'arc' of the 'moral universe' seems unbending; the relentless momentum of persecution continues to shape our history. Are we powerless to stop it?

Notes

1 Gustavo Perednik, 'Naïve Spanish Judeophobia', *Jewish Political Studies Review*, 15 (2003), p.88.

2 Perednik, 'Naïve Spanish Judeophobia', pp.87–110.

3 Jhacova A. Williams, Trevon D. Logan, and Bradley L. Hardy, 'The Persistence of Historical Racial Violence and Political Suppression: Implications for Contemporary Regional Inequality', *Annals of the American Academy of Political and Social Science*, 694 (2021), pp.92–107.

4 Sonja Biserko, 'The Srebrenica Genocide: Serbia in Denial', *Pakistan Horizon*, 65 (2012), pp.1–6; Chaim Kaufmann, 'Possible and Impossible Solutions to Ethnic Civil Wars', *International Security*, 20 (1996), p.163; Damir Mirković, 'Croatian Liberation of Western Slavonia and Krajina', *Peace Research*, 30 (1998), pp.14–24; Norman M. Naimark, *Fires of Hatred: Ethnic Cleansing in Twentieth-Century Europe* (Cambridge, MA: Harvard University Press, 2001), pp.139–184.

5 Herbert Ekwe-Ekwe, *Biafra Revisited* (Reading: African Renaissance: 2006), pp.1–17; Scott Straus, *The Order of Genocide: Race, Power and War in Rwanda* (Ithaca, NY: Cornell University Press, 2006), pp.20–23.
6 Hannibal Travis, 'The Long Genocide in Upper Mesopotamia', *Genocide Studies International*, 13 (2019), p.94.
7 Aldo Zammit Borda, 'Putting Reproductive Violence on the Agenda: A Case Study of the Yazidis', *Journal of Genocide Research* (2022) https://doi.org/10.1080/14623528.2022.2100594 [accessed 29 July 2023];Travis, 'The Long Genocide in Upper Mesopotamia', pp.92–131.
8 Stéphanie Courtois et al., *The Black Book of Communism: Crimes, Terror, Repression*, translated by Jonathan Murphy and Mark Kramer (Cambridge, MA.: Harvard University Press, 1999), p.x.
9 Rushan Abbas, 'International Action to Protect the Uyghur People', *Journal of International Affairs*, 73 (2020), p.215; Ali Çaksu, 'Islamophobia, Chinese Style: Total Internment of Uyghur Muslims by the People's Republic of China', *Islamophobia Studies Journal*, 5 (2020), pp.175–198; Sean R. Roberts, *The War on the Uyghurs: China's Campaign Against Xinjiang's Muslims* (Manchester: Manchester University Press, 2020).

A Guide to Further Reading

Roman Persecution of Christians

The most detailed treatment of this subject remains W.H.C. Frend's *Martyrdom and Persecution in the Early Church* (London: Blackwell, 1965). The motivation for martyrdom is a central theme. This, Frend argued, was an inheritance from the Jewish nationalist tradition, first established by the Maccabees, the family that had opposed the introduction of Hellenic cultic rites into the Temple of Jerusalem in 168 BCE. Readers should, however, be aware that Frend has been faulted for accepting much of his primary-source testimony rather uncritically. The allegation that anti-Christian alliances between Jewish communities and local authorities fuelled persecution, which Frend repeated, is now generally understood to be rooted in the Judeophobia of partisan early Christian authors, such as Tertullian. Frend's broad thesis, that zeal for martyrdom triumphed in the west, but gave way to asceticism informed by Neo-Platonism in the east, has also been criticised as an over-simplification. The Egyptian Neo-Platonist Origen was only prevented from embracing martyrdom during the Severian persecution when his mother hid his clothes to prevent him leaving the house.

More recently, in *Martyrdom & Rome* (Cambridge: Cambridge University Press, 1995), G.W. Bowerstock offered a controversial alternative view of martyrdom. He argued that the concept of celebrating a voluntary death that would be rewarded in the afterlife was alien to both Jewish and Greek traditions and emerged only in the mid-second century CE, shaped primarily by Roman civic spectacle and Roman glorification of suicide. His analysis of martyrdom's place in Roman urban culture, where it achieved the maximum visibility desired by both persecutors and their victims, is illuminating. Yet the overall thesis is unconvincing; even if it was Christians who adapted the word 'martyr' to its current meaning, the underlying concept can be seen in both Greek tradition (in the death of Socrates, for example) and Judaism. There the Maccabees were lauded for their heroism in this world and were rewarded in the next. Daniel Boyarin's *Dying for God: Martyrdom and the Making of Christianity and Judaism* (Stanford, CA: Stanford University Press, 1999) offered a far more nuanced understanding of martyrdom as a fluid

DOI: 10.4324/9781003494331-13

ideology that was shaped by a shared Judeo-Christian tradition enduring into the fourth century CE. The development of this ideology of combative martyrdom, and its potentially dangerous legacy, is also the central theme of Candida Moss's *The Myth of Persecution: How Early Christians Invented a Story of Martyrdom* (New York: Harper Collins, 2013). This very accessible and persuasive work offers an excellent explanation of the problems facing the historian when confronted by the selective, partisan, heavily edited, or even wholly fabricated accounts produced by early Church historians, such as Eusebius, or the anonymous authors of the *Acts of the Martyrs*.

Too narrow a focus on persecution and martyrdom may rather obscure the wider story of Christianity's growth and development which were, after all, the context for much of the hostility, as we can see illustrated by the pressure directed against wealthy and high-status converts in the third century. Those who wish to study Christianity's early history are faced by a daunting array of often very dense accounts. Yet there are books that are both accessible and up-to-date in their analysis. Charles Freeman's *A New History of Early Christianity* (New Haven, CT: Yale University Press, 2009) is characteristic of recent literature in that he recognised the diversity of Christian traditions under Rome and eschewed the old-fashioned and teleological approach organised around the seemingly inevitable triumph of the catholic and orthodox – that is, universal and right-thinking – Church. Gillian Clark in *Christianity and Roman Society* (Cambridge: Cambridge University Press, 2004) presents a remarkably succinct and readable, yet surprisingly comprehensive, coverage of the relationship between the emerging religion and the Roman world. While acknowledging the extent to which Christianity itself came to reflect classical culture, she also devoted a chapter to religious conflict and martyrdom. Willingness to self-sacrifice, alongside charitable instincts towards the poor, and a strong commitment to a clearly defined moral regime, were identified as crucial factors distinguishing Christianity from other elective cults.

In turn, understanding the belief systems of those other cults provides an invaluable insight into the fears and anxieties provoked by Christianity. Perhaps the best guide here is Robin Lane Fox. In *Pagans and Christians in the Mediterranean World* (London: Viking, 1986), he vividly recreated the vibrant and flourishing cults of Roman and Greek cities and explored the lived experiences of dreams, visions, prophecies, and everyday encounters with the divine that shaped ancient lives. In a compelling chapter on persecution, he noted how dangerous Christianity seemed to those who feared the wrath of dishonoured gods. Keith Hopkins took a similar perspective in *A World Full of Gods: The Strange Triumph of Christianity* (London: Penguin, 1999), striving to recapture the lived experiences of religious life in the Roman Empire and find an explanation, in the realms of beliefs and ideas, for Christianity's ultimate success. In pursuing this quest, he used a number of literary conceits, such as an account of the adventures of two young time travellers in pre-eruption Pompeii, that are unusual in a work of academic history. They make for a provocative read though, which promotes in the reader a real empathy for a long-gone culture. Nor should one underestimate the serious scholarship that underpinned this lively account of Roman cosmology and the story of the competition between varied messianic religious ideologies from which Christianity eventually emerged triumphant. The conclusions of this inventive book, however, remained very speculative.

Those seeking a more conventional examination of Roman attitudes towards Christianity, firmly grounded in the analysis of contemporary documentary sources, should look to Robert Louis Wilken's *The Christians as the Romans Saw Them* (New Haven, CT: Yale University Press, 1984). Wilken noted that the fragmentary nature of the surviving evidence from Christianity's detractors had left their ideas marginalised in historical accounts of the early Church. He restored the Roman critique of Christianity, drawing on surviving material authored by politicians, such as Pliny the Younger and Julian the Apostate, philosophers such as Celsus and Porphyry, and from the medical author Galen. Here we can see the intellectual basis of the case against Christianity, whether denigrated as a dangerous and irrational superstition, a fractious and politically suspect secret society, or as apostasy from ancient and respectable Judaism. Beyond merely outlining these allegations, Wilken noted the tenacity of Christian apologists in response and emphasised the constructive significance of discourse between Christians and non-Christians in shaping the philosophies of both. He concluded that the debate catalysed productive cultural, intellectual, and spiritual debates in the Greco-Roman world.

There is, perhaps, in that remark a hint of the once-conventional view that those traditions were moribund by the time Christianity emerged. More recent works on Roman religions have, however, stressed that for all their veneration of tradition, cultic practices often proved enduring because they were capable of adaptation. The religious life of Romans remained dynamic and spiritually fulfilling, and constituted more than just the mechanical performance of empty rituals. Mary Beard, John North, and Simon Price's *Religions of Rome*, Volume 1, *A History* (Cambridge: Cambridge University Press, 1998) is the most comprehensive treatment, surveying over a thousand years of evolving belief systems. The authors included a chapter on policing the boundaries of Roman religion, which is particularly useful to the student of religious persecution. This explores the distinction between proper and improper religious activity, and charts hostility not only towards Christianity but also to the followers of other foreign cults, such as Isis and Bacchus, and the practitioners of sorcery and magic.

Christian Persecution of Heretics and Schismatics in Late Antiquity

Constantine remains an enigmatic figure, despite his importance to our understanding of the development of religious conflict in the fourth century. In *Constantine and Eusebius* (Cambridge, MA: Harvard University Press,

1981), T.D. Barnes challenged a widely held assumption that the emperor pursued a fundamentally tolerant policy. Instead, he depicted Constantine as an active and aggressive enemy of paganism, heresy, and schism, who forged a unified Church with a heavy hand and thus established Christianity as the official religion of the state through coercion. Yet Barnes's argument did not convince all. H.A. Drake, for example, challenged Barnes's understanding of many of the primary sources and, particularly, the emphasis he placed on the (alleged) law banning sacrifice in 324 CE. In Drake's own book *Constantine and the Bishops: The Politics of Intolerance* (Baltimore, MD: Johns Hopkins University Press, 2000), he portrayed the emperor as a pragmatic ruler, with a style akin to a modern democratic politician: tolerant, committed primarily to forging consensus, and willing to be guided by expediency. That expediency led him into an alliance with the bishops, who were bent on establishing their secular authority and controlling religious doctrine. It was principally that relationship that eventually led to the persecution of non-conforming Christians. Understanding Constantine's behaviour within the framework of modern politics allowed Drake to move beyond the (probably insoluble) question of his religious sincerity; others questioned the validity of the analogy. Barnes, for example, accused Drake of creating a new all-American Constantine.

For an overview of the period following Constantine's death and to provide a context in which to understand religious violence, Peter Brown's *Power and Persuasion in Late Antiquity: Towards A Christian Empire* (Madison: University of Wisconsin Press, 1992) vividly illuminated the style and culture of power in the empire as Church leaders emerged as a new ruling elite. Garth Fowden, in *Empire to Commonwealth: Consequences of Monotheism in Late Antiquity* (Princeton, NJ: Princeton University Press, 1993) focused on the utility of universal monotheism as a vehicle for unifying a political empire, and the eventual transition of such an empire into a commonwealth of autonomous but culturally related polities, drawing on the experiences of Rome and Persia and early Islam. The scope of the book, covering nearly a millennium of Mediterranean history, was truly impressive but inevitably this approach led to some over-generalisations. For example, the chapter comparing Christian 'monotheism' with Roman 'polytheism' rather simplified the rather blurred boundaries of religious belief in late antiquity.

Nowhere were those boundaries more contentious than in North Africa. W.H.C. Frend's *The Donatist Church: A Movement of Protest in Roman North Africa* (Oxford: Clarendon Press, 1952) was a landmark text. It was the first full study written in English, informed not just by extensive archival work in Europe, but also by Frend's participation in archaeological excavations at many of the sites he discussed. Frend usefully placed the controversy within the broader secular history of Roman North Africa and provided much valuable detail about the influence of geography and economics on social relations within the province. However, writing during an era of decolonisation, he tended to overestimate the significance of both ethnic conflict between the indigenous Berber population and the Roman and Romanised colonial elites, and the extent to which violence was a reflection of socio-economic grievances.

Perhaps as a consequence of being written in an era of renewed religious conflict, more recent treatments have placed ecclesiastical quarrels and the rhetoric and reality of 'Holy violence' at the heart of their analyses. Those interested in religious persecution in late Roman North Africa specifically should consult, especially, two superlative works: Michael Gaddis's *There is No Crime for Those who Have Christ* (Berkeley: University of California Press, 2005) and Brent Shaw's *Sacred Violence: African Christians and Sectarian Hatred in the Age of Augustine* (Cambridge: Cambridge University Press, 2011). Both works broke new ground in their exploration of the 'communicative strategies' (or, as it might be expressed: 'name-calling') employed by the rival parties in the religious confrontations of late antiquity. Their discussions of the relationship between the violence of the *language* employed in sermons or songs and the actual spilling of blood retains a compelling relevance in the present day, as we still grapple with how to respond to the threat posed by those who incite violence and hatred, whether from a pulpit, or in a *madrassa*, or over the internet. In a bold attempt to examine the theme of religious coercion throughout the empire *c*.250–450 CE, Maijastina Kahlos, in *Forbearance and Compulsion: The Rhetoric of Religious Tolerance in Late Antiquity* (London: Duckworth, 2009), examined the rhetorical strategies employed by those involved in the contemporary debate over coercion, and stressed the growing significance of religious affiliation as an indicator of political loyalties from Diocletian onwards.

Inevitably, and quite correctly, St Augustine looms large in these works. It is unfortunate that this remarkable figure emerges from my chapter principally as the author of a theory of persecution. His legacy to western thought was far greater than that. Although it is admittedly an old text, Herbert A. Deane's *The Political and Social Ideas of St. Augustine* (New York: Columbia University Press, 1963) remains recommended reading as an accessible introduction. Augustine was a prolific writer, yet Deane drew on an impressive command of the full range of his works to discuss his development as a political theorist, whose views on justice, law, statecraft, and the relationship between secular and spiritual authority would influence Europe's kings, popes, and bishops for centuries to come. Deane clearly emphasised the role of the Donatist controversy in formulating concepts of just war and the legitimacy of state violence that would shape European history long after the Donatists themselves were forgotten. Augustine has been the subject of many excellent biographies too. Henry Chadwick's *Augustine of Hippo: A Life* (Oxford: Oxford University Press, 2010) is an outstanding example. Chadwick was capable of combining enormous erudition with an accessible and fluent writing style. This biography provided not simply an account of Augustine's life and times, but also a critical examination of the debates he engaged in with Pelagians, Donatists, Manichaeans, and pagans. It is, thus, a particularly useful preparatory text for any student contemplating reading Augustine's own works.

Christian Persecution of Pagans in Late Antiquity

Arnaldo Momigliano's edited volume, *The Conflict between Paganism and Christianity in the Fourth Century* (Oxford: Clarendon Press, 1963), is a collection of eight essays, now rather dated in their interpretations, but interesting from a historiographical perspective. Momigliano shared the then-conventional wisdom that fourth-century Christianity was dynamic and efficient, and thus its triumph over a moribund and mechanically ritualistic paganism was assured. He sought also to unify the separate essays (which dealt with topics as disparate as the Christian dialogue with Platonism and Neo-Platonism, the conversion of 'Northern barbarians', and the alleged 'Pagan Revival' in Rome in the 380s), by exploring another well-worn theme: the competition between Church and state and its role in the decline of the empire. However, the essays themselves did not really explicitly address this alleged contest between Church and state, nor establish to what extent, or even *if*, Christianity bore some responsibility for the decline of Rome. Indeed, the whole paradigm of the 'decline and fall of Rome' has since been challenged by some historians of the empire, who now stress continuity and gradual development over inexorable decline leading to precipitous calamity.

That question of gradual transition versus sudden change is also relevant to discussions of the Christianisation of the empire: was conversion consensual or coerced? Although some reviewers criticised Pierre Chuvin's *A Chronicle of the Last Pagans* (Cambridge, MA: Harvard University Press, 1990) for being too narrative and anecdotal, it remains one of the best introductions to the subject. Chuvin covered the entire period from the Edict of Milan through to the Justinian assault on freedom of conscience. His was a pessimistic chronicle, focusing on pagan loss of status, social exclusion, the destruction of temples, and physical persecution. Ramsey MacMullen's *Christianity & Paganism in the Fourth to Eighth Centuries* (New Haven, CT: Yale University Press, 1997) offered a similarly sobering account. Having estimated that Christians comprised perhaps 10 per cent of the empire's population in 312 CE, MacMullen posited that urban elites had rapidly converted thereafter, due to the material rewards and social advancement that joining the Church offered during the reign of Constantine and his sons. Others had converted because of the manifest power of the Christian God, revealed in widespread accounts of miracles and healings. In the countryside though, MacMullen argued that force was the means of converting a religiously conservative population. He effectively challenged the idea that paganism was tired and enervated by the fourth century, compared to a dynamic Christianity. Instead, he established paganism's continued vitality;

for example, he highlighted the deep and persistent devotion of ordinary people to their *lares*, household gods.

Controversially, MacMullen also claimed that the Christianised Roman Empire and its successor states in the medieval West were ruled by the anti-intellectual, the credulous, and the superstitious, in contrast to the rational, philosophically trained elites of pagan Greece and Rome. Charles Freeman has made similar claims. In AD *381: Heretics, Pagans and the Christian State* (London: Pimlico, 2009), he identified Theodosius's decree enforcing the Nicene Creed as a pivotal moment in European intellectual history emblematic of a systemic programme of spiritual coercion, resulting in a suppression not just of heresy and paganism but of free thought itself. For Eberhard Sauer, in *The Archaeology of Religious Hatred in the Roman and Early Medieval World* (Stroud: History Press, 2009), the material evidence of smashed icons, defaced statues, and demolished temples (compellingly illustrated in his work) also pointed to religious coercion.

Yet the notion that paganism was effectively hounded to its end by persecution has been forcefully challenged by other scholars. Alan Cameron's *The Last Pagans of Rome* (Oxford: Oxford University Press, 2011) effectively debunked a much-romanticised history of late paganism. He argued that the alleged pagan revival, supposedly sparked by the debate over the Altar of Victory in 382, was essentially a later literary fiction, not a historical fact. Indeed, subjected to Cameron's forensic scrutiny, a number of long-established 'facts', such as Emperor Gratian's repudiation of the title *pontifex maximus*, looked altogether less certain. Given the fragmentary and problematic nature of the documentary record, there were important questions where a definitive answer eluded even Cameron. Yet, on a balance of probabilities, he suggested that paganism's decline was generally orderly and peaceful, and that by the 340s CE, a population that had been moderately pagan was, on the whole, moderately Christian. In *Between Pagan and Christian* (Cambridge, MA: Harvard University Press, 2014), Christopher P. Jones emphasised religious syncretism and assimilation (even in areas as contentious as religious imagery) over confrontation, and demonstrated that neither pagan nor Christian were rigid, fixed identities. For Jones, paganism as a distinct religious system was never really destroyed because it never really existed; it was a rather artificial construct, imagined and re-imagined by its self-proclaimed enemies.

If questions remain to be answered about the extent to which pagans were persecuted in late antiquity, much productive scholarship has now been undertaken to illuminate the period-contingent nature of violence. For example, in late antiquity, religious violence may have been performed in particular symbolically meaningful ways: the targeted blows directed specifically at the face or genitals of a statue of Hercules, or lime thrown by a Circumcellion into the eyes of a 'spiritually blind' priest. (Circumcellions were fourth-century North African Christian schismatics, eventually linked to the Donatists.) Furthermore, incidence of violence would have been written about or described in a particular fashion, or according to an established literary style, such as in the *Christian Acts of the Martyrs*. The researcher needs to understand the era-specific *language* of violence being employed when reading the primary sources, in order to understand the actual events being described. These themes are explored in a superb collections of essays edited by H.A. Drake, *Violence in Late Antiquity* (Farnham: Ashgate, 2006). For the historian of persecution, the six chapters dealing with religious violence, considering such topics as pagan attacks on Christians, the Christianisation of rural communities, the symbolic violence of book-burning, and the murder of Hypatia, are especially useful.

For a genuinely scholarly biography of Hypatia herself, the subject of so much myth-making and romanticism, Maria Dzielska's *Hypatia of Alexandria*, trans. F. Lyra (Cambridge, MA: Harvard University Press, 1995) is much recommended. For that most fascinating and volatile of ancient cities, students are well served by Christopher Hass's *Alexandria in Late Antiquity: Topography and Social Conflict* (Baltimore, MD: Johns Hopkins University Press, 1997). Haas considered the period from Diocletian to the Arab conquests of the seventh century in his study of inter-communal relations between the city's Jews, Christians, and pagans. Drawing on both documentary and archaeological evidence, he revealed both how structures of authority functioned in the urban environment, and the conditions in which they broke down and coexistence turned to violence.

The Medieval Roots of Modern Antisemitism

It is worth bearing three main themes in mind when approaching the literature on antisemitism: the relationship between modern antisemitism and pre-modern hostility toward Judaism; the agency of Jewish communities themselves, and the motivations that have underpinned antisemitism, from 'chimerical fantasies' through to rational calculation. These remain central if contested questions, productive of much valuable scholarship but of little consensus. The collection of essays edited by Albert S. Lindermann and Richard S. Levy in *Antisemitism: A History* (Oxford: Oxford University Press, 2010) is an essential introduction, offering coverage from the pre-Christian era through to the relationship between the Arab–Israeli conflict and the resurgence of antisemitism in the contemporary world. The editors (if, perhaps, not all the contributing authors) of this volume tended towards stressing the distinctiveness of modern antisemitism, evident in its insistent demand that adherents politically organise and act in a putative existential conflict with Jewry.

In contrast, Gavin Langmuir, in *Towards a Definition of Antisemitism* (Berkeley: University of California Press, 1990), has suggested that the fundamentally irrational hostility towards Jews manifested by the Nazis was present, albeit with less devastating effect, in Europe by the thirteenth century. In *Anti-Judaism: The History of a Way of Thinking* (New York: Norton, 2013),

David Nirenberg pursued the origins of this exceptional hatred yet deeper. Beginning his study in ancient Egypt, where resident Jews were resented as an alien and subversive presence, Nirenberg argued that anti-Judaism was not so much a distinctive ideology that emerged at some identifiable historic moment, but rather was a characteristic mode of thinking about the world embedded in the western tradition.

A fuller understanding of the lived experiences of medieval Jewish communities and recognition of their achievements has emerged as a significant counterweight to a long-established focus on exile and persecution. An exemplar of this trend is Robert Chazan's *Reassessing Jewish Life in Medieval Europe* (Cambridge: Cambridge University Press, 2010). Chazan does not ignore hostility towards Jews, but balances his account with a measured assessment of their situation. Jewish demography, for example, was characterised by instability. In part, this was due to expulsion and forced migration but, in other instances, it was voluntary, reflecting the pursuit of economic opportunity. Ranging over economics, politico-legal status, interfaith relationships, and the sustaining of Jewish identity, Chazan's work is essential reading for understanding the medieval Jewish experience *in toto*. In a similar vein, in *Living Together, Living Apart: Rethinking Jewish-Christian Relations in the Middles Ages* (Princeton, NJ: Princeton University Press, 2007), Jonathan Elukin provocatively suggests that *convivencia* was not just a characteristic of the Iberian Peninsula. Similar levels of social integration occurred more widely, even in kingdoms more usually associated with active persecution. Robin Mundill's *The King's Jews: Money, Massacre and Exodus in Medieval England* (London: Continuum, 2010) offers a balanced assessment of one such kingdom's Jewish community, from establishment in 1070 to expulsion in 1290, in an accessible narrative account that serves as a valuable case study.

If we should now recognise that medieval Jews did not live in a constant state of insecurity, the long-term precarity of their situation needs also to acknowledged. Relationship between Jews and Christians were dynamic, and understanding the episodic nature of persecution requires attention to specific contingent factors. In *Early Medieval Jewish Policy in Western Europe* (Minneapolis: University of Minnesota Press, 1977), Bernard S. Bachrach examined the reigns of Visigoth, Ostrogoth, Lombard, Merovingians, and Carolingian monarchs between *c.*476 and 877 CE. He concluded that their Jewish subjects were generally more influential than had hitherto been allowed, and that what persecution had occurred was rooted in politics, as rival kings competed for their support. While Bachrach was criticised for being somewhat selective in his use of evidence, there is a general consensus that the status of Jews deteriorated later, from the eleventh to the thirteenth centuries.

A nuanced and thorough treatment of this period can be found in Anna Sapir Abulafia's *Christian-Jewish Relations 1000–1300* (London: Routledge, 2011). Abulafia argued that the widening circulation of the Talmud was of particular significance in increasing negative attitudes towards Jews, as well as their key economic role, and association with usury. The impact of the crusading movement and the evolution of anti-Jewish libels are also considered as contributing to an environment where, dependent on local conditions, persecution might occur.

In a challenge to teleological interpretations of massacres and expulsions leading inexorably to the formation of a systemic European 'persecuting society', David Nirenberg, in *Communities of Violence: Persecution of Minorities in the Middle Ages* (Princeton, NJ: Princeton University Press, 1996), argued that such violence was actually highly contingent on very specific circumstances. Thus, for example, the attacks on Jews during the so-called 'Shepard's Crusades' occurred because Jews were perceived as the agents of a deeply unpopular royal fiscal policy. Similarly, recurrent rioting on Good Friday, during which Christians attacked Jewish communities, should be understood as essentially ritualised violence, symbolising the triumph of Christianity, while affirming a subordinate role for Jews within society. Yet, while recognising the complexity of both anti-Jewish sentiments and the contingent motivations for episodes of active persecution, François Soyer, in *Medieval Antisemitism* (Leeds: Arc Humanities Press, 2019), has suggested that the essentialisation of supposed Jewish characteristics had created an overarching ideology that was functionally equivalent to the modern concept of race. This ideology might be fairly termed 'medieval antisemitism'.

The Albigensian Crusade

Walter Wakefield's *Heresy, Crusade and Inquisition in Southern France, 1100–1250* (Berkeley: University of California Press, 1974) was one of the first modern scholarly accounts of the Albigensian Crusade in English. Drawing both upon the author's own research and his knowledge of the continental scholarship, Wakefield's volume still repays reading for the skill with which the author charts religious discourse within the broader political, social, and economic contexts that shaped events in Languedoc. He draws out, to particular effect, the conflict between local secular authority and the Church, that was a major factor in driving persecution in the south. Indeed, for Wakefield, it was the lack of cooperation between Church and state in Languedoc, standing in marked contrast to the situation in Capetian France, that explained why heresy had proliferated in the region. Two other surveys with much the same scope followed: Jonathan Sumption's *The Albigensian Crusade* (London: Faber and Faber, 1978) and Michael Costen's *The Cathars and the Albigensian Crusade* (Manchester: Manchester University Press, 1997). These also remain useful and accessible introductions to the topic that seek to integrate the history of the campaign against the Albigensian heresy into the broader regional, economic, and institutional disputes that coalesced around the crusade.

Such approaches may have somewhat diluted the essentially religious nature of the conflict. Thus, historians such as Malcolm Lambert, in *The*

Cathars (Oxford: Blackwell, 1998), and Malcolm Barber, in *The Cathars* (London: Pearson, 2000), sought to re-centre the heretics themselves. Lambert's study is the more wide-ranging, offering coverage of dualist sects in Germany, northern Italy, France, and the Balkans, as well as Languedoc. Barber's focus is very much on the latter. Both offered careful appraisals of the evidence for links with eastern dualists, arguing that there is strong evidence for the transmission of literature and practices from the Bogomils to western Cathars, such as the ritual of *consolamentum*. Yet they were wary of inferring any kind of subservient relationship between western and eastern dualists, or even of over-emphasising their similarities. The heretics of Languedoc developed on thoroughly distinct western lines, adopting Latin as their liturgical language, and developing an episcopate, a hierarchy of offices, before the Bogomils did so.

Both Lambert and Barber, too, offered invaluable explorations of 'Cathar' doctrines, theology, moral systems, and intellectual lives. Lambert stressed the very real and powerful appeal of the Albigensian heresy: the example of a simple, apostolic life set by the *perfecti*, their admirable ethical system, their renunciation of burdensome tithes and clerical venality. Barber also emphasised the appeal of the dualist heresy to ordinary folk, but noted, too, how crucial its noble patrons were to its dissemination and resilience. For Barber, therefore, the most significant factor in the extirpation of the Albigensian heresy had been the eventual reconciliation of the Languedocian elite to the French crown. For Lambert, the inquisitional tribunals loom large in his account of the 'suffocation' of the heresy in Languedoc. Yet he also pays full attention to the long-term fate of the dualist Church in Lombardy. There he attributes its decline not only to inquisition, but also to the influence of orthodox confraternities as vehicles for popular piety, the influence gained by charismatic Franciscan and Dominican preachers, and to municipal and imperial anti-heretical legislation.

These accounts, however much they differ on some points of interpretation, may be regarded as representative of the traditionalist historiography of the Albigensian Crusade. Their authors accepted the existence of an organised dualist Church, with a coherent and distinct doctrine, in late twelfth-century Languedoc. To that rival Church, the Catholic Church responded. A radical revisionist interpretation has now emerged, best represented in the English-language historiography by Robert Moore's *The War on Heresy: Faith and Power in Medieval Europe* (London: Profile Books, 2012) and Mark Gregory Pegg's *A Most Holy War: The Albigensian Crusade and the Battle for Christendom* (Oxford: Oxford University Press, 2008).

They questioned the existence of an organised dualist Church before the Albigensian Crusade. They argued that heresy was an ideological construct projected by a burgeoning class of clerics and bureaucrats onto diverse, local (but basically orthodox) Christian practices. These practices, disturbingly, were outside of their control and their practitioners were resistant to authority. It was, thus, clerical anxieties that populated the landscape of Languedoc with heresiarchs and their deluded followers, who would be denied salvation if the Church failed to act. Those who were, consequently, stigmatised and persecuted as heretics eventually underwent a reconstruction of their own sense of self-identity. They came to equate their torments with their holiness. They embraced the heretical identity that their persecutors had conjured into existence, for it promised martyrdom. A dualist heresy that had been a clerical fiction in 1209 thus became a reality only after 1229. Although a powerful stimulus to debate, many of the traditionalists are dubious of this hypothesis. They continue to argue for the actual presence of dualist heresy, and a dualist Church, in late twelfth-century Languedoc, to which, therefore, the crusade of 1209 was a response. Those interested in this pivotal juncture in the historiography should consult the volume of essays edited by Antonio Sennis, *Cathars in Question* (Woodbridge: Boydell & Brewer, 2016), which includes contributions from leading international scholars on both sides of the debate.

The specifically military aspects of the Albigensian Crusade were long neglected in the scholarly historiography. This is surprising given the conflict's reputation for ferocity and massacre, which it was generally assumed bore some relation to its religious character. There are now two excellent and full military histories of the Albigensian Crusade: Laurence W. Marvin's *The Occitan War: A Military and Political History of the Albigensian Crusade, 1209–1218* (Cambridge: Cambridge University Press, 2008) and Sean McGlynn's *Kill Them All: Cathars and Carnage in the Albigensian Crusade* (Stroud: The History Press, 2015). Both offer very informed and insightful narratives of the war, with due regard not only to battles and (especially prominent in this war) sieges, but also to logistics, organisation, finance, and recruitment. McGlynn, by considering the intervention of the French crown after 1218, offers the more extensive coverage of the war chronologically. Marvin's account is very much centred on Simon de Montfort and his (largely tactical) successes won in the midst of a hostile population, and while leading a rather fragile army of crusaders, most of whom disappeared home after forty days of service. Interesting, while McGlynn very much reasserted the Albigensian Crusade's reputation for a particular savagery, Marvin, while wholly cognizant of the war's brutality, argued that the conduct of warfare in Languedoc was no worse than elsewhere. He was influenced in this regard by the work of the medievalist Daniel Baraz, who had suggested that the idea of 'cruelty' as a philosophical and cultural concept was just emerging in western thought at this time, and the chroniclers of the Albigensian Crusade were thus acutely sensitive to the bloodshed they witnessed. Those in Languedoc were the most horrified of all, for it was their world that had been shattered.

The European Witch-Hunts

Despite the complexity of the topic and the volume of works devoted to it, the witch-hunts are well served by accessible overviews. Brian P. Levack's *The Witch-Hunt in Early Modern Europe* (London: Longman, 1987), offers students a brilliant introduction, comprehensive, insightful, and offering a suitably critical discussion of the established literature. Levack, himself an authority on the Scottish witch-hunts, is especially strong on the legal foundations of witch-hunting as a judicial procedure and in accounting for regional variations, distinguishing the intense 'witch-crazes' of Germany and Switzerland from the more restrained 'witch-hunts' of Italy or the Scandinavian countries. It says much for the strength of the original conception and structure of this book that the author has been able to revise it very effectively to keep up with a changing historiography, and students are advised to seek out the most recent edition. Interestingly, it is another authority on the Scottish witch-hunts, Julian Goodare, who has written a one-volume introduction to the subject to rival Levack's: *The European Witch-Hunt* (London: Routledge, 2016). While, again, offering a comprehensive overview of the topic, Goodare also offers a very thorough coverage of both elite and popular ideologies that explains why both those powerful rulers attempting to build 'godly states', and those struggling farmers concerned about their milk turning sour for no good reason, were equally invested in hunting witches.

Both these authors stress the significance of contingency and locality in understanding any specific outbreak of witch-hunting. Cases studies of regions or nations are thus amongst the most valuable and revealing contributions to the literature. An excellent collection of such studies can be found in Brian P. Levack's edited volume, *The Oxford Handbook of Witchcraft in Early Modern Europe and Colonial America* (Oxford: Oxford University Press, 2013). This comprehensive guide also contains a series of essays on the ideologies that underpinned the witch-hunts and a closing section that considers current themes in witchcraft research. The collection of essays found in Julian Goodare, Rita Voltmer, and Liv Helene Willumsen's edited volume, *Demonology and Witch-Hunting in Early Modern Europe* (London: Routledge: 2020), provided a useful series of case studies illuminating the evolution and dissemination of learned demonology across western and central Europe. There are a number of book-length treatments covering particular countries, of which Lyndal Roper's, *Witch Craze: Terror and Fantasy in Baroque Germany* (New Haven, CT: Yale University Press, 2004), is an outstanding example. This work took the study of witch-hunting beyond the traditional frameworks rooted in intellectual, political, and social history and centred the gendered, cultural, and psychological factors that shaped the belief systems that underpinned both the power and reality of *malefice* and the drive to persecute.

A similarly productive interdisciplinary approach can be found in Edward Bever's *The Realities of Witchcraft and Popular Magic in Early Modern Europe* (New York: Palgrave Macmillan, 2008), in which the author draws upon psychology, neurophysiology, and pharmacology to understand and inform the material historical record. Witchcraft, Bever suggested, was widely practised. He controversially argued that ill-will, expressed through acts of *malefice*, had the potential to do serious somatic harm to its victims (illness, paralysis, even death), because the subconscious mind exercises such influence over the physical body. Bever's work is an essential corrective to any who might still simply dismiss witch-belief as ignorance or superstition, or conclude that all allegations of *malefice* were groundless.

Perhaps more prosaic, but not less insightful, is Robin Briggs's *Witches and Neighbours: The Social and Cultural Context of European Witchcraft* (London: Harper Collins, 1996). Briggs built upon the established historiographical tradition of seeing social tensions, conflicts between neighbours, as lying at the heart of allegations of witchcraft. Yet his account eschewed a dry, materialist approach, and emphasised the emotional states that produced such allegations, and thus how very intimate, personal antagonisms drove widespread persecution. That, disproportionately, women were the victims of the hatred, anger, envy, fear, and resentment that seems to have permeated communal life, is manifest here. Yet Briggs does not offer the fullest explanation of why this should be. Diane Purkiss's *The Witch in History: Early Modern and Twentieth-Century Representations* (London: Routledge, 1996) offered an astute critique of much feminist scholarship on the subject (in which the death tolls of the persecution had been exaggerated to support the idea that the witch-hunts constituted a 'gendercide'), as well of the failure of the established literature to recover the perspective of early modern women themselves. Purkiss considers the witch-hunts in the context of the challenges facing early modern women, related primarily to the management, indeed survival, of their households, and the strategies some adopted to protect both status and self-respect.

Although the early modern witch-hunts need to be considered very much as characteristic of their own time and place, neither witches nor witch-hunts are unique to Europe, or the period 1420–1782. For those who wish to consider the hunts in global context and a longer time-frame, two works are recommended. Wolfgang Behringer, in *Witches and Witch-Hunts: A Global History* (Cambridge: Polity Press, 2004), surveyed the origins, characteristics, and decline of the early modern witch-hunts, covering the whole of Europe, but very much benefiting from his specialist expertise on Germany. In understanding the witch-hunts, he places strong emphasis on environmental factors, particularly climate change in the sixteenth century, in creating an atmosphere of crisis that bred both belief in, and accusations of, demonic witchcraft. Yet beyond this, Behringer offered, too, a global survey of witch-beliefs that brought his study in to the twentieth century and the reoccurrence of witch-hunts, especially in Africa, in the latter half of that century.

The fullest history of the *malefic* witch, though, is Ronald Hutton's *The Witch: A History of Fear from Ancient Times to the Present* (New Haven, CT: Yale University Press, 2017). This opened with a discussion of 'deep perspectives', looking at global definitions, the witch in the ancient world, and the – contested – relationship between witchcraft and shamanic practices. Hutton then focused on continental Europe, considering both the elite and popular beliefs that helped create the early modern stereotype and the final emergence of that stereotype in the fifteenth century. In the final section of the book, he considered the British Isles, with specific references to fairy-lore, witch belief in the Celtic societies, and the peculiar place of animals, or demons in animal form, in British witch-lore.

Race and Slavery in the Atlantic World

Reading around the history of race as an ideology is complicated by the question of definition. On the one hand, race might well be understood simply as the idea that humankind can be divided into distinct and separate biological categories, distinguished by phenotypes (observable physical characteristics), whose physical, intellectual, and moral characteristics are inherited from generation to generation. Yet such a definition does not capture the mutability inherent in specific historical contexts, the permeability of supposed racial boundaries, and the political and cultural negotiations, implicit or explicit, that often took place around inclusion and exclusion. In that sense, race might be considered a socially constructed legitimisation of a prejudice, that was never a straightforward matter of phenotypes, but always included cultural competencies, a sense of belonging and a hostility towards those distinguished sociologically as an out-group. In *Racisms: From the Crusades to the Twentieth Century* (Princeton, NJ: Princeton University Press, 2013), Francisco Bethencourt warns against identifying a single tradition of racialised thinking, recognising instead distinct patterns of prejudice ('racisms') reflecting specific historically contingent circumstances, but related by a common trigger: a political attempt to control economic or social resources.

The collection of essays in Miriam Eliav-Feldon, Benjamin Isaac, and Joseph Zieger's edited volume, *The Origins of Racism in the West* (Cambridge: Cambridge University Press, 2009) offers a very wide-ranging discussion, ranging from antiquity, through the medieval era, to the early modern period. While there is some disagreement between contributors over a precise definition, the editors conclude that racism, as an ideology that provided a conceptual framework for emotional forms of group hatred, existed, in varying forms and with varying degrees of intensity, long before the emergence of modern, so-called 'scientific racism'.

In order to understand the evolving relationship between racial ideologies and the institution of slavery, Robin Blackburn's *The Making of New World Slavery: From the Baroque to the Modern, 1492–1800* (London: Verso, 1997) is a comprehensive treatment that charts the intertwined history of racialised thinking and the evolution of slavery in the Americas, from scriptural origins (with a particular emphasis on a racialised understanding of the Curse of Ham) through to the establishment of race slavery in the 'New World'. The survival of chattel slavery as an institution in the Christian/Muslim frontier zone of the Iberian Peninsula is also accorded an especial significance. The bulk of the book, though, traces the development of plantation societies in North and South America, stressing the emergence of private commerce that developed to satisfy emerging consumer markets as the most significant factor in the scale and rapacious character of plantation slavery.

Herbert S. Klein and Francisco Vidal Luna's *Slavery in Brazil* (Cambridge: Cambridge University Press, 2010) is an enormously valuable study that goes some way to remedying the neglect of Brazil in the Anglophone historiography of slavery. Some 40 per cent of those who survived the Middle Passage were shipped to Brazil, where they laboured not only on sugar and coffee plantations, but in mines, workshops, and transportation. Klein and Luna's account is especially strong on the economics and demographics of Brazilian slavery, and its Portuguese antecedents in the fifteenth-century Azores, but also offers insights into the family structures and cultural life of the enslaved and their sustained history of resistance, rebellion, and seeking refuge on *quilombos*. The lives, and their very struggles for life, of the enslaved are at the heart of Randy M. Browne's *Surviving Slavery in the British Caribbean* (Philadelphia: University of Pennsylvania Press, 2020). Browne draws on extant legal records to recover a harrowing record of how enslaved men and women endured an unforgiving environment, a punishing labour regime, brutal enslavers, and intra-communal violence in a daily battle to survive.

There has been considerable debate around the transition from European indentured servants to a racialised enslaved workforce of Africans and their descendants in the British North American colonies. Explanations have ranged from this being an essentially 'unthinking decision', resulting from pragmatic economic calculations concerning their relative costs, through to a conscious political strategy, with planters emphasising race as a means of undermining solidarity among the labouring classes. Anthony Parent, in *Foul Means: The Formation of a Slave Society in Virginia, 1660–1740* (Chapel Hill: University of North Carolina Press, 2003), argued for a high degree of deliberation on the part of the planter elite. While noting the increasing scarcity of indentured servants, he recognised, too, the emergence of a marked preference for slaves among planters. These could be exploited more ruthlessly than servants and they had experience of land clearance and farming in West Africa that better suited them to plantation agriculture.

While these elite planters sought to carve out great landed estates for themselves, and adopted the trappings of English genteel culture, the plantations were not manorial estates on the 'old world' model. They were ruthlessly profit-maximising business enterprises. Laura Sandy, in *The Overseers of Early American Slavery* (London: Routledge, 2020), provides the fullest account of the management of the larger plantation enterprises, with a detailed analysis of the recruitment, duties, pay, and performance of overseers. While recognising the relentless cruelty of labour management on the plantations, Sandy demonstrated that while some overseers neatly conformed to the stereotype of the brutal ne'er-do-well, others were skilled and aspirational artisans, professional farmers, and 'gentleman overseers', pursuing an apprenticeship in plantation management. And some were themselves enslaved men and women, trusted 'confidential' slaves placed in positions of authority in recognition of their skills and abilities. This question of the management of labour is central to understanding life on the plantations. As Thavolia Glymph demonstrates in *Out of the House of Bondage: The Transformation of the Plantation Household* (Cambridge: Cambridge University Press, 2003), there was no division of 'private' and 'public' sphere in this environment. The plantation household itself was a site of production, where plantation mistresses wielded violent, coercive power, notwithstanding their own subordination to patriarchal authority.

Resistance is now understood as a complicated and multifaceted phenomenon, that characterises a range of activities from prosaic but disruptive and sustained personal assertions of autonomy and flight, through to carefully planned violent rebellions and, in the case of Haiti, successful revolution that not merely ended slavery in the colony but transformed it economically and politically. This wide scope of defiance can be understood at its different levels in these works: Stephanie M.H. Camp's *Closer to Freedom: Enslaved Women and Everyday Resistance in the Plantation South* (Chapel Hill: University of North Carolina Press, 2004), and Laurent Dubois' *Avengers of the New World: The Story of the Haitian Revolution* (Cambridge, MA: Harvard University Press, 2005).

Genocide and Colonialism

For many years, most of Raphaël Lemkin's papers were unpublished. Two of his key works are now available in one volume: Raphaël Lemkin, *Lemkin on Genocide*, edited and with an introduction by Steven Leonard Jacobs (New York: Lexington, 2012). This includes his *Introduction to the Study of Genocide*, which focuses on questions of definition, and outlines the 'techniques' employed in the destruction of groups: political, social, cultural, economic, biological, physical, and by 'racial discrimination in feeding'. The second section of the volume consists of a *History of Genocide* and covers subjects from antiquity and the medieval period through to modern times. Neither work is complete. However, they do give very valuable insights both into the scope of Lemkin's understanding of what constituted genocide and his case that genocide was a recurrent historical phenomenon. This work is not simply of historiographical significance. Given the tendency of scholars of Genocide Studies (a sprawling interdisciplinary field) to attempt (usually problematic) redefinitions of what constitutes 'genocide', and their overwhelming focus on the events of the twentieth century, Lemkin's own analysis still carries considerable weight.

It does however need to be considered critically and with an awareness of how the field has subsequently developed. Donald Bloxham and A. Dirk Moses' edited volume, *The Oxford Handbook of Genocide Studies*

(Oxford: Oxford University Press, 2010), is a comprehensive introduction and overview of the topic. It opens with a section on concepts, including a particularly useful discussion of Lemkin's own background and assumptions, by A. Dirk Moses. This is followed by an examination of interdisciplinary perspectives. William Schabas's discussion of genocide and international law explains why the older concept of 'crimes against humanity' re-emerged in the 1990s as the most useful legal tool to address atrocities. In courtrooms, as opposed to seminar rooms, genocide is currently interpreted in quite a narrow and conservative way, reserved for the clearest-cut cases of phys-ical destruction: the mass murder of groups. The volume then offers a com-prehensive series of case studies of genocide, from the pre-modern to the contemporary world. Three of these deal with colonial genocides: Nicholas A. Robins on Latin America, Gregory D. Smithers on North America, and Dominik J. Schaller on Africa.

A more succinct and accessible book, but one that still offers insightful analysis of genocides from the ancient to the modern period (including an excellent chapter on settler genocides) is Norman M. Naimark's *Genocide: A World History* (Oxford: Oxford University Press, 2016). Those seeking a wide-ranging but manageable introduction to the topic would be especially well served by this volume.

Another very informative collection of case studies is Robert Gellately and Ben Kiernan's edited volume, *The Spectre of Genocide: Mass Murder in Historical Perspective* (Cambridge: Cambridge University Press, 2003). The editors note that their volume offers not merely comparative studies of different instances of genocide, but different theoretical approaches too. For example, Omer Bartov, Marie Fleming, and Eric Weitz all argue for the essen-tial modernity and novelty of twentieth-century genocides, distinguishing them from earlier examples. Differences in approaches can also be seen in that some stress the 'top-down' and agentic nature of genocide, dependent upon a figure like Pol Pot in Cambodia, with the intent and authority to drive a campaign of extermination. Others look for more impersonal struc-tural factors, such as the demands of 'Total War', that Jay Winter sees as integral to twentieth-century genocides. Three essays look specifically at the colonial experience: Isabel Hull on Wilhelmine colonies in Africa, John G. Taylor considers the Indonesian occupation of East Timor, and Elazar Barkan examines genocides of indigenous peoples with particular focus on North America and Australasia.

The attention now being given to colonial genocides is a productive development in the historiography of genocide. For a long time after Lemkin originally defined 'genocide', Anglophone historians were reluctant to con-sider the concept in relation to the fate of indigenous people. The collapse of Native American populations, for example, was held to be a consequence of disease, not deliberate extermination. Without 'intent', there can have been no genocide. Difficult questions about *why* indigenous populations were so susceptible to epidemics could be waved away with reference to their (conveniently) vulnerable immune systems. This ignored the role of enslavement, war, forced relocation, malnutrition, and material depriv-ation, all inflicted upon native peoples intentionally by colonists, and all of which rendered them acutely liable to mass death by disease. A number of works have now categorically made the case for American genocides. These are often polemical and deliberately provocative, but they have opened a necessary debate. For an example, see David E. Stannard's *American Holocaust: Columbus and the Conquest of the New World* (Oxford: Oxford University Press, 1992). Nicholas A. Robins, in *Native Insurgencies and the Genocidal Impulse in the Americas* (Bloomington: Indiana University Press, 2005), took that debate in an interesting direction by arguing that some native peoples themselves committed 'retributive' or 'subaltern' genocides during insurgencies. Given the nature of the asymmetrical relationship between colonisers and colonised, with the former exercising far more coer-cive power over the long term, whether such instances do constitute geno-cide remains contested.

Perhaps the most important development in the historiography of genocide and colonialism has been the (re)discovery by historians of the suggestion by commentators such as Hannah Arendt, Frantz Fanon, and W.E.B. Dubois, that European overseas imperialism set significant precedents for twentieth-century European genocides. Inevitably, perhaps, studies of German colo-nialism have dominated this area. The parallels, in terms of the role of exterminatory racism, the mobilisation of the state and its formidable bur-eaucracy, and the waging of annihilatory campaigns by the military, between the Herero/Nama genocides and the Holocaust have been an irresistible draw for historians. Two edited collections explore these linkages fully: Volker Langbehn and Mohammad Salama (eds), *German Colonialism: Race, the Holocaust and Postwar Germany* (New York: Columbia University Press, 2011) and Jürgen Zimmerer and Joachim Zeller (eds), *Genocide in German South-West Africa* (Monmouth: Merlin Press, 2008).

Zimmerer is the leading scholar in the field and the one who has made the most forceful case that the Herero/Nama genocide was a stepping-stone to Auschwitz and, more generally, a transitional development between the settler-colonialist genocides of the nineteenth century and the state-driven genocides of the twentieth century. Another edited volume, A. Dirk Moses and Dan Stone's *Colonialism and Genocide* (London: Routledge, 2007), while including an essay on South-West Africa by Dan Stone, and another on NSDAP colonialism in eastern Europe by Zimmerer, broadens the scope with studies of the concentration camp (a colonial invention), racial war in Haiti, 1802–1804, and genocides in the Americas and Australia. However, a note of caution is needed here. While the parallels are indeed striking, it would be a mistake to overemphasise the determining role of colonial genocide in seeking the origins of specific twentieth-century genocides. It is, for example, very difficult to demonstrate a clear causal chain between South-West Africa and the Holocaust.

On the other hand, colonialism's genocidal legacy is still playing out in Africa. Herbert Ekwe-Ekwe's *Biafra Revisited* (Reading: African Renaissance, 2006), is a very polemical book, with a clear agenda. He accuses the Nigerian state and the former colonial power, Britain, of genocide against the Igbo people during the Nigerian Civil War (1966–1970). While this remains a very contested case of genocide, Ekwe-Ekwe usefully draws attention to the inherently genocidal nature of post-independence states in Africa. These are former colonies that were created to exploit and violently repress their subject populations. And they have not essentially changed, even though indigenous elites have supplanted the former colonialists in government. The former colonies of Africa are thus, inherently, 'genocide-states'. For Ekwe-Ekwe, this legacy explains why Africa has been the scene of so many genocides over the last seventy years: Uganda, Zaïre/Democratic Republic of Congo, Ethiopia, Rwanda, Burundi, Sudan, especially Darfur.

Genocides in the Ottoman, Russian, and Soviet Empires

Justin McCarthy's *Death and Exile: The Ethnic Cleansing of Ottoman Muslims, 1821–1922* (Princeton, NJ: Darwin Press, 1995) is a detailed demographic history, charting the massacres and mass deportations that afflicted Ottoman Muslims, principally in the Balkans, Transcaucasia, and eastern Anatolia. It is an important counter-narrative to the western historiographical emphasis on the sufferings of subject Christian populations. It also provides a key context for understanding why the multi-ethnic empire collapsed into mutually destructive conflicts, in the century of persecution that began with the Greek revolution in 1821. Its original publication in 1995 was particularly timely, against the backdrop of the break-up of Yugoslavia. The phrase 'ethnic cleansing' had entered the world's lexicon. Bosnian Muslims, descendants of people who had converted to Islam under Ottoman rule, were under genocidal attack. The work, however, is also very problematic, especially regarding its treatment of the Armenian genocide. Indeed, McCarthy did not acknowledge that a genocide took place. He uncritically advanced the argument that the deportations were a military necessity, in response to Armenian revolutionary activity and collusion with the Russians.

There is now an extensive literature which covers the reality of the Armenian genocide in detail, but important differences of interpretation remain, particularly over the question of origins and timing. Some historians have argued that the genocide was instigated before the First World War began, with the conflict merely providing cover to escalate a murderous programme already long underway. Benny Morris and Dror Ze'evi's *The Thirty-Year Genocide: Turkey's Destruction of its Christian Minorities 1894–1924* (Cambridge, MA: Harvard University Press, 2019), treated the sequence of atrocities opening with the pogroms against Armenians in the

1890s, through the wartime deportations and massacres of Armenians and Assyrian Christians, and on to the violent ethnic cleansing of Greek Orthodox Christians in 1923–1924, as effectively the same process.

Raymond Kévorkian's *The Armenian Genocide: A Complete History* (London: I.B. Tauris, 2011) suggested that the unbending commitment to creating an ethnically homogenous Turkish state may have been formulated before the war in early 1914. This was to be achieved through expulsions and ethnic cleansing, rather than mass murder. Under pressure of war, however, a genocidal policy emerged. The particular strength of Kévorkian's work, the most comprehensive history of the genocide that we currently have, is its grounding in archival sources, especially ones – such as those of the Jerusalem patriarchate – that had been hitherto underutilised, and in his use of survivor testimony. A valuable and moving history of the genocide centred entirely around such testimony can be found in Donald E. Miller and Lorna Touryan Miller's *Survivors: An Oral History of the Armenian Genocide* (Berkeley: University of California Press, 1993).

Donald Bloxham, *The Great Game of Genocide: Imperialism, Nationalism and the Destruction of the Ottoman Armenians* (Oxford: Oxford University Press, 2006), makes a similar case to Kévorkian. He argues that the 1890s massacres were essentially acts of political repression, intended to snuff out a nascent nationalist movement rather than destroy the Armenians as a group. The genocide of 1915–1916 was a consequence of the 'cumulative radicalisation' (the phrase is borrowed from the Holocaust scholar Hans Mommsen) of Ottoman policy, arising from a deteriorating military situation. Bloxham's other key contribution has been in highlighting the role of international politics in the genocide. He illustrates how the predatory stance of the great powers, chiefly Britain, France, and Russia, self-interestedly posing as champions of oppressed Christian minorities, served only to raise inter-ethnic tensions within Anatolia.

Taner Akçam is a Turkish historian and political activist, who had to flee his native country in 1977. In *A Shameful Act: The Armenian Genocide and the Question of Turkish Responsibility* (London: Constable: 2007), he provided not only a very full history of the genocide itself, but also a particularly useful section dealing with the war crimes trials held in Istanbul 1919–1922, and the question of Turkish responsibility. He notes that the period of the trials represented a point at which responsibility for the genocide was accepted. Indeed, the phrase 'shameful acts' was originally Mustafa Kemal Atatürk's verdict on what had been done. Recognising this opens the possibility of contemporary Turkey acknowledging the genocide today. Akçam returned to this topic in a volume co-authored with the Armenian historian Vahakn N. Dadrian, *Judgement at Istanbul: The Armenian Genocide Trials* (Oxford: Berghahn Books, 2011). This is a principal published source of legal evidence and first-hand Turkish perpetrator testimony, documenting both the intent and the process of the state extirpation of Anatolia's Armenian population. It also established the significance of the trials themselves. Perhaps because they were soon abandoned, they have not always received the attention they deserve. In the absence of an international criminal court and given the difficult question of whether state officials could be prosecuted for war crimes against their own citizens, they were an important experiment in national legal self-examination.

Cathie Carmichael's *Genocide Before the Holocaust* (New Haven, CT: Yale University Press, 2009) examined the Armenian genocide within a wider general history of the phenomenon, situated chronologically from the 1860s to the 1930s, and geographically ranging across the Habsburg, Russian, Ottoman and German empires. Her work thus provides an invaluable comparative perspective. She explained the rise of (modern) genocidal violence with reference to the disintegration of the old empires and the rise of ethno-nationalist states.

The communist genocides of the twentieth century have presented historians with something of a definitional challenge. Stalin's Soviet Union, Mao's China, Pol Pot's Kampuchea/Cambodia, and a host of African Marxist-Leninist regimes, such as the Ethiopian Derge, all engaged in murderous state-driven campaigns of persecution that aimed at the destruction of targeted groups. Yet these groups were often social categories, putative 'classes', or political opponents, strictly speaking outside the stipulated groups contained in the 1948 UN genocide convention. This is one area where historians ought not allow themselves to be restricted by that definition. Besides, even a cursory examination of these regimes reveals the extent to which they all also quite specifically targeted identifiable ethnic groups, even if those attacks were often camouflaged by the language of Marxist-Leninism. Anne Applebaum's *Red Famine: Stalin's War on Ukraine* (New York: Random House, 2017), discussed the Holodomor as a Marxist-Leninist ideologically inspired, man-made famine, pursued both as class war and as an assault on the very identity and lives of Ukrainians. Stéphane Courtois and colleagues' *The Black Book of Communism: Crimes. Terror, Repression*, translated by Jonathan Murphy and Mark Kramer (Cambridge, MA: Harvard University Press, 1999) is a comprehensive international chronicle and indictment of the Russian and eastern European, Chinese, Cambodian, Latin American, and African communist regimes responsible, in the contributors' estimation, for some 100 million deaths from the Russian Revolution in 1917 through to the Soviet intervention in Afghanistan, 1979–1989.

The Holocaust

Lucy S. Dawidowicz's *The War Against the Jews 1933–45* (London: Penguin 1975) remains a valuable survey that offered a thorough and detailed account of the Holocaust, which concluded with a useful country-by-country summary of the position of Europe's Jews pre-war, and their fate during the Second World War. Readers should, however, be aware that Dawidowicz's central argument, that Hitler was essentially the sole strategist of the Holocaust and that he intended to commit genocide from as early as 1919, has been questioned by many more recent historians.

Dawidowicz's position has been characterised as 'intentionalist', as opposed to the 'functionalist' or 'structuralist' school. Functionalists such as Götz Aly, in *Final Solution: Nazi Population Policy and the Murder of the European Jews*, translated by Belinda Cooper and Alison Brown (London: Arnold, 1999), argued that Hitler, for all his rhetoric, had no clear blueprint for genocide, and that events proceeded haphazardly, driven by low-level bureaucrats, and arising from competing interests within the NSDAP hierarchy and from contingent responses to changing military circumstances.

In *The Origins of the Final Solution: The Evolution of Nazi Jewish Policy, 1939–1942* (London: Arrow Books, 2004), Christopher Browning produced a searching analysis of this question. He concluded that up until the outbreak of war, Hitler's intention was to drive the Reich's Jews out through emigration. That became impractical during the war. Indeed, Germany's conquest brought millions more Jews under their authority. Plans shifted to a territorial solution, whereby Jews would be expelled en masse onto some distant reservation. Administrators in eastern Europe then tried to respond to this policy, while struggling with the practical problems of sustaining the ghettos while the war continued. Attrition through overwork or starvation and disease became for some a 'solution'. The brutality of the *Einsatzgruppen* in the war zone further radicalised thinking; expulsion gave way as an objective to total annihilation. For Browning, this conclusion had been arrived at by the late summer of 1941 and he thus placed little emphasis on the deliberations of the Wannsee Conference.

Saul Friedländer wrote a two-volume history of the Holocaust that constitutes the fullest and most detailed account that we currently have: *Nazi Germany and the Jews: The Years of Persecution, 1933–1939* (London: Weidenfeld and Nicolson, 1997), and *Nazi Germany and the Jews: The Years of Extermination, 1939–1945* (London: Weidenfeld and Nicolson, 2007). He achieved an effective synthesis of the debates over the origins of the Holocaust, re-centring Hitler in his explanation, but noting how his policy evolved from emigration/expulsion up until 1939, to the wartime shift to destruction. His history, however, offered much more than that; he explored Jewish responses to the Holocaust and wrote in effect a full social history of Jewish life in this most tragic of periods. It is worth noting that Friedländer was himself a Holocaust survivor, hidden in a Catholic boarding school in Vichy, and passed as a Christian child. His parents were murdered in Auschwitz.

The question of whether the Holocaust was unique has been as controversial as the debate over its origins. The case that it was unique might be summarised as resting upon the claim that the National Socialist state intended, and attempted, ultimately to kill every man, woman, and child belonging to the Jewish race. This comprehensive, uncompromising, and unmitigated policy of utter destruction has phenomenologically no exact parallel in history. To test that assertion requires a wide comparative knowledge of other genocides. A useful starting point therefore is the collection of essays in Alan S. Rosenbaum's edited volume, *Is the Holocaust Unique?* (Boulder, CO: Westview Press, 2001). This contains a number of essays that examine the claim of uniqueness in relation to, for example, the Porrajmos, the Atlantic slave trade, Stalinist terror, and the Armenian genocide. The essays, on different sides of the debate, by Steven T. Katz, Robert Melson, Vahakn N. Dadrian, and David E. Stannard are especially recommended. Donald Bloxham's *The Final Solution: A Genocide* (Oxford: Clarendon Press, 2009) is an accessible and persuasive comparative study that argued that the Holocaust can only be fully understood along with consideration of NSDAP polices towards other groups, and in the context of the earlier genocides that had shaped the political geography of twentieth-century Europe. He also raised the possibility that not all senior NSDAP figures did conceive of the campaign as requiring the death of every Jew. Eichmann, for example, appeared to think that world Jewry would be sufficiently damaged, so far as to have no meaningful future, by the extermination of its 'biological basis', in eastern Europe.

Belzec, Sobibor, Treblinka: The Operation Reinhard Death Camps (Bloomington: Indiana University Press, 1987), is another work by a Holocaust survivor. Its author, Yitzhak Arad, served in a Soviet partisan unit in Belarus and eastern Lithuania, 1943–1945. He was at pains to challenge the myth of Jewish passivity. While noting that physical debilitation, lack of support from the other Poles, and German success in deceiving deportees of their lethal intent, saw many walk compliantly into the 'showers', he charted also the growing resistance movement and the revolts at Sobibor and Treblinka, which he suggested should be regarded as at least partially successful.

There has been much effort, too, to try to understand the motives of the perpetrators. Christopher Browning's *Ordinary Men: Reserve Police Battalion 101 and the Final Solution in Poland* (New York: Harper Collins, 1992) examined the actions of a unit of reserve policemen, average age 39, educated and socialised in pre-NSDAP Germany, and plucked from normal civilian lives, who massacred thousands of men, women, and children. He noted that the 10–20 per cent who could not bring themselves to participate suffered no punishment and thus concluded that coercive discipline did not explain the willingness to kill. While acknowledging a range of factors at work, Browning emphasised obedience to authority, peer-group pressure, and a growing sense of elitism, over the significance of ideological indoctrination.

Those seeking to understand how Hitler's *weltanschauung* can have led him to pursue such monstrous and inhuman policies, can gain valuable insights from Richard Weikart's *Hitler's Ethic: The Nazi Pursuit of Evolutionary*

Progress (New York: Palgrave Macmillan, 2009). Weikart demonstrated how the Führer's dogmatic and uncritical embrace of evolutionary and eugenic theory led him to develop an ethical code based upon his distorted understanding of 'natural law'. This ethic informed almost every aspect of NSDAP policy, most notably in the areas of euthanasia, racial hygiene, foreign policy, the war for Lebensraum and, ultimately, genocide.

Index

For Product Safety Concerns and Information please contact our EU
representative GPSR@taylorandfrancis.com
Taylor & Francis Verlag GmbH, Kaufingerstraße 24, 80331 München, Germany

www.ingramcontent.com/pod-product-compliance
Lightning Source LLC
Chambersburg PA
CBHW050331270326
41926CB00016B/3412